"Jon Wiederhorn and Katherine Turman know metal. *Louder Than Hell* is an amazing gathering of different breeds of heavy metal rockers telling the tales metal fans want to hear."
—Tom Morello, Rage Against the Machine

"A fascinating, high-octane chronicle of metal mayhem that takes readers on a wild ride, from metal's earliest days to the head-banging present. I'm not saying this just because I'm in the book, but . . . if you love metal, great stories, and music history told by the people who made it, then *Louder Than Hell* is a must-read. This is the book every metal fan should own."
—Alice Cooper

"*Louder Than Hell* is a love letter to the misunderstood genre of heavy metal music, written by trusted companions who had a front-row seat on the devil's roller coaster. The definitive chronological testimony by the people who were there, including some who are no longer with us."
—Mark McGrath, Sugar Ray; cohost of *Extra*

"*Louder Than Hell* comes straight from the twisted minds of rock icons and flows seamlessly through various eras of heavy metal. You hear from the guys that were there on the stage, in the pit, puking in the gutter. It brought back memories, and I even learned a few things I never knew. I really dig this book."
—Riki Rachtman

"This is the best oral history I've read since *Please Kill Me. Louder Than Hell* is the first book that really delivers the brutal truth from the mouths of the artists and key players themselves! I couldn't put it down."

—Matt Pinfield

"An amazingly comprehensive book on all eras and genres of hard rock and heavy metal. The stories and attention to detail make it an instant must for anyone who ever was or is a fan."

—Eddie Trunk, DJ and host of *That Metal Show* on VH1 Classic

"We all know reading is NOT cool. I've said thousands of times that reading 'totally sucks.' But this book does indeed *not suck*. Books on the history of even something as cool as metal can be a bit antiseptic and boring—not this one. It's the story straight from the horse's mouth. Even better is when the horses have experimented with drugs and black out occasionally."

—Brendon Small, Dethklok

"Who likes rock and roll here?? Well, if you do, this is the book for you! Every rock has been overturned, every band has been analyzed, quoted, and lionized, and every page offers a new fact or figure that you probably didn't know. This is *the* definitive chronicle of all that is heavy metal, and I've read them all!"

—Chris Jericho, Fozzy

LOUDER
THAN
HELL

LOUDER THAN HELL

THE DEFINITIVE ORAL HISTORY OF METAL

JON WIEDERHORN
& KATHERINE TURMAN

itbooks

AN IMPRINT OF HARPERCOLLINS PUBLISHERS

*it***books**

LOUDER THAN HELL. Copyright © 2013 by Jon Wiederhorn and Katherine Turman. All rights reserved. Printed in the United States of America. No part of this book may be used or reproduced in any manner whatsoever without written permission except in the case of brief quotations embodied in critical articles and reviews. For information address Harper-Collins Publishers, 10 East 53rd Street, New York, NY 10022.

HarperCollins books may be purchased for educational, business, or sales promotional use. For information please write: Special Markets Department, HarperCollins Publishers, 10 East 53rd Street, New York, NY 10022.

FIRST EDITION

Designed by Renato Stanisic

Library of Congress Cataloging-in-Publication data is available upon request.

ISBN 978-0-06-195828-1

13 14 15 16 17   OV/RRD   10 9 8 7 6 5 4 3 2 1

JON:
TO MY PARENTS, NANCY AND SHELDON, FOR THEIR ETERNAL
SUPPORT, WITHOUT WHICH I WOULD PROBABLY BE WORKING
A REAL JOB.
MY WIFE, ELIZABETH, AND MY CHILDREN, JOSHUA AND
CHLOE, WHO LEARNED TO FLASH THE DEVIL HORNS LONG
BEFORE THEY DISCOVERED THEIR LOVE FOR SELENA GOMEZ.

KATHERINE:
TO MY MOTHER, ANTONIA. THANK YOU FOR THE WORDS.
PROUD, PROUD.

CONTENTS

In my World

SCOTT IAN

I was eight years old, sitting in my uncle's bedroom at my grand-parents' house, going through his vinyl. I pulled out the first Black Sabbath record. There's woods and a witch, and I'm a little kid looking at this going, "What is this? This is scary." And my uncle goes, "That's Black Sabbath. They're acid rock." I'm like, "What's acid rock?"

So I put it on and it starts with the rain and then that riff comes in and I'm like, "Oh my God." I was a little kid, scared, sitting in my uncle's weird dark room with his black light posters, and I had never heard anything like that. Up until that point I lived on AM radio in the car with my parents, listening to whatever was on WABC in New York. This was my first exposure to anything like that, and I instantly liked it. I went, "What else is like this?" And we listened to Led Zeppelin and Frank Zappa and everything heavy and weird he had in his collection.

I started asking my parents to buy me records, and I watched stuff like *Don Kirshner's Rock Concert* on TV, and this other show, *In Concert*, which were about the only places you could see live performance on TV back then. I got way into music. I had a cousin who was twelve years older than me who was a biker and a musician. He lived down the street from us and I used to hang out in his basement when he'd jam. I'd sit there and watch, and I thought anyone with long hair was the coolest guy in the world, and anyone who had a guitar was the coolest guy in the world. That was my introduction to the world of heavy metal.

We were living in Long Island when I was in fourth, fifth, and sixth grade, and up until I started seventh grade, music to me was really personal. None of my friends were into music. They all played hockey. None of them gave a shit about Black Sabbath or Led Zeppelin. So I'd just sit in my house and practice my guitar and listen to songs. It wasn't until I was thirteen and starting seventh grade that I met kids who were listening to Zeppelin and KISS and Aerosmith and Cheap Trick and the Ramones, and that's when I really started to blossom.

All through junior high and into high school I gravitated toward like-minded people, and we were the little clique that all wore leather jackets and had long hair. By that time my parents had gotten divorced and I was living in Queens. Bayside High School had almost three thousand students, and the core of our group was about ten people. With the periphery kids who would kind of hang out with us, we had maybe two dozen people that were into hard rock and heavy metal. Others were just into disco or pop. In 1978 in Queens, you didn't have a lot of people listening to Rainbow. But we were into all this British and European hard rock; it wasn't even really called metal back in 1978.

At lunchtime, my friends and I had a little boom box and we would listen to cassettes and put these hard rock surveys together. We'd have a page and we'd write down the names Ace Frehley, Jimmy Page, Ritchie Blackmore, Joe Perry. Then we'd walk around the lunchroom and try to get people to rate them one to ten and then try to figure out who's the best lead guitar player. This is how fucking nerdy we were at age fifteen! Everything was about music. And there was always the quest to find the next band. You always wanted to be the guy in the group to come in with something that no one had heard yet that was going to blow them away. One day this kid David Karibian came in with the first Van Halen record in his boom box at lunch time. He said, "Listen to this," and put on "Eruption," and we all sat there with our fucking jaws dropping. We had never heard anything like that before. I remember the first time I heard AC/DC. Another time, my friend Golden brought in *If You Want Blood*, and it was the first time I ever heard Bon Scott. Holy shit. We were on a constant quest, looking for the next cool band or the next heavier band—whoever was playing something harder, faster, more intense.

I bought the first Iron Maiden record at the Music Box, which was this record store in Queens, around 1980. I didn't know anything about the band. I had never even heard of them. I bought it strictly based on the album cover because Eddie looked so fucking cool. And then I put it on and heard "Prowler" and lost my fucking mind, and went in the next day and said, "Oh my God, have you guys heard Iron Maiden?" And, like, four dudes went, "Duh, we got that last month."

We thought we were cool, but we were like the fucking plague when it came to girls. I didn't date one girl all through high school who went to my high school. I didn't go to my prom. As a kid in a leather jacket, ripped Levis, Chuck Taylors, and long hair, you weren't getting hot high school chicks. We were the burnouts. That's what the jocks would call us. They never fucked with us or tried to fight us or anything because I think even they understood we were no challenge at all. You could literally blow on even the biggest one of us burnouts and we'd fall over. None of us were fighters. All we cared about was playing guitar.

But the music made us feel strong, and being with other people who were into the same thing made you feel like you weren't alone or crazy. There's a reason I had Ted Nugent, KISS, and Zeppelin posters hanging all over my room. I'm not just some fuckin' weirdo. Look, there's a whole bunch of other dudes just like me.

By '80 or '81, we had already started getting into heavier, more extreme European metal stuff like Venom, Raven, and Mercyful Fate, and it could never get loud enough. At the same time American hardcore punk bands like Black Flag, Fear, and Circle Jerks were emerging. And all of it was starting to cross over because if you hung out at record stores as much as we did, you would pick up anything in the hopes that you were going to find something cool. To me, there were no genres and there were no categories. It was either good or it wasn't.

Then we got into the British stuff like GBH, Exploited, and Discharge because it was the next most extreme thing out at the time. When I first listened to Discharge's *Hear Nothing, See Nothing, Say Nothing*, it sounded like nothing I had ever heard before. There was an intensity and brutality to that record and that band that I had never experienced in any other music. I didn't realize it at the time, but years later I recognized, "Okay. That's hardcore. That's sheer fucking brutality."

A pivotal point in my life was when I met Danny Lilker around '79. He was a sophomore and I was a junior, and we would walk to school together every day and we started jamming because he also played guitar. Danny was in a band called White Heat, which actually played in the city. In 1980, the idea that you were playing in Manhattan at Great Gildersleeves was amazing! I was totally jealous. We would jam all the time. We hooked up with these other friends and got rehearsal time at the Brewery, which was a rehearsal studio at a shopping center across from our houses. I would tell him all the time, "When White Heat breaks up, you and I are gonna start a band." He would be like, "Huh? We're not breaking up. Why would we break up?" Eventually White Heat broke up.

It was July 28 in the summer of '81. We rehearsed with this kid Paul Kahn on bass. Danny was on guitar then and Dave Weiss was on drums. John Connelly, who went on to become the singer of Nuclear Assault, was on vocals. It went so well and sounded so good; right then we decided we were going to form a band and call it Anthrax because Danny had learned about anthrax at school.

Thirty years later, Anthrax is still a band. Metal has gone through as many changes as we have band members, but it's still as addictive, as important, and as exciting to me as it was when I was a nerdy kid in the school lunchroom. As the ultimate fan, I've voraciously read biographies of my favorite bands, watched metal documentaries, and combed store racks for metal mags.

So I'm excited that *Louder Than Hell* strives to tell the definitive story of metal through the musicians' own—often dirty and grammatically messed-up—words. Some credit Frank Zappa with the anti-rock-crit quip, "Writing about music is like dancing about architecture." But Jon Wiederhorn and Katherine Turman approached their book with true objectivity, letting the musicians do the talking. And there are few better qualified for such a massive task. I remember when Katherine sat behind me and vocalist John Bush on a plane from LA to New York for John's first tryouts and rehearsals in Anthrax. She didn't spill the beans or try to eavesdrop (she told me later!) as the info certainly wasn't out in the press yet, and she'd known John since his early Armored Saint days. Then, we were all at Pantera's New York gig that week. And Jon, who I first interviewed with in the mid-eighties for the now defunct *Power Metal*, has been with us nearly every year since, whether for *Rolling Stone, Guitar, Guitar World, Revolver,* MTV, or AOL. We have a mutual respect that comes out of years of journalistic excellence. Jon's critical eye and technical knowledge is only matched by his ability to relate to an artist like a friend, sharing the triumphs and empathizing with the frustrations.

Stories in this book about forty-plus years of metal—some of which I lived through, others of which are new to me—give me the same kind of teenage excited-dork feeling I get when I'm onstage, looking out at the audience and seeing that they feel it too, whether they're fourteen or forty-five, moshing in the pit, hands reaching out for a pick, screaming the words to "Among the Living." That's what makes metal special—no matter how old you get, you never outgrow it—and that's what makes *Louder Than Hell* timeless. It's a living history you can tap into whenever you want. Anthrax sang it first back in 1984, and we'll stand by it forever: "We're soldiers of metal, and we rule the night."

LOUDER
THAN
HELL

HEAVY METAL
THUNDER

According to scientists the world over, heavy metals are highly dense chemical elements that are poisonous at low concentrations. Since 1869, when Russian scientist Dmitry Mendeleyev published the first Periodic Table of the Elements, twenty-three metals have been deemed "brutally" heavy. Some have even inspired bands to adopt their names, including arsenic, cadmium, cobalt, thallium, and vanadium.

As with their musical namesake, heavy metals can be healthy: copper, selenium, and zinc are necessary for metabolism and present in many multivitamins. Similarly, Metallica is ideal for waking up on sleepy mornings, Guns N' Roses hits the spot when driving long distances at questionably safe speeds, and Black Sabbath helps anaesthetize the brain when it's time to unwind.

Counterculture hero and writer William Burroughs made the first literary reference to heavy metal in his groundbreaking 1959 novel *Naked Lunch*. He liked the term so much he used it again two years later in *The Soft Machine*.

"I felt that heavy metal was sort of the ultimate expression of addiction, that there's something actually metallic in addiction," Burroughs said later.

"There was a guy in our road crew named Peter Wagner, who referred to us as the Heavy Metal Kids," said the late Dickie Peterson, front man for the pioneering sixties hard rock/metal band Blue Cheer. "But I think he did that because the heavy metal kids were the junkies in William Burroughs's books. I don't think he was talking about our music."

Ed Sanders, cofounder of sixties underground folk band the Fugs, called his music publishing company Heavy Metal Music in 1965, in homage to Burroughs. The term *heavy metal* was first used in an actual song in 1968, when Mars Bonfire wrote "Born to Be Wild" for Steppenwolf, but again, the term wasn't meant to label the band.

"I used the phrase 'heavy metal thunder' in 'Born to Be Wild' to help capture the experience of driving a car or motorcycle on the desert highway of California," Bonfire said.

In 1968, *Rolling Stone* writer Barry Gifford used the term in a record review to describe Electric Flag's "A Long Time Comin'."

"I made it up," he insists. "I was just describing the sound of the band, who, of course, bore no resemblance to what later became popularly known as heavy metal."

Even Black Sabbath, who, to most fans, epitomize heavy metal, initially didn't like the term.

GEEZER BUTLER (Black Sabbath, GZR, Heaven & Hell): Someone called us "heavy metal" as an insult in some review. It said, "This isn't music. It sounds like a load of heavy metal crashing to the floor." Somebody in England picked up on that phrase, everyone started using it, and we had no say.

OZZY OSBOURNE (Black Sabbath): In Black Sabbath, we didn't care about what we were called. We were backstreet kids and we went on that stage with a fucking mission—to play music to de-ball any fucker—and we could. In the early stages of Sabbath, there wasn't nobody to fucking touch us.

ALICE COOPER: The first time I ever heard music referred to as heavy metal was in *Rolling Stone*—referring to *us*. I thought, " '*Heavy metal.*' What a weird term that is." But I understood what they meant. I think it was referring to our attitude more than our sound. But we were also a very loud band.

ROB HALFORD (Judas Priest, Halford, ex-2wo, ex-Fight): I dare say we were probably the first to start calling *ourselves* a heavy metal band. Word goes around. I think it's fair to say it really started with Priest and Sabbath.

RONNIE JAMES DIO (1942–2010) (Heaven & Hell, ex–Black Sabbath, ex-Rainbow): Once I became part of a heavy metal band, I was as proud as anyone to be that. It's the kind of music I love. The heavier, the better.

EDDIE TRUNK (DJ, Host of "That Metal Show"): The first Black Sabbath record, [1970's *Black Sabbath*], that's where heavy metal was born—with that album and that song ["Black Sabbath"]. People will say Blue Cheer and Iron Butterfly [were metal], but Sabbath were the first band to embody everything that became heavy metal.

ALICE COOPER: We looked at what the Who did on "My Generation" as one of the first heavy metal songs. That, or [Iron Butterfly's] "In-a-Gadda-Da-Vida." If that came out and Metallica did it, everyone would go, "Oh, yeah, that's metal."

LESLIE WEST (Mountain): To me, heavy metal is like pornography. I couldn't tell you what it is, but when I see it, I know it.

LEMMY KILMISTER (Motörhead, ex-Hawkwind): Metal is the bastard son of rock and roll. If Eddie Cochran was playing today, he'd probably be in a garage playing with a metal band.

JOSE MANGIN (Sirius Satellite Radio): Metal is a lifestyle that includes the music, the fashion, the credo. It doesn't matter what bands you like, it's how you live—how you walk, how you move at a concert, how you talk to people, how you get excited about hearing distorted riffs. It's a motivator. It's therapy. Metal is community and it's a group with no doors.

BOB LEFSETZ (Author of "The Lefsetz Letter"): Heavy metal is not made for Wall Street. It's not intellectual—it's something you feel. It electrifies your body, truly plugs you into the socket and makes you thrust your body forward and throw your hands in the air.

BIFF BYFORD (Saxon): When I first met Ronnie James Dio, we talked about the way he uses the heavy metal sign. This is how he explained it to me: in the deaf sign language, the two fingers and the thumb is "I love you." I think that was the first one he used. The thumb went down later on.

RONNIE JAMES DIO: I'm of Italian extraction; my grandmother and grandfather on both my mother's and father's side came to America from Italy, and they had superstitions. I would see my grandmother, when I was a little kid, holding her hand, walking down the street, she would see someone and [make the devil's horns]. I learned it was called the *malocchio*. Someone was giving us the evil eye, so [with the horns, my grandmother] was giving us protection from the evil eye. So [did I] invent it? No, but [did I] perfect it and make it important? Yes, because I did it so much, especially within the confines of Sabbath. Because I've been lucky enough to have done it so much, it's been more equated with me than anyone else, although Gene Simmons will tell you he invented it, but then again Gene invented breathing and shoes.

GENE SIMMONS (KISS): What I started [before Dio] involved the thumb outstretched. Check our first poster in 1974. I started doing it because of comic book artist Steve Ditko, who created both Spiderman and Dr. Strange, who both used the same hand sign. Spiderman used it upside down when he shot out webbing, and Dr. Strange used it as a magic incantation. I was paying homage. Later, I was told it meant "I love you" in sign language.

DAVE MUSTAINE (ex-Metallica, Megadeth): Most people do it wrong, and I'm not talking about outstretching the thumb. For the real devil's horns, when used as a Satanic symbol, you don't close your middle two fingers and wrap your thumb around them. You leave the middle two fingers outstretched and place the thumb between them so it resembles the snout of a jackal.

BIFF BYFORD: Obviously, now, it is the rock and roll, metal salute. It's lost all the devil connotations. It's just a great salute, isn't it? We're all here, we all like one music. Even models on the catwalk, they'll give the sign—"rock and roll."

ROBB FLYNN (Machine Head, ex–Vio-Lence, ex-Forbidden): In high school, we didn't fit in with the jocks or the nerds. We were the outcasts. We had long hair. We were the nonconformists and we didn't have a choice. But we found a community through heavy metal. We met other people who liked the same music and suddenly we were like, "We are not alone!"

RONNIE JAMES DIO: Heavy metal is an underdog form of music because of the way you dress, how you act, what you listen to. So you're always being put down. It's this fringe music and because it pigeonholes the bands and the fans, together we feel strength with each other and become one big pigeon.

JOE ELLIOTT (Def Leppard): It's everything mimicked in *Spinal Tap*. There is an elitist [attitude] among some of us, and I think I put myself in that group. Sometimes heavy metal gets regarded as dumb, and some of us don't like to be regarded as dumb, so we try to distance ourselves from it.

PENELOPE SPHEERIS (Filmmaker, *Decline of Western Civilization II*): I was approached by Harry Shearer and a producer named David Jablin [to direct *Spinal Tap*]. It didn't work out because I felt like it was making fun of metal, and I loved the music so much I didn't think I should do it. Rob [Reiner] kicked ass, though.

LEMMY KILMISTER: For me, it needs to be big and it needs to be loud. In a club, you can have conversations over bands that are playing jazz or pop music. Nobody can ever have a conversation over my kind of music. With my kind of music, [once] we start, you listen or you leave.

1

KICK OUT THE JAMS: PROTO METAL, 1964–1970

Heavy metal was never officially "born." It came together in bits and pieces between the mid-sixties and early seventies, and stemmed from a desire to rebel, shock, and create a level of intensity that did not then exist in pop music.

Strangely, it was British Invasion band the Kinks that captured the earliest sound of metal in 1964 with their third single "You Really Got Me." The band played blunt, repetitive power-chord guitar riffs that they coupled with a primitive style of distortion—guitarist Dave Davies, taking a cue from surf guitarist Link Wray, used a razor blade to cut slits in his speaker cone to achieve the sound. From there, technological improvements allowed guitarists to use effect pedals to make their instruments buzz like swarming bees, or spiral as if caught in the eye of a tornado.

With louder amps, crazier effects, and plenty of social and political turmoil to inspire them, artists like Jimi Hendrix and bands like Hawkwind, Led Zeppelin, MC5, Blue Cheer, the Stooges, and, of course, Black Sabbath set out to change people's perceptions of just how heavy music could be and what was possible with a bit of creativity and a lot of volume.

OZZY OSBOURNE: The first time I ever experienced the feeling I get from my own music was when I heard "You Really Got Me." I got that tickling up my back, and that's what I always go for when I write.

JIMMY PAGE (ex-Yardbirds, Led Zeppelin): A turning point in effects came when Roger Mayer began making his distortion boxes. I [was] playing this gig in the early sixties when Roger came up to me and said he worked at the British Admiralty in the experimental department, adding that he could probably build any electronic gadget that I wanted. He went away and came up with the first real good fuzz box.

WAYNE KRAMER (MC5): Jeff Beck was one of the pillars of pushing the guitar tone. And then there was [Pete] Townshend with [the Who], Hendrix, Jimmy Page, and what I was trying to do with the MC5. We were all trying to push the guitar so we didn't just play the guitar, we played the amplifier as well. It was about getting that overtone sustain out of the amplifier. That was at the beginning of the invention of stomp boxes—fuzz tones and overdrives.

Flamboyant Seattle-born musician Jimi Hendrix developed some of the most inventive early uses for the distortion box, contorting traditional electric blues into flailing, contentious torrents of sound. That he was just as adept at performing beautiful emotional and psychedelic rock songs is a testament to his brilliance as a musician. Tragically, Hendrix died in 1970 at age twenty-seven after consuming sleeping pills and red wine and asphyxiating on his vomit. Yet in four short years he redefined the rock lexicon with three astonishing albums—1967's *Are You Experienced* and *Axis: Bold as Love*, and 1968's *Electric Ladyland*.

RITCHIE BLACKMORE (ex-Rainbow, ex–Deep Purple): I liked [Hendrix's] direct approach, his snarling guitar. He said a lot in one note. Before then, I was very impressed with people who could run up and down the fingerboard. But Jimi was just holding a note sustained, playing with a lot more feeling. His stage presence was unbelievable. He was like a spaceman.

LEMMY KILMISTER: What fans want is somebody that comes down from another planet that you will never possibly visit, and touches you, and goes away again. That's what a real good rock show is like. Aliens from another world come and kick you in the teeth and fuck off quick, you know? Hendrix was like that. He was really a quiet guy, a gentleman. He played the fucking Chitlin' Circuit for years. But by the time he got to where he was going, he was the fucking best. You'll never see a guitar player like him, ever. Van Halen and all them guys don't even get close. The man would do a double somersault and come up playing. I learned a lot about performing working as a roadie for Hendrix. And that's where I learned how to function on five hits of acid. He handed it out like dolly mixtures [British candy], and I used to go score it for him, too. That was part of my job—getting drugs for Jimi.

ACE FREHLEY (ex-KISS): I was sixteen when I heard *Are You Experienced*. I walked around with it all the time and brought it to school with me to show everybody. I brought it to band rehearsals. I lived with that album until someone ripped it off at a party. Of course, I went right out and bought another one. My guitar style was modeled in part after Hendrix. What really influenced me was his attitude—the way he dressed, the way he looked. He was so antiestablishment and nobody wrote music like him. He wrote about LSD, he wrote about sex and drugs and rock and roll. It was all about rebellion, and he was so radical and ahead of his time it ended up swallowing him up.

CARMINE APPICE (Vanilla Fudge, Beck, Bogart & Appice): Jimi Hendrix. Was he heavy metal? Yeah, he was heavy metal, then. But the drums weren't heavy, the drums were light. I think what makes heavy metal heavy is the sound of your drums. That heavy drum sound is what Vanilla Fudge and Sabbath had.

As difficult as it is to define heavy metal, it's even harder to pinpoint the band that started it all. Some cite Led Zeppelin, the eclectic, majestic group that formed out of the collapse of the Yardbirds. The band featured seasoned session musician and Yardbirds alum Jimmy Page, bassist John Paul Jones, vocalist Robert Plant, and his Band of Joy bandmate John Bonham, a forceful, stylistic drummer whose beats were often a hair behind the rest of the rhythm, giving the music a perpetually lunging feel. Although none of the members of Zeppelin ever called their music metal, they had a major influence on countless metal bands, including Black Sabbath, Judas Priest, and Deep Purple.

JOHN PAUL JONES (Led Zeppelin, Them Crooked Vultures): When Zeppelin started, I listened to blues and jazz. The only rock I listened to was Jimi Hendrix.

RUDOLF SCHENKER (Scorpions): I was in the Star Club in Hamburg expecting Spooky Tooth to play, and the DJ was playing an album. I told one of my friends to ask the DJ what the album was; it was Led Zeppelin. It immediately kicked me like the first album by Jimi Hendrix. From then on, I watched Led Zeppelin carefully. Everything they did was a masterpiece.

MARTIN POPOFF (author, journalist): Jimmy [Page] and Robert [Plant] detest being called "heavy metal." It tells you that their heads weren't in that space, and I think when people's heads are not in that space, they shouldn't be rewarded for having invented that thing.

GLENN HUGHES (Black Country Communion, ex–Deep Purple, ex–Black Sabbath): I've spoken to Jimmy Page about [whether Zeppelin is metal]. It's like, there are moments in [Deep] Purple that you would call metal. And there are moments in Zeppelin.

The influence of Led Zeppelin on hard rock and metal is unparalleled (just listen to early Judas Priest, Whitesnake, Guns N' Roses, Soundgarden, and Jane's Addiction). But there are a number of unsung (at least in metal circles) American bands that also took volume and rage to new heights—especially Detroit's Motor City Five (better known as MC5), the Stooges, and San Francisco's Blue Cheer, all of whom performed with frenetic energy and brazen sexuality that defined the otherness of the counterculture.

DICKIE PETERSON (1946–2009) (Blue Cheer): What we were playing was anti-music to a lot of people. They were saying we can't play that loud, and we were saying, "Yes you can. All you have to do is turn up the amplifier, you idiot." There was a time we went out and people weren't kind to us at all. They didn't know how to take what we were doing because we were one of the first bands knocking on the doors of volume. In 1968 we played with Iggy and the Stooges and the MC5 at [Detroit's] Grande Ballroom, and I honestly think to this day it was really the first metal show ever.

IGGY POP (The Stooges): [In 1967], we were a bunch of misfits livin' together in a house saying, "Yeah, we're a *band*!" But we had not played anywhere. We *couldn't* play. I was trying to figure out like, "What's the *key*?" What could *we* do? I didn't want to just go out and be a cover band, because I knew that was death. I knew that, to take it to where I wanted to go, [there] had to be something really creative—something you couldn't get anywhere else. At first, we didn't know what to do, so [we] ended up hanging around the house taking lots of drugs.

WAYNE KRAMER: We would play the kinds of gigs that were available to us—teen dances and record hops. So we'd play what they expected, these tidy three-minute songs—and then for the last song we'd play [the feedback-saturated] "Black to Comm"—our *real* music. We noticed we could empty a room with it. People would be dancing all night, having a ball, and then we'd break into "Black to Comm" and the fucking room would be deserted. The people fled. We came to the conclusion that what we were doing was very powerful, and if the kids were just educated to appreciate and understand what it was all about, then that same power that forced them out of the room would force them into the room. And it did.

IGGY POP: We found a sound based very much on the MC5. They pointed the way—a pneumatic, industrial, valid, corporate jet mixed in with free jazz—Velvets, the Who, the Stones, Hendrix, Muddy Waters, and William Burroughs.

WAYNE KRAMER: We were part of a community with the Stooges. In our time in Ann Arbor, Michigan, we lived close to each other and hung out a lot. We both loved loud, distorted guitars, and the Stooges and the MC5 were equally crazy, equally aberrant—each in our own way. We were friendly and collegial with our fellows, but I never got the sense that many of them really grabbed hold of what we were talking about. We played at the [1968] Democratic Convention and the Chicago police were standing by. The minute we finished, the kids turned on the police, the police turned on the kids, and the rampage was on.

IGGY POP: These guys flew in from New York, saw me, and went, "We don't know what he's doin' but he's weird. People *like* weird things. We're gonna sign him!" So they sign me. And then they left, and I stayed in my little Midwestern town [Ypsilanti, Michigan]. They called me to New York a few months later, and I made a record [1969's *Stooges*], then went back home.

STEFFAN CHIRAZI (journalist): The Stooges were absolutely vital for the development of metal. They had true raw emotion in spades. [1970's] *Fun House* is such a violent record. When I listen to that first song, "Down on the Street," it makes me want to go down the street and smash windows because it really *is* a "fuck you" song.

IGGY POP: You have this leap from *The Stooges* to *Funhouse* to *Raw Power*. It's very rare that you hear a band that grows that quickly and with that intensity and complexity in three years. It tends to be something more like, "Oh, that's Sabbath, and that's another Sabbath, and that's a little different Sabbath. I was doing something based on the logical progressions and extensions of the way we live—of architecture, art, sociology, anthropology, fashion, crime, porno. There was a lot going on there before anyone else paid attention to that shit.

STEFFAN CHIRAZI: I love that famous quote from Iggy that went something like, "I wanted the guy in the front row to want to fuck me, not the girl." It's such an outrageously obnoxious, flip comment. But he didn't care. He wore makeup but would piss on your head at the same time. He was musically very important as well because a lot of the bluesy riffs were given this thoroughly metallic, androidy crunch.

IGGY POP: [We did] "I Got a Right," which is a really intense, up-tempo song. It was thrash before anybody was doing thrash. [But when we played it], not *one* person would move. They'd just sit there and fuckin' stare at us, like "What the fuck is *this?*" When we played, the room would become like a cardboard cutout. After a while, it got uncomfortable; I was putting this stuff out and it wasn't coming back.

JAMES WILLIAMSON (The Stooges): At [the New York club] Max's Kansas City, Iggy cut himself in the chest with a broken martini glass. But we had seen it all at that point. He's dripped hot wax on himself, and he's been so stoned he couldn't stand up, and people thought it was part of the act. The band was kind of desensitized to stuff like that. He wasn't in any grave danger. It was just flesh wounds. But he got a couple stitches.

BOBBY LIEBLING (Pentagram): Iggy Pop was my hands-down idol. When I was using a lot of coke and heroin I was into the shenanigans that Iggy used to do in the *Raw Power* days. One night I made a big cross on my torso with this spiked bracelet I was wearing. I took it from breast to breast, and then from neck to belly button, and took my stomach and ripped myself wide open crosswise and just stood there looking at the people and bleeding all over the floor, and kept singing just for shock value.

IGGY POP: Stooges tours didn't exist. Nobody wanted to tour the Stooges. People would say, "Don't ever come back here!" And then we did one actual tour, which was our death tour, which *Metallic K.O.* was recorded from. Everywhere we went there was some sort of major disaster. Clubs closed, theaters would arrest us. We played Memphis and [on] the front page of the newspaper was a big picture of me and it said, "Vice squad to attend concert." They came to the concert—five uniformed cops, two plainclothes, all with guns. They let me see their guns and said, "You pull any shit, you're going to jail." [So] I just got drunk and fell down a lot.

He never created an album that's entirely or characteristically metal, yet Alice Cooper is essential to the look and mood of the genre. Vincent Damon Furnier dubbed his band Alice Cooper in 1968 and soon after conceived a mesmerizing theatrical stage show that was equal parts Hammer horror film and French Grand Guignol. He allegedly came up with the "Alice" moniker after using a Ouija board to communicate with a seventeenth-century witch of the same name; he changed his legal name to Alice Cooper in 1974. Hendrix may have electrified the flower child, but as Alice says, "I drove a stake through the heart of the love generation." At the same time, other gender-bending frontmen—such as David Bowie and hell-and-hair-fire man Arthur Brown—impacted the antics of future stars, including Marilyn Manson and the members of Mötley Crüe.

ALICE COOPER: I was a fan of Hendrix and a lot of bands, but I knew I didn't want to be anything like them. For instance, I love Paul McCartney, but I can't compete with Paul McCartney on his level. So I thought, "Let me create a character that *he* can't compete with." I loved drama and I loved horror, and I said, "Well, nobody's doing that in rock and roll. Rock doesn't have a villain. Rock has a lot of heroes, but it doesn't have that *one* villain."

KING DIAMOND (ex–Mercyful Fate): I was totally inspired by the makeup of Alice Cooper. It's not that much makeup, but it totally changes his look and the way he came across to an audience. It felt like he was not of this world. If I had reached up over the stage and touched a boot, he'd probably just vanish in thin air. Right there in my mind I went, "If I'm ever going to be in a band I'm going to use makeup" because of what a strong feel it put across.

ALICE COOPER: When the Beatles walked into a room, everybody wanted to be near them. I always said, "When Alice Cooper walks into a room, I want everyone to take a step backwards." So we created this villainous character. I went to see *Barbarella*. The Black Queen, she had all the leather on and switchblades coming out of her hands. I went, "Oh, that's what Alice should look like. There should be a real dangerous sleekness to him." Then I saw *Whatever Happened to Baby Jane*, and there was this old woman trying to look like she's five years old again with the smeared makeup and all the wrinkles.

I went, "Oh, *that's* Alice, too." So if you combine the two you get something that's really creepy and just unearthly.

RITCHIE BLACKMORE: From the beginning, I thought theatrics were really important to this music. I started incorporating pyro into the show in 1968. At the California Jam [in 1974], I wanted to do something sensational. People had blown the guitar up. So I said, "I'll blow the amp up." I told my roadie, "Just pile some petrol on the dummy amplifier and throw a match to it when I point to you." So he did that, and put too much petrol on there, and, of course, not only did we blow a hole in the stage, one of the cameramen went temporarily deaf. [Drummer] Ian Paice's glasses blew off and half the stage caught fire. It looked great—like it was well in control—but it wasn't. The police came after me, and I had to jump into a helicopter to be rushed out of the area.

ALICE COOPER: The thing about theatrics is there needs to be a punch line. In a movie, if it just ends, you go, "Oh." But if it ends with the villain getting his just desserts there's something really satisfying, even for me. So I knew if I was the villain I would have to die at the end of the show, and that's when we started coming up with all these different ways to kill Alice.

Back in those days we were doing tricks that didn't have safety devices on them. We were hanging Alice one time in London in 1974, and the piano wire that was supposed to stop me before I hit the noose failed. If I didn't have the self-preservation button in my head, it could have hung me. I swung my head back so the rope went over my chin and didn't catch my neck. We should have cut the noose, so in case my neck did hit it, it would fall apart. But I went right to the floor and right through the slot in the gallows and hit the floor and knocked myself out for a couple minutes. At that point we started replacing the piano wire with cable.

ROB ZOMBIE (ex-White Zombie): When I was little and I was an Alice Cooper fan, there were so many weird rumors and insanity. The show was larger than life, and the rumors become bigger than the reality.

ALICE COOPER: At a show in Toronto, somebody threw a live chicken onstage. To this day, I can't understand why anybody would bring a chicken to a rock festival. "Let me see, I got my tickets, I got my wallet, I got my drugs, I got my chicken. Okay, I'm ready. Let's go." So there it was, a white chicken onstage. And I threw it back in the audience and they tore it to pieces. The kicker was the fact that the first five rows were all in wheelchairs. So it was the crippled kids that tore the chicken apart. There were white feathers everywhere. I just figured it would fly away or somebody would get a great pet from Alice, not knowing that I was throwing the chicken to its death. The next day I looked at the paper, and I was as surprised as anybody else. "Alice Cooper kills chicken and drinks blood." I was like, "What?" But when you have an image like Alice Cooper, anything's believable.

For many members of Alice Cooper, Led Zeppelin, MC5, Blue Cheer, Hawkwind, and countless others, alcohol and drugs were a vehicle to creativity, a way to cope with hard times, a source of relaxation, and a pathway to easier sexual escapades. Of course, such escapism was a loaded gun that took the lives of Jimi Hendrix, Led Zeppelin drummer John Bonham, and Stooges bassist David Alexander.

JAMES WILLIAMSON: I don't know of anyone [who was more decadent than the Stooges]. The drugs and decadence weren't an act: it was the real deal. It's hard to imagine living a harder life than that and still surviving. And we nearly didn't.

DICKIE PETERSON: I grew up being told, "If you do marijuana you'll be a slave for the rest of your life," and it only took me ten minutes to realize smoking marijuana was pretty cool. Then it was, "If you take LSD you'll be a slave for life." I took LSD, and I wasn't a slave for life. Then it got to be, "If you take cocaine, you'll be a slave for life." There was a time when I thought, "Hey, I've been taking heroin for six months and I feel fine. You know, just on the weekends." I actually believed that you didn't have to become addicted. I was wrong. The most important thing out of this is, don't lie to the kids. If marijuana is not going to make you homeless and addicted, don't tell people it is, because they'll find out it doesn't, then when they get to the stuff that really [will], they ain't gonna believe you.

LEMMY KILMISTER: My view on drugs has always been you can do whatever you like [on] either side of the gig, except heroin. But don't mess up the gig. When it's time, you better show up and you better deliver. That's the only rule I've got.

JIMMY PAGE: I can't speak for the others [in Led Zeppelin], but for me drugs were an integral part of the whole thing, right from the beginning, right to the end.

CARMINE APPICE: Being on the road back then was pretty wild. Everyone's heard about the mudshark incident with Led Zeppelin.

RICHARD COLE (Led Zeppelin road manager): I was in Seattle with Led Zeppelin and Vanilla Fudge, and we started to catch sharks out the window [of the Edgewater Inn Hotel]. We caught a big lot of sharks, at least two dozen, stuck coat hangers through the gills, and left 'em in the closet. But the true shark story was that it wasn't even a shark. It was a red snapper, and the chick happened to be a fucking redheaded broad with a ginger pussy. And that is the truth. [Zeppelin drummer

John] Bonzo [Bonham] was in the room, but I did it. Mark Stein [of Vanilla Fudge] filmed the whole thing. And she loved it. It was like, "You'd like a bit of fucking, eh? Let's see how your red snapper likes this red snapper!" It was the nose of the fish, and that girl must have come twenty times. I'm not saying the chick wasn't drunk, I'm not saying that any of us weren't drunk. But it was nothing malicious or harmful. No way! No one was ever hurt. She might have been hit by a shark a few times for disobeying orders, but she didn't get hurt.

IGGY POP: I think it was the combination of marijuana and alcohol, which makes you very sensual—and the pill. For the first time, [girls] were all gettin' really free. And a lot of them were goin', "Well, let me try this guy, let me try [that] guy . . ." because they *could* try it!

WAYNE KRAMER: We were in San Francisco once and we met this girl who was a total freak and ended up with the whole band—fucked us all to death. We had a friend who was a photographer and he was hanging out at the hotel, and he happened to come into the room while some of the guys were in the middle of getting it on with this girl. And the *Berkeley Bar* published them. When some of the band members' wives saw the photos, there was hell to pay.

CYNTHIA PLASTER CASTER (groupie, penis sculptor): I got Wayne Kramer and Dennis Thompson [from MC5]. Wayne wasn't at his *biggest*. It wasn't his fault at all. It was a mold failure on my part. I only captured his head and a teeny-teeny bit of shaft. But there was more to come. Actually Dennis came in the mold, speaking of coming. That's only happened twice.

LEMMY KILMISTER: Hawkwind was one of the best experiences I've ever had in a band. Sometimes we'd do three hits of acid before we got onstage and sometimes five, because everybody said it doesn't work two days in a row, but we found out that if you double the dose, it does. But I got busted on the Canadian border, and they fired me. The most cosmic band in the world fired me for getting busted. Can you believe it? But the police had to let me go because they charged me for cocaine, and I really had amphetamines, so I was only in jail overnight. The longest time I've ever been in jail was for four days. That was also a bust, but it wasn't me, it was the chick I was going to screw that night. We ride home, and they opened the trunk of the car and it was full of her pills. I've never been sentenced for anything.

JIMMY PAGE: [Zeppelin tour manager] Richard Cole ran into one of the air hostesses on the [Led Zeppelin private plane] the Starship, and she told him, "You know I made a lot of money off of you guys," and Cole asked her how. "Well," she explained, "when people on the plane used to sniff cocaine they'd roll up hundred-dollar bills to use as straws. Then after they were high or passed out, they'd forget about the money. So we would go around and grab all the money that was laying around."

NEAL SMITH (ex-Alice Cooper): I'd fuck a groupie and kick her on the floor. I had more groupies sleep on the floor than on my bed, I guarantee that.

ALICE COOPER: The very first time the band went to Paris, we felt we had to buy prostitutes, because that was what you would do. We're all from Phoenix, and here we are at the Hotel Arc de Triomphe, and French prostitutes seemed like the right thing to do. They showed up and they were all, like, forty-seven years old, and none of us wanted anything to do with them, but we couldn't get rid of them. When I pictured prostitutes, I pictured something a lot better than that. But these girls were almost like World War II prostitutes. It was disgusting. Then we realized that we really didn't *need* prostitutes. The Hotel Arc de Triomphe was the SS headquarters during the occupation of France. So this place was just as decadent as could be. But the traffic of girls coming in and out was a blur and I honestly don't remember much of anything.

NEAL SMITH: There were twins—a brunette and a blonde—in Zurich, who came up to Alice and my room at the Atlantis Hotel after our show in the fall of '72. The blonde was knockout gorgeous. They follow us into our room, the blonde took my arm, the brunette took Alice's. I was having great groupie sex, but even though I was in the next bed, I don't know what Alice was doing because they disappeared under their covers. Not a word had been spoken by the girls. Eventually, Alice and I both emerged and these two gorgeous girls start speaking to each other in Swiss. They didn't speak a word of English. So Alice and I look at each other and just start talking in English. It was the most bizarre, yet in some strange way, wonderful evening that we'd had on the road. But, of course, there were many. I was with two girls several times in the same room.

GENE SIMMONS: Making and playing music is very exciting but it's not a goal in and of itself. Everyone who's ever picked up a guitar did it to get laid. And if they say, "No, I did it just for the love of music," they're lying to your face.

LEMMY KILMISTER: I don't care what people say. They're in it for the pussy. The music's important too, but it's more about the pussy. Chasing women is my biggest hobby. Actually, no, that's the career. The music is the hobby. I've always liked the strip club. Sure, having a lap dance is a tease, but you can sometimes talk them into it, you know? And you can only talk them into it if you have a lap dance. You can't convince them to go home with you from the bar. I've been with five porn stars over the years. It sounds very glamorous and sexy, but they're just the same when they fuck as anyone else. Then again, I'm not as good in bed as the people I usually fuck, so I suppose it evens out.

TED NUGENT: I toured for the girls. I mean, I toured for the music, but if it wasn't for the sexual adventure you couldn't have got me on the road with a gun to my head. I would have taken it away and shot you with it. If all I had to do was look at those unclean heathens in the front row with their lack of personal hygiene and stenchy leather blue jean material, I'd take up crocheting.

CARMINE APPICE: Sometimes there were these mother-daughter situations. The mother was probably my age at the time—thirty-five to thirty-eight—and the daughter was seventeen. It was the kind of thing where you get a vibe, like you're in the room and you're hanging out with the daughter, then you can see the mother acting weird, like she wanted to be there, so you just sort of play it. You play the cards and it just sort of happens. But in those days, there was no AIDS, so anything went.

LEMMY KILMISTER: One time a chick just climbed up onstage and blew me. I was singing—well, I couldn't stop, could I? But that was in the seventies, when women were more liable to do that.

IAN GILLAN (ex-Deep Purple): I had a fantastic experience in Lebanon. I was working in Beirut in a casino with a band for about three months. There was this dancer, Angelo Manchenia, who tried to kill me one night. We were staying at this house in the mountains. Sounds romantic, but it stunk to high heaven. After we finished at the casino we used to party every night. Manchenia would come home and kick the bottles off the table and start dancing. I was sharing a room with [bassist] Roger Glover, and Manchenia was with this super-tall dancer girl with long red hair. The bathroom was not usable, so we'd stand under the moonlight and do what we had to do. I was doing that one night, and Manchenia pulled a big knife out of his boot and said, "I kill you [because he thought I was having sex with his girl]." Then he realized I couldn't be in the room doing what Roger was doing to his girlfriend and outside by the rocks at the same time. He said, "Ah, I've insulted you, now I have to kill myself." I said, "Is there some way out of this?" He said, "Yeah, we can become blood brothers." So we did. We slashed our hands and let the blood mingle, and we went back in and he forgot about his girlfriend being with Roger and we danced the night away and drank more wine.

Some proto-metal icons liked to push taboos even further than sex and drugs, dabbling in occult or Satanic rituals they viewed as a natural evolution of an uninhibited mind.

NEAL SMITH: [Guitarist] Glen [Buxton's] girlfriend was a friend of [guitarist] Robby Krieger and [drummer] John Densmore from the Doors, so we were going to have this séance. It ended up it was the five of us. This is a rental house, and we paint a pentagram on the floor and all sit around the pentagram. It was Glen, Alice, [guitarist] Mike [Bruce], [bassist] Dennis [Dunaway] and me, and [Doors producer] Paul Rothschild, Jim Morrison, and David Crosby. This chick is trying to conjure up spirits on the other side. Believe me, even though everyone had been drinking or smoking, it was embarrassing. She was screaming and moaning and groaning, and everyone was like, "What the fuck is with this woman? She needs some serious medication." She's probably still fucking crazy.

RITCHIE BLACKMORE: I don't believe in any organized religion. But one of my main passions in life is in communication with entities and spirits. I hear from idiots in the business, who go, "Oh, he's a Satanist. He lights candles in his dressing room." I'm not a Satanist. The reason I used to light candles was to have a little bit of meditation before I went on stage, and I hate the lights that you have in those dressing rooms backstage at, say, Madison Square Garden. But people were convinced that I had an altar in there or something, and I was sacrificing chickens.

MICK WALL (author, journalist): I think Zeppelin's mystical interests were more earnest and sincere than most people's. In the case of Black Sabbath, it was slightly more sci-fi. But for Jimmy Page, [who purchased English occultist and author Aleister Crowley's house], magic was something to be taken seriously.

JIMMY PAGE: It's unfortunate that my studies of mysticism and Eastern and Western traditions of magic and tantrism have all come under the umbrella of [Aleister] Crowley. Yeah, sure, I read a lot of Crowley and I was fascinated by his techniques and ideas. But I was reading across the board. It wasn't unusual at that time to be interested in comparative religions and magic. It was quite a major part of my formative experience as much as anything else.

BOBBY LIEBLING: I was practicing all kinds of black arts and occult and Satanism, and I was a member of the Satanic church in the DC area. I did a lot of incantations and was in an actual coven. One night I was at my friend's house. We always kept a couple of copies of Anton LaVey's original *Satanic Bible* around, and books on witchcraft and spells and the occult. It was July 4, and we were completely sober. We were sitting in the basement and reading from the *Satanic Bible,* and all of a sudden I started to blow a little fog out of my mouth. I was into the reading and hadn't noticed that the room had gotten ice cold. All the pipes in the entire basement formed droplets of water that became icicles. The basement windows were covered with frost and the entire room was about 25 degrees. And this was in a matter of 10 to 20 minutes. I got so scared. I'll never forget it for the rest of my life. To me, it was a sign saying, "You're fucking with the wrong thing, man." It scared me so badly that I just dropped that idea and threw all the artifacts away that came along with the game.

JOE HASSELVANDER (ex-Pentagram, Raven): Bobby conjured up something that scared him to death and he ran out of the house and never came back. Of course, you're supposed to close those doors, but they never did. And I think that's part of why he has had so many problems in his life with drug addiction and a lack of financial success. I really believe that, because something like that happened to me. I found these tarot cards dating back to the Salem witch trials that were at a house in New York where we lived with Raven, and they were coated in human blood. They were horrifying. I took about ten of them and they almost destroyed my life. A spirit was found in two of these cards, and the person who was bound to them had invoked demons and was probably responsible for the Salem witchcraft hysteria. He made people go nuts by sending his cursed objects out to them. It caused an incredible poltergeist outbreak in my house and I had to move. I was in Virginia, and that's why I'm in Massachusetts today. The toilets flushed black, there was an infestation of flies. Objects were flying off the counters at us. The house smelled like Rosewater Lavender, which was an old cologne people used in the 1600s. We would tell the spirit to leave, [but] it would go to another room. I was someone who didn't believe in any of this, and in two weeks I had to become an expert or it would have killed me and my son. Finally, I found out who it was, what it was, and I had to return it to Salem, which I did. Since then it's still been a process getting rid of the residual effects. I had an exorcism done—a cleansing of my house— several times, and I was finally able to leave and put miles between me and it. I'm a very religious person because of it today. I won't go into it any further, but I will say that Cliff Burton from Metallica had the other half of the artifacts that I had, and I really believe they killed him.

ALICE COOPER: I was *never* Satanic. In fact, I'm a practicing Christian now. But when I was at the prime of my Alice Cooper notoriety and I was drinking, there was a big gray area where I started and where Alice ended. I had no idea. I was hanging out with Jim Morrison, Keith Moon, and Jimi

Hendrix, and I thought I had to be Alice all the time. Those were times I was so drunk I don't remember anything. One night I was in a Rolls Royce, I was driving, [Aerosmith singer] Steven Tyler was in the car and we had a gun. The next day I don't remember if we knocked over a 7-Eleven. We could have done anything. There were many, many mornings that I woke up after parties with all the wrong people, where I went, "Please don't let me read about something in the paper that I did." Because when you're drunk and you're Alice, you feel like you have the license to do anything. There were times when people said, "You and Jim Morrison were hanging from a balcony to see which one could hang the longest." I don't remember any of that.

WAYNE KRAMER: If the brain's pickled with vodka and heroin it ain't processing so well and you play for shit. Of course, that happened. And it got worse and worse. It reached a point where the show became something to get out of the way so I could get loaded. Then, it was *all* about getting loaded, and who cared about the show? I was very, very lucky. I can't count the number of times I'd wake up in a pile of puke, someone calls 911 'cause you stopped breathing. You wake up in an ambulance. You wake up with the EMS people standing around you.

ALICE COOPER: I looked around and noticed [that] everyone I was trying to be like was dead. I went, "Okay, I get it. Alice has got to be one thing and I've got to be another thing. I can't coexist with Alice; Alice has to be a character I play onstage." When the curtain comes down he really doesn't want to live my life and I don't want to live his. He lives two hours a night onstage. He doesn't want to play golf, he doesn't want to be married, he doesn't want children. He doesn't like anything except what he's doing onstage, and you leave him up there. To this day, we have a great relationship.

LESLIE WEST (Mountain): I don't remember if I had sex with that many girls. I was probably too busy trying to get high, and I didn't care about the sex. One thing the girls were great for is they could go to the record stores and make sure your album was in the stores, and they knew where to eat really late at night, and a lot of them knew where to find drugs, which was useful back then.

2

MASTERS OF REALITY: SABBATH, PRIEST, AND BEYOND, 1970–1979

As heavy as bands like Led Zeppelin, the Stooges, and Blue Cheer were, they lacked the power and sonic impenetrability of the metal bands that followed their lead. More significantly, they could be rugged or mysterious, but they were rarely both, and they were hardly ever frightening. Black Sabbath changed all that. Built on a foundation of dense, simple power chords, tempos that veered from sludgy to fleet-footed, blues-based solos more fiery than anything by Jeff Beck or Eric Clapton, and vocals more akin to a siren than a human voice, Sabbath was immediately loathed by critics and adored by fans in search of new ways to appall their parents. The band surfaced from war-ravaged Birmingham, England, and attacked with previously unheard aggression and ferocity. Moreover, their landmark 1970 self-titled first album was a witches' brew brimming with lyrics about death, darkness, and the devil. Not long after Sabbath introduced the core ingredients of metal to the masses, other aggressive bands, including Deep Purple, Judas Priest, AC/DC, and KISS, conceived their own formulas for metal domination.

OZZY OSBOURNE: When I was a kid, I was hungry. I had my ass hanging out of my pants. I hated the fucking world. When I heard the silly fucking words, "If you go to San Francisco, be sure to wear a flower in your hair" I wanted to fucking strangle John Phillips [of The Mamas & the Papas]. I was sitting in the industrial town of Birmingham, England. My father was dying of asbestos from industrial pollution and I was an angry young punk.

TONY IOMMI (Black Sabbath, Heaven & Hell): When I first met [bassist] Geezer [Butler], he was out of his brain on acid. I saw him at the club and I thought he'd gone mad. This was before we got together. He was in a band and I was in a different band with [drummer] Bill Ward. We saw this guy trying to climb up the wall and we went, "Christ, look at him." Little did I know it was Geez and I'd be in a band with him for the next forty years.

GEEZER BUTLER: I wasn't on acid. I had a big lump of hash with me. I didn't try acid until years later. But we were quite a wild bunch. Ozzy had already [spent six weeks] in prison [for robbing a clothing store and being unable to pay the fine] when I met him. There were two old nightclubs in Birmingham back then. One was a blues club that used to be open all night long that I used to go to, and there was a soul club that Ozzy used to go to. So, at about six o'clock every Sunday morning, I'd be walking home from the blues club because I couldn't afford bus fare, and Ozzy'd be walking home on the other side of the street from the soul club. We sort of made eye contact, but he was a skinhead and I was a hippie, so we never really talked. Then he put an advert in the music shop I used to go to saying, "Vocalist looking for a band." I went around to his house, and it was Ozzy. So we joined up together in the Rare Breed, but we both left that at the same time because it wasn't happening. Then one night I went around to his house and we said, "Let's put a different band together." He knew Tony. So we went around to Tony's house and asked Tony if he knew any drummers. Bill just happened to be at Tony's house that night, and we got together from there.

SHARON OSBOURNE (manager, TV personality): Tony used to beat Ozzy up in school. Tony was big and strong, and his parents had a little bit of money. He was an only child, Ozzy was one of six. He was never a physical fighter kid, so he got kicked around. When Tony had clothes, those clothes were bought for him. He wasn't going to school with his sisters' knickers on. Ozzy came from an abusive home. He came from nothing. A can of soup watered down for six kids—that was dinner. Ozzy didn't have a school uniform. He was sent to school in pajamas and Wellington boots. And they'd send him home because he wasn't dressed properly and he wasn't washed, so he would go sit on a bomb site because, at that time, half of England was still bombed after the war. When he *was* in school, Ozzy was the class clown because that's how he survived. When you don't read and you don't write and you're an idiot at school and everybody picks on you because you're the dummy, you become everybody's friend by being the clown. So he's really learned how to work people, and that's what he's done his whole life.

TONY IOMMI: Ozzy and I went to the same school and he was a year younger than me, so I used to boss him around, but that was one of those things that everybody did at school to the younger students. I don't think we bullied him. I definitely didn't beat him up.

OZZY OSBOURNE: At school, Tony was, like, the bright kid. His mother had a bit more cash because she had a shop, and he was the first guy to have a car. He was always getting into fights with the friends he'd hang out with. He'd bring his guitar to school and the teachers would get really upset about it. He had a reputation for being a really great guitar player.

TONY IOMMI: When I met Bill Ward, he was in a band called The Rest. I had an advert and they read it and came to my house [to talk] about me playing with them. I thought, "Wow, this is great. They've all got good equipment, and they seem like nice guys," so I joined up. Then Bill and I came back to Birmingham and we were gonna start another band [Mythology]. We saw this one advert saying "Ozzy Zig requires gig." I said to Bill, "I know an Ozzy but he can't be the same one," because he didn't sing as far as I knew. Sure enough, we went around to the address we had and his mum answered the door, and she shouted for him and he came, and I said to Bill, "Oh, no, I know this guy from school." A couple days later, Ozzy came to my house. We said, "Well, we're looking for a singer and bass player," and he and Geezer were looking for a guitarist and drummer, so we teamed up.

GEEZER BUTLER: Ozzy was a complete nutter, which you need to be if you're going to be a lead singer. Eventually he became a great performer, but it took him a long time. In the early days, he used to just stand there petrified, and Tony used to shake him to do something. Even more than the rest of us, he was really insecure. His parents were really down on him because he'd been in prison. They just thought he was wasting his life. So it took him a lot of time to build up confidence, because he certainly wasn't getting it from home.

Iommi's doom-laden guitar tone is partially due to an industrial accident he suffered in his youth. As a result, the left-handed guitarist had to alter his playing style, eventually tuning down conventional strings and combining them with lighter-gauge banjo strings, which bent more easily.

TONY IOMMI: I had been playing guitar for a couple of years when I had the accident. I used to work in a factory and I did gas and electric welding. They used to send metal to me from the next department and I'd weld it. One day this person didn't come in that used to bend the metal and send it to me. So they put me on this machine and I had no idea how to work it. I put my hand in to push the metal in and the machine came down on my hand. I reacted by pulling my hand back, and it just pulled the ends of the fingers off. I was due to leave my job that day. I'd joined a band called the Birds & Bees that were going to be touring Europe. There were two girl singers and they were a really good band, just like the Hollies. So I'd gotten the job with them and I was all excited and I was leaving my job. I went into work in the morning and done the first half of the day up until lunch. I said to my mother, "I'm not going to go back this afternoon." And she said, "You go back. You finish off the day properly." So, of course, I went back. If I hadn't have gone back, it wouldn't have happened. It made me look at the guitar differently, for sure. I had to come up with a different way of playing because I couldn't play the conventional way anymore.

GEEZER BUTLER: I used to see Tony playing in his other band around Birmingham, and I saw this thing on his hand, but I didn't realize the tips of his fingers were gone. I just thought he had something there to protect his fingers. Then when we got together I found out his fingers had been chopped off. It was incredible. He used to spend hours and hours making the tops for his fingers.

TONY IOMMI: I got a Fairy Liquid [soap] bottle, melted it down, shaped it into a ball, and waited until it cooled down. I then made a hole in it with a soldering iron until it sort of fitted over the finger. I shaped it a bit more with a knife, and then I got some sandpaper and sat there for hours sandpapering it down to make it into a kind of a thimble. I found this old jacket and cut a piece of leather off it. I cut it into a shape so that it would fit over the thimble and glued it on, left it to dry, and then I tried it and I thought, "Bloody hell, I can actually touch the string with this thing now!" When I go onstage I put surgical tape around my fingers, dab a little bit of Super Glue on that, and then I push the things on. Nowadays, the people at the hospital make the thimble for my ring finger. They actually make me a prosthetic limb, a complete arm, and all I use is two of its fingertips that I cut off.

CORKY LAING (Mountain): I remember running around some auditorium in New Orleans when Sabbath was opening for us once, and we were trying to find Tony Iommi's finger. He couldn't go on without it. We were all on the floor looking for his finger. It had rolled under an amp.

OZZY OSBOURNE: I said to Tony all the time, "How can you know what strings you're touching if you have no feeling in your fingers?" It's amazing to me. Whenever we've been arguing or fighting or whatever, I've always maintained one thing about Mr. Iommi. You will never find another soul who comes up with better hard rock riffs than him. When we'd be together I'd always be, like, there is no way he can top that riff. Then he'd beat it every time.

TONY IOMMI: I didn't start tuning down live until after the first album [1970's *Black Sabbath*]. I liked it because it made the sound a bit darker. I used to experiment to see if I could get a bigger, fuller sound because there was only one guitarist [in the band]. Most other bands had another guitar player or a keyboard player. So the idea was to try to make the sound as big as it could be.

On paper, the odds of ever making a living—let alone becoming heavy metal legends—seemed heavily stacked against the future members of Black Sabbath. Iommi's hand injury would end the careers of most guitarists; Ozzy was a juvenile delinquent and hardly an accomplished singer; and Geezer Butler started out as a guitar player, not a bassist. And the band performed an odd style of progressive blues that earned it little praise.

SHARON OSBOURNE: Ozzy was never taught the graces in life. Literally, he was never taught that you say "thank you." [He did] certain things that would shock you and I. Ozzy had no education. How's he gonna earn a living? He used to go and kill animals in a slaughterhouse. And Ozzy's totally dyslexic. He had a terrible, terrible time at school because in those days [they thought] you were just dumb [if you were dyslexic]. Nobody knew what learning disabilities were. And because Ozzy had such a tough upbringing, his parents didn't give a shit. Ozzy's attention span is, like, two seconds long. But he's as sharp as a tack, and Ozzy has survived all this time on his gut instinct. He can really suss people out. He doesn't give a fuck. He's not looking for adulation or credibility.

GEEZER BUTLER: The first really crazy thing I remember Ozzy doing was defecating on top of a Jaguar. We did this gig in Birmingham at a university, and the [promoter] stiffed us. So Ozzy went out and went to the toilet on top of his brand new Jaguar. That was a taste of things to come.

TONY IOMMI: Geezer couldn't play bass because he wasn't a bass player when we started—he was a guitar player. But I was already playing guitar. So he switched to bass, and in our first rehearsal, Geezer was actually playing the bass notes on his Telecaster guitar. Eventually he got a bass, but even then we didn't seem to be going anywhere. We became a six-piece band, [the Polka Tulk Blues Band]; we had a sax player and a slide guitar player, and it was a horrendous row. We decided we didn't need a sax player and a slide player. Everybody was just trying to get solos in. But the only way we felt comfortable about removing them was to say we were going to break up. We broke up for a week and then we got back together as [Earth, and it was] just the four of us.

GEEZER BUTLER: We used to love bands like Jethro Tull, Led Zeppelin, Cream, and Hendrix. But we knew we had to come up with something different to get noticed. And we discovered that playing blues was a great form of music to use as a base for whatever else you want to do because it was just, like, twelve bars and three notes. You could really improvise when you were playing onstage. Getting into the heavier stuff just came as a natural progression.

Earth's big bang happened in 1968, when Jethro Tull guitarist Mick Abrahams left the band and front man Ian Anderson asked Iommi to join. Iommi was ambivalent but decided to make the move, and appeared with Jethro Tull in the film *The Rolling Stones Rock and Roll Circus*, which remained unreleased until 1996. Iommi ultimately returned to Birmingham to continue with Earth. To this day, he credits Tull for introducing him to the kind of work ethic he brought back to Sabbath.

TONY IOMMI: I told Ozzy, Bill, and Geez, "Look, I've been asked to join Jethro Tull. What do you think?" And they said, "You should go for it." So I did. And when I went up to rehearse with Jethro Tull I took Geezer with me to London because I felt really weird not being with the other guys. I really missed them. I felt a bit out of place. I didn't want to join a band that was already doing well and just be the guitar player. I wanted to be a part of a team.

IAN ANDERSON (Jethro Tull): In his early days, before Black Sabbath was born, we brought Tony into Jethro Tull very briefly because we loved his playing. Tony is what we call the "prototype" of heavy metal. His guitar playing and the monophonic riffs that he came up with were something not entirely unique, but a natural evolution from the more loose, blues-based jamming in bands like Cream just a couple years before.

GEEZER BUTLER: We saw the way Jethro Tull worked, and we couldn't believe it. They used to go in at nine o'clock in the morning and work all day until five, like a regular nine-to-five job. And we realized that's the way you gotta do it. You can't just go to some pub and rehearse for an hour and then get drunk. You gotta really put your mind to it and take it seriously. That's what gave us the kick up the ass that we needed.

TONY IOMMI: That's when I said to Geezer, "Let's get the band back together." We called Ozzy and Bill from London and said, "Look, we're coming back. If everybody is really serious about this, I'll leave [Tull] and we'll get back together again and really work at this."

OZZY OSBOURNE: We were four regular guys with a dream, and we worked really hard and it came true, way bigger than what we ever expected.

TONY IOMMI: I started coming up with riffs and writing songs. I played this really heavy riff one day [that evolved into] "Wicked World." Then I came up with "Black Sabbath," which was a really different thing at that time. That paved the way. When I first played that riff, the hairs stood up on my arm and I knew, "This is it!" It was like being told, "This is the way you're going from now on." The rest of the album came from there, and everything fell into place.

That three-chord riff in "Black Sabbath" has been credited as the first use of the tritone, or *diabolus in musica*, in heavy metal. In the Renaissance era, the tritone was feared by the Church because of its ominous sound. Later on, various classical composers—including Richard Wagner and Gustav Holst—would incorporate the tritone into their compositions.

CHRIS BRODERICK (Megadeth, ex-Nevermore, ex-Jag Panzer): "Black Sabbath" is a classic example of the tritone. It starts with a tonic, goes to the octave, then the tritone. [It's] basically the distance from one pitch to the next; [it's] also known as the "flat five." What this basically translates into is a very dissonant-sounding interval. When they hear it, most people want to cringe a little bit. It's a tonality that invokes a certain mood, a certain attitude. It suits metal.

GEEZER BUTLER: I was a big fan of Gustav Holst's *The Planets* at the time. I loved [the] "Mars" [movement], and that [used] a tritone. I used to always play that on the bass when we were rehearsing and I think somehow that got into Tony's head, and he came up with a different tritone that became "Black Sabbath."

MICK WALL: The very first time they played the song "Black Sabbath" was in a pub called the Pokey Hole in Lynchfield in the middle of the Midlands. They were used to people drinking and talking right through the set every time they played. When they played "Black Sabbath," everybody stopped what they were doing and listened.

TONY IOMMI: We did six weeks in Switzerland and we had a gig in England on the day we came back. We arrived at this place and there was a guy there at the front door with a bow tie and a suit. We thought, "Bloody hell, this is weird," because most of the places we played at were certainly not like *that*. The guy said, "Okay, let's get your gear in and get ready." And as we're getting the equipment in he said, "Oh, I really like your new record." We said, "Oh, thanks," but we hadn't done a record at that time. It turned out that this guy had booked the wrong Earth. There was another band called Earth, and they were a pop band. We played the show and people stood there with their mouths open. We died right there onstage. We said, "That's it. That's never gonna happen again. We're gonna find a name that nobody else has." Hence Black Sabbath. That movie was playing at a theater across the street from where we rehearsed. We thought, "What a great name for the band."

When we went under the name Black Sabbath it opened the doorway to everything for us.

OZZY OSBOURNE: With a name like Black Sabbath, what do you expect? And the album cover wasn't exactly about a bunch of flowers. In the beginning, we decided to write scary music because we really didn't think life was all roses. So we decided to write horror music. Then we started to read books about the occult and we realized that it wasn't just a thing that movies were made from. It was real. There was a *thing* called the occult. We never realized what exactly we were getting involved in until we started getting success and all these nutters started sending us letters. We never dealt with the occult ourselves. Different crazy people asked us to play at their black masses and other ceremonies. I just didn't take it onboard, so it wasn't scary. If you let it in, you're a fucking idiot. If you play with the dark stuff, you're gonna have some bad shit happen.

GEEZER BUTLER: The occult was interesting for me and it was very fashionable at the time. Once, somebody sent Ozzy this really old book about witchcraft. It was all in Latin and it had to be three hundred years old. I got this weird vibe off that book. I was living in this one-bedroom apartment at the time with a shared bathroom. I didn't want this book in the same room as me, so I went out into the hall and shoved it in the bathroom cabinet where the towels were kept, and went to bed. In the middle of the night I felt this presence. I woke up and there was this black shape looming over the bottom of the bed and I couldn't really make out what it was, but I could just see the outline of it. It frightened the pissing life out of me. When I jumped up to turn the light on there was nothing there. I thought, "It's that pissing book." So I went out at four in the morning to get the book to throw it in the bin and it was gone. I told Ozzy about it because it was him that gave me the book, and that incident inspired him to write the lyrics to "Black Sabbath" as a warning to people that were getting heavily involved in black magic. Of course, the lyrics got so completely misinterpreted. If you listen, they're saying, "If you're going to get into it, be serious about it. Otherwise, don't dabble in it." But everybody thinks it's about worshipping Satan.

TOM BEAUJOUR (editor, *Guitar Aficionado*): At that time, messing around with the occult was part of the hipster subculture on some level. But taking that and turning it into a template for a band was such a weird and powerful thing to do.

ROBERT TRUJILLO (Metallica, ex-Ozzy Osbourne, ex-Suicidal Tendencies): When I was a kid, we'd sit there and listen to my friend's older brother's vinyl and play the song "Black Sabbath." We'd look at the album cover and freak ourselves out, totally. It was like watching a horror movie. I would have to say Black Sabbath is the first heavy metal band to kick me in the ass for real, scare the living shit out of me.

LEMMY KILMISTER: Sabbath were fucking great. They seemed dangerous, and basically, you want [your rock stars to seem like] dangerous people. If you read history, you don't read about the fucking medieval agrarian reforms. You read about Attila the bloody Hun and the Norman conquest of Britain— something with swords in it. The subject of evil is obvious for rock and roll. Look at the news every night. That's evil. We're all just singing about it. We're not scared of it.

GEEZER BUTLER: The critics hated us. They totally wrote us off. We thought everybody hated us. We didn't really believe anyone liked us until *Black Sabbath* reached number eight on the UK Albums Chart in [February] 1970. We were absolutely shocked. We knew we had a strong local following, but we hadn't really made it in London. We used to have to play northern England, so we weren't expecting the album to do anything. And we'd been turned down by three or four managers in London. Nobody wanted us. And then suddenly the album came into the charts and everybody started believing in us, especially the nutters. We were invited to the Witches' Sabbath, which was at Stonehenge in England. We refused to go. So, apparently, the head warlock put a curse on us. Then the head white witch of England called us up and told us about this curse and that we had to start wearing crosses to keep the curse away, and that's how we all ended up wearing crosses.

Black Sabbath was the first major metal band to break out of Birmingham, England, and gain worldwide acclaim. However, Judas Priest wasn't far behind. The band formed in 1969 with singer Al Atkins, the same year Earth changed its name to Black Sabbath.

K.K. DOWNING (ex-Judas Priest): The Sabs got an album jumpstart on us, but that was great. It was good to see that a band relatively comparable to ourselves had some success. Everyone was playing it, and that was great news for the Priest because it made us think, "Yeah, if we stick with what we're doing this is really going to happen."

IAN HILL (Judas Priest): There was a nucleus of musicians in the West Bromwich area of the Midlands right outside of Birmingham who were all hungry, all proficient. And they'd form three or four bands between them. If they didn't make it in about six months, they'd all split up. The different combinations of the same musicians would then form another three or four bands. Judas Priest [featuring Al Atkins on vocals] was one of those. They were together for about six months, didn't get anywhere, and split up. And [guitarist] Ken [K.K. Downing] and myself and the drummer John Ellis were in another band [called Freight], and we didn't have a singer yet.

K.K. DOWNING: Alan Atkins was down at our practice room one day with his bass player and he must have been listening out-side the door.

IAN HILL: Al heard us and asked if we needed a vocalist because [his band], the original Priest, had just split. None of us had a very good voice, so we jumped at the chance. We had a couple of very long head-scratching sessions trying to come up with a name for the band, and came up with nothing. Alan said, "Do you fancy calling it Judas Priest? I'll call the other band members and see if they mind." Nobody did, so we took over the name.

K.K. DOWNING: The first show we ever did with Alan as a four-piece was at a workingmen's club. There were lots of cute girls there in hot pants, and we were doing a selection of our own songs and a couple songs by an obscure band called Crater Mass. People didn't know what to think.

IAN HILL: Al's a good singer, but he left the band in 1973 be-cause he needed money and we weren't earning anything. We were living off friends and girlfriends and our families. But Al was already married with a child. So he had to leave, and that's when Rob came along.

ROB HALFORD: I saw Priest play at a place in Birmingham, and at that time the music was a mixture of psychedelic blues and progressive rock. You could sense it was a new band that was getting its legs, but it was difficult to pinpoint what the band was about.

IAN HILL: I don't think either [K.K.] or myself had seen him or heard him, but I was dating Rob's sister [Sue]. And she said, "Why don't you try Rob?" He was in a band at the time called Hiroshima. We went to Rob and Sue's parents' house and Rob came down the stairs doing harmonies to an Ella Fitzgerald song. I went, "Ooh God, at least the guy can do harmonies."

ROB HALFORD: I can't remember what song it was. It could quite well have been [Ella Fitzgerald]. I don't know if I would have been thinking, "Oh, Ian's in the house, I better start wailing." But what's interesting about that is it shows that as a singer I love all kinds of singing performances, no matter what genre.

IAN HILL: Rob brought this drummer John Hinch from Hiroshima. There was some discussion over whether we should use the name Hiroshima or keep the name Judas Priest, seeing as it was a halfway split. Ken and myself voted for Judas Priest and Rob and John wanted Hiroshima. But Priest had been around a year longer than Hiroshima, so we kept the name. I think we made the right choice.

ROB HALFORD: We used to go to this place called Holy Joe's right outside of Birmingham, where we lived. It was this little room, 50-by-50 foot, and it was connected to a high school next to a church. The local parish priest, Father Joe, would rent out this room and we'd give him 5 quid [about $8] to rehearse for the day and night. And the venue itself was nicknamed the Holy Joe, which is kind of cool. Holy Joe and Judas Priest! We didn't have any songs. We were doing a jam with some heavy blues and I would just scat some words together, but it felt so good. It felt like we were all connected, so we decided to keep going forward and write our own material. Then we got to the point where we decided we could do more with the songs if we had two guitarists.

GLENN TIPTON (Judas Priest): My old band, the Flying Hat Band, was with the same agency in Birmingham as Judas Priest. We were on the verge of breaking up when Priest asked me to join. They'd seen me play and perform. As soon as we got together we realized pretty immediately that there was something special there, especially in terms of writing.

While Judas Priest was still finding its feet, Black Sabbath was finishing its self-titled debut, which was recorded live and mixed over two days. Then the band seized the moment, touring Europe and leaving audiences bewildered by their fiercely loud, improvisational, and dramatic sets.

GEEZER BUTLER: We went to Switzerland and Germany for six weeks, and we were literally playing for eight hours a day. We were on tour constantly. But it was good because we got really tight musically. We sort of knew what each other was going to play before we even played it. So we became a really good rhythm section. I loved the way Bill [Ward] always got that kind of swing in his playing. It's great for a bass player to play along with. But since we were playing so much, we only had enough material from the first album, which lasted for about an hour. So we had to make stuff up for the next seven hours. We jammed about onstage and gradually came up with most of the *Paranoid* album. By the time the first album was out, we'd already had 90 percent of the second one written.

TONY IOMMI: The second album wasn't even going to be called *Paranoid*. We hadn't gotten enough songs to fill the album. So we were asked to come up with another song. I sat there during a lunch break and came up with "Paranoid." When the other guys came back, I played it to them. They thought it was good, so we recorded that as a filler. And the bloody thing became the most popular track. The album was originally going to be called *War Pigs*. But that title was banned because of the word *pigs*. We got all sorts of shit from the record company. So they named the album *Paranoid*, which didn't go with the cover at all. There's a guy standing there with a shield and a sword. What's that have to do with being paranoid?

GEEZER BUTLER: The cover didn't have anything to do with "war pigs," either, really. That's like the cheapest album cover the record company could come up with, I think. It's horrible and we hated it, but we didn't have any say in the matter, so we were stuck with it. Also, *War Pigs* wasn't originally called "War Pigs." It was "Walpurgis." It's sort of like the Satanic Christmas. I was writing *Generals gathered in the masses* because that's what Satan is. War was the big Satan, not somebody who lives in the clouds. I was making an analogy, and Warner Bros. didn't like the title because it was too Satanic, so we turned it into *War Pigs*, which is a better title anyway. In the end, they thought "Paranoid" was the standout track, so that's what they called the album, and in England it was the number two single.

MARTIN POPOFF: *Paranoid* is so much more of a trouncing heavy metal album than the first Black Sabbath album, but there are certain things that are done really well with *Black Sabbath*, and that's scary lyrics, a scary album cover, the devil's tritone, and big, bulldozing riffs, but the actual *Black Sabbath* album doesn't do that nearly as well as *Paranoid* or *Master of Reality* do.

GEEZER BUTLER: We didn't want *Paranoid* to have one sound or one tempo all the way through like a lot of bands did back then. "Hand of Doom" was quite a long song. The lyrics came from when we played a couple of American bases in Germany and England. I got to speak to some of the soldiers there, and they had just come back from Vietnam. They told me about the amount of soldiers there that were addicted to heroin because Vietnam was a horrible experience. They had to do drugs just to get through it. You never saw that side of it on TV.

LESLIE WEST: Frank Barcelona was our agent at Premiere Talent. It was Black Sabbath's first tour, and our agent said, "I have a great opening act for you." I said, "What's their name?" He said, "Black Sabbath." I said, "What are they, an R&B group?" I didn't know anything about them, but we became great friends with Ozzy.

OZZY OSBOURNE: Mountain was the first band we played with in America. We used to sit on the side and just watch them. They were amazing, absolutely brilliant. People forget that originally Sabbath was based on a blues-jazz band. Mountain reminded me very much of an American Cream.

GEEZER BUTLER: When we got to America we started seeing some of our success. Once we started getting paid for gigs, it was really rewarding. But you know, you'd end up in hotels with nothing to do after the show except loads of groupies and loads of things to shove up your nose. Then, before you know it, your money's gone. But it was mainly out of boredom, really. There was no television on. There were, like, three channels back then. It was so different when we went to the States than it was in Europe. You meet the *real* groupies in America. The ones who *know* how to party. These people were made for partying, whereas in Europe everybody was miserable. So we loved it. It was a completely new lifestyle to us.

TONY IOMMI: We had our day with [groupies] when we first went to the States, and LA in particular. God, we had all sorts of women. One of the guys that worked with us at the time happened to catch bloody syphilis. That sort of dampened the whole thing.

While U.S. audiences were immediately responsive to Sabbath's foreboding atmospheres, blaring guitars, and trudging rhythms, they were also captivated by the hysteria the musicians engendered, and sometimes took their occult-inspired themes too literally.

MICK WALL: Black Sabbath understood that people were reacting to them in this bizarre way because their music has clearly conveyed that image and message, but they themselves were utterly freaked out at this suggestion. When [Church of Satan founder] Anton LaVey had the Black Sabbath parade in San Francisco when they first came to America, they were watching it on TV and went, "What the fuck is this?" There'd be gigs where witches would show up in black cloaks and Sabbath would play stupid, thicko boy tricks on them. The occultists were being very serious about it, and Sabbath weren't.

TONY IOMMI: You open a can of worms sometimes that you can't control. One time, we were playing at the Hollywood Bowl. We arrived at the gig and on the dressing room door was a red cross. We thought, "Oh, that's odd." As we're doing the show, I was in a really bad mood. I was pissed off because my gear was acting up. I kicked my amp over and went to walk off. As I'm walking off this guy comes behind me with a dagger, and he was about to stab me. He got past security and I just heard this big scuffle on the floor. That's how close I came to being stabbed.

MICK WALL: In those days, they were doing so much coke it was like, "Oh, someone went to stab me, wow! Give us a line then? Cool! Wow! Shit." Going to America was such a foreign concept for them. You might as well have been going to the moon. It's like going from black-and-white TV to color. Anything could happen. "Jesus, of course someone tried to stab me. It's America. It's Hollywood!"

TONY IOMMI: It's funny, because some people think those first two albums were recorded in a haze of drugs, but we didn't have time when we did the first two albums. We were in the studio one day, recorded the first album. And then *Paranoid* was only a couple days and then we were out. There wasn't time to indulge in anything.

GEEZER BUTLER: We couldn't afford anything. When we first started we'd have, like, one joint between us all. We couldn't afford booze either, so none of us drank. The first time I tried acid was unknowingly when somebody spiked me. It was before we went to America. We did this outdoor concert and somebody gave me this pill and said it was speed, and it was actually three doses of acid in one tablet. I got back to where I was living and I used to have all these pictures of Satan and occult pictures on the wall, and all this stuff came to life. There were all these snakes trying to bite me. It was horrendous. I was in my bedroom, but the bedroom turned into the middle of the desert. Then I was a Roman soldier. It was absolutely mental. We had a gig the next day in the middle of this park. And as we were driving through the park, all the flowers were trying to get into the car to strangle me. Later, when we got to America, I tried acid again in California, but that turned bad as well, so I couldn't do it. You can't control yourself. It just turned into a nightmare. For some reason with me, it always went bad.

As with the British Invasion in the sixties, England lit the first heavy metal flames with Black Sabbath and Judas Priest. By 1970, a New York band called Wicked Lester—which, three years later, changed its name to KISS—entered the fray. Although the group was never as definitively *metal* as Sabbath or Priest, it nonetheless altered the face of stadium rock and influenced everyone from Mötley Crüe to Pantera (whose guitarist, Dimebag Darrell Abbott, was buried in a KISS Kasket, the branded casket by the band KISS). Wicked Lester was comprised of bassist Gene Klein (born Chaim Witz, later known as Gene Simmons); his childhood friend, guitarist Stephen Coronel; keyboardist Brooke Ostrander; and drummer Tony Zarrella. At the suggestion of Coronel, they hired Stanley Eisen (later known as Paul Stanley) on rhythm guitar.

GENE SIMMONS: I was going to college and we were practicing at a loft in [New York City's] Chinatown. It was a dump. The stairs were wood and they were covered with carpet, but they weren't very sturdy. You could pull out the step of your choice and use it to start a fire. I'd go to work in the afternoon, then come right there and we'd practice. We were really innocent back then. We were just going forward blindly.

PAUL STANLEY (KISS): It was so hot we left the doors open. One night we were playing and all of a sudden a guy about six feet five was standing there barefoot in a green hospital gown. We said, "Can we help you?" and he said, "I just escaped from the hospital." We didn't know what to do, so we continued playing. He's dancing around and we're rocking, and finally we were able to coax him out the door. For all we knew, he was an escaped murderer. We'd always lock the door after that. We were naïve, but we weren't stupid. We had metal paneling over all the windows, but once, someone very determined clipped the lock and took all our things out the fire escape. We showed up for rehearsal, and it was like a cartoon. The drummer said, "Hey, where are my drums?" The guitarist went, "Where's my amp?" And then we realized we'd been robbed. There was nothing left but a microphone, so clearly we were robbed by an instrumental band.

GENE SIMMONS: Paul used to come in with green high-heeled boots and tight leather pants, with his balls lifted and separated. He prided himself on how he looked and he tried to carry himself as a star. We both did. The other guys never got it—especially Coronel. He was more of a musician, and he used to dig into Stanley, and say, "Who do you think you are, dressing like that? You think you're some kind of rock star?" So Paul turned around one day and said, "Yeah. I have an aura shining over me."

PAUL STANLEY: I told Gene that when I walk around, people notice me, and he was ready to strangle me. I wasn't fucking with him or anything, I was serious. I made this happen. I was a tubby young guy that nobody wanted to know. My pants used to rub together when I walked and they used to wear out between the legs. My ass was as big as my stomach. But I made myself into something else, something that I wanted to be and that I was more happy with. I created my dream.

GENE SIMMONS: We always worked hard, and when we didn't have any [money] Paul and I would busk, singing Beatles and Byrds songs for spare change. We made $9.75 one night and ate like kings when $1.25 could buy you a full Chinese dinner.

PAUL STANLEY: After a couple shows, we were able to convince this guy Ron Johnsen who worked at Electric Lady Studios to record our demo. Everyone recorded at Electric Lady: the Rolling Stones, John Lennon, Bob Dylan. It was incredible. Stevie Wonder used to come in there and take a leak with a girl holding his dick.

GENE SIMMONS: That was where we got our first groupie. We were on the corner just watching people walk by and Paul saw this really tall girl coming down the street in high heels. He dared me to go and pick her up. So as she walked by I said everything I could. I mean, tires and kitchen sinks came out. Before long, she came down with us. She didn't have a clue who we were. We were nobody. But within an hour she was in the sound booth blowing two guys. Then she was with five guys at the same time and everybody lined up to take a look, including the producer and his wife. It was like, "Wow, we're musicians now. This is rock and roll!"

When Ron Johnsen presented the Wicked Lester demo to Epic Records, the label liked the songs, but thought Coronel's afro-and-glasses look distracted from the band's vibe. So Wicked Lester replaced him with session player Ron Leejack and continued working on their debut. A year later, they handed the album over to Epic, which hated it and dropped the band. Discouraged but not demoralized, Simmons and Stanley decided they needed a flashier presentation and brasher sound to succeed. So they fired

Zarrella and Ostrander and finalized their lineup with drummer Peter Criss, who had run a "drummer seeks band" ad in *Rolling Stone*, and guitarist (Paul) Ace Frehley, who replied to an ad Gene and Paul placed in the *Village Voice*.

PAUL STANLEY: The first time we played with Peter, it didn't sound too good. But something made us try it again, and it sounded much better. It was pretty clear at this point that this was going to work. Plus, he totally looked like a rock star.

GENE SIMMONS: Ace came in looking like a bum. He was wearing different-colored sneakers—I think it was red and orange. We were having a conversation with someone else we were auditioning and he walked right by, plugged in his guitar, and started messing with the amp. We said, "Uh, we're talking to someone. Would you wait until it's your turn?" He was totally oblivious to anything else that was going on—just totally rude. So we were like, "Let's let this guy try out and get him out of here." We told him we were going to play "Deuce" and that when we reached the solo part he should let fly. We weren't expecting much. But we started playing and hit the solo part, and Ace blew us away. We could not believe it. We knew that was the sound of KISS.

PAUL STANLEY: We looked like rock stars, we acted like rock stars, but if you had seen our practice space at the loft at 10 East Twenty-third Street in New York, you would have laughed.

GENE SIMMONS: There was wall-to-wall humanity sleeping in the hallways of our loft, and you'd step over whatever needed a good night's sleep to get to your practice space. We were paying $200 a month rent. The place was rat and roach infested. We covered the walls with egg cartons to muffle the sound so we could really play loud, but some of the broken eggs and the shells stuck to the cartons, and the roaches loved it. It was like an "à la carton" feast for them. After we hired

Peter and Ace, we'd rehearse until one or two in the morning almost every day. When the lights went out you'd hear the roaches running all over the place. It sounded like a very bad drum solo. Once I had a girl in bed with me and when she woke up there was a dead roach under her. She didn't appreciate that much.

PAUL STANLEY: I was driving a cab, and I got Ace [a job] doing that too for a while. We'd drive around, show up for practice, and afterwards I'd get back in my cab and make some money. We wrote "Strutter," "Black Diamond," and "Deuce" in that place.

Inspired by makeup-wearing artists like the New York Dolls and David Bowie, KISS started painting their faces in early 1973, but realized almost immediately that the androgynous glam look wasn't for them. So they went the opposite way, creating black-and-white kabuki-style designs that masked each member as a separate character. Simmons was the fire-breathing, blood-drinking demon; Stanley was the starchild; Frehley a spaceman; and Criss a cat.

GENE SIMMONS: We knew we had to move away from the New York Dolls thing. So we bought some black T-shirts and some glittery pants that circus performers wore. Then we went down to the West Village—the gay section of the city—and bought leather items at a hardcore sex shop. I don't know why we did it—as far as I knew, none of us had ever tried the S&M or gay thing. But there was something about the studs and the leather that seemed right to us.

PAUL STANLEY: There were no I-wanna-be-a-rock-star-stores [like Hot Topic] back then. So we had no choice but to go down to the forbidden area of the city and buy our stage clothes. It wasn't easy shopping in these stores, but we knew it would pay off.

GENE SIMMONS: We loaded in for our gigs in the afternoon because we wanted everybody to think we had a road crew. They would show up and, lo and behold, there was our equipment, which consisted of speaker cabinets with no speakers in them, just to make it look like we had a Roland amp, and we would tell the guy not to put a spotlight on them, because if they did, you'd see right through them.

PAUL STANLEY: We never wanted to play the same area too often because we wanted people to believe that we were busy. While the other trendy bands were hanging out at Max's Kansas City doing a fashion show for each other, we were practicing.

GENE SIMMONS: Today, everybody thinks there was this great rush forward and everyone was really believing in what we were doing. The truth is very different. One time, Paul left my bass under the bed before we left for the gig. Well, you know the old adage, "Is there a doctor in the house?" We went onstage and made an announcement, "Does anybody have a bass?" This kid in the audience says he's got one, so he goes home and gets a hack-strung bass guitar no better than the box that you have at home with the rubber bands attached to it—the worst piece of shit you ever heard in your life. Somehow we got through the show.

Once they had fine-tuned their craft, KISS again invited Epic vice president of A&R Don Ellis down for a showcase. The band performed their best new songs, including "Firehouse," "Strutter," and "Deuce," but Ellis was used to the pop-rock sound of Wicked Lester (whose record he had previously rejected), not the pedal-to-the-floor adrenaline rush of KISS. The dramatic embellishments only added to his lack of interest, and Ellis opted out for the second time.

GENE SIMMONS: We played "Firehouse," and at the end of the song we start ringing this bell, and Ellis thinks it's a real fire.

So Paul runs over to the corner and grabs a red pail with the word *fire* on it and throws it at Don, who freaks as a bucketful of confetti goes all over the place. He gets up and starts to walk out, saying, "Okay, thank you, I'll call you." As he's heading for the door, he trips and falls. Then, Peter [Criss's] drunken brother, who was sitting behind Don, throws up on his foot. We never heard from him again.

PAUL STANLEY: Fortunately, Ron Johnsen, who did our Wicked Lester album, still owed us $1,000 for some backup singing Gene and I had done for him. So we called him and he said he could pay us in studio time. We agreed, and we knew Eddie Kramer hung out there and produced. He was the best. He had worked with Jimi Hendrix, Led Zeppelin, you name it. So we said to Ron, "We'll take the money you owe us in recording time, but only if Eddie Kramer produces our demo." After we did the demo with Eddie we got signed by Neil Bogart and ended up on Casablanca Records.

While KISS knew how they wanted to look almost from the start, it took Judas Priest some soul searching—and shopping—to find the leather, studs, and roaring motorcycles that became a template for metal in the early eighties. In the meantime, they honed their sound to a razor sheen.

IAN HILL: In the seventies, we wore velvet and satin and tried to squeeze our girlfriends' shoes on. The way people dressed was still very hippie-based, and that flowed over into our stage clothes.

GLENN TIPTON: If you look at what Hendrix and Cream were wearing, we weren't far from that. We had flares and there were a few Cuban heels on the old boots. Very dangerous on-stage, I may add. Fortunately, we all managed to get through that era without snapping our ankles.

ROB HALFORD: There were tremendous things happening with Priest in the seventies. We got our record contract. We release *Rocka Rolla* [in 1974], which was a good first effort. Suddenly your music is available around the world, which is tremendously exciting. We had great tracks like "Never Satisfied" and "Cheater." But I think a lot of people say it's a band's second release that becomes very, very important to them, and that was certainly the case with *Sad Wings of Destiny* in 1976.

MARTIN POPOFF: It felt like that Jimi Hendrix moment where something just descended from the skies—a bunch of nobodies not even on a major label making a record that just wiped the slate clean with everybody. One of the interesting things about *Sad Wings of Destiny* is that it arrived at a time when all the big dinosaur bands of the era seemed to be faltering somewhat. Judas Priest had very dramatic cover art, very religious and serious-sounding names of songs, this operatic singer that could out-Plant Robert Plant, and above all, the riffs on that album were the best riffs anybody had written to date in heavy metal, and there were twelve of them in every song.

IAN HILL: Unfortunately, our label back then, Gull Records, didn't have enough money to promote and produce their artists. They were waiting for us to make the company [famous] rather than the other way around. They couldn't afford to send us to America and you *do* have to make it in America to become successful, so we remained unknown there for a while. The thing is, when you're starting up you've got nothing, so when someone hands you a record contract, no matter how bad it is, it's hard to turn down.

ROB HALFORD: We all had second jobs. I was managing a menswear shop. I would run home after work, jump in the van, and drive to a gig. We'd load the gear onto the stage, get changed into whatever we had to wear, do the show, break the stuff down, put it back in the van, and drive home, getting back at daybreak just in time to get ready for work.

IAN HILL: I drove a van for five pounds a day, and it kept myself and my girlfriend, Sue, going. There was a time when Ken, myself, and our manager, Dave Corke, lived in a one-bedroom apartment with girlfriends. We couldn't ever afford to get smashed.

ROB HALFORD: We went to Gull and asked for 25 quid (about $38) each a week to live on so we could be professional musicians and not have to keep running back home after shows to our second lines of work, and they turned us down.

GLENN TIPTON: We used to share bags of chips. That was a sheer luxury. I think that helped shape our character.

ROB HALFORD: We'd get in the van and take the ferry to Europe and play any pub shows we could get, then we'd sleep in the van. There was never any question of, "Oh, fuck this. This absolutely sucks. I'm not gonna do it." We were so excited to be on this great adventure.

GLENN TIPTON: When Sony took us over and we left Gull Records, that was a big moment for us. Sony was very supportive and that helped us to address the world stage. In the States we did six weeks alone in clubs and bars, and we played with REO Speedwagon [and Black Oak Arkansas] just trying to get the word out. Then we were offered two shows on the West Coast with Led Zeppelin at the Day on the Green at the Oakland Coliseum. We got very little money and we had to hang around for two weeks in the cheapest motels with no air conditioning and very little food. But we stuck around and did these shows, and that actually helped to establish us. We had a great reaction. The combination of the deal with Sony and those two shows brought us to the attention of a lot of people. America really welcomed Priest with open arms.

Even though they were signed, Priest lacked the finances to mount an extravagant production. By contrast, even when they were eating ramen noodles and Chinese takeout, KISS looked and acted like rock stars. Finally after their fourth release, 1975's concert album *KISS Alive*, produced by Eddie Kramer, KISS achieved mainstream popularity. To perpetuate their success, the band hired esteemed producer Bob Ezrin for 1976's *Destroyer*.

BOB EZRIN (producer): I was at City TV in Toronto doing an interview. As I was going up the stairs, KISS, having been on the same show, was coming down. We met in the stairwell and I said, "If you ever need any help, call me." Within a couple months Bill Aucoin [KISS's then-manager] reached out about doing their next record. I saw them play at an arena in Ann Arbor, Michigan. The place was half full, but everybody in the joint was on their feet from the time the band started until the show was over. The one thing I noticed, aside from the fact that everyone knew the words for every song and were all singing along, was that the audience was all teenage boys. I thought, "This is an opportunity. If they could just get to the girls, this would be the biggest band in the world." I met them in New York and said, "I don't want to make you into softies. You can still be the bad guys, but let's be like Marlon Brando in *On the Waterfront*." When Brando played the leader of the motorcycle gang he was dangerous, scary, and every mother's nightmare, yet underneath it all there was this certain sensitivity and beauty that made him attractive. Every girl in the world wanted to mother, nurture, and fuck him. We went into *Destroyer* with that in mind.

GENE SIMMONS: At some point, I began to keep Polaroid snapshots of my liaisons to remember them. In a certain way, I loved every one of them. But when it was over, it was over.

No fuss, no muss. No agony. To date, I have had over 4,600 liaisons. And I have to say that they were all wonderful, that they all enhanced my life.

BOB EZRIN: The debauchery was part of the culture that surrounded KISS. The day that we arrived at the studio to make *Destroyer*, Gene went into the office where the receptionist was. She was cute. Within twenty minutes we lost him. We didn't know where he was. And of course, he was in the bathroom with the receptionist. That set the tone for the whole project. There were many times when Gene wouldn't be there and I'd know exactly where to find him. I wouldn't know exactly who he was with, but I knew right *where* he was.

While Simmons embraced the opportunity to indulge in his sexual fantasies, he carefully avoided other rock-and-roll excesses; from the start, he believed alcohol and drugs were career-destroyers. In the cases of Frehley and Criss, he was right.

GENE SIMMONS: The most important advice I could give to a band starting out is no booze and no drugs. I refuse to get high, except in a dentist's chair. I never smoked. I have yet to be drunk. People don't believe that. The inference is everybody gets high and drunk. Well, I don't believe you've got to be shot by a gun to know that it hurts. "Oh, you've got to try everything once." What moronic, spineless person ever said that? They're cowards who don't have the strength to live life by their own example.

ACE FREHLEY: There were plenty of times when Paul and Gene got very nervous because I got really drunk the afternoon we had an evening gig. But they didn't know that I had the ability to get loaded, sleep for two or three hours, and wake up ready to play. I used to scare the hell out of them by doing that—but I was always able to put on a great show.

PAUL STANLEY: There is no place—in any quantity—for drugs in what I do or what we do. That's not tolerated, not acceptable. It shows a complete lack of respect for the fans, the music, and yourself, and the people that are supposed to be your family and partners.

ACE FREHLEY: [Drummer] Peter [Criss] and I were both party animals who came from similar backgrounds—we were street kids who grew up in gangs. There was a camaraderie between us right from the start, something neither of us could ever have with Paul and Gene, because they came from very different backgrounds.

PETER CRISS (KISS): There was a lot of coke, and that was my problem. I used to [get coked up] and lock myself in a room with a chick or two—or four or five. It depended on what mood I was in.

ACE FREHLEY: We all started out as friends, but it got to the point where we didn't want to talk to each other. After a gig, we would each get in separate limos and go our own way. We started communicating with each other through our lawyers. I think a lot of [our problems] had to do with our success—the fame, the money and the pressure of the whole business. That kind of stuff changes people.

GENE SIMMONS: Ace and Peter wanted me to babysit them, and I wasn't willing to grow tits so they could suckle on them. In the beginning we had to rent our own trucks, place our own ads, put up our own posters, hump the equipment up and down the stairs, and those guys wouldn't do any of that stuff. That always bothered the shit out of me.

PAUL STANLEY: What bothered me is that once the band made it, did you give 100 percent to your fans? And when that was no longer true, whether or not you hump gear, the ultimate slap in the face is when you start taking your fans for granted or giving them below what you're capable of or what they deserve.

GENE SIMMONS: [Once Ace was wasted drunk, and he went into the bathroom and] wouldn't answer the door, and all we heard inside the room was the sound of water running and music blasting. [We] broke the door down and found Ace soaking in a hot tub with the water running and his nose about a half inch from the surface. He was completely unconscious. If we hadn't showed up when we did, he would have drowned. We took [him] out of the water and put him in bed, and he didn't regain consciousness until the next day.

ACE FREHLEY: No matter how fucked up any of us were—and we were all fucked up in some ways, and not just because of alcohol and drugs—there was a chemistry between us that [could] never be recaptured unless the four of us [were together].

GENE SIMMONS: Talking about stability in KISS is like talking about freedom in prison. It's all relative. Ace had a fascination with Nazi memorabilia, and in his drunken stupors he and his best friends would make videotapes of themselves dressed up as Nazis. Paul and I weren't thrilled about that. But Ace laughed about how funny he was when he saw the tape. Peter, too, was drinking heavily and using drugs.

In some ways, AC/DC were peers of KISS. AC/DC's music was minimal and straightforward. It was fun and often campy, and filled with lyrical wordplay. Both bands knew what they did well and delivered it album after album. AC/DC's founders, guitarists Angus and Malcolm Young, were born in Glasgow, Scotland, and eventually moved with their family to Sydney, Australia, where they found a more vibrant music scene. They named themselves AC/DC after their sister Margaret spotted the electricity-related acronym for alternating current/direct current on her sewing machine. Angus experimented with different looks, including wearing a gorilla suit onstage, before his sister suggested he wear a schoolboy outfit. Margaret later explained she got the idea from Angus himself, who used to rush home from school and jam with his bandmates without changing out of his school uniform.

"The schoolboy thing has always given me the ability to stay young," Angus says. "I put on the guitar and that school suit, and I get on that stage, and there's just this sheer driving force."

In 1974, at the recommendation of the Youngs' brother George (who had played in the successful Australian pop group Easybeats), AC/DC fired vocalist Dave Evans and replaced him with Ronald Belford "Bon" Scott. A wild and expressive performer, Scott's gritty presence and raspy, raunchy vocals put AC/DC on the map as one of Australia's greatest blues-based rock exports.

ANGUS YOUNG (AC/DC): Rock and roll has always had that blues element, and we've always dabbled in blues. I loved Keith Richards and the Stones, but Chuck Berry was the biggest for me. That's how we always wanted to be. Even from the first album, we've done tracks like "She's Got the Jack." Stuff like "Dirty Deeds" and "Ride On"—they've got that blues smell about them.

DAVE EVANS (ex-AC/DC): [Before Bon Scott joined], Malcolm and Angus would have the bare ideas [for a song] and sit down with George at the piano. The three of them would fit on the same piano stool because they are so tiny. George would take the material and get the best out of those ideas.

ANGUS YOUNG: Even when Malcolm and myself were growing up, George showed us a lot of the basic stuff—helping with the songs and explaining studio techniques. When you're a young kid, you don't know the difference between a verse and a chorus, let alone a drum break or a middle eight. He helped with a lot of melody ideas and showed us how you can get the best out of the two guitars without having to resort to layered sounds. And [as a producer of the first four AC/DC records], he gave us that room to be who we wanted to be—not a hit producer's idea of what he thought we should be. From his background, when he was in the Easybeats, he got to work with different legends of rock music, which was invaluable to him.

BRIAN JOHNSON (AC/DC, ex-Geordie): I'd met Bon when he was with a different band, and he was supporting Geordie, the band I was in, and we got to know each other. He was the funniest man and we had a lovely time. But it was all too brief. It was "See ya, mate." He wasn't half as good as he was when he joined AC/DC. They brought something out in him, as they did with me. When they start playing they bring something out in ya that's just inexplicable. I can sing with a charity band, good rock and rollers, all great players, and I'll sing in tune and do me thing, but it just doesn't sound the same. When I sit down with the boys in a rehearsal room, we say, "Let's kick this one around," and boom, this thing comes out that I really can't explain, and I don't want to, because I'm really happy the way it is. That's the way it was with Bon, too.

ANGUS YOUNG: When we finally got to [AC/DC's first gig], Bon downed about two bottles of bourbon with dope, coke, speed, and says, "Right, I'm ready." He got out there and this huge hurricane yell came out. The whole place went, "What the fuck is this?"

MALCOLM YOUNG (AC/DC): We used to finish a gig at about two in the morning, then drive down to the studio. George and Harry [Vanda, of the Easybeats,] would have a couple of dozen cans in and a few bottles of Jack Daniel's and we'd all have a party and rip it up. So it was the same loose feeling like we were onstage, still. The studio was just like an extension of the gig back then.

ANGUS YOUNG: At first, when you're young, a lot of temptation comes at you. Some people get attracted and figure, "Oh, there must be some gold there." There's that feeling of eternal youth going. That doesn't work for me. I think what's eternal is getting a good song. If you can span generations with that song, it becomes timeless.

BRIAN JOHNSON: The one day we got blasted with Angus was when Malcolm's daughter was born and he got a telephone call. Malcolm came down and said, "It's a girl," and that was the first time I saw Angus take a drink. He got a bottle of Jack Daniel's and he went, "Aw fuckin' great mate." And he drank. And he was put on somebody's shoulders and taken to bed. It was the first [and] last drink I ever saw him take, poor sod.

Most rockers didn't stop with one drink. The seeming invincibility of youth brought with it the desire to push the limits and keep the good times rolling 24/7.

ROB HALFORD: Drugs and alcohol are very insidious. They creep into your life and you find yourself doing more and more. It's been there since day one, since rock and roll began. It's like a trial by fire to get through those times of your life. Some of us don't become addicts. Some of us become drug addicts and alcoholics, then clean ourselves up like I've been able to do. Then there are people that succumb and end up in the ground.

GLENN TIPTON: We partied heavily and we performed heavily. The two went hand in hand all through the seventies and eighties. But the one thing we've always felt was important was to give a good performance. People pay to see you, so you have to give them value for their money. So we've never let partying affect our performance. Most of the drinking and partying went on after we left the stage.

ANGUS YOUNG: In the early years, a lot of people thought I was a smack addict. I would lose myself onstage and they'd go, "This guy's gotta be on dope." But the truth is, I've never been a party animal.

OZZY OSBOURNE: There are three things over the years that I have seen destroy more fucking great bands than anything on this planet: women, booze, and drugs. The thing is, you get blinded by the glitter. All of a sudden people start to notice you and you get a buzz. I used to have a cocaine habit of $1,000 a week. I was drinking four bottles of cognac a day. I was just killing myself. John Bonham was a really good friend of mine. He choked on his vomit. I was at a gig with Bon Scott a week before he died. And that didn't change me. When you're young you think that you're never going to die.

TONY IOMMI: The first time I ever tried cocaine, we were playing Madison Square Garden and I felt tired. One of the guys that worked for us said, "Well, just have a bit of this. It'll perk you up and you'll feel a bit better." So I did, and that was *it*. I went onstage and thought, "Wow, this is great." It started from there.

CHERYL RIXON (ex–*Penthouse* Pet): You would go to these parties and there was cocaine everywhere—salad bowls full of it. Every time we went backstage everyone was doing blow. It was like an appetizer.

MICK WALL: In permissive seventies society, cocaine would be like caviar. It would be considered such a delicacy, such a treat, such a marvelous thing to offer your guests. Also, it was expensive, so you're this guy who has come from nothing and suddenly you're being treated like royalty. Sabbath were scum from the council estates [housing projects], the ghettos. And now they're in Hollywood making albums, playing the

Hollywood Bowl, playing Madison Square Garden. "Cocaine? Fuck! You betcha!" It's like saying, "Would you like to travel first class?" "I fucking *would* like to travel first class, actually. Thank you." Of course, the trouble with cocaine is it does make you so high and so edgy. What's the perfect complement to bring you down again? "Have some heroin." And Black Sabbath got well into that. They were all into heroin for a while. It fucked Bill [Ward] up for years. But they weren't unique. Zeppelin—Page and Bonham—were major junkies. Plant did it. Everybody sampled it.

TONY IOMMI: When we were doing [1972's] *Volume 4,* the amount of drugs we were doing was absolutely ridiculous. We were having stuff flown in on private planes. But it was a great period for us. For the next album, [1973's] *Sabbath Bloody Sabbath,* we tried to re-create the same thing and it didn't happen. We went back to Los Angeles, the same house, the same everything, but it didn't work. So we went back to England all disappointed. It was the first time in my life I'd ever had writer's block. We thought, "Well, that's it. We're finished. It's over." And then we rented a castle in Wales and rehearsed in the dungeons, and as soon as we were there I came up with the title track, "Sabbath Bloody Sabbath." Just like that, the riff came up, and I thought, "That's it, we're off again."

While Sabbath and Priest confronted dark, sometimes violent subjects, AC/DC preferred songs about getting loaded and getting laid. "The Jack" is about a girl with gonorrhea; "Crabsody in Blue" is about getting crabs; "Go Down" addresses oral sex. But the band's racy lyrics aren't always so blatant, and their use of double entendres became a trademark. The best example is "Big Balls," a song simultaneously about testicles and fancy parties.

ANGUS YOUNG: I've always viewed our lyrics as a tongue-in-cheek thing—just schoolboy humor. But sex has always been a big part of rock and roll. When I would hear [Chuck] Berry singing, "Riding along in my automobile / my baby beside me at the wheel," it was the same thing. For every rock-and-roll band there's been the cars, the women. The Stones had "Honky Tonk Woman" and "Starfucker." They probably got away with a lot more than we did. Even the Beatles—they had songs like "Why Don't We do It in the Road" and "Lady Madonna." Hell, that's rock and roll.

BRIAN JOHNSON: We had a Swedish reporter who said to us, "Sex, sex, sex! Everything is sex. How would you like it if you were thrown in the back of a car by a woman, and she tied you down and abused you?" I went, "Fucking great! That's me fucking dream come true. Bring a friend." She said, "Do you think that's amusing for the woman?" I said, "I'd fucking love it. Tie me up in a car and get me fucking brains fucked out by some wild rampant tottie" [*laughs*]. Working lads, that's where your head's at.

MARTIN POPOFF: I always thought of AC/DC as the ultimate party band that will kill *somebody* with alcohol poisoning one day, because those records were so intense as soundtracks to partying, to throwing up, to having big drinking parties out in the woods where something bad is inevitably going to happen. There's going to be a car accident or something. And yes, I guess a lot of that is underscored by the lyrics. A lot of them are about drinking and womanizing, and evil women.

From a fan's perspective, Sabbath was still the kingpin of metal. Its first four albums were revered as classics, and the band filled arenas. Behind the scenes, however, Ozzy's chronic substance abuse and unreliability was driving a wedge between him and the rest of the band.

TONY IOMMI: Ozzy used to get out of hand on days off. I used to try to keep myself fairly straight, even though it didn't happen all the time, because *somebody* had to be in control.

Many times somebody phoned me up from the bar in the hotel and said, "Can you get down here and get him out." 'Cause he'd be passed out on the table. So I'd go down and get him and bring him up to his room and put him in bed. We were in the studio once and we went to a real plush club afterwards. We were drinking away and he got absolutely smashed and passed out on this couch. The club was closing and the guy from the club said, "Get him out. Get him out." I went, "I'm not moving him. If you want him out, you get him out." So they picked him up and put him over their shoulders—and of course, I knew what he was gonna do—he pissed himself all over them. And they went, "You dirty bastard," and threw him off. They couldn't wake him up. But I'd seen that so many times, I just knew what was gonna happen.

OZZY OSBOURNE: I really was drunk all the time. I was just fucking crazy, but I was a fun crazy guy, I think. I wasn't a bad crazy guy. I wouldn't hurt anyone intentionally. I put *myself* in danger. But every time you get in a car you put yourself in danger. Every time you leave the house you put yourself in danger.

GEEZER BUTLER: I did everything you can think of and I'm lucky to be alive. But I went off drugs in 1976 once they weren't doing anything for me anymore. They made me depressed more than anything. They were great at first, but once they started taking over my life, I went right off the whole idea. And I saw the way Bill Ward and Ozzy were getting overtaken by it, and I didn't want to get like that. So I was lucky to be content being boring.

TONY IOMMI: Drugs and alcohol eventually take their toll, and Bill was probably the first big sign of it. And Ozzy, of course. We'd all have our times of getting drunk, but Bill actually started drinking onstage. He really got bad. He used to get nervous and take Valium. Then he decided he was too scared to fly and started traveling by road. He'd develop these fears and it was coming out more the more he'd drink and take drugs. It just built up over a while. We'd all go out to clubs and get pissed and come back out of our brain. But Bill was the only one who had to have a drink before he played. The rest of us didn't do that. We *couldn't* do that. I couldn't play drunk. I wouldn't be able to.

MICK WALL: Ozzy told me once, "Me and Bill were like the drug commandos. We would never come through a door if there was a plate glass window we could smash instead." Ozzy told me as far as he was concerned they were all just bumpkins and that "as long as we had a few quid in our pocket, some tarts to fuck, and a bootload of drugs, we were happy." I think in Ozzy's happy-go-lucky world, especially in those days, it was about the intoxication. It was about being permanently out of it every day.

OZZY OSBOURNE: I said to Bill recently, "Can you believe we used to believe having a belly full of alcohol, a bag of pills, and hash and dope was our idea of having a good time?" I can't even think that way nowadays. I figure, "Why did it take me so long to get it?" And he goes, "Yeah, but it worked for a while." That's about right. But when it stopped working, at the end of the day with drinking and me, I'd be miserable. Then I'd have another drink and be even more miserable. Then I'd think to myself, "What am I doing this for?"

GEEZER BUTLER: We played Nashville one time and Ozzy went into the hotel and didn't tell anybody what room he was in. He went to a completely different room than he was registered at, and we thought he'd been kidnapped. We had the FBI come in and look for him. We were playing with Van Halen that night, and they finished their show and then we had to go onstage and say, "Sorry, we don't know where Ozzy is." The next day we all got on the bus and we were really worried. We were saying, "I wonder who's got him and if they've killed him." Ozzy was already on the bus. He went, "Hello fellas, where's the show?" We felt like killing him. As it turned out, he'd had a cough, so he went out and bought two bottles of cough medicine, drank them both, and knocked himself out. That was the last tour we did. It was sort of the last straw.

TONY IOMMI: In 1978, when we went to Los Angeles to write [*Never Say Die*], we had a house and we all lived there. We turned the garage into a studio so we could rehearse and write. We had equipment in the house as well so we could put rough ideas together and then go in the studio and play it. When we were trying to come up with riffs, Ozzy came apart from us. He was going to clubs and getting really out of it and not coming home some nights. It got to a stage where nothing was happening with him.

GEEZER BUTLER: Ozzy didn't show up for six weeks. We couldn't go on with him after that.

TONY IOMMI: It was me that dealt with Warner Bros. in them days. That was my task: to talk to them about the progress of the album, which, of course, we didn't fuckin' have. I'd go over there and they'd say, "How's the album coming?" And I'd go, "Oh, great, great." "When can we hear some tracks?" "Oh, soon, soon." We hadn't got anything, and I was really worried. I had to go and face these people knowing full well that we hadn't got anything to play them. It just got to a real desperate stage. At that point Ozzy didn't want to do anything apart from go out and get drunk. So it came to the point where the other guys said, "Well, look, if we don't do anything we're gonna break up. We're not gonna stand it. We're gonna leave." So that was the decision between the three of us. We said we're gonna have to replace Ozzy, and that's what happened.

That same year, the bottom fell out for Peter Criss, and KISS headed into a decline that ended two years later with the departure of Ace Frehley. After the four members released simultaneous self-titled solo records in 1978, Criss suddenly seemed less interested in the band and began to withdraw. He was credited as the drummer on KISS's 1979's *Dynasty*, but in fact only played on his own song, "Dirty Living." The drummer in David Letterman's band, Anton Fig, played on the rest of *Dynasty* and all of 1980's *Unmasked*. Criss's last show with KISS (until their reunion in 1996) was December 16, 1979.

PETER CRISS: I thought, "God, this is turnin' out to be such a damn business." I was losin' the fun of the early days when we were struggling, and now we were kind of having a lot of money and things we never could afford, we could [suddenly] afford without looking at the price tag. That got scary for me, I didn't like it, and I started thinkin' then about splittin'.

GENE SIMMONS: [When we were making 1978's *KISS Meets the Phantom of the Park*,] Peter [was] in [one of his] car accidents. He skidded 400 feet before he crashed, and he wound up in the hospital. When he did speak in the movie he was impossible to understand because of his thick Brooklyn accent. So his voice was dubbed. Even getting Peter and Ace in front of the camera didn't always work out. Sometimes they went missing. The only solution was to use doubles. For Peter, we had a fifty-five-year-old guy and we put makeup on him. For Ace, an African American stunt double.

PETER CRISS: I decided I wanted to do my own thing, my own music. Ten years in KISS was enough for me. I got tired of playing heavy metal. I like writing love songs. I like playing with strings, horns, and pianos.

ACE FREHLEY: When Peter left, I really felt a great chemical imbalance in the band. Even though I loved Eric [Carr, Criss's replacement], God rest his soul, losing Peter upset the balance of the band a little too much. Plus, I didn't have my drinking buddy anymore, so I had to go drink with my bodyguards and roadies. It took me a long time to realize that I had a serious problem. I guess I finally realized it when I crashed my De-Lorean in '83. I also got busted for drunk driving six months later, and lost my license for a couple of years. That was kind of a wake-up call to me to get help. If I had stayed in the group, I probably would have self-destructed and killed myself. You know, there were plenty of times when, driving home to Connecticut from the city, I contemplated just driving my Porsche into a fucking tree and ending it all. So I had to choose the lesser of two evils.

GENE SIMMONS: We consciously missed Ace and Peter all the time, but in no way, shape, or form did we feel responsible or blame ourselves for what happened to them. Everything is a choice in life and you make the bed you sleep in, and unfortunately, they decided to be self-destructive. That doesn't mean you don't miss them. We've had some great times. Some not-so-great ones, too—and that's why they had to go.

AC/DC seemed unstoppable. Then, on February 19, 1980, Bon Scott tragically lost his life. The band was in London doing preproduction for the follow-up to *Highway to Hell*; Bon was living it up as he always did. The night before he died, Scott went to the Music Machine, a club in Camden Town, London, to check out the band Lonesome No More with his friend Alistair Kinnear, who was driving. After a night of heavy drinking, the two drove back to Kinnear's apartment, and Kinnear noticed the singer had passed out.

ALISTAIR KINNEAR (Bon Scott's friend): I tried to lift him out of the car, but he was too heavy for me to carry in my intoxicated state, so I put the front passenger seat back so that he could lie flat, covered him with a blanket, left a note with my address and phone number on it, and staggered upstairs to bed. It must have been 4 or 5 a.m. by that time, and I slept until about 11, when I was awakened by a friend. I was so hungover that I asked him to do me a favor [and check] on Bon. He did so, and returned to tell me my car was empty, so I went back to sleep, assuming that Bon had awoken and taken a taxi home. At about 7:30 that evening I went down to my car intending to pay a visit to my girlfriend who was in hospital, and was shocked to find Bon still lying flat in the front seat, obviously in a very bad way, and not breathing. I immediately drove him to King's College Hospital, where Bon was pronounced dead on arrival. The Lambeth coroner's report cited acute alcohol poisoning, and death by misadventure.

ANGUS YOUNG: Nobody knew what to do. We were so battered. It's as if we'd had an arm amputated.

PHIL RUDD (AC/DC): His death numbed me. Nobody believed it could happen to us. We were so depressed. We were just walking around in silence.

3

BRITISH STEEL: NEW WAVE OF BRITISH HEAVY METAL SHAPES THE FUTURE, 1980–PRESENT

As 1979 dawned, the metal landscape looked dim for the genre's founders. Black Sabbath had no singer, and its former vocalist was so dependent on drugs and alcohol he could barely function. But even if Sabbath and Ozzy had never returned, the foundation they had built was so powerful it couldn't be destroyed. AC/DC carried on after Bon Scott's death—and reached new heights with vocalist Brian Johnson. Judas Priest was about to release its most highly acclaimed album, *British Steel*. And, inspired by Judas Priest and Black Sabbath, Iron Maiden, Saxon, Def Leppard, and a batch of other UK groups spawned the awkwardly titled but hugely influential New Wave of British Heavy Metal (NWOBHM) movement.

The NWOBHM trailblazers each had their own style, but were lumped together by music journalists. Some, like Def Leppard, were firmly rooted in melody; others, such as Iron Maiden, in galloping, classical-tinged punk. NWOBHM's influence spread across the United Kingdom, and then the rest of Europe, inspiring bands like Germany's Accept and Scorpions, Denmark's Mercyful Fate, America's Armored Saint, and a little band called Metallica.

ROB HALFORD: Metal music gained its foothold on a global level in a short space of time. There were a handful of music papers or magazines, so the way it was growing and the intensity of the focus made us think more and more about how we wanted to look. Really, Judas Priest's biker image started to take shape around the time of [1979's] *Hell Bent For Leather.* You know the way Audrey Hepburn's little black dress in *Breakfast at Tiffany's* shook the world? For me it was the little biker jacket. I wore it to rehearsal and everybody went, "Fuck, that looks really tough. That looks really strong. That looks like the music sounds, almost." We all looked at each other and nodded in agreement and said, "I wonder what else we could do?" I just need a nod of approval and then the walls come crashing down.

IAN HILL: At the time, we were a little bit surprised that other bands started dressing the same way. But the look fit the music. Just imagine us playing "Freewheel Burning" in satin and velvet. It wouldn't fit.

ROB HALFORD: To get some of these bits and pieces of my clothing, I had to go to the local S&M sex shops in the UK. It wasn't like we wanted the S&M part of it associated with Priest, but I could only get the little accoutrements and accessories through these kinds of establishments. I had this whip that went with the outfit. Now these days if I brought out a whip and whipped the crowd I would get litigation left, right, and center. But in those early days that's literally what I would do, and they'd be shouting, "Whip me! Whip me!"

MARTIN POPOFF: When Judas Priest begin to adopt this rough and tough leather look, they begin to get across this idea, subtly, that it's okay to be heavy metal, it's okay to be proud of it, and they slowly begin to become the self-identified, self-aware heavy metal band. You get this metal army forming, and a cult of metal that begins to evolve with the look and the live show that no one had seen before.

ROB HALFORD: We used to do a song called "Genocide," and I said to the band, "Wouldn't it be great if at the end of the song we use a machine gun?" We got in touch with a weapons prop guy, and for that tour he came with us and I used a full automatic machine gun. It shot these blanks. It was really fucking loud, and smoke came out, and these blank brass cartridges would spray all over the stage. Eventually we hit a wall because the local fire marshals were afraid the gun was real and that we were going to cause a riot. They had a point, because there were crowds that looked confused and you could tell they were thinking, "Surely to God, that's not a machine gun. Is it plastic? No, it's real! What's going on? What the fuck is this?" Then I'd look at them and point it straight at them. Nobody knew in advance what was going on, so there was this look that was a combination of sheer horror and, "Oh my God, that's so cool."

While Judas Priest was searching bondage shops and cultivating their dramatic live show, Black Sabbath was looking for a new vocalist. The remaining members were afraid they'd never find a singer as charismatic and iconoclastic as Ozzy—and many fans and critics wrote Sabbath off. Then Sabbath returned with vocalist Ronnie James Dio, discovered through the most unlikely source.

TONY IOMMI: To be honest, it was Sharon [Osbourne, née Arden] that told me about Ronnie; of course, that was before she was managing Ozzy. I met Ronnie at a party and I was talking to him there and I thought, "Well, he's a nice enough guy." Not doing anything [with Ozzy] was getting frustrating, so I talked to Ronnie about doing a side-project album together, but it didn't materialize. Then I called him about joining Sabbath.

RONNIE JAMES DIO: I liked the music they were doing so much. I liked writing with them and I liked them, too. And that took away a lot of the intimidation factor of joining Black Sabbath. But even then, we went through a lot of traumas. The band had to deal with Warner Bros. The label didn't want this band without Ozzy, and that could have been a disaster.

TONY IOMMI: We were arguing with management as well because they said, "Look, it's gotta work with Ozzy. *Make* it work." We said, "Well, it just can't." Ozzy was too out of it and we weren't far behind him, going down and down into the drugs and booze.

RONNIE JAMES DIO: Suddenly, we seemed to have no support, and it came down to us making the record with our own money. Luckily, Tony and Bill had some friends at Warner Bros., and they said they'd listen to the record but they didn't want to bankroll it. The lads spent some of their money, I spent some of mine. It just wasn't the kind of freewheeling experience we were both used to. To make matters more complicated, we went down there without Geezer because he was having some personal problems.

TONY IOMMI: Geezer had to sort his life out. Ronnie and myself put the tracks together with Bill. At one point Ronnie played bass so we could come up with the ideas for "Heaven and Hell" and one or two other songs.

RONNIE JAMES DIO: We eventually had to move to Florida to a city called Criteria because we didn't have enough money to stay where we were. We lived together in a house on Biscayne Bay. After overcoming those initial obstacles, it just worked. The songs were memorable. It was great to bond in the face of that kind of pressure. We tested out the songs by taking them to a local strip bar. We'd have them play it and see if the dancers liked to dance to it. And oh, they loved "Heaven and Hell." That was my favorite Sabbath record because it was a good time that wrested its way out of a bad time.

TONY IOMMI: We managed to have fun, I suppose. Bill used to have this fascination with Nazi Germany. One night he got pissed and wanted to dress up as Hitler. So we got this gaffer tape and taped all his hair down and put a little moustache on him and a swastika on his shirt. It was great until he wanted to take the gaffer tape off. We couldn't get it off of his head. We had to cut all around under the gaffer tape to get his hair out. Oh, he looked a right mess after we were done. When he woke up in the morning, he looked in the mirror and said, "Oh, my God, what happened last night?" Another time, I set Bill on fire. We had this little party prank that started one night in a club. The waiter came up and I said, "Excuse me, do you have a lighter?" Bill had a big beard at the time, and I lit his beard and it went straight up his face and he breathed in all the smoke and went, "Mmm, 1948." And the guy went, "Wow, man, that really freaked me out!" It started at that and just got worse as it went along. I'd tip rubbing alcohol over him in the studio and light him, and, of course, it used to burn off. But this one time, we had producer Martin Birch in the studio, and I said, "Hey, Bill, can I set you on fire?" He said, "Oh, not just yet, I'm a bit busy." And he came over to me two hours later and said, "I'm going home now Tone, do you want to set me on fire or what?" This was in front of Martin, who had never seen us do this. I said, "Yeah." So I tipped a big, full bottle over him and it all soaked into his clothes and when I lit him he just went up like a bomb and then went down on the floor. He was rolling around screaming and I thought he was laughing. Meanwhile, I'm still tipping stuff on him. He had third-degree burns all over his legs and we had to take him to hospital. Then his mum phoned me up and said, "You barmy bastard, Bill might have to have his leg cut off."

MICK WALL: Black Sabbath played with fire and eventually got burned very badly. In 1980, when I went to work for Sabbath, Bill was still in the group and they were finishing up *Heaven and Hell* in Paris. My company, Heavy Publicity, had been hired to do their PR in Britain. I was flown to Paris to meet the group and seal the deal. I met Dio, Iommi, and Geezer, and they all seemed cool. Then I met Bill at the photo session when he went wandering around the Sacré-Coeur in the pouring rain. He was acting strange and we didn't have a proper conversation. In those days it was really important to bond with the people you worked with. You would do drugs and drink and talk, and I hadn't had any of that with Bill. Then at 2 a.m. Paul, the tour manager, called my room and said, "Bill wants to meet you now." I'm like, "Paul, it's 2 a.m. I've just got to bed and I've got an early flight tomorrow." He says again, "Bill would like to meet you now." I got up, got dressed, went to see Bill at the Hotel George Cinq in Paris, and as I arrive at 2:30 a.m. the hotel plumber was leaving Bill's suite. Bill had bunged up every toilet, every sink, every bath drain with vomit so badly that the hotel plumber had to unplug everything. I walked in and Bill's in a robe. It looked like he hadn't slept in weeks. His first wife is with him. She looks like Dracula's wife. I said, "So, Bill, what am I doing here?" He said, "I want to play you the album." None of them had said that to me. I went, "Oh, I didn't know it was finished." He said, "It isn't. We haven't done the vocals yet, but I want to play you what we've done so far." I was thinking, "Great. Just what you dream of doing at 3 a.m. with a guy who's throwing up so heavily because he's a major alcoholic who is doing major heroin." That was in about March 1980. Within six months, by the time the album had come out and we'd got to America, he'd left the band.

TONY IOMMI: Bill left because he had a lot of alcohol problems and he was getting worse and worse. It got to a point where we were on the *Heaven and Hell* tour and [he] had to come off the road and get himself sorted out. He left very abruptly in Denver on the night of a gig. He freaked out, said, "I can't do it anymore," and left. I was panicking and petrified because I had played with Bill for all those years. Ronnie heard about Vinny [Appice], so we tried him out. The next gig we had coming up was in Hawaii, and it was a big festival. I was shitting myself. When I saw Vinny's kit, it was a quarter of the size of Bill's. It just looked ridiculous on our big drum riser. But bloody hell, he really played it well, and we got through the show and I was so relieved after that.

VINNY APPICE (Heaven & Hell, ex-Dio, ex–Black Sabbath): Sharon called me when Ozzy was doing his first solo album and she asked if I was into playing with Ozzy. I was, like, twenty-one, and I knew Ozzy was pretty crazy. I said, "I'll call you back." So I called my brother [Carmine Appice (Cactus, ex-Vanilla Fudge)] and I said, "You know Ozzy. Isn't he crazy? Should I go to England and try this?" Carmine said, "Yeah. He's pretty crazy, so it'll be funny to see what happens." But I turned it down anyway. About a month later, the phone rings and it's Black Sabbath's tour manager, Paul Clark, and they're in Los Angeles at the Sunset Marquis. So I went down to meet him and Tony. I brought an album I played on by a band called Axis. The next day they called and said, "Come down to SIR Studios on Sunset Boulevard." So I went there and they go, "Do you know any of our new songs?" The week before I heard 'Neon Knights'" on the radio driving in my car, so I said, "Let's play 'Neon Knights,' because I knew the tempo. We played for about an hour and then we took a break. They went to the pub, then came back and said, "All right, you're gonna do it." Originally, Bill was gonna come back to the band and I was just gonna play the tour. But as the tour went on we got better and better and we got to know each other. At the end of the tour they said, "We're gonna do an album, you wanna do it with us?" I said, "Yeah!" That's when we started working on *Mob Rules*.

MICK WALL: After he left the band, Bill bottomed out. He told me he went to bed for three months in LA and every morning the drug dealer would come by with his smack and everything else he needed and then leave again. Then they would come back again the next morning. He said the reason he was in bed for three months was his legs didn't work anymore, which was why it was so important that the dealer came to his place. It was at that time that John Bonham died. They were friends, and he found out about it from his dealer. He said his first thoughts were, "I'm right behind you Johnny, I'm right behind you."

RONNIE JAMES DIO: We had a blockbuster hit with "Heaven and Hell" and we suddenly went from "Black Sabbath that is no more" to "Black Sabbath, whoa, check this out!" I think attitudes started to change within the band a little and we went astray. [Our next album,] *The Mob Rules*, is great, but some of us were living a bit more high on the hog, and it was a lot easier not to be together than it was to be together, perhaps.

TONY IOMMI: We found that it was easier to write with just two of us there. It had its ups and downs, but I quite liked that album.

With Dio commanding the band through two albums, Black Sabbath appeared to be back in peak form. However, behind closed doors, egos were growing and tensions were mounting. During mixing sessions for the concert album *Live Evil*, the members of Sabbath reached an impasse.

TONY IOMMI: In my mind, it wasn't recorded right. We had tracks leaking all over the place and we had a lot of problems within the band.

RONNIE JAMES DIO: That was a nightmare. There was so much dissatisfaction and I don't know exactly why. But I do know the engineer told Geezer and Tony that Vinny and I would go in early to the studio and turn up the drums and the vocal, which wasn't true and didn't make sense because we weren't mixing it. Word got back to them and they started not showing up. Then they turned up when we didn't to work on it, and we turned up when they didn't, and that spelled the end of it. So that was a miserable album for me, and at the end I got fired.

Back in 1979, when Black Sabbath was scrambling to get started with Dio, the band's original vocalist had pretty much given up on life. Ozzy Osbourne was broke and living in a hotel, having forfeited all his possessions to ex-wife Thelma Mayfair in a divorce settlement. He felt betrayed by the rest of Sabbath and lost his desire to create, as well as the confidence that came from being part of a successful band. He might have slid into oblivion had his tough-as-nails future wife, Sharon Arden, not picked him up and set him back on the path to rock stardom.

SHARON OSBOURNE: My father [Don Arden] was an extremely successful band manager, but a very violent, very extreme personality. So I had a rollercoaster ride as a kid. I was raised with people who were extreme and outrageous. People would be toting guns, and our door would be broken down at four in the morning and [rockabilly pioneer] Gene Vincent would be lying there on the floor. It was like, "Well, this is the way life is." I hadn't known anything else. So Ozzy didn't frighten me. I had known him in 1970. Then when he was out of Black Sabbath, he was living in a hotel down the road from where I lived. A friend of mine who owed me some money left it with Ozzy. So I went up to see Ozzy, and we struck up a real friendship. He was very down, and I could see that he needed someone to talk to. Over the next year we got together as a couple.

OZZY OSBOURNE: It was love at first sight. She was managing me for a while. She was working for her father. She came in to collect some money and I had spent it on coke.

SHARON OSBOURNE: Ozzy was so lovable. He was so endearing and he had this quality of just being so real. So many times you go out with guys in this industry and they're like Austin Powers. Half of them are wannabes and half of them have made it for five minutes, but they've all got attitudes and they're all full of shit. Ozzy was so honest. I loved that. And he's got a great sense of humor. He's very quick-witted. It was instant love. When we first got together everybody thought, "What could they possibly have in common? He's so outrageous and she's so normal." It's really totally the other way around because I was brought up with such chaos in my life.

OZZY OSBOURNE: When I met Sharon and decided to start making music again, we had nothing. I was broke and an alcoholic and a drug addict. But she made me feel better about myself. That's when her father basically fucked off. He didn't want her to manage me, but she was the only one who could do it.

SHARON OSBOURNE: It was very, very tough for me because I was used to getting up in the morning and picking which car I was going to drive to work and which style of bracelet I was going to put on. I was basically a spoiled, Jewish brat who'd had too much. To suddenly have nothing—not a credit card, not a car—nothing. It was tough. But it made me want to get it back again and it made me fight more.

With virtually no money and only their reputations to rely on, Ozzy and Sharon assembled a band featuring bassist Bob Daisley (ex-Rainbow), drummer Lee Kerslake (ex–Uriah Heep), keyboardist Don Airey (who had played on Black Sabbath's 1978 album, *Never*

Say Die) and practically unknown Quiet Riot guitarist Randy Rhoads, who also taught guitar at his mother's music school, Musonia, in North Hollywood. Osbourne's debut solo album, 1980's *Blizzard of Ozz*, kick-started his solo career, peaking at number 21 on the *Billboard* album chart with help from the hits "Crazy Train," "I Don't Know" and "Mr. Crowley." *Blizzard of Ozz* and its 1981 follow-up, *Diary of a Madman*, put Osbourne's career back on track. But he was still drinking, drugging, and raging out of control—as evidenced by a series of now legendary and well-documented antics. The first took place during a seemingly innocuous photo op at his new label, Jet, owned by Don Arden and distributed by CBS in the United States.

OZZY OSBOURNE: I was at the CBS Records Building for a meeting in 1981. I was very drunk and very stoned, and my wife told me to go in the room and throw these two fucking doves in the air as a peace offering. I was very out of control, and I threw one up and bit the other one's head off and threw it on the table. Before the day was out, it was on the press lines all over the world, and I was the asshole of the fucking year. My wife went fucking nuts when she got home. I was banned from my own record company's building.

SHARON OSBOURNE: That's just an example of how Ozzy's not like other people. He didn't have a normal upbringing; he had to work in a slaughterhouse killing cows. He would shoot five thousand cows in a day in the middle of the head. So for him to take a bird and spit its head out and laugh is nothing. But for people like us, it was, "How could you do that?" It was nothing to him.

In 1982, Ozzy caught more public flack, first in January for biting the head off a live bat in Des Moines, Iowa, and the following month in San Antonio, Texas, where he was arrested for lifting a dress he was wearing that belonged to his wife and urinating on a shrine to the fallen heroes of the Alamo. He was banned from performing in the city for a decade. The bat-related punishment was even more severe.

OZZY OSBOURNE: [Biting the head off the bat] wasn't planned at all. We were touring for *Diary of a Madman* and people would bring meat and throw it onstage. As the tour progressed, it jumped from meat to dead animals and cats. On top of it, I had these Halloween rubber bats on the stage. Unbeknownst to me, I picked one up and I put it in my mouth and it turned out to be a real bat. I bit on the fucking thing and heard a crunch. I had to go to the fucking hospital and get precautionary rabies shots. If you're gonna do something as stupid as me, be warned that these rabies shots are not fucking worth it. It fucking hurts like a son of a bitch. It feels like someone's injected sixty fucking golf balls in your ass. It was nothing short of agony. I made the front page everywhere and I couldn't even get out of the fucking bed to read it.

SHARON OSBOURNE: Ozzy and I were lying in bed watching the news and we were cracking up laughing thinking, "Why would anybody in their right mind find that newsworthy?" It's pathetic and it was on the national news. Somebody at the hospital informed the press because Ozzy went to have rabies shots. There were major events happening in the world, and suddenly Ozzy Osbourne is there with the head of the bat. We were hysterical. To think that it had gone that far and we'd had nothing to do with it.

OZZY OSBOURNE: I do some crazy things, some stupid things. But what right does anyone have to say I've lived a demonic existence? I don't sleep upside down on rafters. I don't nail myself to a cross in my room. I don't burn the first-born child of the person in the next room. I'm not a bloody Satanist. If you listen to [my song] "Mr. Crowley," that's a question [I'm asking]. It's not about [idolizing] Aleister Crowley. It was asking, "Who were you, what were you about, what the fuck were you thinking? I don't know anything about you. Please, somebody tell me." Then it wasn't too long before I started getting letters from the Crowley Society. I got really told off one time by somebody who said the name is not pronounced "Krow-ley," it's "Kroh-ley."

ZAKK WYLDE (Black Label Society, ex–Ozzy Osbourne): When we were recording the *Ozzmosis* album [in 1995], we did a batch of it in New York. There was this occult bookstore called the Magickal Childe, and they had everything in there about Wicca, Catholicism, Satanism, the whole nine yards. I was getting some Aleister Crowley stuff because Jimmy Page owned the castle [Crowley's former home, Boleskine House] and other guys were into him. I'm like, "What's the skinny on this guy?" I'm buying books as if I was doing a book report. I go to get this poster of Aleister Crowley that they had in there. I go, "How much for the poster?" The guy looks at me deadpan and says, "$6.66." I put seven bucks down and say, "Keep the goddamn change. I can't take it, dude." So I hang up the poster and the boss man walks in and he goes, "Zakk, who's the guy up on the wall?" I'm crying laughing and he goes, "Zakk, who the fuck is he?" I said, "Ozz, you don't know who that is?" He goes, "I don't fuckin' know. Who is it?" I go, "You've been singing about him for the last twenty years." He goes, "Well, who the fuck is it?" I said, "Ozz, it's Aleister Crowley, bro." He goes, "Oh, is that what that bald-headed cunt looks like?"

While a growing number of British metal bands were finding their foothold in America, Australia's AC/DC was at Compass Point studios in the Bahamas preparing to make the most important—and successful—album of their career. But first they needed a new singer to replace the late Bon Scott. After numerous auditions, they tried out Geordie vocalist Brian Johnson. His easygoing personality and hell-raising vocals injected new life into the band at the same time that guitarist Angus Young was writing his strongest material to date. The landmark *Back in Black*, which featured pounding, anthemic chart-toppers—including "You Shook Me All Night Long," "Hell's Bells," and the title track—sold more than twenty-two million copies in the United States by 2012.

BRIAN JOHNSON: I auditioned for AC/DC on [Tina Turner's] "Nutbush City Limits." That got their attention. They didn't know it, but Malcolm said, "Thank God for that, everybody else that's been in here wanted to do 'Smoke on the Water.' If we have to play that one more time, I'm going to die." The band [Geordie] I was in was playing the pubs and clubs. We had a big following, and it was a good wage packet every week—not massive, but good. We did "Whole Lotta Rosie" to finish off the set, which we'd just learned a couple months before because AC/DC then had a cult status. So when I joined AC/DC, the lads just said, "Listen, we'll put you on a wage for six months, and if it doesn't work out, then nobody's hurt." I said, "These guys are straight shooters. There's no bullshit." Of course, after three months, *Back in Black* went to number one, and their manager came and said, "I think we'd better talk." I didn't have a contract. I was still on a wage. I signed and they were great. The first thing I noticed about these guys was how straight they were. They wasn't two-faced at all.

DAVID FRICKE (*Rolling Stone*): *Back in Black* is the apex of heavy-metal art. . . . Much of the credit must go to Brian Johnson, a savage screamer who combines the breast-beating machismo of Led Zep's Robert Plant, the operatic howl of Ian Gillan (ex–Deep Purple) and the tubercular rasp of Slade's Noddy Holder into singular, nerve-racking, Tarzan-type shouts.

BRIAN JOHNSON: The cover art for *Back in Black* was a tribute to Bon. The boys didn't want anything mawkish or overbearingly sobby. They said, "Bon's memory must be kept in rock and roll, not as some sort of hymn or dirge. That's not what we want." One day about six songs in, me head was down, and I was spent. Mutt Lange, the producer, came down and he said, "Are you all right, Brian?" I said, "Mutt, I think I'm just dried up on this song." He said, "Well, which song?" I said, "I just got this from the boys and they want to title it 'Hell's Bells.'" I said, "What the fuck? I've already done 'Back in Black.' And that was, like, devilish." Just then there was the mother of all thunderstorms coming in. And it looked nasty out 'cause we were right at the sea [in Nassau, the Bahamas]. I said, "Jesus, the noise of the thunder is coming in." Mutt said, "There you go, there's a start, Brian, the rolling thunder," and I went, "It's fuckin' pouring rain, look at the wind, it's comin' on like a hurricane. And look at that lightning flashin' . . ." Honestly, I was like a reporter: "Across the sky, you're only young, but you're gonna die." I was going on, there was an alarm bell ringin,' so I went, "Got my bell, gonna take you to hell, gonna get ya, Satan get ya, hell's bells." That was it. It was ten minutes. I said, "Mutt, thank you."

While Ozzy and his ex–Black Sabbath bandmates were both undergoing career-changing transitions, Judas Priest was working the formula they built on *Sad Wings of Destiny* into more concise, arena-ready songs. They were also revamping their presentation, cementing their now-iconic biker look. Encouraged by rabid fan response, the danger and drama became more important than ever, and the farther they ventured, the more risks they took.

ROB HALFORD: We played a gig at the Birmingham Odium, and afterwards we said, "Wouldn't it be great if we could bring an actual bike onstage when we do 'Hell Bent for Leather'?" We didn't have our own bikes back then, but bikers would come to our gigs and we would say, "Hey, we'll buy you a couple of drinks if we can bring your bike onstage." We would use whatever bikes were in the venue if "Hell Bent for Leather" was on the set list. I would literally come roaring out onstage on this borrowed bike and the crowd would think, "What the fuck is this? This is crazy!"

GLENN TIPTON: Rob has fallen off his bike or driven it off the stage, but fortunately he usually wasn't hurt. As the productions got bigger, the secret was knowing where *not* to be at a particular point during the show, when a bomb went off or flamethrowers came out.

IAN HILL: A piece of the lighting rig broke off on the *Hell Bent for Leather* tour. The front hinge broke and missed [drummer] Dave Holland by inches. It started the whole truss rocking. If that had fallen into the audience it would have been terrible. Sometimes you're at the mercy of your equipment. On the *Turbo* tour we had a robot onstage that used to pick up Ken and Glenn. There were a couple of occasions where one of them almost fell out or they got stranded in midair when the hydraulics broke.

In 1980, after touring the United States, Europe, and Japan, Judas Priest headed into Tittenhurst Park, the UK house formerly owned by John Lennon, to work on *British Steel,* the album that would cement their reputation as self-proclaimed metal gods. Perhaps most impressively, they wrote and recorded all the songs in less than a month, including the classics "Living after Midnight" and "Breaking the Law," in conditions that could euphemistically be described as hectic.

ROB HALFORD: We were moving at the speed of light, making a record every year, working very, very hard to get all of the music ready in time for release. I suppose as a result of that, we put together a very uncomplicated, uncluttered, very minimally produced bunch of songs that really got the music and the message across in a very quick forty-minute blast. There were some really cool moments on *British Steel,* like "Rapid Fire" and "Steeler," which some people attest to being the early rumblings of thrash metal.

GLENN TIPTON: I was bashing a riff out late one night and Rob was in the bedroom above and came down all disheveled and said, "Hey guys, it's after midnight," and we said, "Yeah, we're living after midnight." And we just went with it. "Living After Midnight" became one of our most popular songs. *British Steel* was a very immediate album like that. But we had a surplus amount of energy and enthusiasm at that time, and I suppose there's a certain argument to be made that if you give yourself a deadline, you've got to come up with the goods, and we actually did. It was done and dusted in twenty-eight days.

ROB HALFORD: I don't recall feeling that much pressure, and it was really cool being in the house where John Lennon used to live. It looked as if John and Yoko had just recently vacated, and there were touches of them all through the house. Glenn's room was where John and Yoko used to sleep, and in the bathroom were two toilets next to each other and each had little plaques with their names on it. You can imagine them sitting there holding hands when they used the loo in the morning. I mean, how far are you prepared to love each other? "I still love you while I'm taking a dump."

GLENN TIPTON: One night [our producer] Tom [Allom] was practically passed out behind the bar and he was playing "When the Saints Go Marching In" on a big hunting horn. We were pouring large vodkas down it and that's the only thing that interrupted his melody. He'd guzzle up and then start again. Most nights, we'd be in the pub and then straggle back to the studio and play in a drunken stupor, and Tom couldn't have been too bad off because he managed to put all that stuff together quite nicely.

VINNIE PAUL ABBOTT (Pantera, Damageplan, Hellyeah): That album was huge for us. My brother [late Pantera guitarist] Dimebag

[Darrell Abbott] wore the Judas Priest [*British Steel*] razor blade around his neck his whole life. It meant everything to him. We were fucking crazy about that album. At the time, we thought, "That's the band we want to model ourselves after."

K.K. DOWNING (ex–Judas Priest): *British Steel* could almost have been called *The Almanac for a Teenage Rebel*. People were a bit down-spirited in the UK. Nothing was going particularly well. So it was the kind of album that sent out waves to everybody that said, "There's good things ahead, and we knew how you feel, and we were all feeling it the same." I think the fans wanted somebody or something to look up to and, lucky for us, they turned to Priest and *British Steel*.

ROB HALFORD: The nation was coming off the back of a number of very turbulent years under Margaret Thatcher. The recession and the strikes and the street riots were very difficult for a lot of people, and we felt a real kinship with them. "Breaking the Law" was almost a political protest song: "There I was completely wasting out of work and down . . . / You don't know what it's like." "Grinder" was about rejecting the establishment. I saw the system as the grinder and it was grinding people up. And "United" was very much about sticking together to get through these tough times.

Over the decades, countless metal scholars have compared Judas Priest to Iron Maiden. Both bands feature dynamic, octave-spanning vocalists, a multi-guitar approach (Maiden upped its "guitarsenal" to three players in 1999) all capable of precision riffs, searing harmonies, and mind-bending solos. Both rigged their stages with more props and pyro than a Fourth of July celebration. Like Priest, Maiden's beginnings were modest, and its growth gradual.

STEVE HARRIS (Iron Maiden): I wanted to be a drummer, but I thought, "I ain't got room and it's just too fucking noisy." I thought I'd do the next best thing and get a bass guitar and start playing along with the drums. I had an acoustic guitar and learned a few chords, then traded it in and got myself a Fender copy bass, 40 quid [about $70]. Once I got going, I started trying to be a bit clever and trying to learn stuff by [Yes bassist] Chris Squire. I was heavily influenced by progressive rock like Genesis, Jethro Tull, ELP, Yes, King Crimson . . . I used to love off-the-wall changes coming out of nowhere.

DAVE MURRAY (Iron Maiden): Like Steve, I'd been a skinhead. Then I went completely to the other extreme and became a hippie. It was a case of finding out more about the music and getting away from the violence. I heard [Jimi Hendrix's] "Voodoo Chile" on the radio and I thought, "Fucking hell! What is that?" I started wearing an Afghan coat, playing guitar, and going to gigs.

Taking its name from a Renaissance-era torture device, Iron Maiden formed on Christmas Day, 1975. The original lineup featured bassist and lyricist Steve Harris, guitarists David Sullivan and Terry Rance, drummer Dave Matthews, and vocalist Paul Day, who was soon replaced by Dennis Wilcock. Both guitarists left the band when Harris met axeman Dave Murray in 1976. Murray, who later anchored the band along with guitarist Adrian Smith, actually quit because he couldn't get along with Wilcock, but returned in 1977, the same year singer Paul Di'Anno joined.

STEVE HARRIS: Dave was the best guitarist I'd ever played with. Still is. After he joined we came up with early versions of "Wrathchild," "Prowler," and "Transylvania." "Purgatory" comes from that time, only then it was called "Floating." If we did a cover we'd make it one that people wouldn't necessarily know. So instead of "All Right Now" by Free we'd do "I'm a Mover." But as soon as an original came in, a cover would go out.

PAUL DI'ANNO (ex–Iron Maiden): They'd been going before me as
a little pub band with a couple of different singers. As I was
joining high school, Steve was just finishing [school]. Dennis
and I had a mutual friend who told me Iron Maiden were
looking for a singer. I said, "Who? Who the hell are they?"
Because I came from punk music. I spoke to Steve and he
said, "Well, are you gonna come out and try out?" I said,
"Well, I'm not really that bothered. I don't care that much."
But I agreed to go to a rehearsal, which is really strange because I knew absolutely nothing about rock music whatsoever.
I had a rough idea of one Deep Purple song, like "Dealer" or
something. I didn't even know the words. I just made them
up as we went along. Later that evening Steve came around
my house and said, "You got the job if you want it." I said,
"Well, not really." Then a couple months later I went over
to his house and he played me some of the songs that became
the first Iron Maiden album. I dunno. Something about it
just clicked. I thought, "Wow, this could be good." Because
it really was so different. It was complicated metal that was
played really fast, and I thought, "Wow, this is cool."

The NWOBHM movement began at the Bandwagon Heavy
Metal Soundhouse, located in a corner of the Prince of Wales pub
in Kingsbury, North London. DJ Neal Kay spun records by emerging bands, and before long it was a hotspot for local journalists.
The place became so popular that Iron Maiden's legendary first
recording with Di'Anno in 1978 became known as the *Soundhouse
Tapes,* and the band struck a nerve almost immediately.

NEAL KAY (Club DJ): I was running and screaming around the
lounge like a lunatic. I just couldn't stop playing [Maiden's
four-track demo]. The combination of speed, power, the key
changes, the melody, and Dave Murray's melody lines bowled
me over. It was definitely the most impressive demo I'd ever
had delivered to me. The next day I phoned Steve Harris and

said to him, "You've got something here that could make you a lot of money." And he laughed at me. He thought I was kidding!

PAUL DI'ANNO: We did the Soundhouse tapes in 1978 [in a single twenty-four-hour session] at Spaceward Studios in Cambridge. We only did five hundred copies of the original. It's like gold dust now it's so rare, and I gave all my copies away. From that, EMI asked us to be on a compilation, the *Metal For Muthas* record, which was put together by Neal Kay. From there on, we were taken over by a real manager, which was Rod [Small-wood] and Iron Maiden was offered a deal on [EMI].

BIFF BYFORD: [I first heard the phrase New Wave of British Heavy Metal] around 1980, about seven years after me and [guitarist] Paul [Quinn got together]. We were looking at all those [Sabbath- and Priest-] type of bands all through the seventies, really. We chose the rock-and-roll rather than the punk route. We were looking at a lot of progressive rock bands like Yes and Genesis, and obviously we were listening to Zeppelin and Cream. But our music was a bit more aggressive, a bit faster. I think the press just coined NWOBHM to make it a bit different from the more established bands of the time.

JOE ELLIOT (Def Leppard): Were we part of the New Wave of British Heavy Metal? Well, from a timing point of view, absolutely. But to me it's as relevant as saying we came out in the new romantic period, too, because that was 1979. So you might as well compound us with Duran Duran. The New Wave of British Heavy Metal was a convenient label created possibly by Geoff Barton at *Sounds* magazine to create a scene and sell more copies.

BIFF BYFORD: I *would* [call Def Leppard NWOBHM], but obviously *they* won't. They seem to think it's a dirty word. But in the early days they were part of it, definitely. Their first EP is a bit Thin Lizzy-ish. Heavy rock, heavy metal. Later on, they became more commercial and had great success with that, but I think in the early days they *were* part of the movement.

GEOFF BARTON (ex-*Sounds*, *Kerrang!*): We ran the NWOBHM feature with Maiden in it in *Sounds*, and the response was just phenomenal. Suddenly there were new heavy metal bands springing up everywhere. Of course, not all of them were as competent or as interesting as Iron Maiden and Def Leppard, but the fact that they were even trying was news back then, and we just ran with it, for about two years in the end.

NICK BOWCOTT (Grim Reaper): Heavy metal got so big at the time that they would actually have heavy metal charts amongst the regular charts printed in the back of magazines like *NME* [*New Musical Express*] and *Melody Maker*. Those charts were invariably put together by guys like Neal Kay, who were doing heavy metal discos. You could send these guys demos, and if they liked you they'd spin it, and if they got a response they would chart you. Three of our songs charted based on a four-track demo because we were motivated enough to get those demos into people's hands and they liked the songs.

BRIAN TATLER (Diamond Head): *Sounds* started raving about Iron Maiden, Samson, Saxon, and Def Leppard. These bands got played on Radio One Sessions and we'd think, "Who are all these young bands our age, nineteen-years-old, doing all this metal stuff?" I bought *The Def Leppard EP* they pressed themselves, and I thought it was really good. Next thing you know, Leppard were signed to Phonogram, and Iron Maiden got signed to EMI. I was thinking this has got to be the next big thing—Diamond Head need to get signed *now*. I thought we'd get picked up on the New Wave of British Heavy Metal thing because after *Sounds* coined the phrase, suddenly it had national coverage and we could play London. We played with Angel Witch and Maiden, and we were able to get around the country and start making our own records.

NICK BOWCOTT: The first small band I ever saw that actually made me fire a drummer was Diamond Head, followed by Raven. I remember seeing them and going, "Holy shit, someone just raised the bar really high." It was a great time to be around. We were going through uncharted territory. It was a rude awakening to come to America and meet bands whose main concern was not their songs, but getting signed. They'd say, "I know this person who works for this record label." It was, like, "What?" It was almost like the music was secondary to getting a deal. Whereas we were just four ugly dudes who think *British Steel* is the best album ever, love Van Halen, write hooks, and have a great singer.

JOHN GALLAGHER (Raven): When we first got together in the seventies, there was a circuit of workingmen's clubs. You'd sign up, get cheap beer. You could play bingo, and there would be bands playing. In the northeast of England a lot of them were hard rock bands, like Son of a Bitch, who changed their name to Saxon. There were a lot of punks there so it was a bit rough. We learned our trade from being three feet in front of somebody who was looking at you going, "Impress me!" If you didn't, they'd throw beer at you or spit on you. We'd do anything to get attention, and we got a reputation as the band that would play and go crazy and throw all our equipment around and smash stuff.

PAUL DI'ANNO: We used to get all this amphetamine sulfate in these different forms. There was one we'd call cat's piss because you'd do a line of it and your eyes was watering and your nose is burning. But if you do a gram you'll be off your face for the good part of two days. We also used to do these pills called

Speckled Blues. Take three of them and you could walk from London to Scotland and you wouldn't even care. I used to stay amped up with it. Unfortunately, that became quite a bad thing for me in the end. Steve [Harris] was always completely straight. Once, he got drunk on the subway going back to East London on about a pint and a half of beer. All of a sudden, he jumped out at Bethel Green completely wasted. We found him on the Bethel Green common half way up a tree.

The quintessential heavy metal warrior, Lemmy Kilmister, may abhor rock labels, preferring to be viewed in the vein of his idols, Eddie Cochran and Jimi Hendrix. However, Kilmister made his most indelible mark during the NWOBHM movement with Motörhead's self-titled debut, which came out in 1977, the same year as the Sex Pistols' legendary *Never Mind the Bollocks*.

LEMMY KILMISTER: Motörhead is primitive brutality, I suppose. It's rock and roll, you know? People always like rock and roll. You can bop to it if you're very quick.

DAVE GROHL (Foo Fighters, Them Crooked Vultures, Nirvana): When I met Lemmy, it was like meeting the fifth Beatle. He was walking out of a strip club and was at the video poker machine. I said, "Hey man, I've got a lot of respect for you." Then I ran away before he could say anything. Years later, when I finally got the chance to work with him, he came into the studio and drank a half a fifth of Jack Daniel's before he even got in front of a microphone. Then he sang [my Probot] song "Shake Your Blood" twice, and it sounded genius. He played bass on it in two takes. Then we were done and he said, "Okay, who wants to go look at some tits?" One time, I asked him to meet me at the Rainbow for a drink. I had never been there. He's been going there since 1971—there's a fucking portrait of him above the bar. He told me a pretty hilarious story about Motörhead drummer ["Philthy Animal" Taylor] being so fucked up on drugs that he tried to climb out of his hotel room through a mirror. Hanging out with Lemmy is a guaranteed good time. He's like a stand-up comedian. If this Motörhead thing doesn't work out, he could do well up in the Catskills.

PAUL DI'ANNO: One time I was standing with Lemmy at this place in Camden Town. He used to go up there, drink Jack Daniel's and Coke, and play the slot machines. I was there trying to keep up with him. I didn't realize I'd been there for nearly six hours, and I wondered why I couldn't move. I was absolutely fucked out of my mind. Lemmy's just standing there talking away to me, and I'm thinking, "How the hell does he do this every bloody day?" He's insane. I'm surprised he's still alive.

Released in 1981 during the heart of the NWOBHM movement, *Killers* was the first of nine Maiden albums produced by Martin Birch. While groups like Witchfinder General, Samson (featuring future Maiden front man Bruce Dickinson), Angel Witch, Girlschool, and Tygers of Pan Tang were still heating up, Maiden was going supernova.

PAUL DI'ANNO: The first big tour Maiden did in England was Priest's *British Steel* tour, which was fun. Then in '81 they wanted us to come over [to America] with them because they weren't selling tickets, as we were the new boys and *everybody* wanted to come and see us. An interviewer said, "How will it be with you and Judas Priest?" and somebody in our camp said, "Ah, it'll be no problem. We'll kick their asses. They're all old men." Apparently Kenny (K.K.) Downing was a bit pissed off. Unfortunately, I got blamed for that.

K.K. DOWNING: All credit due to Maiden that they were gunning to overthrow the mighty Priest or aspiring to one day. We thought that was great because that's all we ever did when *we* supported bands—try to take the stage away from them. And it made us work harder.

BRIAN TATLER: Maiden were a little bit rock star-ish, I thought. They didn't give us a sound check. They would spend hours sound-checking and by the time it was our turn, the doors were open and all the crowd poured in. I think they probably thought we were some Northern upstarts trying to steal their thunder.

MARTIN POPOFF: The New Wave of British Heavy Metal is super important because, number one, it really helped define heavy metal. You had a uniform, you had four or five songs on every record about how great it was to be metal, no ballads, the playing was elevated. Even Black Sabbath sounded simple compared to a lot of these bands. Everything about these bands was heavy metal, so really, if you could go back and find shreds of things that define heavy metal along the way, this was a place where all of them came together.

EDDIE TRUNK: Saxon I still love, but they've never emerged beyond a club act in America. You hear that [NWOBHM] title, you're like, "Oh my god, like fifteen huge bands came from that." But no. NWOBHM was just a scene and a fertile time for British metal. But in America, unless you were really tied in and really a freak for it, it didn't really resonate.

BIFF BYFORD: [Saxon's 1980 album] *Wheels of Steel* came out the same time as Judas Priest's *British Steel*, so it was a bit of a race up the charts at one point. We were one of the biggest bands of that time, from 1980 to 1982. We were probably bigger than Maiden back then. Our first U.S. show with Mötley Crüe was the first time we'd ever played in front of twelve thousand girls and four guys. That was a time of liberation for a lot of young girls, and rock 'n' roll seemed to be the catalyst. There were a lot of girls in America. Not too young. But young enough, and old enough, if you know what I mean.

NICK BOWCOTT: Back then cocaine was a very social drug and the girls were surprisingly willing to do things they probably shouldn't have, on reflection. It was a wonderful time pre any nasty social diseases. Grim Reaper wasn't formed in the hope of getting laid, but it was a nice fringe benefit.

JACKIE CHAMBERS (Girlschool): Girlschool found itself in such a male-dominated arena we were bound to be hailed by some (especially early on) as just a novelty band. But we managed to get past that without being hell-bent on proving a point. I still think a lot of guys felt a bit stupid listening to or admitting to the fact that they liked—and God forbid were playin' air guitar to—a bunch of girls. And no, we never thought of ourselves as anything other than a rock-and-roll band. The fact that we were an all-girl band wasn't an issue to us—just everybody else. Although we weren't really bothered by any outright sexism ourselves.

LEMMY KILMISTER: Girlschool came along about two years after the Runaways. They were a great band and I loved them, but they never became famous because they couldn't afford to tour the U.S. I took them out with us in 1979 when we toured for *Overkill* because I heard their song "Take it All Away" and I thought it was fucking excellent. I always supported them because they were great girls. They loved rock-and-roll, same as me. Their guitarist Kelly Johnson was amazing. It was really sad when she died from cancer [in 2007].

Paul Di'Anno played a major role in Maiden's initial success. But two albums into the band's more than thirty-year career, he was fired for excessive drug use and replaced by Bruce Dickinson.

ALBERT MUDRIAN (author, *Choosing Death*; editor in chief, *Decibel*): Those first couple Iron Maiden records were pretty rough-and-tumble, whereas when they hooked up with Bruce Dickinson the songs became more epic, and you got this overblown and ridiculous presentation. But the thing about Maiden, even when they were playing with Di'Anno, and then were moving on to the style with Dickinson, their presentation was tied together. They had their logo and their album covers with Derek Riggs, which incorporated the band mascot, Eddie, who was in the stage show. That was ingenious. There weren't a lot of heavy metal bands outside of Alice Cooper that had that huge focus on that area of presentation and that was something that hooked people early on. The band was going to sell a lot of shirts no matter how many records they sold just because they had a great logo and this great presentation.

PAUL DI'ANNO: During my last tour with the band, me and Steve almost came to blows right before we went on in Glasgow. He was going, "Yeah, you're fucking up. You can't be bothered anymore." I said, "Oh, fuck you." I was about to fuckin' hit him and then the intro came on and we all forgot about it and went onstage. We finished that tour and [management] says, "Paul, come into the office, we want to have a word." I said, "I think I know what it's all about so I'm gonna tell you anyway what I want to do before you say anything." I said, "I'll just move on. It's the best thing for everybody."

BRUCE DICKINSON: I was with Samson; we all knew each other. Clive Burr, the original Maiden drummer, was in Samson for two years before Maiden. It was a big hodgepodge of musicians who all went to each other's shows and toured with each other. Everybody knew who did what, and who was capable of what. The first time I saw Maiden I was blown away. I was a big Deep Purple fan when I was a kid. *In Rock* [1970] first got me going. The feeling I got off Maiden was like that—no disrespect to Paul, [Di'Anno]—I looked at Paul and went, "Goddamn, I want to be up there. God, if I was singing for that band, wow, what stuff we could do."

PAUL DI'ANNO: I knew Bruce. Fucking hell, they were horrible—Samson, I'm sorry to say. Bruce was pretty good, but the way he used to dress was awful. We used to make fun of him. It always looked like Stevie Wonder dressed him. It was all mismatched and he had this beard. He's all right, Bruce. If he could leave his ego behind he'd be all right.

BRUCE DICKINSON: A year later, I was doing a show [with Samson] at Reading Festival, and Rod Smallwood, who is Maiden's manager, came up after the show, and Steve [Harris] had been in the audience. They'd both come to check me out. Rod said, "We'd like to offer you the chance to audition for Iron Maiden." I was, like, twenty-two, but I was full of piss and vinegar, and I said, "Look, mate, if I audition for the band, I'm going to get the job. So let's not muck about. First, I'm gonna be a bit of an awkward customer, and I'm going to have a lot of opinions, and if you don't want that kind of a guy in the band, tell me now so we don't waste our time." I thought, "Wow, did I really say that?" He went, "Okay, fair enough. That won't be a problem." I went down, I learned both albums. They only wanted me to learn four songs, but I had a couple weeks so I learned everything they'd ever done and walked into rehearsals and we bashed through a big chunk of their entire repertoire. Steve wanted to get me in the studio that day, but one wasn't available, so a week or so later they came back and got me in the studio, and we did four songs so they could have a listen to what I sounded like in the studio. That took a couple hours, and they said, "Right, that's it, let's go get drunk, it's happened." And the next album was *Number of the Beast*.

MARTIN BIRCH (producer): Bruce was capable of handling lead vocals on some of the quite complicated directions I knew Steve wanted to explore. So when Bruce joined, it opened up the possibilities for the new album tremendously—and for that reason, *Number of the Beast* was the turning point for Iron Maiden.

BRUCE DICKINSON: When I was recording *Number of the Beast*, there was that quiet, whispered intro. [There] wasn't a question of [me] not being able to physically sing [right after that], but there was an atmosphere [producer] Martin [Birch] wanted, that I couldn't quite get, and I ended up throwing chairs, and going, "What is it you want?!" We were in the control room and Martin said, "Look, when we were doing *Heaven and Hell* with Black Sabbath, Ronnie came in, and they were all ready to go, and we started recording the song 'Heaven and Hell,' and Ronnie was note-perfect. Then Martin stopped and said 'Ronnie, we need to do this again, rethink it,' and Ronnie said, 'What's the problem, was it out of tune?' Martin said, 'No, no, but if you listen to your opening lines, it says, *Sing me a song you're a singer.* You *are* a singer. It's your life. So I just want those two lines delivered as if your entire life depends on it." That was the way Martin got inside your head.

ADRIAN SMITH (Iron Maiden): The *Piece of Mind* American tour was probably the start of the whole band becoming a little bit more sensible. In the past, touring America had been so easy. We'd do our spot early on and spend the rest of the night having a good time. Now we were headlining and we couldn't afford to piss around. People said we were wrong to go out as headliners in the States so soon; that we weren't ready for it and we'd never be able to pull it off. We had something to prove. We all took it a little bit more seriously.

STEVE HARRIS: For me, [1983's] *Piece of Mind* was the best album we'd done up to then, easily. I carried on thinking that right up until [1988's] *Seventh Son of a Seventh Son* album, five years later. I'm not saying the two albums we did in between, [1984's] *Powerslave* and [1986's] *Somewhere in Time*, weren't good, 'cause there's a lot of stuff on those albums I still think of as some of our best ever. But *Piece of Mind* was just special. It was [drummer] Nicko McBrain's first album. [Di'Anno-era drummer Clive Burr left in 1982.] We felt like we were on a high, and you can hear that mood on the album.

In the wake of the New Wave of British Heavy Metal, two main subgenres emerged: thrash bands—including Metallica, Exodus, and Anthrax—which were heavily influenced by the musicality of Diamond Head and Raven and the speed of Motörhead (and will be addressed in detail later); and doom outfits, which were more drawn to the lazier tempos, psychedelic textures, and sludgier, Sabbathian riffs of Angel Witch and Witchfinder General. Pentagram, which had been around in the Washington, DC, area since 1971, suddenly came alive, and in 1985 released its eponymous debut. Sweden's Candlemass; Chicago's Trouble; Washington, DC's the Obsessed; and LA's Saint Vitus (the latter two of which were fronted by Scott "Wino" Weinrich) weren't far behind. From those tangled roots sprung Down, Cathedral, Kyuss, Eyehategod, Sleep, Orange Goblin, and countless others who valued the intangible journey to the end of a song as much as the elements that brought them there.

BOBBY LIEBLING: I was a huge Sabbath fan. When Tony Iommi first came on the scene, he was the fastest guitar player I had ever heard. Their music was all bummed out and sick, soupy, heavy moan-tone guitars. I was crazy about 'em.

JOE HASSELVANDER (Raven, ex-Pentagram): Sabbath wasn't the first band to do doom metal. There were many other bands at the same time doing the same thing. Most of them were German and Italian: Black Widow, Night Sun, Iron Claw. There's a band called Zior, and the guy who did their first album cover did the first Sabbath album cover. There was a whole lot of sinister riffing. Even Toe Fat had stuff that was as sinister sounding. Sabbath's first album, to me, sounds a lot like the first two Taste records by Rory Gallagher. It's jazz-oriented, but yet it's hard rocking, too.

BOBBY LIEBLING: We started Pentagram on Christmas day, 1971. At the time, nobody knew what the word *pentagram* meant at all—I mean *nobody.*

JOE HASSELVANDER: Bobby had been in bands called Shades of Darkness and Ice. Pentagram was going to be called Stone Bunny as a joke because [guitarist] Randy Palmer said, "Pentagram? You might as well call the band Stone Bunny, it's so stupid."

SCOTT "WINO" WEINRICH (Saint Vitus, ex–The Obsessed): I met Bobby Liebling a pretty long time ago, but he'd already been doing Pentagram for years before I had a working band. He was definitely the first guy from our area to be doing that heavy music that we love. I was coming out of a Motörhead concert and I saw Bobby standing outside asking everybody that came out if they had drugs. I was like, "Wow, that's so radical."

BOBBY LIEBLING: My favorite Pentagram album of all time is [1991's] *Sub Basement,* and that record is extremely bummed out and depressing and horribly difficult to listen to—for me, even. It's total sonic overload and it makes you want to kill yourself. We wanted to do the most depressing album in history. We were going to call the album after *Sub Basement* "Bummer." It was really cool to be suicidally depressed and in absolute hopeless despair.

JOE HASSELVANDER: Bobby got the job done musically on *Sub Basement* because I *made* him. If I hadn't been there, it wouldn't have happened. He had all his drug paraphernalia and sat on the couch downstairs while I'm upstairs in the control room mixing the record. I'd come downstairs. He'd wake up and go, "Sounds perfect. Don't change a thing." How would he know? He's not even upstairs listening. I used to have to wake him up in between lines in the song. He'd fall asleep standing up. But

I would make him do it. I have compassion for people. Bobby is extremely talented. Nobody can take that from him, but he has to have somebody there doing it for him, then he always takes the credit. When you work with Pentagram, he gets the glory and the band who did it gets nothing. I played all the instruments on the entire album. I mixed it. I didn't mind, but when I found out he had taken some of my songs from earlier years and claimed he wrote them, and when I went to BMI and found out that he was the composer and author of my songs, that was it. That was a sign of someone who's desperate and wants to make sure he always has that drug money.

WINO: One time me and Bobby shot drugs together. He had all the connections—anything you wanted any time of day, night or day. He'd say "park here." Five minutes later he comes back with the stuff. He had huge scars all over his body. It looked like somebody held him down and put cigars out on him for about a week. We were in the bathroom one time and Bobby said, "Will this freak you out?" And he just jabs the fucking spike straight down between two tendons in his wrist, right into an artery. I've never seen anything like that.

BOBBY LIEBLING: I should have died twenty-five years ago. I should be dead ten times over. I've been addicted to heroin for forty years and methadone for thirty years. I was on methadone and shooting heroin on top of it seven days a week and smoking $500 to $1,000 of crack every single day around the clock. I've had lots of near-death experiences. The last one I had, I had just taken my methadone. I had been awake around the clock smoking crack for six days straight before a gig. No water, no food, not a minute of sleep. And I was debuting a brand new Pentagram lineup at a packed house at the Black Cat in Washington, DC. I wasn't aware that I came out on-stage twice and then fell into the drum set and blacked out. Then, of course, I seized because of all the drugs. I flatlined twice on the way to the hospital. Next thing I knew, I was going down a tunnel of light. Many people who have died and then been revived talk about the tunnel of light. It's all true. I couldn't believe it. There's a funnel, and at the end of it there are globule amoeba-type things. One had my grandmother's face, but they're translucent and out of focus, and they kind of glob together like an overhead light show projector. Everyone is beckoning you with their hands, telling you to come to the light. And you're sliding down the slide, tranquil as a baby. I almost got through the tunnel. Then it felt like there was a kaleidoscope closing up the hole in the middle with these propeller-like flaps, and I felt like I got sucked back up a sewage pipe, and realized I was alive. God told me I wasn't ready. I'm a very strong believer in God nowadays, regardless of the name of the band.

Even though Washington, DC, was the launching pad for '80s U.S. doom thanks to Pentagram, Saint Vitus, Obsessed and Internal Void, a decade later New Orleans became "doom central." Major bands included Eyehategod, Crowbar, Soilent Green, and Down, a supergroup that featured Pantera vocalist Phil Anselmo and bassist Rex Brown (who quit in 2011), Crowbar front man and guitarist Kirk Windstein, Corrosion of Conformity guitarist Pepper Keenan, and Eyehategod guitarist Jimmy Bower (on drums).

MIKE IX WILLIAMS (Eyehategod): New Orleans is a grim place. It's very hot in the summer, there's lots of poverty and crime. I guess it did manifest itself somehow in the music and with the feedback and the dirty sound. We were huge Melvins fans and we liked Black Flag. But besides being into them, we liked that [doom metal] was easy to play because we weren't very good musicians when we started [in 1988]. We basically played three chords a song, but slowed down with me screaming over it. Our shows were pretty crazy. I used to break a lot of glass and cut myself with it—stupid, childish stuff, really. After we started getting a following, people would put bottles in front of me onstage because they knew I would smash them. One time in Dayton, Ohio, I cut myself really bad on the forehead and I started getting kind of dizzy, but we finished the whole set. It was a weird night because a bunch of the kids in the crowd had brought angel dust and I did that before we played, which made me feel weird to begin with. Anyway, I guess I hit an artery with a shard of glass because my forehead was pumping out blood. A friend of mine, [horror director] Jim Van Bebber, was there with his girlfriend. She was standing a foot or two away from me and she kept getting sprayed by my forehead— all over her chest. We went next door to the fire station and they bandaged me up and told me I had to go to the hospital, and from there I got stitches, which I took out myself three days later.

PEPPER KEENAN (Corrosion of Conformity, Down): We grew up together in New Orleans since we were fucking kids. Phil [Anselmo] and I used to jam in 1992 when we was sixteen years old. We were into Saint Vitus, Sabbath, Trouble, and all this heavy shit, and we were all stoned and drunk so the music came out really doomy. We went in there for a laugh, but ten minutes later we weren't laughing anymore. So we made a tape and started trading it around. Next thing we knew, six years had passed and people were still asking about it.

JIM WELCH (ex-A&R, Earache Records): I've never seen anybody as a collective group take more different kinds of downers than Eyehategod and Crowbar. Guys in New Orleans are really into that, which I never really understood. But shit, you can hear it in their albums.

PHIL ANSELMO (Down, Pantera, Superjoint Ritual) [2002 interview]: For six months after my first real bout with hard dope, I used to have dreams about it. I used to yearn for it a lot. That's where a lot of the depression comes from—wanting something you can't have, and you really can't have it because you damn well know what's coming. That's why I say do it

in moderation—so you don't get caught up in the fucking
game. Don't go chasing it. There's a time and place for just
about fucking everything unless it fucking sucks you in. [After
surviving a crippling addiction, overdoses, and major back
surgery, Anselmo kicked hard drugs. He has since reversed
his stance on moderation and now helps struggling addicts get
clean.]

MIKE IX WILLIAMS: We played at the Covered Wagon in San
Francisco and I drank a lot of Jagermeister and had some dope.
I got back to the house we were staying at and I had the bright
idea to do some more heroin, which was stupid after drinking that much. I was locked in this bathroom and I wouldn't
be here right now if there hadn't been a window in the bathroom. There was hardly anybody at the house, but somebody
said they heard a thump. That was me hitting my head against
the wall when I fell off the side of the toilet overdosed. Mi-
raculously, they heard that and ended up breaking through
this window and pulling me out, and somebody else gave me
mouth to mouth—so I'm still here. I remember I jumped up,
I don't know what I was thinking, but I remember coming to
and seeing all these people standing over me, and they said I
jumped up and started humming as if nothing happened.

BOBBY LIEBLING: When they came out, I wasn't crazy about
Saint Vitus or Trouble. I had been doing that kind of a thing
already for ten years. If I'm to be completely honest, I was
kind of bitter that I had never gotten recognized for anything
and these bands got overnight acclaim and were viewed as
pioneers.

PHIL ANSELMO: There would be no Down if it wasn't for Trouble [who Pantera took on tour in 1992]. Yeah, they play slow,
but as far as their influence goes, it's vast and comes from a lot
of different sources other than Black Sabbath. Eric Wagner had
a miserable quality to his voice. He sounded in pain. It was a

depressing sound going along with these droning, beautifully constructed riffs and great drumming.

DAVE GROHL: What was doubly amazing about Trouble was not only were they heavier than most bands, but they were singing about God. How's that possible? It was cool and off-center and something you'd never expect. Listen to those first two records, [1984's *Psalm 9* and 1985's *The Skull*], and they'll blow your fucking mind. But it's weird. God and metal haven't really had the best relationship with each other.

RICK WARTELL (Trouble): Eventually, a couple of the guys became practicing Christians, but we were *never* a Christian band—by no means. There were some good messages there, and Eric started reading the Bible and using cool quotes from it. But it didn't dawn on any of us that this would become a kinda stamp on us. When we got the "white metal" tag, that really didn't sit well with us. I mean, we did a lot of cocaine and weed—everybody but [guitarist] Bruce [Franklin]. We were rock guys, man. We went out and got drunk and met girls and did things rock guys do. It's how we lived.

JOSH HOMME (Queens of the Stone Age, Them Crooked Vultures, ex-Kyuss): I'm not into Trouble and I thought Vitus was cheesy. I hate both those bands. I was into Black Flag, Minutemen, and the Descendents. That's what was more vital and important. Vitus was just some cheesy guys in pants that were too tight.

While Danzig frontman Glenn Danzig was reclusive and moody in person, his band had an accessible sound that downplayed the punk roots of his earlier groups, Misfits and Samhain. On their first four groundbreaking albums, Danzig combined Elvis-meets-Bauhaus vocals with sustained, sensual guitar chords and pulsing, pounding rhythms, paving the way for the mainstream success of Type O Negative and other so-called gothic doom metal bands.

GLENN DANZIG (Danzig, ex-Samhain, ex-Misfits): Danzig stayed together long enough for people to catch up with it. The previous bands I was in always either broke up or, you know, Samhain turned into Danzig. "Mother," [which first appeared on the band's self-titled 1988 debut], was a live track on [the 1993 EP *Thrall: Demonsweatlive*] and [that's when] it started getting some airplay. Radio guys were calling up Mark [DiDia] over at American Recordings and saying, "You should re-release 'Mother.' "

EERIE VON (ex-Danzig, Samhain): Nobody gave a shit the first time [we released "Mother"], and it was all because of the video, [which depicts Danzig sacrificing a chicken above a scantily clad woman lying on a pedestal]. We gave the video to MTV, which was the dumbest thing we could have done. From that moment on, they were not going to play any video we gave them. They'd give them back to us and tell us what to edit one hundred times, and we'd do the edits. They still wouldn't play it. If we had started out with a video they would have played, we might still all be together. Because everyone loved the live video [of "Mother"], we sold five hundred thousand copies of it in no time. Everyone was saying we were going to be the next Metallica and it didn't happen, so people started to quit. We weren't making a living, so there was no reason to keep going.

The sullen atmospheres and granite-heavy riffs of doom metal were sonically the stuff of internal bleeding, not carefree celebration. And while many bands kept to themselves and reveled in the darkness, others, such as Type O Negative and Monster Magnet, partied like Mötley Crüe. Type O front man Peter Steele even posed as a *Playgirl* centerfold in 1985.

JOSH SILVER (Type O Negative): Peter [Steele] was big and considered himself kind of goofy. He didn't have girlfriends growing up, which was a little rough for him. A lot of Type O music was written from the perspective of someone who couldn't get laid or wanted to get laid. We had songs like "I Know You're Fucking Someone Else." He was able to be very honest about how hurt he was during a lot of these periods. I think that was part of what made us appealing. We told the truth.

DAVE WYNDORF (Monster Magnet): I never thought I could be Sabbath, but when I saw the Ramones I knew I could be *these* guys. It was a real triumph of wit over talent. Focus your psychosis. Even if you've got a psychological problem, whatever is going on with you that makes the energy run through you, use it to create things.

KENNY HICKEY (Type O Negative): We were the premier white trash stripper band. Every night we came offstage [on the Mötley Crüe tour] we had all these desperate fat guys working for us, so they would all round [the girls] up, and you'd go to the front and there would be twenty sets of legs. It was ridiculous, the bus shaking, music blasting, people dancing, every night. It was the exact opposite of what you'd picture the band would be like by listening to our music; it was complete debauchery. Pete Steele partook more than anybody. Nobody could drink as much as him, nobody could do as much drugs as him, nobody could eat as much as him, and nobody could fuck as much as that man.

PHIL CAIVANO (Monster Magnet): One time in New York I fucked this girl on the tour bus. I had my fist in her pussy, and she was slapping me around. When we finished, she pulled out this official police ID and says, "Thank god you were good because if you weren't, I would have arrested you."

KENNY HICKEY: [Peter] saw how many women he was getting after [1993's] *Bloody Kisses* and the song "Black No. 1 (Little Miss Scare-All)," so he decided to design the band towards getting more chicks. *October Rust* was intentionally sensual just to get the high heels in the door. It was a pimp record. He was with two, three different girls a day. It's a great record, but his goal in making it was to fucking wrangle them up.

PETER STEELE (1962–2010) (Type O Negative, Carnivore): Not to be gross, but everybody wants to suck the king's dick 'cause he's top of the hill. I mean look, older men with a lot of money and high positions in government or business always wind up with the most attractive women. As the band did better and better we attracted more and more women.

PHIL CAIVANO: People think AIDS killed sex, but the thing about AIDS is it has forced people to get more creative. You can have a great time without actually sticking it in. Like, there's lots of girls out there who would love to get it on with another girl and have a guy watch and masturbate.

Predictably, the deeper that doom metal musicians got into downers and narcotics, the more dangerous their lives became. Other doom pioneers had already been there and done that, and were persevering with their careers without the baggage of addiction. In 2006, Ronnie James Dio rejoined his Sabbath band-mates after an absence of thirteen years and remained with them for several tours and 2009's *The Devil You Know* album (under the name Heaven & Hell, due to legal restrictions with the name Black Sabbath).

RONNIE JAMES DIO: The band started out with several tracks that we wanted to do for an anthology. The label requested a couple of previously unreleased tracks from the past. Well, we didn't work that way. We always recorded the songs we needed to do for an album and didn't keep anything back. So I went to Tony's house in England, where he has a studio. And we started to work and it was really enjoyable. After long spaces of time not working with people, you forget how good they are or how much you enjoyed being around them.

TONY IOMMI: We did these three songs and had such a good time that we forgot about any of the difficult things that had happened in the past. We were creating something new and that made it all worthwhile. It didn't even seem like we had been apart. You learn to appreciate a lot when you're away from each other. It was the same with Ozzy. When we got back together it was great to do the reunion and you forget about all the other things that went on.

RONNIE JAMES DIO: We should have called the band The Locusts because every twelve years we come back somehow. I'd be a fool if I said I didn't have any reservations, because you remember things that weren't particularly pleasing in the past. It makes you think, "Is it going to happen again?" But once I decided to do another full album, I realized that all those little pebbles from the past had to be left on the beach. I don't think you can bring them along with you on these trips into the water because they're just going to get so heavy you're going to drown.

When it came to the physical and mental dangers of excess and indulgence, generally the famous rockers learned their lessons, or maybe they just settled down. That wasn't always the case for less established, younger, and unmarried rockers, who still hadn't been burned badly enough to mend their ways. Inevitably, some pushed the envelope until they suffered a brush with death that made them at least reevaluate their lifestyle. Type O Negative front man Pete Steele battled a monstrous cocaine habit that threatened his health and career, and Dave Wyndorf overdosed on pills in 2006.

PETER STEELE: I found myself beginning to experiment with drugs about [1997], and that made a profound and unfortunately negative impact on me. I didn't even start with beer or a joint. I went right to the cocaine up the nose and I had never really done it until the age of thirty-five. I'm so ashamed of myself. I had this "it can't happen to me" attitude.

KENNY HICKEY: It's strange, because before that, Pete was ob-sessed with working out. He was a gorilla. We had weights on the road. He was all into the health shit, and then one night he came up to me because he was frustrated about something and said, "Give me a line of that." I was like, "You don't want this shit," and I tried to talk him out of it. And he just broke my balls about it. And yeah, I gave him the fucking first line. I kind of kicked myself in the ass for it, but he would have gotten it anyhow. It was everywhere. Then we all went off the deep end—me, Josh and Peter.

JOHNNY KELLY (Type O Negative): We'd come offstage and the three of them would run like fucking O. J. [Simpson] in Hertz commercials. They would sprint to the back lounge, and all you heard was them bitching at each other, "Hurry up, hurry up," and you'd hear the card cutting the coke.

For Steele, the road of excess didn't lead to poet William Blake's "palace of wisdom." It led to the insane asylum and jail.

PETER STEELE: I was in [Brooklyn's] Kings County Hospital suffering from drug-induced psychosis, and it was actually my own family that got me put away, which kinda made me wish I was part of the Manson family. I had typical para-noia. I thought there were cameras in the light switches and showerheads.

JOHNNY KELLY: Peter came home one day and his girlfriend had packed up and split after a couple of years. So he went to rehab in an attempt to get her back. While he's in rehab, she appears, tells him, "All right, when you come back, everything's going to be fine, we'll work it all out." Peter gets out of rehab, we went to go see him. He'd just gotten home, and we're sitting on Josh's stoop, and he's like, "Yeah, she's on her way over, going to bring a couple of things back that she took that were mine, we're going to talk." She never showed up. Peter found out where she lived and did the Herman Munster in the door, hence his felony conviction for assault. So he's at his arraignment, and the judge or whatever refers to her as Mrs. Whatever, and he's like, "What?" It turned out she was married to this other guy already.

KENNY HICKEY: Pete showed up at this guy's house at four o'clock in the morning, coked out of his mind. He broke down the door, full fangs and everything, chased this guy through his house, and broke his jaw.

PETER STEELE: [I was in Rikers Island jail] about thirty days. In the past, I had done a day here or there for stupid stuff like fighting or pissing on the sidewalk. But this was a rude awakening—twenty-three charges against me, one of which was attempted murder. When you're kicking the shit out of somebody, you really have to make sure not to say, "I'm gonna fuckin' kill you!" because that implies intent. I'm 6-foot-6, I weigh 260 pounds. To be white in jail and to have long black hair and fangs is not an advantage.

KENNY HICKEY: Peter had a couple DUIs. Then one time he calls me at two in the morning and goes, "Can I tell you a story?" At the time he was living with a girlfriend in Pennsylvania, but he had another girlfriend. He goes, "I was at this other girl's house, and then I got a call from my girlfriend that she was going to be home in a few minutes. It was pitch black and I was wasted out of my mind. I got in my Jeep and I'm driving down the road, and a bear jumps out in front of my Jeep and I swerved off the road and hit a pole." So the cops show up and arrest him. His main girlfriend comes to pick him up and she bails him out, picks him up, goes back to her house. He's getting undressed and she goes "What are you wearing?" He looked down and had his other girlfriend's panties on because he got dressed in the dark drunk.

JOSH SILVER: [In 1989 Peter slashed his wrists.] How serious was it? I guess we'll never know. He certainly had a lot of scars and he was always a self-destructive guy. He did press shots of him cutting his arm with a razor around the Type O logo. He had multiple hospitalizations and suicide attempts. But when a lot of them happened we said, "Oh, this is just bullshit," because Pete was a very smart guy. If he really wanted to snuff it, he could have.

DAVE WYNDORF: I couldn't sleep on tour, so the doctors gave me something that would put down a wild animal. I was doing a lot of transatlantic flying, and on a plane one day I just started gobbling them down. All of my paranoias came at me like a giant, three-headed beast. My biggest mistake was not asking for help. I don't recall doing it, but I took the whole goddamn bottle—a hundred pills, man, just like they were a shot glass— and the next thing I knew, I woke up in a fucking loony bin. Drugs are supposedly a gateway into creativity. You know what? It's all a myth. They suck, and they'll get you in the end. They certainly got me.

The doom metal community was dealt two major blows in 2010. The first came on April 14, when Type O Negative front-man Peter Steele died at age forty-eight from heart failure. A few days before he died he felt like he was coming down with the flu. He was clean at the time, but doctors speculate that years of heavy drug use took its toll on his declining health.

KENNY HICKEY: Obviously, Peter wasn't healthy. An aneurysm can just take you at any time, though. He had an ongoing heart condition for years. He said that he always felt the flutter in his heart, even when he was a kid, so he might have been born with it, for all we know. Four or five men in his family have died from heart disease before fifty, so it could have been hereditary.

JOSH SILVER: He lived with atrial fibrillation, which is an irregular heartbeat. Whether that was caused by drugs or something else, I don't know. It was diagnosed years and years ago. But if you take care of yourself and do the right stuff it's something you can live with for quite a while. There are plenty of ninety-year-olds running around with it.

KENNY HICKEY: There was one point when he was in the hospital before a tour. Dude was green from his feet to his head. He had yellow, jaundiced eyes, and eight different surgeons were trying to figure out what was wrong with him, and none of them spoke English. They asked him, "What kind of drugs do you do?" He said, "Cocaine, alcohol, and redheads." I came back three days later and the doctors asked me, "Excuse me, we need to know: What are redheads?" They thought it was a pill or a drug.

JOHNNY KELLY: He calls me up and I go, "What are you doing home, you're supposed to be in the hospital." He says, "I couldn't take the food anymore." I just figured he was like Keith Richards. The guy made a deal with the devil and he's going to live forever. He was the only guy I know who could do two eight balls and eat sixty dollars' worth of Chinese food.

JOSH SILVER: I was sitting at home, and Johnny called me and said "Did anybody call you?" Then he told me Peter was dead—not that he's sick or he's dying—that he's already gone. I was surprised, but to be honest I was shocked that he lived as long as he did. His lifestyle was so unhealthy that I couldn't believe he was as strong as a horse most of the time.

Just over a month after Steele died, a more widely publicized tragedy shook the metal community. Ronnie James Dio, who had been diagnosed with stomach cancer about six months earlier, died from the illness. Dio's last public appearance was at the 2010 *Revolver* Golden Gods Awards in Los Angeles, where he was awarded Best Vocalist.

WENDY DIO (wife of Ronnie James Dio): Today my heart is broken. Many, many friends and family were able to say their private good-byes before he peacefully passed away. Ronnie knew how much he was loved by all. We so appreciate the love and support that you have all given us. . . . Please know he loved you all and his music will live on forever.

TONY IOMMI: Ronnie loved what he did, making music and performing onstage. He loved his fans so much. He was a kind man and would put himself out to help others. I can honestly say it's truly been an honor to play at his side for all these years. His music will live on forever. The man with the magic voice is a star amongst stars, a true professional. I'll miss you so much, my dear friend.

OZZY OSBOURNE: That was terrible. Going through that sort of thing with my wife [Sharon, who battled and survived colorectal cancer], you don't know what to do. I remember when Sharon was diagnosed with colon cancer, I went into an emotional scramble. It always seemed to be something that happened to someone else, and I didn't know anyone who survived from any cancer. So I was walking around thinking, "What am I going to do if I lose my wife?" You start to think that way and it's a very tough situation to go through. When I saw Ronnie, I sent a message of encouragement to him. I was sad, and stunned when he died so quickly. He was a great singer, he had a great voice. A lot of people got a lot of ideas from Dio. Whether you liked him or not, he had his own style, and it was instantly recognizable. When you heard it on the radio, you knew it was him. A lot of people tried to copy him.

GEEZER BUTLER: All the doctors said if he'd have gone in [for a colonoscopy] a year earlier or two years earlier, they could have treated him. If it had been stage one they could have dealt with it. But by the time Ronnie was diagnosed, he had stage four cancer, which was inoperable. The doctor hinted that it was just a matter of time and there was nothing they could do. It's really upsetting to think about that, and hopefully it will encourage people who need to have a checkup to get it done.

4

YOUTH GONE WILD: METAL GOES MAINSTREAM, 1978–1992

While the New Wave of British Heavy Metal was taking over the club scene in the UK and Europe, a batch of bands in and around Los Angeles—triggered by a love for KISS, Van Halen, and glam groups like the New York Dolls and the Sweet—were about to shake Sunset Strip like a 7.0 earthquake. With flashy, androgynous images and brash, solo-saturated songs, the "hair metal" bands were visually compelling and musically engaging. In the beginning, groups like Mötley Crüe and Ratt were almost as heavy as Judas Priest and Dio, the band Ronnie James Dio formed after leaving Black Sabbath. But as the scene gained popularity and a major label feeding frenzy began, many musicians tailored their songs for mainstream radio, retaining some of their heaviness but drawing more emphasis to melody and heart-on-sleeve sensitivity—and sexuality.

With the dissipation of New Wave, MTV latched on to the visually striking glam metal videos—many of which were for syrupy power ballads. Before you could say, "Can I see some ID?"

Skid Row, Cinderella, Dokken, Warrant, Poison, Guns N' Roses, Mötley Crüe, and countless others were storming their way into millions of suburban households around the world. Their videos almost always featured young women in provocative poses, multiple costume changes, and musicians in heavy makeup looking almost as feminine as the girls they stalked. And the stalking didn't end when the tape stopped rolling. Even before the dawn of the eighties, a handful of outrageous LA bands including Van Halen and Quiet Riot planted the genre's seedy seeds.

BLACKIE LAWLESS (W.A.S.P., ex–New York Dolls): I moved to LA from New York in 1975, a lad of nineteen. I was scared to death. [Ex-New York Dolls bassist] Arthur Kane and I moved out; the Dolls were crumbling. We were broke. There was a Ramada Inn that used to be on Sunset Boulevard next to Tower Records. We lived there for a week when we first arrived, and it was like going to another planet.

EDDIE VAN HALEN (Van Halen): In the LA club days in the early seventies, we did some insane shows. Once, we were onstage playing at Walter Mitty's Bar and Grill, and all of a sudden two guys are fighting about whose bike is faster. It got rough, and one of them pulls out a knife, and a minute later the other guy is lying there with his intestines hanging out. It doesn't take too much to figure out which one had the knife—the guy with the Harley, obviously. That was pretty shocking. There was blood gushing everywhere and the guy actually died.

STEPHEN PEARCY (Ratt): I moved to San Diego in 1971. Around '75 we were playing a place called Straight Ahead Sound. Everybody went there, so you automatically played in front of six hundred to one thousand people. You would have Jake E. Lee's band Teaser, [my band] Mickey Ratt [which evolved into Ratt], and Robbin Crosby's band Metropolis. We'd all be competing.

KELLE RHOADS (composer, brother of Randy Rhoads): Randy and I started out in a band called Violet Fox, with me on drums. But that didn't last too long because I always wanted to bash his head in. We didn't get along as teenage boys. Later in his short life I came to really appreciate him, and we formed a really tight bond. The period right up until he joined Quiet Riot was magical for him. If Charles Dickens was around and wrote a story about boys in the seventies going into glam and metal band, I think he would have chosen my brother as a model because it was a real period of discovery for him and he was really good.

KEVIN DuBROW (1955–2007) (Quiet Riot): I was eighteen; Randy Rhoads was seventeen. He walked in and he had hair down to the middle of his back and a really long thumbnail. I didn't hear him play, the first time I met him. Then the second time, I went to his mom's house and I went there just as a joke, because I was playing with Stan Lee, the guitarist of the Dickies. Stan is the one who said, "You should go hear him play; it's going to be funny." You know, we did it as a joke. The joke was on me, because he was amazing. I heard him play and Randy says, "Okay, let's hear you sing," and I was like, "No, not going to do it," and eventually, obviously, I did. But he was brilliant, he was gifted, he was hilarious and a wonderful person.

BLACKIE LAWLESS: The very first show I played in LA was with [Arthur] Killer Kane. The first time we played the Starwood [Night Club], there was a band called New Order—this was half the Stooges and half the MC5. They were headlining, we were playing in the middle, and the other band was, at that point, unknown: Quiet Riot with Randy Rhoads on guitar. Looking back, that was one of those special nights. But that was '75 and disco would start rearing its ugly head, and it was very hard for those bands to get jobs after that.

KEVIN DuBROW: Van Halen got signed a couple of years before Quiet Riot [did, in 1977], and we thought maybe we were going to be the next ones, but we weren't. We were the only hard rock band, pretty much, in town at that time. Mötley Crüe had just gotten started, so they were still in the clubs. We had been out there as Quiet Riot for a number of years. But a lot of bands then sounded like the Knack.

BLACKIE LAWLESS: Van Halen was the very first band I saw in LA. They were the house band at Gazzarri's. They were playing "Running with the Devil" then. I remember hearing that song for the first time and thinking, "That's an okay song."

STEPHEN PEARCY: I used to watch them play in front of twenty people, and they would play like they were at [the LA arena] the Forum. I haul ass home to San Diego. I get tight with guitarist Robbin [Crosby] and we're playing gigs. I tell Robbin, "There's this band called Van Halen," and he comes up to meet Eddie. I'm like, "Look, January 1, 1980, I'm moving to LA." And I did.

EDDIE VAN HALEN: Back in '74, we were playing a club and the public bathroom was our dressing room. I'm changing my clothes in the toilet stall and the guy next to me goes, "Hey, Eddie. Great show. Want some dynamite blow?" I said, "Yeah, sure." So he hands me this paper, and I took my guitar pick and went to town. I didn't taste it first to see what it was. Ten minutes later, I barely made it 50 feet. Alex saw me collapse from across the ballroom and ran to me. I had overdosed on PCP. Thank God [bassist] Mike [Anthony] had a station wagon, because my body was so stiff they couldn't put me in the car. I actually died on the table in the hospital, and when I woke up the doctor said, "Your heart stopped. If it was thirty seconds later, we couldn't have brought you back." I didn't see any light, but I had a vision that I was onstage at the Forum before we ever played there, and when we *did* play there it was exactly as I imagined. The doctor even said to me—because I woke up with my ankles and wrists strapped down because I guess I was violent—he goes, "It's funny, your fingers wouldn't stop moving." That's the only time I ever did any drugs that heavy, and it was by accident.

FRANKIE BANALI (Quiet Riot): I came to LA in 1978 or '79, and I decided to stay and do or die. I took the drum heads off and put all my clothes inside the drums. I took the drums to Fort Lauderdale Airport, my mom dropped me off, and that's when you could pay twenty bucks to get all the stuff on as luggage. I got to LAX, I got my drums, I'm standing on the white zone with my drums, $300 cash. That was my plan. I had no idea how I was going to get to Hollywood. As luck would have it, an SIR [Studio Instrumental Rentals] van comes driving by, and it stops, and this guy goes, "Frankie?" I say, "Joey?" It was a tech I had met in Chicago. He was now at SIR, picking up for some big famous band. He goes, "Get in!" We put my drums in the van and he graciously let me stay at his apartment.

KEVIN DuBROW: Quiet Riot predated [Nikki Sixx's] London by [five] years. London was around about the same time as DuBrow. But remember, Nikki Sixx auditioned for Quiet Riot, when [ex-bassist] Kelly [Garni] left in '77. And those were long years, let me tell you.

By the mid-eighties, LA was populated by wide-eyed, big-haired hopefuls pouring in from all over the country—indeed, from all over the world—lured by the promise of success and the accompanying fringe benefits. Hollywood was just a short commute from major venues like the Forum, Long Beach Arena, and Universal Amphitheatre, and it was home of infamous clubs like the Whisky, Starwood, Troubadour, and Roxy Theatre. Major record companies dotted the city and record stores lined Sunset Boulevard and LaBrea Avenue. A lucky few future rock stars lived in the LA area, where, in the late seventies, they got a bird's-eye view and a jump start on a scene that would overtake their city in a few short years.

VINCE NEIL (Mötley Crüe): The first concert I went to was Lynyrd Skynyrd, with Black Sabbath opening. Then Foreigner, and Eddie Money, I think, at Anaheim Stadium. I was probably fourteen; friends who were sixteen had a car. Everybody was smoking pot. I remember looking around during "Freebird," and it was a stadium, you could see, like, the concrete bending; or maybe it was just me being high, but it was a surreal experience, and that really got the music fired up in me. By the time I was sixteen, I was already in a band playing Gazzarri's.

LITA FORD (The Runaways): I used to hang out at the Long Beach Arena; that was my club! My mother, being from Rome, and my father from London—they were naïve to the bad things in life. It didn't enter their minds. I never had any girlfriends really; I always hung out with the guys. In high school, I would hang out with all the black musicians. We would ditch school and go and jam. After school I'd bring home a half dozen black guys, and my mom would cook everyone dinner, and we'd eat and play music.

DON DOKKEN (Dokken): In the late seventies I'd see George [Lynch's] band the Boyz. Half the time he would pass out. I remember him being carried out at the Starwood; an ambulance came and they hauled him away on a stretcher. Hyperventilate, anxiety. He'd eat a big dinner before the show, get too excited, hold his breath, pass out. I'd be like, "Oh, there's the Boyz, there goes George. They're carrying him off the stage." He passed out, then as they were carrying him out, he was waving at the audience.

LITA FORD: In 1975 in the Runaways, it was hard to be taken seriously as a musician when you're young and dressed like that. Plus, some of the girls were screwing off too much and I didn't like that. I wanted to work, I wanted to jam, I wanted to get paid. I didn't want to fuck off as much as they were. And when I got pissed off about it they would look at me and go, "What's your problem? Why are you so mad?" They wouldn't show up for photo shoots because they'd be too fucked up. Trying to get them off their butts or out of bed or into sound check was difficult at times. I mean, I was into sex and drugs and drinking, too, but it never got in the way of my work. We did well, but it wasn't until after the Runaways that I was really accepted as a musician, and especially a guitarist. I learned from the guys. I never followed any female guitarists because there weren't any. I wanted to play lead guitar, and I put together a three-piece because I didn't want anyone to forget that I was the only guitar player and those were really *my* solos; I could actually play. But I had to work hard in the vocal department because that wasn't my greatest strength.

TRACII GUNS (LA Guns, ex–Guns N' Roses): I started seeing live music when I was about fifteen or sixteen. The first band I ever saw was at the Troubadour. I was a lot younger than those bands I was seeing, but Starwood gigs were more of the beginning of the LA punk rock scene. I saw the Crowd and the Weirdos at the Starwood. Rock bands that were happening played Florentine Gardens and clubs like that. Then I saw White Sister, London, Mötley Crüe, and Sarge, Angelus, Dante Fox—that's my whole rock-and-roll education as far as what went into putting LA Guns together. We came out around 1983, '84, and those bands were all around since '79, '80. Then there were the bigger ones before LA Guns, like W.A.S.P. and Ratt. By the time we put Guns N' Roses together out of LA Guns, we perfected this kind of heavy, but bluesy, but a little bit punk attitude ingredients to make this perfect cake.

SLASH (Velvet Revolver, ex–Guns N' Roses): [Ex–Guns N' Roses drummer] Steve [Adler] started me on guitar. I met him in my early years of junior high and I wasn't doing really well, and he wasn't either, so we started ditching Bancroft Junior High in eighth grade together and hanging out. I went to Steve's house one day, and he had an amp. I didn't know what lead guitar was, but I always wanted to do something musical. He had some KISS records, and the amp and guitar, and we blasted all of it at the same time. I decided I was going to play bass and he was going to play guitar, then somehow we switched and I started playing guitar, and he started playing drums.

STEVEN ADLER (Adler's Appetite, ex–Guns N' Roses): [In my teens] I was the one guy hanging at the Starwood. I was there every day because it was two blocks away from my house. I would hang there for sound check, and that's where I learned to play drums. I never took a lesson until recently. I learned from the drummers in the bands playing there.

SLASH: Steven and I used to get into clubs. I saw Nikki Sixx's band London back then, I saw Snow and Quiet Riot. I never saw Van Halen then, though. Simultaneously, there was this punk scene that was going on, so those were actually mixed, the beginning of the metal scene in LA was the tail end of the punk scene, so I was around for both of those.

For young, impressionable musicians who aspired to rock stardom, Hollywood could be as intoxicating and dangerous as it was for hot eighteen-year-old actress wannabes just off the bus from the Midwest. Rockers rarely ended up in porn but were nonetheless taken advantage of financially, emotionally—even sexually. And if they had an ounce of talent and a taste for drugs and alcohol, their unhealthy appetites were easily sated.

STEVEN ADLER: The Starwood was the first time I met Danny Bonaduce. I was on acid, and I walked into the office at the

Starwood and he was doing a line of coke on the table. I was all, "Oh my God," I'm just tripping on acid, and I'm like, "Danny Partridge, I love you." I was young and naïve. I was a cute little boy hanging out with older people who wanted to take advantage of me, and there's a lot of drugs and sex; it was Santa Monica Boulevard. Still, to this day, West Hollywood is the gay capital of the world.

DON DOKKEN: There were piles [of cocaine] on the tables upstairs at the Starwood. Coke and quaaludes; you just snapped your fingers and it happened—it was free. David Forest was the booking agent. I ran into him years later. He put us with Van Halen and Quiet Riot. I thanked him and he said, "I didn't really like your band, but you got a cute ass." I would see young musicians go into the offices that were above the stage and come out an hour later really wasted on ludes and blow. As far as sexual favors happening, I have no idea, I wasn't there— let's just say a lot of crappy bands got gigs there. There would always be, in the private VIP section upstairs, KISS, Aerosmith, Ozzy, John Belushi on any given night; it was the place to hang, score drugs, and get laid.

STEVEN ADLER: People would pull up beside me in their cars and ask me if I wanted to smoke a joint. I'd be like, "Hell yeah!" The next thing you know, you're completely baked and they're touching you all over and you don't know what the fuck's going on. All you know is that an orgasm feels good. Anybody can make you come, and in that state, I didn't have the presence of mind to give a damn. I was used, abused, whatever. Let's get high, let's party. One time I was walking along Santa Monica Boulevard and ran into two clean-cut guys who must have been in their twenties. We started talking and they said they had some bitchin' weed back at their pad, so I went with them to smoke. We arrived at this dumpy little apartment and there was another guy there, only he was in his forties, a completely scruffy-looking loser. Right away, I felt uneasy. I'll spare you the details, but they hurt me pretty badly. Part of my mind just kind of shut down, and that day my reality became a bad dream. They didn't beat me up, but they did everything else and it was pretty devastating. I was just fourteen at the time.

KEVIN DuBROW: We did a show at the Starwood and someone said, "You wanna do some blow?" I said "Sure, fuck it." But my use of cocaine was no greater than any members of Mötley Crüe or Van Halen. It was less, if anything.

DON DOKKEN: I remember Devo were playing at the Whisky and they came to our show at the Starwood. I asked them why, and they said, "We love Dokken because you're the epitome of what we don't want to be." I didn't know they wore saucers on their heads at that point.

VICKY HAMILTON (ex-Geffen A&R, manager): I cocktail-waitressed at the Starwood when I first moved out from Indiana. That was right when that whole thing went down with Eddie Nash and the murders and Laurel Canyon. [In 1981, Starwood owner and reputed gangster Eddie Nash was charged in connection with the bludgeoning deaths of four people at their home at 8763 Wonderland Avenue in Laurel Canyon. Nash's friend, porn star John Holmes, allegedly helped organize the robbery in an effort to pay back a drug debt to the leader of a crime syndicate.] I can't remember if it was the FBI or what, but they pulled bags of quaaludes from the safe at the Starwood. I lost my job because they closed down the club. [Nash was acquitted of planning the murders but pled guilty to related charges.]

Nash's arrest didn't slow down the LA metal scene, which was growing larger and flashier by the day. In addition to dramatic stage productions, bands featured an ever-growing stable of talented players—most notably lead guitarists—who spent most of their waking hours learning how to play fast, flashy solos. Their early influences included Ritchie Blackmore, Tony Iommi, and Jimmy Page. But the new breed of guitar heroes also bowed at the altars of Van Halen and Randy Rhoads, who had pioneered a variety of lead guitar techniques, including whammy-bar dive bombs, and, more notably, tapping, where fingers on the right hand are used to tap frets like piano keys while the left hand continues to play as normal, creating a rapid succession of notes that varied greatly in pitch.

EDDIE VAN HALEN: I saw Led Zeppelin back around 1970, and Jimmy Page had his arm up in the air, and he was lifting his fret finger off of the string, and I said, "Wait a minute." And I took my right hand and used it to tap on the frets. I just moved it up and kept going up the neck, creating all these different sounds. It developed from there, and I worked with it until I could do it really fast on songs like "Eruption," and it became sort of my thing.

KELLE RHOADS: In the 1840s, Franz Liszt and Frederic Chopin did the same thing that Eddie Van Halen and Randy Rhoads did. They took the instrument to another dimension. The two piano players ushered in an era where the piano became a solo instrument and was used in recitals even without an orchestra. What Randy and Eddie did was they took the guitar, which ten years earlier was mostly a rhythm instrument, and they put it into the perspective of virtuosity. Now you have guitar being extremely important, sometimes, as with my brother, being almost the most important aspect of the song. Like Steve Vai said, Randy didn't only raise the bar, he painted it, too.

STEVE VAI (ex-Whitesnake, ex–David Lee Roth): Guitar is the greatest instrument in the world and it's not that hard to play; some people are just intimidated. Now, if you want to be an elite rock virtuoso, you might have to put some more hours in. But you should shoot to be much greater, much better than the people who are inspiring you, so that the cycle continues.

As Van Halen and Ozzy gained popularity, any guitar player worth his distortion pedal learned to finger tap. The technique fit well with metal's emphasis on showmanship, and flashy solos became a highlight of any metal song. Most bands took extended breaks during their sets to showcase their guitarists and sometimes their drummers. Upping the ante on Van Halen and Rhoads, Swedish-born Yngwie Malmsteen applied classical music theory to his lightning-fast leads and a new breed of players known as shredders developed.

Whether for rising glam acts like Poison or accomplished burners such as Vai, most LA-area clubs in the eighties had a pay-to-play policy, requiring bands to purchase hundreds of dollars' worth of tickets in advance for the privilege of performing. Groups sold the tickets themselves or, just as frequently, gave them away to ensure there was an audience at the shows. While the practice isn't as commonplace as it once was, some clubs still require baby bands and local groups to pay for the right to play.

CARLOS CAVAZO (Ratt, ex–Quiet Riot): Whoever started pay-to-play shouldn't have, because it just isn't right. A lot of people who are extremely talented will never have the chance to become famous because they don't have the money to pay to play.

CHINO MORENO (Deftones): Our first-ever show in LA was pay-to-play. But we went over well because we didn't play shows for a long time. We'd just practice and practice. So when we finally debuted in LA we were tight as fuck and people loved it. But yeah, the idea of the whole thing really sucks.

JAN KUEHNEMUND (Vixen): I believe we paid to play at the Whisky, the Troubadour, and possibly a few other popular clubs. I also remember something about having to "rent" microphones at one club. Pay to play was an awful policy because the clubs weren't hiring bands on the quality of their music and their performance necessarily; [it was more like] whoever had the most money or could pay the most, got the most gigs. We had moved to LA from the Midwest, where we had been *paid* to perform at every show—what a concept, ha ha!—and we had also played the South, Southeast, and Northwest before moving out to LA, and we *always* got paid everywhere else—and sometimes quite well. So you can imagine our shock when we ran into this! It had a negative effect on the scene.

RIKI RACHTMAN (Cathouse founder, DJ, VJ): The Cathouse was never pay-to-play, except one case. I'll never forget [manager] Pete Angelus calling and saying he had a band he wanted to play, and he sent me the CD. He said, "I'll give you $400, and we'll put them on before 10 p.m." I liked the CD and said okay. It was the Black Crowes. I was always really strict on who played.

TOM MORELLO (Rage Against the Machine, ex-Audioslave): Pay-to-play wasn't the only surprise I discovered when I moved to LA. I tried to join bands using the *Music Connection*. This really speaks for that particular time. A metal bass player and I had a good vibe on the phone. I was going to come jam with them. Their manager calls me up and he had a very important question. This guy was all business. He asked, "How long is your hair?" I was like, "It's not that long, but I would like to jam." He says, "Look, we got a lot of interest from agents and we're looking for a specific image." I said, "Let me jam with the band, I mean, I might suck, but I might be the best guitar player you've ever seen." He's like, "Would you be willing to wear a wig?" I said, "I don't want to wear a wig, I just want to jam."

GEOFF TATE (ex-Queensrÿche): We started in 1981 and we were lumped in with the commercial metal thing. We were loud and we could play, but we were from Seattle so we weren't a part of the LA scene. I think that's one of the things that set us apart. We liked some of the same bands, probably, but when we first started out, the progressive bands like Yes, Genesis, and Rush were pretty inspirational. Iron Maiden mixed with Black Sabbath was another area we had interest in. We loved music. We were never into partying. That was never an attraction. The excesses were usually conducted by very young people who were just getting started and also by people that were pretty mentally challenged, honestly.

Ratt was part of the first wave of rock/metal bands to launch the eighties LA scene. Its cutting, trebly guitars, high-pitched melodic vocals, and whirlwind solos, along with a penchant for wild times, epitomized the Sunset Strip. While less over-the-top in image and makeup than Mötley Crüe, Ratt was nonetheless grouped under the "hair metal" umbrella, which also covered Faster Pussycat, Cinderella, Poison, and Winger, as well as latter-day entries like Pretty Boy Floyd and D'Molls.

STEPHEN PEARCY: When Mickey Ratt moved from San Diego to LA, it was a slap in the face. Suddenly we were playing for nobody in these tiny little clubs. I just wanted my name in the paper, and no one wanted to know from us.

WARREN DeMARTINI (Ratt): I moved to LA in the fall of 1982. The late seventies commercially was a pretty hard time if you liked rock. New Wave and disco were selling the best, at least in San Diego. The first change was going to see Mötley Crüe and there'd be lines way up the block on Sunset. You got a feeling you were seeing something that was about to explode. It was fun because at that point it was only LA that knew about them and they were doing so well on their own, in spite of the snobby attitudes of record companies at the time, who felt that rock wouldn't sell.

STEPHEN PEARCY: It started out with Robbin [Crosby] and I. Warren's band opened for us. [Guitarist] Jake E. [Lee] was in the band, Jake E. leaves [and eventually joins Ozzy Osbourne's band]. I ask Warren if he wants to jam, and the rest is history. That was 1982. At the time, I had the members of Rough Cutt, except for [guitarist] Chris [Hager], in my band: [bassist] Matt [Thorr], [drummer] Dave [Alford], and Jake E. Lee made up the first incarnation of Ratt. The scene was still new wave, and Van Halen had just slapped everyone around silly. Then the climate changed. We became this house band at the Whisky [a Go Go] and started our attack on the Strip.

JAKE E. LEE (ex–Ozzy Osbourne, ex-Ratt) [1986 interview]: Stephen [Pearcy] was mainly why I quit Ratt. He was getting ridiculously drunk onstage and announcing songs we'd just played and forgetting words. He was embarrassing.

STEPHEN PEARCY: The first incarnation of Ratt was more metal. The [1983] EP was really aggressive. It made Mötley take notice, and we became great friends. We were a little harder back then with Jake in the band. We wore the studs and chains. Then Robbin [Crosby] pulled in, and he was *way* metal, introducing Priest and Maiden. [Mötley and Ratt] started this street gang called the Gladiators. Everybody had a name. Robbin was King. I was Ratt Patrol Leader. Vince [Neil] was Field Marshall. Nikki [Sixx] was Leader 6. We fed ourselves, took care of each other. They had their place near the Whisky, we had Ratt Mansion West on the west side of LA, and we'd get into a whole lot of trouble. There was a lot of sex, drugs, and rock and roll. It was a good era.

WARREN DeMARTINI: We nicknamed our place Ratt Mansion West as a total oxymoron to the fact that it was a one-bedroom apartment and there were three of us. Sometimes our crew would sleep there, too. Things were pretty lean. Top Ramen, and pick a wall. We weren't arguing over who got what room, we were arguing over who got what *wall* to put your stuff against.

NEIL ZLOZOWER (photographer): I was working with Van Halen at the time Ratt were doing their first EP. [Future video vixen] Tawny Kitaen was Robbin Crosby's girlfriend, and she introduced me to Robbin. He'd always give me a tape of Ratt, and next time, he'd be like, "Did you listen to our tape?" He must have given me that tape ten times. I finally took it home and it kicked me in my fucking ass. I thought it was incredible. I called and said, "I want to work with you guys." They came to my studio and did the photo shoot for the *Ratt* EP, with the rats crawling up the girl's legs. Those were Tawny's legs. That was before she was the famous MTV girl in the Whitesnake videos.

WARREN DeMARTINI: *Too Fast For Love* broke things open for Mötley. The same thing happened for us. We got attention at Atlantic Records because "You Think You're Tough" made its way onto Joe Benson's LA radio show [on KLOS]. I'll never forget Robbin Crosby running into the apartment. I could hear him from almost a block away yelling, "Turn on the radio! It's on!" He busted through the door and by that time we were trying to get the stereo on. Then we just all sat there in silence listening to our song on the radio for the first time. It was a really indelible moment.

STEPHEN PEARCY: "Round and Round" was written on a tape recorder by me, Robbin, and Warren in the front room of Ratt Mansion West. You can't get much less glamorous than that.

BLACKIE LAWLESS: When everyone started coming out [to LA] in '81 and '82, people thought these bands came out of nowhere. They didn't realize they'd been around forever in sweatshop garages writing their little songs. So when the moment was right they exploded. The movement was '82 or '83 but it started in, like, '76.

Mötley Crüe were California locals and couldn't have been more aptly named. Their quest for kicks was legendary, as evidenced by such songs as "Kickstart My Heart," about bassist Nikki Sixx's heroin overdose, and "Girls Girls Girls," the band's paean to strip clubs. Formed by ex-London bassist Sixx and drummer Tommy Lee, an alum of band Suite 19, they were soon joined by guitarist Robert Alan Deal (aka Mick Mars) and lead singer Vince Neil Wharton (ex–Rock Candy). The band would eventually sell twenty-five million albums in the United States alone, but like most rock stars, their beginnings in the LA clubs in early 1981 were humble at best.

DON DOKKEN: Mick Mars was in a band called Vendetta, and he lived in the South Bay, and he played the beach bars, Top 40, five sets a night. The whole band lived in one house. You'd go there at three in the afternoon, and it was pitch black. They had every single window covered in tin foil. Mick sectioned off part of the living room and had his Marshalls and flight cases to build a wall, and that was his invented bedroom. He said he was trying out for this band Mötley Crüe, going, "I don't know. I'm a little older than these guys." I was like, "Eh, don't worry about it. Give it a shot." Mick always looked like he does now: dark hair, pale face, very vampire.

VINCE NEIL: Rock Candy was a party band that played a few times on the Strip. We weren't a big giant band, and Nikki never knew me. Mötley had already found Mick, so the three of them came to see me at the Starwood, and that's when they actually asked me to join the band. The very first day, the very first rehearsal, we wrote "Live Wire," which turned out to be a big hit. So yeah, we clicked completely right away.

STEPHEN PEARCY: Mötley was our only competition, and not really, because they were our friends. They helped us out a lot. We'd open up for them in LA. Nikki and Robbin ended up being roommates. Their big thing was after being successful in

LA, Mötley went to the Ozzy [Osbourne] tour and did that. Right after that, we went to the Ozzy tour when the Crüe started headlining. We shared a lot, including girlfriends.

VINCE NEIL: Girls would go in the front door and out the back windows because their boyfriends snuck in when they were there. There was a lot of craziness. One time we were sitting on the floor with David Lee Roth doing coke and the police kicked in the door and it hit Dave in the head. Our door was kicked in so many times we had to use cardboard to jam it shut. I stole a Christmas tree and decorated it with needles and underwear and beer cans and burned it in the front of the apartment.

JOEY VERA (Fates Warning, Armored Saint): We saw London, with Nikki, then we saw Mötley Crüe's first gig opening for Y&T [originally Yesterday and Today] at the Starwood. Mötley Crüe were awful at their first show. Musically, they were all over the place, not tight, not good, but you could tell that something was there. I remember seeing London and thinking it was kind of spectacular, but this had even more of that. You could tell that something was going to happen.

VINCE NEIL: [As far as umlauts] went, probably nobody else was dumb enough to use them, before us—except Motörhead. They were the first. Ours came from us drinking Löwenbräu and we wanted to seem European. We wanted to have a worldly vibe, even though we'd never been outside of LA.

GEOFF TATE: The umlauts [in our name] absolutely weren't because of Mötley Crüe. They were [guitarist] Chris [De-Garmo's] idea. He thought it looked kind of cool and dramatic, and we were just out of school and didn't have a worldview yet and didn't realize that umlauts actually had a purpose. For a long time, because of the way we spelled the name, and because it wasn't a known word in the English language, people didn't know how to pronounce it. I think we spent the first ten years correcting everyone's pronunciation of the band name.

In the early days of the Strip Scene there was a camaraderie among many bands that later diminished. Established musicians offered tips and even equipment to start-up groups, having no idea that the newbies would soon become major competition in the game to land high-profile gigs and record contracts.

VINCE NEIL: David Lee Roth helped me out a lot, personally. He would come to all our shows. We'd be playing at the Troubadour, and there's Dave—and this was in his heyday. A couple years earlier, when I was in Rock Candy, I was bootlegging T-shirts outside Van Halen concerts at Long Beach Arena, wanting to go in to watch them, but I didn't have enough money. But Dave came because we always had tons of girls. Our audience was 80 percent women. He's a big star, and I'm just a nobody singer, and he said, "Hey Vince, meet me at Canter's on Fairfax, I want to talk to you." I borrowed someone's car and there's Diamond Dave with his black Mercedes with a skull and crossbones painted on the hood. He sat me down and went through all the aspects of the business of rock and roll. He said, "You need distribution, and this, and watch out for this, and be careful of this." He'd go, "Okay, when you find out what your best side is, always use that side [for photos]." For him to take the time to sit down with just some dude, that's pretty cool.

BLACKIE LAWLESS: Nikki didn't steal [our pentagram logo]; I gave it to him. That whole setting himself on fire thing— I gave *that* to him. Nikki and I had played together before. W.A.S.P. was just being put together, but we didn't do shows together. I looked at Nikki like my brother. The pentagram came because I'd left a [Satanic] cult and afterward I didn't want anything to do with it. He came to me after and asked if I was going to use it. I said, "Nope. You can have it." But

I warned him he's messing with very bad stuff. Everyone I know who messes with that stuff, tragedy has fallen on them at some point in life. It's just not something you want to be a part of.

VINCE NEIL: We only used the pentagram for one album, and it's called *Shout at the Devil*—so you use a pentagram! Nobody's really into the devil. It's showmanship, it's whatever image you're trying to project. It's all a bunch of bull, really. Ronnie [Dio] was not a devil worshipper, but he loved medieval history. Same with Ozzy. He is the furthest thing from a devil worshipper I've ever met.

Mötley Crüe earned their bad-boy title with little effort. Even before the overdoses and near-fatal car crashes that could have ended the band's career, they lived for the moment, throwing caution to the wind in favor of cheap, and sometimes costly, thrills.

JOEY VERA: After an Armored Saint show at Mt. Baldy Ski Resort [outside Los Angeles], Tommy Lee's going to a party down the mountain with his sister and another girl who owned the car. Me, in a drunken state, said, "I'll go to the party." That's the last thing I remember. We went down the hill, the car crashed, I cut up both my hands and my head, was in the hospital for a week. The worst thing was that I almost lost my thumb, my right thumb. Tommy was driving. I think he felt really guilty. It wasn't like I held it against him. We were all drunk. I knew what we were doing. It's not like he threw me from the car. I was like, "Dude, whatever, it's cool." But our friendship was done after that. What came out of this was that the girl had insurance, so I got money to pay for all the bills, and there was some chunk of change left—four or six thousand dollars—and with that money, I fronted Armored Saint the money to pay for recording a demo, which turned into the EP that we put out in '83. Our [1982] *Metal Massacre 2* track ["Lesson Well Learned"] is from that session, too. Had that accident not happened, we might not have been able to afford to go in the studio.

DON DOKKEN: The first time I saw Mötley Crüe, we were playing with them, at the Roxy. We both were showcasing. Dokken had done *Breaking the Chains*; it was out in Europe. The whole scene had crumbled, all the rock bands had moved, the Starwood was gone, the Whisky had gone punk, everybody had moved to the Troubadour. It was the only club left. Gazzarri's was waffling. Golden West Ballroom was gone. Clubs were falling by the wayside. I didn't understand Mötley because they didn't have a [major] record deal, yet they showed up in limos, brand new equipment, Marshalls, all these cool stage clothes, big-ass hair. I was like, "How the fuck did they afford that?" Mötley never did a gig with crappy gear. They came on the scene with full-on arena gear because they had [KISS manager] Doc [McGhee] backing them.

VINCE NEIL: If you look at the Mötley Crüe progression of looks, they are all different. When we did [1981's] *Too Fast for Love*, we just wore what we could, because we didn't have any money. We basically shopped at the hardware store, got chains and made our own stuff. Then for [1983's] *Shout at the Devil*, it was a theatrical leather look, not a biker leather look. Then we completely went to the other end and did the glam thing with [1985's] *Theatre of Pain*; there was no leather at all. Then, when everybody started doing that, we changed to the motorcycle look for [1987's] *Girls Girls Girls*. We never pigeonholed ourselves into any look. Entertainment is supposed to be an escape. It's not supposed to let you know how miserable you are.

TOMMY LEE (Mötley Crüe): A lot of bands recently seem to have been there to make the crowd depressed. I could never figure that out. That, to me, is like sitting down at a bar and drinking to remember.

In the early days of hair metal, new bands had to be resourceful to look good onstage even though their wallets were usually empty. For most, gigging and merch sales didn't pay the bills, especially after pay-to-play became widespread. Girlfriends, strippers, or parents sometimes supported the rock star hopefuls. Often, however, musicians sold drugs or toiled at day jobs. One of the most common part-time gigs for aspiring rock stars was telemarketing—boiler rooms of musicians with fake names selling equally questionable goods and services. Tower Records Sunset and Aaron's Records were other spots where Los Angeles's long-haired and hungover could be found trying to earn a buck. The ubiquitous scenario spawned a standard joke. Q: "What do you call a musician in LA without a girlfriend?" A: "Homeless."

JANI LANE (1964–2011) (Warrant): [Drummer] Steven [Sweet] and I were living in Florida and had no money. We had a friend who was a bass player, Al Collins, and he talked his parents into buying him an old '77 Cutlass. I sold my drums, and Steven and I worked at the merry-go-round to make enough money to move to LA. Another guy in Florida was trying to start his own line of children's clothing, so we also worked in his basement making children's T-shirts, like a sweatshop, for about two weeks to save up six hundred bucks between the three of us. We had a car and a U-Haul trailer and we broke down in every state on our trip to LA. Suddenly, we realize that we have $20 left and we're almost out of gas. We get a room at a motel across from the Hollywood Bowl and stayed there for a week. We went down to the store every day and got a jar of peanut butter and a loaf of bread and put the peanut butter on the bread using a Social Security card. That's how we lived the first week in Hollywood.

GEORGE LYNCH (Lynch Mob, ex-Dokken): At one point, I was a liquor delivery driver in South Central LA. I did the routes no one would take [because they were in such dangerous parts of town]. My route was Martin Luther King Boulevard. In fact, on the day I signed my record deal I was in my liquor van, and I had to drive to the Elektra building in LA and sign the contract, and then I went right back on my route.

DON DOKKEN: People had strippers taking care of them, but I really was on that Top Ramen and hot dogs lifestyle. We were way broke.

GEOFF TATE: Living on Top Ramen was the way you survived. You only had a day job simply to keep you in rent money and pay for your musical instruments for your gig.

BLACKIE LAWLESS: I tried telemarketing for about a month and I just couldn't do it. You'd have to cold-call a hundred people a day. I was selling fluorescent lightbulbs over the phone for a hundred times more than you could get them in the store. My phone name was Ted James. The worst thing I ever did was around the summer of '78. I was on my last leg at this place because I wasn't making any sales. I had cold-called this one lady who had a pet shop in Burbank. I said, "Ma'am, let me tell you what's going on. My dad's really upset about what happened to my lil' sister and if you buy a lightbulb it would really help my dad out." She said, "What happened?" I said, "Well, have you heard about the Hillside Strangler? That was my sister." The boss was standing next to me and I thought he'd be mad, but when I got off the phone he yelled out, "You see this? He's genius. Everyone in the room must do that." It's sick, but indicative of Hollywood.

CARLOS CAVAZO: When I was in Snow we opened up for Quiet Riot about four times when Randy [Rhoads] was still in the band. We all lived together. When we couldn't make ends meet, we'd temp. We even lived on food stamps for about a year. We also lived off girls. They would feed us and pay our bills.

SLASH: I got nabbed [shoplifting] at Tower Records on Sunset Boulevard, which was my parents' favorite record shop. I was hired at the very same store six years later in the video division, and during every shift for the first six months I was convinced someone was going to remember that I'd been caught stealing and have me fired.

JANI LANE: We were living nine guys in a two-bedroom apartment. I spent a month shrink-wrapping porno videos in a basement in Canoga Park. I had a paper route delivering the *LA Times* in stage clothes at three in the morning. I was stocking 7-Elevens. I did everything I could to survive. But we were literally starving. We couldn't pay the rent. Steven [Sweet] and I were like, "Maybe we should head back to Florida and regroup. We can play in a cover band for a while there and save some money." Two days later as we're packing, there's a note on the door and it says, "Hi, we're the guys in Warrant. Our band broke up in San Diego last night and we need a singer and a drummer. Can you write music?" I played them "Down Boys," "Heaven," and "Dirty Rotten Filthy Stinking Rich" and they were like, "Wow, he can write." So we formed the band and took over LA.

For ambitious young rockers, the ultimate goal was to score a label deal. Many who were talented or lucky enough to do so didn't bother looking at the terms of the contract and found themselves in financially unfavorable situations. Even those who achieved both fame and fortune often became ensnared in interband rivalries, domestic debacles, and a myriad of other problems.

BRET MICHAELS (Poison): For Poison's record signing I thought there'd be some big party for us with a limo and caviar, and we ended up sitting in a warehouse in El Segundo, California, boxing and packaging and shrink-wrapping our own record, *Look What the Cat Dragged In*. I was sitting on the floor in leather pants.

DON DOKKEN: We thought we'd get rich once we were signed and selling records, but even the Elektra contracts were garbage. For every dollar they made, we made twenty cents split four ways. In Dokken, it was a four-way split, which came back to haunt me, because I wrote most of the hits. That's what started the war between [guitarist] George [Lynch] and I. When I signed that contract, we were at the LA airport ready to go to Japan for our first tour. The deal was still intact—that I owned 50 percent, and they divided 50 percent. They show up at the airport with a contract that says it's a four-way split or we're not getting on the plane. I called [our manager], Cliff [Bernstein at Q Prime] and said, "I can't sign this." He said, "Sign it and we'll work it out." But it never did happen. He just wanted us to get on the plane. I was hijacked. We spent the next five years together getting very famous, and I hated them, and they hated me.

JANI LANE: During *Dog Eat Dog*, everybody was on vacation. I demoed the entire record myself and they showed up and I handed them cassettes and said, "Here are your parts." The band left me alone, and I wrote. In return for leaving me alone, I offered to give them 20 percent of the publishing to split up. Then I would show up at a gig and on my wireless microphone rack it would say, "80 percent Hitler." I'm sure it was done in fun, but it wasn't funny.

Once groups started becoming successful, bands that were more famous began pilfering rising stars. When Black Sabbath broke up and Ozzy went solo, Randy Rhoads from Quiet Riot became Ozzy's first—and prototypical—guitar wunderkind, oft imitated, much worshipped, never replaced.

GEORGE LYNCH: I tried out for Ozzy three times. The initial time was before Randy got it. He and I were up for it. He came to a gig I was playing with Exciter, my band before Dokken. He came down to introduce himself. He knew he got the gig before I did, and he came down with his mom. He said, "I got good news and bad news. Bad news is that I got the job with Ozzy. The good news is you got the job teaching at my mom's guitar teaching school, $5 an hour."

KEVIN DuBROW: When Randy joined Ozzy, I changed the name of the band to DuBrow, because you can't continue to call it Quiet Riot without Randy Rhoads. I realized that Drew [Forsythe] was not the right type of drummer for what I was trying to do, and not the right drummer for me trying to get better as a singer.

FRANKIE BANALI: I was in this three-piece band called Monarch, with Michael Monarch, the original guitarist from Steppenwolf. We were playing a show at the Valley Supper Club, and Kevin came out to see me play. Randy had told him that there was this drummer called Frankie Banali who was a combination of Cozy Powell and John Bonham. We chatted after that show—January of 1980—and about a month later at the Starwood there was a show which had all these future Quiet Riot *Metal Health* lineup members onstage at the same time, but in different bands. The opening band was Monarch with me; the middle act was DuBrow, with Kevin and [bassist] Rudy [Sarzo]. Rudy was just in town on a break from Ozzy—he was already playing with Ozzy and was just sitting in with the band. The headliner was a band called Snow, which [guitarist] Carlos [Cavazo] came out of. About two months into 1980 I started working with Kevin in DuBrow, and it was a huge turnover of musicians. It's unimaginable how many came through that project, and a lot of them have claimed that they replaced Randy Rhoads in Quiet Riot when Randy went with Ozzy, which is clearly not the case, because it wasn't Quiet Riot, it was DuBrow, and most of their tenures were very short-lived.

RUDY SARZO (ex-Whitesnake, ex–Quiet Riot, ex–Ozzy Osbourne): The first face-to-face meeting I had with Randy was at my audition for Quiet Riot back in 1978. He got to show me some of the musical things they were doing, and my first impression was this guy really knows how to teach. I got to teach alongside Randy at Musonia. He really cared about teaching even though it was a monumental task for him. He used to teach ten hours a day and then go to rehearsal for Quiet Riot. Students wanted to learn the popular songs of the day, so he would have to learn Van Halen songs and whatever. But I never heard any other guitar players' influences—especially his contemporaries—on his composition or on his playing.

GEORGE LYNCH: Randy was a good-looking guy and I found out the hard way that all his students were girls and would go there and not care about learning guitar. I went in [to teach in his stead] and they're like "Where's the guy with the polka-dot bowtie?" But you know, I was married and had kids.

RANDY RHOADS (1956–1982) (ex–Ozzy Osbourne, ex–Quiet Riot): Ozzy auditioned a lot of guitar players, and this guy called me and said "Ozzy's heard everybody and he liked [your] playing." He said, "You should go down and audition." At first I said, "I don't know, I couldn't do that." Apparently Ozzy went through every player in LA. I never even knew about it. I never looked for auditions or gigs.

FRANKIE BANALI: When Randy started playing with Ozzy, I get this call, and it's Randy. He was this tiny little guy, but he had a really low, deep voice. "Frankie?" he goes. "Look, I'm playing with this guy. Ozzy." "*This guy?*" I said. "You mean Ozzy, like the Black Sabbath guy?" He goes, "He's putting a band together. He doesn't have a drummer. Do you want to come down and play?" I said, "Sure, but you know, I don't have a car." He arranged for somebody to come and get me, and I threw the drums in his car and went to Mars Rehearsal Studio. I walked in with my drums, and there's a bass player and Randy, and Ozzy is sitting on this piano bench. He was very, very quiet, very nice. He had this little ghetto-blaster he was recording everything on. We sat down and started playing, and we ran down a number of tunes, all of which ended up on the first Ozzy record. For all intents and purposes, I had the gig. But as it turns out, Jet Records had spent a good deal of money on Ozzy, flying him from the UK to New York to LA multiple times looking for musicians, and finally the label decided they were going to record in England, and they were only going to pay to take one musician, and of course, the choice was obvious. It was Randy.

OZZY OSBOURNE: I fell in love with Randy as a player and a person the instant I saw him. He had the best smile in the world. Randy was the best guy in the world to work with. I was attracted to Randy's angelic attitude towards the whole business. I didn't have to teach him anything. All he was lacking was guidance. He listened to every word I spoke to him, and we had a great rapport.

KELLE RHOADS: Randy loved playing with Ozzy. He felt a bit rushed for *Diary of a Madman*. He wished he had a little bit more time. He was a perfectionist. Of course, what's on there is pretty good. Randy's music with Ozzy was absolutely timeless. It's going to be as exciting and vibrant in fifty years from now as it is now.

On March 19, 1982, twenty-five-year-old Randy Rhoads was killed in a plane crash in Leesburg, Florida, along with the pilot, Andrew Aycock, and the Ozzy Osbourne band's hairdresser/seamstress, Rachel Youngblood. The flight was meant to be a short joyride. But as the pilot banked, the left wing clipped the back side of the tour bus and sent the plane spiraling into the garage of a nearby mansion, where it burst into flames. All three bodies were burned beyond recognition. Aycock's autopsy revealed traces of cocaine in his system.

RUDY SARZO: I was on the bus when the plane clipped it. That's how I woke up. It was a thunderous boom. I ran out of the bus and thought that we were involved in a traffic accident.

OZZY OSBOURNE: When the wing hit the bus, Randy and Rachel were thrown through the windscreen, or so I was told. Then the plane—minus its wing—smashed into the trees behind, fell into the garage, and exploded. The fire was so intense the cops had to use dental records to identify the bodies. Even now, I don't like talking or thinking about it. If I'd been awake, I would have been on that fucking plane, no question. But it makes no sense that Randy went up. He hated flying. By the time the fire engines arrived, the flames had already burned themselves out. Randy was gone. Rachel was gone.

RUDY SARZO: Information started unraveling slowly from everybody that had witnessed the crash—our tour manager and Don Airey, our keyboard player. It was one of those chaotic moments. You're wondering what was going on and it was very traumatic.

KELLE RHOADS: I was driving a flower truck, which was a really good job for people in bands. I stopped by my mom's house for a very brief moment to borrow some money, and everybody was crying and my sister was beside herself. My mom was white-faced, but she's an extremely strong woman and she just laid it right out. She said, "Your little brother passed on in a plane accident this morning in Florida." I didn't believe her at first because I thought, "Oh, right. Ozzy bites the bird. Ozzy bites the bat. Ozzy pisses on the Alamo. And now his lead guitar player's dead. I get it. That's pretty sick and fucked up." So I didn't pay attention to it. I got back to the place I worked and my boss put his arm around me and said, "Go home and be with your family. Come back when you're ready." When I got home I turned on the TV and all the channels had pictures of my brother playing guitar. It took me about five hours to accept it. Randy had this charmed Cinderella life and people flocked to do things for him. At twenty-five he's gone in a plane accident? Uh-uh. Can't be. He hated flying. Every single day of my life I miss him so much.

OZZY OSBOURNE: I honestly don't know how we did any of those gigs after Randy died. We were all in a state of shock.

RUDY SARZO: When Randy died he was still living at home. He had not made a major purchase from his royalties. He was still basically the same guy that he was in Quiet Riot. At the core he was a very simple guy and all he wanted to do was be the best he could be and to play. Even though Randy was born with all the goods that you need to be a prototypical rock star—looks, performance chops—deep down inside he was just a great friend, someone who really cared. He helped me so much in the Ozzy days, not only to get the gig but also to understand all the sociopolitics in the band.

DELORES RHOADS (Randy's mother): Ozzy and the rest of the band went to the funeral, as well as all of the people from Jet Records. Members of Ozzy's band and Quiet Riot were pallbearers. My teacher Arlene Thomas, who was a close friend of Randy's, sang and played acoustic guitar. Randy is buried in San Bernardino, which is where I grew up and want to be buried. I had a small bronze guitar put in on one side of his name on the gravestone, and on the other side the "RR" signature that he used. I know he would have wanted that.

After a short grieving period, Osbourne returned to the road, first with a fill-in—British guitarist Bernie Tormé (ex-Gillan) for a few weeks, then with Rubicon guitarist Brad Gillis (Night Ranger), who played on the 1982 live album *Speak of the Devil*. The band found some stability for a few years when Ozzy discovered ex-Mickey Ratt guitarist Jake E. Lee, who played on 1983's *Bark at the Moon* and 1986's *The Ultimate Sin*.

BRAD GILLIS (ex-Ozzy, Night Ranger): I got my stage presence together on the road with Ozzy. I'd been thrown to the wolves. I went from playing to five thousand people a night to twenty thousand a night with Ozzy. The main thing I learned was professionalism and showmanship, and of course I grew from playing Randy's parts as well. It was quite a learning experience and definitely the heaviest time of my life.

GEORGE LYNCH: I got closest [to joining Ozzy after] Brad [Gillis] left. I did the audition tape; they were interested in me. I was still working at my liquor delivery job when I got the call from Ozzy. I flew out to Ireland with their publicist and toured a little bit with them. Then I came back and rehearsed with them in Dallas. I remember that Sharon and Ozzy came walking in with their big giant bags of money and fur coats looking like royalty. They started whispering to each other and I was told by their handlers that they didn't like my guitar because I built my own guitar, a green tiger. Sharon thought it looked like a booger.

JAKE E. LEE: At first I said no [to the audition] because I didn't want to step into Randy Rhoads's shoes. It's hard enough to replace a good guitar player—and I don't want this to sound callous—but when they die they turn into a legend. I'd make it on my own and I didn't want to be compared to somebody else for the rest of my life. But I went down there anyway. I think there were twenty-five guitar players, and we all spent fifteen minutes in the studio. We had our pictures taken and they were given to Ozzy, and he picked three of us: George (Lynch) was one of them, and he was flown to England and given first crack at it. And there was me and Mitch Perry (ex-Heaven, ex-Keel) left in LA. Ozzy came down and we auditioned at SIR and I got it. And I was forty-five minutes late! [Bassist Dana Strum] said that Ozzy almost walked out the door; he said, "Fuck it, if this guy doesn't care enough to show up on time and he's going to be this kind of problem, forget it. I don't care how good he is." But [Dana] kept him there.

GEORGE LYNCH: We went to Hollywood to do more rehearsals and someone was pushing them to try Jake E. Lee, because they hadn't 100 percent committed to me. I walked into the practice room and there was Jake E. Lee jamming on stage with the band. He looked the part, all decked out in leather from head to toe. He looked great, but the problem was he sucked. He admitted that to interviewers. He went up to me later and said he played horribly. I went backstage and saw Ozzy. It was kind of like *The Blair Witch Project* at the end, where that lady is staring at a wall and not moving. Ozzy turned to me and said, "Oh yeah. We got someone else." That was it. There was no "Sorry." Or "Sorry you quit your job and are behind two months of rent and filing for bankruptcy." But what they were going to give me for the gig, if I got it, was $250 a week. So much for those rock-and-roll fantasies.

Some thought Quiet Riot was through when Rhoads left to join Ozzy's band. Actually, it was just getting started. A quick audition later and Carlos Cavazo was the band's new guitarist. (The two albums Quiet Riot recorded with Rhoads were only released in Japan but are widely available on the Internet.) DuBrow hit the Strip hard with his new group, gaining the attention of Pasha/CBS Records. Much to everyone's surprise, the band's first album for the label, 1983's *Metal Health*, shot to number one on the *Billboard* album chart, knocking the Police's *Synchronicity* out of the top spot. By 1995 it had sold more than six million copies in the United States. What seemed like overnight success to the rest of the world were the rewards of years of dues-paying for the LA veterans. As bassist Rudy Sarzo noted, "From October 1978 until

October 1979, Quiet Riot performed approximately three dozen shows at various Los Angeles nightspots. We watched a number of New Wave bands get signed to major record labels as apathetic record executives passed on Quiet Riot, dismissing us as local rock dinosaurs."

FRANKIE BANALI: I don't agree with the notion that *Metal Health* is the first "glam metal" album, because we really were not a glam band by any stretch of the imagination. It wasn't until later in the band's history that the hair got bigger and the show got bigger and the stages got bigger. I've always had the Sicilian poodle hair thing; it's much tamer these days. The whole idea of wearing the tights and stuff, that was really not a fashion statement, it was something that was light, easy to pack, and would dry overnight when you hung it up at the local Super 8 or Motel 6 or whatever terrible place we were staying at. We weren't traveling on a tour bus, there was no wardrobe girl to make sure that the next day's stuff was nice and fresh and clean. Sometimes we'd wear it for two or three weeks before we had an opportunity to wash it, which would be Woolite in the sink. Kevin would room with Carlos [Cavazo] and I'd room with Rudy [Sarzo] and it was a blessing when we got into a hotel that had two sinks because that meant that we could both put our clothes in the sink and Woolite it at the same time instead of, "I got dibs on the sink!"

CARLOS CAVAZO: We were on tour with Black Sabbath on their *Born Again* tour with Ian Gillan when *Metal Health* went number one. The guys from Black Sabbath came into our dressing room with cocaine and champagne and we drank up and snorted up before the show. I went onstage and I felt so crappy I decided I would never play on this crap again. It was the worst feeling.

FRANKIE BANALI: I will always, forever be grateful that [producer] Spencer [Proffer] recommended we do ["Cum On

Feel the Noize"]. Spencer felt that Kevin's vocals and [Slade singer] Noddy Holder's vocals were very much alike, something that Kevin never agreed with. Kevin and I were aware of Slade because we both appreciated English bands from the sixties and seventies—although I will say that they were not on our top list of bands we looked at, because our bar was set so high—we're talking the Who, Led Zeppelin, Free. So Kevin flat-out refused to do it. In order not to make waves we decided not to rehearse the song at all. Spencer would call the rehearsal studio, always, and whether it was the beginning, middle, or end of the conversation, he'd say, "Are you working on 'Cum On Feel the Noize'?" The answer was always, "Oh yeah, absolutely, every day." Of course, we never played it. We planned to go into the studio and play it so poorly that Spencer was going to say, "You know, it's a great idea, but maybe not for this band." So we go in to record and Spencer goes, "Okay, let me hear 'Cum On Feel the Noize.'" Now, earlier that day, knowing that this day was going to come, I said to the engineers, "Do me a favor. When we play 'Cum On Feel the Noize' hit record, because whatever we're going to play, it's going to be awful, and you'll have it for comedic value." So here we are in the live room at Pasha. I'm behind the drums, Rudy's on bass, Carlos is on guitar, Spencer's sitting on a stool about two feet away from the drums, and Kevin is in the far corner, and you can just see him smirking because everything was about to fall apart. I didn't even have an intro for the song because we hadn't worked on it. So I start an intro and Kevin's smiling away, waiting for the total train wreck. Well, I can't do anything intentionally poorly, so I'm playing the song, and I'm not making any mistakes, and I'm powering through it, and slowly but surely, Rudy and Carlos are finding their way through it, and now they're joining in, and there were some errors there, but I kept playing. About halfway through, Kevin's smirk turns into this scowl, and he's angry. He's trying to mess me up, so he's making all these faces, he's pulling his eyelids down, pulling them up. I'm laughing, but

I'm powering through it. We get to the end of the song, and Spencer goes, "That sounds great; I wish we'd recorded that," and the engineer says, "We did." So what you have on the record is the first time we actually ever played that song! Kevin grabbed my arm, almost pulled it out of its socket, takes me out of the room, and goes, "What the fuck was that?" I said, "I don't know, I went into autopilot." And he goes, "That was great, but what am I supposed to do now?" I said, "You could always sing it shitty. You know how to do that, don't you?" He kind of had a smile on his face, but he was pissed off, and it was quite a while before he actually came to terms, after everyone else had put their parts on. He finally just said, "It's just another song," and he sang it and sang it great.

The stretch of West Hollywood's Sunset Boulevard, from Doheny to Fairfax, where the hippies had frolicked in the sixties, was mostly dormant for much of the seventies. But by 1983, the year Mötley Crüe released *Shout at the Devil* and Ratt put out its first EP, a colorful crew was giving the Strip a new identity and the kind of popularity it hadn't experienced in years. Clubs and bars like the Whisky a Go Go, Roxy, Gazzarri's, Rainbow, and the nearby Troubadour and Starwood on Santa Monica Boulevard were ground zero for the Strip scene, a musical and social movement based on excess, theatricality, and decadent fun. Men and women decked out in spandex, liberally applied makeup, and Aqua Net strutted the streets like high-strung transvestite gangs. Any night of the week, "flyering," a ritual in which musicians handed out flyers and chatted up women about their gigs, was the predominant pastime of the Strip-hangers.

BRET MICHAELS: If we were fortunate, [guitarist] C. C. [DeVille] had a car that ran. He would pick us up in the Volvo, flyers in back. We went to the Strip, parked halfway between the Troub and Roxy, and took off in different directions. Until we became friends with Steady at the door at the Rainbow, we stood in the parking lot and waited for it to dump out. We would start at 10, and get together at 2 a.m. at the Rainbow parking lot. If we were lucky, someone was having an after-party. We were below poverty level, but I think it was one of the absolute best times in my life.

VICKY HAMILTON: I had worked out a deal with the Troubadour so that they would pay Poison's rent and phone bill every month if they did one show a month there. I think they still owe them a show. They were due for a show in ten years and then one in twenty—and I think they did the ten year, but the twenty year one they still owe, I think.

VINCE NEIL: We were each pseudo-famous in each one of our previous bands, so we wanted to let people know we were *together* in this band called Mötley Crüe. We flyered a lot. We'd walk down Santa Monica Boulevard in our high heels and dog collars flyering anything and everything that was there. It worked. It got people to come to see us, and that really started the word-of-mouth.

PHIL LEWIS (LA Guns, ex-Girl): There were times you could walk down the street and you couldn't tell the difference between the curb and the streets because there were so many flyers. It was like a ticker-tape parade. From Doheny down to La Cienega.

JANI LANE: You'd be on Sunset Boulevard on a Tuesday night and there would be four hundred people in the street, let alone the clubs being packed. Afterwards, it looked like Armageddon. All these flyers blowing in the wind. What was the city going to do with all this mess? The police just started cracking down.

VICKY HAMILTON: Eventually, West Hollywood outlawed poster-ing on the Sunset Strip, so the kids couldn't stand out there and free-bill. Those telephone and light poles were like three inches thick with posters and things.

DEE SNIDER (Twisted Sister): I definitely don't feel connected to the LA scene. I didn't even know about it until we were heading out on our first tour—it was Blackfoot, Krokus, Twisted Sister. We were driving our Ugly Duckling rental cars out of the desert to Los Angeles for a show at the Hollywood Palladium in '83, and at ten in the morning I hear "The Trooper" [by Iron Maiden] on KMET, and I'm like, "Where are we? I'm in heaven!" I found there was a whole scene going on, and we were welcomed with open arms. They were very aware of Twisted Sister coming out of New York. Clearly, we were inspiring people with our independent singles. Out there, they weren't inspiring us.

JOEY VERA: In the early eighties there was really no splintering. Heavy metal was just heavy metal—one blanket of the same kind of thing. You could be a fan of the LA Overkill and you could also be a fan of Black 'n Blue, and it didn't matter. By '86, '87, '88, these huge lines were being drawn. There were heavy bands on the one side, which was driven more by thrash metal, and on the other side were the hair bands, the glam bands. We were totally in the middle. We kind of wanted to be both.

TOM MORELLO: My first trip to the Strip predated my moving to LA. I had a girlfriend in Granada Hills, [California]. I was a Harvard University student and I visited her one summer and, of course, the first stop we made was the Whisky, where there were some eye-opening, unpleasant surprises. The admission price was higher than I could afford: $12 a ticket. The show was very underattended, the musicians were not great. I had anticipated this glut of Steve Vai-caliber axe-slingers up and down the Strip, and it was more a hair metal thing. I don't even know if Poison was out yet, but that was when the scene was coming out—Jailhouse, bands like that. It was more pomposity than musicianship. I moved to Hollywood for one reason—because that's where you went to get signed and put a band together. I didn't go there for the party scene, which I always felt a complete stranger to.

TRACII GUNS: A lot of people were into blow, and then there was a whole other group of people I was friends with that were into heroin. I didn't want to get involved with that. I watched a lot of people do a lot of drugs and end up in bad places, and watched people get into horrifying fights over drugs and money. There was a seedy underbelly, because LA Guns is like half of the LA [hip college rock station] KCRW scene and half the rock scene, so we would play at these clubs like Lipstick Fixx and the Red Light District, as well as doing the Troubadour, Roxy shows. A lot of our fans are more of the hair fans, but the people we were hanging out with were more of the older punk rock scene.

JOEY VERA: In the late eighties the scene turned into what you see in [the Penelope Spheeris 1988 documentary] *Decline of Western Civilization*.

PENELOPE SPHEERIS: I watched the metal scene develop. There was a certain struggle going on: the punk movement was waning, and the metal scene was moving in. The Strip was packed shoulder to shoulder with glammed-out dudes. Just as with the first *Decline* [Spheeris's 1981 LA punk documentary] when I saw such a powerful music scene developing, I felt compelled to document it. I never looked at any of the feedback as negative. For chrissakes, the movie helped them go down in history. What's so bad about that?

CARLOS CAVAZO: Obviously, we were achieving major success, and all our friends—Dokken, Ratt, Great White, Mötley Crüe—were also doing great. I used to see all these guys in clubs playing in front of twenty or thirty people. I saw Vince in his band Rock Candy before Mötley. I did shows with Don [Dokken]. He opened up for the band I was in, Snow, a couple times. I've seen the guys in Great White when they were Dante Fox. All these guys were going through the same things. So to see that evolution was amazing.

BLACKIE LAWLESS: Once, during a show at the Troubadour, someone opened the doors and I got a glimpse out of the corner of my eye. There must have been two hundred people standing on the grass median on Santa Monica Boulevard trying to hear what we were doing. I had them open all the doors and I went back to the microphone and sang to them out there. That's when I knew we were a part of something that was going to be really special—not just W.A.S.P., all the bands involved.

For musicians in their twenties, "major success" meant having a record deal, a devoted fan base, and a tour schedule. It was also mandatory to have your own place when you were home, a plentiful supply of booze and drugs, and, most importantly, as Mötley Crüe so succinctly put it, "girls, girls, girls."

STEPHEN PEARCY: The three P's: pussy, party, paycheck. There was so much out there, there was no competition. At one time I had a quota. I had to have three different women a day. It was like an addiction.

CARLOS CAVAZO: I got into music for the love of guitar, not girls, but the girls were a great consolation prize. They were everywhere, and so were the drugs, and it just got worse as the money and fame came along. I had friends who would bring over big bags of coke and a bunch of women and we'd stay up all night doing blow and getting laid. Sometimes I'd be up for a day or two from all the coke. I hated that feeling. I gave up the drugs in the late eighties, but it took a little while.

PHIL COLLEN (Def Leppard): I was twenty-four when I joined the band, and we had our first platinum album. We're touring the

States. There's chicks coming up all the time, and you're going, "Wow, this is fucking great. This is why I got in it." You're doing three girls in a day, and two the next day. It's like, "This is absolutely great." You're a young kid and you're having a blast. This was the eighties—pre-AIDS. It didn't seem wrong at all.

JOE ELLIOTT: The stories of us getting blowjobs under the stage are absolutely untrue. [Girls] used to get invited under the stage and have a Polaroid taken with the band, and there were more chances of success if they showed their tits. People don't talk about the *real* debauchery. The myth is always more fun than the reality, so just let the myth get bigger, and we'll just keep denying it.

PHIL COLLEN: Pussy passes? Oh, we had those. Those were for girls who gave blowjobs to the road crew to get backstage passes. It could be a lighting guy or someone who sells T-shirts in the crew. If they went down on them, they would get this special pass that said "Dick Licker" in the logo. On our first headline tour, we had a code. There was a picture of an eye, then a little bird, and a ship with a sailor, and it stood for "I swallow semen." So you would know how the girl got back-stage. But we didn't do anything with those girls. If anything, we reeled back in horror because we knew exactly how they got these passes.

CARLOS CAVAZO: I think every band had guys who would look out for girls and give them passes. The ones that would suck cock to get backstage, they'd give 'em a pass with a special code so you'd know not to kiss her. They also had special codes if someone was reserved for another band member or something and we weren't supposed to mess with her.

NEIL ZLOZOWER: I like to consider myself family to most of the bands: Mötley, Ratt, Poison in their day. I'm the guy they used to give forty passes to go out and get chicks for the bands, because they always appreciated my taste in women. You don't want to give it to the fucking road crew, 'cause they'd get anything—fat, ugly, no teeth, smelly, disgusting. They knew I would get legal girls of the highest quality. Ever since AIDS, it doesn't happen as much. I don't think they have the guys anymore who go out with forty passes. This was the age of fuck-me pumps, fishnet stockings, little short dresses, spandex; skintight clothes that let it all hang out.

DON DOKKEN: I saw [guitarist] George [Lynch] put a girl's high heel up a girl's hiney while I was banging a girl right next to him. She wasn't too happy about it. She was beautiful but on acid. Everybody including the crew saw it because it was on film, but I erased all that crazy stuff years ago to protect my kids in case I croaked and they'd find it. You're laying there, and you whip out a high heel and shove it up her butt. Why do they accept it, how much can you dehumanize and humiliate?

RUDOLF SCHENKER: The eighties were like a big party. In the sixties and seventies, the music was very much connected to political situations in the world—Vietnam, flower power. The eighties became more and more a kind of party music. A girl on the left side, a girl on the right side—let's party. We were involved, of course. Pure rock and roll: it was the best time in our lives.

EDDIE VAN HALEN: I got into the groupie thing in the beginning, but I was kind of shy, so I wasn't a smooth operator. But Dave [Lee Roth] would have these girls come backstage, and half the time Alex would end up with them. We were bunking together, Alex and I, so I'd hear everything. Once Alex was banging this girl all night, and I was sleeping, and then he had her wake me up by sitting on my face. I woke up to this red, engorged pussy on my face. I didn't know what it was. It fucking smelled so bad, I sat up ready to punch whoever was doing that to me.

ALEX VAN HALEN (Van Halen): Put it this way: everything you've ever heard about rock-and-roll bands and pussy passes and orgies and experimentation is true and then some. Everyone knows Connie as "Sweet Connie." Grand Funk had that song she was in. ["We're an American Band."] She came to a lot of our shows. We had multiple partners and crazy scenarios. We made movies and other shit. Those were the days, man.

"SWEET CONNIE" HAMZY (groupie): Eddie does all right in bed; Alex is fabulous. He was very warm and affectionate, which is unbelievable, because when you meet him he can be an absolute dick.

STEPHEN PEARCY: We were playing Little Rock, somewhere around 1985, and we'd heard the famous stories about Connie. So me and Robbin Crosby were out on the bus with her after the show. She's blowing Robbin, and she looks up at me and says, "You want some of this too?" She's a force, man. You gotta have some big nuts to hang with Connie.

CONNIE HAMZY: Me and another girl blew David Lee Roth at a production office in Barton Coliseum. I've [blown] Geddy Lee and Alex Lifeson [from Rush], but I have not had Neil Peart. That I regret, but Peart doesn't give it up very easily.

JEANNIE CRANE (groupie): The high is being with these rock stars because you feel that you're important and you're famous, too, even though you might go home in the morning to your simple life. [After I was handed a backstage pass by someone in the crew] Vince Neil was like, "Why don't you come back and party with us?" I was [sixteen] and was so nervous, and I was shaking. I went, "Yeah, I'll be there!" I went back to the hotel and was up all night partying with the band. You'd have sex with them and then they'd very candidly ask you to leave.

CHERYL RIXON: I always loved rockers. They're more honest and straight-ahead. There's no pretense about what they want. But when it comes to the sex and groupies, I think it's more a case of being alone on the road away from home and needing some companionship.

ROXANA SHIRAZI (groupie, author): I tend to really surprise rock stars, as I can easily conduct an orgy or get a band to do me at once, and the next minute I can start talking about political theory. *Groupie* to me is very one-dimensional. Man, when I go to hang out with bands, if they don't give *me* fun or get me off sexually, I leave or tell them to go and find me someone who will. I genuinely don't [understand] girls who do things just to please these guys. What do they get out of it?

BRET MICHAELS: I do not consider myself sleazy. I consider myself a good host of a good party, and some sleazy things may occur, but it's all in the eyes of the beholder. It looks great on TV, if they were slapping themselves in the ass and sticking stuff up the vajayjay every two seconds. But eventually you gotta cook, have dinner, and talk about what's going on in the world—"How about Obama, is he working?" There's gotta be some amount of intelligence going on.

While bands and groupies had no ethical qualms with the lifestyles they led, others were appalled by the unbridled hedonism in metal videos and song lyrics—especially a group of Washington, DC–based politicos who banded together in 1985 under the name Parents Music Resource Center (PMRC). The group included Tipper Gore, wife of future vice president Al Gore, and Susan Baker, wife of ex-U.S. Treasury Secretary James Baker. Metal was far from their sole target: along with W.A.S.P., Twisted Sister, and

Judas Priest, the group also took aim at Frank Zappa, Prince, and Madonna.

FRANK ZAPPA (1940–1993) (1985 speech to the Senate): The PMRC proposal is an ill-conceived piece of nonsense which fails to deliver any real benefits to children, infringes the civil liberties of people who are not children, and promises to keep the courts busy for years dealing with the interpretational and enforcemental problems inherent in the proposal's design. It is my understanding that in law First Amendment issues are decided with a preference for the least restrictive alternative. In this context, the PMRC demands are the equivalent of treating dandruff by decapitation.

SUSAN BAKER (PMRC): The material we are concerned about cannot be compared with "Louie Louie," Cole Porter, Billie Holliday, et cetera. Cole Porter's "The birds do it, the bees do it," can hardly be compared with W.A.S.P.'s "I f-u-c-k like a beast." There is a new element of vulgarity and violence toward women that is unprecedented. While a few outrageous recordings have always existed in the past, the proliferation of songs glorifying rape, sadomasochism, incest, the occult, and suicide by a growing number of bands illustrates [this] escalating trend that is alarming. Judas Priest [wrote "Eat Me Alive,"] about forced oral sex at gunpoint, [and that] has sold over two million copies.

ROB HALFORD: [For "Eat Me Alive"] we were all fucking pissed out of our minds in a little studio in Ibiza being very hedonistic, and I was writing whatever came to mind. I don't know where the title came from. We were falling about in the studio because we all thought it was really funny. I don't think we knew that song was going to end up on Tipper Gore's hit list. It was just a moment that had a lot of repercussions, and I'm glad it did because that's what rock and roll is about. I still think it's very important that rock and roll carries that title and energy, and vibrates and irritates.

IAN HILL: Tipper Gore and the Washington Wives were trying to get rock and roll banned, and it was real right-wing Nazi-type stuff. Obviously, that was never going to work. The thing is, heavy metal bands aren't the establishment. The establishment is people like Michael Jackson, Bob Dylan, and Barbra Streisand. And that's the kind of thing the people in power listen to. They don't understand anything else. And some of them think, "Well, if I don't like it, nobody else should either," and try to put a stop to it, which is rather ludicrous. I've got no problem whatsoever with rating records. It's the same thing with movies. But trying to ban it as something that's detrimental to the country—I mean, c'mon.

After a well-publicized Senate hearing, the Recording Industry Association of America (RIAA) agreed to place "parental advisory" labels at the bottom right hand corner of records deemed potentially inappropriate for young, impressionable ears. Some outlets, including Walmart, refused to carry albums with warning labels. But the titillation that accompanied obtaining an album with a parental warning increased the marketability of many metal bands. Still, in the post-PMRC climate, some had to compromise. Poison and Guns N' Roses were forced to change album artwork to appease conservative lobbyists. Neither band suffered. Poison's 1988 sophomore offering—*Open Up and Say . . . Ahh!*—went quintuple platinum in America, and GN'R's *Appetite for Destruction* had sold eighteen million in the United States. The two groups were on opposite ends of the glam/Strip spectrum, of course. Poison had a happier, less abrasive aesthetic. Vocalist Bret Michaels, bassist Bobby Dall, guitarist Rikki Rockett, and original guitarist Matt Smith moved to LA from Mechanicsburg, Pennsylvania, in early 1984, changing their name from Paris to Poison before adding guitarist C.C. DeVille and exploding with flashy neon intensity.

VICKY HAMILTON: Poison did several Reseda Country Club gigs with guitarist Matt Smith, prior to C.C. I tried to get Slash in the band. Slash actually auditioned and got the job. He said, "Yeah, I'll take the job, but I'm not gonna wear all the fucking makeup. And I'm not gonna say, 'Hi, my name is Slash.'" You know, Poison had that whole thing in the early days where it was, 'Hi, I'm Bobby.' 'Hi, I'm Rikki' . . ." Slash was like, "I'm not doing that. Sorry." Enter C.C., who would do anything.

BRET MICHAELS: Poison is not a resurgence of the glitter rock scene of the seventies; we're just products of the music and bands we were influenced by. The first two records I bought were Led Zeppelin *II* and Lynyrd Skynyrd [*pronounced 'lĕh-'nérd-'skin-'nérd*]. And then I stole KISS's *Alive* from Sears. That went over big when my dad made me return it after I bragged that I stole it. My first influences were those guys, the Beatles, and the Stones. And then I bought a Strat [guitar] because I thought Jimi Hendrix was the bomb, and he played one. That's where I was coming from. Poison has three things onstage: attitude, image, and most of all, that down-to-earthiness, that rolling-in-the-mud attitude of being with the crowd.

WILLIAM HEIN (founder, Enigma Records) [1986 interview]: [Their songs] might tend to cut off the more intellectual side of the market. I can't see too many Philip Glass fans going crazy over Poison. I'm not too concerned. It seems obvious to me that this band is going to have huge appeal. I think, actually, Poison is going to end up selling more records than KISS.

BRET MICHAELS: I first realized I was a rock star the day I got to play Texas Stadium when we shot the "I Won't Forget You" video. Paul Stanley was onstage with us jamming. Steven Tyler was in the wings with David Coverdale, and we were playing to 83,000 people on our first album. Afterwards I got completely hammered and dove into what I thought was a really deep fountain at Texas Stadium at the Cotton Bowl, but it had a shallow bottom and I banged myself up pretty well. I faked my way through the injury because I didn't want anyone to know I was hurt. The night ended at Carl's Corner truck stop to eat. There were probably six people in there and I don't think anyone knew who we were. So the same day I realized I was a rock star was also the same day that humbled me. I think that's what's helped give me such a long career. Every time something good has happened, I've sort of gotten a kick in the teeth that came with it. That's what helped make me a fighter.

RONNIE JAMES DIO: All Poison had to offer musically was a load of crap. They were just a hair band with makeup, but they were supposed to be heavy metal. I laughed at all that. Heavy metal bands, to me, were always Deep Purple and Black Sabbath. Sabbath created that form of music and I was in that band. So when you're in a band that pioneers a style of music, you look at everyone else who tries to emulate it and go, [sarcastically] "Yeah, sure. You're a *real* heavy metal band."

Though they shared some of the same audience, Guns N' Roses was grittier, heavier, nastier, and more self-destructive than Poison. The road to GN'R's formation was long and convoluted, encompassing the bands LA Guns, Hollywood Rose, and numerous other musicians before the group's "classic" lineup solidified in 1985 with the addition of Indiana-bred vocalist Bill Bailey (aka Axl Rose) and his friend, guitarist Izzy Stradlin.

TRACII GUNS: I met Axl through Izzy, who I first met in 1982 or 1983. He was playing with a friend of mine's band, Shire. We became good friends, and within a year he was living at my mom's house. He kept telling me about Axl. He showed me pictures: "He's my best friend, I'm going to get him out here and do this band." Axl came out to LA a couple of times. He went back and forth between Izzy's girlfriend's house, my mom's house, and guitarist Chris Weber's house, until he ended up in LA Guns. We were best friends for a couple of years. Then, when I went back to do LA Guns, I tried to do a heavier version of Guns N' Roses.

STEVEN ADLER: Tracii had LA Guns, Axl and Izzy had Hollywood Rose, and then they got together and turned into Guns N' Roses. That was with Rob Gardner on drums and Tracii and that was only for about a week.

TRACII GUNS: The first LA Guns show was 1983, or '82. I recall the very first show we did with Paul Black singing. It was the closing night of the Cathay de Grande. One of the highlights for me was Mentors singer El Duce right in front of me all night, with his pants around his ankles, going, "Tracii Guns is god!" He was the sweetest man.

IZZY STRADLIN (ex–Guns N' Roses): This lineup started with Duff, Steve, Axl, Slash, and myself like two days after rehearsal. Duff said, "I got a West Coast tour—Oregon, Seattle." We had six people in his car [and] a U-Haul trailer. We made it to Bakersfield and the car broke down. But we made it. We played all the shows. That's how the band really cemented. It's a survivalist band. I ran away from home when I was almost seventeen. I've been out in LA ever since. Same with Axl.

STEVEN ADLER: Tracii and Rob weren't ready to be road dogs. And me and Slash had already played with Axl, Izzy, and Duff, and we're like "fuck yeah, we'll do it." We were in this guy Danny's car, this big old Cadillac, with a U-Haul, and we're driving through Bakersfield and the car caught on fire, and I got some truck driver to give the band a ride. We had our guitars and our bags and we're in this big eighteen-wheeler, and he takes us to Medford, Oregon. It must've been the coolest scene ever, to see five guys with their guitars and suitcases standing on the freeway hitchhiking. Then these two hippie girls picked us up. That was our first show as Guns N' Roses. But we did shows as Hollywood Rose and Rose. Actually, the first GN'R show was at the Troubadour. That was on a Thursday night, and Friday morning we were on the road.

JERRY CANTRELL: At a Guns N' Roses concert, me and [vocalist] Layne [Staley] were trying to pass a demo tape to Axl Rose, through the fucking gate. When we first met, Layne actually had this other band. [Late bassist] Mike Starr and I were in this band called Gypsy Rose. We got canned after a week 'cause I couldn't do squiggly diddlies on my guitar and they found a bass guitarist that could do better Steve Harris impersonations than Mike.

VICKY HAMILTON: Axl called me when I worked at Silver Lining Entertainment as an agent and said, "You come highly recommended. We want you to book some shows for us." I was like, "Cool, send me a demo." He said, "No—can't I come and play it for you?" I said, "Well, you could if I had a stereo system here." He said, "That's okay, I have a ghetto blaster." A few hours later, he and Izzy showed up with "Back Off Bitch" and a lot of the songs that were on *Appetite*. I was like, "Shit. This is good." I actually booked them at the Music Machine without even seeing them live. It was like this slo-mo moment where I was introducing Slash to Axl. Slash says that he met Axl before that and he probably did, but I thought I introduced them. Whether I did or I didn't, I *did* reintroduce them that night. They stood there talking for quite a while. Chris Weber was basically leaving the band. His parents were shipping him off to England or whatever. At that point, Steven Adler was in the band, too.

PHIL LEWIS: I didn't see Guns N' Roses early. We did a couple shows with them, like Perkins Palace in Pasadena, but Slash and Tracii didn't get along and there was some shenanigans with the amps. Slash doesn't like Tracii at all. He mentioned it twice in his book, and one of the reasons is something to do with that show.

SLASH: There were a few Iron Maiden dates for us to do in California to end the tour. But Axl's throat was such that he just couldn't do them. LA Guns was hired to play the opening slot as long as enough of us showed up to jam with them. Duff, Izzy, Steven, and I showed up reluctantly—at best—to play a few songs. We got up there and our crew told me after that LA Guns had tried to sabotage our gear; they'd turned down all the amps to make us sound bad. I guess Tracii was worried that I was going to outplay him. That show ended any sort of civil relationship between Tracii Guns and me.

Early on, one of Guns N' Roses' favorite haunts was the weekly rock club Cathouse, which helped popularize glam metal in the same way the Soundhouse spearheaded the NWOBHM.

RIKI RACHTMAN: We went to this party, six of us, and Taime [Downe] was one of them. We started talking and totally hit it off. I was DJ-ing this regular club; he came down and hung with me in the DJ booth. I said, "I should start a rock club." He said, "I'm starting a band called Faster Pussycat." I said, "I'll call it the Cathouse and you can do it with me." We called it Riki and Taime's World Famous Cathouse. He was a very important part for the first couple months. The Cathouse is not to be confused with Gazzarri's. We were more the gypsy/junkie thing, as opposed to the [hair metal thing]. I wanted a place for everybody to hang out. The very first live performance at Cathouse was Guns N' Roses, Jet Boy, LA Guns, and Faster Pussycat, all taking turns playing acoustic; nobody had record deals. We probably had five hundred people there. Nobody knew Guns N' Roses would become the biggest band in the world.

VICKY HAMILTON: [GN'R] ended up living with me because Slash called one day and said, "The police are looking for Axl [on rape charges]. Can he come sleep on your couch for a couple of days?" This was before I was their manager. Axl moved in, then a few days later they were, like, "The police are still coming around. Can we move in?" So the rest of Guns is living with me, with the exception of Duff, who always lived with his girlfriend. I felt like I was having a heart attack every day because there was always something going on— the cops were beating at my door, or whatever. At one point, Howie Hubberman, who backed me on Poison and Guns N' Roses financially, said, "Here's a few hundred dollars. You and [roommate and concert promoter] Jennifer [Perry] need to go check in a hotel. I think you're gonna have a nervous breakdown and die." [The rape charges against Rose were ultimately dropped.]

STEVEN ADLER: We lived there for three months; the five of us and Vicky and Jennifer. We destroyed this apartment. The last day we were there, Axl and I got into a fight and he pushed me into this fire extinguisher outside the front door. The glass broke and then I grabbed him in the living room, because he pushed me out the door. I pushed him on this coffee table; everything was destroyed.

VICKY HAMILTON: The building we lived in was the first apartment building on Clark Street, across from the Whisky. I wasn't present when that fight happened, but I did return to the broken window and my apartment being even more trashed than when I left. Once Steven was trying to help me pick up empty Jack Daniel's bottles and beer cans while Axl was sleeping on the couch. We woke him up and he was so mad he picked up the heavy wood coffee table (which I still have, complete with cigarette burns and water rings) and heaved it at Steven with everything on it. Then he started punching him. It was the day before a showcase and I said, "Great, you want to kill your drummer the day before an industry showcase. Perfect!"

SLASH: I hated Gazzarri's. I never would set foot in there. But

I did actually play there with Guns N' Roses, once, right after we got a record deal, and Paul Stanley did sound for us, because he was courting us to produce us at that time. When [Geffen A&R man] Tom Zutaut was bending over backwards trying to find people to work with Guns N' Roses in '85, '86, no one really wanted to work with us; anybody that we met would disappear. They'd show up at a meeting and go to the bathroom and never come back.

DUFF McKAGAN: Finally, at the end of April of 1986, we got signed. There was heavy interest by all the majors, five or six. We were personally dealing with them.

IZZY STRADLIN: We were staying at a place with a phone, and they'd call and leave messages. We'd say, "Yeah, we've been talking to Capitol, EMI, and Geffen, but we'll meet you down at, uh, yeah, Le Dome. Yeah, for dinner. We'll talk some more." We went from eating fucking bean burritos to steak and lobster in a matter of a few days. That lasted about two weeks, and we got bored with that, so we said, "We'd better sign with somebody." Geffen was very hip to what was going on. They know about rock and roll. There were labels we went to who wanted to sign us but they didn't know who Aerosmith was. We're in this office with big plants and desks and something came up about Steven Tyler, and the chick goes, "Who's that?"

VICKY HAMILTON: John Kalodner said to me after I went to work at Geffen, "Yeah, you brought me Stryper, you brought me Mötley Crüe, you brought me Poison—then of course the day you wanted to bring me Guns N' Roses at Columbia, I wasn't here." I took 'em to Tom Zutaut at Geffen at that point.

W. AXL ROSE: We got two firm, and a six-album deal. That's good, because they wanted a lot more, and we didn't want to be tied for that long. The deal is the best thing we could have fucking hoped for from any label, and we wouldn't have gotten any more support from another label.

SLASH: I know David [Geffen] from when I was a little kid. My dad used to work for Geffen & Roberts, a management company, and we lived next door to Joni Mitchell. Any time Guns did anything bad—I wrecked our apartment, I wrecked our van—I'd call David and go, "I'm not such a bad guy and the band really likes this company."

W. AXL ROSE: I spent my advance on clothes. I took out everybody I'd known for the last few months. Every time we went out, I paid for it because everybody used to do that for me.

RIKI RACHTMAN: Axl was the guy; the key word is *was*. If there was an opportunity for him to help a friend, he would. Axl and [GN'R manager] Doug Goldstein called MTV to get me the audition for *Headbangers Ball*. For the audition, Axl came with me to New York. We flew together, he paid for the hotel—the Mayflower Hotel. When I walked into my audition, I walked in with Axl. I was horrible. Is it who you know? Yeah. Did I care? No.

VICKY HAMILTON: The last time I saw Axl was at Hamburger Hamlet and he acted like he didn't even know me, which was better than him screaming, "I'm gonna kill you, bitch!" He left [*that* message] on my answering machine. I took the tape out of my machine and said to [friend and journalist] Janiss Garza, "Put this somewhere. If I ever end up missing, take this to the police." I think she still has it somewhere.

STEVEN ADLER: I love Vicky. We got signed because of her. She got us a record deal, and then Axl and the guys wanted to get rid of her. I was devastated because I loved her and she did everything for us, and they didn't want her working for us because she was a girl. It was the eighties and some people still thought women weren't as strong or powerful as men. It was bullshit. I was very disappointed in the band because she deserved to be with us.

VICKY HAMILTON: The day that Axl was screaming he was going to kill me was over something I said to *Musician* magazine. I believe the quote was, "Axl has two very distinctive personalities; one is a sweet, fun-loving boy, and the other is a demon dog from hell." But that wasn't what caused the break. The break happened when Tom Zutaut brought in Alan Niven to manage the band. The reason according to Tom was, "The band needs *major* management." Funny how I was *major* enough to do A&R for a *major* label [Geffen] but not major enough to manage the band I brought in.

Guns N' Roses' trailblazing debut, *Appetite for Destruction*, was released in July 1987. From its opening salvo, "Welcome to the Jungle," which describes Axl's and Izzy's intro to the surprisingly mean streets of sunny LA, to the prophetic drug anthem "Mr. Brownstone," the album chronicled the band members' down-and-dirty LA lives through incendiary yet accessible songcraft.

W. AXL ROSE [1986 interview]: We went through so many producers; we dealt with Spencer Proffer, Bill Price—who did the Pistols—then we found this guy [Mike Clink]. We weren't so into him at first, but he made some cool comments, so we kept negotiating. We went and did some test tracks. He doesn't necessarily go, "I think you should change this." He'll say, "I don't know about that one part," but he'll fucking cause a scene about it. So we totally analyze something [and] we show him why it works perfectly the way it is, or we come up with a better idea. That's all they wanted—to make sure we are giving 100 percent. Geffen was really worried, but then they heard *Appetite* and they think we're great. Tom [Zutaut] told me if I lost my voice it was okay, I could leave my rough tracks.

Ozzy Osbourne performs with Black Sabbath in Detroit, 1972. Photograph by Robert Matheu.

Iggy Pop on a "Search and Destroy" mission in 1973. Photograph by Robert Matheu.

Rob Zombie demonstrates his firm grasp on the music of Alice Cooper. Photograph by Stephanie Cabral.

MC5 kicks out the jams. Photograph by Robert Matheu.

Jimmy Page bowing with the mighty Zeppelin. Photograph by Robert Matheu.

Alice Cooper makeup: the eyes have it. Photograph by Kyler Clark.

KISS's Gene Simmons shows off his licks.
Photograph by Stephanie Cabral.

Klassic KISS. Photograph by Stephanie Cabra

...as Priest performs 1980's
...ish Steel *in its entirety on a*
...tieth-anniversary reunion tour
...ones Beach, New York.
...tograph by Jon Wiederhorn.

*Judas Priest, hell-bent for
leather.* Photograph courtesy
of Jayne Andrews.

*Neither Priest's then-closeted
Rob Halford nor ex–Penthouse
Pet Cheryl Rixon was aroused
during the taking of this photo.*
Photograph by Steve Joester.

British nineties stoner metal pioneers Cathedral get lit. Photograph courtesy of Nuclear Blast.

Maiden front man Bruce Dickinson takes a leap of faith. Photograph by Stephanie Cabral.

Ra
pr
ur
Ph
Ke

Ozzy, locked and loaded.
Photograph by Robert Matheu.

Guitar legend Tony Iommi of
Black Sabbath. Photograph by
Jon Wiederhorn.

Black Sabbath (left to
right): Bill Ward, Ozzy
Osbourne, Geezer
Butler, Tony Iommi.
Photograph courtesy
of Rhino Records.

Birmingham brothers Ozzy Osbourne and Rob Halford chat it up at Revolver magazine's Golden Gods Awards in Los Angeles. Photograph by Stephanie Cabral.

Maiden's Steve Harris shines under the lights. Photograph by Stephanie Cabral.

WASP's Blackie Lawless sings like a beast. Photograph by Stephanie Cabral.

The late Ronnie James Dio, "devil horns" pioneer, strikes a metal pose.
Photograph by Stephanie Cabral.

Saxon warrior Biff
Byford stresses the
importance of
bandanas in metal.
Photograph by
Kevin Hodapp.

Axl Rose, big hair, buttless chaps.
Photograph by Janiss Garza.

The eternal schoolboy shreds: AC/DC's Angus Young.
Photograph by Bill O'Leary.

Rockin' with Dokken. Photograph courtesy of Rhino Records.

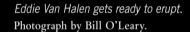
Nikki Sixx and Mick Mars: the young and the restless. Photograph by Michele Matz.

The late guitar great Randy Rhoads. Photograph by Ron Sobol.

Eddie Van Halen gets ready to erupt. Photograph by Bill O'Leary.

Hanoi Rocks front man Michael Monroe gets his wings.
Photograph by Kevin Hodapp.

Hollywood hell-raisers Mötley Crüe.
Photograph by Robert Matheu.

A. Guns' wild bunch—sleazy come, sleazy go. Photograph by Nick Charles.

Twisted Sister's Dee Snider: pretty in pink. Photograph by Kevin Hodapp.

Late Ratt guitarist Robbin Crosby lays it down. Photograph by Kevin Hodapp.

Ratt's Stephen Pearcy demonstrates his admiration fo Jackson Pollock. Photograph by Kevin Hodapp.

Late Quiet Riot front man Kevin DuBrow and guitarist Carlos Cavazo before metal health drove them mad. Photograph by Robert Matheu.

Poison's Bret Michaels: look what the cat dragged in. Photograph by Jon Wiederhorn.

The late Dick Clark with Guns N' Roses front man Axl Rose at the American Music Awards.
Photograph by Nick Charles.

Slash, Sebastian Bach, and John Conley from Scar Culture at the Rainbow Bar & Grill in L.A.
Photograph by Stephanie Cabral.

DAVE MUSTAINE (ex-Metallica, Megadeth): I remember when Guns N' Roses just came on the scene and I used to listen to "Mr. Brownstone" every day after I scored heroin. I'd hear it on KNAC and go, "All right, these are my kind of guys—me and Keith Richards and Guns N' Roses."

W. AXL ROSE [1986 interview]: They were going to ban our record cover, a picture by the artist Robert Williams. It's this picture of a big red monster jumping over a fence, in armor. There's a lot of energy, and there's like an old man robot, and his brain's exploding, and he's smashing little pink robots. I found the painting by accident in a book. . . . It's called *Appetite for Destruction*, which is also what we're going to call the record. The picture is really strange; you can't quite figure out what's going on, and that always bothers you. But it captures the band. I submitted it to the band as a joke, and they all went "this is it." The girl, her shirt's open, she was abused by somebody; I don't know if it's the robot or the monster.

LONN FRIEND (ex–*RIP* magazine editor, author): We had the *RIP* magazine Park Plaza Hotel party in 1989. In a day and a half, Guns N' Roses is opening for the Rolling Stones, four nights at the Coliseum. I say to management, "Why don't you play the *RIP* party? You can use it as a warm-up in the club for the Stones shows." By some miracle, everybody is into it. About two hours before GN'R are supposed to go onstage, the fire department shows up. The place was so full that the fire department starts to kick everybody out from downstairs, including Alice Cooper and Steve Vai. I'm wondering if we're gonna be shut down. Then the curtain opens, the band hits the stage—bedlam. They must've played an hour and forty minutes; it was an epic performance. How prophetic that Axl Rose is onstage a couple days later, threatening to break up the band because his band members won't get off of drugs. "Dancing with Mr. Brownstone," in front of eighty thousand people at the Coliseum, which, right there, is a microcosm of why Guns

N' Roses was a completely unscripted, apocalyptic event in the history of rock and roll. You could not, with your finest craftsman, choreograph that chain of events, those personalities, and the collision of those guys.

One of Axl Rose's big musical and style inspirations was Finnish band Hanoi Rocks. In fact, GN'R's vanity label, Uzi Suicide, re-released all of Hanoi Rocks's albums on colored vinyl. But Hanoi's first visit to LA was tainted with the tragedy that ultimately resulted in the band's demise. Drummer Nicholas "Razzle" Dingley was accompanying an already wasted Vince Neil on a beer run when Mötley Crüe's front man lost control of his car and it hit an oncoming vehicle, killing Razzle instantly. It was yet another chilling illustration of the recklessness and vulnerability of many young rock stars.

MICHAEL MONROE (ex–Hanoi Rocks): At the end of 1984, Hanoi started doing our first American tour, and that's when I broke my ankle in Syracuse, [New York]. We should have cancelled the whole tour and gone home, but there was an executive decision at CBS that we should go to LA to do some press, because there was a big following there. That's when we first came to LA. That's the last time I saw [drummer Nicholas] Razzle [Dingley]. The next day he went out partying with Mötley Crüe, and he died.

VINCE NEIL: As the car rounded the curve, I shifted into second gear for the final stretch home. But as I did so, the wheels chirped and the car slid sideways into the water to the left—into oncoming traffic. . . . Something was coming over the hill and heading straight for us. That's the last thing I saw before I was knocked unconscious. When my head cleared, Razzle was lying in my lap. I lifted his head up and shook it, but he didn't budge. I kept yelling "Razzle, wake up!" because I assumed he had been knocked out, too. . . . At the police station, the officers kept glaring at me. They kept asking me to tell them what had happened, but I just kept saying, "Where's Razzle?" The commanding officer left the room. He came back and said coldly, "Your friend is dead."

NEIL ZLOZOWER: When I got back to LAX from Club Med with Nikki Sixx and Robbin Crosby, my assistant told me about Vince killing Razzle. Nikki probably didn't know yet. He got to Florida and someone said, "Aren't you the guy in Mötley Crüe who killed someone this weekend?" He was, like, "What?" He had to fly back to LA; then all the shit hit the fan.

MICHAEL MONROE: After Razzle's accident, me and [lead guitarist] Andy McCoy stayed in LA for a few days. We hung out with Nikki Sixx and Tommy Lee, and it was a devastating time. Then we came back to London. That was my first experience in Hollywood. The first time I saw the Hollywood sign was when I was on my way to see Razzle's body. It was like a wax doll. For years I had the creeps whenever I saw the sign.

VINCE NEIL: It was a very depressing time; everybody hated me. It was one of those experiences you hear about and go, "God I hope I won't have to go through this." I was looking at seven years in prison. It took a lot of smart people to help me through it. It was devastating to lose a friend like that. Of course [my bandmates] turned against me. It was an accident, but they thought I deliberately did it to fuck them over and they wanted me out of the band. I had no one to lean on. I was pretty much alone. We went on and did the *Theatre of Pain* tour. I was put on probation. I tried to be sober during the tour. The guys weren't supportive at all. It was hard sitting on our airplane and having me pass cocaine and beers to somebody. There was no support there.

DON DOKKEN: I said, "There's a person who murdered somebody and he never quit drinking." [Vince Neil] did, what, one day in jail? I saw him about four days before it happened. He bought the Pantera. He sold me his other car—a 240Z. And he lived in Redondo Beach, on the Esplanade, the same street that he killed Razzle on. Mick [Mars] and I were renting a house in Hermosa, about a half mile away. Vince was always driving wasted, and he'd always make it the ten blocks home. Then Razzle died. Over the years, it's not been any secret, everybody has seen Vince completely wasted out of his mind. It didn't shake him at all, because he didn't have to pay any punishment. The system doesn't work when it comes to celebrities. I was shocked when he didn't go to jail. I remember Mick saying, "Well, the band is fucked. He just killed somebody." But [legendary manager] Doc McGhee got him out. Then Doc got busted too [in 1988, for drug smuggling].

Skid Row was one of the more popular latter-day hair bands. The Jersey boys formed in 1987, the year Guns N' Roses released *Appetite*. Photographer Marc Weiss had shot front man Sebastian Bach's former band, Madam X, in Phoenix, Arizona, and was so impressed he invited Bach to his wedding in New Jersey. During the event, the singer stepped onstage and performed a cover of Led Zeppelin's "Whole Lotta Love" with the wedding band. Jon Bon Jovi's parents were there, and since they knew that their son's friend Dave "Snake" Sabo was looking for a singer, they asked Bach for his contact information. The singer sent Sabo a tape and was invited to audition for Skid Row. Mentored by Bon Jovi and his manager, Doc McGhee, Skid Row inked a record deal with Atlantic in 1988.

"Youth Gone Wild" was an iconic anthem of the waning hair era, and Bach's bad-boy antics were as much a part of the band's presentation as its music. However, his words and actions—even his attire—caused major controversies and engendered several lawsuits. On one occasion, he injured a young female fan with a bottle he threw from the stage. Another time, he was excoriated for wearing a T-shirt onstage that read "AIDS Kills Fags Dead."

SEBASTIAN BACH (Skid Row): I'll never forget Kurt Loder coming on MTV News and saying, "If homophobia was a restaurant, Axl Rose would be the proprietor, Ice-T would be the bell-man, and Sebastian Bach would be the garbage man in the back." That was fuckin' ridiculous.

KURT LODER (MTV News): I might have said something like that, but not in those words. And hey, the guy was onstage wearing a T-shirt that said "AIDS Kills Fags Dead." I've always liked Sebastian, and I liked his band. The T-shirt might have been just bad judgment on his part—a bad joke he should've kept to himself. But I don't think he should've been shocked about getting grief for it.

SEBASTIAN BACH: I'm Mr. Homophobe!—the horrible guy that wore "the shirt." Please! If I'm a homophobe, how could I do four fuckin' Broadway shows? Whoops. Of course I regret anybody getting hurt.

KURT LODER: I actually saw him perform in a Broadway show several years after that incident—he was good—and I hung out with him a little bit after the show in his dressing room. He was still miffed about the T-shirt story, but as he explained, that was mainly because MTV went on to put a lot of rappers into heavy rotation on the channel who were sometimes pretty serious about their homophobia, although maybe some of them were just judgment-impaired young kids, too.

More than most touring rockers at the time, glam bands were notorious for their destructive extracurricular activities, which were often triggered by alcohol, drugs, and the desire to reenact or one-up the antics of their peers.

BRET MICHAELS: C. C. DeVille and I have been through three well-publicized knock-down, drag-out fistfights. Onstage at the MTV Awards was one of 'em. And in New Orleans I broke his nose. Bobby and me got in a huge fistfight in Atlanta a couple years ago onstage. He took his bass off and winged it at my leg. I ended up with twelve stitches; we were pissed off about songs in the set list.

EDDIE VAN HALEN: We thanked the people at the Madison, Wisconsin, Sheraton Inn on our second album because we damaged the seventh floor to the point where the people on the sixth floor had to check out. We turned on the fire hose and water leaked through the floor. Alex and Dave got my room key and took the table and fucking threw it out the window. I come back to my window. There's no screen, the table's gone. I looked down and the fucking table's laying seven stories down in the snow. I went down to the front desk and said, "I'm Mr. Roth, and I lost my key." I went into Dave's room, grabbed his table, and put it in my room. The cops come, and everyone pretends they're asleep. I had to try so hard not to laugh. It was like two Barney Fifes. They walked into the room and I could hear them talking. "I don't get this. There's no screen in the window, but there's a table. In the other room, there's no table, but there's a screen." They couldn't figure it out. In the end we had to pay something like $70,000 worth of damage. We had to pay for the people who checked out, plus the damage.

ROB HALFORD: By the mid-eighties I was a full-on drunk and drug addict. I really was losing control, doing the classic smashing TV sets, pulling telephones out of the wall. For some reason, when I was drunk and high on cocaine, I used to have this thing about setting off fire extinguishers, whether they were in elevators, hotel rooms, or corridors. In Japan, when I came home from a night of sake, I was fumbling around trying to find all the fire extinguishers in the hotel to set them off. I had this idea to stick a tube from one of the fire extinguishers under the door of our tour manager at three or four in the morning and set it off. I ran

back to my room, laughing hysterically like a complete idiot.
But it wasn't a water fire extinguisher. It was one of those
extinguishers that shoots out pink powder. So I set it off and
ran. People were yelling and screaming. I surreptitiously
opened my hotel room door and looked down the corridor
to see all these Japanese hotel employees, and this guy, who
was not the tour manager, but a Japanese businessman, covered head to toe in pink powder. I'd put the hose under the
wrong door. This poor guy's room was just destroyed and he
had to be moved.

GEORGE LYNCH: Monsters of Rock [1988] could arguably be considered the height of our rock stardom, but at the same time
we were all strung out on drugs and the band was breaking up,
we all knew it; the end was in sight.

DON DOKKEN: I have footage from Monsters of Rock; you hear
George go into a solo, the cameras are scrambling looking for
him, but he's hiding behind his amp, sitting down at a table
doing lines of coke. His roadie is holding a straw up to his nose
as he's playing.

SEBASTIAN BACH: When we were on tour with Guns N' Roses
in the early nineties there was a lot of partying going on. Slash
said to me, "Hey, Sebastian, man. You can party all fuckin'
night and drink and smoke and snort and then you can still
sing the next day. I can't fuckin' do that. When I drink I can't
sing." I said to Slash, "Well dude, maybe you should think
about cutting out the partying so you can sing better." He
goes, "Naah. I think I'm gonna try to sing as little as fucking
possible."

ROB HALFORD: The craziest times for Priest happened in Ibiza,
where we recorded [at Ibiza Sound Studios] from 1981's [*Point
of Entry*] through 1984's [*Defenders of the Faith*]. There, Ian
[Hill] went through twenty rental cars and drove motorcycles

in ponds in death-defying feats, and K.K. [Downing] got run
over by a taxi and Glenn [Tipton] was on an acid trip so he
plunged his hands into some boiling water while he was trying
to wipe [K.K.'s] wounds. K.K. was wrapped up in so many
bandages he looked like an Egyptian mummy. He couldn't
walk for a week. We had to escape from Nassau because we
were literally chased out of town by the locals because I got
into a fistfight after we brought some boat rentals back that had
damaged propellers. I got into a scuffle with the owner. We
had people chasing after us throwing bottles and bricks. In the
end, we had to escape from Nassau back to Miami so we could
finish *Turbo*.

EDDIE VAN HALEN: I continued doing blow through 1984. I knew
it wasn't good for me. The last time I did some was with David
[Lee Roth]. But it was just a one-off kind of thing. As soon as I
did it, I went, "Aw, God, why did I do it?" That creepy feeling. It was not a problem stopping the shit because I used to
end up hating it. After that first bump, it's never the same. It
just got worse and worse to the point where your skin starts to
crawl and you feel uncomfortable. So that was an easy one to
give up. Drinking was a lot harder.

ROB HALFORD: There were nights when I would do so much
alcohol and cocaine I literally thought I was on the verge of
crossing over. Then you wake up the next day and literally feel
like walking death for three or four days. And you don't learn,
do you? People still do that today. History hasn't taught us
any lessons. [What made me stop drinking] was a cataclysmic
event. The boy I was dating back then had a cocaine problem.
We had one of those bombastic physical attractions and there
was a tremendous amount of violence. We used to beat the
crap out of each other in drunken and cocaine rages. One day
we were fighting, and I left for my own safety and called a
cab. As I was getting into the cab, he came up to me and said,
"Look, I just want to let you know I love you very much."

When he turned away, I saw that he had a gun. Moments later he put the gun to his head and killed himself.

DAVE MUSTAINE: There is a line down the middle of AA [Alcoholics Anonymous]. There's people who believe in God and those who don't. The people who believe in God are the ones who get that spiritual enlightenment. Those who don't—the ones who joke around and say God stands for "group of drunks"—well, those are the ones who are gonna continue to piss their pants on a curb for the rest of their life.

ROB HALFORD: I finally got clean and sober in 1986 [after my boyfriend's suicide]. For me, it was life or death. It was a simple choice, really. I was getting to that place of complete self-destruction, where if I kept going I would do something really stupid, either intentionally or unintentionally. The great people that we've lost in rock and roll, either deliberate suicide like Kurt Cobain, or choking on vomit like Hendrix or Bon Scott, that's the way some of us are destined to end up. I turned to spirituality to get me out of that dark place, and that side of me is what gets me through the day and I'm always in touch with it.

Some who couldn't clean up their acts met with tragedy. In 1984, Def Leppard drummer Rick Allen, known at the time for alcohol and substance abuse, was speeding to a New Year's Eve party in his hometown of Sheffield, England, when he missed a sharp turn, lost control of his Corvette Stingray, and rolled his car, sustaining an injury that severed his arm below his shoulder. Seven years after Allen's accident, Def Leppard guitarist Steve Clarke died from an overdose of codeine, valium, morphine, and alcohol; his blood alcohol level was twice that which killed Led Zeppelin drummer John Bonham. The GN'R camp lost several friends. In 1987, former Jetboy bassist Todd Crew OD'ed and died in his friend Slash's hotel room. Then, in 1997, Guns N' Roses collaborator West Arkeen (co-writer of "Patience," "Yesterdays," "It's So

Easy," and others), was found dead in his LA home from a drug overdose. And in 2002, Ratt guitarist Robbin Crosby died of a heroin overdose, after having contracted AIDS.

WARREN DeMARTINI: Robbin definitely reached a point where he was really, really mixed up with drugs, and it was extremely difficult, because no one knew what he was going through. One quote I never forgot is he said, "Quitting heroin is like quitting breathing." I had no idea to what extent he was struggling, because it was such a secretive thing to begin with.

ROBBIN CROSBY (1999 VH1 *Behind the Music*): What has drug addiction done for me? It's cost me my career, my fortune, basically my sex life when I found out I was HIV positive. I had spoken to somebody . . . [whose] opinion mattered to me, and he said, "Do you wanna be remembered as the guy . . . [from] one of the premier groups of the eighties? Or do you wanna be remembered as the guy who has a disease and who is dying out in Hollywood somewhere?" I feel like if I can help just one person to avoid what got me into this maelstrom of hell, then it's worth it for me.

STEPHEN PEARCY: It hit me really, really hard when Robbin told me he had AIDS, and then when he died from the heroin overdose. It shook us up. It made me want to really pull it together and try to get things moving with Ratt again—otherwise I would still be a solo artist.

WARREN DeMARTINI: Missing Robbin doesn't get any easier as time passes. It's not something I can hope to get over as much as it's something I try to get used to daily. There's no closure. When we play the old songs like "Scene of the Crime," although it's a happy thing, I think back to when we would play that song and the band was just breaking—seeing Robbin in the spotlight playing the intro.

STEPHEN PEARCY: You look at any successful band and there's always a terrible thing that's gonna happen or has happened to wake you up. It happened to us with Robbin's death. It shows you're successful, but also it shows you how vulnerable and how short life can actually be and, how quick it can end.

Quiet Riot front man Kevin DuBrow's life didn't end as early as Crosby's, but the cocaine overdose that killed him at age fifty-two was clearly preventable. While DuBrow left and rejoined the band over the years, and battled his bandmates for the rights to the group's name, he seemed to be in good spirits and was officially in the band at the time of his death. His last recording with Quiet Riot was its eleventh album, *Rehab*.

CARLOS CAVAZO: I loved Kevin a lot. He was like my brother. When he got around Frankie, that's when he got bad. Those guys were bad medicine. They really wound each other up and would cause problems. But when I was one-on-one with Kevin we got along great. He was like my big brother. I miss him dearly.

FRANKIE BANALI: When [Kevin and I] were at each other's throats, we were as vicious as we were friendly. The test of a true lifelong friendship is we always managed to sort out our problems, shake hands, hug, and then continue. I can tell you without any reservations, the last five years of Kevin's life was the happiest I had ever seen him. The last three years in particular, he was so up and so positive, feeling great and looking great, there were bright things on the horizon for us for 2008. Then on November 25, it all ended.

STEPHEN PEARCY: There's two entities of sober: the dabbler—someone who was the extremist and [then only] dabbles; and the person who really makes a conscious effort to be sober. I can speak on something like that for Kevin. When you're into something as heavily as he was, then you just stop and then you start to do it again, your body's not used to it. When you get clean, you can't just jump in and do it like you used to.

LONN FRIEND: He was never without a smile on his face or a bounce in his step. It didn't matter what rug he plopped on his head or what folks might be saying about the guy he was in the spandex-clad past. Kevin didn't give a fuck anymore. He was content playing his own rock, venturing out to see his musical peers shred it loud and hard, and totally enjoyed the second half of his life.

By comparison, Warrant singer Jani Lane struggled with his and Warrant's declining popularity in the last years of *his* life, sometimes showing up wasted onstage. He left Warrant for the last time in 2008, and toured in place of ailing Great White front man Jack Russell for a few months before dying from acute alcohol poisoning in August 2011 at a Comfort Inn in Woodland Hills, California.

JANI LANE: The only thing that made me a bit of an odd duck was that it was a known fact that I wanted nothing to do with drugs and I didn't want them around me. If anybody was caught with them in their possession or doing them, they were immediately fired. Code words were used around me, which for one tour, I found out. Everybody kept going, "Have you seen Fred? I saw Fred. When'd you see Fred?" I'm asking the whole tour, "Yo, what's goin' on?" At the show before the last one, this tour guy goes, "You do know what *Fred* stands for, right?" I said, "No." He was like, "Blow." I didn't tolerate any of that stuff. But drink 'til you puke, pass out, get up, and do it again!

As Guns N' Roses wrote in "November Rain," a song from the ambitious 1991 double-CD set *Use Your Illusion I and II*, "Nothing lasts forever." By the early nineties, hair metal was on its way out. MTV abruptly canceled its weekly metal show, *Headbangers Ball,* and once-ubiquitous songs like Poison's "Every Rose Has Its Thorn," Skid Row's "I Remember You," Warrant's "Heaven," and GN'R's "Don't Cry" disappeared from the airwaves, replaced by the more stripped-down and angst-riddled fare of Nirvana, Pearl Jam, Soundgarden, and Alice in Chains.

JAY JAY FRENCH (Twisted Sister): Over time, I found the eighties metal thing to be as pretentious and phony as "Championship Wrestling." Hair bands fell apart because kids were dying for something real, and they got so sick of the pretentiousness and the "let's party on dudes" vacuous music garbage that was coming out of the eighties. [So] when Nirvana and Pearl Jam hit, it was a dose of real emotion. The songs are better, the message is more real.

CHRIS CORNELL (Temple of the Dog, Soundgarden, Audioslave): [The "grunge" scene] was the right mood at the right time. We were getting bludgeoned with one kooky-haired commercial metal band after another, and they would present themselves as people you could never be: they had loads of expensive cars; hung out with scantily clad supermodels with bolt-on breasts; wore leather suits and huge gold watches.

GEORGE LYNCH: We were like sheep—very short-sighted—a product of our environment. We'd all go to the same clothing designer, Ray Brown, wear the same makeup. We'd go to others and go, "How do they get their hair up that high? I've got to get mine higher." Everyone just chased each other's tail until it exploded on itself. Grunge exposed it for the silliness that it was. [The attitude of grunge was] "I don't care if I can play a fucking guitar solo or if my guitar is even in tune."

PHIL LEWIS: Everybody was throwing their crap in the back of a Camaro and driving west. It glutted up the city. There was a "rock zone," "Rock & Roll" Denny's and "Rock & Roll" Ralph's [on Sunset Boulevard]. It diluted it. There were bands getting signed that shouldn't have gotten signed. It was a fad, like Pretty Boy Floyd.

LITA FORD: I really wanted to get away from all the evils of the music industry, so my then-husband and I packed up and moved to a little island in the Caribbean. Everything was changing so fast and metal was getting ruled out all over the place. It just didn't fit anymore. What really pissed me off was that "eighties metal" got labeled as a dirty word. All these grunge guys were speaking out against everything we did. It was like, "Hey man, you wouldn't be here if it wasn't for us." I felt like we led the path for these people, so why would they label us as something bad?

RUDOLF SCHENKER: When I first heard grunge music . . . I think Mother Love Bone was the first grunge band inspired by Led Zeppelin, but they also had this more kind of fucked-up kind of feeling, very dark. Nirvana, I liked them very much. I called my manager, Peter Mensch, and said, "Peter, what do you think about this Nirvana thing?" He said, "You know, it's a one-day thing." I said, "I tell you one thing, Peter, I like the stuff. I hate the lead guitar, but I love the composing and also the attitude."

HARRY CODY (Shotgun Messiah): I heard *Nevermind* and thought it was just brilliant. But great albums come and go without scenes dying because of it. I didn't feel a sense of impending doom. I don't think grunge killed the scene as much as MTV turning on a dime and making fun of everything up til that time they had helped create.

SEBASTIAN BACH: Yes, [the Seattle scene's dominance] definitely sucked and it was a bummer. But between 1989 and 1991 Skid

Row sold twenty million records. We were all wealthy as fuck, so it really didn't suck that bad. It sucked, but I bought a five-acre estate and I could walk around in the woods and ride on a boat. So my attitude was, "Fuck it, who cares?" It gave us a chance to buy some shit and have some fun.

5

CAUGHT IN A MOSH: THRASH METAL, 1981–1991

At the same time as the hair metal scene developed, a handful of young, defiant bands were creating a new, more aggressive counterculture that would quickly go mainstream. Metallica is most often credited for pioneering the thrash movement, and there's no underestimating its contribution. However, if it weren't for the thundering tempos of Motörhead, thrash bands wouldn't have had a bar—or a Jack and Coke—to rise above. By combining the speed and ruggedness of Motörhead, the attitude of the Sex Pistols, and the precision and complexity of Judas Priest and Iron Maiden, groups like Metallica, Slayer, Exodus, and Anthrax birthed a scene diametrically opposed to everything that made commercial metal popular. By 1984, Metallica had moved to San Francisco and become huge; ex-Metallicat Dave Mustaine had formed Megadeth and started making his mark in LA; Anthrax was carving its niche in New York; and, before long, San Francisco's Legacy (soon to be Testament) and New Jersey's Overkill joined the fray. For almost a decade, these bands composed the fastest, heaviest music on many of the nation's major labels, at the time a significant accomplishment. Along with the speed, groove, and aggression came plenty of stage diving—and a new audience activity borrowed from hardcore known as moshing: members of the crowd rotating like clothes in a washing machine, colliding with, and sometimes inflicting damage on, anyone who dared enter the mosh pit.

RAT SKATES (ex-Overkill; filmmaker): Thrash was a spinoff of the music coming from the New Wave of British Heavy Metal, and it was an example of what American kids do. We take everything to an extreme. That's always been the mindset of heavy metal as it's grown. We took what we were hearing and made it faster, heavier, and more intense.

KERRY KING (Slayer): Before we came out, what was popular? Glam. Men looking like women. I knew that's what I *didn't* want to be. We definitely missed out on a lot of good-looking groupies that way, but I've still got my credibility, and where are all those other guys?

GARY HOLT (Exodus): I think the thrash bands and the hair metal bands needed each other. We were mutual enemies, and it gave us ammunition. They were the pretty boys in the makeup and we were the guys in the denim vests with Motörhead patches on the back. But by the same token, we always went to the hair band shows because we knew that's where the girls were. So we appreciated them at the same time as we hated them. If I wanted to get laid I went to a Faster Pussycat show, not a Saxon gig.

DAVE MUSTAINE: The hair bands turned metal into a farce or a joke. You had the video [for Whitesnake's "Here I Go Again"] where Tawny Kitaen is trying to swallow a Jaguar with her vagina. That kind of stuff cheapened everything. You've got guys like us who live heavy metal. It's what we eat and breathe. Then there were bands like Warrant and Poison, and when people thought of metal, they thought of *them*, which did a terrible disservice to the music. But at the same time, there was a loyal following of thrash fans who hated that shit, and it made them want to be even heavier and less commercial.

DAVE ELLEFSON (Megadeth, ex-F5): During that whole era, there was so much confusion because guys were dressing up like chicks and chicks wanted to be with rockers. You didn't even have to be any *good*, you just had to be in a band and you were getting laid. So what happened? Well, every guy I know instantly got into a band—and most of them sucked.

CHUCK BILLY (Testament, Dublin Death Patrol): In the eighties, San Francisco was known for its glam bands, too. So when metal was rising in the Bay Area, the whole theme for us was "kill posers," and, to us, the posers were the guys who were into glam. I think our crazy, young madness and all our threats eventually drove all the glam out of San Francisco, and that's why San Francisco rose as more of a thrash metal center. The glam bands went to LA and we had the Bay Area metal scene pretty much to ourselves.

SCOTT IAN (Anthrax, S.O.D.): Motörhead were so important to the development of thrash metal because they were so fucking fast and heavy. When Anthrax started out, we were listening to Motörhead nonstop. We'd be writing a song and going, "No we should play that one *faster*. That's how fast Motörhead plays. We have to be faster than them."

LEMMY KILMISTER: As far as the tempos go, well, we were all doing speed when we started, but then again, I was doing it in Hawkwind. I've just always been in a hurry for everything. I'm a very impatient man.

DIMEBAG DARRELL ABBOTT (1966–2004) (Damageplan, Pantera): Motörhead—man! Songs like "Ace of Spades" and "Love You

Like a Reptile" just tear your head off. The uniqueness of that band changed the way a lot of people looked at their sound. Lemmy's bass—cramming it through a Marshall cabinet on twelve—was real unique. His voice was very raw, and so was their whole way of jamming. The music didn't have to be all pretty and polished. It's like they set up, jammed it one time, and said, "Okay mix it, we're done. We're going to drink. See you later."

Metallica quickly became the most influential thrash band and one of the most inspirational metal bands, period. But they weren't the *first* to play thrash metal. A year before Metallica drummer Lars Ulrich met guitarist and vocalist James Hetfield in Los Angeles, San Francisco quartet Exodus was playing an early form of thrash with a lineup that featured future Metallica guitarist Kirk Hammett, drummer Tom Hunting, and a revolving door of players, before the band's future architect, guitarist Gary Holt, entered the fray.

GARY HOLT (Exodus): I met Kirk Hammett when Exodus played in my high school band room, and we became friends. He taught me a couple chords, and six months later I was in the band. The Kirk-era of Exodus was definitely thrash, but it had a more Iron Maiden-ish bent to it. Tom [Hunting] used to play drums *and* sing because we couldn't find a singer at first. Then we met Paul Baloff at an outdoor party we were playing. He came down because Lääz Rockit played with us and he went to school with those guys. Paul couldn't sing at all, but he was more metal than anybody I'd ever met. We believed in him, so he became our vocalist, and he became a guy many people still consider the voice of the band, even though he only sang on one studio record.

RAT SKATES: In the heavy metal underground, even before Metallica, Exodus was definitely huge. We had recordings of all their live shows, which they didn't know people were making.

The tapes got copied and passed around. We all knew what
they were like live way before we saw 'em.

GARY HOLT: The live shows were a big thing for us from the
start. But a lot of the real excitement always happened offstage.
One time, Kirk, Tom, and our former manager got frustrated
with their lack of quality equipment and robbed the band
in the rehearsal storage shed next to them. I wasn't even in
Exodus when this happened, but sometime between the actual
theft happening and me hooking up with them, I let them rehearse in my parents' garage. The guitar player I replaced—my
high school buddy Tim Agnello (ex–Blind Illusion)—ratted the
band out because he was one of the founding members and he
was so mad at them for firing him. They got caught, and I got
called in for questioning. The police considered me an innocent patsy until I got caught hiding the remaining stolen gear,
which cemented my guilt. So I spent one night in juvenile
hall. That's the only time I've actually spent in jail.

At first, thrash was deemed way too heavy for radio or MTV
airplay, so bands played out as much as they could and sent demo
cassettes to musicians, fans, and industry insiders in the hopes that
their music would be embraced by fanzine editors, mom-and-pop
record stores, and ambitious start-up labels. This was the early-to-
mid-eighties era of tape trading, the primitive method of peer-
to-peer music sharing that existed almost twenty years before the
dawn of Napster and BitTorrents.

RON QUINTANA (San Francisco radio DJ, ex–fanzine editor): In 1980,
there was no metal in any real magazine in America. *Circus*
would maybe show pseudo-metal bands like Scorpions or
Ozzy, and an occasional Black Sabbath. They hardly ever
showed Motörhead or Iron Maiden, or anything coming out of
Europe. And the New Wave of British Heavy Metal was pretty
big hype for England in 1979 and 1980, so we'd read about it
if we could ever find any of the British papers—*Sounds, New*

Music Express, or *Melody Maker.* That's why a lot of fans started their own fanzines.

LARS ULRICH (Metallica): The scenes were all centered around stores that imported a lot of records and driven by word-of-mouth, grassroots movements, and tape trading. By the time you got a copy of a demo, it was like the fourteenth generation of it. You could barely make it out, but man, you knew it was the thing: "Hey, guess what, I got a demo you don't have, ha-ha. I'm super extra cool." It was sort of like the early version of the Internet.

RON QUINTANA: I met Lars on the streets of Berkeley on Telegraph [Avenue] going into a record store. Back then, anybody wearing jackets with buttons and patches of underground bands from Europe was pretty noticeable. My friend ran over and talked Lars into coming up to our party spot in the middle of Golden Gate Park. Since Lars was from Denmark and knew all about the New Wave of British Heavy Metal, we all accosted him and pointed at his patches for Silverwing or Demon Pact, because we had only read about these bands. He told us all about the groups, and we all listened intently. It's funny, because Lars was a total metal guy, but he was also this tennis kid down in LA in Newport Beach. So he went back to LA after our party to play tennis, and then he'd come up every once in a while and we'd go on record trips to Tower Records and this store in Walnut Creek named the Record Exchange. Those were the only places you could buy metal imports. It was an hour east of San Francisco, so it was quite a trek. Lars would pick us up in his little green Pacer. It was kind of like the Wayne's World car. Not very metal at all.

BRIAN SLAGEL (chairman/CEO, Metal Blade): I hadn't started Metal Blade Records yet when I went with my friend John Kornarens in December 1980 to see the Michael Schenker Group at the Country Club [in Reseda, California]. While we were there, he saw a kid wearing a European Saxon T-shirt, so John ran up to this kid and said, "Do you know who Saxon is?" The kid turned out to be Lars Ulrich. I'll never forget hanging out at his family's condo in Newport Beach. He had a drum set sitting in the corner. It wasn't even put together. He said, "I'm going to start a band," and we're like "Yeah, sure you are." He was a crazy little kid. When we went to the record store with him, he'd be out of the car and at the metal bin before we even shut the engine off. He had to get there first.

While Tower Records and the Record Exchange were selling vinyl and tapes to California metalheads, a less flashy but even more influential mom-and-pop retail outlet was taking root in Clark, New Jersey; it would indirectly help launch the careers of Metallica, Anthrax, Overkill, and others.

JONNY ZAZULA (Megaforce Records founder): Before thrash metal started taking off, my wife Marsha and I had a flea market store in New Jersey, where we were selling predominantly picture discs from Europe by bands like the Kinks. But there was one picture disc I really loved, and it was Judas Priest's *Sad Wings of Destiny*. Someone gave me $200 for it. I said, "Wow, this is amazing." I realized there was a real market for metal, so I started bringing in other things like that. And then I met Maria Ferrero [longtime Megaforce Records publicist and the current owner of Adrenaline PR]. She came knocking on my door to buy Motörhead and I really didn't know much about them, but I found the album and I got it for her. We got to the point where all we would buy was metal, nothing else.

MARIA FERRERO (Adrenaline PR founder, ex–Megaforce publicist): Jonny and Marsha were the champions of metal. They brought us the goods and we ate it up.

BOBBY "BLITZ" ELLSWORTH (Overkill): Jonny's flea market was part of a big supermarket that sold everything from Indian tapestries to cleaning solutions. Overkill wasn't a band at the time yet, but we would all go out there and be exposed to things like Raven and Anvil. Jonny slowly became this local guru because he held the *gold*.

While Zazula was selling Saxon and Motörhead albums, across the country in Los Angeles, Metallica front man James Hetfield was just getting started. And Ulrich was learning to keep a steady beat—initially with limited success.

RON McGOVNEY (ex-Metallica): James and I went to junior high and high school together. In high school we had our lockers by each other. He was the rocker kid with the Aerosmith shirt, and I had an Elvis Presley sticker on my notebook, so he'd always make fun of Elvis and I'd make fun of Aerosmith, but we became friends. James had a band called Obsession and I was one of their roadies. We started going to clubs when we were seventeen and seeing Hollywood bands. That's when I really got into Mötley Crüe, because they were so different. We just looked at their ad in *BAM* magazine, and I was like, "Hey man, this band looks cool—let's go watch them." So James and I went down and saw them, and he was like, "Yeah, whatever," but I thought it was awesome.

RON QUINTANA: On one of his trips to San Francisco, Lars said he was a drummer. My friends in Metal Church—at the time they were called Church of Metal—were looking for a drummer. They had made this amazing demo, and back then they were probably the heaviest band in America. So I set up an audition for Lars with them in early '81. But he disappeared and he didn't show up for months after that. We didn't know what happened or if he could actually drum.

As it turned out, Ulrich was in the UK following some of his favorite bands. Having grown up in an art community in

Copenhagen with ultra-liberal parents, he retained worldly per-spective as a teenager and was allowed to travel back and forth to Europe on his own.

BRIAN TATLER (Diamond Head): Back in 1981, Diamond Head still hadn't gotten a record deal, so we decided to sell our first album ourselves via mail order for 3 pounds 50. We advertised for six weeks in *Sounds* magazine, which Lars regularly read, and he ordered his copy. Well, he loved it and he wrote back to the fan club address, which was at [vocalist] Sean Harris's house, and said how much he loved the band. He even phoned Sean and Sean's mum a few times. Next thing you know, he shows up at this gig in London at the Woolwich Odeon in 1981, and he introduced himself and said he flew over from California to see us. That was astounding to us—that a seventeen-year-old had flown over from America to see us in England. I asked him where he was staying, and he hadn't ar-ranged to stay anywhere yet. So I said, "Well, come stay with me." He literally jumped in the car with the rest of the band and we drove back up to the Midlands, and he slept on my floor in my bedroom. I still lived with my parents, so he slept in my brother's old sleeping bag on the floor for a week. Then he went and stayed with Sean for four weeks.

LARS ULRICH: In the fall of 1981, after coming back from a trip in England, I wanted to put a band together. I put together an ad in *The Recycler* saying, "Heavy metal drummer look-ing for other musicians. Influences: Tygers of Pan Tang, Angel Witch, Saxon." Most people would call up and be like, "I'm into heavy metal but I've never heard of any of those bands. But I like Journey and I like REO Speedwagon. Does that work?" One of the guys that called up was a guy named Hugh Tanner. He came down with his rhythm guitar player, this James Hetfield guy, who basically spent the whole afternoon not saying one fucking word. I mean, I'd never met anyone that shy in my life. We had a bit of a jam and nothing much materialized out of that. My ability on the drums at that time was basically zero. I think they were secretly laughing at me. But there was something about this guy Hetfield. The way he played, his aura, his vibe.

RON McGOVNEY: James and I were in Leather Charm; I played bass. We only had "Hit the Lights," which we played in Metallica. And there were riffs from three different Leather Charm songs that James put together later to make the Metallica song "No Remorse."

LARS ULRICH: I called up Hetfield and I said, "My friend's putting this [heavy metal compilation] record together. Do you want to take another shot at it?" He came down and we started hanging out pretty much every day. I started subjecting him to every single New Wave of British Heavy Metal thing, from Praying Mantis to Black Axe to Silverwing. Then we basically wrote a song together—"Hit the Lights."

RON QUINTANA: Me and Lars prepared band names and magazine titles. I had *Metallica* on my list for magazine names, but I liked *Metal Mania* better, and, of course, he liked Metallica better. It came from the *Encyclopedia Metallica*, an English book that was hard to find in America that was all about English heavy metal bands.

BRIAN SLAGEL: So Lars finds out I'm doing this record [*Metal Massacre I*] and he says, "If I started a band, would you put me on your compilation?" I said, "Sure." Him and James had been jamming for a while but couldn't find anyone else who liked what they liked. So they'd stopped jamming. Typical Lars. He was scattered. They recorded that song, "Hit the Lights," the night before the very last day [of the deadline for the compilation]. I kept pressuring him, saying, "This record is going to press. I need your track." So they recorded on [a

Fostex four-track tape recorder] and he brought a cassette to the mastering session, and the engineer told him, "It has to be on quarter-inch reel," which would cost $50 to transfer—but I didn't have $50, Lars didn't have $50. So my friend John Kornarens actually paid for it because if he didn't, it wasn't going to get on the record.

RON McGOVNEY: When this thing from Brian Slagel came up about doing a song for *Metal Massacre*, Lars didn't have a complete band and I thought Lars was a horrible drummer, so I told James and Lars, "You guys just go ahead and do whatever you want." But they were at my house, so I'd sit there and watch them play. They would try out bass players, and one night I'm watching a guy try "Hit the Lights," and I'm like, "Wait a minute, let me plug in here and I'll show you how to play it." And James and Lars go, "Why don't you just be in the band?" I said, "OK." When *Metal Massacre* came up, Lars knew [guitarist] Lloyd Grant from somewhere. I didn't know him. So, there's a knock at the door and there's this black Jamaican dude standing there, and it's Lloyd. He plugs in, and he's a ripping guitar player. He did lead guitar on the first pressing of *Metal Massacre* for "Hit the Lights," and James played my bass and did vocals, and Lars played drums. My name is misspelled and Metallica is misspelled. When they reissued *Metal Massacre*, we had already done the *No Life 'Til Leather* demo, and they just took the song off of that. Of course, by then Mustaine was in the band.

DAVE MUSTAINE: I was leafing through *The Recycler* and an ad caught my attention. It was the first to reference, not one or two, but three of my favorite bands: Iron Maiden, Motörhead, and Budgie. I would soon discover Lars was an avid collector of music from the New Wave of British Heavy Metal. Deep down inside, a very long time ago, we really were kindred spirits. We met a few days later at Lars's condo in Newport Beach. We shook hands and went right upstairs to his bedroom. Lars played me a rough demo of "Hit the Lights." The song wasn't bad. The afternoon ended with a handshake. Lars called again a few days later, wanting to know whether I'd be able to meet him and the other guys in Norwalk, where Ron McGovney lived. There was a weird vibe almost from the moment I arrived. While I set up, everyone else went into another room. I plugged in my amp and warmed up. I kept playing, faster and louder, figuring somebody would walk in and start jamming with me. But they never did. Finally, after a half hour, I put down the guitar and opened the door into the house. The entire group was sitting there, drinking and getting high, watching television. Lars smiled at me and waved [and said] "You got the job."

RON McGOVNEY: I remember Dave calling my house, and I answered and this guy starts spouting off about all these guitars he's got and all these amps and everything, and I remember saying to James and Lars: "If either one of you want to take this, this guy's head's not going to fit through the door." Within a couple of hours he was over there, and he had a B. C. Rich guitar and a fake Marshall amp spray painted with a Marshall logo on it. He plugged in, and we were like, "Wow, this guy's smokin'." But all he did was rattle on about himself.

By the early eighties, Metal Blade was the premier West Coast indie label for underground metal. As ambitious as it was financially challenged, the label released four *Metal Massacre* compilations before 1983, and soon after, put out albums by Bitch, Slayer, Voivod, Fates Warning, Hellhammer, and others. The East Coast equivalents were Jonny Z's Megaforce, initial home of Metallica, Anthrax, Overkill, and Testament; Combat Records, which released albums by Megadeth, Possessed, Dark Angel, and others; and Shrapnel, which focused on shredders like Steeler (which included a young Yngwie Malmsteen), Cacophony (featuring future Megadeth axeman Marty Friedman, and Racer X (showcasing Paul Gilbert). In the UK, Music For Nations distributed Exciter, Manowar, and Metallica; and Neat Records released Venom, Raven, and Tygers of Pan Tang.

JOHN GALLAGHER (Raven): Neat Records was a little project studio [in England] that used to do recordings for the local bands playing the workingmen's clubs so they could have a 45 vinyl single to sell at shows. In '79 they put out a record by Tygers of Pan Tang ["Don't Touch Me There"] that did really well. Tygers manager Tom Noble saw us play and said, "Would you like to do a record, too?" and we said, "We certainly would." We did the "Don't Need Your Money" single [in 1980] and it took off, so we never looked back. Except, by the third record we were still unsigned, and we were making no money and getting zero promotion, and we were really frustrated. Then we got the opportunity to come to America with Metallica.

JONNY ZAZULA: The owner of Neat was a jolly good fellow named Dave Wood, and when I brought Raven over to America, Dave wanted to come too, so I had to pay for Dave. From that, he gave me approval to book concerts for Venom, who had never done any American shows. In fact, they had done six shows in their life. When their first album came out, they weren't even a band. Dave stayed in our house in a room across from my bedroom and one night at about 3 a.m., he wanders into my bedroom and starts peeing all over my wife Marsha. He thought he was in the bathroom.

CONRAD "CRONOS" LANT (Venom): We always used to say that Venom was all of our favorite bands thrown into a pot and mixed up—the stage show of KISS, the lyrics of Sabbath, the speed of Motörhead, the look of Judas Priest. We were trying to use as many influences as we could to make the ultimate metal band, but also be original.

JOHN GALLAGHER: Venom's vocalist and bassist, Conrad—or Cronos, as he called himself—was the tape operator at the studies at Neat. That's how he eventually got recorded. He bugged the guy who ran the studio: "Can we do a demo? Can we do a demo?" So, of course, they finally did. But Venom had a master plan, which was to never play live and just build this mystique, and to a large degree they succeeded. There was such a demand for them to play live. When they finally did, they got paid outrageous amounts of money. But they were terrible and did stupid things. When they first came to America, they brought black [explosive] powder over on the airplane. You try that now and you're in jail for twenty-five years.

JONNY ZAZULA: They brought all this pyro that they were told not to bring. But they convinced me it was safe. Kids waited for them for two and a half hours while they were busy stringing bombs to everything. When the bombs went off the whole front row turned black. I went up to the balcony to get my head together, and two of the explosives were up on the balcony. [That pyro] could have taken kids' heads off.

SCOTT IAN: For me and all my friends, [1981's] *Welcome to Hell* was our first exposure to Venom, and it was a huge eye-opener. It was one of those "holy shit" records. Like, "Jesus Christ, listen to this. These guys are fucking insane." There were songs like "Sons of Satan," and the title track. It was so, so evil. This was a new kind of insanity.

JONNY ZAZULA: We brought Venom over to our house. When they came in, Cronos took glasses out of the kitchen cabinet and started chewing them and everyone freaked out. He left a few of the broken glasses in my cabinet as souvenirs. He wanted me to have them one day to put in the Rock and Roll Hall of Fame.

CRONOS: Venom was unlike anything at the time. People credit us with starting [the thrash metal] movement and all, but the truth is, I think it was inevitable. Punk had died. Metal was lame. There could only be one new way to do this—for metal bands to get some fucking balls again.

Venom's pyrotechnic performances, Satanic lyrics, and occult imagery were hugely inspirational for Slayer, Possessed, Hellhammer, and others. However, Venom was musically limited, and when they tried to be anything but a really evil Motörhead, they fell on their snarling faces. It took Metallica's blend of razor-edged New Wave of British Heavy Metal riffs and hardcore punk to really ignite the thrash movement. But first they had to break out of the cock-rock scene in LA.

JAMES HETFIELD (Metallica): So we get this gig—our first ever. The crew at sound check steal a keg from the place. The venue calls us up and says, "Well, you're canceled." We said, "Oh, we'll bring the keg back, hold on!" It was our first run-in with what you were supposed to do and not do in the music business. But yeah, basically seek and destroy. Drink, smash stuff up, feel good.

LARS ULRICH: Initially [for our fans] it wasn't just about identifying with the songs. It was also identifying with what the band represented. We were the antithesis to what most of the bigger bands were doing at that time. In '83, '84, '85, the music scene in America was still dominated by the major labels. We were the big fuck-you alternative to Loverboy and Journey and REO Speedwagon. At that time we were pretty fucking vocal about it, too. We made sure that everybody understood that we were the anti-Mötley Crüe.

RON McGOVNEY: In the beginning, James just wanted to be a singer. I was the only Metallica bass player who had to play without a rhythm guitarist. But James was really not comfortable. He needed something in front of him, so he decided, "You know what, I don't want to be the singer anymore, I just want to play guitar." We started auditioning singers. We wanted to get John Bush from Armored Saint, and he wouldn't do it. Finally, James said, "The heck with it, I'll just play *and* sing."

JOHN BUSH: Lars was a real big Armored Saint fan so he asked me to join Metallica, and the reason I was reluctant was that Armored Saint was *happening*. The wheels were going and we were moving. I was like, "These are my buddies I grew up with, I'm not going to just quit Armored Saint. Yeah, Metallica's happening too, but this is *my* thing."

KIRK HAMMETT (ex-Exodus, Metallica): We were all looking for the most extreme stuff, and back [when I was in Exodus], the most popular music was Mercyful Fate, Venom, Motörhead. . . . Then this band came into town called Metallica. That was the sound that everyone was looking for but no one could actually execute until Metallica came along and showed everyone how to do it. There were pockets of bands in LA and New York that played heavy metal, but it was Metallica that brought it up to the next level.

LARS ULRICH: We played faster and heavier and louder and more obnoxious and more out there than any of the rest of them. And slowly people started taking notice. In the beginning, it's not that they actually appreciated what we were doing. It was more like, "What the fuck is that?"

BRIAN SLAGEL: We'd go to Hollywood and drink, and then we'd end up at Betsy Bitch's mom's house. We'd have big, gigantic parties: Bitch, Armored Saint, Metallica, Savage Grace. We're all drinking heavily. One night they were playing "Ace of Spades" by Motörhead [on the stereo] and there was a huge dog pile. That was the thing back then. You'd tackle somebody and everybody else would jump on top. Literally, there'd be thirty people. At the end of the night we noticed that [guitarist] Phil [Sandoval] from Armored Saint was limping. He had broken his ankle in the dog pile. He claims that Dave Mustaine broke his ankle on purpose.

JOEY VERA: I think Dave saw Phil in the pile and jumped on his leg in a way where he knew that it was going to cause some hurt, which is why he felt guilty about it for so long. I thought it was an accident for the longest time. We were all pretty drunk, and he was no exception.

DAVE MUSTAINE: Harmless verbal jousting gave way to nasty, personal insults, paving the way for a physical confrontation. They targeted Lars, probably because he was the smallest. . . . As the guys from Armored Saint dog-piled on top of Lars, I ran across the room and applied a side kick to the first person in my path, Phil Sandoval. The first thing I heard was a loud *crack!* Like the sound of a branch snapping in half. I'd broken his ankle. I tell this story not to brag, but simply as a way of pointing out how I felt about Lars, James, and Cliff. I would have done anything for them.

RON McGOVNEY: LA was kind of a bust. I remember playing a gig at Lars's high school. It was an auditorium. The stage was set up for a school play, so it looked like the inside of someone's house. Lars was in the living room, I was in the bathroom, James was in the kitchen. The place was full when we started, and by the time we ended, there was probably about ten people there. They all walked out. In LA, everybody was trying to do the Mötley Crüe thing, standing there with their hair teased, and we'd come out looking like we just walked in off the street. But every time we made trips to San Francisco, the audiences went wild. There would be more and more people, until we were headlining.

KIRK HAMMETT: When people say thrash started in LA, it really didn't start in LA. Metallica was kicked out of LA because they weren't understood. I'm sure that after the fact, it was really convenient for people to say, "Oh, yeah, it started in LA." But no, it started in San Francisco.

BRIAN SLAGEL: As Metallica got better, Lars called and asked if I knew a bass player. We had just signed Trauma from San Francisco, which Cliff Burton was in. I put them on *Metal Massacre II*. They played a show at the Troubadour. Cliff was just amazing. I told Lars about him, and Lars and James went to see the show and Lars said, "That's going to be our new bass player." Cliff wanted them to move to Frisco and they said, "Fine." They'd had a huge reaction up there that they didn't get in LA, so they moved. In fact, when Metallica was playing in LA they were deemed too punky. They got banned at the Troubadour for being too heavy.

CLIFF BURTON (1962–1986) (Metallica): Trauma went down to LA and while we were there, Lars and James saw us and decided that they would like to have me in their band. They started calling me, and I came to their shows when they played Frisco. Eventually Trauma started to . . . annoy me. They were starting to get a little commercial in different ways, so I said, "Later."

RON McGOVNEY: At one of my last gigs in San Francisco, Cliff [Burton] was hanging out quite a bit. I knew who he was and I knew they were looking at him, and I saw that was pretty much the end of it right there. One time I wasn't at rehearsal but my bass was sitting there and Mustaine says, "Well, I just fucking hate Ron," and he took a beer and poured it into my bass. Me not knowing that, the next time I go to practice, I plug it in and it shocked me. At one gig I had a bass stolen. The last time I saw it, it was behind Dave when we were playing, and one of our roadies was supposed to pick it up and bring it on. Well, our roadies were his friends, so it disappeared. All this stuff started to be too much for me, so I quit in November 1982. What bothered me most was that James and

Lars threw a blind eye to it. They just didn't even recognize or realize what was going on. A couple days after I quit, they left for San Francisco.

In the early eighties, San Francisco was a fertile landscape for thrash. Not only were there hordes of fans to support the music, there were several clubs that understood the marketability of the new genre. The most famous was Ruthie's Inn, located in Berkeley, on the east shore of the San Francisco Bay. In the same way CBGB was the New York City breeding ground for punk bands like the Ramones, Blondie, and Richard Hell and the Voidoids, Ruthie's broke countless thrash acts, including Exodus, Metallica, and Testament.

GARY HOLT: Ruthie's Inn was kind of our home. It started out as a blues club; we were the first metal band to ever play there. At the show, the band before us was just some rock band and their family members' friends stood at the front of the stage with their drink glasses and left them at the front of the stage. Then we came on, and in no time there's broken glass everywhere and blood all over the stage. One girl that was part of that rock band crowd liked us so she was up front rocking. Suddenly, [our vocalist] Paul [Baloff] put his hand in a puddle of blood and smeared it on his face. This girl ran screaming for her life.

BRIAN SLAGEL: We did the *Metal Massacre* show at Ruthie's with Bitch and Cirith Ungol. But Cirith Ungol dropped out, so I asked Metallica if they wanted to play and they said, "Sure, why not?"

BETSY BITCH (Bitch): After the show they provided each band with a case of beer backstage and Dave Mustaine stole our beer.

CHUCK BILLY: After every gig at Ruthie's, everybody would venture back to Paul's house because it was the closest place.

We'd roar there all night. One day he got evicted, so instead of having a house-leaving party, we had a house-*wrecking* party. Me and six friends walked in and there wasn't a lot of damage done yet, so we threw a twelve-pack of beer right through the front window, and then we went up and down every hall and put our fists and legs through every wall. That really spread the madness and everybody went off, and in five minutes the whole place was taken apart.

HARALD OIMOEN (D.R.I., photographer): Ron Quintana from *Metal Mania* once printed a picture I took of James and Kirk in bed together. And they stuck El Duce's from the Mentors' head in the middle of the bed, like they were sleeping with El Duce, as a joke. I didn't realize I was supposed to keep those pictures for myself and James got so upset. I showed him the magazine and he had this smile, then the smile turned into a frown. He said I would never take photos of them again and he kicked me in the stomach. It was this really bad scene, but that was also the alcohol talking. Lars, when he would drink, would get really obnoxious. He punched me in the face one time at an Angel Witch show for no reason. And then he started urinating right in front of me at the bar.

In 1982, shortly before McGovney left the band, Metallica recorded the legendary *No Life 'Til Leather* demo, which electrified the tape-trading underground and led to a recording contract with Megaforce Records.

JONNY ZAZULA: A guy came by [my record store] who had just come back from San Francisco and he played me the Metallica tape, and I thought it was unbelievable. The song "The Mechanix," especially, took me by storm. Then I saw an article in [Brian] Slagel's magazine written by K. J. Doughton [the original head of the Metallica fan club]. So, KJ got Lars to contact me. He sent me a letter and I called him up. The next thing you know, I had twelve shows booked for them with

Venom, Vandenberg, the Rods, Twisted Sister. That brought the Metallica family and the Zazula family together.

SCOTT IAN: I was hanging out at Jonny Z's record store and he puts on this tape, and I'm like, "Holy fuck, what's that?" He says, "It's this band Metallica from San Francisco. It's their demo." I'm looking at this cassette case *No Life Til Leather.* I'm like, "Whoa, this is crazy." He says, "Yeah, I got it a week ago. I'm bringing them to New York. I'm gonna start a label and put out their record."

BRIAN SLAGEL: My friend John Kornarens got *No Life Til Leather.* We used to have parties at the record store I worked at in Woodland Hills. So, he put in this cassette tape and tried to make me guess who it was. I was like, "What, some band from England?" He goes, "No, that's Metallica!" I was like, "Man, they've come a long way in a short period of time."

TOM ARAYA (Slayer): We were doing the same thing at the same time, so it wasn't really groundbreaking to us. It was, "Dude, check out this tape, *No Life Til Leather.* Kinda sounds like *us.*" We were like, "Who the hell is *this?*" The same thing with Exodus. We had heard of them, but when we got up to San Francisco and saw them they blew my mind because we were so similar.

BRIAN SLAGEL: Megaforce were flying bands like Raven and Anvil in to audition them, and we were trying to do the Metallica thing. Metallica came to me and said, "We can do a record for ten grand." I said, "Where am I gonna get ten grand?" I had a little money I had saved from working at Sears, and I borrowed $800 from my aunt, and that's how I paid for *Metal Massacre.* I was only twenty years old, just doing it as a fan.

JONNY ZAZULA: I sent Metallica $1,500 figuring the money would get them to New York. But I never thought about what's gonna happen when they get here. So they come over in this U-Haul, and three of the guys were sleeping in the back and two of the guys and a tour manager were in the front. They traveled through the desert and everything with that door closed in a U-Haul truck. That reality hit me—these guys will do anything to make it. But Metallica fell in our lap. We didn't know what we had and we didn't know what to do because they were young and they were wild. The first second we were together, they raided everything there was out of the liquor cabinet in my house. They drank all the bottles down without even using glasses. They were all raging drunk and Dave Mustaine is throwing up all over the place. I was like, "Hmm, this is going to be interesting." They stayed with me and Marsha for a little while, but that wasn't working out.

RAT SKATES: Jonny Z bullshitted Metallica to get them. He didn't have any of the things he was promising them. The only thing he got was a couple of shows booked. It's actually beautiful when I think of it now because everyone's spirit was so intense and so strong. Lars went on the phone and was like, "This dude I don't know called from New Jersey and says he's going to book us shows and he's got a record label going, so he's going to send us some money. We can get a Ryder truck and drive out there." They don't have anything on paper. They don't even know where they're staying, and they didn't ask questions. They just got into the truck and drove.

SCOTT IAN: Not long after I first heard Metallica, Jonny Z says to me, "Hey, Metallica's on their way. They're in a U-Haul and they're driving across from San Francisco with all their gear. I got them a room at the Music Building where you guys rehearse." Now, the Music Building was a burnt-out squat in South Jamaica in the worst neighborhood in Queens that would rent rehearsal rooms. You'd pay $250 a month and have a room 24/7, but you were risking your life getting in and out of this place. So Jonny's like, "Do you mind meeting Metallica at the Music Building? It would be great if you can show them around." I said, "Of course," because me and [ex-Anthrax bassist Dan] Lilker (Brutal Truth, ex-Nuclear Assault) were there every day anyway. So Metallica shows up and we were instant friends. We were probably the first people they saw when they got to Queens. Mustaine was still in the band and they were still rehearsing and finishing the songs for *Kill 'Em All*. We gave them a toaster and a refrigerator. They used to come to our houses to shower. These guys had nothing.

JONNY ZAZULA: Anthrax had a practice place in the Music Building. It was a very nice room. And since Metallica had no place to stay, we told them, "Don't you worry. You can stay in Anthrax's room." Then the manager [of the Music Building] came up and said, "No, no one can sleep in these rooms. If we get caught, they'll close us down." But he felt sorry for the band so he puts them on the roof in a giant storage area with broken furniture. It was really shitty. When I went up to see them, James was making a bologna sandwich and trying to put a bullet belt together, and everyone else was just jamming away to escape the reality of where they're staying.

SCOTT IAN: Lars knew how to play drums, but he definitely wasn't the most accomplished drummer. But James [Hetfield] and Dave [Mustaine] were both sick guitar players already, and Cliff was the maestro. I used to listen to them jam the songs that would go onto *Kill 'Em All*. In the beginning, Lars had a hard time keeping up, that's for sure. He had no problem playing fast, it was just a case of *what* he was playing. It was a mess. I would definitely say Lars learned on the job, and he learned how to play drums *for* Metallica by *being* in Metallica. Even today, Lars's drums only work in the context of Metallica. You couldn't put Lars's playing in any other band. Lars plays specifically for James's rhythm style, and in a way, that's amazing.

JONNY ZAZULA: Metallica started working in the Music Building with Dave Mustaine. He was a big part of that band. He co-wrote four of the songs [on *Kill 'Em All*], including "The Mechanix." But Dave drank an awful lot. I think he did everything a lot. The problem was he was Dr. Jekyll and Mr. Hyde, and when he got drunk, you never knew if you were gonna have this happy-go-lucky guy or this sloppy, terrible guy with a bad fuckin' attitude. A lot of times he was just out of it and played all the wrong shit. It got to the point where he was in a real bad mood all the time and they were all just paranoid. There was a big black cloud walking around with Dave and I think the band felt it, too.

SCOTT IAN: Metallica were the only ones there in the middle of the night at the Music Building in their shitty room drinking beer. Mustaine would get super-drunk and fuck with other people's rehearsal rooms. A band would show up the next day and there'd be a mountain of garbage piled up in front of their door because Mustaine would go get all the garbage cans and dump them in front of the practice room door of a band he didn't like. Of course, everybody knows who did it because Metallica was the only band there overnight. Once, Metallica was opening for the Rods and Vandenberg at L'Amour. Vandenberg is sound checking at 4 p.m. and Dave is ripped. He's screaming at Adrian Vandenberg, "Get the fuck off the stage. You suck." The other dudes in the band are trying to run and hide. Metallica didn't even have a record out yet.

RAT SKATES: Dave had a reckless drinking problem and it was very obvious. He would say stupid things onstage into the microphone and he wasn't the front man. James was supposed to be the man talking to the crowd and Dave would just embarrass them.

RON QUINTANA: As much of a problem as Dave was, he was still the most charismatic guy in Metallica. He was way ahead of

James at that time. He was the guy who would yell out be-tween every song and get people involved and into the show.

DAVE MUSTAINE: Right before things went south for me and Metallica, James kicked my dog. I was selling pot [at the time]. When I would go play a concert, people knew that my pot was sitting in my apartment saying, "Come keep me company." Y'know? So I was broken in on. People stole everything that I had—all my stash. I figured, "Screw this. I'm gonna get some dogs to stay in the apartment when I leave. So I got two dogs and I took one of them up to re-hearsal one time. She put her paws up on Ron's car. James kicked her right in the side. I said, "What'd you do?" [And James said,] "She put her paws up on Ron's car." [I said] "It's a dog. That's what they do. You don't kick animals." So, we went into the house, we started arguing some more, I ended up punching him in the face, and I think that was the root of why I lost my job.

KEVIN HODAPP (photographer): I was shooting Metallica, and before the show Lars came up to me and said, "Don't take any pictures of Dave Mustaine." I said, "Why?" He said, "Well, we're getting rid of him." I knew Mustaine was getting kicked out of the band before he did.

RON QUINTANA: We had a going-away party for Dave, but he didn't know that's what it was [*laughs*]. Dave always got drunker and crazier earlier than everybody else. That night, Dave was already drunk and passed out. So somebody drew dicks all over him and we took pictures around his drunk body. Dave would outdrink all of us, and if he didn't get in a fight, he'd pass out. But a lot of the fights he got in weren't his fault. A girl would suddenly fall in love with Dave and he got hassled by the boyfriend and they'd be fighting. But when they kicked out Dave, I really thought it was over for Metallica because Dave was such an outrageous, crazy guy. It was really fun to see him onstage with the band. And [guitarist] Kirk [Hammett] didn't have that kind of personality.

RAT SKATES: The night Dave knew that he was kicked out, he came up to me when they opened for Venom, and he was holding, like, twelve beer bottles and was pretty wasted. He said, "Hey man, I'm Dave." We kind of already knew each other from the flea market, but he said, "I'm looking for other musicians because we feel it's really important to know other guys, especially out here in New York, that are into the heavy stuff like we are." But what he was actually trying to do was get another band together.

SCOTT IAN: I show up at the Music Building at two in the afternoon. Cliff's standing outside having a smoke, and I'm like, "What's up, buddy?" And he says, "Eh, not much. . . . We fired Mustaine." I'm like, "Yeah, *right*," 'cause Cliff was a ball-buster. He goes, "No, for real, dude. He's on a Greyhound bus right now back to California." I'm like, "Get the fuck out of here. We're playing gigs together next week in Jersey." He goes, "I'm totally serious, dude. We've been planning it for a month. We just didn't want to say anything to anybody 'cause we didn't want him to find out." Then he says, "Go upstairs and ask James." It's funny to think that Mustaine was too drunk to be in Metallica because they were all big drink-ers. But the difference was Dave was a troublemaker when he was drunk. So we're sitting there in the room and they're telling me, "Yeah, we want to be a professional band and that was never gonna happen with that guy because he's just always gonna get us in trouble."

DAVE MUSTAINE: I'm gonna assume full responsibility for my part in the whole Metallica thing. I talked a lot of shit, but I was really hurt because I got fired. I didn't really believe that I got a chance. At that time, if someone would have sat me down and said, "You know, Dave, you've got a fucking problem. . . ." But no one said that to me. I didn't hear from anyone's lips that I had a problem until probably 1988. I *knew* I did. I had a problem with *everything*. I just think being a loose cannon and not having anybody to answer to since I was fifteen, you get on autopilot, and you don't really care. In a nutshell, I was a violent drunk, and I was more drunk than sober, and I jeopardized Metallica's safety. Looking back, I would have asked me to leave, too.

KIRK HAMMETT: I distinctly remember getting the phone call to come to New York to audition for the band. Exodus's manager called me and said, "Hey man, Dave Mustaine is on his way out and Lars and James are interested in auditioning you." It was very peculiar, because prior to that I knew I had some sort of connection with the band. I had some sort of feeling before that I would be involved with Metallica in some way, but I didn't know it would be as a member. So when I got that call it made sense to me in a very strange way, like it was fulfilling a destiny.

GARY HOLT: Kirk [Hammett] was the principal songwriter for Exodus through all the early years. Then he told us he was gonna join Metallica. When he told us, we had a big party for him. There was no bad blood anywhere, partly because when I joined the band, it was basically *his* band. So when he left to join Metallica, that's when I started sowing my own creative oats. Not to say his stuff wasn't good, but the *Bonded by Blood* Exodus was my thing, and when Kirk left, it put me in the driver's seat. I was able to point the band in the direction Paul and I wanted, which was much more violent and brutal and faster.

KIRK HAMMETT: The first time I ever saw James and Lars and Metallica was in 1983 at the Stone in San Fran. I was totally blown away. They were the fastest band I had ever seen up to that point. I went up to the front of the stage in between songs. Dave Mustaine was talking and I screamed out, "Sweet Savage!" which was a New Wave of British Heavy Metal band, and Dave heard me and said, "Fuck you!" into the mic. Fast forward six months later: I was sitting around with Lars listening to a tape of that very show and I heard myself scream out while Dave was talking. I said to Lars, "Hey, that was me!"

SCOTT IAN: At the same time as Metallica told me they'd fired Dave, they said they had this guy named Kirk from Exodus flying in and asked if I could pick him up at the airport. I'm like, "Sure, of course." The next day I picked Kirk up and he goes, "So, where are we staying?" I'm like, "Uhh, they didn't tell you?" He had no idea they were in this shithole at the Music Building. Not long after that, Kirk came down with this terrible eye infection, probably from sleeping on the floor of this fucking hovel. So I take him to Long Island Jewish Hospital emergency room to get checked out, and after having us wait around forever, they give him some cream. So we're in my car back to the Music Building, and he starts putting this cream in his eye, and he's like, "What the fuck? My eye's burning. My eye's burning!" We drove all the way back to the emergency room and we wait again and they finally take us in and it's the same doctor and he goes, "Whoops, I gave you the wrong stuff." That's where Kirk and I bonded.

JOHN GALLAGHER: Jonny Z calls me up and says, "We want you to come over from England. The biggest band out of San Francisco is going to open up for you." We were like, "Who, Y&T?" He says, "No, Metallica." We're like, "*Who?*" He gave us this demo tape, *No Life Til Leather.* I put it on and it was like 400 miles an hour Motörhead on 78 [rpm]. We were like, "All right, I guess these guys will do." It was a no-frills tour—seventeen people in a six-berth Winnebago. The only one who was an old soul and had a good head on his shoulders was Cliff. Lars was a shyster, a mover and shaker—always looking for an angle. James didn't say very much at all, always had a permanent smile on his face, always drinking. Kirk was so young and quiet. We played two days in a row in Boston at a place called the Rathskeller, a real hole-in-the-wall. We had been on the road for three days—they hadn't given us a hotel. So, we get to the Rat, we play this gig, and the woman who ran the club said, "Here's my apartment key. Go and crash." So, we get to this apartment and the place is absolutely skeevy and disgusting. It was filthy. Of course, the guys in Metallica came in and made themselves right at home in all this rot and dirty bed linens, and we went, "Oh god, get us back to the dirty Winnebago."

Metallica recorded its full-length debut, *Kill 'Em All*, at Music America Studios in Rochester, New York, between May 10 and May 27, 1983. The album was coproduced by Jonny Z and Paul Curcio, who later worked with the Doobie Brothers and Carlos Santana. Some immediately adored the album; others didn't know what to make of it.

JONNY ZAZULA: Cliff Burton was the originator of the title *Kill 'Em All*. It was basically a disparaging comment about our distributor, Important. We wanted to call the album *Metal Up Your Ass!* and they wouldn't allow that. There was a fellow at the company named Barry Kobrin, and after Megaforce was successful, he started his own label, Combat. But at the time he felt that I didn't have a chance of getting this record anywhere past some small independent stores with the name *Metal Up Your Ass!* The cover was supposed to be a picture of a sword coming up through a toilet bowl. Cliff Burton was sitting there with the whole band when they got the news that they couldn't call the album *Metal Up Your Ass!*, and out of frustration he just said, "Kill 'em all, man. Just kill 'em all!" I think James and Lars said that should be the name of the album.

SCOTT IAN: You can't say enough about that record. It was definitely influenced by bands like Anvil, Raven, and Motörhead, but Metallica took all that and turned it into the new wave of American thrash metal. They broke the door wide open. They didn't get big off of *Kill 'Em All*, but it definitely got the ball rolling.

DIMEBAG DARRELL: *Kill 'Em All* was the first really consistent thrash album where every song was just a razor blade and the whole record was one direction. James's fuckin' rhythm playing is unbelievable, especially for his first record. They wrote fantabulous songs and it made me motivated. It made me want to tear something up.

EDDIE TRUNK: In 1983 I was one of the first people doing a heavy metal specialty show on commercial radio. I used to go to Jonny Z's flea market store, and one day Jonny showed up at the radio station while I was on the air. He walked in and said, "I need a favor. I've got this band, they're going to be huge, I can't get anyone to even consider playing it on the radio. No one understands what this is. Will you please give this an opportunity?" He pulls out an early pressing of *Kill 'Em All*. That night I played "Seek and Destroy" or "Jump into the Fire." I'm not going to lie and say, "I heard the future." I was more, "I don't know what I just heard."

JOHN GALLAGHER: When we toured with Metallica, Lars didn't know one end of the drum kit from another. Once, he broke the skin on the bottom of his snare drum and didn't know how to get at it, so he got wire cutters and cut the snares off rather than unscrewing them and releasing the skins. Another time, Lars was in the middle of a show and he turned to our drummer Rob ["Wacko" Hunter] and said, "Can you tune my drums for me?" Rob was like, "What? Now? In front of the crowd? Now? No! You couldn't pay me enough [*laughs*]." Also Lars was always like, "LA sucks, it's for posers. LA sucks, LA sucks." Then we get to LA and he unwraps his brand new cymbals to use for the show. I went, "Oh, you've been holding them all tour and you bring them out now?" He says, "Well, you got to look good in LA."

JONNY ZAZULA: I mortgaged my house twice to put out *Kill 'Em All*. Plus, I didn't pay my record distributor $18,000 I owed him. I already had to pay everybody else, so I would mortgage something or use a credit card. I thought I was gonna get the record done on spec and we would pay for it as we were getting royalties, but the guy thought spec was two weeks. So I had to go get the money for that, plus I was feeding everybody and giving per diems. Marsha and I weren't making any money. We had just gotten into our first house and all of this was happening as our children were being born. One time, the Old Bridge Militia boys [a group of diehard working-class fans from Old Bridge, New Jersey] came to feed Metallica, Raven, and Anthrax. Everyone was at the house. So they came in with some fresh-killed venison, and without asking permission they cooked it on my stove. Well, they didn't know what they were doing and they ended up burning down my kitchen. There were flames everywhere, and by the time they put it out it was charcoal black. The house was spared, but my kitchen was destroyed.

DEE SNIDER: Metallica opened for Twisted Sister for a while. Then, there was one show in Holland where we arrived and the audience was clearly there for them. The bill said "Twisted Sister" in the smallest letters "AND METALLICA" with their logo. I went to them and said, "Guys, you're headlining tonight." It gave me a chance to finally see the band live. I stood on the side of the stage with my bass player, Mark "the Animal" Mendoza, and I watched them do "Whiplash" and "Seek and Destroy," and I turned to Mark and said, "These guys have a lot of heart, but they're never going to go anywhere." It wasn't that I didn't think they were good, it's just I thought they were so heavy—who knew that people would eventually become desensitized, like horror movies, they're able to handle heavier and heavier stuff.

It didn't take Dave Mustaine long to get back on his feet after being kicked out of Metallica. Back in LA, he formed Megadeth with bassist David Ellefson and worked with a bunch of other players before hiring guitarist Chris Poland and drummer Gary "Gar" Samuelson.

DAVE MUSTAINE: When I left Metallica, I was on the bus and I was looking for paper to write lyrics on because I was trying to keep myself from going insane on a four-day ride [from New York back to California]. I was writing lyrics on the back of anything I could get my hands on, and one of the things I was writing on was on the back of a handbill from Senator Alan Cranston that was talking about nuclear armament, and it said "The arsenal of megadeath can't be rid." I thought, "What a fantastic song title." That song later became "Set the World on Fire." So, in the midst of having a problem naming the band, it was suggested that we call ourselves Megadeth instead of the song. With extreme lack of foresight, I decided to go with that, not knowing what a professional setback the name would be for us. No one imagined this band would become this successful at the level where the name would affect us. When you're thinking about ruling the club circuit and playing the arenas, and unsafe sex and drugs and alcohol and parties and fighting and speeding down the roads, the thought of someone not liking your band because the name's "Megadeth"—it's like, "Fuck you, it's your loss." But when you're trying to get on the radio that's something else entirely.

DAVE ELLEFSON: I met Dave in the apartment complex we both lived in. I had just moved to Los Angeles from Minnesota, where I grew up. I knocked on his door and said, "Hey, where can you buy a pack of cigarettes?" He slammed the door in my face like I was some annoying vermin. I knocked again, and I said, "Hey, where can you buy some beer?" and then he let me in. I was only eighteen, and he was twenty-one. Once we settled on a case of Heineken, he started telling me about

Metallica and played me some songs. Then he started playing some new songs he was working on, "Devil's Island" and "Set the World on Fire." I was blown away. I was like, "I have to be a part of this."

KERRY KING: I did the first five shows with Megadeth after Dave left Metallica. Basically, we both played B. C. Rich and we had the same guitar contact, and somebody suggested we should play together. I had seen him play with Metallica when they were still doing clubs. I was flattered that he would even consider my dumb ass, because, fuck, I was, like, nineteen then. I also thought it was a good way to promote my own band while helping him out and maybe learn something on the way. After five shows I went, "All right, it's time for you to find somebody that you're gonna keep 'cause that ain't me." It would have flown fine if I had stayed in Megadeth, but I had way more evil ideas to get out.

TOM ARAYA: It weirded us out when Kerry played with Megadeth. Me, Jeff, and [drummer] Dave [Lombardo] were like, "What the fuck?" But we didn't talk to him about it at all. We just waited to see what he was going to do. And whatever he decided, it wasn't going to affect what we were going to do.

DAVE MUSTAINE: When I first met Kerry he was making that fabulous spiked pentagram belt and he was putting on that nail gauntlet. I was watching him do that stuff in his front room, and his dad is a sheriff, so his dad was sitting there watching TV and Kerry's assembling this fucking evil belt. Who would ever think that Kerry would come from a really normal family with a sheriff for a dad? One of the funniest things Kerry King has ever said to me was when we were driving up the freeway and I was rolling a joint. I said, "Would you hold this?" So Kerry put his hand out and I put a couple of skunk buds in it and then rolled the joint. Then he smelled his hand and said, "Wow, this smells neat." We were just kids at the time. As far as I could tell, he really respected his parents because he waited until he was in his twenties til he started doing any [partying]. He wasn't even drinking back then. It was really funny because we'd all be drunk, [ex-Megadeth drummer] Gar Samuelson's doing heroin, and there's Kerry over there blazing away on guitar—sober. I remember thinking, "How can you get up there and play like that without having some kind of stimulant?"

BRIAN SLAGEL: When Megadeth started, Dave [Mustaine] wrote me a three-page letter about what Megadeth wanted to do. He wanted Metal Blade to sign them. It was between us and Combat. They offered him nine thousand dollars and we offered them eight thousand. So they went with Combat.

SCOTT IAN: Dave played me the demos to Megadeth's first album, *Killing Is My Business . . . and Business Is Good*. We were on tour with Raven, and we were playing the Country Club in LA. We were sitting in someone's car and he was playing me "Skull Beneath the Skin," and we were just like, "Holy shit," banging our heads. That record still absolutely holds up. To be able to get kicked out of Metallica after having written a lot of *Kill 'Em All*, and then come back with *Killing Is My Business . . . and Business Is Good*, churn out all those great riffs and songs, is no small accomplishment.

Megadeth recorded *Killing Is My Business . . . and Business Is Good* at Indigo Ranch Studios in Malibu, California, between December 1984 and January 1985. The record is universally regarded as groundbreaking for jazzy, technical thrash, despite its poor audio quality, which was largely the result of the band spending most of its recording budget on drugs and therefore being unable to keep producer Karat Faye on to finish the album.

DAVE MUSTAINE: Even after we were signed, we were so broke. I was selling dope to try to finance the band, and then I became one of my customers, and then I became my best customer, and then I became my only customer. I went from girl's house to girl's house to live. When we couldn't find some tart that would feed us, we would take turns living in a car. At one point we lived in a studio with no windows, no toilet. The only time we could shower was when our manager would take us to the gym. We'd go there high on whatever we could find in order to not feel the pain and misery of starving to death, or acknowledge the lifestyle we were living, as shaming as it was.

DAVE ELLEFSON: I was flat broke and I knew I couldn't get any dope. So out of boredom one day I went down to the mailbox and checked my mail, and MasterCard saw fit to send me a brand new credit card with an $8,000 limit, of which $3,000 was available at ATMs. So I went right to the ATM and just watched $20 bills fly out of that thing, so I could go cop dope.

DAVE MUSTAINE: We had [guitarist] Chris [Poland] and Gar in the band, and every time we turned around they would pawn some of our equipment for heroin. We had nowhere to turn. So, yeah, we would get high whenever we could.

DAVE ELLEFSON: During the *Killing Is My Business* era I was a raving maniac, drinking moonshine when I couldn't score dope. One night I had sex with some girl on a sidewalk outside of a gig in Austin, Texas, and she even had to pull her tampon out before we could do it.

DAVE MUSTAINE: I was into black magic and witchcraft when I was a teenager. I put two hexes on people and the result was what I was asking for. It took forever to get that Satanic depression off of me because it's just like playing with a Ouija board. You open the doorway to the dark side, spirits come through. It took almost twenty years to get rid of it. You ask yourself, "How is it possible that all this bad stuff is happening to me?" Well, because you flirted with the devil and you owe him. That's what the lyrics to "The Conjuring" was about. That's why I have a problem playing that song today. Fortunately, I'm saved now so I don't have to deal with that, but God, man, I was going through so much turmoil from what I had done.

Impaired by substance abuse and past dabblings with the occult, but hardly incapacitated, Megadeth entered the studio in 1986 to record its second album, *Peace Sells . . . but Who's Buying?* It was originally funded by Combat and produced by Randy Burns. Impressed by Mustaine's charisma and the band's songwriting, Capitol Records bought out Combat's deal, signed Megadeth to a multi-album contract, and re-produced the album, which would catapult Megadeth to the upper tier of the thrash hierarchy. The video for the title track became one of the first big thrash clips on MTV's *Headbangers Ball*, and the song's rapid-groove bassline was used in the opening theme music for *MTV News* for years.

DAVE MUSTAINE: Things were looking up, but we were still living like junkies. David Ellefson was living with the singer from Détente [the late Dawn Crosby]. Dave told me nightmare stories of him being over there and her making him sleep on the floor while she had sex with another girl.

DAVE ELLEFSON: In '86, we had just made *Peace Sells . . . but Who's Buying.* We had a rehearsal studio downtown in LA. We built a loft there, and I'd sleep between there and any girl that would have me. One of them was a prostitute in LA; she told me she was a cleaning lady. I'm thinking, "This chick really likes me," and then I find out she's shooting pornos and then copping heroin from a taxi driver. The day that I had to take her down to do a photo shoot with [porn star] John Holmes was when I knew my days were numbered.

DAVE MUSTAINE: [In 1988], we canceled seven Monsters of Rock [support-slot] shows in [European] soccer stadiums. Why?

Because Dave Ellefson ran out of heroin. When I ran out, I would tough it out. I'd be sick for a couple days, I'd drink some Jack Daniel's, and I'd be over it. He came up with some excuse that he sprained his wrist in the shower and the tour ended. So did our run for a long time. We took the gnarliest hit to our credibility.

DAVE ELLEFSON: I was fucked up for a long time. I was lucky I never got busted for drugs. But there were times I'd be copping bags of heroin, swallowing them because the cops came along—and then getting interrogated by the cops and getting away with it. Then I'd have to stop off at a Mobil station and puke my guts out and weed through my barf to get the balloons of heroin out. I'd immediately pop them open and get high, and celebrate the victory of not getting busted. After a while, I was hanging out in apartment bathrooms smoking crack and doing heroin with people I didn't know. And I was looking around and thinking, "How did I get with these people? I hate these people."

DAVE MUSTAINE: We just did not want to, no matter what, quit or give in. And sadly, we encountered some situations that were of the magnitude that other people would probably say "forget it." We ran over a person in a taxi going 60 miles per hour—creamed the guy dead as a doornail. The driver in the taxi said, "Whoa. Huh. I hit that sucker clean in the head. Better send a meat wagon." He had an absolute disregard for life, and that kind of stuff affects people, and it affected us very badly. But the thing is, we kept making good music through all this. We just put our heads down and stuck it out.

DAVE ELLEFSON: When Dave set out to start his band after Metallica, there was a lot of pressure on him. It wasn't until the early nineties that we stepped out of that shadow. People had to get their mind around the idea that Metallica didn't have to fail in order for Megadeth to be successful. Once that happened, people embraced Megadeth and the competition stopped.

STEFFAN CHIRAZI: For some reason, Dave seems to never have gotten over being kicked out of Metallica. It's like he's got some sort of illness. I could never understand why he could not move on. If you've been tremendously hurt in a relationship, I think you're allowed a few years to work it through. Whenever I would interview Dave, I would turn the tape recorder off when he would start complaining about Metallica. I would say to him, "Dave, I'm not here to talk about that. I don't want to write about it." Then I'd turn it back on when he was done. It's weird because Dave is a unique and wonderful guy and yet, to this day, he's so tortured that he was kicked out of Metallica. To the best of my knowledge, he still gets his publishing [royalties] from the songs he helped write.

While Mustaine was wrestling with the shadow of Metallica, his former bandmates were proving why they were the kingpins of the healthy West Coast thrash metal scene. After touring for *Kill 'Em All*, Metallica flew to Copenhagen to work with producer Flemming Rasmussen (Morbid Angel, Evile) at Sweet Silence Studios. There, the band tracked *Ride the Lightning*, which was more musically intricate but just as heavy as *Kill 'Em All*. In September 1984, less than two months after Megaforce released *Ride the Lightning*, Elektra Records signed the band, making Metallica the first thrash act on a major label. It reissued the record on November 19 with the wheels of promotion spinning faster than the churning guitars on the opening track, "Fight Fire with Fire."

LARS ULRICH: We wrote *Ride the Lightning* in a garage in El Cerrito, California, with egg crates on the walls and no heat. The last four songs of that were done in a cold cellar in nowheresville New Jersey at my friend Metal Joe's house, where we were cold and hungover all the time. So there was no luxury there. We just wanted to tear everything up and play shows and get drunk.

MICHAEL ALAGO (ex-A&R Elektra, Geffen): I picked up *Kill 'Em All* at Jonny Z's record store and I was blown away, so I went to the Stone in San Francisco to see them play, but I didn't tell anybody I was going. . . . It was amazing. James [Hetfield] was an extraordinary, raw ringleader. He has the most charismatic, wild smile. And those songs! I was sold. I was friends already with Jonny and Marsha Z at Megaforce, and when I came home and told them I had been to see Metallica and I wanted to sign them, they lost their minds. They were furious.

JONNY ZAZULA: Metallica played in New York at the Rio Theater and that was a big show. Everything came together perfectly, and they were the greatest band in the world. There were about 800 people there. The next night was the Roseland Ballroom where we had Metallica, Anthrax, and Raven and had 3,500 sales. I think it only held 2,500. That's the night Metallica got signed with Elektra.

MICHAEL ALAGO: I knew there were other A&R people there from other labels, so I bolted the door shut and wound up being the only one backstage early in the evening. I said, "Look, I'm freaking out. I love you guys and you have to come to my office tomorrow." They got there bright and early. I ordered Chinese food and beer for them and we talked. I think they liked that I was their age and I was that enthusiastic, and that I would take the right care of the band. And I did, from day one.

MARIA FERRERO: We had Metallica, Raven, and Anthrax playing that show at Roseland, and that night Jonny and Marsha signed Metallica to Elektra, Anthrax to Island, and Raven to Atlantic. I was like, "Wow, that's a big deal," 'cause those are big, mainstream companies. So for me, that was the moment I said, "Oh, wow! This is real."

Despite the hype surrounding Metallica, Anthrax seemed to come out of nowhere with their 1984 ragged-but-raging Megaforce record *Fistful of Metal*, which led to their deal with Island Records, where they released four critically and commercially successful albums. But Anthrax was hardly an instant success. When high school classmates Scott Ian and Danny Lilker formed the band in 1981, even Jonny Z repeatedly tried to shoo them away. At the time, Anthrax was a rotating door of musicians with dreams of greatness and just enough talent to leapfrog the obstacles they kept creating for themselves. Steadily, though, they improved, and with the help of Megaforce and a never-say-die mentality, they were able to clamber their way into metal's Big Four, alongside Metallica, Megadeth, and Slayer.

SCOTT IAN: Dan Lilker and I were always totally about metal. We used to drive sixty miles from Queens to this metal bar called 516 in Old Bridge [New Jersey], and that's where all the guys in the Old Bridge Militia used to hang out. We'd all stand there in this shitty little bar, sometimes with fake cardboard guitars, drinking beer and headbanging. That's what we did for fun—listen to this music and bang our heads and jump around like idiots. It was so nerdy, but it was the greatest feeling ever.

DAN LILKER (Brutal Truth, S.O.D., ex–Nuclear Assault, ex-Anthrax): The first show we did was a battle of the bands in a church basement. Cease Fire was the other big band, and we won by doing Priest and Maiden covers, and we might have had a few originals.

CHARLIE BENANTE (Anthrax): In the early eighties, I had some friends in Queens who knew of this band called Anthrax that played locally in schools, but they hated them. There was talk of me auditioning for them, and my friends were like, "Don't you dare do that, dude. They suck." I was like, "Well, lemme just go try." Scott and Danny came over to my house and we jammed and it wasn't perfect, but I could see there was a lot of potential.

SCOTT IAN: We were looking for a drummer because our old drummer [Greg D'Angelo] had left. Someone recommended Charlie, who was in Throgs Neck in the Bronx. We went to Charlie's house and he had this drum kit up in his little room at the top of this four-family house. We jammed "Fast As a Shark" by Accept and "Invaders" from Iron Maiden. We said, "Can you play double bass?" and he went *dumma-dumma-dumma-dumma-dumma* with his feet flying. We said, "All right, you're in the band."

JONNY ZAZULA: Anthrax would constantly bring their demos to us at the flea market and they were a real royal pain in the ass. One of the only reasons we even allowed them to hang out there was because Danny Spitz was the lead guitarist for Overkill at one point, and he was quite a character. But I wouldn't even listen to their stuff. One day I went to breakfast with Marsha at an IHOP in East Brunswick, New Jersey, where [the] flea market was, and parked there waiting for me at the IHOP was a car that had "Anthrax" license plates. They asked if they could play their tape during my meal. I told them after I ate I'd meet them in the store and we'd talk. That's when we put it on. They were so persistent. I liked production by Ross the Boss (ex–Manowar, Dictators) on "Soldiers of Metal." I didn't really want to release it, but Scott had used $2,500 of his bar mitzvah money to produce the song, so I printed up two thousand singles and sold all of them in two and a half weeks. That was really surprising, so we signed them.

SCOTT IAN: [Ex-lead guitarist Dan] Spitz was working at a guitar store on Forty-eighth Street before he joined. I used to go in there all the time. He was this cocky little fuck, and one time he said, "Yeah, I've heard about your fucking band. I'll fucking blow away your lead guitar player. You should have me in your band." I was like, "Uh, dude, I just came in here to check out an amp." A month later we auditioned him. Before him was a guy named Greg Walls. He did a bunch of demos with us, but he just wasn't into it.

JONNY ZAZULA: The money that came from Metallica went to Raven and Anthrax. Then Raven got signed [to Atlantic Records], so I placed everything on Anthrax and stayed with them. Metallica were gone. They'd been signed by Elektra. Then Anthrax got signed [to Island]. So everybody was signed and Anthrax owed me $250,000 from [recording, traveling, everything I had paid for in their career to date]. I never took a dime for the first three or four years. Then we did a merchandise deal for $1.5 million, and not only did I make myself a very good commission, but they paid me back that day. That's the moment I made money with Megaforce.

SCOTT IAN: Our first tour was the summer of '84 with Metallica, and [ex-vocalist] Neil Turbin took it upon himself to make that decision that Danny Lilker wasn't going to be in Anthrax anymore. Granted, when I got the call from Danny saying, "Hey man. What's going on? Neil just called and told me I was out of the band," I was like, "What the fuck?" But I kind of knew it was coming. Neil so had it in for him at the time because he didn't think Danny was responsible, and I know this sounds crazy, but truthfully, Danny was taller than Neil and Neil didn't want someone in the band taller than him because he was the front man. But Neil did have a point. When it came to the responsibility department, Danny was a bit lax. It's one of those things that eats me up to this day. I wish I would have stood up for my friend and told Neil to go fuck himself, but Neil gave us an ultimatum and said either Danny went or he went. We couldn't afford to lose our singer. We had a record out and he had us over a barrel. Finding a new singer would have been impossible at the time.

DAN LILKER: Three days after *Fistful of Metal* came out, they asked me to leave the band. Ninety-nine percent of the reason was because they wanted to keep Neil and he couldn't deal with me because he had no sense of humor. When I realized he could never take a joke, that made it more fun to poke fun at him. In the end they decided it was better keeping the front man than the dude who wrote three-quarters of the record. So I got the short end of the stick.

NEIL TURBIN (DeathRiders, ex-Anthrax): Even though I have no regrets about doing *Fistful of Metal* or the first tour, there was nothing pleasant in any aspect about it. Scott had aspirations of wanting to be the central figure in the band, being the front man—and the guy is not even a lead guitar player. And there weren't lots of song ideas coming from him. This was my agenda: I was there to rock. I came there to kick some ass and thrash. Scott admitted to the rest of the band that Dan Lilker had to be let go, but it was a lot easier for him to use me as a scapegoat, especially after I wasn't there anymore. Everybody knew that Dan just wasn't cutting it on a number of levels. He took thirty takes to play the [Alice Cooper cover] "I'm Eighteen" in the studio. But there was this great resentment because I was getting a lot of attention, so I was completely undermined. I was foolish because I decided to weather the storm. But the momentum that was created, the excitement level was definitely something that I contributed to, and that can never be taken away from me.

SCOTT IAN: We did a tour with Neil, opening for Raven in the fall of '84, and we realized we could not survive as a band if he was our singer. He was a dictator. It was his way or the highway. The rest of us all bonded on the road and he was this total outcast. He would bring two huge suitcases out with him, one for his stage stuff and one for his day-to-day clothing. We were doing the tour in a van that we would take turns driving. He would take the backseat and put his suitcases there and wouldn't allow anyone to sit back there with him. And he couldn't sing past the first song. He'd blow his voice out. So we knew right then and there, "You gotta go."

CARL CANEDY (producer, the Rods): Neil is a tough singer to replace. Matt [Fallon, who later sang for Skid Row, prior to Sebastian Bach] was inexperienced and really not the right fit for the band. But we were now past the preproduction stage and several weeks into recording their [second] album [*Spreading the Disease*]. I was very surprised by their decision to hire Fallon, and I admired their choice to let him go. They called me and asked me to get Jon and Marsha on the phone. Jon simply said, "Put him on a bus" [as he had with Dave Mustaine]. In that short, three-minute meeting with their manager, Matt's career with Anthrax was ended. They'd just made the ballsiest move I'd ever seen a band make, and now they needed to get back to work with a new singer right away. I put out the word, and as luck would have it my good friend Andrew "Duck" MacDonald (the Rods, Blue Cheer) told me about this kid [Joey Belladonna] who was a great singer he was considering for *his* new project.

SCOTT IAN: We had everyone looking for singers for us. Our plan B was to have me and [bassist] Frankie [Bello] sing. But Carl said, "I saw this dude play in a band here. Let me see if I can find his number." He ended up getting a hold of Joey Belladonna, who was living in upstate New York. We were recording in Ithaca and he drove down a day or two later. He had never heard of us. He didn't know who Metallica was. We just put him in a studio and said, "Sing what you know." He was singing Journey, Foreigner, and Deep Purple. And we were like, "Wow, he's got an amazing voice." As much as we loved hardcore and other thrash bands, we came from the Judas Priest/Iron Maiden school of wanting a real singer.

NEIL TURBIN: With Joey Belladonna, I didn't think they put in someone who could sing with more passion than me, or who had the range I had. I don't think they put in someone who had a connection with the fans or audience, or someone who is a writer. Basically, they hired a puppet.

JOEY BELLADONNA: I had no clue who Anthrax were. I had never even sung anything remotely in that kind of range. But it was cool to me because I came up with my own vocal twist that sat overtop the music. I wasn't sure about the heaviness of the music at first, but once we got going it was great.

SCOTT IAN: [1985's] *Spreading the Disease* was just the right record at the right time. Everyone was waiting for that kind of music to surface, and we were suddenly the big kids on the block in New York.

DIMEBAG DARRELL: The sound on *Spreading the Disease*, with songs like "Gung Ho" and "Medusa," and Charlie Benante's feet flying off the handle—that was huge for me. It was like somebody hit you with a two-by-four across the face.

In Los Angeles, the city that initially shunned Metallica, something faster, heavier, and more sinister was congealing. Slayer—bassist and vocalist Tom Araya, guitarists Kerry King and Jeff Hanneman, and drummer Dave Lombardo—formed in 1981 as a classic metal cover band, but over the next five years they took the intensity of Metallica and combined it with the ferocity of hardcore and the occult lyrics of Venom; to date they remain one of the most brutal, uncompromising bands on the scene.

KERRY KING: [Slayer bassist] Tom [Araya] was in a band with my guitar teacher and their guitarist got the axe, and they got me in to play, probably just to fill space. But I knew the songs, so I stayed. I was sixteen at the time, and then that band fizzled when I was seventeen. So I was looking in the *Recycler* for bands to jam with. I tried out for this band that was rehearsing right above where [guitarist] Jeff [Hanneman] worked. They were these Spinal Tap dudes—old guys that had no business doing anything. But I heard Jeff practicing guitar during some downtime at work, and he was playing songs I knew. So I got Jeff's number and we started hooking up. [Drummer] Dave [Lombardo] lived right down the street from me. One day he stopped at my house and said, "Hey, you got some guitars?" I guess he heard me playing. And I said, "Yeah, you wanna see?" So me, Jeff, and Dave jammed in his garage a couple times. I got back in touch with Tom, and we jammed, and that was it.

JEFF HANNEMAN (Slayer): We were in LA, but we all hated glam. I was listening to a lot of hardcore, but I still loved classic metal like Judas Priest and Iron Maiden. Kerry was more into the metal. So when we started writing songs, we combined the best of both.

KERRY KING: When we started Slayer, we did a lot of Priest covers, but then we heard those first two *Metal Massacre* records and we knew we could write songs that were better than those, so we progressed rapidly.

TOM ARAYA: We met the folks at Metal Blade and they said, "Listen, we'll put you on this *Metal Massacre III* album. So we did "Aggressive Perfector" for *Metal Massacre III* in 1982, and that was the birth and beginning of the Slayer sound. We wrote that song just for that record and we rehearsed it for weeks. We recorded it in one day. We listened to it and compared it to everything else on the record, and we thought, "This fucking rocks!" The only thing we kept saying was, "This needs to be a little faster." So we kept trying to do stuff that was faster and heavier and more violent.

BRIAN SLAGEL: That was back in the days of no money. Tom's dad scrounged up $3,000 to record their full-length debut

[1983's] *Show No Mercy*, and I mixed and produced the record out of necessity. Usually, by the end of a record, you don't want to hear it again for at least a month or two. But with Slayer, I kept listening to it over and over. I took it to Enigma [our record distributor] and said, "This is going to be the biggest record Metal Blade has ever done."

KERRY KING: For our first publicity photo we all gathered around this "dead" girl covered in blood. It was supposed to be some girl Tom dug, but she backed out at the last minute. So we ended up using Jeff's woman.

JEFF HANNEMAN: Yeah. After that, I had to marry her. But we were into the whole Satan gig, so it seemed appropriate. "Ahh, kill the virgin!"

RAT SKATES: You look at the back of the first Slayer record, *Show No Mercy*, the band have this Misfits kind of makeup and you're going, "Man, this must be the most incredible thing I could possibly go and see." But the makeup came off really quick, I believe, because Mötley Crüe was breaking at that time, too, and it was confusing. Bands are always extremely influenced by the fans, especially in thrash, because everyone was so tight-knit, so a few guys too many coming up to you saying, "Man, Exodus kicked our ass last night and they didn't *need* makeup." That's all it took.

KERRY KING: We may have been young and naïve, but we were determined as fuck. We knew we had good songs, and we knew if you want somebody to look, you have to get their attention. We wanted a wild stage show with explosions. But we didn't have the budget for that kind of shit, so we improvised. We stole floodlights from any apartment building we could find. We had a fucking agenda—with no money.

TOM ARAYA: Kerry and Jeff would go out at night and rip off lumber so they could build stage platforms by day. We ended up with a smoke machine and live explosions. The stage was like a minefield.

KERRY KING: We used gunpowder with a tube and nails and wire in between. And we just had a switch to turn it on and ignite the gunpowder.

TOM ARAYA: We never knew how much gunpowder to use. Kerry fried his back one time and I almost got a face full of flames. We burned a few ceilings. I'm surprised we didn't burn any clubs down.

KERRY KING: One time we had a burning trough that was supposed to be a wall of flames, and it only went up about an inch high. It was total *Spinal Tap*. But the look of the band was really important and I started making these wristbands with nails and spikes. Everyone knows me for wearing this gauntlet full of long nails, and the first time I had that armband on was when we played with Bitch at the Roxy. I had these big-ass fucking nails, and by coincidence, their bass player came out with a wristband of baby nails.

TOM ARAYA: There were times I'd come up behind Kerry, and—scratch! "Fuck!" I'd be bleeding. I probably coulda used a tetanus shot after some of those. We knew we wanted to do something theatrical because we were from LA, and that was the thing.

While Slayer was building a following, Metallica was becoming an international phenomenon. *Ride the Lightning* received rave reviews across the world, and Elektra, intent on promoting their rising stars, provided the money and resources to back the band, taking out numerous magazine advertisements and pushing the near-ballad "Fade to Black" at commercial radio.

JAMES HETFIELD: One of the first moments I realized things were really happening for us was at my girlfriend's house right when *Ride the Lightning* came out [in 1984]. I was waiting for her while her sister was home, and I don't think she knew I was there. I could hear "Fade to Black" blasting out of her speakers in her bedroom. She was just listening to that because she liked it and it spoke to her. That was pretty big for me. "Fade to Black" was one of those pivotal songs where we had the hardcore fans that said, "Screw you, you sold out, you did a ballad." That was their simplistic thinking. Then you had the other people that said, "Wow, I totally relate to that and it has helped me."

GENE AMBO (photographer): Metallica played with Dokken, Aerosmith, Ted Nugent, and Armored Saint at this big outdoor festival called the Iowa Jam. The show was in the afternoon, so by that night everyone was really fucked up. And we all got invited to see Van Halen at the big arena. Eddie [Van Halen] came into the back room before the show, and we're all standing around drinking. It was really funny because James was all shy, creeping over to Eddie. We just drank and drank and in the morning James was running around the street bashing parking meters after completely trashing Armored Saint's dressing room.

HARALD OIMOEN: [On August 31, 1985] they played the Day on the Green festival at a stadium in Oakland [California], which was their biggest show yet. They only had two or three photo passes for the concert and they said if I wanted one I'd have to do their dishes. I found out after that they were just winding me up. We all got shit-faced after the show and they drew a bunch of stuff all over my shorts. I thought they were autographing my shorts, but literally they were drawing big dicks on the back of my leg and they wrote, "Fuck me, I'm tight with AIDS" on the back of my pants. They drew this big hairy butthole on there. I was just clueless. I went to a Nations, a burger place, afterwards, and a cop came up behind me and said he doesn't appreciate my pornographic garments. I was so drunk I had no clue.

JAMES HETFIELD: When we got back from the *Ride the Lightning* tour that we did with W.A.S.P. and Armored Saint, it felt like the scene had grown so big. There were at least two gigs every week in the Bay Area that were full-on metal. We had parties at our house. Me and Lars and a friend of ours, Mark, lived in this one house. We would pull all the furniture out of the house and onto the lawn and we would have this big brawl mosh-a-thon in the living room.

As Metallica climbed the ladder of success, Exodus continued to seal their reputation as the Bay Area lords of destruction. While this made for some great stories, it underplayed the artistry of the songs on their 1985 full-length debut, *Bonded by Blood*. The album was rife with eviscerating hooks and ecstatic chant-along choruses. At the same time, a host of other bands, including Dark Angel, Possessed, Vio-Lence, and Forbidden emerged and happily moshed in the rubble.

RON QUINTANA: Exodus put out the demo for *Bonded by Blood* the year before it came out. Everyone had a copy and was listening to those songs. If it had come out when it was really done it would have scooped Metallica. If they had followed up with their second album, that one should have been better than *Ride the Lightning*. But it's tough being a Bay Area band because there isn't that label push that Metallica got immediately. Exodus really stop-started, stop-started. By the time [Paul Baloff was fired and Steve] "Zetro" [Souza] was in the band, they should have been on their fourth album like Metallica, and if they had, they probably would have been as famous.

GARY HOLT: I don't have any sour grapes about what happened.

We had a lot of fun doing *Bonded by Blood* at this studio about ninety miles north of San Francisco, and we were living there in these cabins for two weeks while we recorded. We had a steady stream of friends coming up for parties. Windows got broken, fights broke out everywhere. The guy who owned the place was mortified.

SCOTT IAN: People talk about the Big Four all the time, but back then it was really the Big Five because Exodus were just as important and just as influential as everybody else. For me, when it comes to debut records, *Bonded by Blood* might be better than all the rest of our debut records.

GARY HOLT: We were the last people you'd want to invite to your party. We'd kill fish in people's fish tanks and we'd piss in their shampoo bottles. Awful stuff. We were total juvenile delinquents and I think the reason Exodus got away with it at the time was we all looked like sixteen-year-old angelic figures. We were able to smile and give that "Who, me?" look. We just didn't look malicious. But there was a lot of evil behind those big, winking eyes. There was a party at this female photographer's house once, and we took these nicely framed photographs in the hallway and destroyed them.

KATON W. DE PENA (Hirax): Paul Baloff was one of the greatest front men who ever lived. His personality alone could carry any band. He used to carry a baseball bat and beat the shit out of TVs. No TV was safe.

GARY HOLT: Our entire image from the day the band became mine and Paul [Baloff's] was based on violence, and the crowd lived up to the musical imagery. At Ruthie's, there was a lot of blood. We had members of our inner circle that we referred to as the Slay Team, and they were legendary for the amount of destruction they would commit at a show. If someone pissed the band off, they would just start beating them in front of everybody. There was a guy named Toby Rage, and he would jump off the front of the stage and make it 20 feet walking on the tops of people's heads. He was the star of the video we did for "Toxic Waltz." One person left that shoot in an ambulance with a broken arm. Another had a concussion. And we were just lip-synching. It wasn't even a real show. We all got into the violence thing as well. We left a party once in San Francisco, and a few of us were heading to my friend's car and we saw a bunch of guys jumping some dude. At first we ran up to help the guy and it turned out the guy was just some crazed lunatic homeless guy. So we ended up joining in on the fun and next thing you know the cops showed up and we scattered into Golden Gate Park and hid until the cops left. I guess we kind of encouraged violence.

PAUL BALOFF (1960–2002) (Exodus): These two kids in high school were wearing Exodus T-shirts, and right in the middle of the class they got up and were clubbing their teachers with chairs and they were singing "A Lesson in Violence" while doing it. We play and people fight.

GARY HOLT: We preached killing posers, and if somebody happened to show up at Ruthie's wearing a Ratt shirt, we thought nothing of it to pull out a pocket knife and walk up to him and demand that they let us slice that shirt off their back. It was like, "You can either let us do it or we'll do it with you wearing it." If you look at a lot of the old pictures of Paul, on his left wrist he'd have five-inch pieces of cloth tied around it and those were all hair-band shirts. The funny thing though is years later all of us guitar players finally came out of the closet and admitted how much we coveted all of [Dokken guitarist] George Lynch's and [Ratt guitarist] Warren DeMartini's licks.

GENE HOGLAN (Dethklok, Testament, ex–Strapping Young Lad, ex–Fear Factory, ex–Dark Angel): Exodus was a big influence. Their whole "kill the posers" approach was big for Dark Angel. We went to parties in the Bay Area with those guys, and yeah, they were crazy psychos. You hear stories about them kidnapping a poser and tying him to a chair and setting him on fire and sticking knives in him. That could have all been great hype, but we thought that was awesome. Our road crew would do the same thing in LA. They'd get their raiding parties on the Sunset Strip. They'd grab a poser and set his hair on fire. A couple of our crew got sent to juvie because of stuff like that. If they didn't like your band they would go onstage and beat you off the stage.

HARALD OIMOEN: Baloff had these parties where he would invite a bunch of people to somebody *else's* house and they'd show up and totally trash the place. He was like the leader of a gang, the Slay Team, and he'd have these guys destroy people's houses or steal things from them.

KATON W. DE PENA: Speed was a very big thing in the scene. I think that made the music a little bit faster because a lot of people were playing on that stuff. One night I was getting ready to go onstage and I was in the bathroom. And this guy came up and ripped this mirror off the wall. I looked over and it was Paul Baloff. He ripped the mirror off the wall to put it on the bathroom sink so he could do lines off it.

GARY HOLT: We fired Paul because he didn't have his shit together. We were more successful eventually with Zetro, but I think about how fucked up my own personal situation became much later with alcohol and drugs, and I wish I had been more understanding about Paul's problems. It says a lot about what a thrash metal icon Paul was because he only recorded one album with us, and then he did the same record again live with us in 1997 [before he died of a heart attack], and he's viewed, as he should be, as a thrash metal legend.

Every thrash fan knows the Big Four: Metallica, Megadeth, Slayer, and Anthrax. If, as Anthrax guitarist Scott Ian suggests, Exodus should be included in the mix, then it's not much of a stretch to add Testament as well. The band is widely regarded as one of the top bands from the second wave of Bay Area thrash. Actually, Testament was around just as early as Metallica and Anthrax, forming as Legacy in 1982 with guitarist and songwriter Eric Peterson; vocalist Steve "Zetro" Souza; his cousin, guitarist Derrick Ramirez; bassist Greg Christian; and drummer Louie Clemente.

ERIC PETERSON (Testament): We were all in eighth grade and we used to cut school and go to San Francisco. One day we were sitting at this park and we bumped into [ex-drummer] Louie [Clemente]. He had a jean jacket with Iron Maiden patches on. He goes, "You know where I can get a nickel bag?" We ended up jamming together, and we wrote "Secret Agent," which became the Testament song "First Strike Is Still Deadly." Then [my cousin, guitarist and vocalist] Derrick Ramirez left and we met Alex [Skolnick].

ALEX SKOLNICK (Testament, Alex Skolnick Trio, Trans-Siberian Orchestra): When I tried out for Legacy, I was just fifteen. I was a totally nervous, shy kid, and they didn't help me feel comfortable. They didn't function on that level back then.

ERIC PETERSON: Alex was real awkward, and he wouldn't look at us. But he picked up his guitar and he was like Yngwie [Malmsteen]. He was in a band called Blackthorn, and he said, "Well, I dunno if I want to leave them." Then he came to one of our shows and he really liked "Cursed Are the Legions of Death." So he joined, and me and him wrote "Burnt Offerings" straight off. It was an epic song with all these nooks and crannies [that was on our 1987 album *The Legacy*]. We made a great team. I had a lot of the darkness in my sound, and he knew more about playing scales on the guitar than I did.

CHUCK BILLY: Steve "Zetro" Souza was my friend from the scene and he called me up and said, "Hey, I just joined Exodus. Here, call Alex Skolnick and tell him you wanna try out." I was taking vocal lessons and I really wanted to sing. I went to college for vocal and guitar. I didn't know much about thrash metal. I called him and he said, "Yeah, come on down. I brought this hella PA and a case of beer, and they had a little tiny room. I had to sing in the hallway because I couldn't fit in the room with them.

ERIC PETERSON: We were tripping because we knew Chuck was the huge guy from Dublin Death Patrol [violent peers of the Slay Team], and we were all scared of him. Me and Louie went, "No way! He's crazy!" But we went to see the [melodic metal] band Guilt that Chuck was in. Chuck was ripping it out and calling everybody in the crowd pussies. We were like, "Hey, he's a cool front man."

Although Testament was on the scene nearly from the start of thrash, it took Metallica's 1986 landmark album *Master of Puppets* to expose them and other Bay Area bands to the masses. *Master* was a watershed album: the band combined the brutality of thrash, technical wizardry of prog-rock, and epic grandeur of cinematic composers like John Barry and Ennio Morricone with the urgency of hardcore, and did it all in a framework of angry, infectious sing-alongs. It was the first album the band recorded specifically for its new label, Elektra, and, ultimately, it was the disc that legitimized thrash for the mainstream.

LARS ULRICH: Metallica was never just a thrash band. I accept that we had a lot to do with the way that whole scene took off; we were the first band to sound like that. But we never thought of ourselves as a "thrash" band. We were always an American band with British and European metal influences. It's just that until *Master of Puppets*, nobody took us seriously.

KIRK HAMMETT: The cohesiveness from one track to the next made perfect sense to us. It was almost as if the album created itself. From the beginning, when we started writing the songs, all the way to the end, really great ideas were just moving and coming out of nowhere in a nonstop flow.

LARS ULRICH: Cliff and Kirk brought incredible depth into the band. Cliff went to music school. We would sit there and talk about Venom or Angel Witch. He'd sit there and talk about Bach, Yes, Peter Gabriel. I guess we slowly started feeling that the fast stuff needed dynamics because if it was all fast, none of it really stood out.

JAMES HETFIELD: On *Master of Puppets*, we started getting into longer, more orchestrated songs. It was more of a challenge to write a long song that didn't seem long. The riff for "Master of Puppets" was pretty messy—constantly moving. It works good live. People love to scream "Master!"

By the time Metallica was opening for Ozzy in 1986, big things were happening for other bands as well. Megadeth was about to release *Peace Sells . . . but Who's Buying?*; Anthrax was touring for its major label debut, *Spreading the Disease*; Slayer was being courted by Rick Rubin and Def Jam Records; and Testament was on the verge of its first big break.

ERIC PETERSON: We were talking to Megaforce about doing a record as Legacy. All these people wanted to sign us because of our 1985 demo.

MARIA FERRERO: Elliot Cahn, a lawyer, sent a cassette, and I was like, "Oh my God, this is great!" I kept playing it over and over, and Jonny was like, "Get it the fuck off, you're driving me crazy!" Finally he said, "OK, we'll sign this, we'll sign this."

CHUCK BILLY: Jonny Z was like, "Send me a demo of the new singer." So I went and did a demo of "Over the Wall" and "The Haunted." He's like, "Okay, we got a deal." So Jonny and Marsha flew out to San Francisco to see us at this little tiny room. They looked beat up and were all down because the night before they got a call that Cliff Burton had died. And we couldn't be excited either because Cliff was our good friend.

JONNY ZAZULA: We were completely devastated. We didn't believe it at first—then we found out it was true and that Cliff had died, and we had already made this appointment to go out and listen to Testament. We already knew we were going to sign them and this was just to seal the deal. So they did this showcase, and they were a lot better with Chuck Billy than they had been with Zetro. We told them they had a deal. But everyone was just too upset about Cliff to celebrate.

Cliff Burton's death is one of the metal world's greatest tragedies. Metallica was enjoying breakthrough success, and Burton was in his prime as a musician. Some say he was the main force behind Metallica's sound. Sadly, the world will never know what Burton would have contributed to a post–*Master of Puppets* Metallica. On September 26, 1986, the band was in the middle of a European tour and heading to a show in Copenhagen. Shortly after 5 a.m., their driver skidded on black ice and lost control, and the bus rolled over into a ditch. Burton was ejected through his bunk window while he slept and crushed under the bus.

JAMES HETFIELD: I saw the bus lying right on him. I saw his legs sticking out. I went to pieces. The driver tried to take Cliff's blanket and give it to someone else. I just screamed "fuck that!" I wanted to kill the guy. I don't know if he was drunk or if the bus had skidded on ice. All I knew was Cliff was dead.

SCOTT IAN: We were on tour with Metallica when that happened. We left halfway through their set the night before.

I said goodbye to them before they went onstage because I knew we weren't going to see them when they got offstage. We got into the hotel that morning and I saw our tour manager Mark talking to some guy. I walked up all bleary-eyed looking for my room key, and he's like, "There's bad news." I said, "What?" He goes, "Metallica's bus crashed on the way here last night and flipped over and Cliff was killed." It didn't even register in my brain. It made no sense. I said, "Bullshit. They probably just got super drunk and made up some story about a bus accident because they're going to be late or they can't make it to the gig." I was in complete denial. Then fans started showing up as the word got out. There were hundreds of people around the hotel because somehow people knew this is where both bands were gonna be staying. Later that day, James and Kirk got brought to the hotel and they told us the whole story of how Lars had broken a toe, but outside of some other scratches and bruises that was it. Cliff was killed. It was completely insane. We spent a really horrible night in Copenhagen with James and Kirk. James was inconsolable and uncontrollable. He was smashing things in the hotel. So we took him outside to walk him around and he started smashing things in the street. We didn't know what to do. Obviously, we didn't want him to get arrested. The cops don't give a fuck that his best friend was just killed. So we stayed up all night with those guys in disbelief, and then they got on the plane the next morning to fly home.

MARIA FERRARO: Marsha [Zazula] called me from California to tell me. I was standing in my old house where I grew up, on the steps in my kitchen on the phone, and I sunk to the floor. The first person I thought to call was Mustaine, because, you know, he wasn't in Metallica anymore, but I knew he cared. I called him, and I know he mentioned that in his book.

DAVE MUSTAINE: Maria told me all about it. I just stood there clutching the phone, feeling like someone had punched me in the stomach. I hadn't talked to Cliff in a while but still considered him to be a friend. If I harbored some lingering anger toward Lars and James, well, it was impossible to work up the same degree of animus toward Cliff. He was just too decent a person. For whatever reason—guilt, anger, sadness—I hung up the phone, got in my car, and went out and scored some heroin. I got loaded, sat around and cried for a while, then picked up my guitar and in one brief sitting I wrote an entire song, "In My Darkest Hour," which wound up on Megadeth's next album, [1988's *So Far, So Good . . . So What!*]

SCOTT IAN: I was out there with those guys for the funeral and then with them for days in San Francisco, and the mood was very much, "Who are we gonna get and what are we gonna do and how are we moving forward?" They set their minds to it immediately because they felt that the last thing that Cliff would want would be for the band to end, and that's absolutely 100 percent true. So they charged right back into it and we were back out doing shows together in February of 1987 when Jason [Newsted] was in the band. We went back and made up some of these dates that got canceled, and that's just six months after Cliff died. So they never took the time to grieve. Maybe in retrospect taking three months off and dealing with it would have been the thing to do. But they were Metallica. At the time, how could they have stopped? They were on this path that led them to where they are now and there was no way to stop the machine.

MICK WALL: [Cliff] was incredibly important [to Metallica]. I think without him, there would be no *them*. But because he died, people trot out a lot of clichés about what happened. And the biggest cliché is that they had to carry on, because that's what Burton would have wanted. That's bullshit. They carried on because that's what Ulrich and Hetfield wanted. The other thing [about Burton] is how his death freed them to become the monster success they became. I think had he stayed in the band, they would have made a much more interesting album than . . . *And Justice for All*. But the fact that he wasn't around really did leave Ulrich and Hetfield to run the show without any interference. And Ulrich and Hetfield have run the band ever since. That's how the *Black Album* came about. I have serious doubts that the *Black Album* would have happened had Burton not died.

JOEY VERA: People think that I auditioned for Metallica, but the truth is that they were basically having cattle calls and it was depressing for them. I think that they just wanted to play with people that they knew personally, to get more friends to come out. Armored Saint were my buddies from school and we were on a major label, making our third record, *Raising Fear*, even though, in hindsight, maybe the business wasn't going so well. Still, you can look at it as some sort of job security, because you're still signed, you're in a band that's working. So I declined the invitation because I wasn't in a place in my mind to say about Armored Saint, "This is enough, I'm done with this. I need something different."

MICHAEL ALAGO: Lars called and said, "We're going to move forward. Do you have anybody in mind?" Funny enough, I had just signed Flotsam and Jetsam. I was crazy about them. [Bassist] Jason Newsted was their spokesperson. It bothered me for a moment because I knew it was going to upset the apple cart with the boys in Flotsam, but he had that same kind of charm, integrity, and his bass playing was wild and animated, and I knew he would be the perfect fit for the guys. I also suggested Phil Caivano, who was playing bass in Blitzspeer [and later joined Monster Magnet as a guitarist].

LARS ULRICH: I called up my friend [Metal Blade label owner] Brian Slagel, who had given Metallica their first break. I asked him, "Who are the hot young cats out there?" All roads were leading to this guy Jason Newsted. We were auditioning bass players right down where Cliff used to live in Hayward. And Cliff's mom and dad were hanging around the rehearsal rooms. It was a pretty beautiful thing, but it was also a little intimidating for the bass players. Jason Newsted came in and he didn't look a day over fourteen. He was very serious and fired up and knew all the songs. He had tremendous energy, enormous tenacity. He was the kind of guy that you could tell, "Okay Jason, you'll get the gig in Metallica on one condition. You have to go lay in the street and get run over by a truck." I mean, he would have done that.

Metallica persevered with Jason Newsted and started working on its most progressive album up to that point, the schizophrenic . . . *And Justice for All*. At the same time, Slayer was injecting thrash with a new degree of intensity and malice, thanks to the blinding ferocity of *Reign in Blood*, which was released October 7, 1986. It was Slayer's fastest, most lyrically vicious and controversial album. Produced by Rick Rubin, *Reign in Blood* featured graphic cover art and ultraviolent lyrics—especially those in "Angel of Death," a song about the grisly human experiments performed in concentration camps by Nazi doctor Josef Mengele during World War II. Largely because of the song, Def Jam's distributor, Columbia Records, refused to release the album. *Reign in Blood* ultimately came out on Geffen Records, a more daring label. It became Slayer's first gold album.

DIMEBAG DARRELL: Slayer's *Reign in Blood* was groundbreaking. They did shit that was unorthodox. They did shit that was out of the books, but somehow it wasn't out of place. There were two wild-ass crazy guitars, and you're going, "What key are they in and what kind of lead playing are they doing?" But it's just so *bad*, dude. Nobody can play it because nobody can figure it out.

SCOTT IAN: *Reign in Blood* defines thrash metal. If anyone ever has a question of what thrash metal sounds like, just put on

Reign in Blood. The songs are amazing, the riffs are sick, and it's heavy as hell from start to finish.

TOM ARAYA: At the time we did *Reign in Blood*, everyone was all about being politically correct. We got accused of being neo-Nazis because of "Angel of Death." If you look at it, the song just tells a story. It doesn't glorify anything. Anyone who thinks we're Nazis isn't paying close attention because I'm originally from Chile, so I'm a minority, and that would have to mean I hate myself.

KERRY KING: We like being the bad guys. We branded ourselves as that years ago because we write about shit no one else will. It's better than singing about posies. When I go to movies, I always cheer for the bad guys. The thing that pisses me off is the bad guys always get killed in the end of the movies. I just like to ignore that part.

JEFF HANNEMAN: We're not praising Mengele or terrorists or serial killers. We just write from their perspective. I've got some German war artifacts, and a lot of people don't understand it. They say, "Why would you have that in your house?" But it's cool. It's evil. It's part of what being in Slayer is. And it's a major part of history. It doesn't mean I'm a Nazi, because I'm not and I don't want to be one. Since we did "Angel of Death" I've had three occasions where somebody will go, "Psst, hey. I'm part of this Aryan world nation group and we're thinking of having you speak." I'm like, "Why?" And they'll go, "*You* know." I'll be like, "No, why?" And they'll go, "Aren't you . . . ?" I'm like, "What? No. Go away. You don't get me at all."

LEMMY KILMISTER: I collect German war memorabilia because the Nazis made the best shit. I've often said if Israel made the best stuff I'd collect that, but they didn't. The Germans had the best uniforms. The bad guys always have the best stuff—the

Confederates, Napoleon. I've been collecting ever since I first came to America because this is where all the stuff is. GIs were allowed to ship anything home. And now it's worth plenty. It isn't skinheads who are collecting this shit, it's dentists and doctors.

DAVID DRAIMAN (Disturbed): That's super-duper taboo and offensive to me. It's the most provocative imagery, and that's why people utilize it. If that's their goal, I guess they're achieving it, but just know there are going to be repercussions. I don't give a fuck who you are. If you're going to brandish Nazi symbolism, I'm going to have a problem with you because I don't understand how anybody could think it's okay to wear something on their body that symbolizes the annihilation and genocide of my people. There is no excuse for that and there is no explanation.

Numerous German thrash bands were greatly inspired by Slayer, but they stayed away from any sort of nationalistic imagery because it hit too close to home, instead embracing tried-and-true tales of death, dismemberment, monsters, and demons. The main players in the Kraut metal kingdom were Sodom, Kreator, and Destruction.

GENE HOGLAN: We were all fans of Destruction, and we liked Sodom because they were so bad and could barely play their instruments—kind of like Venom. And Kreator were just trying to do the hyper-blur thing that was really cool.

MILAND "MILLE" PETROZZA (Kreator): Being fifteen-year-old kids when we started the band, we were like, "Man, we gotta be Satanic like Venom." So we got books and tried to celebrate the black mass. The Satanic thing was a gimmick to me that was really entertaining. Of course we thought for maybe a year or so that we were real Satanists, but then we were like, "Ah, this is all bullshit. It doesn't work."

TOM ANGELRIPPER (Sodom): I read a lot of books by and about Aleister Crowley, like *The Beast: 666* and *Equinox*. I was really inspired by his lyrical writing, but by the time we did our 1986 debut *Obsessed by Cruelty* I realized that it gives me nothing. We never practiced any of the rituals. We had some black candles and skulls in the rehearsal room, but I think it was just funny. By 1987 we did *Persecution Mania* and I wanted to write more political songs that were heavier and faster than Venom.

While the German thrash bands Kreator, Sodom, and Destruction played an important role in building upon the sounds of Slayer and Venom, it was a group from Brazil, Sepultura, that ultimately became the most innovative and influential non-American thrash band.

IGOR CAVALERA (ex-Sepultura): My father used to tell me that I didn't pick drums, the drums picked me. Once we went to a restaurant and they had drums there for some old people to play jazz, and I couldn't eat. I would just stare at the drums. I started playing right around that time. I was seven.

MAX CAVALERA (ex-Sepultura): Igor never actually got a drum kit until after [Sepultura's 1986 album] *Morbid Visions*. He used to practice on the sofa, and then he used pots and pans. I really wanted to be a drummer, too, man, but he was so much better than me. Guitar was my second choice, but I was never completely serious because I'm a drummer at heart. I only use the four lowest strings. One of the strings broke once, and I was like, fuck it, I don't use it anyway, so I just got rid of the two high strings.

IGOR CAVALERA: That's something I look at in a very positive way. Max doesn't treat the guitar like a lot of players do. He's a lot more percussive.

MAX CAVALERA: Our first jams were crazy. Igor's drum kit was a broom with one cymbal, a snare from marching band, and a bass drum from school band. Our first bass player, [Roberto] "Gato" [Raffan], had a dad who was a missionary Canadian preacher. We had a guitar player, Julio [Cesar Vieira Franco], and he was a full-on doctor doing surgery. He was thirty-five and we were, like, fifteen. Then we had another guitarist Roberto [UFO] whose mom wouldn't let him go out after ten. He missed one of our very first shows because it was too late.

At first, Sepultura's ambition substituted for their lack of talent and experience, but it didn't take long for front men Max and Igor Cavalera to hone their musical chops and songwriting skills. The band's 1986 full-length debut, *Morbid Visions*, was brutal and primitive, and the more refined 1987 follow-up, *Schizophrenia*, set the stage for its deal with American indie label Roadrunner.

MAX CAVALERA: I got a meeting with Roadrunner in New York, and a friend gave me an employee airline ticket. I had to travel with a tie and my hair pulled back and say I worked for Pan Am Airlines. It was the only way for me to get to America. And when we got there, they signed us.

STEFFAN CHIRAZI: At first, Sepultura were a little messy, but when *Chaos AD* came out [in 1993] it brought everything into focus. Then, of course, there was *Roots*; it was percussive, it was conscientious. These guys weren't just singing about darkness and violence. It was relevant shit. That's one thing you can say about Max Cavalera. He's one of those guys you would point a stranger to if you wanted to explain how this music can actually be a really positive and educational force.

MAX CAVALERA: The music is angry and pissed off, but it's also very personal and passionate. I don't want to write songs about serial killers, and I get really angry when people think we're a negative influence or blame us for something violent. We played this big show in São Paulo and one of our fans got killed with an axe by some skinheads. I realized, "Fuck, we were the soundtrack of that brutality." The next day every newspaper was blaming us, and we had nothing to do with it. We just did a show. That was so upsetting to me. Our fan took a fucking axe to the chest.

While Anthrax launched around the same time as Metallica, it took them a few more years to reach a serious level of critical and commercial acclaim. That era began with their groundbreaking 1987 album, *Among the Living*, which featured speed-freak tempos, propulsive yet memorable riffs, and plenty of sing-along vocals.

SCOTT IAN: We were really on a roll in every way business-wise, creative-wise, emotionally. We played London and Lemmy from Motörhead came to our show. Every little thing was a huge fucking deal. I remember [drummer] Charlie [Benante] coming in with the riff to "I Am the Law," and I was like, "Oh, my god. Fucking huge." That and "Indians" were the first two songs we wrote for *Among the Living*, which a lot of people consider our best album. We were already playing them on the *Spreading the Disease* tour. Our confidence was so high. It's almost like we were being guided by the power of metal. It was out of our hands. We were being used as the tool to make the record that needed to be made.

DAN SPITZ (ex-Anthrax): That record was Anthrax to a tee. Charlie and Scott come from a hardcore background and they're bringing that to the music, and me and Joey are connecting musically, inflicting a lot of melody into the band, and [bassist] Frankie [Bello] is barreling right down the middle filling every gap.

SCOTT IAN: In 1986, we were suddenly the big kids on the block in New York. We had a record on a major label; we were all-original. Coming up, you could never get gigs unless you were a Van Halen cover band. But here we were in '86, we almost had a hundred thousand records sold, and we could sell out the

Ritz. It was kind of a big "fuck you" to a lot of people who stood in our way for years.

For all the tragedy, turmoil, controversy, scuffles, addiction, and shake-ups that plagued the thrash metal community, there were plenty of good times; many, many memorable moments; and the kind of sexual misadventures non-glam bands had once only dreamed about—thanks in part to the coverage of the music by MTV's *Headbangers Ball.*

GARY HOLT: When we did the MTV Headbangers Ball tour [with Anthrax and Helloween in 1989], it was about as close to a Mötley Crüe kind of scene as we were ever gonna know. We'd roll into town every day and there'd be thirty or forty women hanging outside. The real beauty of it was the other bands on the tour weren't debauched like us. We were fuckin' chicks every day, all day, multiple amounts, and really thinking it was ridiculous because we're not a hair band. "Why is this happening? Who cares? Just enjoy it!" The really crazy stuff usually involved the road crews. You look at some of these guys and go, "Okay, he has never been laid in his life." And all of a sudden he has the power of the backstage pass. I've seen chicks with flashlights up their pussy drinking beer out of dog dishes and girls blowing, like, twenty guys just to get that fuckin' pass. Everybody in the band knows what she did to get it and no one's gonna touch her! No one wants to give her a hug. She blew all these dirty old guys instead of the dirty young guys.

KIRK HAMMETT: I couldn't figure out why all of a sudden I was handsome. A fat bank account will make you look handsome. No one had ever treated me like that before in my life.

LARS ULRICH: We all had some pretty slutty moments. I don't think there's anybody in this band who hasn't had crabs a couple times or the occasional drip-dick.

LEMMY KILMISTER: I don't care what people say. They're in it for the pussy, you know? The music's important too, but it's more about the pussy.

DAVE MUSTAINE: I think that heavy metal is obviously very sexual. Rock and roll itself is Negro slang for having sex. But there was a time before I got married when I couldn't fuck just one girl. I had to have two fucking each other for me to even get excited. That's when I started to think, "Man, I'm losing my perspective on things because pretty soon I'm gonna have to get a whole girl scout troop in there just to get an erection."

JAMES HETFIELD: We had our battles with spandex, that's for sure. You could show off your package: "Wear spandex, dude. It gets you chicks." On the first tour through America, my spandex were wet from the night before, and I was drying them by the heater. A big hole melted right in the crotch. I opted to keep my jeans on, and that was the best thing that ever happened. Lars wore spandex up through the *Black Album* tour, though he might tell you different.

CHUCK BILLY: On our first tour ever we were out in a van, and me and [guitarist] Alex [Skolnick] got a couple ladies in our van in Richmond, Virginia, and we were hammered on Jack Daniel's. One of the girls started mouthing off to me and I got pissed off. We were parked right on the boat dock so I opened the door and flung her into the water. It was about a twenty-foot drop into the bay, with no stairs to get up. So she's holding on to the wooden pier. The water's hitting hard. She's crying. She keeps getting rubbed up and down, and she's getting slivers all over her arms and her chest. She's getting cut up. So we got ropes and hauled her out of there. She was so pissed, and all the fans were around the van cheering us on.

When they weren't hooking up with groupies, thrash musicians amused themselves in other ways: drinking to excess, taking recreational drugs, and playing stupid pranks.

BOBBY "BLITZ" ELLSWORTH: One night I set [Slayer front man] Tom Araya on fire at a party. I just lit him up, man. He had on a T-shirt with a rat with a joint in his mouth, and I had the idea that I was lighting the joint. Suddenly the flames are running up his shirt, and we had to pat him down. I spent the next day looking for a replacement for the shirt, and I found one.

TOM ARAYA: I would think I'd remember that, but I was totally wasted drunk all the time and that was not a good thing because I was a belligerent drunk. I was total rage. They told me I would do all kinds of crazy shit. I had a lot of blackouts, which were not cool. Do you wanna keep waking up every day apologizing for all the stupid things you did that you don't remember? No way, man.

JEFF HANNEMAN: One of my favorite things that [drummer] Dave [Lombardo] ever did happened when we were going to a gig and we pulled over because Dave had to shit and we didn't have a tour bus at that time. Dave went out and took a Big Gulp cup, shit in it, wiped his ass with a leaf and then got back into the car. I was in the car behind him. We're driving along and he reaches out the window and throws the cup of shit at us and it hit the windshield. There was shit all over the windshield. And of course, you turn on the wiper and it just smears all over the place.

GARY HOLT: When we went for our first tour in Europe supporting Venom, we loved nothing more than cock-blocking each other. Someone's trying to get laid, and just for fun we'd come up and spit all over the girl until she ran away screaming. Then someone's really pissed off and we know the next time we're gonna try to get laid the same thing's gonna happen to us. On the last show of the tour, I pulled off one of the most amazing catches since Willie Mays's basket catch [in the 1954 World Series]. I was 30 feet from the stage on the floor, and the stage was 5 feet high and 30 feet deep. Venom's drummer Abaddon is 20 feet up on a platform and he spits towards me, and I caught that shit in my mouth and swallowed it. It was so gross. That completely outgrossed Venom, and that was quite a feather in my cap at the time.

TOM ARAYA: I did crack in 1987 out of boredom, but that was a one-day thing. At the end of the night I was like, "I'm glad I don't have any money, I can't control myself." I was searching around for little things on the floor. The stuff's just too good for me. The high was fucking awesome, and I can see why people get hooked.

KERRY KING: There was a time when we did crank, stuff like that. It's ridiculous. Mostly for us though, it's just been about drinking.

TOM ARAYA: There was a time in Montreal in 1988 that went down as "Tom's Supersonic hurl." It was two-for-one happy hour, so we were pounding beers. I walked out and my stomach's sloshing. There was snow all over the ground, and I just said, "Watch this." I opened my mouth and spewed all over the snow, and the snow melted. We walked a little further, and I'm like, "Check this out." It was a four-foot arc of puke. They couldn't believe it and they were like, "Do it again! That was intense." The last time I did anything as fucked up as that was in Japan, and that was just me in my hotel room. It was scary because I woke up with a pizza pie circle of puke around my bed. I was like, "Man, who the fuck stinks?" and then I realized it was me and I thought, "Damn, I did that in my sleep." That freaked me out because some people who do that don't wake up.

GARY HOLT: For a long while, we'd snort anything you'd put in front of us, but back then it was much smaller amounts. It was mostly booze, and when we dabbled with methamphetamine we'd get a half gram and the whole band would get wired all night on it, which allowed us to keep drinking. Decades later it got to the point where some of us were smoking it and we'd burn up a half gram in thirty minutes. The only good thing methamphetamine ever did for me was I had about one-sixteenth of speed hidden in my rehearsal room. I had no money, and before I left on tour I let the repo man come get my car. I got dropped off at a rehearsal studio and I lived forty-five minutes away. I went in the rehearsal room and pulled out the bag of dope and used it to barter a ride home. That was about $180 of speed and the last time I ever held any in my hand was when I gave it away.

TOM ARAYA: Me and Jeff made a pact in '88 that we would cut the crap that we were doing. So I stopped then. You find yourself driving down the road doing fucked-up shit without a care in the world and then you realize that's a real good way to get yourself killed.

GARY HOLT: We all had bad methamphetamine habits—me, [vocalist] Paul Baloff, drummer [Tom Hunting], and [ex-guitarist] Rick [Hunolt]. I had to bury five friends who died from that. Eventually, you realize it's a dead-end street. That's why we parted ways with Rick. He'd get clean to tour, then go back home and start again. And I love Rick to death. I want nothing more than for him to straighten up his life. But when you're smoking that shit, it's a whole different ballgame. And he was in deep and wouldn't stop.

The glory (and gory) days of thrash came to an end because there were hardly any new ideas being generated, and the glut of bands didn't seem to care as long as they were partying and getting laid. By the late eighties and early nineties, thrash was on its way out—and a new form of heavy music brewing in Seattle was about to redefine the musical landscape. But before grunge took over, thrash had one dramatic last gasp. In 1990, a promoter put together the first Clash of the Titans tour in Europe, which featured Slayer, Megadeth, Testament, and Suicidal Tendencies. The tour was named after the 1981 Desmond Davis fantasy movie about the Greek myth of Perseus. Before the tour even began, Megadeth front man Dave Mustaine accidentally started a rivalry with Slayer that would last until their Carnage tour in 2010. The tension wasn't noticeable from the audience, however, and all four bands delivered jaw-dropping performances before stadium crowds. The shows went over so well that the tour continued in 1991 in North America, with Anthrax replacing Testament, and a then-unknown Alice in Chains taking Suicidal's spot.

DAVE MUSTAINE: This was way before stuff like Ozzfest, so having Slayer, Megadeth, and Testament on one bill was really special. Then when you add Anthrax in the States, nothing like that had ever happened. It should have been really fun, but before we started the European run, we had to do a photo shoot for *Rolling Stone*, and [Slayer front man] Tom [Araya], myself, [Testament vocalist] Chuck [Billy], and [Suicidal Tendencies vocalist] Mike Muir were supposed to all be there, and Mike couldn't make it. I said something and it got back to Mike, and he didn't like it. That started a shit storm.

MIKE MUIR (Suicidal Tendencies): Before we left, someone said, "Hey man, you sitting down?" I'm like, "No, why?" He said, "I wanna read you something." He read me a couple interviews Dave Mustaine did. I was like, "Why [is he talking shit about me]? I don't really know this guy." When I finally saw him a few days into the tour he told me, "Hey, I never said any of this stuff. It's the press. They're trying to get me. Why would I say that?" I went, "I dunno, man. It seems like a little bit too heavy of a conspiracy to me, you know?" The next day he came open and went, "I said some stuff I shouldn't have said. I got some problems. I don't know why I did it. All I can say is I shouldn't have and I was wrong." And that was the end of it.

MIKE CLARK (Suicidal Tendencies): Dave Mustaine is a jerk. I'm not one to put people down and talk behind people's backs, but during that tour he publicly stated in some magazine interviews that we were unprofessional, not good enough, and did not deserve to play the Clash of the Titans tour. He said Mike couldn't sing—"sings like a frog," something stupid like that. Then in his usual manner he said he was very drugged out at the time and apologized. Dave was lucky that Mike actually didn't beat the shit out of him, because he *did* deserve it. You can ask anybody.

DAVE MUSTAINE: We got overseas and we were in an airport and there were some guys that were drinking and having a good time. I wasn't drinking. I was newly sober and in that AA police thing, so I was miserable, and as I was suffering silently, my lips gave way and I spoke out. I said something about [Slayer guitarist] Kerry [King] that I shouldn't have said and that I regretted. I think it's probably better left unsaid because it's water under the bridge now.

KERRY KING: That was the beginning of me and Dave Mustaine being at odds, because he was just a pompous ass back then. We had never had any problems before. Over the course of a tour you find out stuff about people that you didn't know when you were just hanging out at a show or a party. It was funny because he said in an interview that he was angry about us drinking in the hallways, farting and burping and having a good time. I'm like, "You're just making us sound fun, dude."

TOM ARAYA: We were stoned and drunk in a hotel in Scotland. We were goofing around and my hand ended up hitting the side of the elevator. So Chuck decided he'd punch the side of the elevator. There was a display there with glass and he put his hand through it. Blood was running down on the floor of the elevator and I was like, "Dude, we need to take care of that."

ERIC PETERSON: Tom grabs Chuck's wrist and goes, "You stupid idiot. Look what you did to yourself!" He's slapping Chuck in the face—and Tom's the only guy that could get away with that; Chuck's got a lot of respect for Tom. So Tom went, "C'mon, we gotta get you to the hospital." We got a cab to the hospital, and while Chuck's getting stitches in the emergency room, these old Scottish people are looking at us all funny and someone says something to Tom about our long hair. So he gets up on the top of the table in the waiting room and yells, "Satan rules your soul!" He totally freaked those people out.

TOM ARAYA: They stitched up Chuck's wrist in the emergency room. And there were some old people there. I must have been pissing them off because this old man was yelling at me and started coming at me, attacking me. The hospital staff had to get him away from me. Then the doctor came out and said, "Chuck won't let me do anything. He wants you back there with him." I sat with Chuck while they stitched him up. The doctor was scared shitless. I'm not a small guy and Chuck's this big Indian dude, and we're being loud and stupid. We got out of there to get the cab back to the hotel. I realized I didn't have any shoes on. I was barefoot the entire time and I didn't realize it.

DAVE MUSTAINE: The rumor mill went crazy. It didn't help that Chuck Billy cut his hand, and then I walked underneath the curtain and some idiot didn't raise the lighting truss and I ran right into it and split my nose open. So there was a huge chunk of skin hanging off my nose and Chuck's hand's bloody, and everyone's thinking he punched me in the face.

RICK ERNST (director, _Get Thrashed_): A lot of people don't know that Alice in Chains weren't originally going to be on the

U.S. Clash of the Titans tour. The last spot was given to
Death Angel, but they got into a horrible bus accident and
couldn't do the shows. So if you think about it, the tour
symbolized the end of thrash and the torch being passed to
something else.

ROB CAVESTANY (Death Angel): On November 28, 1990, we got
in an accident that ended everything for a while. We had
just done a show in Mesa, Arizona, and were traveling to a
show in Vegas. It was 6:30 in the morning, and instead of
a normal bus our management chose to save money and go
with a mobile home. The soundman was driving and he fell
asleep at the wheel doing 90 down the highway. We went
into a ravine, tipped over, and slid for 300 feet. It looked like
a bomb blew up. Our drummer Andy [Galleon] was injured
really badly. We didn't even know where he was at first. He
had been thrown against the side window, and then when the
bus flipped over on its side, he was against the pavement of the
street with a mattress and a big TV on top of him, and it literally pressed his head to the pavement while we slid. It took a
year for him to recover [from severe head trauma].

JERRY CANTRELL (Alice in Chains): I never felt at home on Clash
of the Titans. It was never our audience, but it was an opportunity to play in front of a big crowd. We took some serious
abuse on that tour.

SCOTT IAN: We'd stand onstage every night and watch Alice
get pelted with everything those crowds could throw at them.
[Vocalist] Layne [Staley] would be jumping into the audience
and punching people. But they never once walked off the
stage. Every night they finished their set. They stood there and
they took it.

KERRY KING: At Red Rocks [in the Rocky Mountains, near
Denver] somebody had a big gallon jug that they had pissed in,

and they dumped it on Alice in Chains more than once. I was like, "Goddamn, that sucks."

JERRY CANTRELL: As soon as we hit the stage shit just started raining down; it was insane. It was like that movie *Three Hundred* with all the arrows. The sky was black with coins and bottles during our whole forty-minute set. Somebody threw a gallon jug of something that crashed down on Sean Kinney's drum set. You had to keep your eye out, just dodging shit. Then Layne got pissed off and was like, "Fuck you, mother-fuckers!" We kept playing, and he jumped the barricade while people were spitting on him. He was spitting back. They were hitting him, and he was kicking and hitting back, and we did the same thing. We were right there, but we kept playing, like, "Fuck you, we ain't goin' anywhere." We finished the set and we were like "Jesus Christ, that was insane." We're waiting to get in the bus to leave, and there were a bunch of Slayer fans backstage that had passes and they started walking toward us. We're like, "We're gonna get our fuckin' asses kicked." But they walked over and went, "Okay, man. You didn't puss out. I guess you're all right."

6

---

†HE AGE OF QUARREL: CROSSOVER/HARDCORE, 1977–1992

In the mid-eighties, thrash metal and hardcore fans who had once been bitter rivals realized they had a lot in common. Once the barriers between the two subcultures had broken down, the foundation for crossover was established, and bands from across the country began constructing their own blends of metallic hardcore.

ROGER MIRET (Agnostic Front): Back then, there wasn't much difference between metal and hardcore scenes. Everyone dressed in black, everyone was walking out of step with society, because whether you were a punk rocker, a skinhead, a hardcore kid, or a metal dude, you didn't fit in. You were a weirdo, and nobody's mother wanted their kids hanging out with you.

BILLY GRAZIADEI (Biohazard, Suicide City): We formed our own culture because we weren't accepted by society. It wasn't like now, where everyone's listening to Green Day and you can buy the latest punk fashions in Hot Topic.

DAVE GROHL: Bands like Cro-Mags, C.O.C. [Corrosion of Conformity], and D.R.I. [Dirty Rotten Imbeciles] went from being strictly hardcore to adding more metal riffs and getting even heavier. That crossover period of music really allowed both hardcore and underground metal to grow because everyone was feeding off each other's ideas and sharing each other's audience.

HARLEY FLANAGAN (Harley's War, ex–Cro-Mags, ex-Stimulators): If it were not for Venom and Motörhead, the Cro-Mags would not have sounded the way we did. That, along with the Bad Brains and Discharge, were our main influences. I wanted something to set us apart from the other hardcore bands, period. I was hanging out with violent skinheads with crazy pentagrams and swastikas tattooed all over them, listening to Venom and Discharge, huffing glue, trying to invoke demons. Our idea of fun was, "Hey, let's go out and stomp people," not, "Let's go out and have a few drinks."

While bands like Black Flag, Dead Kennedys, and Void laid the groundwork for the new subgenre, the Misfits were the first to draw both a hardcore and metal following.

GLENN DANZIG: We were the first hardcore band to experiment with speed metal, and we got a lot of flak for that. I never saw why the two weren't connected. They were both about power, rebellion, violence.

EERIE VON (ex-Danzig, Samhain): The Misfits were playing superfast. They had this occult image. Those were metal signposts. You could see these metal kids showing up with long hair. Later on, we'd see all these bands and we'd say, "This is just like hardcore, but with long hair and guitar leads."

JONATHAN ANASTAS (DYS): The Misfits were the first ones to lean in a rock star direction. Even when they weren't playing a

show, [guitarist] Doyle [Wolfgang von Frankenstein] and [bass-
ist] Jerry [Only] would show up in full regalia, six-foot-eight
in those heels, in the lobby of a Minor Threat show, and they'd
be mobbed.

GLENN DANZIG: The funny thing is that the Misfits weren't really
popular when they were around. Also, they weren't very good
live. I was as good as you can be at eighty-million miles an
hour. I don't think a lot of people got what I was doing. The
guys in the band didn't even get it.

EERIE VON: Some people thought it was a joke, but Glenn took
the occult stuff pretty seriously. The Misfits once got arrested
for going into a graveyard in New Orleans with two hundred
people following them, thinking they could just reach in and
grab skulls and take 'em home.

GLENN DANZIG: People like to use the word *occult* like it's going
out of style. It can cover parapsychology, witchcraft, Satanism,
black magic—everything. It's an unfair word. You don't have a
cover-all word for Catholicism. My words and music are made
to fit a certain mood, and my lyrics accompany that.

EERIE VON: Glenn wanted the band to be his life. And the other
guys—their dad worked in a machine shop. One day he said to
them, "Well you have to run the family business. I'm retiring."
So they couldn't go on tour very often. They could do a show
but they'd have to fly there and then fly back to be at work,
and at that point they might as well have just played for free.

GLENN DANZIG: The Misfits didn't break up on good terms. I cut
myself loose because it was a dead end. They were holding me
back.

EERIE VON: Glenn eventually said, "We have one more Misfits
show in Detroit and then I'm telling the guys I'm quitting,

and when I get back I want to start this band with you." He wanted the timing of the rhythms for Samhain to be different and didn't want to play fast. And he wanted it to be weirder. We did two or three rehearsals, but I couldn't play the drums for that stuff. It was beyond me at the time. So he said, "Why don't we get Steve [Zing] from Mourning Noise to play drums, and you play bass? Anybody can play bass. Besides, you're a ham, you should be out in front." We played a little too slow for some people. They'd be like, "Play a fast song!" and Glenn would say, "You wanna hear a fast one? Okay, here's another slow one." But we had fun. We did the first show that probably anybody's ever done all covered in blood. People would show up and give us deer heads and tombstones. But what do you expect from a band covered in blood?

The progenitors of crossover formed during the conservative Reagan administration. Most were white and working-class, and saw little hope for a better future. Some were political, though not always well informed. Few had backgrounds in music, and some were street brawlers and troublemakers with criminal records. Ironically, the band most commonly cited as the era's greatest influence is Bad Brains, composed of four talented black musicians from the ghettos of Washington, DC. Bad Brains was raised on funk and R&B, and even when they cranked their amps, ramped up the tempo, and integrated fleet-fingered metal runs, their songs were fueled by messages of peace and love.

IAN MACKAYE (Fugazi, Minor Threat): From the start, the Bad Brains were really constructive. They were encouraging, they were inspirational, and their music was undeniable. They made you want to do something. And [their singer] H.R. was a visionary who made things happen. Plus, the way they played was so incredible that if you were on the same bill and didn't at least try to put on a show, you had no business having a guitar in your hand.

HENRY ROLLINS (Rollins Band, Black Flag): H.R., to me, is still the ultimate front man and a huge influence. At one point, I was at a Bad Brains show, and he went, "You are gonna be a singer," and I went, "Oh, c'mon, H.R." He went, "Nope, you're gonna be a singer and tonight you're gonna sing in the Bad Brains." He had me come up and sing along and that planted the seed in my mind that, "Okay, maybe I'll do this."

JOHN JOSEPH (Cro-Mags): If you want to know the baddest front man who ever stepped onstage, I'll say, hands down, it's H.R. He's athletic, and he can sing his ass off. I've seen him smoke an ounce of ganja and go onstage and put out more energy than anybody, hit every note perfectly and do a backflip and land precisely on the last note of "At the Movies."

SHAVO ODADJIAN (System of a Down): There probably wouldn't be a System of a Down if it wasn't for the Bad Brains. They were so influential, and not just musically. They paved the way for artists to not give a fuck and do what they want to do.

EARL HUDSON (Bad Brains): We were ahead of our time, at least beat-wise. I can say from the jump that people were really into the speed thing. It was different, and it was hitting them hard.

H.R. (Bad Brains): From the start, my spiritual advisors gave me good advice and expressed how much they wanted to see, breathe, and hear. What we wanted to do was an amplification of the inner thoughts of people's hearts and their minds so they could work on their motor skills and find themselves a little creative immortality and focus on the supernaturalistic gifts that God has offered them in the fine arts impulses.

On the East Coast, the toughest of the new breed were New Yorkers Agnostic Front and Cro-Mags, bands whose lifestyles contrasted starkly with those of their straight-edge hardcore influences, including Washington, DC's Minor Threat and Government Issue, who didn't drink, take drugs, or have sex. Cro-Mags and Agnostic Front had no such ethical concerns. They didn't just take drugs, they sold them, and never backed away from a fight.

JOHN JOSEPH: The first time I met [ex-Cro-Mags bassist] Harley [Flanagan] was in Washington, DC, when [the band Harley played drums for], the Stimulators, played with the Bad Brains at the 9:30 Club. After that Stimulators show, we hung out all night and I told Harley, "I'm originally from New York," and he said, "If you ever come back up, let's hang out, I'm on the Lower East Side."

HARLEY FLANAGAN: Our original singer, Eric Casanova, was fifteen and a real B-Boy skinhead. The dude would breakdance, do a floor spin, and then kick into some crazy hardcore shit and do a stage dive. But he had a kid at fifteen, and he tried to do the right thing, which meant leaving the band. We auditioned Roger from Agnostic Front and John Joseph ["Bloodclot" McGowan], and really, John was just a better salesman. One of the first times I hung out with John he was wearing a T-shirt that said in magic marker, "Fuck you Bitch, I'm Celibate." And he had T-Boots with bandanas around his ankles and spurs, and a chain around his waist and his head shaved, trying to look all tough. John and I were good friends. The thing is, I'm five years younger and that's quite a difference when you're fifteen. So I was probably a little bit gullible even though I *did* grow up on the streets and had a pretty rough life. John really taught me how to be a hustler. He had already been in prison and I can honestly say he led me more astray than most people did. We used to lay down in the snow with fake guns, then we'd jump up and rob weed dealers. He was already in his twenties. I'm not saying I'm any less at fault, but he took advantage of my youth.

ROGER MIRET: [Vocalist] Vinnie [Stigma] and I have been

together longer than most people in marriages—thirty years, at least. We've always got along, but he's a different creature than I am; Vinnie's very laid back and just goes with the flow, and I've always been more outgoing. They started with another singer, [John Watson] for a few months, but once I got in there, Agnostic Front became more established. *I* started doing all the records, put the band on the road. I'm just more motivated than he is. And he's very grateful for me being who I am because I gave him his career. And at the same time, I am very grateful that he is who he is. He's like my Eddie—like [the zombie mascot] in Iron Maiden. People love him.

HARLEY FLANAGAN: We were street punks, selling weed on the Lower East Side. When we weren't working on the band, we'd shoplift our food. Sometimes friends who worked at restaurants would feed us out the back door. Otherwise, we wouldn't eat. So there was a certain realness to our music that didn't come from practicing in your parents' garage. We lived in squats with no electricity and we toured with a pocket full of quarters and a map to get from city to city.

ROGER MIRET: Back in the days when we did the *United Blood* EP [in 1983], everyone was doing acid and angel dust. But we didn't have any money, so we used to rob drug dealers. Me and [drummer Raymond] Raybeez [Barbieri] had big meat hooks and one of us had a gun. We'd sneak up and rob these machine gun toting dealers because those guys had the best angel dust. When you put a meat hook to somebody's throat, they forget they're holding a machine gun. We'd play shows and these same drug dealers would be dancing to the band after we robbed them because they liked the music and they didn't know it was us.

JOHN JOSEPH: The vibe in Tompkins Square park, [where we hung out, was one of] drugs and guns. It became a daily occurrence to find people either overdosed or murdered, but everyone took it in stride—just life in the city, y'know? I mean, I was *raised* on the streets when it was really fucking dangerous. The band was an outlet to express what I was feeling from being on the streets, and it was cool because we had this spiritual message about looking for meaning in life. But we were unlike bands who delivered their message with a flower. Cro-Mags delivered it with a baseball bat.

HARLEY FLANAGAN: We used to surf on the hoods of cars, tripping our faces off. We used to get in fights all the time. But honestly, John was just a little bit less fucked up than everybody else. John just didn't get in fights. He's good at putting on a big show. Like, "What? Yo! I'll fuck you up." He does that ghetto-ass bullshit—talks a lot of shit and everyone panics and nobody wants to be the one to step up. But I don't remember him being in more than a couple fights in the thirty years I've known him. I remember my high score though. I put nineteen motherfuckers in the ICU in one night. I was a fuckin' hooligan. But that all started because I was a target in my neighborhood. Once I started fighting back I got respect.

JOHN JOSEPH: One time me and Harley went to see the Bad Brains at L'Amour and all these metal dudes were there, and one of them punched Harley. Me and Harley fucking fought eight of these dudes and fucked them up. See, the metal dudes didn't know how to get down in the pit. They didn't understand moshing was like an art form. You had people creepy-crawling, coming within six inches of each other but never smashing into each other. The metal motherfuckers didn't understand that, and they'd just be like, "Oh shit, he bumped into me, let me run up and punch him in the back of the head," and next thing you know they'd get the shit beat out of them. Then the next week they'd show up with a fucking shaved head.

HARLEY FLANAGAN: On Avenue A [in New York City], there was a private club called A7, where we all hung out and played. Imagine a small room full of insane people who have angel dust, bags of glue, and 40-ounce bottles of alcohol and you'll see a little bit of what it was like. I was always drinkin' there because having a 40-ounce bottle in your hand meant that not only did you have a buzz on, but you were armed. If anybody fucking said shit, you could smack them in the head with the bottle.

ROGER MIRET: One day, Raybeez was tripping on angel dust and he tried to commit suicide by the East River. He had a gun and he pulled it out and started yelling that he was gonna kill himself. All of us being on angel dust didn't help diffuse the situation, but I managed to get the gun away from him. We had to kick him out of the band after that because he was too unstable. But fuck, man. We used to get so high on angel dust and sometimes we'd get in our old bass player, Rob Kabula's, car and see how many red lights we could get through before we hit another car. Then, after the accident, we'd take off. The Lower East Side was our city, our town. Whatever we did went.

MIKE DEAN (Corrosion of Conformity): Agnostic Front were very good and very tight, but there was always an aura of violence. It gets good marks on the authenticity level. They're not pretending to be anything they weren't. But if I'm thinking, "Do I want my sixteen-year-old going out and running with these dudes, basically marauding and getting into fights and fucking people up?" Hell no, I wouldn't. That's some real street shit and not something I want to be involved in.

ROGER MIRET: We didn't wise up for a long time. Our music was political, but we were doing acid the whole first tour and then we'd go into a military recruiting center and try to join: Army, Navy, whatever. We never got called on it. I think the recruiting people thought it was entertaining. When we were on the road, we'd just pull over randomly and shoot guns at the farm animals on the highways or shoot at a train as it went by. One time going into New Jersey I had a bunch of ammunition in my bag, and cops pulled us over and decided to search the whole band and fortunately, they searched through every bag but mine.

One of the biggest internal schisms within the crossover scene took place between Cro-Mags bassist and founder Harley Flanagan and vocalist John Joseph. Both insist they started as friends. But a gulf erupted when Joseph left the band after they were signed and recorded 1986's legendary *The Age of Quarrel*, an album that brimmed with the speed of Motörhead and the attitude of the Sex Pistols. Unable to coexist, Joseph and Flanagan bounced in and out between lengthy hiatuses. Then, in 2003, Joseph re-formed the group without Flanagan, who was furious at Joseph both for using the name Cro-Mags and for making disparaging comments about him in his 2007 book, *The Evolution of a Cro-Magnon*. Ironically, Joseph and Flanagan once both adopted the ideals in the *Bhagavad Gita* in a quest for inner peace, and the Cro-Mags are widely regarded as the first major Krishna-core band. The Krishna tag made for a great marketing hook, but it wasn't one the Cro-Mags fully embraced. Even as they preached enlightenment, they smoked bales of weed and continued to bust heads.

JOHN JOSEPH: I once got beat up by six guys. I had beaten up one of them, and then they came back in Cadillacs with baseball bats and took me out. To be honest, I got my ass kicked lots. I called a gigantic black guy the N-word one time and he beat me so bad I had a black eye for two weeks. But eventually, I matured and grew spiritually because I wanted to be a better person.

HARLEY FLANAGAN: John came on all spiritual, but there were times when I'd be fucking up people, and he'd be going through their pockets saying, "Give up your shit or my man's gonna fuck you up." When John first got into the Krishna consciousness, people on the scene totally made fun of him. One time at one of our illegal basement crash pads, Apt. X on Norfolk Street, everybody was high on angel dust and they burned all his books and pamphlets and he threw a fit and threatened to kick everyone's ass. And everyone's giggling. But me and some of our roadies wound up kicking the piss out of a few people and putting them really close to death.

JOHN JOSEPH: Shit got out of hand when Harley got into this whole skinhead gay-bashing thing because some gay dudes took out a contract to get him fucked up. I got in a fight with those guys, but then we became friends, so I was able to squash that whole thing. Then I was like, "Yo, Harley, concentrate on the music, that's what your thing in life is. It's not about running around like an idiot all the time and kicking people's asses."

HARLEY FLANAGAN: Man, John tries to demonize me by blowing up some ill, dumb shit, when the fact is Allen Ginsberg was one of my mom's best friends and I grew up around Allen. I knew plenty of homos growing up. I didn't beat *them* up. I got in way more fights with the local Puerto Ricans, drunk yuppies, and bridge-and-tunnel motherfuckers. I'm not homophobic, and I could fuckin' play you tapes of the Cro-Mags playing at CBGB where John was on a complete anti-homo rant between every song. I've had singers and managers who were gay, and I've had friends that were gay. It's not something I'm really concerned about. The thing is, when I was a kid on the streets a lot of the people that were out at that hour were freaks and pervs. You're fifteen and you got motherfuckers trying to take advantage of you sexually. They'd offer you drugs, get you to their house, feed you, hook you up. So what are you going to do? You're gonna rob the motherfucker. Okay, that ain't right or politically correct, but is that less correct than some pedophile trying to pick up some homeless kid who ain't got nowhere else to be?

The schism between Joseph and Flanagan continues to this day. During a celebration of the legendary club CBGB in summer 2012, Joseph was arrested after a violent conflict.

NEW YORK DAILY NEWS (July 7, 2012): A former member of the Cro-Mags slashed two current members of the band as they were set to take the stage in Manhattan, police sources said. The show at Webster Hall, part of the CBGB Festival, was canceled and two members of the band were taken to Bellevue Hospital. One was treated for a bite mark and a cut to the face and the other for cuts to his arm and stomach, the sources said. The attacker was also taken to Bellevue Hospital to be treated for a broken leg, according to police sources. Harley Flanagan, a founding member of the New York band who has a history of strained relations with newer members, is believed to be the attacker.

HARLEY FLANAGAN: I, being the sentimental fool that I am, thought that if I actually saw John face to face and got to speak to him that maybe it would rekindle some of that friendship that we had. [I was invited backstage to speak to John, but instead of being greeted warmly, I was attacked.] I was getting the shit beat out of me; it was like an old-fashioned biker beat down. So what I did was defend my life.

JOHN JOSEPH: Harley's been watching too many sci-fi movies. First of all, Harley was *not* invited to the show. He was given a CBGBs laminate to attend another event, then used it to sneak into the show. He just wanted to come on the stage during the show and do something to gain press—well, he got his press, all right. We were onstage about to go on; he was asked to come into the dressing room. When Harley was grabbed to be searched for weapons, the fight ensued. He pulled a knife and began stabbing people. When the security finally arrived, he wouldn't drop the knife and they banged him up.

Californian crossover may not have been as blatantly violent as the East Coast scene, but the more urban bands came of age in an era of gun-toting gangs like the Crips and Bloods. In Venice, California, crossover pioneers Suicidal Tendencies became the go-to group for metal-loving gangsters of all stripes. While the band members claim they weren't in a gang, they sure looked the part—and they didn't discourage violence at their shows. There was, however, more to Suicidal Tendencies than blue bandanas, flipped-up baseball caps, and an open invitation to mayhem. Their self-titled 1983 album is a smarmy, sarcastic hardcore classic, featuring the single "Institutionalized," which was included in the 1984 cult film *Repo Man*. That same year, the band boosted its metal cred with the addition of guitar shredder Rocky George, who remained with the band for eleven years and whose riffing style was often imitated. As lynchpins of LA crossover, Suicidal was watched closely by the police and feared by other, less well-armed bands.

MIKE MUIR (Suicidal Tendencies): We've always been the outsiders. There are certain people that *try* to be outsiders. We never did. We just *were* outside. We realized that, and everywhere we went there were people watching us warily. Even when we were in a room, the people there were afraid we were going to trash the place. You could see the way they were talking, and then when we came in they talked differently.

MIKE CLARK: From the start, the status quo were scared to death by our lyrical content. And we had a certain style of dress where we come from, which is Venice Beach, California. All the skateboarders, surfers—we call 'em *eses* or *vatos*—the Mexican gangsters—we all dressed the same. We wore khakis or blue jeans, Pendleton button down shirts and bandanas, and these shoes called Rhinos. We were getting arrested, literally, a few times a week, just because of the way we looked.

MIKE MUIR: All these people told us we needed the proper "etiquette" for the massive punk rock goal of being an individual. I always loved that shit—individuality. Their definition of individuality was looking like *they* do, having the same haircut, thinking the same way, and then, you become an individual. I always thought that was a little strange. I'm not too smart, but somehow that concept went right over my head.

KATON W. DE PENA: Suicidal Tendencies had their own record label and they wanted to sign us. The only reason we didn't sign with them was we didn't like the gang element of their music. I love Mike Muir, and Rocky George is one of the most underrated guitar players. We got along with those guys beautifully, but Hirax is all about bringing people together, not dividing them. Suicidal had such a gang mentality following their music that it just wasn't the right fit.

The two biggest crossover bands outside of New York and Los Angeles were Dirty Rotten Imbeciles (D.R.I.), which formed in Houston, Texas, before moving to San Francisco, and Corrosion of Conformity (C.O.C.), which hailed from North Carolina and released three slabs of fierce, powerful crossover before transforming into a Southern rock–influenced doom metal band. Since they came from scenes far removed from the major crossover action, both adopted a strong DIY mentality. The major problem with doing it yourself, as they discovered, is that you quickly run out of money, gasoline, and food.

KURT BRECHT: We started the band in 1982 and created our own record company, Dirty Rotten Records, just to put out our own first seven-inch [the twenty-two-song *Dirty Rotten EP*]. The mosh logo for the label came from a project my brother [and original drummer] Eric and I did when we were both in commercial art school. We had to do a project called "signage," where we made three or four signs using different logos. One of his was "No Moshing." It originally had the "anti" line through it, and the guy [on the sign] had a Mohawk. But we decided the logo would be good for Dirty Rotten Records, so we took the "anti" sign and the Mohawk off.

MIKE DEAN: We got together in 1982. The name Corrosion of Conformity was our response to the conformity within this scene—this milieu that was supposed to be anticonformist. It immediately turns out that it's an alternate conformity. We wanted to be semipolitical as well. Music-wise, we liked the Necros, SS Decontrol and Void as much as Motörhead and Black Sabbath. We were totally DIY at first. We put out our first album [*Eye for an Eye*] ourselves [in 1984] because it was the only way we could release it. We got a really good artist, Errol Englebrecht, to do our logo [which was used in the cover art]. I think he got a pittance for drawing that and is probably pretty irate about that to this day. But it's been great for us in a corporate way, ironically, because it's been good for merch.

KATON W. De PENA: C.O.C. was one of those bands that released their own records and then finally got a deal. That was really inspiring. A lot of those bands, including D.R.I., would tour most of the year on next to nothing. What was different about the crossover bands and a lot of the metal bands was that they really did do it DIY. They were booking their own tours, surviving on the road, selling their own merchandise, screening their own T-shirts, pressing their own vinyl. Those bands taught a lot of other bands how to run their own business.

KURT BRECHT: We played one show where we asked everybody to bring a can of food for us so we'd have something extra to eat. We toured for years before we found out that you could ask for food at the venue—that you could tell them in advance that you wanted a pizza or a deli tray. G.B.H. were the first ones to tell us that. They were like, "Yeah, all you do is give them a rider, tell them you want beer and food and water, and they'll have it all for you when you get there."

REED MULLIN (C.O.C.): Since we were in North Carolina, which is the textile capital of the world, we could buy T-shirts and print them for cheap. We'd sell them for $5 to $10 a piece. We financed our road gigs that way—that and stolen credit card numbers we got from different people. We'd also sell sperm, blood plasma, and hair when we were out of cash. One wig shop gave us $45 for our discarded hair. But I found out, much to my chagrin, that I have a pointy head like a golden retriever. And, of course, we'd stay with anyone we could when we were on tour because we couldn't afford hotels. Once a dog took a big dump beside my head while I was sleeping and I woke up to the smell of dog shit. That's when you wish you had slept in the van in a parking lot, which we also did a lot.

KURT BRECHT: We had to donate blood plasma on tour and get, like, $7 each, which was usually enough to get us to the next city. The problem is you can only do it a certain amount of times before you run out.

MIKE MUIR: I have all these old punk fanzines from when the first record [*Suicidal Tendencies*] came out [in 1983] and they all said we suck, [that] we're metal. Punk rockers had a real hard time when we came out because we didn't dress the way they did. We had [guitar] leads. We broke a lot of the punk rock rules.

ROGER MIRET: A lot of metal kids that got into Suicidal branched out and discovered bands like us, Cro-Mags, D.R.I., and Corrosion [of Conformity]. We worked really hard to spread the word because it was all still very underground.

MIKE DEAN: We could play really fast like Motörhead, but also slow like Black Sabbath. The timing was good because other bands were doing the same thing at the same time. SSD put out *How We Rock* [in 1984], and Black Flag were playing slower and sludgier as well.

REED MULLIN: We played with Slayer in 1984 on their very
first tour. They were cruising around in [drummer] Dave
Lombardo's Trans-Am and a U-Haul truck. They were on
the *Haunting the Chapel* EP tour and we played with them in
Baltimore. It was the first time they ever saw us, and they dug
us. After the show, they said they were gonna get us a record
deal. Two days later, we got our very first record label deal
[with Metal Blade offshoot Death Records], which we glee-
fully signed—probably prematurely.

MIKE DEAN: It was good for us even though we didn't see any
money from it. I mean, businesswise, it was a bad move. We
were young and dumb and signed the worst thing ever, because the lawyer we paid assumed that was the *best* we could
do. But I think it was ultimately positive because it got us
known on the West Coast. We had a really good experience
playing all those shows in Los Angeles with Slayer.

KURT BRECHT: When *Dealing With It* came out in 1985, we had
already started mixing slower songs into our set, because we
had forty songs that we played in about twenty or thirty minutes. We wanted to start letting our old, slower metal influences seep back in. This was the time the New York hardcore
bands were doing slower mosh parts, so we started incorporating that as well, and the metalheads liked it. They heard influences from bands like Exodus and Metallica and Slayer and
Anthrax coming out in our music.

SCOTT IAN: When we toured for the *Spreading the Disease* in
1986, we had a guitar tech named Arnie Ring, who was a
really small guy. He's the last dude who would ever want to
be out in a pit. We played a show in Denver and there were
kids all over the stage. At one point, Arnie ran out to grab this
kid who was stepping all over [guitarist] Danny Spitz's pedal
board and both him and this kid got tangled up and tumbled
out into the crowd. I could see Arnie stand up and there were

kids going in a big circle-pit bashing into him, and he's just getting destroyed. He looked like a pinball. The next morning everyone was waking up on the bus and Arnie's moaning and groaning and he's covered in bruises. He goes, "Oh, God, I got caught in a mosh." We thought that was the funniest thing. That's where we got the title for "Caught in a Mosh" on the *Among the Living* record.

Some crossover shows in big cities were booked at established rock clubs. But in regions where the bands weren't as popular, the gigs went down on the outskirts of town at gymnasiums, community centers, VFW halls, and rickety warehouses. Whether that exacerbated the violence at the concerts is unclear, since some shows in well-known clubs also erupted in chaos.

MIKE DEAN: We played a show in Spokane, Washington, in a disused industrial building downtown that probably should have been condemned. We were on the second floor. It's getting hazier and hazier, and the room is full. Suddenly, the fire marshal comes in and makes them take some people outside. We're still playing, and pretty soon I'm like, "That smells electrical, we've got to stop." So we stopped. Everyone leaves. It's smokier and smokier, and as we get the last of our gear down the fire escape and I'm going up to get a check from the promoter, we open the door, look up one last time—and the entire drop ceiling falls in like a firestorm. There's rafters and all this material on fire. It all just fell in, literally ten minutes after the room had been full of 350 people.

ROGER MIRET: It was a white minority thing. You'd put on this show in a full-on black ghetto in California. Someone says something to somebody outside, and next thing you know it was a full on black-against-white riot, and the whites happened to be the punks. Once this guy came up to a kid and sliced him from the bottom of his neck right across. He was going out with a friend of ours, Terry, and she comes running in. Next thing you know, a riot's happening and this guy's bleeding to death. We threw this guy in our van and drove him to the hospital. One of our good friends was a nurse and she saved his life by holding him together while we took him to the hospital.

BILLY GRAZIADEI: We played a show at the Marquee [in New York], and these dudes ran up to one of our boys and stuck this huge Rambo hunting knife into his abdomen and sliced him up the center and left him there, saying "Payback, motherfucker." That was pretty sick, and our boy was on the verge of death for weeks, but he recovered. That seemed to be a common thing. Your boys jumped me, my boys are gonna jump you. Next time you come back with bats, then knives. It just escalated.

MIKE MUIR: A lot of people, if they lived in the suburbs, their only exposure to blacks and Mexicans is on TV robbing and raping people. The first time a lot of white people saw blacks and Mexicans was at our shows, and they freaked out and assumed they were all in gangs. You'd have all the [police] units there and they could say, "Oh, we were beating people up in the show because there were gang people there."

MIKE CLARK: People don't realize that, for the most part, we were an incident-free band. It was the crowd that started the melees. We were never troublemakers. We never got into drugs. We did some beer drinking, but we never got off on being wild.

JOHN JOSEPH: Harley had some beef with Mike Muir early on. They beat Harley up, and then when [Suicidal] came here [our guys] beat [Mike] up. The shit all got settled. Then, years later I'm walking Venice Beach and twenty motherfuckers surround me. One of 'em shouted, "You, you're in the Cro-Mags," and they were ready to do some fuckin' damage. I went, "Yeah, but I'm not the one who had the fuckin' problem. That's been squashed for years." They seemed to accept that. I mean, shit, [ex-Suicidal Tendencies] guitarist Rocky George *played* in the Cro-Mags.

MIKE CLARK: I think the Harley and Mike thing was probably the first East Coast/West Coast rivalry. I don't know what started the situation, but one time when we were leaving town, Cro-Mags dudes were chasing the bus, shooting at it and throwing bottles. I think Louiche [Mayorga], who was our bass player at the time, got into an argument with one of their members, and then that escalated. But we have no problems with them now.

Of all the rock clubs around the country that promoted crossover, the venue that became synonymous with the movement was New York City's legendary CBGB, which had spawned the punk and No Wave scenes years earlier. By 1983 the club had established a Sunday afternoon matinee that featured a lineup of hardcore bands. The matinees were a ritual until the shows became too violent and club owner Hilly Kristal canceled the series. Before the good times came to an end, many bands released concert albums or DVDs called *Live at CBGB*, including Bad Brains, Agnostic Front, D.R.I., and Cro-Mags.

ROGER MIRET: All these bands like Anthrax and Metallica would come and see us at CBGB. It was like the welcoming home of all these bands, and I think meeting each other and seeing each other's bands really cemented the crossover scene. [Our second album,] *Cause for Alarm*, which came out in 1986, is a landmark crossover record for us. I don't remember sitting down and saying we have to make this metal, it was just what was happening. We were rehearsing in the same room with Carnivore and Biohazard, and we had the same management as Carnivore, Crumbsuckers, Whiplash, and King Diamond. We all watched each other rehearse and went to each other's shows and hung out. We didn't know we were influencing each other, we just were.

PETER STEELE: [Carnivore's second album, 1987's] *Retaliation* was extremely influenced by my discovery of hardcore music at CBGB in '85 and '86, which instantaneously I was attracted to. What I strived to do was create an album that was half Black Sabbath and half Cro-Mags, Agnostic Front, Murphy's Law, Sheer Terror, Black Flag, stuff like that. I loved the heaviness, the slowness, the dirge of Sabbath. But at the same time, going to CBGB on Sundays for the matinee, there was so much unbelievable energy in there. It didn't even matter if bands were not in tune.

SCOTT IAN: I used to go to the CBGB hardcore matinees and that got me totally into Agnostic Front, C.O.C., and D.R.I. You'd have all these hardcore and metal kids coming together to see these bands and there were definitely fights, but at the same time you felt this sense of community.

Bands like Agnostic Front and Suicidal Tendencies may have been a gateway to metal for hardcore fans, but it was the thrash band Anthrax that did more than any other metal band to connect metal kids to crossover. Their hardcore metal side project, Stormtroopers of Death (S.O.D.)—which featured guitarist Scott Ian, drummer Charlie Benante, ex-Anthrax bassist Dan Lilker (Nuclear Assault, Brutal Truth), and vocalist Billy Milano (M.O.D.)—recorded the legendary 1985 album *Speak English or Die*, which was brutally fast but loaded with tight, metal riffs and slow, crushing breakdowns. The politically incorrect, tongue-in-cheek lyrics only added to the defiant quality of the project. Cro-Mags' debut, *Age of Quarrel*, shared the same rebellious spirit, but the lyrics of songs like "Street Justice" and "Hard Times" were instead rooted in the musicians' reality.

SCOTT IAN: [S.O.D.] was a sociological experiment. I used to read *Maximum Rock and Roll*, and you always heard people like Jello Biafra (Dead Kennedys) picking on the New York scene and calling it fascist. We figured, "Okay, like the Bonnie Raitt song says, let's give them something to talk about." So we had a little fun and went over the top by saying shit that we didn't really mean because we thought it would be funny to see their reactions. It was really a one-joke thing and it blew up. But being the guy that created it, I never wanted it to be a real band. I was already in a real band. And eventually, S.O.D. became everything I didn't want it to be. We were saying, "Speak English or Die" and "Fuck the Middle East" and a lot of people misinterpreted it and really thought we held those views, which we certainly didn't.

DAN LILKER: With S.O.D. there was the concept to mesh hard-core and metal. It was hardly original. D.R.I., C.O.C., and Suicidal were just a few of the bands doing it already. But we were the first band coming from the metal side to do it, which is why it got all the recognition and people were like, "Holy shit! Never heard this before." If you look at [my next band], Nuclear Assault, it was more long-lasting, and it took the music more seriously. We were like Slayer one second and Minor Threat the next, with all this other stuff mixed in.

JOHN JOSEPH: At the time the crossover thing started exploding, we never really rehearsed, and I was like, "If we're going to do this, let's do it full on, and practice all the time." So that's what happened. I started booking shows and we started blowing up. I liked metal, but I couldn't relate to the shit they were singing about. I was singing about what I knew. And that's why you can feel every groove of *The Age of Quarrel*.

HARLEY FLANAGAN: *The Age of Quarrel* sucked. Our [1984] demo, [later released as *Before the Quarrel*] was better and I never thought we captured our live performance in the studio, even on the next album, [1989's] *Best Wishes*, which was even more metal. People base their whole perception of Cro-Mags on

The Age of Quarrel, and we had a lot of bad blood recording
that. I blew out my bass amp and I had to play through the
board without effects on my bass, and it sounded like dog shit.
The manager, [Chris Williamson], said, "Don't worry about
it. We'll do the bass tracks over through an amp." I played
my runs like shit and I did a lot of them in the wrong places.
I didn't care because I thought I was gonna get to do it over.
Of course, I never did. Also, when we were recording, John
had a cold and that was the sound that he became legendary
for, but it was really him at his *worst.* And during that session,
a friend of mine got in a fight with these metalheads, supposedly because they said the Cro-Mags sucked and they liked
Anthrax. One of the metal guys tried to gouge my friend's
eyes out, so my friend bit the dude's thumb off, which got spit
out into the sewer, so he never found it. Then, this one hardcore dude outside grabbed what he thought was a metalhead
and started kicking him in the face, holding him by his leather
jacket—and then he realized it was a chick. We'd go from
recording back to our life on the streets, and then go back in
and try to record again. I guess we captured the intensity of
our lives in those songs, but the highlight definitely wasn't our
performances.

GENE HOGLAN: There was so much violence before the crossover
scene blew up. Once, Dark Angel played an all-day hardcore
festival in San Diego with Dr. Know and Ill Repute. I was
always goading our singer, Don Doty, into calling the audience names and getting in their faces. Before that show Don
came to me and said, "Dude, do you realize we are really
outnumbered here. Do you want me to do that shit onstage?" I
was like, "Yeah, it'll be awesome." So here's a bunch of longhairs yelling at a bunch of skinheads, "You fuckin' suck. You're
a bunch of fucking assholes." They put up with it for about a
song and a half, and then somebody got kicked in the face and
all hell broke loose. We were brawling onstage with a crowd
full of angry punk rockers. It was 10 longhairs against 150

pissed-off punks. I refer to this incident as "the night Gene's balls blew up" because I jumped off the stage to help my drum tech, who was being absorbed into this crowd of punks, and this guy grabs me and knees me in the nuts as soon as I got offstage. Usually when that happens you go down. But I had so much adrenaline going, I just punched his fucking face off. I didn't even notice my balls were swollen like grapefruits until after the cops came. Thank God they did or who knows what would have happened.

MIKE CLARK: We played the Whisky [a Go Go] in 1987 with Fuhrer and Black Flag, and there was a police riot on Sunset Strip in front of the venue. The guys from the Rainbow and the Roxy came down and they were backing the cops. There were a lot of built-up hostilities on both ends and there was a lot of bloodshed. That led to a seven-year ban of Suicidal playing Los Angeles, which really sucked. The closest we could play before 1994 was Ventura, San Diego, or Orange County.

MIKE DEAN: We never liked violence and we didn't like skinheads. On the sleeve of 1987's *Technocracy*, [drummer] Reed [Mullin] wrote something like, "The best thing about skinheads is that they're biodegradable." We got death threats for that. In Miami, at this place beside the Jackie Gleason Theater, we had all four of our tires slit and our van windows broken by skinheads while we were inside playing the show. But I guess the rest of the skinhead community got drunk and forgot about wanting to kill us. Somehow we dodged a bullet on that one.

Hardcore diehards will point to the Bad Brains' 1982 energetic, positive, and aggressive self-titled album (originally only available on cassette) as their breakthrough moment, but it wasn't until 1986's *I Against I* that the band was embraced by headbangers, thanks to the crisper, crunchier riffs of guitarist Dr. Know and the slicker, brighter production of Ron St. Germain, which gave the band a more metallic tone that served as a major influence for Living Colour, Faith No More, System of a Down, and countless others.

DARRYL JENIFER (Bad Brains): We always tried to be progressive. It's not something we contrived. So by the mid-eighties we gained a certain amount of popularity and we started to think more. We were keeping it moving. So the riffs became more metal because we were really trying to bring more funk and bounce to the rock.

DR. KNOW (Bad Brains): The metal thing was popular at that point in time and we were all somewhat influenced by that.

H.R.: One of the priorities is being able to teach people the new concepts firsthand—having the sisters and brothers come to the shows, see the group and also the improvements of our students and our loved ones, hear their approaches and their ideas and also their new languages. A lot of people in the early days came from Ethiopia, and they couldn't really speak English too well, and their handwriting was kind of scribbly. But now, through the years of work and its teachings, including myself, we can abide in our humble abodes and also through these concerts and have a very groovy, right-on, soul-responding communication that's just hip. Some people are not hip, they're just squares. So we're trying to avoid the squares, show them that they can take a square, turn it into an A-plus response, and get an A-plus performance.

DARRYL JENIFER: If you notice, H.R. can be a little eccentric. But he's always got his own motivations, and a lot of times he's trying to protect his brothers. He chased [legendary photographer] Annie Leibovitz off the tour bus when she was shooting us for *Esquire.* He stood up and said, "That's it. You and your people get your stuff, we got a gig. Get off the bus." And he stood there like the enforcer. The lady was pregnant. I was embarrassed. So they leave, and he goes, "I'm sorry Darryl,

I know they were bothering you and we gotta play a show tonight. The last thing you probably want is a camera in your face." A lot of times, he thinks like that. He's got different ways and deeper missions and, of course, he's weird and wacky. But there's still a lot of positive and deep insightful things that this dude possesses.

One of the most controversial New York–based crossover bands came from the bowels of Brooklyn. To some, Carnivore embraced all the political incorrectness that S.O.D. had only joked about. The group was fronted by hulking, self-deprecating bassist and vocalist Peter Steele, a sanitation worker for the New York City Department of Parks and Recreation, whose dark sense of humor was often mistaken for racism, misogyny, homophobia, and anti-Semitism.

JOSH SILVER: Peter liked to annoy people and get a reaction—[and] whenever you write a song [like] "Jesus Hitler," you're going to get some kind of response. He liked to push buttons, and humor was his coping mechanism.

KENNY HICKEY: When Carnivore played L'Amour they used to throw out . . . lamb's heads during their show because [their friend] Sal Abruscato's father worked in a meat factory. The raw meat was dripping blood and it stunk. The owners of L'Amour banned it. So Peter goes up to the mic at the next show and goes, "[L'Amour owners] Mike and George [Parente] said we can't throw out meat at this show, so we're going to throw out fifty White Castle hamburgers." Peter was Henny Youngman dressed up like Herman Munster. He was a one of a kind.

HARLEY FLANAGAN: He was one of the more talented guys to come out of the New York scene. He was a total longhair; then he showed up at CBs one day with his head shaved and combat boots on, totally skinheaded out. We all laughed about that.

KENNY HICKEY: Peter cut his hair short because he'd just filled out all these forms to try to be a cop in Nassau County. He thought he was going to give up the rock-and-roll thing and become a policeman. But of course, he started Type O Negative instead.

Once places like CBGB, L'Amour, and Ruthie's got too small for crossover shows, promoters packaged hardcore bands with major thrash acts at bigger venues. Motörhead and Venom were some of the first groups to take crossover acts on the road; generally, the response was good. Then bands from other subgenres of metal booked gigs with popular crossover acts—but with mixed results.

JOHN JOSEPH: We terrorized metalheads who would come up with attitude. We did a show with Helloween and they started erecting fake castles onstage. Our skinhead fans ate these motherfuckers alive. It was a straight Spinal Tap situation. We were getting ready to sound-check and they told us we had to set up in front of the stage. I said, "Are you fuckin' kidding?" and I started throwing kicks at the castle, trying to dismantle it. These guys started panicking. We were contracted to co-headline, so we compromised and wound up playing on their castle. It was hysterical. We went on first but it was mostly Cro-Mags fans there. So you had this band that had this real pompous rock star attitude, and after we got offstage everyone left and there was one row of metalheads in the front row and a big fucking empty club.

BILLY GRAZIADEI: Anthrax acted like they were all down with hardcore. So our manager gave them a Biohazard T-shirt, and [drummer] Charlie [Benante] said, "Oh, great. Another T-shirt I can wax my car with." When we heard that, we wanted to fuckin' kill them. Our manager said, "No, you don't fuckin' understand. They probably get fifty T-shirts a day." We were like, "We don't give a fuck. We're Biohazard. Don't disrespect us like that." Of course, years later we were all friends.

JOHN JOSEPH: We did a lot of shows with Megadeth, and if Dave Mustaine wasn't on drugs he was the nicest guy in the world. But the first time I met Dave I was helping out the Bad Brains and Dave was fucked up, and he was a complete asshole. The show was at the old Ritz in New York, and the Bad Brains were headlining and then it was Megadeth and Slayer. So Megadeth had to walk through Bad Brains' dressing room to get to their dressing room. Dave comes in talking like, "Fucking bitches, suck my fucking cock"—just being vile. And the Bad Brains had their wives and kids there eating hummus and cake and being all peaceful. So I was like, "Yo dude, can you fucking chill out with that shit. There's kids here." Dave goes, "Man, fuck you! Who the fuck are you? You're just a fucking roadie." I didn't tell him who I was, but I was thinking, "Yeah, you're going to get taught a lesson in a minute." Then when Megadeth got offstage, Dave picks up a big tub that all the beer goes in that's full of melted ice water, and he throws it in the air all over everybody in the Bad Brains dressing room. So I grabbed his fucking hair and slammed his head into the wall, and H.R. got in his face and goes, "You want fucking violence? We'll show you violence!" You do *not* want to fuck with H.R. when he's pissed off. I went, "Just give me the word and I'll deck this dude." But H.R. said, "No, we'll let him go this time." Then, sure enough, Cro-Mags are touring with Motörhead and Megadeth not long after. I was thinking, "Let's see if that motherfucker remembers me" because he was really high when he did that shit. And Dave comes in and goes, "Hey, man." He was sitting in the middle of the floor of the venue on the road cases and he says, "You want to come and smoke some bud?" So we're sitting there and he rolls up a few, and he's like, "You look really familiar—do I know you from somewhere?" And we're all like, "Nah, man. Never met you before." And Harley and our [guitarist] Doug [Holland] are cracking the fuck up. Finally I was like, "All right, I'm going to give you one hint and if you don't get it I'm never telling you." So he goes, "All right," and I say, "Remember this?

'Fuck you. You're just a fucking roadie.'" He turned white and was real apologetic.

KURT BRECHT: Even after things caught on and people started coming to shows and buying our records, we still didn't make any money. I lived in the van as long as I could, then I had to move into a tree in Golden Gate Park around the time we did *Crossover* [in 1987]. One night after we played a huge show in LA with Slayer, we drove back to San Francisco and they dropped me off in front of my tree. The reason I was in the tree was because no one could see me up there, so they couldn't fuck with me. Most of the bums slept on the ground, which is really dangerous. Anyone can come up and attack you. I would hear somebody if they were climbing up the tree.

MIKE CLARK: I noticed things were taking off big-time when we were headlining, and even more when we were on the radio. Because getting radio play back then was pretty much impossible, and then they started playing "Waking the Dead" statewide. That's when I noticed, "Okay, there's other bands like us, now," which is the best compliment you can ask for, basically.

By 1992, crossover had hit critical mass. Suicidal Tendencies' *Controlled by Hatred/Feel Like Shit . . . Déjà Vu* went gold, as did 1994's *Lights, Camera, Revolution*. And Biohazard's second album, *Urban Discipline*, eventually sold more than one million copies worldwide. The Brooklyn band was a bit of an anomaly, mixing syncopated beats, crushing metal riffs, and flailing solos with barked hip-hop-influenced vocals. But the band came from the streets and embraced the ideals and lyrical themes of hardcore, which gave them cred. Moreover, Biohazard didn't just surface out of a sea of flames and broken bottles to claim the crossover throne. The band formed in 1987 and shared stages with Cro-Mags, Carnivore, and Agnostic Front long before breaking into the mainstream.

EVAN SEINFELD (ex-Biohazard, Attika 7): When I was seventeen, I roadied for Carnivore, which was probably the single biggest influence on Biohazard because Carnivore played thrash metal, but they were somehow fused with the hardcore scene because they had the best skank parts, slow parts, and dance parts. One day I went down with Carnivore to the rehearsal studio to see Agnostic Front. They all had shaved heads, tattoos, and were more punk than Carnivore, but they were starting to play a metal style. I was totally sucked in. I thought, "Wouldn't it be great to have all of these styles in one band."

BILLY GRAZIADEI: I was playing in hardcore bands in Manhattan and I was just about to try out for a band called Breakdown when a buddy of mine said, "Oh, I know a metal dude who is looking for a guitar player. He works at Crazy Eddie's [electronics store] down the street." Back then, I was doing security at Flip, a famous punk rock/metal clothing store. So I met Evan and we bullshitted for a bit. I played some guitar for him and we decided to form a band. We got together with a drummer who wanted to bring in guitarist Bobby [Hambel]. But Bobby had gotten drunk and had gotten in a fight with a cabbie, then a bunch of other cabbies stopped and jumped him. So we had to wait for Bobby to heal before he could join us.

EVAN SEINFELD: I was a street kid from Brooklyn, but I got what Biohazard wanted to do because after I went away to college to SUNY Oneonta, my friend Ian gave me the Cro-Mags demo and it totally made sense. That, and Agnostic Front's [1984 album] *Victim of Pain* blew me away. I knew I wanted to do something that had that vibe, but mixed with Carnivore and early Black Sabbath, Judas Priest, and Iron Maiden. The rap thing wasn't contrived at all. Me and Billy were kind of shy about our vocals, so we started this rhythmic delivery because it sounded hard and you didn't have to worry about sounding too happy if you were singing. We were definitely not happy guys. We wanted our music to portray our anger, our dismay, our dissatisfaction with the world. When I heard metal, I really wanted to say fuck the world—not just fuck the world, but blow it the fuck up! Biohazard was perfect for that.

BILLY GRAZIADEI: We didn't exactly fit in anywhere. When we played with bands like Exodus and Slayer, we got the vibe that we weren't *metal* enough. Then, we would play with hardcore bands and we were *too* metal. We were outcasts. So we just did our own thing and created our own style, which eventually became popular.

JOHN JOSEPH: A lot of people hated on Biohazard when they started blowing up. But I always thought, "God bless the dudes" 'cause they were a good band. And they were good guys. You can't hate on people just 'cause they have success.

EVAN SEINFELD: As productive and successful as we were, I was so fucked up on drugs. I was really into coke. I used to smoke crack before it was known that crack was a bad thing to do—like it hadn't hit the news yet. The vibe was, "Hey, there's this new thing! It's like freebase, but it's five dollars." And I was like, "Wow, that's great, I got $20. Let's go."

BILLY GRAZIADEI: All of us were into drugs and alcohol. Evan used to deal coke, and he was doing a lot of it himself. We were young and amped up, and the violence was crazy. We once played Riverside, California, and there were these Latino white power dudes there. I was going, "Why are they *sieg heiling*? They're Mexican." So we went off on them and it erupted into a big brawl. New York shows were crazy too, because we were pretty solid in Brooklyn, but we played a lot in Manhattan. So a lot of DMS [gang] guys would come out. There was another crew in Brooklyn called BYB. It seemed like whenever we played, that was the meeting point for all the different gangs in the hardcore scene to have beef. A lot of kids used to hold razorblades in their knuckles and then when they were dancing they would just start slashing people. I'd see all these kids leave the pit with slices down their back.

EVAN SEINFELD: In England, a fight broke out with the bouncers and I punched this guy in the head and broke my fucking hand, like a boxer's break. Now I'm trying to fight with one hand. I can't even raise my other hand. We ended back in the dressing room. They emptied the club, pulled down the gates, and locked us in, and we were terrified. I thought they were going to kill us. There's twenty of these football hooligan bouncers and eight of us. All of a sudden there's a knock at the door and we hear this Irish brogue, and the guy says, "We'd like you to send out one representative." Our tour manager was a Scottish guy named Rush Duncan and he says, "I'm your manager. I'll go out." So he opens the door and we're waiting for an ambush. We got a refrigerator blocking the door and we're holding these chair legs. It's like *The Warriors*, and the head guy, the guy I broke my hand on, his head has got a big fucking giant lump, and he says, "Well, we talked it over. We think you are stand-up guys and we want to buy you some drinks." We ended up having the coolest night ever.

BILLY GRAZIADEI: We'd score heroin at night after work and party, drink beer, and cause trouble. And then the next morning you'd snort crystal meth and go to work all day. You'd do that three or four days in a row. And then you'd take three days off and call in sick because you couldn't do it anymore. I lost a lot of friends and saw people wither away. I had a friend Hal, a skinhead from the Lower East Side. He had this big heroin problem and he hung himself. It shocked me because, I was like, "You don't hang yourself. You're a junkie. You die. You OD. That's how you go out when you're a junkie." That's when I realized, "You know what? Living like this is way more dangerous than I ever imagined." At first you're like, "I'm only snorting" or "I'm only smoking." Then it's, "I'm only skin-popping, I'm not mainlining." But you end up getting to a place where you think it's the bottom, and there's always one step lower. When Hal hung himself, I said, "You know what? Making music is getting me more excited than doing dope." And we started straightening ourselves up.

EVAN SEINFELD: For a long time, everything was still all about sex, drugs, and violence. We were in Phoenix, Arizona, on tour with Sick of It All and Sheer Terror, and a brawl broke out between these kids and these skinhead guys, and some guy whips out a hammer in the pit and cracks some kid in the head. We all went out to the Winnebago and the kid comes knocking on our door, and he's got a dent in his head that looks like it goes back into the middle of his brain. It had to be six inches deep. He's like, "I don't feel so good." I'm thinking, "You don't feel so good because you're probably going to die any second." Over what? Over a rock concert. The night turned into a full-on ballroom riot. Every guy in every band was standing back to back in the club fighting these dudes. One guy from our crew had two cue balls in a woven sock and he started cracking people in the head. One of my friends had two glass beer pitchers he used as weapons, and I had a broken pool cue. It seemed like it made sense back then. We were like warriors of the wasteland. But I look back and I try to think of what we were fighting for. We had a positive message in our music and we were trying to fight ignorance. But we were all acting like thugs. So we thought, "Well, maybe we can find some positivity and use our music as a positive release to all this negative energy and let other people use it to vent their frustration, and we ended up taking this thing that started really negative and turning it around.

BILLY GRAZIADEI: Our judgment was clouded because of our lifestyles. Evan was still doing tons of coke, but then he had a heart attack [on May 31, 1988]. He thought he was gonna die. They rushed him to the hospital. After that he went through rehab and straightened out. Evan was the first to clean up his shit and I followed suit, and what kept us straight for a long time was trying to help [guitarist] Bobby [Hambel]. Well, how do you help your buddy with a drinking problem while you're sitting there holding a beer? The first time we toured with Pantera we were straight, and they thought we were the most boring band ever. But Evan wasn't going to just straighten out and be this normal guy. As soon as he was clean and sober he jumped deep into the other vices of life and got heavily into sex.

Today, Seinfeld is as notorious for his life as a porn star as he is for being a metal icon. In 2004, after doing some professional acting work, including the HBO series *Oz*, Seinfeld married pornographic actress Tera Patrick and became her manager. The couple performed in fifteen movies together, Seinfeld under the name Spyder Jonez; he has been involved in more than thirty-five in total. In September 2009 the couple divorced. Seinfeld launched his own website, RockstarPornstar.com, in March 2010, and after nearly a three-year break, Biohazard reunited with now-sober guitarist Bobby Hambel to tour and work on the follow-up to 2005's *Means to an End*. In June 2011, Biohazard announced that Seinfeld had left the band amicably. He has since become the vocalist for Attika 7, which also features celebrity motorcycle builder Rusty Coones.

EVAN SEINFELD: I was always obsessed with pussy and girls. The very first video I saw was "The Beatles at Shea Stadium." Girls were screaming and pulling their hair, and I thought, "Fuck, I want somebody to scream for me like that." When I got my first bass guitar, all of a sudden all these new girls that I didn't know before were suddenly interested in me. Playing in a metal band and going on the road is almost like being an urban land-pirate swashbuckling your way across the earth, raping and pillaging. To me a good concert was like this: there'd be a fight, I'd get laid, and the show went well.

BILLY GRAZIADEI: One time I ended up in the hotel room with two girls. We're hanging out and the girl to my left says to the girl on my right, "I can't believe we were in this same hotel last week." One of them goes, "I was with Phil," and the other says, "I was with Dime." I'm like, "Aw fuck, two friends of mine." The funny thing about that is we just did a tour with Unearth and the same thing happened to them regarding us. One girl they were with said, "I was with Evan." And the other goes, "I was with Billy."

EVAN SEINFELD: If I was in it for the money, I would've been in a commercial band. I'm a smart guy. I could've been a lawyer. For me it was about having a good time and living that rock-and-roll outlaw lifestyle. I ride choppers and Harleys, I drive hot rods, I'm tattooed. I like brutal heavy metal and fast times with easy women. And I love girls who know what they want and aren't uptight.

BILLY GRAZIADEI: Evan had "the book." Really, it was Biohazard's book, but he likes to take credit for it. The way it started was we'd get a girl to consensually show us her tits and we'd take a picture of her. At first, there were ten Polaroids on the table. And then somebody decided to put them into a photo album. The album gets bigger and bigger, and it progresses from, "Oh, shit, this girl showed her ass" to, "Oh, shit, this girl showed her landing strip for her Brazilian wax." Eventually, it turned into a full-on porno book. There were volumes and volumes of these things.

EVAN SEINFELD: I heard that Gene Simmons had a photo album of naked girls and I thought that was the coolest fucking thing ever. I thought, "This guy is documenting his role as a super-pimp." So my friend Drew Stone says, "You should take it a step further and take pictures of chicks sucking your dick." I said, "That's really funny, but how are we going to get them developed?" He goes, "We won't, we'll get a Polaroid." So we got the camera and one day I said to Drew, "When I get her back in the bus just come in with the Polaroid and I'll ask if she minds taking a picture." A lot of girls were into it, posing with my cock, and it became really funny. Then Billy and I hosted MTV's *Headbangers Ball* and we had to interview all the bands who we were on this festival tour with, including KISS and Ozzy Osbourne. After the interview, Gene says to me, "So, I heard you have a book." I was floored. I said, "I *have* a book, Gene. Actually, you inspired my book because I heard about *your* book." So Gene, who's in KISS makeup, in his full demon outfit, reaches into his shirt, under his wing, and pulls out a photo album. I'm looking at this book, and there's hundreds of pictures of naked girls. He goes, "This is just one volume from the last tour, but there's hundreds of volumes." I was impressed. Then he says, "So, can I see *your* book?" I felt it was like a meeting of the minds, and I sent one of the guys from my crew to get it. So he brings it back and Gene opens the book. It has facial cum shots and girls with my dick stretching their mouth. Gene's face was somewhere between shock, disbelief, envy, and disgust all at the same time. I'm thinking to myself, "I'm on to something here" because if you can get that kind of reaction from Gene Simmons, then porn is the new punk rock. And that's when I decided to enter the porn business.

BILLY GRAZIADEI: Once, Evan got in a fight with one of the girls he was dating. He threw a bunch of his Polaroid books out in the garbage and said, "I don't give a fuck about these girls. They mean nothing to me." After he sorted out his shit with his old lady he called one of my boys and asked him to go through his garbage and pick up the books because he threw them out just to save face with his girl, but he really wanted to keep them.

EVAN SEINFELD: We were filming the movie *Load Stories* in our bus, and between takes, two of the girls gave me a blowjob, but it wasn't on camera. And [porn veteran] Ron Jeremy, who was my idol as a kid, walks in and goes, "Wow!" I'm like, "What do you mean, 'wow'?" He goes, "Those chicks were totally sucking your dick." I'm like, "Dude, you fuck a different couple of girls every day. You're Ron Jeremy!" And he goes, "Yeah, but they fuck me because they *have* to. They fucked you because they *wanted* to. They weren't getting paid." It's definitely the most validating thing—someone wanting to have sex with you, giving themselves to you because they think you're hot or they admire you.

BILLY GRAZIADEI: One time we were on tour with Pantera, and they were having a party on the bus. There were two naked blond girls on the couch kissing and licking each other. And there were twelve people cheering them on. It was all of Biohazard, Pantera, and our tour guys. Then this girl takes a banana and starts inserting it in the other girl. I'm thinking, "This is fucking crazy." There are eighteen dudes here all screaming and yelling, and more people kept piling in the front door. Morally, I thought this was kind of fucked. All of a sudden, Evan stopped and went, "Hold on. Everybody stop. Chill the fuck out," 'cause guys were reaching over and grabbing the girls' breasts and it was getting a little out of hand. As soon as he said that, I was like, "Fuck yeah, man. Stand up for these girls. Tell these guys they're being disrespectful and they should be cool." Then all of a sudden he reached down, head first, and eats the banana out of the girl's crotch. And I was like, "Ah, man. All decadence. Rock and roll."

EVAN SEINFELD: My signature trademark is something I invented in Biohazard called the "dickfold." It looks a little humiliating, but it's done in good sport. And now, every time I shoot a porn scene, after I do my patented facial cum shot, I blindfold the girls with my cock by pulling my dick across their eyes and holding their head tight with it. That's the "dickfold."

By 1995, crossover had run its course. Biohazard had transformed the genre from a counterculture vehicle for rage and non-conformity into a mainstream entity that embraced the traditional hedonism and debauchery of rock and roll. Cro-Mags broke up for an extended period after the prophetic 1993 debacle *Near-Death Experience*. Suicidal was on hiatus, and when it returned in 1997 it was without guitarist Rocky George and bassist Robert Trujillo (Metallica). And Corrosion of Conformity slowed down and embraced doom metal. The last gasp came when Bad Brains, the group that had sparked much of the excitement and revolutionary activity that spawned crossover, began to self-destruct. Vocalist H.R. struggled with the decision whether to continue with Bad Brains or pursue a reggae career. Then, in 1990, after the fierce and metallic *Quickness*, H.R. abruptly left the band and was replaced, first by ex–Faith No More vocalist Chuck Mosley and then, in 1991, by Israel Joseph I. The following year, Jenifer convinced H.R. and drummer Earl Hudson to return to the Brains. The band recorded its first album, *God of Love*, for Madonna's record company, Maverick, with which the band had reportedly signed a lucrative deal. But H.R. was in no mental condition to be back on the road. He was still ambivalent about playing hardcore and metal, and in Lawrence, Kansas, during an opening slot for the Beastie Boys on the *Ill Communication* tour, he self-destructed, clubbing two fans with the mic stand in the middle of the set. Police arrived, closed down the show, and arrested H.R. for battery. One fan required five staples to repair his fractured skull.

DARRYL JENIFER: There were skinheads at that show with suspenders, boots, sideburns. He thought those skinheads were out to get us. Basically, a kid spit on him in the spirit of punk, and H.R. smacked the kid with the mic stand and told us, "Get 'em, soldiers." He thought we had to battle the skinheads that night. Turns out the skinheads were our biggest fans. They weren't Nazi skinheads. It was a big confusion and what went down was horrible. I don't even think the people who got hit with the mic were the people that were spitting. When

I saw that shit, I just put my bass down and left. I went out the back door of the club and walked down the alley like I was a bystander. The police came and it was a mess.

H.R.: It wasn't really catastrophic, but a momentary absence of the objectives and the reward that one receives once they are able to tune in with what is happening in the matter of expansion of the soul, rebuilding the nation, and learning to love I and I. It was a temporary expression of communication in the nation [that] had been withheld for natural purposes, being that some of our artists visiting were still learning how to walk at that time. They're a lot more mature now, a lot more responsible, and can receive the information not from secondhand individuals or a subculture, but from someone who knows what's going on and has proven time and time again that we can survive.

DARRYL JENIFER: Whenever we got to that point when it looked like we were gonna get big, something would occur that would seemingly look like H.R. was behind it. He would walk out or do something crazy. People wanna say, "H.R. fucked you all up." But when you look at the Bad Brains as a cosmic musical force, it's the great spirit's work. That's why Living Colour can't do what we're doing right now. The mild attention that we're getting for being who we are, the respect that we get, the respect our records get, a lot of bands don't have that. Maybe they have platinum plaques, but do they have lasting significance?

7

FAR BEYOND DRIVEN: THRASH REVISITED AND REVISED, 1987–2004

Arlington, Texas, doesn't seem a likely spawning ground for one of the most important bands in the history of metal. And in the mid-eighties, when Pantera were teasing their hair, wearing spandex, and putting out LPs that sounded like a hybrid of Van Halen and Mötley Crüe, the band was barely on the radar outside of Dallas. Then they discovered thrash metal, hooked up with a new young singer from New Orleans named Philip Anselmo, and transformed into the heroes of the second generation of thrash. While other thrashers in the nineties (with the exception of Slayer) were either breaking up or becoming slower, grungier, and more alternative, the Cowboys from Hell stuck to their guns, holding the metal torch aloft and inspiring a new generation of underground bands that would later dominate the metalcore scene. Even traditional metal heroes like Rob Halford and art-metal pioneers such as Rob Zombie were moved by Pantera's energy.

ROB HALFORD: Pantera changed the playing field for a lot of people. They were so heavy and aggressive, and their songs had amazing melodies. And there was this unbelievable guitarist who was in your face and played with incredible skill.

JAMEY JASTA (Hatebreed, Kingdom of Sorrow, Jasta 14, ex–MTV's *Headbangers Ball* **host):** They were *so* heavy, and they still got so big. You could always hear Pantera on mainstream radio. They'd play "This Love" and "Cemetery Gates" on big rock stations, and I remember thinking, "Damn, that's *huge* for metal."

SCOTT IAN: At the top of their game, no one could touch Pantera. Dime was the sickest guitar player and Vinnie and Rex lay down these grooves that were unreal. With Phil screaming overtop and really venting all his poisons, they were, like, the greatest band ever.

Vinnie Paul Abbott and his brother Darrell had music in their blood. Their father, Jerry, was an established country and blues producer who owned his own studio, Pantego. Every step of the way, he was instrumental in teaching his sons the ropes and encouraging them to pursue a career in music.

DIMEBAG DARRELL: My brother Vinnie came home from school one day carrying a tuba, and my dad said, "Son, take that thing back. Play the drums or do something that's gonna make you some cash." When I was about ten years old, I used to go down to my dad's studio as much as I could. I was lucky enough to see guys like Bugs Henderson, Jimmy Wallace—all these great Texas blues players.

VINNIE PAUL ABBOTT: We have the same story as the Van Halen brothers. I started on drums and Dime started on drums a couple weeks afterwards. I got better than him, so he asked my dad to give him a guitar. I used to walk by his room and see him with his Ace Frehley makeup on standing in front of the mirror holding the guitar. I said, "Are you ever gonna learn to play that thing?" I never thought he would. One day he comes into my room and says, "Are you ready to jam?" He plugs in and starts playing "Smoke on the Water." We played it for five or six hours, and we were hooked forever.

TERRY GLAZE (Lord Tracy, ex-Pantera): We all went to Bowie High School in Arlington, Texas. In eleventh grade my best friend [bassist] Tommy Bradford and I had a band. We wanted Vince to join because he played in the high school band and was awesome. Vince was like, "Me and my brother are a package deal." Darrell was in middle school, and we said, "We'll take your little brother, who's *not* that good a guitar player, but you have to take our singer [Donnie Hart], who owns a PA." So the five of us started a band.

REX BROWN (Pantera): When I first met Darrell he must have been fourteen. Me and Vinnie were in high school and Darrell could barely hit a bar chord [*laughs*]. But he learned fast. He was a natural.

DIMEBAG DARRELL: When I was thirteen that's all I gave a fuck about. I skipped school and sat in my room and worked my fuckin' ass off. That's all I did for five years. My dad showed me some scales. Musicians in his studio would show me the hot lick of the day, then I'd go home and turn it into my own thing. I'd try to play something, and make a mistake, and hear some other note come into play. Then I'd start moving it around and find the beauty of it.

VINNIE PAUL: Once he learned a little, his desire never stopped. A lot of people start playing to chase chicks or do dope. For us it was always about the music and the musicianship. Before long, here he is fifteen years old, and instead of *imagining* he could play "Eruption" by Eddie Van Halen, he's playing it, and playing it good.

DIMEBAG DARRELL: I didn't get no pussy. I didn't drink no booze. I didn't do *nothin'* until I was seventeen. I tried a guitar lesson one time and never went back for the second. I figured out I was on my own road.

TERRY GLAZE: Darrell went in his room and woodshedded when he was sixteen, and about six months later, he came out fully evolved. He started doing [guitar store] guitar contests and won the first two. It wasn't even close. After the second one, he wasn't allowed to enter anymore. He became a judge as a teenager.

REX BROWN: Vince calls me and goes, "Dude, you gotta come over and check out my brother." So I go and suddenly, there's this total virtuoso. He knew all of Randy Rhoads's licks. He won so many guitars and Marshall stacks in these contests— hands down.

DIMEBAG DARRELL: It would sound egotistical to say I'm a natural guitarist, but I'm gonna have to say it [*laughs*]. I know for a damn fact, dude. It just came too quick. Three months and it was there. I knew that was my calling.

TERRY GLAZE: Pretty early on, we were called Pantera, and we had a picture of a cat and there was a race car [in the logo]. [The Abbotts'] dad [Jerry] was our manager, and we'd drive out to Abilene and play behind chicken screens like in *The Blues Brothers*. Their dad got us a Suburban, and we each made $150 a week. We all lived at home and put the money back into gear.

JERRY ABBOTT (Dime's and Vinnie's father, manager, producer): I was *always* a Pantera fan. I would look anybody dead in the eye and say for the first five years of that band I was the fifth member. When they were kids, I helped them restructure their songs: first verse, chorus, instrumental bridge, chorus. They did some things that were off the wall and needed to be honed.

DIMEBAG DARRELL: We started getting tired of doing covers, so we began writing more originals. We did our first record, [*Metal Magic*], in 1983, and it didn't sound anything like we ended up being, but we were just kids.

TERRY GLAZE: I played guitar on *Metal Magic*, but after that, Darrell was getting better at a crazy rate. From then on, he played all the guitars. Going into our senior year, Tommy decided he wanted to be the drum major for the high school band, so he bowed out of Pantera and we got Rex Brown. He went to the high school closest to us. He was a bad boy and he partied. By that time, we'd pushed out Donnie Hart because I wanted to sing my own songs. We were playing skating rinks and parties, and sold our first album off the bandstand.

Throughout its major-label career, Pantera downplayed its self-released glam and commercial metal albums because they contrasted so vividly with the thrash-and-burn sound they pursued through the nineties. The shift was hardly disingenuous—Pantera was always true to the music they loved. They grew up on KISS, Van Halen, ZZ Top, Ozzy Osbourne, and Judas Priest before discovering Metallica, Slayer, and Anthrax. They recorded three credible and diverse mainstream metal albums with Terry Glaze between 1983 and 1985 before Phil Anselmo joined in 1987. Silly as it might seem today, at the time their glam image matched their commercial sound.

JERRY ABBOTT: A guy from Mechanic Records in New York City told me he wanted to sign the band. After we talked a bit, he said, "Do you want me to tell you what's wrong with this band?" I said, "Fire away." He said, "They're too diverse. You get one song that's speed metal, one song classic metal, and then one that's almost commercial pop. Get your band to hone what they're doing. That's my advice." That's exactly what they did later when Phil came into the band.

PHIL ANSELMO (Down, Pantera, Superjoint Ritual): Before I joined Pantera, every band in a bar had to look like Mötley fucking Crüe. I would come home from school and sing *Unleashed in the East* from Judas Priest front to back. Then I ended up in the bar scene, and out comes the spandex. Here I was, a metal and hardcore fan, and I'm standing up there [in New Orleans band Razor White] looking prettier than a goddamn girl. I'm going, "Fuck, I can't do this, man." I was sixteen. I had quit school and left home. For the entire year I was doing between four and six gigs a week, three to five sets a night. That's how Pantera heard about me.

TERRY GLAZE: Me leaving Pantera after 1985's [*I Am the Night*] had nothing to do with music. I loved the music onstage two hours a day. It was the other twenty-two hours that was difficult. I loved playing with those guys. But I wanted [the business to operate] slightly differently than they did. The Abbotts [including Jerry] never split their vote, so if one of them wanted something, that's what we were doing, and there was no negotiating. I said, "I'm quitting in two weeks unless things change." Nothing changes. The last show I played with them was in Louisiana. Afterwards, I took my stuff and drove home, and it was really weird, because I'd been with them forever.

JERRY ABBOTT: When the whole band decided to go in a heavier direction, Phil was perfect for that. That, to me, is what brought Pantera from a band that wasn't quite on the scene yet to a powerhouse.

PHIL ANSELMO: When they lost Terry, they lost a lot of the identity of the band, and Dimebag became the focal point. It was just Dimebag and these fill-in guys. They had four different singers before I even showed up [David Peacock, Matt L'Amour, Rick Mythiasin (Steel Prophet), and Donnie Hart (who returned briefly)]. The first time I ever tried out for Pantera, I flew in from New Orleans to Dallas-Fort Worth [airport], and we jammed all night on Priest and Maiden. Then we went back to Darrell and Vince's mother's house, where they were living at that time, and we drank tequila, which I almost puked because I was definitely not a tequila drinker. We smoked some weed and they played me some demos from *Power Metal*. I wanted to make sure if I joined that we would be going in a heavier direction. And they were like, "Oh, totally." So they played me these demos, and sure, it is more aggressive than their old stuff, especially the opening track, "Power Metal." They gave me a tape of the fuckin' thing, and I wrote lyrics in about half an hour—*obviously*. I went in there and nailed that motherfucker. And yes, Rob Halford was a huge influence for me on that album. But it was a good start and it was a natural evolution from that to [1990's] *Cowboys from Hell*.

DEREK SHULMAN (president of 2PLUS Music & Entertainment, ex-president/CEO of Atco Records and Roadrunner Records): I was quite aware of Pantera when Vinnie and Darrell had Terry Glaze in the band because I visited Dallas in the mid-1980s from time to time, where my in-laws resided. They had built a following in the area and were regarded as a band to watch. I had listened to their third self-produced album, *Power Metal*, with their new singer Philip Anselmo, when I was at Polygram, and although I thought it was a well-crafted, heavier album with fantastic playing, it still did not have that unique quality that they would ultimately acquire. It was not, at that time, particularly distinctive from the artists that I was involved with, like Bon Jovi, Cinderella, and Kingdom Come.

REX BROWN: Phil was a scrappy dude—a young kid who had left home to live in the back of his car. His temper was out of control. He'd fight anybody at the drop of a goddamn hat. He made sure that when he walked into a room people would know it, and he had that whole "don't look at me" attitude he still has to this day, but it was way worse back then.

PHIL ANSELMO: I had just joined Pantera. Now, they hadn't told Donnie Hart he was out of the band again and I was in. I didn't know Donnie, and we were out one night at this bar and Dimebag says, "Yo dude, you better watch out." I was like, "For what?" He goes, "Our old lead singer is here and he's pissed off." Then I see this guy, an oddball, from across the bar. Now, I'm not one to turn away from a glare so I glared right back until he took his eyes off me. The night goes on. Next thing I know, he walks into the bathroom while I'm in there. I go, "What the fuck are *you* looking at?" He charges me and tries to wrap me up around my waist. I beat the ever-living fuck out of him with rapid combinations. Then the bass player [of his new band Boss Tweed] grabs me, and I spin his ass around and KO him with a sweet right hand and somehow the whole place gets pushed out the back door. Then the guitar player charges me and I toss him on his head on the gravel. His other guitar player charges. I punch him square in the chest, took his air out. I kicked the whole fucking band's ass right in front of everybody, and they're like, "Whoa man, you can fight." Donnie came up to me a week later and was like, "You should be a boxer, man." I was like, "Man, I've been boxing for years. Maybe that's why you shouldn't have fucked with me to begin with." But we became friends after that.

VINNIE PAUL: After we finished *Power Metal* (1988), we took a good look at ourselves and said, "You know what? These fancy clothes and all this crazy hair stuff ain't playing music for us, we are." We decided to drop all that and focus even more on the music, and just fucking kick ass as much as possible.

PHIL ANSELMO: We were down in Houston, Texas, in '88, and I had fucking had it with our look. I told them, "Fuck this. I will quit the band," and I was dead serious. I was not going to do another show in spandex. We had a huge argument—a knock-down, drag out fucking huge fight that spilled over into Fort Worth. I finally said, "Fuck it. This is my last gig." I laid down the law, and we had crowds coming, so what were they going to do? It was ugly at first, but it proved that the brotherhood was there. I could jump onstage in the same clothes I wore all day and sing the fucking songs. That bred confidence and a new fire in our bellies. The rules were torn down. Kids are stage diving. There's skanking. Punks start showing up. Suddenly we've got a new audience that wouldn't have gone to see them before.

By 1988, Pantera was beginning to develop a foothold in the speed metal community, thanks to Anselmo's rugged delivery and a new series of influences—including Slayer. That band's 1986 album, *Reign in Blood*, was rightfully received as the pinnacle of thrash metal, and with their next two releases, 1988's *South of Heaven* and 1990's *Seasons in the Abyss*, Slayer firmly established themselves as champions of evil, penning songs about Satan, serial killers, and the evils of war, all motivated by their disgust for mainstream society and their general misanthropy.

KERRY KING: The world's a really stupid, fucked-up place, and it drives me crazy. I swear, man, I'd be the first one out there shooting people if it was legal.

JEFF HANNEMAN: If I didn't have this outlet, I think I would have snapped by now. I'm more pissed now than I was at twenty-four. The older you get, the more you see what's going on in the world and how fucked-up things are. There's nothing you can do about it unless you want to spend the rest of your life in jail, so you just have to find a way to deal with it.

TOM ARAYA: We can apply all this anger to our music and our lyrics. Others just get mad and punch people. We're able to use our energy constructively. That's why we can be kind of mellow and normal in our daily lives.

KERRY KING: Some people have said that Slayer's music doesn't change and grow. Fuck that. We do it 'cause we like it. I'm a true fan of what we do, and that's why my music has stayed very similar over the years. You know Slayer when you hear Slayer. It may not be the most technically advanced thing, but there are plenty of places to go if that's what you want to hear.

JEFF HANNEMAN: I used to be totally into Steve Vai and Joe Satriani and other shredders, and I tried to emulate what they did and really grow as a guitarist. Then I said, "I don't think I'm that talented, but more important, I don't care."

TOM ARAYA: We were doing all this great shit, but we were having problems with our original drummer Dave [Lombardo], so that made things a little bit stressful. It was a repeat problem. The first time was when we did our first semiprofessional tour in 1986 [for *Reign in Blood*]. Then Dave just quit. We had just got done doing a tour with W.A.S.P., and he fucking bailed on us on the second half of the tour. We finished the rest of the tour with [Whiplash drummer] Tony Scaglione. He did a decent job. Then Dave wants to come back. At that point I had lost trust in him. It took a lot of convincing from [Rick] Rubin and our manager [Rick Sales]. But Dave stayed in the band until the end of [1990's] *Seasons in the Abyss*. Then, at the end of *Seasons*, he bailed again. Actually, we bailed *him*. He just didn't have his shit together. [Paul Bostaph joined the band, until Lombardo's 2006 return.]

DAVE LOMBARDO (Slayer): When I was originally in Slayer, I didn't feel like I needed to explore other avenues. But once

I started being pigeonholed in that metal scene, I was like, "Forget this. I am more than just a metal drummer." When I heard the first record they did without me, I was a bit upset because on the first drum roll of the first part of *Divine Intervention* the tempo drops, and you hear it. It's *obvious*. It goes from, like, 160 beats-per-minute down to about 140. I was like, "Wow, and they picked on *my* drumming?"

Ozzy's legendary guitarist Randy Rhoads was a huge influence on Dimebag Darrell's playing. Nonetheless, after immersing himself in early Metallica and Slayer, Darrell decided to take a heavier approach to songwriting. With Anselmo as a raging, antiestablishment, hardcore-and-thrash flag-waving front man, Pantera finally had the attitude and direction to go along with their musicianship. They began crafting the songs that would eventually comprise the pivotal thrash-groove album *Cowboys from Hell*. Whatever they lacked in corporate muscle and money, they made up for in drive, determination, and the confidence to persevere at a time when the market was already glutted with thrash bands and major labels were about to purge their metal holdings.

VINNIE PAUL: In '83 when Metallica played at Harvey Hall in Tyler, Texas, me and my brother drove to see those guys. They were opening for Raven and there were maybe twenty people there, and we're all standing up against the stage going crazy. James and Lars ended up coming back to the house and hanging out with us for a couple days. It was such a thrill to be around them. *Kill 'Em All* had just come out, and it was a whole new thing.

TERRY GLAZE: James and Lars came back and hung out in Arlington a couple times. I think they possibly were interested in Darrell joining Metallica, but he wouldn't leave his brother. Same thing with Megadeth. He said, "Not without my brother."

VINNIE PAUL: Megadeth called Dime and asked him to audition. Dave Mustaine actually offered him the job. They offered him health insurance, a Nike endorsement, lots of money, and an opportunity to play on the big stage. He came back and said, "Look man, this ain't gonna happen. The only way it could happen is if they wanted to hire you and they already got a drummer. So let's fuckin' knuckle down." That really caused everyone to focus and get on it.

DAVE MUSTAINE: I had just asked Nick Menza to join Megadeth when I called Darrell and asked him if he wanted to play with us. Darrell goes, "Well, yeah, man. Love to come play with you, but I gotta bring my brother." I went, "Uh, okay. What's your brother do?" I didn't know who Vince was and I thought he was Dime's guitar tech. He goes, "No, he's my drummer." I went, "Oh shit man, I just hired Nick Menza." He said, "Well then I can't come." I went, "Ah fuck. Okay, well nice talking to you." Later I was thinking, "Man, if I would have just hired both of them I would have had the greatest band in the world."

VINNIE PAUL: We always felt like our musicianship enabled us to be more than just a thrash band. The groove thing was something we didn't want to lose, even though we got heavier. We wanted people to be able to move to the music. Being from Texas, we were always fans of ZZ Top and bands that had big grooves.

DIMEBAG DARRELL: I fit the kind of music I play. I'm rowdy, I like to tear into shit and drink shit and have a good ol' time. I can't imagine playing something laid back that didn't fit who I am. I'm lucky I found myself. A lot of people don't until the day they die. As for our Southern thing, everybody in Texas is laid back. There are places like New York where everybody's in a rush to hurry up and get things done. That's not good for your health—not that booze is either [*laughs*]. That more relaxed thing goes into the music. You can hear the bends, you can hear the Southern rock parts.

RITA HANEY (Dimebag's longtime girlfriend): Some of the things Dime would play off the cuff were amazing. There was always a song going on in his mind. Even when he brushed his teeth, it was to a song. I asked him one day, "What are you doing? You're roughing your gums up pretty good." He goes, "Oh. I'm brushing my teeth to Metallica's 'Whiplash.'"

With 1990's *Cowboys from Hell*, Pantera reemerged as a vicious, razor-clawed beast. The album was a new kind of thrash—a bit of Slayer and Metallica crossed with a crushing Southern rock–tinged power groove. Songs like "Domination," "Psycho Holiday," and of course the title track were devastating and heavy, combining Anselmo's love of hardcore and thrash with Dimebag's ability to rip, squeal, and crunch.

PHIL ANSELMO: The biggest thing was when I befriended Kerry King from Slayer [in 1988], at the beginning of their *South of Heaven* tour. Slayer played Dallas on a Saturday night, but they get there the night before when *we* had a gig. So that Friday, Tom, Jeff, and Kerry came to our show and got up and played "Reign in Blood" with us—well, not Tom because he had had a little bit too much to drink by then. Afterwards, Kerry and I exchanged phone numbers. He called out of nowhere a few months later. I didn't even believe it was him. He's like, "Well, fuck, how many Kerrys do you know?" He came down and we had a good time partying. Then he calls me again and says, "Hey, I want to come down, but I don't want to do it for nothing." I said, "What's on your mind?" He said, "I wanna jam, man. You got a gig this weekend?" I'm like, "Fuckin'-A, man." We built our set around a two-guitar player situation, which is something we had never done. We did "Reign in Blood," "South of Heaven," Judas Priest songs with guitar harmonies, and all kinds of shit. I know in my heart the fact that Kerry King came down and him and Dimebag Darrell jammed for hours and hours together was a *big*-time experience for everybody in the band—a major turning point.

VINNIE PAUL: A lot of people think that [Phil] was the driving force behind the heaviness. That's not true at all. My brother wrote the guitar riffs. I wrote the drum parts.

PHIL ANSELMO: I showed them the fucking *path*, man. It would be a lie to say anything different. But I gotta say you can't force-feed anybody anything. Dimebag came over to the first house I lived in Texas in early '88 and I said, "Look here. This is what we're gonna do. We're gonna smoke this bowl and you're gonna sit down and listen to a song." I put on the vinyl of "At Dawn They Sleep" from Slayer's *Hell Awaits*. He sat there and stared at the turntable, and by the middle of the song that big curly head started to move a little and groove, and by the end of the song he's like, "Damn, son, that's badass!" Vince was more skeptical. He's a look-before-you-leap kind of guy. Sometimes he would need a little shove.

REX BROWN: We were writing almost continuously at that point. We'd sound-check at a place called Joe's Garage, where we used to play every other weekend. We'd sit there in the club and write. The first three songs we did that way were "The Art of Shredding," "Heresy," and "Domination." It took us six months to write those songs on *Cowboys* because we were so particular about every detail.

PHIL ANSELMO: We wrote *Cowboys* from late '88 all through '89. The first demo had "The Art of Shredding," "The Sleep," and "Cowboys from Hell." Very shortly after, we did "Psycho Holiday."

REX BROWN: "Psycho Holiday" is all about Phil. I was trying to get him out of town because he was a fuckin' mess. We were all drinking way too much and his temper was out of control. He was getting in fights all the time and no one could calm him down. I was sitting there going, "Well fuck, man. We really need to send him home and let him chill a little." I wrote on a pad "Psycho Holiday" because he was psycho and he was going on a holiday. I went, "Okay, Delta, American. What's the cheapest flight we can get. Southwest?"

PHIL ANSELMO: Rex and I were living together at the time and I come back to the house after this vacation—which I really needed—and I looked next to the telephone and written there is "Psycho Holiday" scribbled out with all these flight times. *I* was the psycho. It became an inside joke, and Vinnie said, "Man, that's a great fucking song title." I guess I was fucked-up back then. I went through a big LSD phase. I quit washing my hair. I put peanut butter in my hair when I was tripping, and I didn't take a fuckin' bath for the longest time.

REX BROWN: The noise at the beginning of the first song "Cowboys from Hell" was totally a Dime thing. That's what he was hearing in his head. We made a loop of that crazy echo sound for Dime to play over. It was repetitious and very fuckin' annoying for a long while. But he just played this thing called "in-the-box scaling," and he got that from all the great blues guys we'd see recording at his dad's studio. We wanted the song to be this anthem that said, "We are here to take over your fuckin' town, so step aside or join in."

PHIL ANSELMO: "Clash with Reality" is a true story. We had a New Year's Eve party on a Saturday night. We played on a Friday. After the gig, we went to a friend of ours whose mother owned an apartment complex. I guess in our minds that meant we could do whatever the fuck we wanted. Well, that proved to be false. . . . We showed up to this one-room apartment with about thirty fucking people. I walked straight into the bedroom and there was a Marshall half-stack there.

I just turned that motherfucker on and started playing god knows what on "10." The people next door were sound asleep. They fucking freaked out. Next thing you know the place is crawling with cops and Darrell and Vinnie are down on the ground. I was upstairs in this apartment and this cop told me to stay put or I was going to jail. I'm watching what's going down in the parking lot, and I see this fucking cop whip out a steel baton and start beating Darrell.

RITA HANEY: Darrell wasn't fighting or struggling. He wasn't like that. Phil came running from across the parking lot and kicked the cop off him. They both wound up going to jail that night. The cops were telling them they were gonna keep 'em, saying, "Don't even worry about doing your New Year's show."

In 1989 after a chance meeting with an ATCO Records A&R man, Pantera evolved from an unsigned Texas group with plenty of firepower to a major label buzz-band with the marketing push to go global.

VINNIE PAUL: Mark Ross, who worked under Derek Shulman at ATCO, was flying to North Carolina to see a band they signed called Tangier. Then Hurricane Hugo hit and they landed in Dallas. So Mark called up Derek and said, "Hey, I'm stuck here in Dallas. Are there any bands you want me to go see?" We had been turned down by every label on earth twenty-three times. Derek says, "I've been following this band called Pantera for three or four years. Why don't you see if they're any good live?" Well, I got a phone call from Mark Ross, and he said, "Hey, I'm from Atco Records. I need to see you play tonight." I giggled because I'd met with so many of these A&R guys and was ready for the same old bullshit. I said, "Dude, we're not really playing a gig tonight. We've got a birthday party that we're playing for this chick at this Mexican restaurant in Fort Worth. If you really want to come see us, come by and check it out." I kind of cracked up about it and told the guys that this dude was coming out. None of us took it seriously. We get to the party and I see this tall guy with curly black hair who looks really out of place. I go up to him and say, "You're Mark Ross." He says, "Yup, I just got here."

PHIL ANSELMO: To add to the ridiculousness of it, there were only about forty people there. We set up in the corner on this slick dance floor. The girl had her cake, and we did the birthday thing. The cake smashed all over the fucking floor and there's icing, so it's slippery as shit. We're up there scared to take a step 'cause we thought we were gonna fall and break our fucking necks.

VINNIE PAUL: We were killing, man, throwing down as hard as we can. About four songs into it everybody looks up and goes, "Hey man, he left. He's gone." We're like, "Ah, fuck. I guess he didn't like us." So we just started drinking and partying, throwing birthday cake all over the place. Dime's sliding all over the dance floor while we're playing. Four songs later, Mark comes back. Everybody's like, "Oh, shit. Get serious again." As we get done he walks over and I said, "What'd you think, dude?" He said, "I loved it. It was incredible." I said, "Well, why'd you leave?" He said, "I went out to the car to call Derek and tell him we're signing you guys."

VINNIE PAUL: We were huge fans of Ozzy's *Diary of a Madman* and this band Malice, and they're all produced by Max Norman. So we thought we *had* to have Max Norman. He flew to Houston to see a gig, and he loved the band. We were ready to go. But our recording budget only allowed for $30,000 for the producer. About two days before we were supposed to start with Max, he got offered $50,000 to do Lynch Mob. He calls us up and said, "Guys, I gotta take this. I need the money. I'm out." We were like, "What the fuck?" So Mark Ross goes, "I got this guy named Terry Date who just finished doing Soundgarden and Overkill." We were like, "Man, I don't know." He said, "Well, let's find out."

REX BROWN: Me and Dime would sit there with Terry and do what we'd call "the microscope." We'd turn everything else off on the tracks except for me and him and a kick and a snare. That's the way we'd make sure every guitar and bass note was picked the way it should be. That's how we got that real tight sound.

PHIL ANSELMO: The last song we wrote for *Cowboys from Hell* was "Primal Concrete Sledge," and we did that in the studio in '90. Vince came up with that drumbeat and then Dime added the riff around the beat. It was the sound of us really discovering ourselves, and as good as the rest of *Cowboys* was, it really paved the way for us to develop musically.

DIMEBAG DARRELL: We were in Texas, and we heard "Cowboys from Hell" on the local radio station. It was a trip, man! My first tattoo said "Cowboys from Hell." I thought to myself, "Well, fuck, man, even if I'm fifty years old I'll be able to look at the tattoo and say, "I made it that far at that one point, dammit."

PHIL ANSELMO: We were on a mission, man. There were some slim crowds in some bleak cities in places like North Dakota, where nobody had heard of us. There would be people just sitting at the bar tables, and I would charge them and kick their fucking tables out from underneath them and scream in their fucking face. They were not getting out of there without remembering us one way or another.

REX BROWN: We wanted to be feared—be as brutal as we could possibly be. When the four of us walked in somewhere it was always like an old saloon—the Jesse James gang was there. That was one of the things we worked on. Being those bad guys wearing black, just like the lyrics of ["Cowboys from Hell."]

In 1990, just as Pantera was about to blow up, original heavy metal madman Ozzy Osbourne was working on songs that would escalate him to a level of popularity he hadn't experienced since the death of Randy Rhoads—thanks to the addition of nineteen-year-old New Jersey shredder Zakk Wylde, who played with Ozzy for much of the next two decades and continues to front his own band, Black Label Society. With Wylde's songwriting help, Ozzy crafted some of the most popular music of his career. The quadruple-platinum 1991 album *No More Tears* featured the Grammy-winning "I Don't Want to Change the World" and the hits "No More Tears" and "Mama, I'm Coming Home." As successful as the pairing with Wylde was, the nineties were a tumultuous period personally for Ozzy, who was back to the excesses and indulgences that got him dismissed from Black Sabbath.

ZAKK WYLDE: This guy Dave Feld saw me playing in some shit hole in New Jersey called Close Encounters. He said, "Hey man, have you ever thought of auditioning for Ozzy?" He goes, "My buddy Mark Weiss is a legendary photographer and he just got done shooting them." He said, "Take some pictures of yourself and record some shit, and I can get it to Mrs. Osbourne." I had nothing to fuckin' lose. I was working at a gas station, mowing lawns and teaching guitar. So I put together a cassette of me playing "Mr. Crowley," "Crazy Train," and "I Don't Know," and playing classical guitar. My sister took some Polaroids of me with the Instamatic camera on my parents' porch and sent them to him. Then Ozzy was up in the city and they called me up to meet him, but I ended up missing him because he went out drinking with André the fucking Giant and got blitzkrieged. They were out all night. I was like, "Man, that sucks." I would have just liked to get an autograph. Next thing you know, I got a call from Mom [Sharon Osbourne]. I thought it was one of my friends putting their mom up to it. She was talking to me and I was waiting to hear my fuckin' friends laughing in the background. But she just kept talking. She said she wanted to fly me out to Los Angeles to audition. Next thing you know, I'm in Los Angeles. I jammed and when Oz walked into the room I was like, "Aw shit, it's fuckin' Ozzy!" I had just seen him with Jake at the *Bark at the Moon* tour at the Spectrum in Philadelphia. Ozzy goes, "Where have I seen you before?" He goes, "Have you lived out here?" I went, "No, I'm from New Jersey." He went, "I know I've seen you before." He said my picture was the only one he picked out of all those fuckin' thousands upon thousands of boxes of audition tapes. He said, "I looked at the picture and I said, "Oh, look at this little kid. He loves Randy Rhoads. That's how I remember seeing you." I auditioned, and after that Mom was like, "We gotta get your passport because we gotta see if you can write with Ozzy." Then they wanted to see if I could play live.

BRIAN FAIR (Shadows Fall, Overcast): Zakk is an amazing character; his personality is over the top and he's a total cartoon, yet he can play a guitar like nobody's business. The combination makes him a heavy metal superhero.

ZAKK WYLDE: The first show we did was at Wormwood Scrubs Prison in England. All lifer inmates are in this fuckin' place. I had long blond hair, I weighed 144 pounds, and I go, "Dude, I'm about the closest thing to Farrah Fawcett that these motherfuckers are gonna see for the rest of their fuckin' lives." I was like, "If I don't pass this audition, what the fuck are they gonna do, leave me in this fuckin' hellhole?" So we ended up playing there so no one would be able to see me audition, and if things didn't pan out they'd get another guitar player. It was fuckin' hysterical. My first gig with Ozzy and I'm in a fuckin' prison.

SCOTT IAN: We were in Tallahassee, Florida, opening for Ozzy on Zakk's first tour with the band. I was walking across the arena parking lot towards this backstage door. The door opens and some dude in bell-bottom jeans and work boots with long blond hair walks out. And he goes, "Hey, Scott," so I said, "Hey, man," and I kept walking because I was late for the Anthrax sound check. A couple hours later, Ozzy's band is onstage and there's that same dude with the bell-bottoms and the work boots up onstage shredding. And I was like, "Oh, that guy was Zakk Wylde." I had no idea. So, I see him backstage after that and immediately he goes, "What's up? I say hi to you, you won't even talk to me." I said, "I didn't even know. I had no idea. I don't know you. I didn't know what you looked like." I was all apologetic, and he started laughing and said, "I'm just kidding. I'm just fucking around." But then the rest of the tour he busted my balls incessantly. At sound checks he'd be onstage at the microphone and he'd see me and go, "There's that cunt Scott Ian. Too big to say hi to the little guitar player." And this went on until about, oh, three years ago.

VINNIE PAUL: Outside of him being an amazing guitar player, he truly is a comedian, man. He likes to cut up and laugh and have a really good time. He has the same spirit and energy my brother Dime had. I just love hanging out with the guy.

Joining Ozzy's band was Wylde's big break for sure, but the original madman of metal couldn't have chosen a more skilled or compatible wingman. Wylde could outdrink most anybody except his boss, and he was crazy enough to stand by Oz no matter what tumbled his way.

ZAKK WYLDE: Me, Father [Randy] Castillo, Phil Soussan, and John Sinclair and Oz were coming up with riffs for "Miracle Man" and "Demon Alcohol" [for 1989's *No Rest for the Wicked*]. But every day at 10 or 11 a.m., like clockwork, Oz would go straight to the Wheatsheaf pub and have about five vodkas and OJs and a couple cognacs and a couple pints to start the day off. Then he'd have a little something to eat. Then we'd jam for a little bit before we went back to the pub for dinner. Same shit. Rifling down cocktails like it's nobody's fuckin' business. Oz had a beige jumpsuit on and people would go, "Oh, man, it's fuckin' Ozzy Osbourne." Oz was trashed out of his mind. He's got his round glasses on. They're crooked as fuck. He's got piss running down his whole leg from the jumpsuit into his shoes. And we'd be like, "There he is, our fearless leader." Whenever this shit would go down, Mom wasn't too happy. She'd see him in this condition, and Oz would be like, "Uh-ohh."

OZZY OSBOURNE: The word *one* doesn't exist to me. I should start at twenty-five drinks, you know. I never went out for *a* drink—ever. What I really meant was I was going out to get shit-faced and you won't see me for the rest of the week.

SHARON OSBOURNE: Ozzy started to get violent, and I could deal with it to a point. He would hit me, and I'd hit him three times. I can stand up for myself. It was very violent. Our fights are legendary to people in this business. We'd hurt each other a lot. We had a great fight once at the Hard Rock Cafe in New York. We beat the shit out of each other. That's how we were. If Ozzy would throw something at me, then I would destroy the fucking room. I was used to that because I was brought up with a lot of violence. So it didn't faze me.

OZZY OSBOURNE: I'd become what they call a blackout drinker. I didn't know what I was doing, and it was fucking horrendous. Waking up and thinking "what the fuck have I done now?" You wake up covered in blood, and you don't know where the blood's come from.

SHARON OSBOURNE: The worst it got was when he tried to kill me [*laughs*]. I had him arrested, and the court put him in a treatment center for three months. That must have been '89. He was on an unbelievable roll of drug-taking, drinking, making drug concoctions that were hidden all over the house. He would take it with the booze, and he was on an outrageous roll for a week. On the seventh day, he tried to kill me. He seriously tried to strangle me. I got to the panic button for the alarm, and the alarm system went off, and the cops came within a few minutes.

DAVE MUSTAINE: There was a period where I kept thinking, "Hey, it's cool to be crazy and drunk and on drugs. Ozzy does it, look how popular he is." It wasn't really a great approach for me to take because it gave me a reputation for being a loose cannon for a long time. I thought, "Shit, the guy pisses on the Alamo, he bites the head off a bat, he's out of his mind, and people love that. He's always in and out of insane asylums professing to be mad. Then I realized that the world isn't fucking insane. Just some people are.

Ozzy and Pantera were peaking at the same time that Ozzy's peer and Pantera's hero—Judas Priest vocalist Rob Halford—was growing weary of singing with the metal titans. He would record one more album with the band, 1990's *Painkiller*, before quitting the group for more than a decade to pursue other metallic avenues with Fight, 2wo (with Nine Inch Nails' Trent Reznor), and Halford (which featured future Damageplan vocalist Pat Lachman). His exit from Judas Priest was hardly civil and his last stage appearance with Priest in the nineties could have been his last show ever.

K.K. DOWNING: Rob got his head knocked off in Toronto. When he came onstage on his motorcycle, metal stairs rose up and Rob would drive underneath the stairs. On this particular occasion, the intro tape started but everyone but Rob was late to the stage, so the guy who started to lift the stairs up in all the smoke brought the stairs back down because we weren't ready to start the show. Rob was already riding the bike toward the stairs and they were halfway down, so he literally drove into them and was knocked unconscious. We'd started "Hell Bent for Leather," and, of course, there were no vocals. We didn't know where Rob was. He was actually on the stage and so was the bike, but it was underneath all the dry ice and smoke. We played the whole song with no vocals, but he came around and managed to do the show. Afterwards, he went to the hospital and that was the last time I saw him for a long time because , after that—it wasn't because of that incident—but that was when he actually quit the band.

VINNIE PAUL: After *Cowboys from Hell* came out, Pantera did a European tour with Judas Priest. Apparently, Rob was a huge fan. We heard later that was around the point when he was thinking of leaving Priest and was going to put together Fight. I think he kind of modeled Fight after Pantera, his favorite, heaviest band at the time.

ROB HALFORD: There was supposed to be a time where I could be in Judas Priest *and* do stuff outside of the band, and go back and forth. That's when confusion started, because I had to send what is commonly known as a "leaving member document," which would have effectively removed me from Judas Priest on paper in the world of lawyers, but let me stay in the band. That's when Priest went, "Well, hang on. What does this mean? You're gonna leave?" One thing led to another, and it got very bitter. There was a lot of screaming and yelling, which I don't like. So I just started sending faxes as opposed to trying to communicate via the phone or in person. The big Grand Canyon of disruption started to happen, and suddenly that was it, I was out of Priest. Initially, I was apprehensive because I wondered, "Is this suicidal?"

IAN HILL: We had no argument whatsoever with him going to do a solo album, but he said he wanted three years, which is a long time for a band like Judas Priest to stay dormant. We were going to take a year off anyway. For the previous twenty years we'd done an album and tour every year, but three years was just a bit too long. As it turned out, we were out for quite a bit longer than that.

ROB HALFORD: In the world of metal, there's this fierce, loyal, devoted, almost conservative approach from the fans that will not accept you doing anything more or less than what they love you for. It's that Sylvester Stallone syndrome. We only want him to be Rocky. We won't give him the chance to be anybody else. So Fight might not have been as successful as it could have been because people only wanted to hear me in Judas Priest. But for my personal sanity, I had to explore these other areas before I could return to the mighty Priest.

From 1990's *Cowboys from Hell* tour until its 2000 swan song *Reinventing the Steel*, Pantera was unstoppable. Not only did the band proudly support metal after others abandoned or corrupted the musical form, they engaged in so many antics and practical jokes that they were able to release three VHS videos of shenanigans filmed by Dimebag and his best friend, Bobby Tongs. The material was rereleased in 1999 as the *Vulgar Videos From Hell* DVD. According to Dime's girlfriend, Rita Haney, the Pantera videos inspired pro skateboarder Bam Margera and his demented friends Johnny Knoxville, Steve-O, and Ryan Dunn to launch their cringe-inducing reality show, *Jackass*, which debuted on MTV in 2002. Despite Pantera's constant revelry, the nineties were almost as unkind to thrash metal as to hair metal. To be considered relevant in an age of grunge and alternative rock, many bands were forced to rethink their sonic approach. Of the Big Four, only Slayer stayed the course. Even when they changed drummers, as they did several times through the nineties, their core sound and controversial subject matter remained consistent. But the members discovered that there are sometimes consequences to writing songs about death, the devil, and devastation.

TOM ARAYA: Because we speak our minds and don't try to say things nicely, we get blamed for all the stupid shit that other people do. In late 1995, some guy killed a girl and blamed it on us. Apparently, he had a black metal band and he fashioned it after us. They wanted to sacrifice a virgin, but they messed up because they fucked her and *then* they killed her. It's like, obviously everyone knows who did it; what more do you need, and why blame it on someone else when it's clearly your fault?

San Luis Obispo Tribune, **April 14, 2010: On the evening of July 22, 1995, 15-year-old Elyse Pahler left her home to hang out with three teenage boys, who had promised her drugs. Later that evening, the three, aged 14, 15 and 16, held her down, stabbed her and later had sex with her dead body. . . . One of the boys, Royce Casey [later] led authorities to her badly decomposed body. The three boys pleaded no contest and were sentenced to 26 years to life in prison. . . . The case garnered national attention after Pahler's parents filed a lawsuit against the band Slayer, [whose music they claimed] incited the murder. In 2001 . . . a judge said lyrics written by the heavy metal band may have been offensive, but they did not incite three teens to murder. "Slayer lyrics are repulsive and profane," [Judge Jeffrey] Burke wrote in his 14-page decision. "But they do not direct or instruct listeners to commit the acts that resulted in the vicious torture-murder of Elyse Pahler. . . ."**

BRIAN COGAN (professor, author): The connection between certain kinds of metal and violence is nebulous in terms of influence. Did thrash lead to more aggression? Sure. But to try to say that violence is connected to music is a stretch at best. The Swedish and Norwegian black metal scenes *did* have their share of grotesque violence and murder, but that was mostly some fairly twisted individuals using racist and dubious neo-pagan ideology in order to justify their actions. For most other metal heads, a pentagram necklace or a "metal up your ass" poster was as likely to be the source of any kind of violence as a Bee Gees poster. However, if the fan is an asshole to begin with, all bets are off.

KERRY KING: It's funny how quick somebody points a finger at a band rather than the fucking bingeing of drugs that was going on at the same time. Things like that and Columbine have happened before and they're gonna happen again. It's the result of not taking responsibility for what you do, then trying to pass the blame. When you leave your kids to be brought up by MTV and Jerry Springer, you're asking for trouble. Parents today are fucking idiots. And maybe some crazy fucker says he was set off by movies or music, but if you're raised with no values and no sense of right and wrong, anything can set you off. Don't blame the fucking entertainment industry.

The Pahlers weren't the first to put metal on trial. In the mid-eighties, in two widely publicized cases, other parents blamed rock stars for their sons' suicides. In 1984, depressed California teenager John McCollum held a loaded .22-caliber handgun to his head and pulled the trigger while listening to songs by Ozzy Osbourne. His parents filed a lawsuit in a California civil court against Osbourne and CBS Records, alleging that the song "Suicide Solution" encouraged their son to end his life. In 1986, an appeals court dismissed the case, claiming Osbourne's First Amendment right to free expression exonerated him from blame. Then, in 1985, two teens in Reno, Nevada, James Vance and Raymond Belknap, were smoking pot and drinking beer while listening to Judas Priest's 1978 album, *Stained Class*, which features a cover of the Spooky Tooth song "Better by You, Better Than Me." The teens later attempted a dual suicide in a church playground.

San Francisco Examiner, September 29, 1989: . . . Near dusk, the two went to the playground of a local church with Raymond's sawed-off 12-gauge shotgun. Raymond Belknap, seated on a merry-go-round, placed the end of the shotgun under his chin and pulled the trigger, killing himself. A few minutes later, James pointed the same gun at his chin and fired. Somehow, the blast missed his brain and he lived. [Vance died in 1988 from medical complications.] Four months later, Raymond Belknap's mother went to attorneys with James Vance's letter connecting the death pact to heavy metal music. Reno attorneys Ken McKenna and Tim Post began to examine the music, lyrics and album cover for suicidal messages. They say they found references to blood, killing and the implications of suicide in the lyrics, but no explicit directives to take one's life. Those they claim to have found in the music and album cover's subliminal messages. [The case went to trial in 1990 and after a bizarre hearing involving all five band members, an aggressive prosecutor, and supposed audio experts, the case was dismissed.]

IAN HILL: With all due respect to the families involved, we treated it as an immense joke until we were actually sitting there in court. The use of backwards masking is protected by the Constitution. So they came up with this weird idea of subliminal messages. They play you a song, and you go, "Well, I can't hear anything." They say, "Well, that's because it's subliminal." Then it's up to you to prove that the message *isn't* there. It was absurd. There was a sound on there that was a combination of a high-hat cymbal and Rob exhaling, and it sounded like "Do it!" But anybody that actually wants to go out and murder their own clientele has got to have some commercial death wish.

ROB HALFORD: It was a very sad experience. We've never been a band that has or ever will make music that will hurt people, and we were enraged that we were being accused of something we didn't do. It caught the public's attention. It was like a very bad *Jerry Springer* episode. But it was very serious. We couldn't just make it go away. It was a very important and sobering reflection on some of the things that happen in families where kids aren't given the right love, care, and attention, and they go off the rails. The irony was those two boys loved Judas Priest. So we couldn't figure it out until we got to the courtroom, and within the first couple of days we went, "Oh, we know what this is about. This is about making a fast buck on something that's so tragic."

As Pantera was enjoying the success of *Cowboys From Hell*, the members' pals in Anthrax entered their third phase as a band. With the departure of Joey Belladonna after 1990's *Persistence of Time*,

Anthrax hired Armored Saint vocalist John Bush. The timing was peculiar. Anthrax was coming off the momentum of having played the legendary 1991 Clash of the Titans festival with Megadeth, Slayer, and Alice in Chains, *Persistence of Time* had gone gold, and Anthrax had just inked a lucrative deal with Elektra Records. Moreover, the band had broken boundaries by collaborating with Public Enemy front man Chuck D for a cover of the hit "Bring the Noise" and touring with their hip-hop heroes—moves that helped set the stage for the evolution of nu metal a few years later.

SCOTT IAN: Public Enemy had never gotten groupies before, and our crew guys would always have chicks on the bus getting naked, and they'd take pictures of these girls. [Public Enemy rapper] Flavor Flav was out of his fucking mind for that. He couldn't get on our bus fast enough to see what was going on because that didn't happen on Public Enemy's bus. But it was a weird time for us. Everything seemed great from the outside looking in, but inside we were miserable because we didn't even know how we were gonna write another record. We just couldn't move forward with Joey [Belladonna] because he didn't represent us musically anymore. It wasn't personal. Creatively, we felt like we were going somewhere else, and his voice wasn't going to work.

JOEY BELLADONNA (Anthrax): I wasn't ready to go anywhere. I thought I was doing fine, and I think I could have continued with them even when they changed the style of their music. But it's like being in a relationship. If someone wants to move on you can beg them not to leave, but I didn't want to do that. I didn't want to overstay my welcome.

SCOTT IAN: Changing lineups sucks. It's a horrible thing to deal with, but any time we've ever done it, we did it to move forward, whether or not the fans liked it or it helped us commercially. It was what we had to do in order to continue.

JOHN BUSH: At first, I was thinking, "I don't know if I want to replace Joey Belladonna." He did so much with the band, and fans associated his voice with the Anthrax they loved. When I joined Anthrax, my attitude was, "Once I'm in, let's go for it." The guys always embraced me and I never got much negativity from the crowd. Maybe the people that weren't into it just stopped listening. But the thing that bummed me out the most is that the [four studio] records I did with Anthrax will probably never get the fair shake they deserve because we went through a bunch of management changes and label debacles, and all of that took over how people saw the music. Those records were really unfairly looked at in comparison to the success that Anthrax had in the eighties.

SCOTT IAN: We signed a deal with Elektra, and we had a team of people working with us all the way from the head of the label, Bob Krasnow, down to people in the mailroom. But between '93 and '95 there was a huge corporate shake-up and everyone we worked with was let go, and they brought in Sylvia Rhone to run the label. The first meeting our manager had with Sylvia, she put our contract on the table and said, "I never would have done this deal. I wouldn't even have signed this band. What do you want me to do for this next record?" That was the attitude from the label on *Stomp 442*. That record sold about 150,000 copies, and I'm surprised it even did that well. They did nothing. They put it out and we toured our asses off, but at that point in time, if you didn't have someone fighting for you as a metal band, you were fucked in the face of the grunge world. Look at Pantera in '95. EastWest [Records] was going to bat for them. We were basically thrown out in the trash.

JOHN BUSH: The band's sound *did* change a little, but it needed to change. Times were changing and we were changing with it. I hear *Sound of White Noise* and I think of the influence it had on so many bands. I listen to a band like Godsmack, and so much of it sounds like it was influenced by *Sound of White Noise*.

In 1991, Metallica also reinvented itself by writing a batch of new songs that eschewed the amphetamine-freak tempos and complex rhythms that were the hallmark of earlier albums. The eponymous record—which became widely known as *The Black Album* because of its black cover—was produced by studio veteran Bob Rock (Aerosmith, Mötley Crüe), and featured simple, heavy songs filled with strong melodies and instantly memorable hooks. There were even two fairly traditional but well-written ballads, "The Unforgiven" and "Nothing Else Matters." Old-school followers were divided on the record, but *The Black Album* garnered the band millions of new, loyal fans and spawned five hit singles. By November 2009, *The Black Album* had sold more than fifteen million copies in the United States.

LARS ULRICH: . . . *And Justice for All* was on the thin side in terms of its lyrics and its sound, so we decided to track down this Bob Rock guy who had made this Mötley Crüe album which really sounds beefy and see what his story is. The first thing that he told me was that he felt that we had never made a record that was up to his standards. That was a bit of a battle cry. We had never been challenged before, and nobody ever really said, "Well you can also do it this way, and you can also try it in a different key, or why don't you try this kind of drum fill." [We were like], "Why don't you go fuck yourself and stop telling us what to do. Just get us that bass sound like the Mötley Crüe album." But as the process wore on we very reluctantly realized that maybe this guy had some relevant suggestions, and he won us over.

KIRK HAMMETT: We gave Bob a bunch of gray hairs. There's a twitch in his eye that won't go away. But Bob, what did Mötley Crüe give you? We gave you gray hair and a twitch! They'll stay with you forever.

LARS ULRICH: Me and Bob almost came to blows on that record. All of a sudden he's saying, "If you want to come across sounding lively, you have to start playing like a band, acting like a band, being more like a band," because it was very much the James and Lars show up til then. Me and James used to guard it like the fucking crown jewels. We would tell everyone, "Yes, it *is* a band," but I think everyone knew that me and James were pretty much taking care of everything.

BOB ROCK (producer): I think what makes these guys what they are is the fact they weren't content with just making another *Justice*. They said, "Okay, that's fine, but now let's go on. Let's make something new." That, to me, is the sign of a really great artist. It would have been so simple for them to have just done what they had already done.

LARS ULRICH: To turn it around, instead of saying [*The Black Album*] is more accessible to more people, you can also say it turns fewer people off. Seriously. It was less annoying to more people.

EERIE VON: I think we definitely had an influence on Metallica. When James played me . . . *And Justice for All* before it came out, I was like, "Meh. It's not that good." I just didn't like it. We talked to those guys like real people, not superstars. We spoke our minds. We were always telling 'em, "Dude, you've got seven parts in this song. Fuckin' seven parts, and the tempo changes ten times." I was like, "Why don't you take each riff and write a good song?" So when James played me "Enter Sandman," I was like, "Yeah, this is what I'm talking about." I was so happy. Of course everyone thinks they sold out on that album.

LARS ULRICH: I think of course, when you go [from] making ten-minute songs that travel between ten different musical landscapes to songs like "Enter Sandman," it's no secret that people will point to you and go, "Oy, what's going on here?" I know deep in my heart and soul that it was the direction we wanted to try and go, the only thing we hadn't explored.

KIRK HAMMETT: *The Black Album* sold fifteen million, which freaks me out. It's still selling. I can't figure out who the hell is buying it. My theory is that people are just wearing out their CDs and buying it for all their friends.

For Metallica, *The Black Album* was a commercial breakthrough. For Pantera, it was an opportunity. For years they had dwelled in the shadow of their favorite band, Metallica. When their heroes were no longer the heaviest game in town, Pantera saw an opening and vowed to capitalize on it; they did so with 1992's *Vulgar Display of Power.*

REX BROWN: I heard [Metallica's] first single, and it didn't sound like Metallica at all. We just went, "Oh, Jesus Christ. Man, we gotta do something. We gotta blow some people's minds." When that record came out, we could tell the direction they were going and it just seemed like a letdown, so we went, "Well, there's this big, huge fucking gap to fill."

VINNIE PAUL: We felt like, although it was a great record, they had moved away from being a total metal band. I remember thinking, "Wow, we can step up to the plate and move up with the likes of Megadeth and Anthrax and these bands we eventually toured with."

ZAKK WYLDE: I used to goof with Dime, "*Vulgar* is like with the *Spinal Tap* album, except instead of it being 'you can't get none more black' it's 'you can't get none more heavier.'" It was the most brutal thing. It took heavy to a whole other place. But what made it so brilliant was the musicianship. It wasn't just heavy for the sake of being heavy. The songwriting and the way they put everything together was slammin', and so was the production. It was just extreme fuckin' great, heavy shit.

VINNIE PAUL: To us, heavy metal had to sound like a machine. The guitar had to have a buzzsaw sound to it, the drums had to have an edge to it, and Dime and Terry [Date] spent many hours getting the guitars "ass-tight." My brother was a complete perfectionist.

REX BROWN: We did 250 dates on the *Cowboys from Hell* tour with hardly any breaks at all. We had maybe a month off before we went back into the studio. Darrell and Vinnie were still at their mom's house. Me and Phil were still broke, so I bought myself a bike. I'd ride up to this place that was like a 7-Eleven, and we knew a guy there who would leave us beer and sandwiches behind the back of the place so we had something to eat after we finished at the studio.

TERRY DATE (producer): There were two things they wanted to do with *Vulgar*. They wanted it to be a little heavier than *Cowboys from Hell*. And they wanted to make the heaviest record of all time. They went in with that perfect combination of confidence and security.

REX BROWN: Sometimes I thought that I'd played something real intense. Then we'd listen back and realize that wasn't the case. So we'd come in and start punching in, which means you had to cut the tape [to edit the song]. I was playing the same stuff that Dime was, and that's the reason that sometimes you don't hear the bass. I'm playing just dead on the money with Dime and it makes the guitar seem like it has this lower frequency to it. That's just one of the things that we were really focusing on, and that's when we became the machine.

TERRY DATE: We doubled and sometimes tripled Dime's rhythm guitars, and he wanted the double to be perfectly tight with the first guitar. With songs like "Walk," that meant every downstroke, every attack of the pick, and every palm mute at the backside of the riff had to be exactly on time with the first track. That took hours and hours.

REX BROWN: When we weren't working, Dime had pranks up the fuckin' ass. We always wanted to stay and be a whole part of production, but we'd get so fucking stoned and be such jackasses that we weren't really good at being ears late at night, and we'd have to leave.

VINNIE PAUL: We used to play this game called "chicken brake," where you grab the fuckin' emergency brake. As soon as you hit it, the whole car came to a screeching halt. We'd do it in the streets of LA, down Hollywood Boulevard; you could be going 5 miles per hour and there would be a bunch of people walking and all of a sudden, "*scree-ee-ch*!" and it just scares the shit out of 'em. One time in Texas we were hauling ass down the highway in the pouring rain in Terry's rental car, and all of a sudden Rex thinks it would be funny to reach over and hit the chicken brake. When he hit it I was doing, like, 60 miles per hour, and the car went into a 360 spin, and spun and spun and spun, and then it came to a stop in the middle of the highway. We both looked at each other pale white and went, "Okay, that didn't happen," and kept going. Later that night we went to a place called the Basement, and we were really ripped when we got back. We went through this neighborhood and ran over every fuckin' mailbox there. I don't know how we didn't go to jail or blow the radiator out, but we pulled up in front of the studio. Terry comes running out and sees the headlights all busted out, the fucking front end was all bashed in. There was steam coming off the motor. He never yelled at us like he did that night. We were like, "Dude, just chill. We'll make enough money on this record to pay for it."

REX BROWN: Everybody had a nickname in those days. Vinnie Paul was Riggs. They called me any number of things, just depending on the day, [including Rex Rocker]. Darrell called himself Diamond, then Dimebag.

RITA HANEY: Philip is the *reason* why Darrell is named Dimebag. Diamond is the name he picked when he was thirteen or fourteen. But when Philip first joined the band, he and Darrell really connected. Phil moved to Texas from New Orleans, and he didn't know many people at all—just the guys. And he smoked weed. Philip would always hit Darrell up, going, "Hey, man, you know where I can get some weed?" And Darrell would always give Philip half of whatever he had, which was two joints—about a dime bag. Vinnie and Rex always called him Dime, and it was one of those stoner moments. Darrell was bringing weed over to Philip, and instead of Dime it became Dimebag.

PHIL ANSELMO: For *Vulgar Display of Power*, we stripped away all the raw, non-songs. Take "Cowboys From Hell." I sang from the ravaged gut. But the interesting thing is, after going out on tour for *Cowboys* opening for bigger bands, after being the band that's stared at, and not the main attraction, and fighting for recognition, I realized that, man, I am no different from any motherfucker out there in the audience except that I had a microphone in my hand. And if I had a microphone in my hand, I was going to speak the language of the people out in the audience.

While Metallica was becoming more popular than ever, former cofounder Dave Mustaine was falling apart. In 1992, stressed out by the sudden changes in his label and management, the mounting pressure of success, and the mainstream breakthrough of his former band, Megadeth's front man came close to his own extinction. Then he found salvation.

DAVE MUSTAINE: We had to cancel the tour because I was eating so many Valiums I was totally out of control. See, my wife didn't like the smell of alcohol on me, but I was much keener than to be defeated by something as simple as the smell of alcohol. So I got Valiums. I took a bunch and overdosed, and my heart stopped. It wasn't near death, it *was* death. All I remember was going up to Phoenix, driving out to a little place called Wickenburg. and then just laying down. I didn't see a light or a tunnel or anything like that. The hospital actually called my wife to say I had died. After that, I started to improve my life and get things together, but I ended up going back to treatment two more times before quitting.

DAVE ELLEFSON: I managed to get cleaned up from dope a year before that, but it was the hardest thing. I was like, "Fuck, I don't even know if I ever want to touch my bass anymore." That was scary, 'cause that's all I had—my dope and my music. Fortunately, everybody got their act together and we continued making albums. We've had more second chances than any other band I know. We're way beyond nine lives.

DAVE MUSTAINE: My biggest problem was that I had all this success, but my life was not very enjoyable. I had a lot of self-doubt. I hurt from loneliness and anger, or I hurt because I didn't have something I wanted, or I hurt because I was afraid I wasn't going to keep something I had. I tried the whole religious trip and I found it really wanting. Then I went into this spiritual thing with the gurus and the Filipino priests laying on hands. And that was even more empty. Then I went back to going to church, and I went with a new set of ears. I started listening for the stuff that applied to me instead of the stuff I found fault with. My life started to get better. I attribute that 100 percent to finally having God in my life.

Sensing a changing of the musical guard, Iron Maiden's Bruce Dickinson left the band following the tour for 1992's *Fear of the*

Dark. Three live albums recorded during that cycle, *A Real Live One*, *A Real Dead One*, and *Live at Donnington*, were meant to signify the end of an era. Dickinson pursued a solo career, flew commercial airlines, fenced, and wrote books. He was replaced in Maiden by Wolfsbane vocalist Blaze Bayley, but with metal already on the decline, the last thing fans wanted to hear was a new Maiden vocalist.

BRUCE DICKINSON (Iron Maiden): I thought, "If you want to, you can stay with Maiden, but things are sure not gonna change." Or I could take a chance and go somewhere else. Potentially, I knew I could be facing the prospect of commercial oblivion, which didn't scare me at all, because I've had a great career out of Maiden, which is more than anybody could possibly ask, and also I thought, "If that's as far as I'm supposed to go in this lifetime, if that's all I'm destined to do, then that's fine with me." But I wanted to find out.

NICKO McBRAIN (Iron Maiden) [1993 interview]: [I] love the geezer—I've worked with [Bruce] for ten years. I'll always be there for him, but I still feel hurt 'cause I know he don't like the band anymore. At this stage, that ain't fuckin' cool.

STEVE HARRIS: The reaction was disappointment, sadness, being pissed off—all at once! But we've all felt that he's been doing so many different things, that something had to give eventually. The thing is that if he can't give Maiden 100 percent, then we don't want him in the band.

The tidal shifts in the music industry that made Pearl Jam, Nirvana, Soundgarden, and Alice in Chains the new leaders of heavy music inspired Pantera to rage like never before, and in 1994, the band's slugfest *Far Beyond Driven* entered the *Billboard* album chart at number one, an indication that their loyal fanbase had grown. Along with mainstream success came the cash and recognition that allowed them to be more wild and destructive than ever.

VINNIE PAUL: When all that alternative stuff started coming out, that's really what propelled us into *Far Beyond Driven*. Before we even wrote a note, we went, "This album has to be the most over-the-top metal record ever made." After *Vulgar*, everybody expected us to go the Metallica route and put out a "Black Album," and we did the opposite. We even went more extreme and pushed it to another level. Bonnie Raitt and Ace of Bass were bummed the fuck out when that record entered *Billboard* at number one. The entire music world thought, "Who the fuck is this overnight sensation?" We went, "Fuck, we've been on the road for four years nonstop and we've got the best fans in the world, and they're the ones that made this record number one."

DIMEBAG DARRELL: It's kinda funny, I wear a giant razor blade around my neck, and a lot of people think it's for crank or cocaine. I've never touched either of those things. I've smoked some dope, I've done some V's, and I've drank millions of gallons of whiskey. But the cover of Judas Priest's *British Steel* has a picture of a fist holding a razor blade, and that thing rearranged my whole way of thinking about a whole lotta shit. So my chick got me this necklace. Me and Vinnie never did cocaine or heroin. We drink booze. We get drunk, we fall down. We do stupid shit and that's the end of it. Dude, I'm crazy enough already. I don't need to fuck with that kind of crap.

VINNIE PAUL: Some of the greatest music in the world was inspired by Jack Daniel's, Crown Royal, marijuana. If you look at most musicians who were just outstanding and then they cleaned up, all their songwriting ability went away with it. Music sounds better to you when you got a buzz. You feel more creative and a little less inhibited to try things.

JOE GIRON (photographer): They definitely relished hearing those stories later on about what happened to people who went out with them drinking. One night, one of the record company marketing guys ended up passed out in a field, and they were so proud of themselves for that. I think they got that tolerance from their club days, because they would play six nights a week every week. They were probably chugging ten or twelve shots a night.

PHIL ANSELMO: Everyone knows there was a lot of sex. Everyone knows there was a lot of drinking. Everyone knows there was a lot of drunken sex. Yeah, I was single then, and there were some incredible times where I caught myself in the middle of a situation and I look around me and put my arms in the air and said, "I'm the fuckin' king of the world!" I've had five women in bed at one time for long periods of time. Just group sex constantly. They used to call me "Manson without the Murder" because I had my harem. They would make my food and suck my cock and do whatever else as well as being with themselves. Ain't nothing wrong with double chicks in bed that are down with it.

RITA HANEY: I have so much respect for the strong person Phil was. Not his morals, because some of his morals were totally crappy when it came to trying to fuck everybody's wife or girlfriend. But that's kind of a New Orleans thing. Those dudes kinda did that, and it was okay. That bros-before-hos kind of thing.

BOBBY TONGS (videographer): Occasionally, Vinnie would bring chicks on the bus, but me and Darrell always had girlfriends back then, so we didn't get involved. But they'd get on the bus and act like they owned it, and we didn't appreciate that. Vinnie would always pass out first, and then we'd have these chicks riding with us, and me and Darrell would have to sit there and listen to them all night. Finally they'd pass out, and usually they'd leave their shoes or something up in the front lounge. So we'd take their shoes and microwave them and bend the little buckles every which way. We'd fill the pockets of their jackets with chili or put a chicken wing in there. We'd be crying, laughing for hours, passing the camera back and forth and filming this shit.

For Anselmo, partying on the road didn't end with booze and broads. Throwing himself into his performances night after night for eight years left him with two painful ruptured discs in his back. Exercise helped to a point. Drugs were more effective. He started with prescription painkillers like Vicodin and codeine, but discovered that the most helpful narcotic was heroin. For a while, Anselmo kept his drug use in check. As his back pain worsened, however, his usage increased and he began to withdraw from his bandmates. Then, two months into a tour for 1996's *The Great Southern Trendkill*, Pantera received an alarming wake-up call following a show at the Coca-Cola Starplex in Dallas.

VINNIE PAUL: Phil was raging, but he kept to himself, and the performances were good, so we felt that was okay. To me, *The Great Southern Trendkill* was the most extreme record we'd ever made. It came out in '96 when the rap metal thing was going down. We thought, "This is the biggest bird finger we can give the whole industry." We still sold almost a million copies. It's hard for me to listen to. It's not very musical. It is the most abrasive and darkest record Pantera's made. We didn't know it at the time, but Phil was going through a lot of mental distress and drugs. And it's all on that record. You can really feel the pain—you can see it and you can hear it. It's just crushing.

PHIL ANSELMO (1996 press release): I, Philip H. Anselmo, immediately after a very successful show in Dallas, injected a lethal dose of Heroin into my arm, and died for four to five minutes. There was no lights, no beautiful music, just nothing. And then after 20 minutes (from what I heard later) my friends slapped me and poured water over my head, all basically trying to revive me. The paramedics finally arrived and all I remember is waking up in the back of an ambulance. From that point on I knew all I wanted was to be back on the tour bus, going to the next gig. Instead I was going to the hospital where I was released very shortly. You see, I'm not a heroin addict. But I am (was) an intravenous drug abuser. The lesson learned here is that every nightmare ever heard about O.D.ing and/or Heroin is terribly true. And for my friends and family as well as myself and our fans (Pantera, Down Etc.), I since then have recovered completely, the Pantera Tour uninterrupted. I intend to keep it that way! Special Thanks to my Family and Friends who supported me, and the fans who pump me up to the hilt. One message to everyone in this fucking world. I am not a weakling groping for sympathy. I WILL NOT DIE SO EASILY! I'm here to piss off the music press for a long time to come.

VINNIE PAUL: None of us knew he had a problem with heroin. Then, bam, we do the biggest show that we've done in years—twenty thousand people in our hometown—and somebody comes up and says, "Hey, man, something's wrong with Phil." I went over to the next room and he's blue and lying on the floor. The paramedics are working on him. You talk about shocking. We all sat down, cried together, talked together. It made us better as people, it made us better as a band. We thought those days for him were over.

REX BROWN: This type of music is intense shit. It drains you, man. And if you can't go any further, you can't go any further. At that point, we were starting to become unhinged.

VINNIE PAUL [2003 interview]: It wasn't a "one for all, all for one" thing, the way it used to be. It was me and my brother in one bus and then Phil and Rex had their thing. I don't know if he was using [heroin] the whole time, but it got to the point where I didn't know which Phil was gonna show up to the gig. One night he would walk in and be a fucking animal. The next night, I'd walk backstage and he'd be lying in the corner and he'd say he was tired or his back hurt. I will never take anything away from that dude from when he was at the top of his game, but where he's at right now, yeah, I think he's much less than subpar at what he does, and I have a hard time watching him when I see him on MTV talking about Superdope Ritual [sic] or whatever they're called, and he can't keep his fucking eyes open.

PHIL ANSELMO: I felt like heroin couldn't kill me, man; there was no way heroin was stronger than me. Come to find it *could* kill me and *did*, and no fucking way is *anyone* stronger than heroin. Heroin—definable, evil. You're a liar. The most wretched liar. I've had friends whose wives had just miscarried and they're racing to the hospital to be with their wife and their stillborn child . . . but they need to stop off at the junkie house and get a quick fix. I've had friends at other friends' funerals who have overdosed and died, and they're lying in the cold fucking earth at twenty, and they're going back and forth to the car, shooting up. Not pissing on their friend's grave, fucking opening the coffin up and ripping the corpse apart. Man, I've [overdosed and] died three times and been brought back each time. And it was *still* a hard thing to give up.

RITA HANEY: There was an incident [when Pantera was] in Australia in 2001—and that's why Darrell started compiling footage—because he wanted to show it to Philip and go, "Dude, look at you. What are you doing?" It was an interview where he was so out of it and he said so much shit that they got [Phil's friend] Jimmy Bower [Eyehategod, Down] to run into the room and steal the tape recorder from the press guy because Philip had made such a fool of himself in the interview and he didn't even know what he was saying. Darrell came back and said, "Dude, we actually had to steal that guy's shit. I bought him a whole new recorder because I felt bad, and I told him I didn't know who did it."

VINNIE PAUL: We all flew out of New York City six hours before 9/11 happened. We landed in Dublin, Ireland. I got off the plane and I had never felt such a cold vibe in my life. I didn't know what was going on. I went to my hotel, got checked in, and my tour manager called and he said, "Are you watching TV?" I said, "No, what, do they have the Cowboys game on?" He said, "Turn it on." I turned it on. The second plane flew right into the tower, and I went, "Wow, what fucking movie is this?" He went, "This ain't no fucking movie, dude. This is happening. The tour's canceled." We were stranded there for fourteen days before we got to fly home. During that time, I didn't speak to Phil once. He turned into a recluse and went into his room. We came home. Two weeks later he called me up and goes, "I got all these side bands I want to put out. If you don't want to help me get them out, I quit the band." I said, "What are you talking about, dude?" He said, "Elektra's not gonna help me do this, and if you don't help me, I quit." I'm like, "All right, I'll do what I can for you." I did every-thing I could to get the guy squared away. We'd been doing Pantera for twelve goddamn years and we already agreed to take six months to a year off. Next thing I know, Phil's off doing Down. There's no communication. We went a whole year without being able to get in touch with Phil through his management. He was talking shit about us every night on Ozzfest. His attitude was totally destructive.

RITA HANEY: They tried to help Philip every step of the way. They called Sylvia Rhone at Elektra, and said, "Hey, let the dude go ahead. We'll take six months off and then you'll have your new Pantera record." Vinnie sent Down a brand-new drum kit. Darrell sent Down a PA, monitors, everything they would need for a studio. And he was leaving messages on Phil's machine saying, "Hey man, I was just trying to see if you got the equipment we sent." They were *that* supportive. That's another reason why later on when they found out Phil was doing heroin again and talking shit about them, Darrell started wondering, "Did I help the demise of my band by supporting him?" I said, "No you didn't! All you did was just love him." But he felt betrayed.

PHIL ANSELMO: Once you start using, drug addiction is past, present, and future. You remain addicted. When someone says, "I've kicked drugs," well fine, but for how long? That's the question that would probably loom in any addict's mind. I'm an extremist. With me it's all or nothing. Sometimes it takes a certain getting somewhere in your brain to live the moment. In order to do [*Down II: A Bustle in Your Hedgerow*] I had to torture my soul. No matter how cheesy it may sound, it's the fuckin' truth.

RITA HANEY: We got stories about how Down were at Elektra to play the record for the label and they were completely ridiculous and wasted, saying things like, "We're the next Led Zeppelin. We don't need the Abbott brothers. We're gonna be huge."

VINNIE PAUL: Phil has no respect for anything and perceives other people to be less than he is. After hearing him talking so much shit, I looked at Dime and we went, "You know what? I think this might be the end of this. We better start doing something because the only thing we know how to do is play music." So any kind of rumors about a Pantera reunion back then are total bullshit. Maybe the other guys thought there was gonna be one, but me and Dime were done.

PHIL ANSELMO: Truth be told, me and the boys hadn't talked in a while, I had been doing Superjoint, wasted out of my mind. Superjoint was on its last legs and I knew this, then I heard about [Vinnie and Dime's new band] Damageplan. I called up Vince. He said, "I don't know if Dime wants to talk to you, man. He's pretty angry. You've been out there doing Super-joint, we've been sitting here for over a year wondering what the fuck is going on." He said, "You can try and call Dime back, but I don't know." So I called Darrell. I said, "Sorry I haven't been in touch. Happy to hear you're jamming, man. What's going to happen with Pantera?" He said, "I'm not worried about that anymore. I got this new shit going on." I said, "Really? So, no more Pantera?" He said, "Man, you've been doing this and that." I said, "Yeah, I know what I *have* been doing. Here's the question once again: No more Pantera?" He said, "Nope." He was doing Damageplan and that was the last time I spoke to him.

Pantera or no Pantera, metal remained in a state of flux through the nineties. Old-school heroes like Dokken, Ratt, and Queensrÿche could barely fill clubs, while others, like Skid Row and Lita Ford, left the industry for years. For Iron Maiden, who longed to return to stadiums, the only way to move forward was to return to the past. In 1999, vocalist Bruce Dickinson rejoined the band after a six-year absence, and Maiden released the progressive return-to-form *Brave New World*, which they followed with a triumphant reunion tour.

BRUCE DICKINSON: It was [manager] Rod [Smallwood] who took me aside and said, "How do you feel about getting it back together?" [I told Rod,] "Well, you know there are a couple of things that concern me, but 90 percent of things I think are massive opportunities."

STEVE HARRIS: I've always had the view that you don't look back. You look forward. The thing is, we know Bruce and we know what he's capable of, and you think, "Well, better the devil you know." We got on well professionally for, like, eleven years, and so . . . after I thought about it, I didn't really have a problem with it.

BRUCE DICKINSON: I told him, "This is why I left." I can't remember exactly what I said, but at the end, I said, "Does that make sense?" He went, "Well, yeah."

As Maiden was regrouping with Dickinson, Rob Halford was collaborating with Nine Inch Nails front man Trent Reznor and John Lowery (aka John 5) on the industrial metal band 2wo. Additionally, in 1998, Rob Halford, then forty-seven, dropped a bombshell during an interview with MTV news producer Jim Fraenkel—although most of those who knew him were hardly surprised.

ROB HALFORD: I think that most people know that I've been a gay man all of my life, and that it's only been in recent times that it's an issue that I feel comfortable to address, and an issue that has been with me ever since recognizing my own sexuality. A lot of homophobia still exists in the music world—in all kinds of music. . . . I think it's difficult for everybody, you know, in making the decision to come forward and be who you are, based on peer pressure, especially if you're a teenager. That's where a lot of the anxiety begins, and so maybe people like myself and others that do step in front of a camera and let the world know. Maybe it's of some help when there's an individual that's been successful, that's been able to achieve dreams and visions and goals in life and not let the issue of sexuality be something to hold them back, so I think it's an important thing.

MARK McGRATH (Sugar Ray; TV host; DJ): Before Rob came out, I didn't know he was gay. One day, I was at Riki Rachtman's [*Headbangers Ball*] barbecue. Riki's parties had a mix of the real metal dudes and the guys that were kinda new, like Alice in Chains and [Faster Pussycat's] Tamie [Downe]—but also Rob Halford. Back then as a joke, I used to wear daisy dukes, heavy metal jean shorts, rolled up, with my nuts hanging out. Then I see Rob Halford, and I've never met him before, so I am over the moon. I went to him with such enthusiasm—I looked like "Play the Game"-era Freddie Mercury, I go, "Rob, I'm such a big fan." I'm overly friendly, touching him. [Film director and McGrath's best friend] McG is there with me. We were hustling, trying to get a record deal. So I gave Rob my number, told him if he ever wanted to hang out. . . . He took it that I was cruising him, so he started calling my number, which was the house hotline for my band the Shrinky Dinks. First message was [*in British accent*] "Hello Mark, it's Rob here, I'm currently in Phoenix but I'm promoting the Fight record right now, and I'm going to Los Angeles, back and forth, back and forth, back and forth." He said, "I'd like to fly you out to Phoenix so we could see each other." The way he said "*so we could see each other*," I went, "*He's gay!*" I look at McG, and he goes, "You gotta go. Now! It's *Rob Halford*. He's the Metal God." I was too freaked out. He left a few messages, but he speaks so eloquently, I almost turned gay. I wish I had a gay inclination, 'cause it would have been Rob Halford if I was going to get down with a dude. Believe me. I felt bad if I misled him in any way. I was like, "Why would he think I'm gay? Oh, the shorts and the touching and the phone number."

IAN HILL: We used to call it the worst kept secret in heavy metal. We knew from day one that Rob was gay, and it was left up to him whether he wanted to come out or not.

ROB HALFORD: Unless you're a gay person, you can't really explain why you need to [come out]. I let myself out of jail. For those people who live in that straight world, who have no connection with gay people or the culture, they were probably surprised. But I think many of those people went, "I don't think it's important. It's the music that matters."

KERRY KING: I wanted to be in denial, but shit, you can only hear it so many times. He's hanging out with a certain type of guy every show. Yeah, it just had to be made public. I personally don't fucking care for fucking homos of either sex, but as long as they ain't in my face, fine. It wouldn't be a problem if they weren't so fucking petty about getting it in the public. If you want to go fucking suck a dick, go suck a dick, but I don't need to know about it.

ROB HALFORD: [Before I came out] they had their girls, and I had my right hand and a bottle of Dermalube and a porno mag [*laughs*]. It's fucking sad, man. No one was willing to face the truth. I was scheduled to do a photo shoot with Cheryl Rixon, who was a *Penthouse* pet of the year, on the roof of a hotel near a swimming pool. Cheryl was in this skimpy little tits-and-ass bathing suit and I was in full-on leather S&M gear. I loved it. I never got a boner, but it was hysterical. Of course, the implications of the picture are enormous. It was a difficult time. It's part of being in the closet. It's difficult, but my music helped me survive all that.

CHERYL RIXON: I did the shoot with Rob by the pool at the Parker Meridien in New York. We had a blast. We were really comfortable together because I knew he wasn't sexually attracted to me.

While Halford was busy with Fight, 2wo, and his eponymous solo band, his former bandmates hired singer Tim "Ripper" Owens, from an Ohio cover band. The 2001 film *Rock Star*, which starred Mark Wahlberg and Jennifer Aniston, was based on an article about Owens that appeared in the *New York Times*. At first, Priest were consultants for the movie, but they backed out when they realized the screenplay didn't accurately reflect their story. Owens sang on two Priest albums, the thrash metal–inspired *Jugulator* in 1997, and the slower, more straightforward *Demolition* in 2001.

TIM "RIPPER" OWENS (ex–Judas Priest): At one point in high school my whole room was nothing but Judas Priest stuff. I wouldn't allow any other band pictures on my wall. Then fifteen years later, I'm in the band. I [auditioned with] "Victim of Changes." I sang the first line and Glenn Tipton said, "Okay, Owens, you got the gig."

IAN HILL: We went through thousands of tapes and videos trying to find someone to fill Rob's very large shoes. We didn't find anybody until [drummer] Scott [Travis] came along with a videotape of Tim singing with a cover band. We thought, "At last we have someone who can not only handle the notes that Rob hits, but he knows the songs. He's singing them already."

RIPPER: At the time, there was never any intention of getting Rob back. Their intentions were, "Rob's doing his thing, we're gonna do ours." But as time goes on, you see the wheels turning. You start thinking, "Uh-oh, here it comes." [In the early 2000s] Judas Priest was starting to get a lot of good offers to reunite with Rob. I got an e-mail that read, "Listen, we decided to get Rob back." Even though it was an e-mail, it was still handled in a good way.

Vinnie Paul and Dimebag Darrell's new band, Damageplan, featured ex-Halford guitarist Patrick Lachman on vocals along with bassist Bob Zilla (Hellyeah). They released their debut album *New Found Power* in 2004. The music was less abrasive and confrontational than Pantera's, but it maintained the group's trademark groove and blended midtempo thrash with some more accessible elements. It also featured some high-profile guest stars.

VINNIE PAUL: We got some special appearances from Corey [Taylor] from Slipknot and Zakk Wylde. Dime fuckin' loved Zakk, man. They had some of the best times together. One time, Dime and Zakk were doing a cover for *Guitar World*, and Zakk had only heard a little bit of the music from the Damageplan album. So Dime goes, "Zakk, man, come down to the studio and check this shit out." He heard it and went, "Yo, bro! I wanna play lead on this motherfucker right there." He had, like, ten minutes before he had to go to the airport. He said, "Go get my guitar out of the car." He comes back and starts fucking shredding. He heard the song "Reborn" twice and he played it twice and he smoked.

PATRICK LACHMAN (Damageplan, Halford): We all started doing shots and next thing you know Dime says, "You want to hear the diversity in the record?" He puts on "Soul Bleed." Zakk's people are going, "Zakk, you gotta go, you're gonna miss your plane." And he says, "Yo, I gotta go and sing backups on that, real quick. Turn the microphone on." He wound up missing his plane.

Damageplan's album came out February 10, 2004, to mixed reactions. Some Pantera fans were stoked to hear the Abbott brothers rocking again, but many felt it wasn't brutal enough and missed Phil Anselmo's vocals. Anselmo, who was admittedly often under the influence at the time, took stabs at the Abbotts in the press. At first, Vinnie and Dime turned the other cheek; however, they soon started returning the jabs. Vinnie Paul remains convinced that Anselmo's venomous tirades contributed to Dimebag Darrell's murder on December 8, 2004, by schizophrenic ex-marine Nathan Gale, a Pantera fan who, it was alleged, blamed the Abbotts for Pantera's breakup.

Dime, who was performing onstage with Damageplan at the Alrosa Villa in Columbus, Ohio, was shot three times in the head by Gale. Also shot and killed were Jeff "Mayhem" Thompson, the head of Damageplan's security; Erin Halk, a club employee who tried to stop Gale while he was reloading; and Nathan Bray, a Damageplan fan who was administering CPR to Darrell. The band's drum tech, John "Kat" Brooks, was shot, but survived; Damageplan tour manager Chris Paluska was injured, but also survived. The bloodbath ended when undercover police officer James D. Niggemeyer entered through the back of the club and killed Gale with a shotgun round to the face. In the aftermath of the shooting, accusations flew, and more than eight years after the tragedy, Anselmo and Vinnie Paul Abbott still hadn't spoken to each other.

VINNIE PAUL: We were two shows away from the end of the tour and we were really looking forward to going back for Christmas, blowing up New Year's Eve, and getting to work on the next Damageplan record. We played the demos all the time on the bus. The night before all this shit happened, we played Buffalo, New York, and we always liked to go gambling. We finished the show, and we were like, "Man, we're gonna run up to Niagara Falls and gamble. Let's go." Dime was like, "Man, I'm too smoked. We got two shows left. I wanna just take it easy and kick some ass and go out strong." I'd never seen Dime turn down a night of gambling. So me and Mayhem went gambling and had a blast. About two-and-a-half hours later, we called the bus to come pick us up and as soon as we hopped on I figured everybody was gonna be asleep. But there was Dime sitting in the front lounge with half a dozen people, partying. I was like, "Dude, I thought you were smoked and going to sleep?" He was like, "Dude, I couldn't let these people down, man. They wanted to fuckin' party, so I brought them on the bus."

RITA HANEY: He really, really wanted to cancel those last four shows and come home. They were coming off of the Slayer run in Canada and he was like, "Man, do we really have to play these shows on the way down? Can't we just keep going and get in the studio?" He was so fired up on the new stuff.

VINNIE PAUL: We got to the gig the next day in Ohio and Dime gets up and goes, "Man, we gotta go and do a sound check. I was having a problem with my rig last night." We only had two shows left in the tour, but that's how much he cared about his shit. We had played the club back in the early Pantera days. Dime went around and found the club owner and said, "Thanks for having us back. We're glad to be here." There was this band playing in front of us that was doing Parliament songs heavy metal style, and they were all dressed up like G.I. Joes, and we were catching such a nut on them. We were back there doing shots and peeking out and cracking up. We were all in a good mood, and we had a full house. I went up on the deck and right before we went on, Dime was warming up his hand and putting his lip gloss on. The last thing I ever said to him was "Van Halen?" He gives me a high five and says, "Van fuckin' Halen." That was our code for letting it all hang out and having a good time. That's the last thing he ever said to me, man. A minute, forty-five seconds later he was gone. It's insane. . . . Insane.

RITA HANEY: I can't help but think things about Phil—like Darrell wouldn't have even been playing this shit hole if you hadn't done what you did before the demise [of Pantera] or put him where he was. All kinds of things run through your head. I even think stuff like, if I hadn't gone home, I would have been in the front videotaping right in front of him. Would I have seen this guy coming? Could I have jumped on him and stopped him? I've had time to think about it to where there's only one person to blame for what happened, and that's the person who did it. I do have resentment toward [Philip] for hurting Darrell. But if I blamed Philip for Darrell being in that shit hole I could easily turn around and say, "Vinnie, why didn't you cancel the show like he asked?" It just doesn't get you anywhere.

VINNIE PAUL: There's no doubt the guy who did this was out of his fuckin' mind. He's somebody that should have been in-carcerated. When you've got somebody with obvious mental problems, it's not a great idea for him [to own] a gun that's used for killing people in the military. And obviously, he knew how to use it. He wasn't just some ragtime dude who grabbed a gun. I saw what happened, and I knew exactly that the dude was on a mission, man, for whatever reason.

Some of the lingering animosities between Vinnie Paul Abbott and Phil Anselmo stem from an antagonistic interview Anselmo did with the UK magazine *Metal Hammer*, which came out shortly before Dime was killed.

PHIL ANSELMO [2004 interview]: There was never a point when [Dime] could not get drunk, which was pretty much every day. Now I'm hearing it's worse than ever. He would attack me, vocally. And just knowing that he was so much smaller than me I could kill him like a fuckin' piece of vapor, you know, he would turn into vapor—his chin would, at least, if I fuckin' smacked it. And he knows that. The world should know that. So physically, of course, he deserves to be beaten severely. . . . But of course, that's criminal and I won't do such a thing. . . . Really, I just let him prattle on. I grew very tired of it very quickly, and in all honesty I really wish that [the Abbotts] would be men, which is very hard for them, figuring that they were living in their mother's house until they're thirty years old. In comparison, I was on the street by choice at the age of fifteen, living anywhere I could.

VINNIE PAUL: He said it word for fucking word. He was not coerced into saying it by the interviewer. And the kind of shit he said in there is the kind of shit that might incite [Nathan Gale] to do the kind of things he did. Phil called me when he was trying to get into the funeral and left me a message that said, "I can prove to you I didn't do that interview." I got the fucking audiotapes, man. Anyone that wants to hear them, I'll be happy to play them for you. Him sitting there and talking in a calm voice, saying the shit that he said. So he ought to feel really fuckin' guilty, any way you slice it.

PHIL ANSELMO: The press did wind us up. We were both guilty of taking the bait. Very guilty. There was the unfortunate article, there was Dimebag's death, and, in my view, if there's anyone that does not know any of us, nor was in the fucking band, if they're going to take a stand, I say "Who are you, motherfucker? You don't know me. Therefore you do not affect me." That's how I see it. I am not bothered by it. I've moved on. I've found my peace. Do I understand it all? Fuck no. Will I? Fuck no. I'm sure I won't. Who can fully understand the acts of a maniac who murdered someone close to you? You can't understand that. You accept it. It's a done deal. Do you wear it on your heart? Yeah, probably forever.

Anselmo, who says he quit heroin in 2002, was lying in bed in New Orleans when he heard that Dimebag had been shot and killed. Devastated that Vinnie Paul and Rita Haney did not want him at the funeral, he made a raw, emotional video speech to his fans, during which he struggled to hold back tears.

PHIL ANSELMO [from Internet video]: This isn't about me or some motherfucking psycho that happened to destroy the most beautiful fucking person, one of my best friends in the world. It was the heavy metal goddamn media that destroyed Pantera. This is about Darrell, my brother of seventeen years, whose music changed people's lives, man. We weren't just some band. He was not just some guitar player. I wanna say bless his family and all his close friends and I never got a chance to say good-bye in the right way and it kills me. And I'm so sorry. I wish to God I could have gone to his funeral, but I have to respect his family's wishes. And they do not want me there. I believe I belong there. But I understand completely. I'm so sorry to his band members. I'm so sorry to the whole fuckin' world that loved Dimebag Darrell because let me tell you something. There was not one motherfucker like him. Vinnie Paul, my other brother. I'm so sorry. I'm so sorry.

VINNIE PAUL: Phil likes to blame the heavy metal media for breaking up Pantera. I've never felt betrayed by the media in any interview I've done. They've printed what I've said word for word, verbatim, and I never felt like they were out to get me. He did his interviews, he said what he said, and all they did is write what he said. If he really wants to place any blame, he needs to look in a mirror.

RITA HANEY: When I saw Phil at the Download [Festival in London years after Dime's murder], I looked in his eyes and I asked him, "Why?" It was the first and only time that he didn't make an excuse. He looked me in the eye and said, "I don't have an excuse. I'm a junkie. I was an idiot." He didn't say, "Oh, my back hurts [so I took drugs that made me say stupid shit]" or anything else.

PHIL ANSELMO: What made me finally quit drugs was a good friend of mine overdosing right in front of my eyes. Right next to me. Time stopped. We were in a speeding truck in the middle of fucking nowhere, heading to nowhere. There was no motherfucking hospital. Just a dude next to me who I've known for fifteen years whose heart had stopped. I fucking freaked. I pulled this dude's beard, slapped his fucking face, grabbed ice from the ice chest and put it down his pants, punched him in the balls. Nothing. I said, "No way! No fucking way!" and I reared back and I punched this motherfucker in the chest as hard as I could and his eyes opened. His pupils were like the actor Marty Feldman's, completely fish-eyed apart. I punched him again in his chest and his eyes came together and he was back. Shortly after, I met Kate [Richardson], my lady, and that's another hard one to explain, because the first time I met her I fell in love with her. It fucking got me. The rules were laid. "You want me as a partner, no drugs allowed. I'm not gonna share you with that fucking church of hypodermic." So I made that choice.

VINNIE PAUL: My life has been one gigantic comic book, and on the other hand it's been one gigantic book of laurels and amazing accomplishments, and on the other hand it's been a book full of horror stories. It's a big book.

8

HİGH-ŦECH HAŦE:
İΠDVSŦRİAL, 1980–1997

The descriptors of some subgenres of metal, such as "death" and "black metal," are nebulous at best. But the word *industrial* conjures up vivid imagery of the music and lyrics it designates: the filth of coal mines, the unrelenting whirr of a sawmill, and, especially, the buzz and grind of automotive factories. Before industrial metal morphed into industrial dance music, its sound was indeed rooted in the sounds of the factory. The term stems from the name of the pioneering band Throbbing Gristle's label: Industrial Records. Emerging from Kingston upon Hull, England, in 1976, Throbbing Gristle strove to emulate the clatter and clamor of industrial machinery by combining performance art with primitive electronic beats and analog samples. Like-minded artists—Sheffield, England's Cabaret Voltaire, Sydney, Australia's SPK, and others—took a similar path to sonic annihilation. Then in 1980, West Germany's Einstürzende Neubauten emerged with a more percussive style of music that took a fairly literal approach to the term *industrial*, combining actual machinery—including jackhammers, barrels, and chainsaws—with harsh Teutonic vocals. The next wave of industrial bands, including Skinny Puppy (started in Vancouver, Canada, in 1982) and KMFDM (launched in West Germany as a performance art project in 1984), incorporated Neubauten's dissonant assault with a variety of keyboard melodies and dance beats. (KMFDM was originally called Kein Mehrheit für die Mitleid, which translates as "No pity for the majority"; the acronym was not short for Kill Mother Fucking Depeche Mode, as was widely believed.) As industrial became more structured and technology advanced, bands added distorted electric guitars and caustic samples, making the sound more conventionally metallic.

TRENT REZNOR (Nine Inch Nails): I don't mind the term [*industrial*] applied to us, but I think the reason people cringe is what it connotes—Throbbing Gristle, Test Department—bands Nine Inch Nails have very little in common with. What is industrial, then? I'd basically define it as dance music that's a bit harder, a bit tougher, definitely with a drum machine and maybe some distorted vocals.

ADAM GROSSMAN (Skrew): When I think of early industrial bands, I picture that guy Dieter from "Sprockets" on *Saturday Night Live*. There was this whole kind of intellectual philosophical based thing that was underground and elitist.

BILL LEEB (Front Line Assembly): To me, industrial music is six guys onstage with shaved heads, pounding viciously on metal drums. They have sheep's heads and blood and power drills. There's a film of an autopsy playing in the background, and there are no effects, no tapes, or samples, or anything.

SASCHA KONIETZKO (KMFDM): We did an early KMFDM show in Paris and we had a fire-eater onstage, and we would blow up TV sets and bang on sheet metal and air conditioner ducts. We had twenty people onstage, and everybody wore funky outfits. There was fake blood and we were shooting animal intestines around the stage. We've changed a lot since then.

Legendary Danish face painter and black metal progenitor King Diamond is bad to the bone. Photograph by Stephanie Cabral.

Conrad "Cronos" Lant spews Venom. Photograph by Ray VanHorn.

Brazilian thrash hero Max Cavalera (Sepultura/Soulfly) frets and screams. Photograph by Stephanie Cabral.

Anthrax's Scott Ian poses with late Metallica bassist Cliff Burton at London's Marquee Club in 1984.
Photography courtesy of Scott Ian.

Overkill's Bobby "Blitz" Ellsworth conjures the magic.
Photography by Bill O'Leary.

Slayer assembles the war ensemble. Photograph by Kevin Hodapp.

Megaforce Records founder Jonny Z at Rock n Roll Heaven record signing with Raven. Photograph by Kevin Hodapp.

Lemmy entertain you. Photograph by Jon Wiederhorn.

Early Megadeth lineup: Chris Poland, Dave Mustaine, Gar Samuelson, Dave Ellefson.
Photograph by Kevin Hodapp.

Anthrax guitarist Scott "Not" Ian before beard and baldness. Photograph by Kevin Hodapp.

Jonny Z welcomes Alcoholica into the Megaforce family. Photograph by Kevin Hodapp.

Early Megadeth and Slayer: best buds? Photograph by Kevin Hodapp.

Former and current Anthrax vocalist Joey Belladonna. Photograph by Nick Charles.

Blond bombshell sacrificed at the altar by future husband Jeff Hanneman and bandmates, circa 1983. Photograph courtesy of Metal Blade.

LAYER

THE
HOLLYWOOD PALLADIUM

GOLDENVOICE presents

The Masters of Black Metal

from England

venom

from L.A.

SLAYER

from S.F.

EXODUS

LP—Bonded by Blood—out Apr 5

Friday··April 19··7·30 pm

IN ASSOCIATION WITH *Avalon*

(213) 480-3232 AND (714) 740-2000.

Dream bill for hell-bound metalheads!
Courtesy of Todd Nakamine.

Testament vocalist Chuck Billy bares his bling. Photograph by Stephanie Cabral.

Chuck Billy wants YOU for Testament Army! Photograph courtesy of Nuclear Blast.

James Alan Hetfield: some kind of monster?
Photograph by Jon Wiederhorn.

Metallica founders James Hetfield and Lars
Ulrich slay on the Death Magnetic tour.
Photograph by Jon Wiederhorn.

New York hardcore pioneers Agnostic
Front. Photograph by Todd Huber.

Thrash and crossover collide in downtown Los Angeles in 1985. Courtesy of Todd Nakamine.

After leaving Anthrax, bassist Dan Lilker broke new ground with Nuclear Assault. Photograph by Bill O'Leary.

Type O Negative's Peter Steele: gothic in green. Photograph by Stephanie Cabral.

Suicidal Tendencies' Cyco Miko Muir. Photograph by Jeremy Saffer.

Pantera front man Phil Anselmo shows how high Pantera can get with the #1 Billboard Album Chart debut of Far Beyond Driven. Photograph by Stephanie Cabral.

Rhythm guitarist Mike Clark displays his suicidal tendencies. Photograph by Stephanie Cabral.

DRI's Kurt Brecht: original imbecile. Photograph by Bill O'Leary.

Biohazard bassist/singer Evan Seinfeld lays down the urban discipline. Photography by Bill O'Leary.

...tera guitarist Dimebag Darrell dressed to impress the 1994 Type O Negative tour. Photograph by ...ephanie Cabral.

Longtime Ozzy Osbourne guitarist and Black Label Society front man Zakk Wylde hits the Bullseye. Photograph by Stephanie Cabral.

After Dimebag Darrell's murder, his brother Vinnie Paul resurfaced in the new band Hellyeah. Photograph by Jon Wiederhorn.

Dimebag Darrell: struck by lightning.
Photograph by Stephanie Cabral.

Dimebag Darrell's last run with Damageplan.
Photograph by Jeremy Saffer.

Pantera's Phil Anselmo strikes his Jesus Christ pose at the 2001 Ozzfest.
Photograph by Stephanie Cabral.

The *"Metal God" screams for vengeance.* Photograph by Stephanie Cabral.

Slayer guitarist Kerry King fiddles while Rome burns. Photograph by Jon Wiederhorn.

Burton C. Bell bares his soul during Fear Factory's heyday. Photograph by Stephanie Cabral.

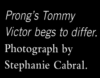

Prong's Tommy Victor begs to differ. Photograph by Stephanie Cabral.

Nine Inch Nails mastermind Trent Reznor smells the glove. Photograph by Stephanie Cabral.

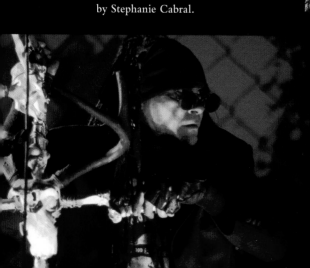

Rammstein vocalist Till Lindemann plays with fire. Photograph by Stephanie Cabral.

Ministry vocalist Al Jourgensen, industrial metal deity. Photograph by Stephanie Cabral.

Marilyn Manson: Antichrist Superstar. Photograph by Stephanie Cabral.

Marilyn Manson lends bandmate Twiggy Ramirez a hand. Photograph by Stephanie Cabral.

Killing Joke's Jaz Coleman dares others to follow the leaders. Photograph by Greg Cristman.

Rammstein's stroke of genius. Photograph by Stephanie Cabral.

Early Rob Zombie: the devil's reject.
Photograph by Bill O'Leary.

*Longtime Marilyn Manson guitarist John 5
finds a new home with Rob Zombie.*
Photograph by Stephanie Cabral.

*Onstage blood bath with
Skinny Puppy's Nivek
Ogre.* Photograph by
Greg Cristman.

BRANDON GEIST (editor in chief, *Revolver* magazine): At one point, mixing dance music with metal was about as taboo as you could get. It was one thing for metal and punk to start cross-pollinating, because those seem like natural bedfellows. But it took real balls for a metal band to start collaborating with an electronic dance music producer or start making dancey metal.

The most successful artists to create hybrids of metal and industrial are Ministry, Nine Inch Nails, and Marilyn Manson. But the first band to incorporate tangible elements of industrial and metal in their music was London's Killing Joke. The band formed in 1979 and blended rigid, repetitive riffs, regimental drumming, and aching vocals with strident keyboards and sound effects.

JAZ COLEMAN (Killing Joke): When we started Killing Joke, we looked to all the outcast philosophers, guys like Nietzsche, Spinoza, and Aleister Crowley, for inspiration. At the time, we were all very cynical about punk. We would listen to dance music and seventies disco music and heavy, dark reggae. Of course, we liked a lot of high-energy music like AC/DC, and it was there that our tradition started.

TONY FLETCHER (journalist): [Killing Joke] was stark, dark, minimal, confrontational, loud, and not a little violent. And that was just their reputation as interviewees. But there was something truly fascinating about Killing Joke's apocalyptic vision, and their arrival on the London scene upon the dawn of the eighties was impossible to ignore.

JAZ COLEMAN: One time in 1981, we had two thousand people at a concert and they were all fighting. It was like the music was a soundtrack to the violence. That's when I questioned whether I was part of the problem or the solution.

TOMMY VICTOR (Prong, Ministry): To me, [Killing Joke's 1980] song "Change" [from their second album, *What's This For . . . !*]

started the whole danceable metal thing, which, eventually, we really used for [our biggest single,] "Snap Your Fingers, Snap Your Neck."

JAZ COLEMAN: One of the funny things about Killing Joke was we were intense and things could get violent, but we weren't one of these self-destructive bands. We'd have gallons of tea and the occasional reefer, but we never drank. Our first gig in America was in 1981 at the Rock Lounge [in New York City]. [Ronald] Reagan had just gotten into office. We were backstage, and this junkie guy came up to [drummer] Big Paul [Ferguson] and said, "Hey man, can I use your belt?" This guy was gonna jack up. Paul took off his belt and started whacking him with it. The guy yelped like a dog and ran out of the dressing room, and the promoter came in and said, "You don't know what you've done. That was Johnny Thunders [late guitarist for the New York Dolls]."

The first industrial band to be openly accepted by metal audiences was Chicago's Ministry. Ironically, the group began as a dance band, and their first record, 1983's *With Sympathy*, was lightweight synth pop with syrupy vocals. It would be another three years before Ministry evolved into the most carcinogenic industrial band with the guitarless but unnerving *Twitch*. The keyboard-only mandate didn't last long, and by 1988's *The Land of Rape and Honey* Ministry had added caustic metal riff samples to the electronic mix, creating the template for groups like early Nine Inch Nails, Rammstein, and Static-X.

AL JOURGENSEN (Ministry, Revolting Cocks): I started playing guitar in the seventies, and I did it to get laid, but I wasn't that great of a guitar player. I was into MC5, Nugent—anything loud. Then somebody taught me a little bit of synth and I figured, "Well, I can actually play this better than I can play guitar." Then I got into Throbbing Gristle and Cabaret Voltaire and realized I wasn't as good as them on synth and I wasn't as good as the metal bands on guitar—but I could do both. So it was a case of [being a] jack-of-all-trades, master of none. I roped the two together out of necessity.

JAZ COLEMAN: I remember Al [Jourgensen] coming to our Boston Channel gig in 1980 dressed like he was in Duran Duran. Of course, he ended up later marrying my ex-girlfriend. There's nothing like flattery, is there? He married her and they both became junkies. Happily ever after [*laughs*]. I love Al. He is the cuddliest, nicest person you could meet. It's just that people die around him.

AL JOURGENSEN: Really? C'mon. I was never involved in anyone's death. [Killing Joke bassist] Raven died after he played with us, but he was working with Treponem Pal in Geneva, Switzerland. And I was devastated.

ROB ZOMBIE (ex-White Zombie): When I was in White Zombie, people were always saying to me, "Oh, man you gotta see Ministry. They're the most insane thing." I was like, "Wait, weren't they that disco band?" I didn't get how they could suddenly be really heavy.

AL JOURGENSEN: I started as a metal and industrial dude before anyone knew what the fuck industrial *was. I* didn't even know what it was. Then I signed to Arista, and they made me become Milli Vanilli, like a pop artist. So I sued them, got off their label, and hooked up with Wax Trax!, and I started doing my own music. A lot of the stuff that Arista rejected [for *With Sympathy*] wound up on *Twitch* and [1988's] *The Land of Rape and Honey.* I was doing that in 1980, but they said, "No, we don't want *that,*" even though *that's* what I was playing live in clubs. Arista said, "You need to get a nice little haircut and wear suits and be British." So it wasn't a real big switch for me to go heavy. The unnatural progression was doing that Arista album.

PAUL BARKER (ex-Ministry): In the early eighties a lot of people were just making straight electronic music. We brought out guitars because we weren't interested in being enslaved by our machines. We grew up loving rock, and Al was a really good guitarist. So we're like, "What are we doing? Why are we trying to make just noise records?"

AL JOURGENSEN: What I did notice about the difference between our electronic and metal stuff is the kind of chicks I would attract. When I was doing the synth stuff I got fat chicks with runny makeup. When I was doing metal I had skinny chicks with puffed up hair. When I put both together I kind of got a midway chick with runny makeup and puffy hair.

KEVIN OGILVIE ("NIVEK OGRE") (Skinny Puppy): At first there was a kind of a competition between us and Ministry. We were following each other around. Al was cutting himself for real [with a razor blade], and I was faking it. Then I started cutting myself for real, and Al started faking it. We asked Al to produce our [1989] album *Rabies*, and that's the first time our two worlds merged and we had a lot of these metal guitar sounds. Then when I was touring with Ministry, our crowds converged. Touring with Ministry was definitely like boot camp. In Salt Lake City, Al beaned somebody with a bottle by accident. Afterwards, I came back to the hotel in a cab with a bag of weed in my pocket to the tune of six police cars with their high beams on, and everybody was out of the bus with their hands up. But it all ended up fine. There were apologies made and a T-shirt given and all was fine.

AL JOURGENSEN: Chaos followed me everywhere. When I was in Tennessee during Lollapalooza '93, I bought this gigantic pyrotechnic from some toothless guy behind a truck stop. [Butthole Surfers front man] Gibby [Haynes] was with us and lighting off m80s in the back of the bus. I decided to one-up him. I lit the firework thing, which was like a bazooka that's

larger than a man's arm. It was a professional pyrotechnic that
you're supposed to light on boats, away from people, and it's
supposed to make a pirate ship in the sky. So the fuse is lit and
everyone was freaking out, but I was just joking and I went,
"All right, enough's enough." I tried to put it out and I didn't
realize it was an underwater fuse. The only way you can put
that out is to cut it, and we didn't have scissors. So we passed
it around back and forth to each other, freaking out. Then
the thing went off. There were all these pellets that shot out
down the length of the bus, and everything it touched started
a different color fire. Just the recoil of this thing going off
sent me flying back four feet through the air into the back
lounge. People are diving out of the way of the sparks and
the bus driver pulls over and says, "Get off my bus. I'm calling the police." He called the cops. We had put the fire out
by this point, but there's still so much colored smoke coming
out of the bus it looked like *Apocalypse Now*. The cops pull
up and they looked at the bus driver, and he's going, "Throw
them in jail. They blew up my bus." This Texas state trooper
was chewing tobacco. He spits, looks at the bus driver and
goes, "Well, what do you expect? This ain't Mozart, it's rock
and roll. Now get these boys back on the bus and get off my
highway."

JAZ COLEMAN: The Ministry thing was based on this idea that
it's cool to be sick. They used shock for shock's sake. You'd
have Ministry videos with people jumping out of buildings
and scenes from *Faces of Death*.

AL JOURGENSEN: What people don't get is the macabre shit is
absolute parody. I make fun of people who have a fascination
with the macabre. When we were on Lollapalooza, [Pearl Jam
front man] Eddie Vedder said to me, "Look at the Pearl Jam
dressing room." I did and there were all these clean-looking
boys and girls. Then he said, "Now look at your dressing
room, Al." There was a one-legged lesbian with a patch over

her eye, and she's asking me who I'm gonna vote for. All I can say is, "Are you a girl?" Then she hits me and walks out. We get some real fucking strange-os, but it's all right; it just means we have to carry more weapons. That's the only difference between us and Pearl Jam. We're more heavily armed.

One of Ministry's biggest rivals was White Zombie, who, like Ministry, defied the rules of industrial metal long before it helped define them. When White Zombie launched in 1985, it was an offbeat, psychedelic noise-rock band. Over time, however, Zombie evolved into a carnivalesque arena metal band equally influenced by Sabbath, the Ramones, Alice Cooper, and B-movie horror films.

SEAN YSEULT (ex–White Zombie): Me and Rob Zombie met at Parsons School of Design in New York City, and our first drummer went to Parsons. Rob and I were both oddballs, so I think we were drawn to each other. We started the band within a month of meeting, and basically lived together for seven years. We both had dyed black hair; he had a stenciled Misfits leather jacket and I had a bunch of animal bones tied onto a necklace.

ROB ZOMBIE: At the time, there were two scenes going on. There was the New York shit like Foetus and Sonic Youth, and that was the scene we were stuck in. And then there was all the good hardcore that came out of DC, like Minor Threat, Bad Brains, Scream. We took those two scenes we were influenced by and formed White Zombie.

SEAN YSEULT: When our first [full-length] record *Soul-Crusher* came out in 1987, people called us art-noise/dirge/psycho rock. We liked Sabbath and Black Flag, but we were also into Butthole Surfers and the Birthday Party, and we were trying to mix a lot of those things together. People didn't really get it. We would play this really heavy music in clubs in the East Village, and all these hipsters just stared at us and scratched their heads.

ROB ZOMBIE: Even before we found our sound, I knew that going to a show had to be worth leaving your house for. In the eighties, there were so many years of bad shows. A band would make a million-dollar video that looked insane, and then you would go see them live and they didn't do jack shit. My big thing was to give people something for their money.

SEAN YSEULT: Back when we played at CBGB, we used to rig our own pyro. It was totally illegal and very *Spinal Tap*. Either we'd pack too much gunpowder and everyone in the front row would get singed, or we'd use too little and just get this non-impressive fizzle. We were buying all this stuff at these industrial stores on Canal Street—all these cop lights and rope lights. We'd put them all over the stage and wrap them around the amps—anything we could do to be a little more outrageous and obnoxious.

ROB ZOMBIE: People would hear our music and see the show and go, "My God, you guys must do so much dope." I was like, "Why, because we like flashing lights and our pants are dirty?" I've always had so much stuff in my head that I wanted to get done that doing drugs didn't interest me. That whole lifestyle always seemed stupid and contrived. Heroin became popular in LA, and everyone was trying to pretend they were Iggy Pop or Lou Reed. It's one thing if you're the first guy to do it and you don't know what's going on. But if you're just copying what you think is the rock star lifestyle that someone else invented, that's just pathetic.

SEAN YSEULT: We didn't drink, and we certainly never did drugs. We were really straightlaced, which you might not expect from the music and the imagery we used.

ROB ZOMBIE: People used to tell me my goals weren't possible, and I always had that stubborn streak where I'd try to do the exact things that people told me I couldn't do. Every review of

White Zombie in the beginning said, "This is the worst band ever. They should quit. They suck." That was so great. It motivated me to keep going.

SEAN YSEULT: Around the time of [the 1989 album] *Make Them Die Slowly*, we started going in a more metal direction. And we started getting asked to play [Brooklyn metal club] L'Amour by bands like Cro-Mags and Biohazard. These were crossover punk bands that were going kind of metal, and we were really surprised they liked us. I thought they'd want to beat us up, but they gave us the thumbs up and their crowds knew that, so they liked us also. It didn't seem like a place we would survive, between metal heads and skinheads, but everyone dug it, and it was a lot better than playing for East Village crowds.

ROB ZOMBIE: Everything got larger than life because I would go, "Okay, I'm bored. What would make me not bored? I know! Let's do a show where there are 60-foot flames and giant robots and go-go girls. Why can't I do that? No one else is doing it. I guess I'll have to do it." The thing with the theatrics is it will never be a trend because it takes too much work for most people. I could have made ten times the money that I've made if I had no show because it costs a fucking fortune and it all comes out of your pocket. I do it because I love it. That's the world inside my head that I have created on a stage. It just costs more than the world inside my head.

In the late eighties, two more industrial acts surfaced that won over metal audiences: Birmingham, England's sluggish, corrosive Godflesh and New York City's faster, spite-laden Prong. While both were hugely inspired by Killing Joke, the former played crushing, repetitive riffs accompanied by a pummeling drum machine, while the latter went through a hardcore phase before perfecting a mid-paced, staccato thrash sound propelled by serrated riffs and sing-along choruses. While Prong arrived on the scene first, Godflesh was more deeply rooted in industrial music. In 1982, before Godflesh was even a thought, front man Justin Broadrick was tinkering with tape loops in his makeshift project Final, which resembled some of industrial music's forefathers.

TOMMY VICTOR: We started as a hardcore band [in 1986] with noise and metal influences. I liked Killing Joke, Black Flag, Big Black, Die Kreuzen. We just added that into a hardcore framework and then metalized ourselves after the fact. I was working [as a soundman] at the Sunday hardcore matinees at CBGB. I put together a show with Prong, Warzone, and White Zombie when we were trying to solidify a signing with Epic, and nobody [at the show] got along and there was a lot of fighting. . . . It seems like there was always a lot of violence at Prong shows.

JUSTIN BROADRICK (Godflesh, ex–Napalm Death, ex–Head of David, Jesu): I was eighteen and living in a flat with Benny [G.C.] Green, the bass player for Fall of Because. As soon as I was kicked out of Head of David, I said to him, "I'm playing drums for Fall of Because anyway, and I've already got a bunch of songs I've written for Head of David. Why don't we buy a drum machine? You play bass and I'll sing and go back to guitar." So Benny borrowed money from his mum to buy the machine, I programmed the drums I would have played for these riffs anyway, and that's how we got the first set of Godflesh songs.

RICHARD PATRICK (Filter, ex–Nine Inch Nails): The day I met Godflesh I was with Ministry and I was so drunk I ended up puking tequila everywhere. But Godflesh are the reason I knew I could use a drum machine in Filter and it would work. I heard their [1989] record *Streetcleaner* and I said, "This is what we should do!" It's obviously programmed, but the beauty of it is you can do anything. We had seventeen tracks of cymbals being played in [Filter's 1995 hit] "Hey Man, Nice Shot."

JUSTIN BROADRICK: When we started the band, we were doing magic mushrooms and Benny was reading a lot of Aldous Huxley. We had just seen the film *Altered States*, which we watched on acid and got totally obsessive about. Hence, the picture we took from it, which is the front cover of *Streetcleaner*. We took peyote also, which was almost physically transforming. We were obsessive about attaining really extreme hallucinogenic states at that time. Benny read that peyote was referred to as "God's flesh." We were like, "God's flesh, what a wicked name for what we're doing."

TOMMY VICTOR: There was a period of five years where I don't even remember what was going on. The alcohol consumption was incredible, and we were a really angry bunch. When we went out with Pantera, these fun-loving, crazy, wild Texans, we felt so different from them because we were from the Lower East Side and we felt like nobody liked us and we were miserable all the time. It was a totally different vibe than the "Gimme high five!" metal thing that Pantera had. We felt isolated, and as we went along we hated everybody.

JUSTIN BROADRICK: We became quite obsessive about psychedelic death trips and creating music that conveyed that death-trip angle 'cause the trips we shared watching movies like *Apocalypse Now* with our faces four inches from the screen were so heavy. We were just like, "Bring it on!" We really enjoyed how much larger than life these things appeared, and I think that became the influence for making music that felt larger than life.

TOMMY VICTOR: In London, we stayed at the Hilton. It was right by a cricket field. [Ex-drummer] Ted [Parsons] destroyed the place. He was pulling lamps off walls, completely out of his mind. We had a little area of five rooms that we ruined, and it quickly spread from there. We threw garbage cans around the balcony and smashed the glass doors. By the end, we had destroyed a good half a floor of the hotel. We didn't have cell phones at the time, so we had to disappear because we were afraid to be seen anywhere near the hotel while the cops were looking for us. I walked around London for two days because we had no place to stay. That was when I realized we had to change our destructive ways.

JUSTIN BROADRICK: At first, people did not get Godflesh at all. We wanted to mix real industrial music—like Throbbing Gristle, Whitehouse, SPK, and Test Department—with intensely tuned-down guitar and bass and create a dirgey, rock-based cacophony. The situation became more confusing after we signed with [extreme metal label] Earache Records. The label had just started to establish itself with Napalm Death and Carcass, and then they presented Godflesh to a death metal audience that was looking for further metal extremes. It was amazing how outraged a lot of people were by what we were doing.

TOMMY VICTOR: Our crowds were as angry as we were. Every time we played, the mic kept getting smashed in my face [by the crowd], and over time my front two teeth started deteriorating. I'd be spitting blood and trying to sing and play. Eventually I had to get my teeth filed down to make them even.

JUSTIN BROADRICK: We toured in late 1988 supporting Napalm Death, and jaws hit the ground when we started playing. People would dive onstage and yell, "You suck! Where's the drummer?" The same audiences that were berating us at that point came to every Godflesh show two years later to beat the shit out of each other.

Most industrial bands—with the exception of Killing Joke and White Zombie—partied pretty hard; some took raging to dangerous extremes. Cocaine, speed, and psychedelics were abundant, and for many, heroin was more than a recreational activity: it became a deadly maintenance drug.

AL JOURGENSEN: When you make the kind of music we make, drugs can drag you into the music. I don't think it's the other way around. I used to get wasted to the point where I didn't even know I was on this planet. I didn't even know if my soul was in my body—and I came up with some of the best riffs. The drugs and the music went hand in hand because it let me levitate and get out of the mundane. When I was eighteen to twenty-one, I had long hair and I was into Skynyrd. So if I did a band, I'd be Skynyrd, but if I did *drugs*, I'd be something *else*. It was a good thing—at first.

KEVIN OGILVIE: I definitely had a needle fixation. I'd inject cocaine to get hyped and then I'd do heroin to come back down. I suppose shooting up is the closest way a male will get to being a female. There's erection, insertion, ejaculation, and orgasm. When you're injecting, you can't get much higher. Once a person gets addicted to cocaine, it changes the whole chemistry in your head. Wrong becomes right, and right becomes left. In a weird way, all my paranoia gave me fuel for a lot of writing and art.

TRENT REZNOR [1994 interview]: I'm not out to promote drug use, but I think the right drugs used with the right amount of intelligence can be a very important tool in self-awareness and learning about your own mind. I don't ever sit down and write lyrics when I'm high, and when I've tried, it's nonsense. It seems like a great thing at the moment, then you realize later it's gibberish. But I think there's a real importance in the experience. The first time I hallucinated with mushrooms, I was changed for the better in the sense that I realized that all these things I'd been trained to believe in don't make any sense. I found a connection between nature and my mind and everyone else's mind, and everything being under one umbrella in some very obscure and nonliteral way.

AL JOURGENSEN: At the start, the drugs bring out this incredible creativity. They let you free and let your mind wander to discover all these incredible things. That's the open door. But then the door slams shut. The drugs take over and the creativity goes away. And pretty soon you're thinking more about the drugs than the music. That door that was once open to you is locked and you don't have the key anymore. The drugs take over and then you're not "something else" anymore, you're just this babbling idiot.

TRENT REZNOR [2005 interview]: When *The Downward Spiral* tour ended I went straight into doing *Antichrist [Superstar]* with [Marilyn] Manson, and I realized I get fucked up a lot. Pretty much every day. But I was functioning. I didn't realize at the time, but that was the beginning of a pretty intense struggle. I was drinking, but a few drinks in me, if someone suggested getting some cocaine it would seem like a fantastic idea. It still seemed like a great idea twenty-four hours later, picking through the grains of the carpet looking for more. After a while I realized I wasn't in control. The price wasn't just feeling bad the next day; I was starting to hate myself.

KEVIN OGILVIE: When I was heavily into heroin, I went into convulsions several times and I *did* almost die. But even when I had a death wish, there was a very strong base desire to survive. I was once in an apartment building with a friend and I was shooting up in her bathroom. Suddenly, for no reason, I became sure that she was trying to poison me. I went out and lit a pair of my pants on fire and left them on a lamp in one of her rooms. I had the closet door rigged with a wire coming out from the lamp and wrapped around the door, so if anybody came through this door, I thought I could plug in the lamp and electrocute them. I was fucking whacked! I grabbed a pair of pliers and ran around each floor of the building snipping as many electrical wires as I could find. I must have snipped one too many, because the fire alarms and the sprinklers went off and they had to evacuate the whole building.

AL JOURGENSEN: One time, [Skatenigs front man] Phildo [Owen] had a party and I OD'ed on heroin. He starts giving me mouth-to-mouth because I have no pulse. I'm ashen, gray-white. I'm not breathing. He's beating on my chest. I had been out for five minutes and somehow he got me alive again. The first thing I did when I woke up is I punched him out for being a homo and trying to make out with me while I was passed out. Two years later he OD'ed and I had to do the same shit to him—only he didn't wake up swinging.

TRENT REZNOR: By the end, when I was high all the time, I couldn't think, and I didn't want to think. [My attitude was,] "If I can't think, and I can't write, well, I might as well just get fucked up, because what else am I gonna do?"

AL JOURGENSEN: I was on and off drugs, and I got off them for the last time when I realized I was making music in the studio that wasn't really challenging anymore. I couldn't come up with a song to save my life. I was completely broke because I had spent all of my money on drugs. Then I woke up on some crack dealer's couch pawning my last guitar for drugs. But in the long run, I wouldn't change a thing. I'm not pro-drug or anti-drug. I'm pro-human spirit. You do what you need to do to get by.

KEVIN OGILVIE: In 1991, on the first day of the Pigface tour . . . [drummer] Martin Atkins and [guitarist] Mary Raven helped me go cold turkey. I would be sick and throwing up and I'd sleep all day and perform at night, then collapse in cold sweats after the shows. I finally got clean, but for the longest time I still had dreams about scoring and shooting up.

TRENT REZNOR: I finally realized I had to come to terms about becoming an addict—for a long time, I lied to myself about [it] until I couldn't lie anymore—'cause I was either going to die or get better.

Before Trent Reznor went on his downward spiral of depression and heroin abuse, he was an anonymous musician with a background in classical piano. Raised in rural Mercer, Pennsylvania, he moved to Cleveland after a year at Allegheny College, and began playing in local bands. He also wrote music at home on his computer. And when he wasn't writing or jamming, he worked as a janitor and assistant engineer at Right Track Studios, where he recorded the demos that got him signed to TVT Records.

RICHARD PATRICK: Trent and I were both in weak New Wave alterna-bands in Cleveland; his was the Exotic Birds and mine was the Act. We kept tabs on each other and went to see shows like Skinny Puppy and Ministry. Then we ran into each other again at the Fantasy at a concert by [Al Jourgensen's side band] Revolting Cocks. Trent goes, "See that guy up there? That's Al Jourgensen; he's my fucking idol!" It was really Al Jourgensen's [1986] album *Twitch* and sound design from Skinny Puppy that were the building blocks for Nine Inch Nails. Trent liked *Twitch* because it was a little more pop-oriented and it used traditional songwriting, but it was still weird and had rough edges and was jagged and scary.

TRENT REZNOR: If anyone ever asks me about influences, I always say Ministry. I'm not embarrassed by that, but I also don't want NIN to be the Ministry wannabe band. Al's been a hero of mine. But I have to admit, before I met him, I thought, "Is he going to fucking throw a bottle at me?"

AL JOURGENSEN: I love Trent, man. Before he got all famous he was a roadie for Ministry. He was this kid and he rode with us in our bus and we used to fuck with him all the time. We'd throw firecrackers into his bunk and scare the shit out of him. At my studio, we had a rule that you couldn't fall asleep or you'd get fucked with. So one time when he was passed out I took out a razor and shaved his head. I thought he looked pretty good that way.

RICHARD PATRICK: Trent came up to me one day and was like, "Hey listen, I finished up this new record. I actually have a record deal." Now, for kids of our generation, being in an alternative band from Cleveland and getting signed was unheard of. It was probably the most one-sided, most horrible record contract in existence. He signed away his entire publishing, everything. But still, he had a record contract. He goes, "I'm going to go on the road. Wanna be in the touring band?" I had just disbanded the Act, so I was like, "Sure, let's go for it."

TRENT REZNOR: What I was trying to say with [my 1989 debut] *Pretty Hate Machine* was that the world sucks and everything around me is a piece of shit, and everything's depressing me, but I've still got myself. Through that whole Lollapalooza tour [for *Pretty Hate Machine*] I felt overwhelmed. When an underground band starts to get big, some of those initial supporters start to turn on you because now you're too big to be cool anymore. I thought Nine Inch Nails was getting out of control in terms of how big we were getting. I felt like everything I've worked on my whole life I'm starting to get, yet it was all falling apart because the record label we were on did everything they could to fuck it up. I didn't really like myself or what I had become at that point. In my personal life, I didn't know who I was. I looked back at what I'd done, and I realized that's not the me I thought I was. That really fucked me up. I've done some shitty things and abused some people, and taken people for granted. I've done nice things as well, but when you finally have a moment to sit back and think, "Well, what am I now?" I mean, the normal me is the person who's not on tour, that's at home, but is that really me?

RICHARD PATRICK: The highlight of being in Nine Inch Nails was when I sat down by myself and wrote [the breakthrough Filter single] "Hey Man, Nice Shot" because I knew I would soon be out of the insanity and the pure emotional hardship of being in that band. I was paid next to nothing. Trent would smash $40,000 worth of equipment, and I came home from his huge Lollapalooza tour with maybe a thousand bucks. I lived at home with my parents, and that's when I was like, "Something's not right."

By the end of Lollapalooza, Reznor was emotionally shattered. He responded by writing the 1992 EP *Broken*, which featured his fastest, heaviest, and most metallic songs to that point. It was both an attack on TVT Records, which was taking the lion's share of his earnings, and a cathartic release of the stress and insecurity that had consumed him since "Head Like a Hole" became a hit single.

TRENT REZNOR: I wanted *Broken* to be really angry through and through, like a punch in the face. I didn't want to convolute that message with slow parts or dance tracks. Basically, *Broken* was me saying "fuck you" to everybody. There's a lot I don't enjoy about the competitive and backstabbing nature of the music business. Fame—being put on a pedestal just to be immediately taken off—is a drag, and I don't think my skin is tough enough to deal with it most of the time.

RICHARD PATRICK: When Trent saw the Jane's Addiction electronic press kit [video] that came out, in which Dave Navarro and Perry Farrell were making out, he was into the shock value of that. So he just found a little part of subculture that hadn't necessarily been exploited yet—the whole S&M thing—and he grabbed it and attached it to his own aesthetic. He put out a video for "Happiness in Slavery," which had a meat grinder tearing this guy apart.

TRENT REZNOR: A lot of times sadomasochistic imagery works as a good metaphor. Sometimes I know what I'm writing about, sometimes the truer meaning becomes apparent to me later. But dominance and submission, and power in relationships, whether physical or mental, is interesting to me.

RICHARD PATRICK: He was never, like, this wild S&M guy or anything. Trent was very conservative sexually. He would always have a regular girlfriend. There were no groupies or anything. Al [Jourgensen] was the one who was completely, totally, and utterly into everything. At one point, Trent hired Al to help him and Al was like, "Sure, I'll take your money." Al had no respect for him, but Al sure had a good time. He was banging dope right in front of us. And he'd fuck any girl right in Trent's house. Al came down from Mardi Gras and had all these crazy goth girls with him that were part of the subculture he created. Trent would hear things going on in the next room as he was sitting there with his then-girlfriend and he would say, "What the fuck is happening?" In the morning, Al would wake up and go, "Okay everybody, we're having margaritas." He'd put in a little bit of a margarita mix and a whole ton of tequila. And he'd go, "What else you got, Trent?" Trent would go, "Well, I think that's pretty much it, margarita mix and tequila." Al goes, "No, no, no. Where's the washing machine? There you go, a little Clorox." And he would pour a little Clorox into the blender. Then he'd say, "You got any motor oil?" Then he would mix it up and fuckin' drink it and serve it to everybody. It was not enough to hurt anybody, but you still knew there was Clorox in your margarita.

With both metal and alternative camps firmly supporting him, Reznor holed up in the home of the late Sharon Tate, who, in 1969, had been murdered by the Charles Manson clan in that same house, and wrote *The Downward Spiral*, a bleak, haunting album that balanced pop hooks and warped keyboards with progressive arrangements and just enough guitar angst to remain heavy. Angular and angry, it's probably the only album ever released with a mega-hit single that features a sing-along chorus with lyrics as extreme as "I want to fuck you like an animal."

TRENT REZNOR: I was living in New Orleans and couldn't find a house and studio that was the right size and distance away from other houses. So we came to LA and saw the Tate house. It was the coolest house—very centrally located but still fairly isolated, and it was on a beautiful piece of property with an amazing view. When we later found out it was *that* house, that just made it more appealing. It's a cool piece of history. I wasn't consciously thinking of what great media stories I was going to get, it was just an interesting place to be—a cool house in a very uncool city.

RICHARD PATRICK: When Trent started working on that album he was freaked. There was a lot of money flying around, and he was in that house way too long. I went to play "Hey Man, Nice Shot" for him and say, "Hey, what do you think of this?" He said, "Yeah, fits really good," and that's huge for him to even say because he's so competitive. I offer it to him and he says, "Maybe I'll take the riff and we'll do something cool." An hour later, [Reznor's ex-manager] John Malm calls me and says, "You can never own it, you can't have any publishing, but we'll give you credit." I said, "No, I think I'll keep it for myself." Now, being out of that camp and owning 100 percent of that song has literally paid my mortgage, paid for my life for the past fifteen years.

TRENT REZNOR: Going into *The Downward Spiral*, the safest thing I could have done was make another *Broken* that was tough and mean and would show everybody how many great metal riffs I can write. It would have been the least artistically challenging thing, so I wasn't going to do that. I started *The Downward Spiral* on guitar but ended up using a lot of computer instead of guitar to write because it was a lot more inspiring to me. I was also trying to make a record that was fairly broad in its scope musically, rather than everything being really hard and fast.

RICHARD PATRICK: While he was working, Trent was nice enough to let me record demos. But there was always this belittling vibe with him and John [Malm]. I was getting paid $400 a month. After a while, I called John and said, "I don't think $400 a month is gonna be able to cut it." I will never forget this. I was in my brother's guest room talking to John on the phone and he goes, "Well listen Rich, we know you want some extra money. We found a great little pizzeria down the street and saw a 'Help Wanted' sign, and we think it'd be in your best interest if you got a real job to see how hard it is out there in the real world." I said, "For $400 bucks a month you want me to go deliver pizzas so I can learn the meaning of the word *respect*?" That was the final straw for me. Fortunately, the next phone call I got was [from my own manager], going, "Warner Bros. and Atlantic are interested in you. Are you available?" I'm like, "Are you fucking kidding? I'm *so* available."

TRENT REZNOR: I'm on a quest to figure out what the fuck is in my own head. I think a lot of the stuff that's addressed on my records is from a fairly confused standpoint, and one that I know is incorrect, or maybe looking for solutions in the wrong things. With *The Downward Spiral* I wanted to really examine the debris of that negativity and see what I could make out of it. And maybe that involved being a bit more musically diverse with a lot more moodiness and atmosphere in the music, and maybe a bit more lyrically vulnerable. When you peel back the skin, sometimes you find that what you see is not always the person you thought you were.

CHUCK PALAHNIUK (author): I listened to *The Downward Spiral* and *Pretty Hate Machine* constantly while I was writing *Fight Club*.

There were cuts on it that I would put on repeat to the point that my housemates were just insane. "Hurt" was one of the big ones. The lyric "I hurt myself today / To see if I still feel" might as well be one of the novel's mantras.

TRENT REZNOR: Before it came out, I thought there was a danger that there weren't any real singles on the record, and people that really liked *Pretty Hate Machine* wouldn't like *The Downward Spiral*, and people that were more into the metal sound of *Broken* wouldn't like it. That's when I caught myself saying, "Am I a marketing product or am I trying to make a piece of art? This is the record I wanted to make." I thought I quite intentionally may have shot myself in the foot commercially. I didn't do that just to fuck myself up, either. It's what popped out of my head and was the strongest statement I could make. Fortunately, people identified with it.

CHRISTOPHER HALL (Stabbing Westward): When Nine Inch Nails got really popular, people compared us to them. We're not really influenced by them, but more by people who *influenced* them, like Ministry and Skinny Puppy. But I always thought melody was missing from industrial music. That's why we did songs like "What Do I Have to Do" and "Shame."

At the height of his commercial and critical success, Reznor formed the vanity label Nothing, which released future NIN records as well as albums by Prick, Meat Beat Manifesto, and 2wo, a collaboration between Reznor and Rob Halford. None was particularly successful, but one superstar—or rather *Antichrist Superstar*—bankrolled every failure. Before being courted by Reznor, Marilyn Manson (aka Brian Warner) was the leader of the Florida-based performance art/shock metal band Marilyn Manson & the Spooky Kids. Impressed by his nihilism and perversity, Reznor signed Marilyn Manson and produced his 1994 debut *Portrait of an American Family*, the 1995 EP *Smells Like Children*, and the 1996 breakthrough *Antichrist Superstar*, on which Reznor is credited with playing Mellotron, Fender Rhodes piano, and guitar, as well as programming and mixing. But Manson didn't want to be someone else's protégé, and by the time *Antichrist Superstar* was a hit, he had burned bridges with Reznor and lashed out on his own. In no time, Manson was the new antihero for a generation of postmillennial misanthropes, the bogeyman for terrified parents, and a whipping boy for conservative America. The more heat he took, the more outrageous he became in his show, cutting himself, dressing in outfits reminiscent of Nazi soldiers, and tearing up the Bible. For Manson, spitting in the face of the mainstream was as enjoyable as having a hit single.

MARILYN MANSON: "Marilyn" came to me in about 1990 from watching a lot of talk shows and reading *Hollywood Babylon*. I realized Marilyn Monroe and Charles Manson were some of the most memorable people from the sixties. I thought—in the tradition of philosophers like Hegel—about the juxtaposition of diametrically opposed archetypes: taking two extremes, putting them together, and coming up with something totally different. It's male/female, good/evil, God/Satan. That kind of defines my personality and represented the lyrics that I was writing. I met Trent Reznor, and over the growth of Marilyn Manson, I always passed along demo tapes [to him]. When he got the opportunity to start his own label, he contacted us.

TRENT REZNOR: From a business point of view, Marilyn Manson was wildly successful. I think he's a talented guy, and I'm not taking credit where it's not due. If there was a valid role I had, it was helping provide a framework to allow him to do what he wanted to do.

MARILYN MANSON: A lot of people think that Trent was very involved with our songwriting and the direction of the band. [Our second album,] *Mechanical Animals*, not only proved that we can do things on our own, it proves that what we've done in the past was still very much our own creation. The problem with *Antichrist Superstar* was I was put in a position where I was made very unsure of myself. I was questioning everything I did because at the end it really fell apart, and I had to make a choice whether to accept someone else's opinion or my own. Trent is a very heavy-handed producer, but I've always been my own songwriter. I have no animosity against Trent. I don't think that we'll ever work together again—I think that's obvious. But that doesn't mean we can't be friends.

TWIGGY RAMIREZ (Marilyn Manson): We come from a different place than Trent. I want to make music that people can put on if they feel shitty, and it will make them feel even more shitty. I like to write stuff that makes people want to go out and do drugs and fuck shit up. If I can motivate someone to go out and destroy something, I accomplished my goal.

JOHN 5 (Rob Zombie, ex–Marilyn Manson, ex–David Lee Roth): When I was in 2wo with [Rob] Halford, we were supposed to do a festival in Germany with Manson that was canceled. I was so bummed because it was the last day of the festival and I never saw Manson. I get home from Germany, put my bags down, and the phone was ringing. It was Tony Ciulla, Manson's manager, saying, "We're looking for a guitar player. Would you like to come meet Manson?" I was like, "Absolutely." We met at Gaucho Grill [in West Hollywood] and he had a Loverboy shirt on and big sunglasses. He asked me to be in the band right there. He gave me the name [John 5] there in the restaurant. He wanted me to rerecord the guitars on *Mechanical Animals* because they hated ex-guitarist Zim Zum so much, but the record company was like, "We can't, we've got to put this out."

A volatile, confrontational performer, offstage Manson abused himself and others as well. He developed a hearty appetite for cocaine and other drugs, and relished every opportunity to stretch the limits of his libido.

MARILYN MANSON: I met Alyssa at a showcase we did for Maverick Records. I immediately realized she was deaf because of the way her voice sounded. A year later we were at South Beach Studios in Miami, and I went outside to get something to eat and I ran into Alyssa. I said, "Why don't you come by the studio?" It was ironic because just that day [ex-keyboardist] Pogo [aka Madonna Wayne Gacy] was saying that one of his fantasies was to have sex with a deaf girl. Pogo shouted, "I'm going to come in your useless ear canal," and it seemed to echo through the room as maybe one of the darkest things we had ever heard. Alyssa went to take a shower because she was covered in meat [we had thrown at her while she was naked] and assorted body fluids from the act of filth. So since she was going into the shower anyways, I asked, "Can we urinate on you?" She said, "Just not on my boots, and don't get it in my eyes. It burns." Twiggy and I put one leg on the stall and one leg on the toilet and hosed her down with urine.

JOHN 5: Every single night, every single day [there was debauchery]. It was disturbing, to say the least; it was unbelievable. The very first night of [2000's] *Holy Wood (In the Shadow of the Valley of Death)* tour there were tons of girls, and this girl had to go to the bathroom. Someone said, "Hey, why don't you just go in the trash can." I had the video camera, we're all giggling. She starts to pee in the trash can, but she has a dick. It's on film if you look on [2002's] *Guns, God and Government* DVD in the behind-the-scenes section. And a black girl was smoking a cigarette with her vagina—and this is just the very first night of the tour. This stuff happened every night. I was upset if I didn't [have sex with] two girls a night.

MATT PINFIELD (TV host, *120 Minutes*; DJ): We're partying under Roseland, doing blow and drinking. It was before a trip to rehab for me. I see Twiggy and Marilyn, and they're sitting there, and Marilyn just looked at me and goes, "Pinfield, you scare *us*."

ALICE COOPER: When I first saw Marilyn Manson I went, "Well, I can understand this: a new Alice Cooper for a new generation." It was sort of like, "Hmm, girl's name, makeup, tall, slender, theatrical"—except that he found different pressure points and anger points within the audience. "I'm gonna be a devil worshipper. I'm gonna tear the Bible up. I'm gonna do all this Nazi stuff." This was going to irritate every parent and every church in America. I totally got it [though] I was surprised that he went with a girl's name, only because that just made it *totally* Alice Cooper. When I saw his show, I realized it was different. But at the same time, I could not buy into his theology at all. The guy was in the Church of Satan. When I announced that I was Christian, he suddenly disowned me saying, "I hate Alice Cooper because he's Christian."

MARILYN MANSON: I'm completely unlike a lot of other performers in the past who have been forgiven or come to terms with the real world because they tell everyone their performance is just a show. So people say, "Oh, it's okay then. We don't care. He's not really a bad person." It's not just a show for me. It's my life. I live my art. I'm not just playing a character onstage. Anyone who thinks I'm just trying to be this weird or shocking guy is missing the point. I've never tried to be merely shocking because it's too simple. I could do a lot more shocking things [than I do]. I've just always asserted myself as a villain because the villain in any walk of life is the person who refuses to follow blindly and always wants to question things.

ALICE COOPER: Manson and I had about twenty-five rounds of dueling against each other in the press. But we finally did meet in Transylvania at a festival around 2008. He walked by the dressing room and knocked on the door and opened it as I was getting ready, and he said, "Can I come in?" I said, "You know what? It's about time we met." We got along very well. But I still held to the point that my belief in Christianity was something where his show did offend me in a lot of places.

Tearing up the Bible and throwing it in the audience—that was very offensive to me. But he came up onstage and did "Eighteen" with us and then I did "Sweet Dreams" with him. I understood that for this generation there needed to be a new villain, and he was that villain.

MARILYN MANSON: I was born to be a rock star, so I'm just trying to be the best one that I can. We're in an era where rock music is gradually becoming extinct, and I think it's important for me to ensure that it survives and that it survives with a personality and an attitude, and not mediocrity. The only rock music that exists right now isn't doing what the people that created the music form intended for it to do. Now I feel I can balance perfectly because I can be as sober as I want, or I can out-drink Frank Sinatra or Jim Morrison, and I could do more drugs than Andy Gibb, and I could still get up and look better than all four Spice Girls.

JEFF HANNEMAN: When we toured with Manson [in 2007] I went onto his bus one time and he says, "Hey, Jeff." I go, "Hey, what's up?" He says, "Hey, come kick me in the balls." I told him, "I'm not gonna fuckin' kick you in the balls." I was like, "This is too weird. I gotta go."

TRENT REZNOR [2009 interview]: Manson is a malicious guy and will step on anybody's face to succeed and cross any line of decency. Seeing him now, drugs and alcohol rule his life and he's become a dopey clown. During the *Spiral* tour we propped [Manson's band] up to get our audience turned on to them, and at that time a lot of the people in my circle were pretty far down the road as alcoholics. Not Manson. His drive for success and self-preservation was so high he pretended to be fucked up a lot when he wasn't. Things got shitty between us, and I'm not blameless. The majority of it, though, was coming from a [resentful] guy who finally got out from under the master's umbrella and was able to stab him in the back.

MARILYN MANSON: A doped-up clown sounds kinda fun. It sounds like something you'd send to a kid's party and be really upset you've hired the wrong person. Which is kinda me. Lipstick, drunk sometimes. . . . Since I've known Trent he's always let his jealousy and bitterness for other people get in the way. I'm not talking about me—I sat back and watched him be jealous of Kurt Cobain and [Smashing Pumpkins'] Billy Corgan and a lot of other musicians. I stopped thinking about him a while back, but I know that every day I have a song played where the money will go to him, forever. As long as I have a record deal it will be attached to him financially. In the words of his own song, you shouldn't bite the hand that feeds you—you should take that hand and punch yourself in the face.

Around the same time that Trent Reznor was falling out with Marilyn Manson, White Zombie was heading for the grave. The band, which started as a tight-knit group, had become a business entity, and the bond that once united them was splintering.

ROB ZOMBIE: The last seven years of the band were pretty shitty. No one got along, no one ever wanted to do the same thing. It was like when you have a group of friends, and everyone outgrows each other. But when you've got all this money involved and these expectations about what you're supposed to do, it forces all those people to stay together and you drive each other fucking crazy.

SEAN YSEULT: It's weird that he would say that because we were together eleven years, and most of that time was really good. But when we were in the middle of a tour with Testament in 1992, [drummer] Ivan de Prume and Rob got in a big fight onstage. Ivan made a slipup and Rob got mad and spit on him. Ivan was like, "I quit!" Rob said, "Okay, quit!" I thought we could work things out, but at that point it was irreconcilable. That was sad because we were like a gang or a family of misfits. By that time the band and business had really taken over our relationship, so Rob and I decided to call it quits as a couple. That was when we started working on *Astro Creep 2000*, [which came out in 1995].

ROB ZOMBIE: When we recorded the last record, I don't think the four of us were in the studio at any point. I would ride on a separate bus at all times. Separate dressing rooms. It was just four people who didn't work at all. That was beyond stressful. Everything about it should have been great. We had finally made it, we sold millions of records, we were playing in big, sold-out arenas. On the outside, it looked so fucking great, but on the inside it sucked.

SEAN YSEULT: I dated Al [Jourgensen] for a while in 1995, and I don't think that helped my relationship with Rob any [*laughs*]. Al and I packed a couple of years into a whirlwind couple of months. He almost drove us off a cliff at Johnny Depp's house. It was late one night and Al was backing up. I told him he should back up a little slower 'cause we were getting ready to go off a cliff, and he proceeded to back up really quickly. It was just like in a Looney Tunes cartoon. The car was teetering back and forth and we had to delicately leap out of the Taurus back onto safe ground and spend the night there until we could get a tow truck.

ROB ZOMBIE: Now [as a solo performer with a new band], I'm finally in a place where I'm with a group of friends doing this weird thing and we're all on the same page. I never had that before. This feels like what that was always supposed to be.

SEAN YSEULT: The end for White Zombie came because Rob wanted the band to go a little more techno. He hired [programmer] Charlie Clouser from Nine Inch Nails to write techno tracks, and [guitarist] Jay [Yuenger] and I had to create riffs over them on a couple of songs. Rob can be really controlling. Whoever's on his team, it's them against the world. Once Jay and I didn't want to go along with him creatively, he kind of considered us against him.

Most industrial bands that formed in the eighties had played electronic music and alternative rock prior to integrating their music with metal. One of the first extreme metal bands to tinker with samples and electronics was Fear Factory.

DINO CAZARES (Fear Factory, Divine Heresy): I first heard [vocalist] Burton [C. Bell] singing in the shower. In the late eighties, we both lived in this eight-bedroom house in Hollywood that this guy rented out to starving musicians. Burt's in there singing some U2 songs and I thought, "Hey, it sounds pretty good." Later, we met and started talking and I found out he was into some heavy, heavy industrial shit. I was into grindcore, death metal, and speed metal, so he turned me on to stuff I didn't know and we decided to start a band together.

BURTON C. BELL (Fear Factory): The reason I moved into that house was because I was in this industrial noise band called Hateface and my other bandmates lived there. When we broke up, Dino said, "Hey man, I know this great drummer. We're gonna meet and jam. Come with me." That's when we went and met Raymond [Herrera].

DINO CAZARES: I said to Raymond, "Yo, I'm trying to put a band together. Let me know if you're interested." He said, "Well, I know a band looking for a guitar player. Why don't you go jam with them?" So I went and joined this grindcore band called Excruciating Terror. But I was like, "Eh, I need something a little more experimental." One day I was at rehearsal and the drummer didn't show up. Raymond happened to be there to watch us rehearse, and he got behind the kit and I was like, "Oh, man, this guy can play double-bass pretty good. Maybe I can see something going on there." So

I quit Excruciating Terror after two shows. And Raymond goes, "Well, *our* guitar player quit. Wanna join *my* band?" His band was horrible. They were called Extreme Death. But I saw the potential in Raymond. So I asked him to join forces with me. I said, "We already got a singer," because Burton was on board. So we formed the band Ulceration, and later, three of those songs came out on Fear Factory records.

BURTON C. BELL: Dino was friends with [producer] Ross Robinson, and Ross wanted to get into producing. He had an investor and he was engineering at Fort Apache, which was [W.A.S.P. front man] Blackie Lawless's place. Ross heard our demos and said, "Hey, I love your sound. I want to start my own label. I want to produce." We went, "Okay." So we went into Ross's studio and recorded sixteen songs in a week and a half, and it sounded killer. Then he handed us this contract [which would have given him ownership of everything]. We showed it to our lawyer, and he was like, "Don't sign that!" We didn't, so basically, Ross owned the masters, but we still owned the songs, we just couldn't use the versions Ross produced. So we sent the DAT of those recordings to Road-runner, and that's what got us signed. Later, Ross played our demo for Korn to show them he knew how to produce bands. He played them "Scapegoat," and then all of a sudden you hear a song called "Blind" coming from Korn. I think Ross was a real helpful inspiration to them by showing them that sound.

ROSS ROBINSON (producer): I kind of got jacked and I thought, "Oh gosh, maybe I should have a band sign a piece of paper *before* I record them." The next band I worked with was Korn. At least [Korn] signed something, and they could've jacked me too, but they stuck by me, where the Fear Factory guys just jacked me. I mean, I love those guys now; we were all just kids, doing the best we could.

DINO CAZARES: On the first album we didn't have a bass player, but we got [Andrew Shives] after the record was done, so we put him on the album cover and used him for touring. But he and Raymond didn't get along, so after the record came out we needed to find another bass player. A week or two later, Christian [Olde Wolbers] came in. Our rehearsal room was in South Central LA, a heavy gang area. Sometimes we'd open the door and hear "pop, pop, pop." And we knew someone was getting shot at. So we'd close the door and wait til it was over. During the Rodney King riots the owner of the place put "black-owned business" on the door so the building wouldn't be burned down. The day we auditioned Christian, we had a few bass players waiting outside, including him. He was like, "Man, where the fuck am I? I'm gonna get jumped. I'm gonna get killed!" We liked him—not because he could play that well, but because he was different. He wasn't from the LA scene.

BURTON C. BELL: The first record, *Soul of a New Machine,* was definitely an introduction to Fear Factory. I have been told a few times that the whole metalcore vocal style [death metal vocals leading into a clean, melodic chorus] is all my fault. When we started out, it definitely took people aback.

DINO CAZARES: When *Soul of a New Machine* came out, some people were like, "Whoa, this is new." Other people went, "He's singing melodically? That shouldn't be on a fuckin' death metal record!" I've heard a lot of people say Burt ripped off [Killswitch Engage singer] Howard Jones's style. I'm like, "Uh, well, that was Burt's thing. He was doing that *before* Howard."

BURTON C. BELL: It wasn't until we did the remix of *Soul of a New Machine* [called] *Fear is the Mindkiller* [1993] that we met (ex-Front Line Assembly programmer) Rhys Fulber, and we went, "Wow. This is a great sound. We could really move this forward." We were always fans of Ministry and KMFDM, and we thought we should integrate some of those more industrial elements into our sound. That's where our second album, *Demanufacture*, came in. We brought Rhys in to co-produce and do the soundscapes for it, and it was that union that really helped create the sound that we're known for.

Fear Factory's albums abounded with experimentation, innovation, and mathematical precision that required endless hours of intense studio time. However, perfection came at a price. The members argued frequently and grew further apart with each release. On the road, tempers flared, and the musicians antagonized one another out of boredom.

RAYMOND HERRERA: Dino would get under Burt's skin pretty frequently. They would argue about the color of the sky. That created a lot of tension. Then we had some misfortunes that didn't help. In 1994, we had all our gear stolen in Philadelphia. We show up at the hotel. We had a long night. We wake up. Our truck is gone. All our shit was gone. We had to cancel the tour and go home. Also, the rest of us liked to party and Dino didn't get high at all. His only real vice was having sex with whoever he could find.

DINO CAZARES: I didn't do drugs and I hardly drank. I was definitely a sex addict. I never had a girlfriend for that reason. I was into full-on orgies. Once, I had four chicks at one time. I was picking girls from the audience and pointing them out to my personal assistant, who had a red bandana. He'd go through the crowd and when he found her he'd wave the bandana. I'd give him the thumbs up, and he would talk to her. Nine times out of ten, the girl I wanted would come back. I had some girls waiting on one side of the stage and other girls on the other. During the five-minute wait before the encore, I'd go backstage and get a quick blowjob and then come back on and start the next song. On average, I'd have sex with two girls a night.

RAYMOND HERRERA: The rest of us had girlfriends or were married, so we didn't get into that. But there was plenty of it around. Seeing the same girl with three different guys from three different bands in one night just comes with the territory.

DINO CAZARES: In 1994 we were out with Sepultura and we had this tour manager whose communication skills were horrible. He talked to everyone like they were pieces of shit. I knew I had to get him back some time and I knew he was a really big stoner. One day this kid came to the show and said, "Hey Dino, can you let me in? I got some weed for you." I walked him in the back door and took the weed. All of a sudden I had an idea. I picked up a girl and took her to the bathroom. She gave me a blowjob and right when I came, I pulled out of her mouth and shot my load on this weed. The girl thought I was fuckin' weird. She bolted, but I didn't care. I put the weed back in the foil, let it sit for a few days and ferment. I told everybody on the whole tour, "Look, I'm gonna give this nugget that I shot a load on to our tour manager when he's behind the soundboard." That's exactly what I did. Everybody was watching. He opened it up and put it in his pipe and took a hit, and everybody's like, "Oh, my fucking god!" He blew it out and went, "That's some really good weed." Everybody just blew up laughing.

Fear Factory's commercial peak came with 1998's *Obsolete*, a bruising, well-crafted industrial metal album laced with enticing melodies. Ironically, the springboard that launched them into mainstream success was a collaboration with Gary Numan on a cover of his 1979 hit single, "Cars," which was left off the first pressing of the album. The record went gold. Fear Factory's management and label, hoping history would repeat itself, encouraged the band to work with nu-metal producers and add hip-hop elements to their sound for their 2001 album, *Digimortal*, which featured a collaboration with Cypress Hill's B-Real on the song "Linchpin." For Bell and Cazares, it was the beginning of the end. During the tour, a rift developed between them, and the band broke up. They later regrouped without Cazares, while the guitarist played with underground death metal groups Brujeria, Asesino, and Divine Heresy. But without Cazares's catchy, ripping guitar riffs, the band fizzled. In 2009, Cazares and Bell mended fences and re-formed without Herrera and Olde Wolbers, and Fear Factory returned heavier than ever.

RAYMOND HERRERA: [Before the first breakup] I was in the back of the bus playing video games. We were getting ready to leave to the next city. Our tour manager had to delay our departure. Dino crawled up his ass. Burt went to defend him. All of a sudden it went from Dino arguing with the tour manager to Burt arguing with Dino. Then some personal stuff came up and before you know it, they're throwing punches. Burt's really reserved and quiet and private; he's just not the kind of guy who gets into fights. So when Burt went to punch Dino, I knew this was a different situation than we had ever experienced. We had another four months to tour. And man, it was uncomfortable. These guys wouldn't eat at the same table, sit in the same room, or look at each other. Then in Tokyo Burt said to me he would finish Japan and Australia, but after that he was out.

DINO CAZARES: After Burt quit the band, we all broke up. Then a little while later, Raymond said, "Hey, I have a plan. Let's put the band back together." At first, Burton went, "I don't want nothing to do with it." But then he finally agreed. But the plan from Raymond was Burton could come back and they'd get rid of me and put Christian on guitar.

RAYMOND HERRERA: We still had a contract with Roadrunner as a band and individuals for three albums, and if we didn't write any music for them then we were in limbo [as musicians] for who knows how many years. Me and Christian were already doing another project, and we couldn't do anything until the Roadrunner issue was resolved. Our lawyer told me to go back to Burt and say, "Look, dude, can we write two or three songs?" Because if we did that and got Roadrunner a demo, the ball would be in their court and we could say, "Okay, do you want the next record? Give us our advance." So Burt said, "Okay, if you get rid of Dino I'll think about it." I sat down with Dino and told him what happened. Dino never quit. We got rid of him. Then we did the songs and got them to Roadrunner, but it still took us eleven months to get off the label. Most people think Roadrunner dropped us, [but] we were trying to get off the label, and it took a long time and cost us a lot of money.

DINO CAZARES: Burt agreed to go back to the band for a little while until he realized Raymond was taking control and was having an affair with Christian's wife Christy [Prisque], who was also managing the band. That's when things started to go sour. Burt said, "Look, we need to get a real manager, not some woman both of you guys are banging." I can understand why Burt had a problem with that, but they didn't want to change things. Also, they didn't want me back in the band. They made that clear.

RAYMOND HERRERA: I told Burt many times, "Why do you want to fire her? I don't fire people for no reason. We've gotten sued for firing people for no reason." As far as me going out with Christy, yeah, I went out with Christy after Christian had already found another girlfriend. I was spending a lot of time with Christy because we do a lot of business together, and we became intimate. Now the funny thing about that is Burt had no problem with it after Christian knew and everything was cool. Everything's been cool. If there was really an issue, don't you think me and Christian would be the ones not talking? Me and Christian are the best of friends. What does that have to do with Burt? Furthermore, Burt has gone out with every female manager that we've ever had and I never said anything about it. I never cared.

BURTON C. BELL: In October of 2008, I extended an olive branch to Raymond, stating that I would like to bring Dino back into the band. Raymond said he would never work with Dino or me ever again.

RAYMOND HERRERA: I didn't want to work with Dino because I know how Dino and Burt are. Burt coming back and saying, "I want to work again with the guy I hated most out of everybody in the world and even quit over" was just ridiculous. If Dino's bummed out or hurt because I said I don't want to work with him, it's nothing personal. It's just that I've been there when they fight about the stupidest shit. I don't have time for that anymore.

BURTON C. BELL: Dino and I were good friends for a long time. [And when we weren't] I was talking to mutual friends and asking about him, hoping he was well and relaying messages. Then, at a Ministry show in LA, there he was. I just said, "Hey, how you doing?" It felt really good. We started keeping in touch over the phone and through e-mails. I felt comfortable with the idea of, "Hey, how'd you like to do this again?" Of course he was down. And since then, we've done two albums together that sound the way Fear Factory is supposed to sound without all the bullshit.

During Fear Factory's absence, an East German band swept across the scene like a brush fire, adding a new level of theatrics to industrial metal. Rammstein's six albums are packed with militaristic guitar riffs, operatic vocals, melodic keyboards, and lyrics about control, submission, and sex—both heterosexual and homosexual. But the totality of their vision can only be experienced in a live setting. Their shows are rife with pyrotechnics that make KISS concerts look like candlelight vigils. Effects include towers of fire, flame-throwing muzzles, exploding babies, and a giant mechanical penis vehicle that launches foam twenty rows into the crowd. In part, the band's hunger for thrills stems from an upbringing starved of pop culture.

RICHARD KRUSPE (Rammstein): When we formed in 1993, the music scene in East Germany was divided. One part was the professional, educated type of musician, and the other was the so-called amateur, and the amateur was not allowed to play onstage without having another job to get money from. We had to play in front of a jury to get a document that allowed us to have concerts for a certain amount of money. Even then, no one wanted to let us play. So we just played wherever we could.

CHRISTOPH "DOOM" SCHNEIDER (Rammstein): We never tried to be anything in particular, but we have our influences. Ministry had a considerable impact on us, especially the fact that their music is very hard and monotonous. But pop music has also had an influence, so we make hard, monotonous music that's catchy. There's a lot of different emotions and sexual expressions and things that [most] metal doesn't have. For example, we hate the guitar solos of the metal music.

RICHARD KRUSPE: The low frequencies of Till [Lindemann's] voice forces us to arrange our music differently. We've tried to develop that with a German type of groove, plus, the vocals are in German—and there's the theatrics. The visual aspect of the band comes from our own insecurity. From the beginning, Till was very unsure of his own abilities. He was afraid of singing in front of people and he didn't know what to do onstage, so he decided to set himself on fire.

CHRISTOPH "DOOM" SCHNEIDER: He started to bring along fire equipment and play with dildos. It grew from there, with flamethrowers and different props. Now, what we perform onstage isn't just musical, it's visual as well. An audience can't be bored during a concert.

RICHARD KRUSPE: Everything that we do is controlled by fire police and gets approved by special permissions. In the early days, we weren't so careful. A burning backdrop fell on the drummer's back in about 1995 in Berlin, and his drum set burned. That was the moment we said, "Okay, this can't happen again. We are not professional pyro workers so we need to hire people who are." Even now, there are always small things, like a piece of the floor catching fire and you have to put it out quickly. When I heard what happened to Great White [at its 2003 concert at the Station nightclub in West Warwick, Rhode Island, when one hundred people died after the band's pyrotechnics set the venue ablaze], obviously it hit home. It was very sad and [we were] grateful that nothing really terrible happened to us in the early days when we were young and irresponsible.

CHRISTOPH "DOOM" SCHNEIDER: In the beginning and even now, some people don't understand that there's no political approach at all to what we do. But because we're German, we often get confused with having some sort of extremist tendencies. We're making hard music, we've got short hair, and we're German, so people immediately associate us with fascism and the right wing. That frustrates us.

ALEC EMPIRE (Atari Teenage Riot, EC8R): I think they're not a fascist band at all, but I think in Germany there's a lot of misunderstanding and that's why they sell records, and I think that's dangerous. You just can't [use footage from Leni Riefenstahl films] in your video [for "Stripped,"] and say it's just a joke, because my grandfather died in a concentration camp and for me, that's not a joke at all.

TILL LINDEMANN: I am fed up with allegations of being a right-wing band. My daughter—my dearest in my life—came to me to ask, "Tell me, do you play in a Nazi band?" At this point I knew we had overstepped a border.

Today, more than twenty years after Ministry started a metallic revolution, the industrial movement has petered out, but the music is still going strong. Rammstein continues to set sold-out venues ablaze, Marilyn Manson still pushes pressure points and reaps the rewards, Fear Factory released its second album since Cazares's return to the band, and Ministry has returned from a five-year hiatus (during which Jourgensen almost died from a ruptured ulcer). In addition, non-industrial bands, including Korn and Asking Alexandria, are adding more industrial samples to their songs and inviting dubstep DJs, including Skrillex, Excision, Borgore, and Big Chocolate, to remix their music.

BEN BRUCE (Asking Alexandria): Even Slipknot and Korn have a lot of low, grimy industrial sounds. We've taken influence from that, and at first we worked with our producer [Joey Sturgis] to program the beats. But then we went, "Well, none of us are DJs, and that [dubstep] stuff mixes well with metal," so we got a bunch of guys to remix a lot of our songs for [2011's] *Stepped Up and Scratched*. It just adds another cool element to the songs.

BRANDON GEIST: The crossover between dubstep and metal is pretty big right now. Korn's the most obvious example of that, but lots of younger bands like I Wrestled a Bear Once and Periphery have done these collaborations with dubstep artists as well. It might seem weird because dubstep is really dance music, but a lot of these guys really know metal. Even Cameron Argon, from the death metal band Disfiguring the Goddess, is better known as the electronic dance music producer Big Chocolate.

Industrial metal also still thrives in the underground, as evidenced by groups like Blut Aus Nord, Aborym, and the Shining, which have added samples and electronic beats to death metal, black metal, and jazz.

JORGEN MUNKEBY (The Shining): I thought it would be interesting to combine free-jazz with black metal, but both kinds of music are kind of dirty and messy, so I decided to add the catchiness and the polished aggressiveness of American industrial pop. I didn't know how to do that, so I read through all these album liner notes and found this guy, Sean Beavan, who was the engineer, mixer, and producer for all the Manson and Nine Inch Nails albums. I sent him our demos and he was really into what we were doing. He mixed *Blackjazz* and made it sound better than I could have imagined.

MALFEITOR FABBAN (Aborym): Nine Inch Nails are still an important band for me and Aborym even though they have nothing to do with black metal. I love those kinds of electronic sounds, and we have been able to apply them to the music we make to sound ominous and scary, but also different than other bands. We're free to do anything because we have no commercial aspirations. Aborym is a band that doesn't play to make money. We only play for artistic satisfaction.

9

ALL FOR THE NOOKIE: NV METAL, 1989–2002

As sonically different as metal and rap were when Ice-T put out the singles "Body Rock" and "Killers" in 1983, the two genres were fated to merge. Both were loud and percussive, tended to attract confrontational musicians who thrived on creating controversy, and were dismissed as "noise" by those who didn't appreciate them—especially parents. Even before the Beastie Boys broke the hip-hop–race barrier in 1986 with *Licensed to Ill,* some metal fans were already vibing to the distorted guitar samples of Run-DMC's 1984 hit "Rock Box." It was only a matter of time before groups like Korn, Limp Bizkit, and Deftones would emerge, guided by collaborations between Aerosmith and Run-DMC ("Walk This Way") and Anthrax and Public Enemy ("Bring the Noise"), as well as the creative hybrids of Faith No More and Rage Against the Machine.

ICE-T (Body Count): White kids have always been intrigued by black culture. It's something they're taught by their families is very taboo. They think, "Oh, black kids are going to rob you." Most of the white kids from Christian fundamentalist homes get pushed this Christian doctrine so hard, so that the first bit of them rebelling is going, "I like Dio, I like Slayer." That pisses mom off. Then a double rebellion is them saying, "Yo, I don't even like Slayer, I like Ice Cube and Ice-T."

REVEREND RUN (Run-DMC): When we made "Walk This Way" with Aerosmith [in 1986], people was wondering, "Why?" "Why?" isn't a good question when it comes to bands collaborating. Music is music, and I think they can cross each other at many paths, and I think musicians tend to think the same, so they get along well. Working with Aerosmith was exciting, and it was even more exciting when so many other people liked it. We had no idea it would break down so many barriers.

ICE CUBE: I used to always watch what the Beastie Boys was doing, which was kind of like, to me, the birth of something new. They started as straight rap, but as they went along they mixed different styles in their music and that led directly to the kinds of things that lots of rock bands would mix into their music to create this metal and hip-hop blend.

The Beastie Boys were the first rap outfit to appeal to metal fans on a large scale—probably because they shared similar roots. The New York trio started as a hardcore group, but thanks to their behind-the-scenes virtuoso, Def Jam cofounder Rick Rubin, they soon morphed into a rowdy rap group that colored its songs with brash Led Zeppelin and AC/DC samples. To boost the Beasties' metal cred, Rubin hired Slayer guitarist Kerry King to play a solo on the groundbreaking *Licensed to Ill* track "No Sleep till Brooklyn," named after the Motörhead live album *No Sleep 'Til Hammersmith*.

KERRY KING: That was such a whim thing to do. We were in the studio at the same time. They were on Def Jam and they needed a lead and I went, "Okay!" I got to be in their video, which was cool because we didn't have any videos at the time. I think I got, like, two hundred bucks or something. I had no idea who they were or if they would be popular.

CHINO MORENO (Deftones): The Beastie Boys' *License to Ill* was when I realized, "Damn. I can rap now." So I started rapping right away. Before that, I'd go to the high school football games and I used to rap in a big circle, and there would be beat boxes, but nobody would really take me seriously because I wasn't black.

The Beastie Boys opened the floodgates for the marriage of rock and rap, yet they weren't the first to blend hip-hop and metal. Outside of the spotlight, Faith No More had been cultivating a volatile mixture of metal, alt-rock, rap, and hardcore for several years, and in 1985, a year before *Licensed to Ill* came out, the band dropped the underground radio hit "We Care a Lot." The same year, Megaforce founder Jonny Z got together with members of the Rods to write "Metal Rap," a hastily constructed song about the history of metal that featured rapping by Z and a choir of children on the off-key gang vocal chant, "metal music."

CARL CANEDY (ex-Manowar, Thrasher, Rods): Jonny always had his finger on the pulse of the emerging metal scene, so he wanted to do a tribute to the bands he was working with. That song got a little bit of attention, but it didn't break open any doors—like Faith No More, who merged rock and rap successfully. It didn't seem like it was two interescting right angles. It was more like a *T* in the road. Everything had a hook and made sense, which made it powerful.

JONATHAN DAVIS (Korn): It all started off with Faith No More. I can't give them enough credit. They had groove and they were heavy and weird. They were a huge influence to all of us.

BRIAN SLAGEL (founder, Metal Blade Records): Faith No More brought down a lot of the barriers. Before them, you couldn't like Queensrÿche and Slayer at the same time. Suddenly, all these different styles are being integrated in the music, and fans are getting into it.

BILLY GOULD (Faith No More): I moved from LA to San Francisco in '81. There was an ad in a record store; somebody was putting a band together. I met these guys and we found drummer Mike Bordin through a mutual friend. We played for a year as Faith No Man, and then the keyboard player, Wade [Worthington], left, and Roddy [Bottum] came in. We went through five singers, including Courtney [Love, in 1983]. We originally thought Courtney was cool because she wasn't afraid to get in front of a microphone and assault people, and that made the shows interesting. But she was really high-maintenance. People would call us up because she would go to their houses and burn up their phone bills and not pay them. We got kicked out of a rehearsal space because of her being fucked up and leaving doors unlocked when we were sharing the room with another band. After six months of this, it seemed better for her to go. Also, her singing wasn't very good. But during all this time with different singers we were discovering how to play in rhythmic patterns and make grooves heavy. We didn't even know what kind of singing should go over it. But I was friends with Chuck Mosley, so we tried him out and he stayed in the band [for five years].

CHUCK MOSLEY (ex–Faith No More): People always credit Red Hot Chili Peppers for being the first to mix rap and metal, but they weren't doing metal, they were playing funk. We were more mixing metal and hardcore with rap. Mike and [guitarist] Jim [Martin] grew up with Cliff Burton from Metallica, so they brought in more of a metal sound. A lot of early Faith No More was all rhythm, with Billy and Mike pounding out beats. I had no idea what to do over that. I wasn't a natural singer, and I was a fan of rap anyway, so whatever I couldn't find a melody for, I would just pound out vocal rhythms to the beat. And I was a lousy rapper, so it turned into my own version of freestyle.

BILLY GOULD: Chuck is a funny, sharp guy with a lot of charisma, but he couldn't sing, so there'd be a lot of tension within the band. When something mattered, we'd always wonder if we'd be able to pull it off. And he didn't seem to care. We lived in San Francisco and he lived in LA, so we'd have a show and he'd come up from LA. We'd go onstage and start playing and we wouldn't even know if he was in the city yet. Whenever he arrived, he'd walk in the front door, jump up, and join us onstage.

CHUCK MOSLEY: They were real serious about the band, and I didn't take it as seriously as they did because I *knew* I wasn't really a singer. I was more into partying and being crazy and fucking with people. I'd dress in drag, put on skirts and dresses and not have anything on underneath. Then I'd go onstage and find the most macho, headbanging, punk rockin' dudes in the crowd and I'd teabag them. I wanted to shock people. Someone in England said I was gay and I said, "I'm not an AIDS receptacle," which was really stupid and juvenile. I'm not a homophobe. I was just trying to be offensive, and this group of people got *really* offended. [Keyboardist] Roddy [Bottum] got yelled at and attacked. He's gay and he gets attacked for *my* anti-gay remarks. I thought that was hilarious. We thrived on that kind of tension and humor.

BILLY GOULD: We signed to Slash Records and had a big debut show. Half the club were press people, and the record company was saying, "This is our new band, we're expecting big things." Chuck was drunk, and he passed out and fell asleep for three songs. Because of that show, the press thought we sucked. It took us two years to crawl out of that hole.

CHUCK MOSLEY: There were a couple shows I was drunk at, but not many, because once I heard myself singing drunk I put an end to that. I tried to stay focused. There wasn't that much revelry when I was doing the band. But right before I left, I had a girlfriend and I was missing her, so I complained a lot. I was complaining about not getting paid and playing shitty places, and the guys got sick of me. They wanted to fire me before one of the tours, but they couldn't cancel the tour, so they waited until after we got home. Me and Roddy were the closest in the band at the time, so they got him to call me up and tell me I was fired. I was pissed and kind of shocked. I expected it, but I was still hurt. Part of the reason they fired me was I was more into change and growth, and they wanted to find a sound and stick with it.

JIM MARTIN (ex-Faith No More): [Chuck] was very stubborn and resistant to change or growth. He would resist everything for some reason. We'd argue about almost every little thing, right down to where we were going to stop to get gas.

BILLY GOULD: I quit the band, actually, then everybody else said, "We still want to play with you," and I said, "I can't deal with Chuck." Turns out, *nobody* wanted to play with Chuck. What started off by me quitting the band actually ended up with us firing Chuck. We went for a year after we fired Chuck before we found Mike Patton. We wrote songs during that year not knowing what they would sound like with vocals. Then we heard the first Mr. Bungle tape [with Mike Patton singing] and we thought we'd give Mike a try. Judging by the insane music, I thought he would be some fat guy with a leather jacket. Turned out he was this little twenty-year-old kid, and we were all eight or nine years older than him. He came to rehearsal and we started playing these songs we'd been working on for the past year. He got on the mic and started singing, and he was just nailing them. The first time he heard them, he came up with great stuff. He's a real musical guy, extremely talented. And those songs turned into *The Real Thing*.

MIKE PATTON (Faith No More) [1990 interview]: Some people praise my singing, but I just see my job is to jump up and down onstage and to have long hair and look like a rock and roller. When I first joined the band I had short hair, and I had to go into hibernation for a while before they would let me join.

On 1989's *The Real Thing*, Faith No More combined hip-hop rhythms with heavy guitars and Patton's soaring vocals. Thanks to the straightforward rap-metal anthem "Epic"—which was structurally similarly to "We Care a Lot"—the album took off. The video for "Epic" received regular airplay on MTV, which surprised both the band and its label, and the album quickly went platinum. As influential as Faith No More has been in the evolution of nu metal, bands like Korn, Deftones, and Limp Bizkit might never have heard of Faith No More if Warner Bros. hadn't let them shoot three videos for the album.

BILLY GOULD: We did videos for "From Out of Nowhere" and "Falling to Pieces," and they didn't go anywhere. Then Warner Bros. said, "We're going to let you do one more video, but this is the end of the record cycle—it didn't work. What song would you like to do?" They had basically given up. We wanted a video for "Epic," which we all thought was the best-sounding song on the album. It had *nothing* to do with what the record company wanted. They thought it would go on *Headbangers Ball* for a couple of weeks and that would be the end of it. But it blew up, and we were on the road for a year and a half, which really screwed with our heads. We got back and we didn't have any money. We couldn't even pay rent. The record company spent a lot of money making videos and doing promotions. We didn't clear a lot in royalties right away, so we were broke, but everybody thought we were huge.

Suddenly, we have to deal with people in the neighborhood giving us shit for being "rock stars." We realized our popularity was a fluke, so we didn't really respect it. People wouldn't even review us before and all of a sudden we were everybody's darlings. It was very hard to take seriously. So, sometimes, we just got more obnoxious to get a rise out of people.

JIM MARTIN: Being on the road is kind of boring, so we have a good time by being violent. Violent acts don't come out of anger anyhow. It's more for entertainment value.

MIKE PATTON: Masturbation is a lot easier to do than relating to someone. It's like playing a video machine. You can relate to a machine a lot easier than a human being. You can just pound yourself for hours and hours and not think about it.

BILLY GOULD: There was a lot of shitting backstage [and not just in toilets]. Mike [Patton] did that all the time. The thing about shit is that it's cheap. It's hard to explain to people, but it's part of our sense of humor. We're a lot different from each other, but we have a shared sense of humor conventional people don't quite understand. But after touring so much for *The Real Thing*, which was our most conventional record, being conventional stopped being exciting. We had a real need for rediscovering music again, and we did that with *Angel Dust*. I know there was a lot of discouragement for us to take that approach, but I think that was the only approach as artists that we could possibly make.

Angel Dust was skewed, bizarre, and acerbic, featuring songs with titles like "Jizzlobber" and "Crack Hitler" and ending with a cover of John Barry's "Midnight Cowboy." While the album went gold on the back of *The Real Thing* and the band remained critical darlings, fans who wanted to see Patton rapping and rolling "Epic"-style were sorely disappointed, and Faith No More drifted away from the mainstream. The next great evolutionary step in rap-metal came from a collaboration between Anthrax and rap act Public Enemy. The New York thrash band had already toyed with hip-hop on its 1990 spoof "I'm the Man," but in 1991 Anthrax got serious, inviting Public Enemy to contribute to a re-recording of their 1988 song "Bring the Noise" from *It Takes a Nation of Millions to Hold Us Back*.

SCOTT IAN: Public Enemy was my favorite rap band from the first time I heard the demos for [1987's] *Yo! Bum Rush the Show*. All I could think of was, "How the fuck can we work with these guys?" It took until 1990, when we were recording *Persistence of Time*. We were done tracking. I told [drummer] Charlie [Benante], "I wrote this riff based around 'Bring the Noise.'" I played it for him, and he started playing a beat. Within twenty minutes we had recorded it, and we were like, "Wow, this is so fucking heavy." I called Chuck and told him we wanted him and Flavor Flav to come in and do vocals. He said, "Ehh, I don't know. We already did 'Bring the Noise.' Why don't we do something new?" I said, "You just gotta hear this." He said, "Well, lemme talk to Rick [Rubin]." He did, and told me, "Rick thinks it's redundant." But we Fed-Exed Chuck the tape anyway, and two days later he called up and said, "This is fucking slamming. When can we do this?" He and Flav did vocals, and we shot the video on a day off during the Clash of the Titans tour in Chicago. At the shoot, we had so much fun we said, "We should do shows." Chuck said, "When and where?" So we toured the world for four months.

WES BORLAND (Limp Bizkit): "Bring the Noise" was the main reason I got into Public Enemy, and that's what got me into hip-hop. I got [their 1990 album] *Fear of a Black Planet* and went back and listened to all their old records. Then I checked out N.W.A and Ice Cube, which a lot of my friends hated because they were metalheads.

SCOTT IAN: I loved what we did with "Bring the Noise," and that tour with Public Enemy was so fun. They had never gotten groupies before, and our crew guys would always have chicks on the bus getting naked, and they'd be taking pictures. Flavor Flav was out of his fucking mind for that. He couldn't get on our bus fast enough to see what was going on. But to me, Rage Against the Machine were the ones who created the whole rap-metal genre. "Bring the Noise" was a collaboration between a metal band and a rap band. It wasn't one band creating something new. Whereas, when Rage came out, they weren't like anybody else. They took something organic and they made the Rage Against the Machine sound. We might have opened the door, but they drove the fucking truck through it.

In the fall of 1992, Rage Against the Machine's self-titled debut was the album rock and rap fans had been longing for, a seamless combination of aggressive rock influenced by Led Zeppelin and Helmet and political rap that drew from Public Enemy and N.W.A. Rage wasn't just provocative, it was motivational, as demonstrated by the chorus from "Killing in the Name": "Fuck you I won't do what you tell me," which audiences chanted with the fervor of football fans screaming Gary Glitter's "Rock and Roll, Part 2."

TOM MORELLO (Rage Against the Machine): I moved out to LA with a Harvard guy, Ivy League mentality. I wanted to form a band that combined Sabbath and Run-DMC with some Aerosmith, and we put an ad in *The Music Connection* for a socialist lead singer. I wanted to play the music I really love and make a statement at the same time. As a band, we have a realization that from top to bottom the system is corrupt and that's essentially what our songs are about. As Chairman Mao said, "You learn to make revolution through the process of revolting."

FRED DURST (Limp Bizkit): When Rage Against the Machine came out in 1992, that was fucking huge for me. I came from

this break-dance and hip-hop background, so to see this
band that put a lot of hip-hop into this heavy rock was really
inspiring.

TOM MORELLO: I have a complete love for Led Zeppelin, KISS,
and Black Sabbath, as well as funk and hip-hop, and I love to
express myself on guitar. Tony Iommi was one of the biggest
influences on me as a riff writer. Early on, as a fledgling guitar
player, I was trying to learn some Black Sabbath songs, and I
asked this guy to show them to me and he almost didn't want
to lower himself. He was like, "It's so easy, why would you
want to learn them?" I said, "Dude, because they rule!" That,
to me, is absolutely as much a part of this band as any political
agenda. But the fact that we've been able to extend the message contained in the music into the realm of political activ-
ism has been extremely rewarding. It's really the barometer by
which I measure our success, rather than units moved or tickets
sold.

Between Rage Against the Machine's solid debut and its craftier
1996 follow-up, *Evil Empire*, numerous rap-metal outfits emerged,
but few mixed politics and rock as powerfully, and none stood
behind their words so vehemently. As it turned out, many metal
fans weren't ready for such populist polemic, preferring instead to
rage against their parents and ex-girlfriends rather than the government. Groups like Korn, Deftones, and Limp Bizkit met their
needs, creating hybrids of rap and metal that focused on youthful
angst and emphasizing the hedonistic vibe of their favorite hip-hop.

TOM MORELLO: Unfortunately, I'd say I played a large part in
the evolution of nu metal. There was a wave of bands that
composed the first Lollapalooza nation: Tool, Nine Inch Nails,
Rage Against the Machine, Nirvana, etc., that were artistically forward-looking, combining elements of arena rock with
artistry and punk. But they all had qualms about playing the
same arenas that Poison was playing. It took those Lollapalooza

bands four or five years to make a record because they were busy kvetching. I'm quite confident that at the same time, record company executives in boardrooms across the nation were saying, "If only we can find a Rage Against the Machine that would make five videos per record and have songs about chicks and show off."

REGINALD "FIELDY" ARVIZU (Korn): Everyone in our circle was listening to a lot of West Coast hip-hop, and a lot of that stuff was real minor key and dark anyways, so with the music it was almost like, if you could take that to the next level, you could make it heavy metal.

STEPHEN CARPENTER (Deftones): When I was in high school, I couldn't get enough heavy metal. There were so many good bands in the eighties—Van Halen, Priest, Iron Maiden, Metallica, Anthrax. I was fifteen when I first played a guitar chord. I used to watch videos, and most of the time everyone's faking it. I was watching Ratt's "Round and Round" where they were on a table soloing out. [Warren DeMartini] played a power chord, and I copied his finger positions, and went "Whoa, what the hell!" It was just a matter of playing it up and down the fretboard and learning to stay on time with my right hand. It was just fake-it-out city from then on. I learned to play to Anthrax, S.O.D., Metallica. I didn't learn another chord besides a power chord until I had been playing for four years.

CHINO MORENO: I didn't grow up on heavy music at all. I grew up on new wave and bands like the Cure and Depeche Mode, that were really moody and had a lot of sorrow. My heart has always been really into sad music, and I incorporate it naturally into our songs. That's what sets us apart.

JONATHAN DAVIS (Korn): When I was a kid, I was into death rock, industrial, and Duran Duran. Bauhaus, Christian Death. I was called a fag because I wore eyeliner and had my hair up in the air. I was a nerd. I was picked on, and that shit's never gonna change. I'm a rock star now, and people still call me a fag. There's all these things on message boards about how I suck dick and fuck guys, and you know it's never gonna change. So fuck it. I'm just who I am.

FRED DURST: I'm definitely not a happy person, and I don't sing happy songs because I fuckin' don't like them. I don't have a positive fuckin' message. My message is, "If you've ever been pissed off and felt like shit, it's okay, because you're not the only one."

JONATHAN DAVIS: My lyrics have always been dark because the things I get off on are all morbid, and my whole life I've collected and done dark things. When I was seventeen, I was a senior in high school and I got into this job placement program that hooked me up at the coroner's office doing autopsies. I was like, "Oh, cool, I'll be able to see dead bodies and cut them open." I'll admit I was white the first day and it freaked me out. But after the second and third time, I was totally into it. I liked trying to figure out how people died, and seeing the anatomy of the body was amazing. Just the fact that you're cutting a fucking person open and you're not going to jail, that's awesome. So after high school I went to mortuary college. I was an apprentice embalmer at a funeral home, and that's where I was in my first band, Sexart.

By the mid-nineties, bands were no longer flooding the Sunset Strip the way they had in the heyday of hair metal. The most exciting scenes were coalescing away from the city and manifesting suburban angst more than urban hardship. The first city to gain attention for its music community was Bakersfield, California, an area known for its country music scene in the fifties and, forty years later, home to Sexart, Korn, Videodrone, and Adema.

RYAN SHUCK (Sexart, Orgy): The whole Bakersfield scene started with Sexart [which featured Shuck, Davis, and future Adema bassist Dave DeRoo]. Jon [Davis] came down to our studio and then I went down to his house and partied with him. Jon played with us for a few years. One of the first songs I ever wrote [for Sexart] was "Blind," which ended up being a pretty popular Korn song. But there's only one chord in that song. It's all conceptual. It's all about feeling.

JONATHAN DAVIS: When I was in Sexart, [Korn guitarists Brian] "Head" [Welch] and [James] "Munky" [Shaffer] were in a bar in Bakersfield, California, watching us play, and they thought we sucked, so they were getting ready to leave. Then, suddenly, they heard my voice and flipped out. [Bassist Reginald] "Fieldy" [Arvizu] called me and asked me to try out. Me and Fieldy grew up together. His dad [Reginald Arvizu Sr.] and my dad [Rick Davis] had been in a band. From the first note, when I heard their sound, I was like, "Oh my god, this is insane!" I got my PA and I sang the first song all the way through, and everyone's mouths dropped open and they were like "This is it! Let's do it!" Two weeks later, we did a demo tape with [producer] Ross [Robinson] that started getting shopped around. But at first, no one wanted to have anything to do with us. We played clubs in San Diego up the coast of California for about a year before anyone noticed us.

FIELDY: Most bands that get together are just a bunch of musicians. We weren't a bunch of musicians. We were all friends always having fun together anyway. So we thought, "Why don't we get in a band so we can all drink in a band together and get crazy?"

JONATHAN DAVIS: When I write, there's always that sense of sex there. I have a lot of fantasies I like to write about. It's just the other side of human nature. But at the same time, I'm a vulnerable guy. I'm not trying to go up there and say, "Fuck this, I'm a bad motherfucker." That's not me.

JAMES "MUNKY" SHAFFER (Korn): I started using a seven-string guitar to make the music really dark and different-sounding and lower. [A Korn guitar tone has] gotta be heavy, but with clarity. When we record, sometimes we layer three or four different tracks to get the right sound—a clean tone, a really dirty tone underneath, and then something between the two. Then we use lots of sound effects to make it sound even weirder. But I don't know how to play a standard six-string guitar anymore. It feels like I'm missing a finger when I try.

JONATHAN DAVIS: Alternative music was a depressing time in rock. I'd go to those shows and just fall asleep. I just wanted to wake people the fuck up. I didn't even know what Black Sabbath was until I joined Korn. The thing that changed my life was when Pantera released *Vulgar Display of Power* [in 1992]. Then Fieldy turned me on to Sepultura. But we never wanted to do anything that was typically metal. If we ever write something that sounds like Judas Priest or Iron Maiden it's out the door.

FIELDY: If Jon even tried to sing the word "die" with lots of vibrato, we'd have to kill him. We're heavier than heavy metal.

Around the same time Korn was honing their chops in Bakersfield, further north, in Sacramento, Deftones were writing in a similar style, combining jagged metal riffs influenced by Helmet, Prong, and Faith No More with hip-hop rhythms and subtle, haunting melodies. But like Korn, Deftones were innovators, not imitators.

STEPHEN CARPENTER: A major thing happened to me when I was fifteen. I got hit by a drunk driver. I was skateboarding to a friend's house, and *boom*! I should have died. The guy was doing, like, 60 miles per hour and I destroyed his car. I had an out-of-body experience. I never saw or heard or felt the car hit me. I just recalled not being here and floating above the treetops in Sacramento, and seeing the buildings popping up downtown and going, "Oh, this is really cool. What's going on?" Meanwhile, there's this voice repeating like a scratched record, "Man, you're gonna be all right. You're gonna make it, man." I was like, "Who the hell is telling me this? And why the hell are you floating above the trees?" My final question was, "While you were skateboarding, did you fall asleep?" And I woke up instantly. I had fallen off my skateboard and there was reality. I wasn't in pain, but I was right there in the moment and totally conscious of everything. There wasn't a smell, a color, or an angle that I wasn't aware of. I acknowledged everything at once at that moment, and I've been that way ever since. I felt totally normal—other than the fact that my leg was snapped in half. I had a compound fracture and I was in the hospital for two weeks. From that point on, I didn't care about skateboarding anymore. I just wanted to have a good time and live and make music. I got a bunch of money as a settlement and I used it to buy equipment for the band. When we started Deftones, [drummer] Abe [Cunningham] and [vocalist] Chino [Moreno] were fifteen going on sixteen. We grew up together, and spent our teen years doing what we wanted to do, making music together. And we sucked for a long time.

CHINO MORENO: I knew Abe because we used to skate together. Abe and I lived ten miles away from Stephen, and bus number 68 went right from Abe's house to Stephen's house. So we went over there one day after school. Stephen was sitting on his porch with his guitar on, and all his cabinets were in the garage plugged in and he was just rocking out.

ABE CUNNINGHAM (Deftones): I had been playing since I was seven, and I knew what I was doing. But I was clean-cut and Stephen probably thought I was some wuss. There was a drum set in the garage, and he's like, "The drums are in there." He stayed out on the front porch with the garage door shut and started jamming. I'm like, "What a prick. He doesn't want to jam with me, he's out here sitting on the fucking porch."

STEPHEN CARPENTER: Abe started playing along with me and I was blown away. Everyone I knew my age or younger, nobody was as good as Abe. He was fifteen and he was like [Rush drummer] Neil Peart. The first Deftones show was hilarious. Our bass player at the time showed up late, and he was in cut-offs and a W.A.S.P. shirt that was mesh and sleeveless. He didn't have enough sense to take the cord up through the strap and plug it in, so he'd step on the cord and it would unplug and he'd be playing and it wouldn't be working. They built a stage for us to play on in the backyard, and it was, like, 4 inches high. Chino used to sound like Gomer Pyle singing. He was trying to sound like Danzig. That's why he became our singer, because we could do "Twist of Cain" and sound just like Danzig.

CHINO MORENO: We knew we needed a new bass player. Chi Cheng and his older brother Ming put up an ad, and it said, "Brother bass players. One plays metal, one plays funk." Stephen called them up and talked to Ming first. Ming asked Stephen what kind of band he wanted to make. Stephen said, "Well, we sound kind of like Primus or Faith No More." Ming said, "You want my brother, then. He's a funk player." So Chi came over to Stephen's house. We saw his long hair and thought, "Yeah, this dude's a straight rocker. We gotta get him." We wrote a new song the day he came in.

Even though they cultivated a solid live set and were getting booked in and around Bakersfield, Korn were broke and scraping to get by. In Los Angeles, Coal Chamber were suffering a similar fate, and in Sacramento, Deftones were only slightly better off.

JONATHAN DAVIS: Before I joined Korn I had a good career working as a mortician. Then I was in the band and had no money, so I worked for Pizza Hut and became a manager and got paid next to nothing. Before we got signed, I had that Top Ramen case kicking. I lived in a friend's garage with a mattress on the floor because it was all I could afford. He built a carpet partition in the garage, and that was my room. I had to hang my clothes on pipes.

DEZ FAFARA (Coal Chamber, DevilDriver): We were all living in my one-bedroom apartment on Melrose and Poinsettia in Los Angeles. [Bassist] Rayna [Foss] was sleeping on the floor in the kitchen. We were all eating Top Ramen. We would go into Trader Joe's and steal food any time we could. LA was a musical dead zone. Before we came along, there were one or two other bands and us, otherwise there was no scene. Labels were not signing bands from LA anymore, whatsoever. Poison and all these hair bands came in and killed the Sunset Strip and killed LA. We fought like hell to bring the scene back to life.

JONATHAN DAVIS: To spread the word, we'd scrounge up some money and go to Kinko's and make flyers in Huntington Beach. We'd buy a bunch of 40s, get drunk, and flyer cars all night. Then, we got a printing press, bought all this sticker paper, and stickered every stop sign in town. People started hearing the name Korn. They knew the logo and wanted to know what the hell it was about.

CHINO MORENO: We played a show in Bakersfield, and Korn's producer [Ross Robinson] was at the show and he really dug our band, so we gave him a tape. A couple days later, the Korn guys called and said, "Dude, we want to play shows with you guys." We had never heard them, but we went to LA and both played. They played first and we played last. I tripped out and said, "This is kind of like what we're doing." Except their shit is a little more dark.

FIELDY: It was a trip. Jon and Chino were doing almost the same moves and wearing Adidas jumpsuits. But we didn't give a fuck. We liked them 'cause they were good, and we all became friends.

ROB HALFORD: The way I view a Korn/Deftones situation is much the same way I viewed Judas Priest and Iron Maiden. Two very, very different bands, but they just happen to be from the same kind of mode, and they popped up in the same general time. It's unfortunate that the media tries to pick up on the supposed conflict, because a lot of bad information gets put in people's heads, and then you have to try to explain how it's not true.

CHINO MORENO: There were a lot of times when the press said we were talking shit about each other and we'd call each other up and straighten shit out. It was really stupid because we were all friends even before all this started, and it seemed like people were trying to make us enemies.

JACOBY SHADDIX (Papa Roach): When we were coming up, the Deftones was *the* band we looked up to. I'd go to their shows and I'd leave going, "Man, I want to start a band."

DEZ FAFARA: When things started happening again in LA, you had Coal Chamber playing the Whisky one night, and Korn would play the Roxy the same night. Both were unsigned. But Korn brought buses of people from Huntington Beach up to LA to make sure their shows were packed. And they weren't the only ones. I remember Lynn Strait kept bringing Snot from Santa Barbara to fucking LA, which pissed a lot of people off. So I walked up to Lynn in front of the Roxy one night and said, "Fuck you, go back to Santa Barbara." And he said, "You know what? I like you and I'm a huge fan of Coal Chamber. Let's go get high." We ended up in a car smoking a joint. Then we went into the Roxy and did shots of whisky. We became friends from that point on.

RAYNA FOSS (Coal Chamber): Korn got signed and blew the doors wide open for us. Snot got signed, System of a Down got signed. Fear Factory and Machine Head were already signed. Everything was happening.

DEZ FAFARA: Everybody would go into clubs every single night and you'd run into every single person from every band. Most of the time people would have backpacks on and be handing out demo tapes and stickers. Promotion was key at that point. And the shows were really intense.

JONATHAN DAVIS: Most of the time, I had no clue what I was doing up there. I blackened my eye so bad from smacking my microphone against it one night. I stuck my teeth through my lip, bloodied my nose, I looked like Blackie Lawless from W.A.S.P. for a whole set 'cause I was bleeding all over myself. I fucked myself up left and right all the time just trying to do the best show we could.

DEZ FAFARA: There was a lot of nepotism, which I was a little wary of. We got a deal after Korn and Deftones and Ross Robinson was supposed to produce our first record, but after hearing people compare us to Korn I ran away from Ross and straight to Jay Baumgartner and Jay Gordon [of the band Orgy] to do our first record. But Ross is the one who brought us to the attention of Roadrunner, and Fieldy lent all of his bass equipment to Rayna for our first record.

MONTE CONNER (ex-VP A&R, Roadrunner): Coal Chamber got some grief because they had a similar sound [to Korn]. Hundreds of bands came after that, but Coal Chamber was the first to follow Korn—I would say Coal Chamber's first record was the second nu metal record ever to come out.

FIELDY: When we started out there was nobody to tour with, and now we have all these bands out there that we can put tours together with. Back in the day we were like, "Fuck, we want to go on tour. Who can we do this with? Megadeth? I don't want to go on tour with fucking Megadeth." But we did.

While Los Angeles was developing into a musical hotbed again, a band in Jacksonville, Florida, was bubbling under. Limp Bizkit would eventually eclipse the popularity of all the West Coast bands by combining the volcanic guitar eruptions of Korn with straightforward rapping, courtesy of part-time tattoo artist, former break-dancer, and future entrepreneur Fred Durst.

FRED DURST: I started break-dancing in 1982, and I got real good around 1984. I started rapping, doing talent shows and break-dancing contests at the mall against crews, battling and rapping with a beatbox. Then I got turntables and a mixer and learned how to DJ in 1985. Most nights I went skating or went into a break-dance contest at some little club.

WES BORLAND: I grew up in Nashville and bought my first guitar with lawn-mowing money when I was twelve. I started taking blues lessons because I had to take what was offered, which was fingerpicking, blues, and country. But I wanted to play electric and was listening to Minor Threat, Circle Jerks, Black Flag, Metallica, and Testament. I would bring in something, and my teacher would go, "I've never heard of the Damned. Don't you want to play Merle Haggard?" When I was thirteen I really got into Metallica's *Kill 'Em All*. At the same time I liked a lot of New Wave. I was always the weird kid. I got beat up a lot by jocks in high school. It was a really

racist school, and my locker was in the "black" hallway. So I
got hit a lot out of nowhere 'cause I was a little white skateboarder kid. Then we moved to Florida and I started going to
a school of the arts, which was much safer. Fights there were
like little gothic girls saying they were gonna cast spells on
each other. That's where I met [drummer] John Otto. He was
going there for music.

FRED DURST: Before Limp Bizkit, I was in an alternative band
called Malachi Sage, and Sam [Rivers] was the bass player.
They wouldn't listen to me so I said, "Fuck them," and I
started 10 Foot Shindig, which was more of a rap/rock thing.
Sam was still in Malachi Sage, and one night after they opened
up for us, I said to Sam, "You need to quit this band and start
a band with me." He said, "I wanna call my cousin John. He's
a jazz major in school." The first day we jammed with John I
was playing guitar and rapping. It happened right there. We
wrote three songs.

WES BORLAND: John brought me into the band. I guess I was the
artsy guy. In the beginning I dressed in drag and I wanted to
look like a girl who was trying to be hard. Everyone thought
Limp Bizkit had a butch female guitar player. Then I started
wearing masks onstage to look like a cartoon or turn myself
into different characters. I played in my underwear and painted
my head jet black from the neck up when I didn't feel like
doing anything else. That was my "burnt match" costume. All
you could see was teeth 'cause I had big black contact lenses.
And I had a couple of skeleton suits and an oversized kung
fu suit. The artiness was always meant to be a big part of the
band. The goal was to have musicians who could cross over
into as many different styles of music as possible and mix them
all together.

FRED DURST: At the same time as I liked rap, I liked Ratt. And
Nirvana and Soundgarden were big influences to me. The

people who slam us as being on some bandwagon are the people who don't care about growth. They don't care about reality, and they don't want to listen to music evolve. They just want us to be removed. And as long as those people keep writing shitty stuff about us, the more people become curious, and the more it's good for us.

WES BORLAND: Fred's really unpredictable. You never know when he's gonna freak out and totally lose it. It happens all the time. He will just explode and try to knock the monitor guys over the head with a microphone stand. He has attacked people onstage, kicked entire speaker stacks over. He's walked offstage after one song. Sometimes we'd be at a huge show and he'd break every single microphone that was handed to him and not sing. Or he'd sing for a minute and then break it on purpose. And he's paying for all of it, but he doesn't care. I've done the same thing. We would all get in these zones where we would freak out and you just can't stop.

JONATHAN DAVIS: I've flown off the handle like a motherfucker. I've screamed at everybody and become a real dickhead because I love this music so much. It's my fucking baby, and I take it really personally. I'm known for having fits. I've smashed lots of stuff—picked up my equipment in the studio and chucked it across the room, thrown chairs, knocked over things. It just gets frustrating when stuff isn't working out the way I want.

WES BORLAND: Korn was one of our influences, and I think some of the guitar tones and a few of the rhythms sound like Korn, but it's not the same band at all. Fred raps most of the time and Jonathan doesn't rap at all. They were our big brothers. They helped us out insanely in the beginning, but we quickly got to the level where we didn't need to always have their name tagged on to everything we do.

FRED DURST: I met Korn at a show they did opening for Sick of It All. There were twenty people there, and afterwards I tattooed Fieldy at my house. We became real good friends, and I gave them our demo, and they loved it, so they gave it to Ross and he helped us get signed.

FIELDY: Fred ended up tattooing "Nor" on Head's back. It's supposed to say Korn, but it looks like "Nor."

FRED DURST: They fucking liked the tattoo the night they got it! Fuck Head, that motherfucker. He was fucking begging for the tattoo. I drew it up and we were all fucked up. It was real late. And Fieldy was going, "Yeah, get it man, get it, get it."

FIELDY: We took Limp Bizkit under our wing and brought them on tour because we liked them. If we like a band and we get along with them, they're gonna tour with us and we're all gonna get crazy. We paid Fred $500 to go out onstage naked and play "Faith" by George Michael, so he went out and did it buck naked. And the stage was only about 3 feet off the ground, so people's faces were right up against his dick. We just sat back and giggled our asses off.

JONATHAN DAVIS: He had his dick tucked for the first part of it, then he popped the thing out and it was just slapping against his body. The people up front were all talking about how he had a small dick. You could see them all putting their thumb and forefinger like two inches apart to show how small it was. It was fucking embarrassing. That was funny.

Once the first wave of nu metal bands proved they could sell records and draw crowds, labels clambered to snatch up other similar-sounding groups. With the help of their musician friends, Orgy, Staind, and, of course, Limp Bizkit were soon hot commodities.

FRED DURST: We got an offer to sign to Mojo/MCA, and then we got in a major car wreck and all of us almost died. It was weird. Before the car wreck, we were on our way out to California, and we said the only way we *won't* be on Mojo [and go with an earlier offer we'd gotten from Jordan Schur & Flip] is if we flipped the van or something. We were asleep, and the driver fell asleep at 6 a.m. in the middle of the desert. He over-rotated and tried to correct. The van flipped five or six times. My feet got crushed. Everybody got banged and cut up. One guy who came along with us broke his back and was just lying on the street in the freezing cold desert. I took it as an omen and we went with Flip.

WES BORLAND: We'll never be able to repay Korn for what they did for us. All we can do is show that love to other bands, which is what we did for Staind. Then Staind wanted to move away from us and do their own thing, which was fine.

AARON LEWIS (Staind): [At first,] Limp Bizkit didn't want anything to do with us. Fred thought we were devil worshippers. He was freaked out by our first CD cover [*Tormented*], which was a bleeding Bible with a knife in it. But we worked that out and explained we weren't devil worshippers or anything. Then he heard our music and liked it.

WES BORLAND: Staind's demo tape blew us away. Fred brought them to Florida, let them stay at his house, brought in some DAT recorders, and did a demo with them and sent it out. They played a showcase in LA at the Opium Den, and a bunch of major labels started drooling. It was kind of the same thing Korn did for us and Orgy. We've all looked out for each other.

RYAN SHUCK: We had never really played in front of a bunch of people as Orgy when our first record came out. We'd all been in other bands and played clubs—guitarist Amir Derakh was in the hair metal bands [Rough Cutt and Jailhouse]—but when Orgy got together we threw a curveball with our approach to music and it caught on. We didn't have to play a lot of clubs and go through that whole drawn-out play-for-three-years thing. Korn signed us to their label Elementree. So after [1998's] *Candyass* came out and we started touring, we became the band that we are. We did things a little backwards.

JAY GORDON (Orgy): Some people freaked out about our name, but back in the Roman days people didn't used to feel that was a problem. And it's not about group sex. It's actually definitely a musically based name and it all came from how the different styles in our music work together. It's a word I put on a bass case one day, and the guys loved it, and I thought, "Cool. We'll just call our band that," not even thinking of what would happen down the road.

While Korn and Limp Bizkit were excited to embrace a music scene of like-minded bands, Deftones didn't want to be associated with a musical movement. When Korn organized its own "Family Values" tour in 1998, Deftones turned down an offer to play; the maiden voyage of Family Values featured Korn, Limp Bizkit, Orgy, Incubus, Ice Cube, and Rammstein.

FIELDY: If someone tried to tell us for a year straight we sounded like the Deftones, I'd be pissed off, too. They never sounded like Korn. Not even their early stuff. It's not the same shit. It's just the same vibe.

CHINO MORENO: When angst-ridden, heavy music goes out of style, I don't think we're gonna go out with it. There are a lot more elements to our music that separates us from that scene. As far as the other bands, I respect them and I dig them, but the minute we get pigeonholed in a scene, basically everything we've worked for years for is out the window. Suddenly you're reliant on all these other bands, when you should just rely on yourself and what you're doing.

Nu metal bands dismissed the profeminist and anti–rock star stances of Rage Against the Machine and Nirvana. Instead, they indulged in the Babylonian excesses that had motivated the Sunset Strip hair bands. Getting laid became almost as important as getting paid. At the same time, a new synergy developed between the adult entertainment world and the music industry that made debauchery more acceptable to the mainstream.

MIGUEL "MEEGS" RASCÓN (Coal Chamber): There is definitely a connection between the porn and metal worlds. This kind of music is all about unleashing. It's a creative purge. It's all about rhythm, and sex is all about pulsing rhythms. The people in the porn industry and the music industry have the same kind of values. The two groups are debaucherous. It's hard for a rock guy to date a normal nine-to-five banker. They look at us like we're fucking out of control, while someone in the sex industry, they look at us as normal because that's the way *they* live. So it's not a big secret that porn girls date rocker guys or strippers or any type of sex industry people.

BOBBY HEWITT (Orgy): My wife [Shane] used to be in the adult industry, so she understands what happens out on the road. And with her being so fine with all that, it makes it easy to not want to fuck around. But when we're together, me and my wife get together with her girlfriends, and we always have a great time.

JONATHAN DAVIS: We're rock stars. We go out on the road for years at a time. We're never home. We have tons of beautiful women trying to fuck us all the time. There's a lot of things going on and you just have to find that special lady that can deal with that. I was really lucky to find my wife, Deven Davis, and we have two kids together. She was a porno actress and she used to do girl-girl movies, which I have no problem with. She didn't take dicks for a living like the other girls. But then she stopped to become a spokesmodel and go out on the road and do signings and interviews with the starlets while they're on set. So it keeps her involved in the business, but it takes that aspect of the sex out. I'd describe our relationship as a liberal, free thing and I love it.

LYNN STRAIT (1968–1998) (Snot): We're not gonna mention any of my porn career [*laughs*]. We went through a lot of strippers. We practiced two doors down from a strip club, so between practice we'd go over there. We'd have a soda on our break and get a lap dance and go back. Then all the strippers would hang out at practice. Then everyone in the band was dating one for a while at one time or another.

DEZ FAFARA: Lynn Strait's girlfriend Karen was a porn star, and he did a scene with her in [Matt Zane's] *Backstage Sluts 2: No Ass, No Pass*. We were all, at that point, getting interviewed by porn magazines and porn videos, and it was cool to be a part of that because, as a single dude, there was just endless pussy. Lynn was the guy backstage in the shower, with everyone looking at him getting his dick sucked by two chicks and then going out and getting tattooed. We both got our hands tattooed the same day by Paul Booth. I got a big huge black-and-white pumpkin, and he got a big skull. In between sessions he's getting up, going in the bathroom, getting his dick sucked by two bitches. It was total rock and roll, bro. That guy was on fuckin' fire.

WAYNE STATIC (Static-X): My wife Tera Wray was a porn star [with Matt Zane's Zane Entertainment], so when we're on tour it's a party with a million people. After we got married [in 2008] she retired from the business. The first thing she said to me when we met onstage at Ozzfest in front of twenty thousand people was, "I masturbate to your music every day." I was like, "Wow, I love you. Let's get married." Now she lays around and masturbates when I'm writing.

DEZ FAFARA: One day you'd read in *Hustler* magazine that some *Hustler* chick loved you, loved your band. The next day she'd be at your show with six women and everybody'd be having sex up on the bus with handles of Jack Daniel's and cocaine and meth.

FRED DURST: It you're a heterosexual guy, you're a horn dog whether you're with one person or not. Whether you sleep with your girlfriend once a month or five times a day, you love tits and pussy and pornography. I believe in God. But I love titties. I love seeing girls in panties more than I like seeing them naked. That's what makes a lot of guys be so good to their girlfriends, 'cause they're so guilty in their minds all the time.

JONATHAN DAVIS [1999 interview]: I'm the kinkiest motherfucker you'll ever meet. I do freaky, weird shit and people enjoy it. I've had a girl for a birthday present. I've made girls piss in cat boxes, I've taken a drill gun and put a rubber on the end of a screwdriver handle and drilled out a bitch's pussy. You name it, dog, I've done it. Just try watching an all-deaf orgy in the back of my bus. That was in Florida. They had a threesome in the back of my bus. They were all eating each other's pussies and it was the damndest thing watching a deaf girl get off because the sound is like no other.

DEZ FAFARA: It wasn't uncommon to walk up to our bus, open the door, and see any of us naked having sex in the front or back lounge. It wasn't uncommon for four, five, six girls to be riding the bus on a nightly basis and for us to be getting down with all of them at the same time. Me and Meegs had orgies. It was not uncommon to usher in and usher out women and to share women. As a matter of fact, that was *more* common because it was like, "Dude, we're bro-ing down on this right now."

MEEGS RASCÓN: It was like *Caligula* on the bus. Everyone's running around naked, and if you weren't involved you were just sitting there and it wasn't a big deal. We had two bass players who were girls, Rayna [Foss] and Nadja [Peulen], and they never partook. They knew we were all doing crazy things in the next room or the next bunk. They'd hear noises and they'd hear porno on the DVD player, but they just laughed and shook their heads.

RAYNA FOSS: I was recording the original version of "Unspoiled," and everything raunchy that happened in one room came through my bass speakers, and I'm the only one who has it!

JAY BAUMGARDNER (producer): Let's just say there were bits of that track that needed to get edited out. It's like the Watergate tapes, actually—the missing five minutes somewhere! It involves spanking, I think.

FIELDY: With some of the shit I was doing, I think it was pretty safe to say the girls I was with the night before were never gonna call me again. Either I kicked them out of my house or I was actually at a club with another girl right in front of them. I even kicked some of them off the bus while we were rolling. We'd just stop the bus—"Get the fuck out." But the thing is, you really couldn't get as freaky as you could back in the day. I wasn't gonna go down on some chick, and I wore a condom all the time. And I didn't kiss girls because you didn't know how many other dicks they'd been sucking.

FRED DURST [1999 interview]: We brought strippers out on one tour, dressed them up as nurses, and had them strip down and eat each other out on the last song. Not naked, but I know there are a lot of fifteen-year-old kids out there who've never seen any shit like that, so why not see it at my show? Every guy out there probably wishes he had a fine girl he could tie up and blow a load all over them and they would love it—some crazy kinky girl. But I make sure, when I do the chicks, they're all over me and they're into it.

JONATHAN DAVIS [2002 interview]: One time, I was in the shower and these three girls came up to me with a bag full of dildos and whips. They went at it in the shower. I got tied up and got the shit beaten out of me with Judas Priest belts and about fifty people watched. They beat me up pretty badly. That was pretty cool. Then some other people took beer bottles and used them in both of these girls' orifices. It's not like I look for it. Usually, I walk into my dressing room and, hello, there it is. I've seen girls bend over and guys hock loogies on their assholes and whoever gets the asshole gets to fuck her. I've never regretted anything I've done. It's been all fun. No one was hurt. It's sex, man. You gotta explore and do things that are different, and these girls want to do that with you. Short of beating on someone—that's wrong—but if they like to be beat in a sexual way, I'm all for it.

ICE-T: In the rock-and-roll world, it's not unusual for a girl who wants to meet someone like Marilyn Manson to be told, "Okay, but you gotta suck the bus driver's dick and the light man's dick," and they'll do it. It's amazing. But after you see that, it fucks your head up because people will do low shit, and there's no limit. For the average dude, sex is so hard to get in the normal world. Then you go into a power game like a rock concert and you see the same chicks that would make a normal guy take them on twenty-five dates before they gave it up, and they'll lick your bus driver's ass in a second. It really gets to your brain.

EDSEL DOPE (Dope): One of my old drummers has some good video footage of him with some chick that is sucking his cock and then pukes all over it, and then goes back to sucking it again. But he liked that. Another time, *I* puked while this girl was giving me head and then she puked. And then she kept giving me head. It was a mess.

ICE-T: I'd see guys that would loan their girls to the group for autographs. But the weirdest thing I ever saw was on the Lollapalooza tour, where there was some chick in a trailer giving blowjobs. I was on the bus, and everybody was like, "You gotta see this," so my curiosity took over. I went to the place and there were like fifty cats in a line, and this had been going on for hours. This chick must have done five hundred head jobs. When I went in there it was dark, and someone introduced me as Ice-T, and the girl said, "Oh, you're back." So apparently guys had been telling her that *they* were Ice-T.

MEEGS RASCÓN: Even when we did our record, there were girls everywhere. They were running around the recording studio and between takes, us and other bands were going in and out of these rooms that weren't being used for music and doing drugs and getting laid. Before I would track, we would go into the restrooms and get blowjobs and then we'd go back out and record.

MORGAN LANDER (Kittie): We'd always see stuff like guys bringing back strippers and banging them, and we encourage that for our crew members 'cause we're living vicariously through them. I think honestly we're more apt to be objectifying women just because they're asking for it. There are male groupies, I guess, if you can classify them as that. I've seen some interesting stuff in my day, but most of the time they come off as gross. No one wants to have some dude breathing in their ear or saying disgusting things. "No, I don't want to fuck you on the bus, that's weird, just go away."

More often than not, alcohol and drug abuse accompanied the debauchery. Cocaine, methamphetamine, and hallucinogens were main ingredients for the raging party. And as in past eras, the musicians had little awareness of or concern for the damage they were causing themselves and their bands.

DEZ FAFARA: It says it best on Coal Chamber's first record on the license plate of the ice cream truck: "Sex, drugs, and rock and roll." That's what we lived. We did every kind of drug: coke, sniffing ketamine. Our rider had four bottles of whisky a day, and after that was gone we would go out to the bar drinking. Meegs and them did so much meth. I don't even know how they're alive. I saw balls of meth get mailed to them that would have lasted meth heads a year, and they would do it in three days.

MEEGS RASCÓN: We kind of re-created the eighties but in the nineties. The music was darker, heavier, and angrier, but the amounts of drugs, alcohol, and girls was out of control. I was doing a lot of what we called drug salads. It was every type of drug at once—coke, speed, weed, Special K, GHB, ecstasy. There were times I would do way too much blow and I would sit in my hotel almost praying because my heart felt like it was coming out of my chest. I always sweated it out, but there were some instances where I felt like I should have been dead.

DEZ FAFARA: I would take handfuls of Somas, mixed with Xanax, mixed with red wine and whisky. And then at two in the morning I'd decide to eat an eighth of mushrooms. I once did two weeks straight on the road on mushrooms every day.

FIELDY [1997 interview]: Munky likes to pee on us when he's drunk. We were too busy laughing to kick his ass. He didn't know what he was doing. He thought he was taking a piss in the bathroom. I've only tried to piss on someone one time, when I was in New York drinking Jäger. These Korn fans came up to me, and I was taking a piss. They're all, "Yo, G," and I said, "Get the fuck out of here," and I tried to piss on them. They ran. We don't drink Jäger anymore. It turned us into dickheads—especially Jonathan. We'd go on the bus and we'd look down, "Here comes Jon," and we'd all get in our bunks and act like we were asleep.

JONATHAN DAVIS [1997 interview]: It's true. When I walked into the bus everything stopped. I think it was because I'd get fucked up and bite people. I bit everyone in the band. I would party and get drunk and do cocaine or crank. Then I'd get all horny and wanna be tied up and fuck some chick, but I've got a wife. So I'm fighting inside, and I drink more. And for what? The whole thing is fucked-up anyway. I always wake up in the morning feeling bad from doing drugs, so why do I keep doing it?

MUNKY: I think you wind up drinking so much because you're covering up some sort of pain. And then when you stop drinking, you start feeling that pain and you don't know what to do. And that's when you start freaking.

JONATHAN DAVIS: I definitely freaked, but I kept drinking because they tried to kick me out of the band if I didn't.

BRIAN "HEAD" WELCH (ex-Korn): No we didn't. Fieldy did.

JONATHAN DAVIS [1997 interview]: He said, "If you don't drink beer, it's not gonna work out." But then I got to the point where I had to stop. I was like an alcoholic bulimic. I'd drink mass quantities of alcohol, go puke in the toilet, and then keep drinking. And one day I just looked at myself and I saw I was gonna die. My baby was about three at the time, and I came home drunk one night and he saw me and gave me this fucking look that I'll never forget. I felt like the biggest piece of shit. I was like, "I'm not gonna do this to my son. I gotta be there for him." So I sobered up. The thing is, I stopped drinking because I thought it would make me feel better, but it didn't, and that's when it really started to scare me.

HEAD: Jon would be happy for a few days, and we thought, "Oh, cool, he's doing better," but then he'd be in his room all fucking depressed. It was like this rollercoaster, and it depressed all of us.

JONATHAN DAVIS: Dude, I'd wake up and I'd literally want to kill myself. I wanted to jump out the window.

MUNKY: It was so sad. I felt so helpless sometimes 'cause I wanted to help him and I couldn't. I'd sit next to him in bed and he'd shake and I'd go, "Dude, are you all right?" But nothing I could say or do would make him come out of it. I'd tell him I love him and hold him and hug him. I'd say, "Jon, man, all this great stuff is happening to us." But it just didn't matter.

STEPHEN CARPENTER: Between the time we were eighteen and twenty-five, me and the guys in the band drank everything we could get our hands on, and I realize now I did that because it was the path of least resistance. But to go that way made me not ever concentrate on anything because otherwise I was focused on everything all at once and it was way too much to handle. I was stressing out. But when I was twenty-five, I weaned off the alcohol and went to weed, and that really made me feel good and allowed me to focus on everything, and I gained respect and appreciation for the fact that I am everything that is.

DEZ FAFARA: We got in lots of fights. Once we were sitting in the front of the bus at three in the morning. I was yelling at Meegs, telling him he was a fucking junkie, and he threw a whole gallon handle of whisky at me. I ducked, it hit the front windshield of the bus, broke out the glass, and the driver stood up, took the keys out of the ignition, said, "I quit," and walked away.

MEEGS RASCÓN: When fights would erupt, I would be right there in the middle. We just knew how to push each other's buttons. So I'd push Dez's buttons and he'd push mine and before you know it, we were throwing punches.

JONATHAN DAVIS: It was fuckin' bad, dude. I was going insane, literally. The only time I felt good was the hour that we were onstage. Other than that, I was in fucking hell. We did the first Family Values [in 1998] and we had just done *Follow the Leader*, which blew up so big with "Freak on a Leash" and "Got the Life." That freaked everyone in the band out. We went through a crazy adjusting period. No one was getting along because of all this sudden fame. We used to be able to go out in the crowd and talk to people, and suddenly I needed a bodyguard to go anywhere. Then I got a cocktail of Prozac and Dexedrine and it changed my entire life [for the better]. I still party like a motherfucker with all my friends; I just don't partake. If you see me at a party, I'm sitting there chopping lines and giving people drinks and rolling joints—whatever my homies want. But for me, it's just something I can't do any-more. I don't even drink caffeine.

WES BORLAND: At first, I drank beer and hung out, and we did mushrooms on the road and X. One night I tried a couple of heavier drugs, but then I realized, "Whoa, that's bad. That's so bad. 'Cause if I keep doing this, it's so easy to take this and fill up the loneliness hole so fast." I was like, "Boy, I could just fill up with this every night, and then I'll find something like coke or heroin that will fill it up even quicker," and if you do that the hole just gets bigger and it takes more of it to fill. There's another way to fill that hole more permanently, and that's by reading books on the road or going sightseeing—being a little tourist for a day. You've been given a chance to learn and go to all these different places and take advantage of that instead of nursing a hangover.

Capitalizing on the nu metal fever, Ozzfest assembled a cutting-edge lineup in 1998 that included Limp Bizkit, Sevendust, Coal Chamber, System of a Down, Incubus, Ultraspank, Snot, and Sepultura front man Max Cavalera's new band, Soulfly. But the year ended in tragedy when Snot front man Lynn Strait was killed on December 11, when his Ford Tempo collided with a truck on an off-ramp on California's 101 Freeway near Santa Barbara. In tribute, many of Strait's friends and peers—including Slipknot's Corey Taylor, Jonathan Davis, Sevendust's Lajon Witherspoon, Sugar Ray's Mark McGrath, System of a Down's Serj Tankian, and Incubus's Brandon Boyd—contributed vocals to an album of unfinished Snot songs and released it as *Strait Up* in November 2000.

It didn't take long for the nu metal community to rebound from Strait's death. For much of 1999, rock radio blared Korn, Limp Bizkit, and Deftones, and in June nu metal went supernova when Limp Bizkit put out its second album, *Significant Other*, which featured the sex anthem "Nookie." The disc debuted at number one on *Billboard*, selling 834,000 copies its first week. In 2001, the album was certified seven times platinum; it has sold over fourteen million units to date worldwide.

FRED DURST: Everything on *Significant Other* blows me away. We nailed it. Every song is its own entity. I can't think of a song that I'm not excited about. I think maybe I wanted to redo one chorus that I didn't get to do, but I was happy about everything else. We just went in and did it, real natural.

WES BORLAND: It was a hard record to make mentally and emotionally. We were constantly going, "Is this right? Is this the best we can do?" We were constantly second-guessing ourselves. We had a lot to live up to, and we were thinking about what our fans wanted and how to make that without compromising what *we* wanted.

FRED DURST: I really dug into myself and pulled a lot of stuff out. There are songs about sex and breaking stuff, but a lot of my lyrics come from betrayal and the way I've been treated by certain ex-girlfriends, because those scars don't go away. When I was in relationships, I was so naïve. I'd think everything was okay because we cared about each other. I'd spent all this time to prove I liked her, so I think everything's okay [and I stop pampering her]. And suddenly she feels rejected, and she thinks I don't like her or respect her, and she'll start fucking my friends. That's the worst thing. Your close friends have the best connections to the lonely girlfriend, so they act all sympathetic just to get her in bed. It became really hard to trust anybody.

When *Significant Other* blew up, Durst started to believe his own hype. He became a regular on MTV's *TRL* and an A&R man at Interscope, signing Staind, Cold, and Puddle of Mudd. He wrote songs with pop princess Britney Spears and boasted about the two allegedly having a sexual relationship. He dated celebrities Carmen Electra and, reportedly, Halle Berry, who shot a romantic scene with him for the video of Limp Bizkit's cover of The Who's "Behind Blue Eyes," a song from the appropriately titled 2003 album *Results May Vary*. Such Hollywood antics undercut his metal cred, and when Durst bad-mouthed Slipknot and even Korn in the press, boasting about how the student had eclipsed the sensei, there was a major backlash. In an online chat, Jonathan Davis said, "It's time for me to put that little bitch in his place. Never bite the hand that feeds." Ironically, Durst expressed similar sentiments—albeit more graphically—in a message he left on the answering machine of Stephen Richards, the singer for Taproot. Durst felt betrayed after the band, whom he'd offered a deal at Interscope, signed with Velvet Hammer/Atlantic for their debut album, *Gift*, in 2000.

FRED DURST (phone machine message): Hey man, you fucked up. You don't ever bite the hand that feeds in this business, bro, and your fuckin' manager so-called guy is a fuckin' idiot . . . a loser motherfucker goin' nowhere. You have just chosen that path. Took you under my wing, brought you to my house, fuckin' talked about your ass on radio, on press, and you embarrassed . . . me and the Interscope family. Your association with Limp Bizkit does not exist. Your manager slings that name around, he's gonna be blackballed and probably be erased . . . and you will, too. He's a fuckin' idiot. You're gonna fuckin' learn from this time right here. I hope you let your band know that you just fucked yourself. You need to be associated with somebody in this business. You need somethin' to get you out there, put you out there, and believe in. Now you got enemies and you're fuckin' yourself already. Tell your friend that. Don't fuckin' show up at my show, 'cause, if you do, you're gonna get fucked. All right? You and your fuckin' punk ass, man. You call your fuckin' manager, David Manifestease-whatever, ask him what he's done and doin'. You're a fuckin' dumb motherfucker. You're learnin' right now exactly how to ruin your career before it gets started. All of the luck, brother. Fuck you.

MIKE DeWOLF (Taproot): The deal Durst offered wasn't too good, and in the long run we were glad we found out what we would've been dealing with. That's putting it mildly.

JONATHAN DAVIS: There was one time when Fred was a really cool guy. Then fame hit and went to his head. I miss the old Fred.

WES BORLAND: Fred really wanted to embrace celebrity and stardom and become that character, just as I was hoping to become the character of the weird Mike Patton-y guy. We've always polarized people. There's not a lot of dismissive gray area when it comes to Limp Bizkit. A lot of people that were polarized to the hatred side were in complete disbelief that anyone would actually like us. That's one of the reasons I left the band. A lot of the people I had looked up to my entire music career were bashing something I was a part of.

TOM MORELLO: For me, Woodstock '99 [which included Rage Against the Machine, Limp Bizkit, Korn, and Kid Rock] was the low point of nu metal—the rapes in the pit, the trashing of the sites. It just seemed like it distilled the worst element of metal—the misogynist jock buggery—and the message wasn't announced as "this is a horrible thing." It was more like, "This is our new Woodstock generation—[a] bunch of idiots."

JONATHAN DAVIS: We rocked that place that first night. Everybody had fun. The second night, Limp Bizkit fucked it up for everybody.

WES BORLAND: The conditions at Woodstock were really shitty and overpriced. The organizers were running out of cash and water. People were getting crazy, anyway, but the shit didn't hit the fan until the day *after* we played. When we played it was a crazy show but all we could see were endless people going onto the horizon. If there were fires, I didn't see them when we were onstage. People were surfing on pieces of wood and Fred went out and started surfing on a piece of plywood, but I don't feel like he encouraged anyone to riot. It felt like our normal set. We weren't even at the venue when the rioting cranked up.

MATT PINFIELD: I think Fred burned a lot of bridges with friends, with other bands that he was actually associated with and helped out. It was personal. There are obviously people who didn't like him. They thought it was a dumbing-down of rock. In the industry, there were people who had it out for Fred, and therefore had it out for nu metal.

Some bands were happy to be considered part of the explosively popular nu metal movement. Others were dragged kicking and screaming to the carnival. The four most visible were Los Angeles's Linkin Park, whose 2000 debut, *Hybrid Theory*, was a commercial feast of rapping, melodic screaming, and industrial metal rhythms; Des Moines, Iowa's Slipknot, whose 1999 self-titled debut featured rapping and syncopated beats within a sea of experimental guitar riffs, samples, scratching, and percussive clatter; Chicago's Disturbed, who started out combining rap and vocal melodies with abrasive guitar riffs; and Lawrence, Massachusetts's Godsmack, whose 1998 self-titled debut featured plenty of staccato drop-D riffing and vocals that sounded like a blend between front man Sully Erna's favorite singers—Layne Staley (Alice in Chains) and James Hetfield (Metallica).

MIKE SHINODA (Linkin Park): When we came out with *Hybrid Theory*, the other stuff that was even remotely close to it was what we were calling behind closed doors "frat rock." It was really aggressive male, testosterone-filled, "I'm in your face, I'm a badass," alpha-male shit. Our stuff was not that. We came out with a flavor of hip-hop, but there was also a flavor of Depeche Mode and the Cure and stuff that was a little more introverted, and we exposed insecurities that those other bands would not touch. Our own A&R guy at the label was telling [vocalist] Chester [Bennington], "We need to kick Mike out of the band, we need to put you in front and do less of that other shit." He wanted our DJ to wear a gimmicky outfit to look like a mad scientist because other bands had gimmicks.

CHESTER BENNINGTON (Linkin Park): The second we heard it, we were like, "Fuck that." We had this repulsed reaction to that. We thought of ourselves as a band that was on the forefront of doing something original that had not been done before. Granted, a couple of bands we had no connection with had done a similar thing to what we were doing, but to be lumped into that nu metal thing felt wrong. We felt at that point that we either needed to embrace this or separate ourselves, because if we're going to be expected to make this kind of music for the rest of our lives, that's not very exciting.

COREY TAYLOR (Slipknot): We had elements of nu metal, but that was because we wanted to do everything. We were so much beyond that, and it took ten years for people to figure it out. We were the heaviest, craziest fucking band on the stage. Everyone gave us attitude and we were like, "Put it the fuck away. We don't give a fuck. We're not here to make fucking friends or suck up to anybody. We're here to destroy and move on."

JIM ROOT (Slipknot): I'm not really sure what nu metal is. I grew up listening to thrash bands like Overkill, Flotsam & Jetsam, Slayer, Venom, Metallica, Megadeth, and Anthrax. So to me, the guitars, other than the fact that we're tuned down real low, are real riffy like that. Sometimes that gets a little bit convoluted in the mix with all these auxiliary drums, but I really think we're our own thing.

SULLY ERNA (Godsmack): Unfortunately, we got lumped into the nu metal thing, and we were never that. We weren't rap-rock. We weren't doing all that weird shit and weird sounds like Korn was doing. We were just a rock band. It's because at that time Korn and Limp Bizkit were blowing up so big that they just had to categorize us. But you can't compare Godsmack's "Keep Away" to "Nookie."

DAVID DRAIMAN (Disturbed): The one thing that seems to unify nu metal bands is that they're all focused on issues like self-development and individuality and things that are strong and inherently a part of the human condition, which is definitely something I'm proud to be associated with—as opposed to old metal, which sort of dealt with content that was somewhat flimsy, nonsensical, meaningless. On the other hand, I don't see how rap–metal and what we do can be categorized together. As nu metal became defined as this fusion of hip-hop and metal, we began to feel like the odd stepchild, going, "Why are we being lumped in with this?" Granted there's a rhythmic vocal delivery, but truth be told, I borrow a lot of the vocal rhythms more from reggae than from anything else. And I'm always sure to fuse them with very strong melodies, unlike most rappers. We certainly benefited from the momentum of the movement at the time, but years later it's frustrating to be labeled as one of those bands when we didn't really have anything stylistically to do with it.

The first nu metal pioneers to implode were Coal Chamber. By 2002, after the release of their third and final album, *Dark Days*, the band members were traveling in different buses and there were fights almost daily. Some of the friction stemmed from the death of Drowning Pool front man Dave Williams, who succumbed to a heart attack on the road in Virginia on August 14, 2002, at the age of thirty.

DEZ FAFARA: Dave was so over the top he made me look *not* over the top, and I was *over the fucking top*. When we lost Dave, it was a huge wakeup call. I started to straighten out my life, and to do that I had to get my own tour bus to get away from the drugs and the craziness. I had just gotten married, so the orgies weren't gonna work. And being surrounded by people that don't go to bed for days wasn't gonna work either. Those guys were on meth so hard. These days, I'd rather have a glass of wine, smoke five joints, and talk about dragon mythology than be off my head and blowing shit up.

MEEGS RASCÓN: The final point came when we all decided without Dez to end our relationship with Sharon Osbourne, who was our manager. We felt like we weren't going anywhere with her. It had run its course and we needed another point of view.

DEZ FAFARA: They had a meeting in a hotel room one day behind my back. Some of the guys had been up for four or five days straight on meth. They called Sharon and fired her. And she's not only our manager, but also my second mom.

The only reason we had a good shot in the business is because she was behind us. They fired my business manager, and that night at a gig they handed me contracts that would have signed the band name and the whole band over to them. Normally I would just take a piece of paper and sign it and walk out, but I looked at it and showed it to my fiancée, Anastasia. And she went, "Whoa, this is fucked up. They're trying to take the band."

MEEGS RASCÓN: I don't think it was quite so dramatic. I don't remember any of the details 'cause I was too fucked up. But I know we got to Lubbock, Texas, and from the morning to the evening we were all fighting. By the time I got onstage we had both drank a lot and we were taunting each other, and before you know it we were throwing shit at each other and punching each other.

DEZ FAFARA: I booked every show. Came up with every song, came up with the name of the band. And people on drugs wanted to take over the band. I watched them spinning on meth before we went onstage, and people in security came over and said, "Hey, they're really cranked out over there. Crazy shit's gonna happen." Sure enough, Meegs tried to stab me with the guitar headstock for the first song. I realized, "Wait a minute, this guy's trying to actually fuckin' hurt me." I said, "That's it," and we started roughhousing. I grabbed the mic and said, "This is the last Coal Chamber show ever." Then I walked into my tour bus. Meegs came in ten minutes later and we exchanged blows. I think I got the better of him because he was on the bottom when they pulled me off.

MEEGS RASCÓN: We literally wanted to gouge each other's eyes out and break each other's bones. The band was a ticking time bomb and that was the moment where it exploded.

After Coal Chamber's career came to an abrupt end, Fafara continued as the front man for the more thrash- and death metal–oriented DevilDriver. Other nu metal pioneers also went through major life changes. Weary and depressed from years of drug and alcohol abuse, and newly committed to a life of Christianity, Head left Korn in 2005. Drummer David Silveria quit and opened his own restaurant. Unable to express himself fully musically or coexist with front man Fred Durst and his ever-growing ego, guitarist Wes Borland left Limp Bizkit in 2001, effectively crippling the band. He rejoined briefly in 2004 and played on *The Unquestionable Truth (Part 1)*, which was inexplicably released without any advertising or promotion. Borland quit again, and Limp Bizkit began a long hiatus, which they ended in 2009 for a European tour. Their first studio album in six years, *Gold Cobra*, came out in 2011 and received a lukewarm response from fans and critics. The band from the nu metal scene that has enjoyed the greatest longevity is unquestionably Deftones, which, ironically, has endured some of the worst trauma. When the band was working on its fourth album, *Deftones*, Moreno was drinking too much and drifting away from Carpenter creatively, and Cheng, who had just gone through a divorce, was in the throes of drug addiction. But things were about to get worse.

CHI CHENG (Deftones): I was so fucked up I don't even remember writing *Deftones*. Before I came in I'd crush up some mushrooms and put them in some hot-and-sour soup. I wouldn't remember playing in the studio at all. I was doing every kind of drug except heroin. I was just broken up because of my divorce, and I was going the irresponsible route. I'm not proud of it, but I decided to go gonzo style and see how far one man could push it. It was pretty much 24/7 for a while—until they threatened to get all Betty Ford on my ass.

CHINO MORENO: The next record, [2006's] *Saturday Night Wrist*, was a fucked-up time for me. I had never worked on a record without [producer] Terry Date. He's like another father to me. And suddenly we're with [producer] Bob Ezrin, and I didn't have anybody that I trusted, so I was completely lost and I started not having faith in my own singing. Plus my head was all messed up and I was trying to self-medicate any way I could to deal with the pain. Basically, I had a child with another girl. This happened around the time when we started writing the record. I found out and I didn't know what to do, so I didn't tell anybody in my band. I spent the whole summer in Malibu with all this weight on my shoulders. Then one morning I woke up and said, "Why am I living like this? It's affecting my creativity. No matter what, I just have to be honest with myself." So I told everyone. My marriage didn't last through it, and we'd been married since I was nineteen.

CHI CHENG: After I got clean, I was trying to work out and get in shape, too. Our guitar tech, who is one of my best friends, was going, "You never drink with me anymore." It was a Sunday morning. So I get on my beach cruiser with him. We get breakfast, get some mimosas, end up at a bar at 10:30, drink until about 12. I was coming down the PCH highway in Malibu at full speed, and this car whips out of his fuckin' driveway out of nowhere and I blasted into him head-on. I crushed the front of their car, blew in their hood, smashed up the windshield. They had to airlift me out. I never lost consciousness, but I couldn't move at all. I was laying in the road and the people there were saying, "No, we can't move you." I was like, "Someone's gonna come drive by and finish the job. Pull me out of the road." I thought I might die, but I was pretty comfortable with it. I thought it might be a drag for my wife and kids to go on without me. They flew me out *M*A*S*H*-style and I had this big thing around my neck so I couldn't even enjoy the view. I was like, "Fuck, push me into the ocean." I was beaten to shit and my knees and shoulder were blown out. I chipped my spooky tooth. But they were shocked I wasn't way worse. When they landed, they were like, "Ooh, this guy's done."

The incident wasn't Cheng's last near-fatality. The bassist was almost killed on November 4, 2008, in Santa Clara, California, when he and his sister Mae were driving away from a wake for their older brother, who had died the year before. Cheng, who wasn't wearing a seatbelt, was thrown from the car and suffered severe head trauma. When they saw the mangled vehicle, three off-duty EMTs called an ambulance to take Cheng to a Northern California hospital. There, doctors managed to regulate his vital signs, but the bassist was comatose. As of early 2013, Cheng remained in a minimally conscious state, but was able to lift his leg on command.

ABE CUNNINGHAM: I got a call at 3 a.m. from someone who wouldn't have had my number and I figured, "This can't be real." So I went back to bed. But I thought about it all night long, and the next morning I called Chino really early to see if he had heard anything.

CHINO MORENO: The night before, I had been at the studio working on vocals. I got home and crashed out. A couple hours later the phone rang and it was Abe asking me if I heard anything about Chi being in a coma. I figured, "Well, this has to be a rumor or someone from my management or Chi's family would have called me." So I tried to go back to sleep, but it just felt weird. I called my management and told them Abe had called me. They said they hadn't heard anything. At that point, I figured nothing was going on and I really did go back to sleep. Then I got a call back and they said, "Yeah, Chi was in a really bad accident."

ABE CUNNINGHAM: They removed part of his skull to make some room because of all the swelling. It's just such a strange situation to be in because he's here, but he's kinda not here. I don't think he's going somewhere any time soon. I don't think he's leaving us.

After Cheng's tragic accident, Deftones shelved *Eros*, the nearly completed album they had recorded with him, and quickly wrote a fiercer, more direct collection of songs. *Diamond Eyes*, produced by Nick Raskulinecz, came out in May 2010, and effectively resurrected the band.

STEPHEN CARPENTER: I never considered breaking up, but I was perfectly comfortable with starting a brand-new band—just come up with a whole new name and start from scratch. People would know who we were, but we could be ourselves and do something else without trying to make something without Chi.

CHINO MORENO: We could have gotten all depressed and said, "Fuck this, everything is pointless." Instead, we made new music. It was our appreciation for life and a celebration of the fact that we still have each other that kept us going. We just took that zest for being alive and poured it into the record.

STEPHEN CARPENTER: The alternative to us having a good time and doing music was being bummed out, and that's tough. It's still there now at this very moment. It's like, I'm divided. One half of me is having a great time in life, the other half can't have that great a time because my friend can't have a great time.

While Deftones was reinventing itself with producer Nick Raskulinecz and ex-Quicksand bassist Sergio Vega, Korn was taking a step back in time. In the wake of nu metal's apparent demise, the band released two albums that were funkier and more experimental: 2005's *See You on the Other Side* and 2007's *Untitled*. Both were well received by their devout fan base. Nonetheless, for

2010's *Korn III: Remember Who You Are,* Korn recruited their original producer, Ross Robinson, and strived to recapture the tortured
sound that had started the nu metal revolution.

JONATHAN DAVIS: It was just like old times. Ross would sit and
talk to me about the most personal shit and bad memories and
use any kind of ammunition he had to get me into that headspace where I feel like I want to run away and get the fuck out
of there. But it gets the message across for what I'm singing
about and the vibe, and you definitely can feel the emotion.
I basically went fucking crazy. It was very painful to do the
vocals and it totally damaged my psyche. But what isn't painful? In life we got a lot of great things and a lot of bad things.
But I chose my art and my art is to sing about pain.

STEPHEN CARPENTER: I've been in the same headspace with our
music for the past ten years. I don't ever question whether
we're in or out. I feel like our first three records have proven
our consistency. I think the self-titled record is just as great
as the first three, I think [2006's] *Saturday Night Wrist* is just
as great as the first four. [2010's] *Diamond Eyes* is our sixth
record, and when I reflect on all the records, they are all good
to me. I don't ever feel like I have to prove myself to someone
anymore.

JONATHAN DAVIS: It's pretty fuckin' crazy that we're still around.
I feel truly blessed. Even though the music business is dying,
we're still going strong. . . . People counted us out a long time
ago and we keep coming back. We're tighter than ever. I love
Fieldy and Munky. They're still my brothers.

FIELDY: We're getting along better than we ever have and that
has a lot to do with me. I was a lot of the problem when I was
drinking and doing drugs. Since I've become Christian I'm a
lot easier to get along with. It's been about eight years for me
since I've changed my life. When I first made my change I was

pretty quiet. Because everything that happened with Head, I kinda just was taking everything in and chilling out.

In 2011 Korn released the dubstep-saturated *The Path of Totality*, and in 2012 Deftones recorded their second album without Chi Cheng, *Koi No Yokan*. Both were critically and commercially successful. Yet both bands have effectively transcended the genre that spawned them. As a movement, as a subculture, nu metal no longer exists. Even though sounds from the scene continue to thrive in the more hectic music of modern death metal groups like Suicide Silence, Carnifex, and Job for a Cowboy, many musicians and critics look back at nu metal as an embarrassing moment in metal's history—an era colored more by style than substance, and one that encouraged misogyny, violence, and mindless rebellion.

JACOBY SHADDIX: It was cool to be a part of the nu metal scene at first, but after a while it became watered down because it was oversaturated by so many bands. So we said, "Okay, now we want to have our own identity." Us, Incubus, Deftones, Korn, we all broke out of all being tagged as the same thing, and now we're still doing our own thing.

SULLY ERNA: Korn's first couple records were fuckin' great. They were so different and so unique and their live show was phenomenal. Them and Limp Bizkit hit a moment where they really influenced this certain generation. But it kind of went by fast because the generation they hit were in their late teens and early twenties. They were wearing crooked hats and baggy pants down to their knees. And then those kids grew up and started having families of their own. So suddenly they're thirty and they have this wife and kids and it wasn't so cool to wear pants down to your knees anymore and crooked hats. I don't really think it was their music that got bad, I think it was their fan base that grew up and grew away from it.

COURTNEY LOVE (Hole) [2010 stage banter]: I have to say, as much as I like Fred [Durst], he brought about the worst years in rock history. That just be a fact, okay? That just be a fact. "I did it for the nookie!" I did not do it for the nookie, I did it for the rock. . . . I see [a] guy with [a] backwards baseball cap. "Dude, you! You scare me! You make me feel like you're going to rape me or something, and all my children. You did it for the nookie, dude in the red baseball hat? I'm so sorry you're here for the nookie. I could beat your ass."

10

HAMMER SMASHED FACE: DEATH METAL, 1983–1993

Tampa, Florida, isn't generally thought of as the kind of city that breeds great art. In 1990, its artistic community was at least 10 percent less active than that of most major American cities, according to National Science Foundation statistics, and it ranked just .08 percent above the national average for employed musicians. The city has a large conservative community of retirees, and, aside from the abundance of strip clubs along North Dale Mabry Highway, there's little indication of anything terribly sordid going on. Yet from the mid-eighties to the mid-nineties, Tampa was unquestionably the death metal capital of the world. Groups including Death, Morbid Angel, Obituary, Deicide, and Cannibal Corpse played blazing, savage, and lyrically graphic music that abounded with frantic double bass and blast beat drumming, down-tuned bee-swarm guitars, and low, guttural, and largely unintelligible vocals that made Slayer sound like Bad Company.

JIM WELCH: Everybody always wants to push extremes to the greatest degree, and that's what drove death metal. Thrash was fast and heavy, but death metal was faster, more extreme, and more out there.

BRANDON GEIST: The vocals became so inhuman, and that was a big step. It's like, "I'm no longer going to sing as a person. I'm going to sound like a demon." Thrash bands were pissed and that's why they shouted. Death metal bands were possessed. It was a whole other level of evil.

JOSE MANGIN: Death metal is about mixing insanely fast blast beats with slower grooves. With the good bands, there's musicianship and technicality there along with these vicious vocals.

For almost two decades, the origin of the term *death metal* has been fodder for late-night drunken arguments among fans. Some credit hyper-thrash band Possessed, which put out a demo called "Death Metal" in 1984. Others swear on an inverted cross that Mantas front man Chuck Schuldiner (later of the band Death) called his music "death metal" to separate it from thrash even before recording the 1984 demo "Death by Metal," and thus deserves the credit. Regardless, everyone agrees the scene was motivated by misanthropic rage and violence, and that it spread like a pathogen across the globe.

JEFF BECERRA (Possessed): The first singer for Possessed, [Barry Fisk], committed suicide by shooting himself in the head as his ex-girlfriend opened her front door, so [drummer] Mike Sus and [guitarist] Mike Torrao came to my high school and asked me to join [on bass]. I had just gotten out of a band called Blizzard and wanted to play Motörhead-type music. This was a perfect opportunity. We couldn't find a singer, so the guys asked me to sing. Later I went back to my old band and got [guitarist] Larry LaLonde (Primus), and with a little help from the devil we became Possessed.

RICK ROZZ (ex-Death, ex-Massacre): The death metal scene totally started in San Francisco with Possessed because there was nothing going on [in Florida] yet. The first time Death played a show at Ruby's Pub with Nasty Savage in '84, there were at least two hundred people there, but there was nobody in front of the stage. They were clueless, and I *know* Possessed were already playing in front of people in California. The thing is, there was never a thrash scene in Florida. Savatage wasn't thrash. Nasty Savage wasn't thrash. Exodus and Slayer were ruling in California, so crowds there were already used to the growly vocals, and this was just the next step for them.

JEFF BECERRA: I came up with [the term *death metal*] during an English class in high school. I figured *speed metal* and *black metal* were already taken, so I said "death metal" because the word wasn't associated with Venom or anybody else. We wanted to piss people off and send everybody home. And that can't be, like, "flower metal."

PAUL MASVIDAL (ex-Death, Cynic): Chuck [Schuldiner] heard [Possessed vocalist] Jeff Becerra and said, "Whoa, that's where I want to go." Chuck definitely was labeled as the godfather of death metal, and in some ways he was. He kept going and making records and developed the whole sound.

ALBERT MUDRIAN (author, *Choosing Death*; editor in chief, *Decibel*): Some people say Possessed's [1985 album] *Seven Churches* is the first death metal album, and it *may* be, but I feel like it's the first proto-death metal album. I feel like it's the last non–death metal because it's about as close as you can be without being all the way in. And the fact that they have a song called "Death Metal" on the record sold it to a lot of people. But to me, there's a clearer delineation when these bands that are recognized as death metal starts. If you listen to Obituary's first album [1989's *Slowly We Rot*] back to back with *Seven Churches*, you can tell the difference.

JOHN TARDY (Obituary): My family moved from Miami to Tampa when we were young, and the first people we came in contact with in our neighborhood were the guys in [speed metal band] Nasty Savage and [power metal group] Savatage. So, those were the bands that got us interested in playing music. And me, my brother, [drummer] Donald, and [guitarist] Trevor [Peres] all lived in the same neighborhood, so we started jamming when we saw Nasty Savage playing out. We didn't sound anything like them, but they were real motivational. We started Xecutioner [the predecessor to Obituary] in 1984 just to have fun in our garage. We had no idea what we were doing, but it didn't take long to develop the sound we wanted.

JAMES MURPHY (ex-Death, Disincarnate): Nasty Savage and Savatage got all the Florida bands going because they were making records, playing clubs, and going to Europe, and they showed us, "Hey—you too can start a band and get signed."

JOHN TARDY: We were getting off the school bus and going in my parents' garage and jamming until my mom said, "Come in and eat." Xecutioner tried to do a gig with Nasty Savage at Rubies in Tampa. We showed up and went to load in and they went, "You guys can't play here. You're not old enough." So we turned around and left.

JAMES MURPHY: As great as Nasty Savage and Savatage were, they were far from death metal. Chuck deserves the credit for that. He was an avid record collector and was into obscure European bands like Demon Eyes, Sortilège, and H-Bomb, as well as early [German thrash bands like] Sodom, Kreator, and Destruction. Nobody else was listening to that at the time. And that really helped shape his sound. In 1983 when he did the first Mantas demo, ["Death by Metal,"] he was doing something unique, and it hit a nerve with people who were looking for something heavier than thrash.

KAM LEE (ex-Death, Massacre, Bone Gnawer): It was 1983 and we were all in high school. I knew Rick [Rozz] because we had art class together. I was a little punk kid and I was always drawing skeletons and spooky stuff 'cause I was a Misfits fan. So, Rick would come over to look at what I was drawing and we started talking about music. One day he came into class with a copy of Iron Maiden's *Killers* album and he threw it down on my desk and said, "Do you think you could draw that?" I was like, "Yeah, man, that's easy." So I drew Eddie and gave it to him. He goes, "Hey man, I know we're not into the same music, but I'd like to give you some stuff to listen to." I was a punk drummer. I really wasn't into metal. But he got me listening to Motörhead and that pulled me in. One day he goes, "I met this guy Chuck at a party and we were saying we can't find drummers who can play this stuff. Would you like to come in and try it?" He had seen my other band, Invaders from Hell, which was very Misfits-influenced, so he knew I could play fast.

RICK ROZZ: The three of us got together a week later and all dropped out of school within a week of each other to spend seven days a week in Chuck's garage working on music. We started with covers of Slayer, Metallica, and Savatage and then we wrote originals. We had the same taste in music and wanted to do stuff that was heavier than anything.

KELLY SHAEFER (Atheist, Neurotica): Chuck Schuldiner put the stamp on death metal and said, "Hey listen, my band is gorier and darker than anything else." He stepped out on a limb at a time when that wasn't fashionable. He had already cooked his dinner, and we were all just on the burner. Kam Lee was the first one to have that low death metal growl when they called themselves Mantas.

KAM LEE: Chuck and Rick introduced me to Venom's first album, [1981's] *Welcome to Hell*. We didn't have a name yet and someone said, "Why don't we call ourselves Mantas after the guitar player in Venom?" We started doing rehearsal tapes on weekends and recorded the first Mantas demo in Chuck's garage. Since we didn't have a singer I was like, "Well, I could play drums *and* sing." I was fourteen and I hadn't gone through puberty yet. But by '85 I knew I didn't want to go in the same direction as all those other vocalists who were singing in high-pitched screechy voices like Jeff Becerra from Possessed. So I started singing lower. Then, other people took what I did and made it deeper and deeper and that became the template of death metal.

CHUCK SCHULDINER (1967–2001) (Death, Control Denied): I'd only been playing guitar for six months—I couldn't even play a lead. I just wanted to bash out the most brutal riffs ever with the most brutal guitar sound ever, but I always had an urge to become a better guitarist.

RICK ROZZ: The first gig we did was at a Knights of Columbus hall opening for a band called Tempter. Everybody was like, "What the fuck is this?" We were a three piece, we had no bass player. We tuned really low to C, and Kam was growling. At the time in Florida, promoters were only booking hair metal cover bands for clubs, so there was no way we were gonna get a gig at a real venue. We played this pizza place in Orlando. We played at a restaurant at the salad bar—anything we could get.

KAM LEE: The heaviest thing most people in Florida were exposed to back then was probably Ozzy. So when we started playing everyone was like, "Oh, these teenage kids are terrible." And that's the reaction we got until the late eighties when bands like Kreator started gaining popularity and the San Francisco thrash scene caught on.

RICK ROZZ: Chuck wanted to get more serious and he wanted us to have our own identity, and that's how the name Death came into play. I was really into tape trading, and we knew Possessed were out and had the song "Death Metal." And we had our song "Death by Metal." So we went with Death.

KAM LEE: I left Death before they got a record deal. It wasn't a business falling out, it was teenage kids falling out. I liked a girl; Chuck liked the same girl. I made a move; he didn't. He got mad at me. Also, at the time, I was homeless and living in the street. I was kicked out of my home and when he could, Chuck would let me stay at his house, but I couldn't live there permanently. So finding a place to live became a priority and they wanted to keep doing Death.

CHRIS REIFERT (ex-Death, ex-Abcess, Autopsy): Chuck was about to broadcast a radio ad saying he was looking for a new drummer, and a friend at the local radio station told me about it before it went on the air. I was completely in shock because I had been collecting the demos and ordering the live tapes from the band. So I was super excited. I called him up and we got together, and things clicked immediately.

RICK ROZZ: Combat signed us because they liked what they heard on the [1986] "Mutilation" demo. I was in and out of the band several times. I was let go before any recording was done because Chuck met a bass player, [Repulsion's Scott Carlson], and the guy would only join if his guitarist [Matt Olivo] came, too. So I was let go and didn't record on the first album, [1987's] *Scream Bloody Gore* [which wound up featuring Schuldiner on guitar, bass, and vocals]. Then I came back to tour for *Scream Bloody Gore* and help write [1988's] *Leprosy*.

SCOTT CARLSON (Genocide, Repulsion, ex-Death): We knew Chuck [Schuldiner] and Death from tape trading, and he liked the Genocide demos, so when Kam and Rick left Death, Chuck asked me and Matt to move to Florida to work with him on Death. We sat around trying to write demos, but we could tell very quickly that our writing styles were going in different directions. Matt and I started writing faster and faster with more primitive riffs, and Chuck's riffs kept getting more technical and melodic. So we decided to go back to Michigan and continue what we were doing as Repulsion.

CHRIS REIFERT: We feasted on gore movies every night—the more blood and heads and guts flying, the better. A lot of the songs on *Scream Bloody Gore* were based directly on horror movies. "Torn to Pieces" is about *Make Them Die Slowly*, "Regurgitated Guts" is about *Gates of Hell*, and "Evil Dead" is about *Evil Dead*. "Scream Bloody Gore" is about *Reanimator*. It was just gore for the sake of gore.

RICK ROZZ: For all the extreme music that Death made, we were a bunch of mellow guys. There was no substance abuse—hardly any alcohol. It was all about the music. But there was lots of chaos. Our first time in Europe, we came back twenty-seven shows early because Chuck wasn't happy with traveling. We were in a shuttle van instead of a tour bus, and I went, "Dude, we're saving money. Let's go with this," but Chuck wouldn't have it. What do you say when your singer says, "We're out of here"? You can't say, "No, we're not leaving." We went home.

CHRIS REIFERT: After the record came out, Chuck moved back and forth between Florida, California, and Canada. I wasn't a big fan of Florida and the heat and humidity. So I stayed behind in San Francisco and started Autopsy.

JIM WELCH: Chuck literally thought he was making more money [than he was], so he held everything hostage. He'd say, "I'm going home unless you write me a check." He canceled multiple tours over time because of that.

RICK ROZZ: I was fired from the *Leprosy* tour. Maybe I was a lazy guitar player because I didn't feel like shredding. Chuck always asked me if I was practicing and if I had my guitar with me. I read between the lines, and when I was let go there was no fuss.

PAUL MASVIDAL: I missed my high school graduation to go on tour with Death. I was eighteen, and Chuck had just kicked Rick Rozz out and needed a guitarist to tour Mexico. I became his emergency guy. When he kicked out [James] Murphy in 1989, he called me again. Although I was committed to Cynic, as a friend I was willing to lend a hand.

JIM WELCH: Chuck was definitely the most difficult artist I ever dealt with. He was a violent, angry, irrational person. From day one, he thought the record company was ripping him off and that he was owed all this money. He was actually broke and in debt, but he didn't understand that. Every day he'd have a tantrum, then he would be calm and morose. He never threw a punch at me, but did he throw shit around the room? Absolutely. I certainly felt like he could've gotten physically violent. He'd have fits all the time, and his mom would call up and apologize. It says something when one band goes through so many different musicians—twenty-seven—over its eighteen-year career.

RICK ROZZ: We never really fought, even after I was out of the band and they kept using my stuff. I co-wrote the whole *Leprosy* record with Chuck and have a lot of writings on *Scream Bloody Gore* and *Spiritual Healing*, but I'm not credited. Even when Chuck was alive, I didn't complain. But people would ask me all the time, "Did you write any of that? That sounds like you." I was like, "Yup." That's just the way it was.

As word of Death began to spread, another seminal Florida death metal band arose from the fetid earth. In 1983, accomplished guitarist and occultist Trey Azagthoth formed Morbid Angel with bassist Dallas Ward and drummer Mike Browning. Like Death, the band endured several lineup changes while Azagthoth searched for musicians who complemented his blasphemous vision. Then in 1989, after the demise of grindcore pioneers Terrorizer, bassist and vocalist David Vincent and maniacal drummer Pete Sandoval entered the Morbid fold, giving the band the boost it needed to carve its diabolical path. Still, it took the rest of the community a while to catch up to the band's ferocious tempos.

DAVID VINCENT (Morbid Angel, ex-Terrorizer, ex-Genitorturers): The letters of rejection that we got from various labels from our first few demos were amazing. One label went so far as say, "You do for music what King Herod did for babysitting." But we always looked at it as though we were in battle, and every time someone said, "Slow it down, make it more melodic, write less controversial lyrics," our response was always, "Fuck. You. You don't like that one? Great. You're definitely not gonna like the next one 'cause it's worse."

MITCH LUCKER (1984–2012) (Suicide Silence): The first time I heard Morbid Angel, [drummer] Pete [Sandoval] fucking blew me away. He was doing these completely blisteringly fast blast beats in triple time. I had never heard anything like it—that insane speed was totally sick.

ALBERT MUDRIAN: Morbid Angel's debut album, [1989's] *Altars of Madness*, was so Satanic and over the top. You had bands like Possessed that would dabble with stuff like that, but Morbid Angel took it a step further. It felt fucking serious.

DAVID VINCENT: We heard some of those other bands from tape trading, but Morbid Angel was really shut off from everything else. For us, it was about the inner spirituality amongst the members of the band. We never saw ourselves as part of any scene and I don't think we sounded anything like any of the bands we were associated with.

TREY AZAGTHOTH (Morbid Angel): Morbid Angel assembled in 1984 to lift ourselves with [a] celebration of the gifts from the triumvirate: the spirit, true will, and creative faculty. That's always been our purpose, to be their instrument on this earth and let their influence flow through us, and simultaneously be the sharp-edged weapon that destroys the influence of the enslaver and the falsifications, and also helps establish a new foundation to build upon once the limits of the paradigms have been shattered and the rubble is cleared out of the way.

DAVID VINCENT: Me and Trey are very different people and we see things different ways, but I think that's a strength. We have things we see eye to eye on and things we don't. It makes for a bigger, more complete project, and although we look at things differently we'll often arrive at the same conclusions, but for totally different reasons.

Why Florida? The question has been asked repeatedly, but never definitively answered. Clearly it had something to do with the boredom teenagers felt roaming strip malls, and their desire to create their own culture. The fact that Schuldiner was there to plant the seeds of hate was also a factor. But as much as anything it seemed to be a matter of right place, right time.

PAUL MASVIDAL: Central Florida is a hyper-conservative, religious retirement community. So it's a weird place to begin with, and then you have these kids with no place to go. So maybe death metal happened as a reaction to that, or maybe it's just some energetic physics thing—a spirit that's in the air that kids just tune in to if they have an artistic bone in their bodies.

PHIL FASCIANA (Malevolent Creation): The heat in Florida makes you fucking crazy, man. And between that, all the old people, tourists, and the fucking drunks, no wonder everyone wanted to make really extreme music.

GLEN BENTON (Deicide): All the bands in Tampa were practicing in these metal storage units that you could rent. It was the only place you could rehearse, and there was no air conditioning. You get there and you're totally sweated out before you even start playing. It builds endurance and feeds your anger.

MONTE CONNER: I don't know that there's anything specific about Tampa that caused death metal to blow up there as opposed to anywhere else. If Chuck Schuldiner lived in Michigan, it could have been the Michigan death metal scene.

KELLY SHAEFER: Chuck Schuldiner was a really competitive guy who was very protective of anybody being trendy. One of the main reasons Atheist ended up being such a strange band was we were trying so hard not to sound like anybody else that we went way overboard. We were outsiders in an outsider's scene, so we made it doubly hard for ourselves.

PAUL MASVIDAL: Atheist and Cynic were really the prog bands in the scene. We were nerdier kids and we had been into all kinds of music since we were really young. In late high school and early college I was really getting into jazz and fusion. When we worked with Chuck [Schuldiner] on the [1991] Death album *Human*, we didn't see it as making death-prog, we saw it as doing what we do, but on Chuck's tunes. It was how we would approach a death song and still have that [jazzy] sensibility. And it really inspired him to take his music in a new direction that was further from the growly, more simplistic stuff he started out doing.

JAMES MURPHY: To be honest, the early Tampa scene was very divisive, and a lot of the bands didn't like each other or talk to each other because it was extremely competitive. No one knew that literally every single one of their bands was going to get signed. There was an overall feeling that there were only so many record deals to be had.

The actual death metal album *sound*, characterized by crisp, rapidly thumping bass drums that cut through walls of roaring vocals and buzzing guitar distortion, was conceived at Tampa's Morrisound Studios by owner Tom Morris and then-fledgling producer Scott Burns.

TOM MORRIS (founder of Morrisound Studios): We opened up in 1981, and two of the first bands we recorded were Nasty Savage and Savatage. Obituary was the first death metal band that came to us at our studio, and that's when they were kids in high school going by the name Xecutioner. They cut a demo in a little eight-track studio we have and that's what got them signed to Roadrunner. But when [vocalist] John Tardy and [drummer] Donald [Tardy] first came in, I almost told them to just go home. I had never heard death metal prior to that and I thought they were wasting their time and money trying to do it. But they were pretty insistent and went ahead and finished it, and, obviously, they knew something I didn't.

SCOTT BURNS (ex–Morrisound Studios producer): Xecutioner were doing their first album and [Morrisound engineer] Rick Miller was in an accident. I knew the guys from working sound at their shows, so I finished up their album. About the same time, Atheist came in and did *Piece of Time.* I'd also engineered for producer Dan Johnson. He was doing *Leprosy* for Death, so I met all those guys. After that, I was always either engineering or assisting.

JOHN TARDY: Our first record, [1989's] *Slowly We Rot,* wasn't even something we planned on doing. Roadrunner heard our demo and said, "Do you wanna do a record?" and we were like, "Sure." At the time, I really wasn't interested in writing lyrics. I just liked making sounds that went along with the music. So, the low, growling vocals weren't planned, they just happened. There were so many vocal parts on *Slowly We Rot* that went from a couple of real words to a jumbled mess of screams and growls that I couldn't have written the lyrics out if I wanted to.

KELLY SHAEFER: When I listened to Obituary's demo I went, "Holy shit, you can hear everything!" Whenever we had gone to a studio before, we terrified everyone. And none of their engineers knew how to capture double bass drums or death metal vocals the proper way. Morrisound was the first studio in the country to record death metal without it sounding like a bunch of shit. They had a great way of tracking bass drums in particular.

GLEN BENTON: Everybody wanted to record with Scott. He's the George Martin [legendary Beatles producer] of fuckin' death metal. He was good at getting the right sounds and he was also dealing with a lot of record labels, so he helped get a lot of bands signed.

SCOTT BURNS: I always thought it sucked that you would hear some kid playing extreme double bass or fills and it sounded like a muffled echo. We spent a lot of time figuring out exactly how to mic everything to get the drums to sound good. When everything's in a blender at 200 miles per hour, it takes a little bit of time to figure out how to get all the stuff to fit in. On the downside, I got typecast for the Morrisound sound. And it's not like I got rich off it. I made more money than the bands, maybe, but I don't think I ever charged more than $5,000 for a record, and I didn't take any [percentage of royalties] off bands. I was offered royalties on two records and I gave them back to the bands at the beginning because they were getting screwed by their labels.

Between Schuldiner's leadership, Burns's diligence, and the persistence of musicians wanting to make insanely heavy music, the death metal scene grew. Bands with records out launched low-budget national tours to spread the word, and groups from out of state immigrated to Tampa to be with like-minded individuals.

ALEX WEBSTER (Cannibal Corpse): We started in Buffalo, [New York,] in 1988, but we didn't move to Florida until 1994, and we went there strictly because of the death metal scene and Morrisound. Even before we did *Eaten Back to Life* there in 1990, we were listening to stuff like [Morbid Angel's] *Altars of Madness* and [Death's] *Leprosy*, which had been done there. We did four albums in Tampa before we finally decided to move there.

TREY AZAGTHOTH: We knew we had to tour to spread the word, so we gutted out a school bus and made a cargo area in the back with heating in the front. It didn't have any air conditioning. We went to Texas in the summer, and the heat was crazy. We didn't have any money, so we slept in the bus and a lot of times we could only buy food or gas. We looked at it like we were a special forces unit going into enemy territory.

RICHARD CHRISTY (ex–Death, ex–Public Assassin, Charred Walls of the Damned): Even though bands were doing well in Florida, not a lot of people around the country knew about death metal. Some promoters would book death metal bands to open for popular nationwide acts because they didn't know any better. When I was in Public Assassin, we got booked to open for Molly Hatchet in Springfield, Missouri. We got up there and did a sound check of blistering, blast-beat death metal. And then the club owner went, "I'll pay you guys $100 *not* to play." We were like, "Screw that, we're gonna open for Molly Hatchet!"

CHRIS REIFERT: Autopsy played plenty of shows for ten or twenty people. There wasn't a lot of mass acceptance of death metal in the Bay Area at the time. People just thought it was dumb. We weren't being political or singing about banging your head in the mosh pit like all the thrash bands, so people looked down at it. I would try to explain to people what we were doing and I would get ridiculed, but I didn't care. I wasn't going back to Florida.

Death, Morbid Angel, Obituary, and Deicide all made their mark in Tampa, but it was Cannibal Corpse that first exposed death metal to the mainstream, and it remains the most popular death metal band. Thanks to original vocalist/gore freak Chris Barnes (who was in the group from 1988 to 1995), their lyrics were uglier and more graphic than those of most of their contemporaries, often dealing (in their early days) with zombie invasions, serial killers, and the mutilation of women (in explicit detail). Their brain-in-a-blender riffs were so furious they would have sounded nearly nonsensical were it not for drummer Paul Mazurkiewicz's precision playing. Cannibal Corpse struck a nerve with audiences seeking the ultimate in extremity. Song titles like "I Cum Blood," "Entrails Ripped from a Virgin's Cunt," and "Post Mortal Ejaculation," all from 1992's *Tomb of the Mutilated*, were deemed so offensive that the album was banned in Germany until 2006. Ironically, the Jim Carrey movie *Ace Ventura: Pet Detective* included a cameo of Cannibal Corpse playing "Hammer Smashed Face," which is from the same album.

MARK "PSYCHO" ABRAMSON (VP promotions, Roadrunner Records): Even in the beginning, you could tell they were great. Their stuff was a lot more simple than other bands, but they never had a problem with a catchy hook. And everything they did was always intense. Plus, they combined it with a twisted sense of humor that made it brilliant.

ALEX WEBSTER: A lot of bands in Florida had a darker, anti-religion thing going on, so we decided to focus on gore. Most Western music is people singing from the heart, singing to a girlfriend, so a lot of people are freaked out by our songs. But our lyrics have nothing to do with our personal lives. It's just storytelling, and it came from the kinds of movies we all used to watch, like *Evil Dead* or *Gates of Hell*. We knew it was going to be controversial, but we didn't know to what extent.

FORMER SENATOR JOSEPH LIEBERMAN (I-CT) [1997 Congressional speech attacking entertainment industry]: The death metal band Cannibal Corpse . . . [has] one song describing the rape of a woman with a knife and another describing the act of masturbating with a dead woman's head. I apologize for expressing—describing these lyrics, but this is what we are talking about. We are not overstating. This is extreme, awful, disgusting stuff that millions of kids are listening to.

JEREMY WAGNER (Broken Hope, author): Some lyrics I write for Broken Hope are over-the-top in violent imagery, horror, and explicit sexual content. That said, here's the scary part: many of my lyrical ideas come from real life. Songs like "Bag of Parts," "Coprophagia," "Decimated Genitalia," "Preacher of Sodomy," "Penis Envy," and more were all drawn from actual events that happened in the news and in some highly respected medical journals. Society is much more horrifying and strange than any fiction I could dream up.

PAUL MAZURKIEWICZ (Cannibal Corpse): When a crime is being committed against a woman, it's generally more disturbing to people. Like, some people have been really freaked out by our song "Fucked with a Knife." But, damn, it's just a song.

CHRIS BARNES (ex–Cannibal Corpse, Six Feet Under): When those guys wrote music, it presented such a violent image to me I felt like I had to match it with the lyrics. And I was able to pull from my imagination some sick qualities of mankind and put it down on paper. For example, "Entrails Ripped From a Virgin's Cunt" was based on a true story my friend told me, and I twisted the facts in my head and filled in the blanks.

ALEX WEBSTER: Some people saw Chris's lyrics as misogynistic. He is not a misogynist and neither are the rest of us. But I can understand how people who didn't know us might misinterpret that.

CHRIS BARNES: My lyrics almost got me killed at gunpoint in 1994 before a show in East LA. Some gang members got on the bus somehow and told me they didn't like my lyrics. One of them had just got out of San Quentin, and he had a .38 stuffed into his belt lining. He picked up his shirt and showed it to me and said, "We're gonna kill you if you keep writing about this shit." I tried to talk to him calmly and say, "Hey, I respect your opinion." Luckily, we had a really good tour manager, who somehow got those guys off the bus.

ALEX WEBSTER: I don't buy the argument that our music makes people violent because with our stuff you always have that comfort zone—that separation of reality. That's something most people know about our lyrics. They're just for entertainment. They're not condoning real violence. They're about zombies and serial killers. It's like a horror movie. So for people to focus on it just because it's so lurid is ridiculous. Maybe one or two bad things have happened over the twenty-five years thrash and death metal have been around. How many bad things have happened involving fans of country music, rap, or R&B?

PAUL MAZURKIEWICZ: I find real violence extremely disturbing. I watched the movie *Faces of Death* years ago, and it wasn't at all entertaining. Real gore is a completely different and upsetting thing.

The insane speed and aggression of death metal probably had more appeal to audiences than did the brutal lyrics. Nonetheless, the music attracted a violent and rowdy crowd. Those brave enough to enter the pit risked bodily harm from fans treating the floor like a gladiatorial arena. And some musicians fed off the brutality.

GLEN BENTON: There's a lot of motherfuckers in this world walking around with teeth missing because of me. If you came up on the stage, I'd be the first one kicking the shit out of you. I had a three second rule. You turn around, you jump back off—otherwise your ass is mine. A lot of people fell prey to that. With all the armor, spikes, and nails, I was a human meatgrinder, man. I was into the whole making of the armor. One night, I made this armband with .308 spitzer [bullet] heads on it, and I went through the crowd sticking that thing into people's backs. At the end of the night there were all these people walking around with big bloody spike marks.

CHRIS BARNES: Our first club show almost started in a riot, and the last show I played with Cannibal Corpse in Australia ended in a riot. It's been a pretty wild ride.

PHIL FASCIANA: We played a club in Hallandale, Florida, called the Treehouse, with Obituary, and when I went outside to cool off I seen a kid with a towel on his face. It was covered in blood. When he took off the towel I could see somebody had bitten off his top lip. It was gone. Up until almost his nostrils there was nothing, and you could actually see the grooves from the person's teeth in this guy's fuckin' face. This poor kid's chances of playing the trumpet or growing a fucking moustache are not there anymore.

JOHN TARDY: The fucked-up thing is he was laughing about it. I'm like, "Dude, I can see all your front teeth and your mouth's closed. That ain't right."

KELLY SHAEFER: When the New York hardcore scene mixed with metal, fists started flying. There were lots of broken jaws and knocked-out teeth. I saw someone get their eye poked out of the socket at a show with Solstice. The eyeball wasn't just hanging out, it was pushed out to the side and the guy stayed in the pit with that fucked-up eye like that. I saw a guy get his ear half ripped off from the top. The whole top of it was flopping down from his head. That's when I was like, "Shit, I'll never get back into the pit."

GLEN BENTON: I saw Marilyn Manson get the living shit kicked out of him by twenty skinheads at one of our shows in Fort Lauderdale. After the gig, I went outside and him and his buddies were lying in the parking lot, makeup all fucked up.

KAM LEE: I knew a guy in Arizona who was in a band, and he would eat human bones. I met him at this club called the Mason Jar. He would raid cemeteries and dig up bones. He invited me to his house, so I went, and he was wearing a black robe, doing the whole Satanic thing, trying to impress me. Then he brings out bone fragments and starts chewing on them, saying they're human bones. I was like, "Okay, I guess if that's cool to you, that's how you get your thing. I'm not gonna chew no human bones. Just give me a Heineken."

Some death metal bands accompanied their music with occult-themed theatrics. As with early Venom and Slayer, such drama was usually just for shock value. But two bands, Morbid Angel and Deicide, took their odes and gestures to Satan seriously.

GLEN BENTON: By the definition of Christianity, I am a Satanist. Am I putting my goatskin leg pieces on and dancing around the fire? No. Am I a free thinker? Yes. I'm ordained at several Satanic institutions. I didn't pay $99 to get my card. I think any organized religion is hokey. If you've got to pay to belong, fuck that. I don't believe in God as far as putting my trust in him. So I don't know what that makes me. It makes me Glen

Benton. If Satan jumped up right now and asked me to do something, nine times out of ten I would probably do it.

KELLY SHAEFER: I was walking backstage in the early days and seeing the guys from Morbid Angel sitting around a chalice, cutting themselves and bleeding into the cup. I thought, "That's fuckin' nuts." We played crazy music, but we didn't roll like that.

JIM WELCH: The first show Morbid Angel ever played was at the Sundance in Long Island. Their manager introduced me to [vocalist] David Vincent, and he seemed like a really charismatic guy—a little off, but nothing too strange. So we walk into the dressing room and Trey [Azagthoth] was warming up on his guitar. When you look into his eyes you can tell there's a lot going on in there that you're never gonna decipher. Back in the day, every night before he went onstage, he pulled out a knife and sliced his left arm open. He's bleeding all over the fucking place, and he grabs his guitar and goes onstage, walks up to the front of the crowd, and bleeds all over everybody. And he's bleeding for most of the set. I mean, the wound was so big, you could tell it had been opened up so many times, that it just doesn't stop. He'd get to the end of the show and there'd just be fucking blood everywhere. He did that for years.

DAVID VINCENT: He *did* go for it. I don't think he ever did enough damage to where he had to be hospitalized, but he wouldn't have gone anyway. He's not a fan of the medical profession. I don't think he did it for shock value. It was an artistic expression.

GLEN BENTON: One of the first shows we did was at the Sunset Club in Florida. We had a teenage mannequin onstage, and I packed it full of $60 worth of chitlins and beef livers and brought it onstage. And this wasn't fresh meat. I left that shit outside in the sun to rot. A few of my friends attacked this thing while we were playing. Next thing you know, it was a slaughterfest of meat! One girl started screaming, "You're killing him!" She thought it was actually a person. The club owner was mortified because the place reeked of decayed meat. The next day the sheriff's department was in there taking samples and checking to see if they were human remains. Then the health department started sending people to my shows.

TREY AZAGTHOTH: In New Jersey on one of our school bus tours, we got pulled over and thrown in jail because our whole appearance to them was questionable, and they found guns, a human skull, and occult stuff on the bus. I think they were wondering if we had killed this person and were carrying around his skull.

GLEN BENTON: Deicide were up in New York and the clubs were saying, "If you bring any of that meat shit in, you're out of here." I had to bury a whole 30-pound beef liver in a shallow grave in the backyard of the place we were staying at. The cops came and dug the thing up because there were a million blowflies coming out of the ground and they thought I buried a dead body.

TREY AZAGTHOTH: It was a time of tearing down the walls. For me that's the only thing that Satanism is, and what it's useful for. The most important thing for us is to use our music to lift up and give praise to the Ancient Ones, and then we take this stuff and share it. I am the living act of God. My true will cannot be denied. I create myself as well as my world. I want to be the instrument for the most high element of the living continuum and let their magic flow through it. As far as the death metal scene goes, I think that the bands that come from someplace of a high, beautiful, complimenting arrangement of values and purpose, and that use imagination and are of a high standard, they will be brilliant, too, and the rest, well, they will just be the trees in the forest.

JIM WELCH: Trey had all kinds of demons in his head that he conversed with, and he would tell you that. There were names for them. And they *did* propel him to make music and perform in the same way that they would propel a killer to do what he does.

GLEN BENTON: I think I put a little bit more into my art than [Morbid Angel]. They used to slice themselves up, but so do teenage girls. Whereas I would just all-out splatter the place. I've got an inverted cross branded in my forehead. I used to use a scarring effect [with makeup] to create the scar years ago. Then one day in 1992 I decided to burn it into my forehead. So I heated up a piece of jewelry and pressed it in. I showed up the next day with this big huge red fucking sore of an upside-down cross in my head. Everybody's like, "What the fuck have you been doing?" You burn it and then you peel the dead skin off it and then it dries tight. And then it's all red. I re-did it eight or nine times at least to make it more visible. The last time I did it, you could see the arteries underneath, so I didn't really want to go too much further.

RICHARD CHRISTY: There was this big rivalry between Glen Benton and David Vincent about who was more evil. They were the Vince Neil and Axl Rose of death metal. You always wanted to see them get in a ring and duke it out.

DAVID VINCENT: I don't feel that there was any competition between us and Deicide. If they look at it as competition and that's what fuels them and makes them stronger, that's probably healthy for them.

GLEN BENTON: In the beginning, there was a little rivalry with Morbid. But after a confrontation at an airport, all that came to an end. We got on a plane together and I went, "Hey man, what the fuck is this shit-talking about?" And there was an about face. "Oh, we didn't say that, man." But we have some mutual friends, so we *know* what they said. I said, "If you want to take it to the next level, we're ready." And we made peace after that and realized we were all on the same team.

KELLY SHAEFER: When he first came out [with Amon in 1987], Glen Benton was pretty convincing. Now he comes across as pretty pathetic and not somebody I see as a real champion of our scene. [By comparison,] David [Vincent] was confident and deserved to be at the top.

Like most forms of rock, death metal attracted groupies—but not many. Usually, the musicians looked for other distractions after shows. Since the longhairs looked like derelicts compared to the other twentysomethings in conservative Tampa, local law enforcement was only too happy to harass and arrest, so bands partied at private houses or at the strip club Mons Venus, infamous for stimulating lap dances and death metal pole dancing.

GLEN BENTON: Mons Venus used to have all the local metal bands on the jukebox. You'd walk in and you'd need a fuckin' stick to get out. All the bands who came to town to record would head to Venus after they finished their session at Morrisound.

PHIL FASCIANA: It's strange to go into a club that's dark and gloomy and you've got crazy strippers running around dancing to fuckin' Morbid Angel.

RICHARD CHRISTY: The only death metal groupie I remember was this real muscular woman who used to come to lots of shows, and one of my old band members banged her one time and he said afterwards, "She was throwing me around like a rag doll." It was pretty much a sausage fest. I knew if I went to a death metal show I was going home with my right hand.

KAM LEE: Once in Germany, the members of the opening band, Demolition Hammer, gangbanged these chicks. There were two girls, and the dudes were passing them back and forth, like, "Okay, I'm done. Here, take her." They did everybody in the opening band. It was like, "Okay, I'm not here to watch a live sex show," but when you're backstage, what can you do?

CHRIS BARNES: I saw some guy fucking his girlfriend in the front row up against the barricade during our set. I was like, "Is he really doing that?" So I looked again. Shit, man, yes he is.

JEREMY WAGNER: Former Deicide guitarist Eric Hoffman and I were solicited by some prostitutes outside an apartment building in Montreal. Eric said something about getting free oral if the hookers couldn't accommodate his dick. The hookers laughed and said, "Sure," thinking he was joking. Eric said he'd be right back and walked over to our tour bus. He used a penis pump on himself, and once his cock was inflated to, like, Hulk size, he limped back to the hookers. I was two blocks behind him when I heard the screams.

JOHN TARDY: As extreme as the music is, most of the guys in this scene are pretty normal. Everybody likes to party and smoke weed, but I don't see them getting mixed up with hard drugs.

PAUL MASVIDAL: Half of us were still living at our parents' homes, including Chuck, so there weren't any huge scene parties. There was a lot of pot smoking and beer drinking, but nothing like the parties that happened in the glam scene.

ERIK RUTAN (ex–Morbid Angel, ex–Ripping Corpse, Hate Eternal): The music we were playing was fast and precise and required you

to be on your A-game, which didn't leave much room for
being totally obliterated.

PHIL FASCIANA: We were on a U.S. tour in 1999 and our bus
got pulled over in Little Rock, Arkansas, at 8 a.m. We all got
out, and there were six cop cars behind us. They searched the
bus and found three ounces of weed, so they took us and our
small crew to jail for four days. They charged us with drug
trafficking and they took everything—all the merch money
we had, saying it was drug money, and threw us in fuckin' jail
and they tore the bus to shreds looking for drugs and weapons.
Since they found the weed our bail was $12,000. When they
first booked us and gave us our jail uniforms, they put us in
a holding cell with these huge black guys, and one cop yelled
out, "We got a bunch of bikers coming in here and they hate
niggers." I thought that our lives were over. The inmates were
the meanest looking, baddest guys you ever saw, but they knew
the cops were just busting our balls. They actually hooked us
up with cigarettes and got us a couple joints. We spent a lot of
time playing poker. Then, luckily, my brother was able to wire
down 12 grand to get us out of jail. The whole thing cost us
over $20,000.

For Atheist, the party ended in tragedy at the close of a 1991
tour with Swedish doom band Candlemass. Atheist was in Los
Angeles and had three days to get its van back to Florida. On the
way, they planned to stop at Mardi Gras. But right outside New
Orleans, disaster struck.

KELLY SHAEFER: Our driver had driven for twenty-nine hours
and couldn't do it anymore. We were all sleeping in the van at
the time. He was going 85 miles per hour and then changed
lanes to pass a truck. When he went back into the right lane
the wheels went off the road and got caught in the gravel,
and we flipped six times. I injured my foot and my elbow and
[bassist] Roger [Patterson] was thrown out of the vehicle. He

had been leaning against the window, and when we flipped the first time the window came out in one piece and just left him on the road, and we rolled over him at least once. But he was still alive. We were both laying in the middle of the street. We went and got his leather jacket and put it on him because it was about 45 degrees. He got up and looked at me, and I remember thinking, "God, he's gonna be fuckin' hurting," but I thought he was gonna live. When we got to the hospital and they came and told me he had died, we all fuckin' lost it. He was my best friend in the world, one of the most talented metal bass players ever. But he had a great time the last thirty days of his life, that's for sure.

Atheist didn't want to continue without Patterson, but they were almost done with their next record, so they finished the jazzy, proggy *Unquestionable Presence* with bassist Tony Choy (Cynic, Pestilence) in 1991. When they told their label they were breaking up, they were told they still owed the company an album. So after a brief hiatus, they wrote and recorded 1993's syncopated but more melodic *Elements* and then split up. Although they reunited for 2010's *Jupiter*, when *Elements* came out many believed death metal had dug its own grave.

KELLY SHAEFER: At one point the scene got so big that kids from Europe were coming to Tampa on vacation to see what it's all about and get their picture taken outside of Morrisound, and hopefully have a brush with one of the bands. It was just ridiculous, and it couldn't last.

MONTE CONNER: For me, death metal really peaked in 1992 when we put out Obituary's *The End Complete*. You could sell between 100,000 and 125,000 records at that time. After that, bands started stagnating and repeating themselves. Between 1994 and 1995 the whole scene started to crash, and death metal started to wane.

CHRIS BARNES: There were a lot of bands popping up, but it didn't really affect bands like Cannibal, Obituary, Morbid, and Death. Our attendance and record sales kept going up year after year. All the bands that were big back then are still around and do pretty well. I think the labels just started to see a lot of generic recycled stuff, and they eventually leaned away from signing new death metal bands because they weren't seeing anything exciting that hadn't been done and done better.

KELLY SHAEFER: So many bands were going to Morrisound and recording, and that was the beginning of the end because everything started sounding exactly the same. Then bands like Soundgarden came out, who were heavy in a different way, but they were also marketable. At that point, death metal had run its course.

JAMES MURPHY: I can tell you exactly what happened: Seattle. The big metal record labels all decided they needed to sign bands like Gruntruck. I was working at a record store and I witnessed it firsthand. Over the course of a couple years, guys I knew from the death metal scene came into the store wearing flannel and selling all their death metal CDs.

ERIK RUTAN: When I started Hate Eternal, I had labels telling me there was no market for extreme death metal anymore and that this would never sell. We were trying to bring the music to a new level of extremity, and a lot of that was out of the frustration and rage of hearing, "Oh, death metal's dead." I just thought that was a bunch of bullshit. You don't kill a whole genre of music if it's good. I knew death metal would come back around.

To death metal fans, Death front man Chuck Schuldiner will always be a legend, but when he was diagnosed with a brain-stem tumor on May 13, 1999, on his thirty-second birthday, death metal had gone so far underground that his illness was largely ignored by the mainstream media, which had embraced his acolytes, Cannibal Corpse, just five years earlier. In the beginning stages of his illness, Schuldiner was still able to perform and record with his new band, the more power metal–oriented Control Denied, whose only album, 1999's *The Fragile Art of Existence*, shed new light on Schuldiner's depth as a musician.

To battle his tumor, Schuldiner underwent radiation therapy and an operation. In October 1999, his family announced that he was recovering, but the cancer returned worse than before. On December 13, 2001, the forefather of death metal died, leaving an entire community in grief. In some ways it was the end of an era. Yet in the underground, death metal refused to die. Cannibal Corpse replaced vocalist Chris Barnes with George "Corpsegrinder" Fisher for 1996's *Vile* and continues to release an album every couple of years, as do Deicide, Six Feet Under, Malevolent Creation, Nile, Immolation, Incantation, and others. At the same time, technical death bands inspired by Death, Cynic, and Atheist have captivated the underground community; these include Necrophagist, Arsis, Decapitated, Origin, and Psycroptic.

GLEN BENTON: Every ten years the whole metal thing takes a hiatus and then it kicks back up again. So what's happening now is a lot of kids are tired of this fuckin' emo metal bullshit, and they're making new hybrids that incorporate death metal. They've learned their lessons from what we did fifteen years ago from their uncles or parents and are mixing it with this new shit to create new sounds. Good for them.

ERIK RUTAN: I knew death metal would come around, and it did. Now there are so many hybrid death metal bands. And a lot of these kids weren't even born when [1989's] *Altars of Madness* came out.

To most, death metal began as an American phenomenon in Tampa, Florida. However, at the same time as Death, Morbid

Angel, and Deicide were damaging eardrums in the States, a close cousin of death metal, grindcore, was brutalizing audiences in the UK; a savage punk-rooted form of the genre was battering Stockholm; and just a road trip away, a more technical and listener-friendly version of the genre was sweeping through Gothenburg, Sweden—one that would greatly influence the American metalcore scene that dominated the landscape in the early 2000s.

The heralded UK grindcore movement—popularized internationally by its hometown label, Earache Records—started in Birmingham and eventually brought two of the heaviest bands ever, Napalm Death and Carcass, to major label Columbia Records as part of a distribution deal. Other UK grindcore groups, including Extreme Noise Terror and Bolt Thrower, also developed international fan bases. It was, however, a Michigan metal band, Repulsion—whose bassist and guitarist worked briefly with Death's Chuck Schuldiner—that helped trigger the UK grindcore scene.

MARK SAWICKIS (Impetigo): Repulsion was one of the main gore/grind pioneers. They were so fast and brutal and their lyrics were sick and twisted, and that was way before Carcass. They were definitely one of our influences.

SCOTT CARLSON: A lot of our speed came from our drummer Dave "Grave" [Hollingshead], and we actually hired him because he was convicted for grave-robbing. He was seventeen at the time, and he decided he wanted a skull for his drum set. So he and one of his knucklehead friends decided the best way to get one would be to steal it; so they broke into a mausoleum and stole a skull out of a coffin. But then Dave took the skull to high school and bragged about it, and someone got freaked and called the authorities. It was in all the newspapers. We didn't know him when it happened because we were in Florida playing with Death. After we came home, Kam Lee played drums for us, but that fell apart also. So Matt and I went back to Michigan, and we're hanging out at the local record shop thinking, "Who are we gonna hire to play drums?" And we see this article tacked up on the bulletin board about this kid who was busted for grave-robbing. And we were like, "Hey man, I remember that guy. He was in a skate punk band called Bloody Coup. Let's get him." So we called him up and jammed with him, and next thing we knew we had this infamous grave robber in the band. We changed our name to Repulsion and started writing new songs.

KORY GROW (journalist): Everything about their one album, *Horrified*, was done to the extreme, with songs about everything from being eaten alive to odes about various states of decomposition. The songs literally could make you feel sick, even if they were played at human speeds, which they weren't.

SCOTT CARLSON: As the scene got bigger, it started to attract more weirdos, and I saw people that were taking it way too seriously, which was a bit disturbing. In Detroit, this kid picked a cockroach off the floor and bit it in half in front of me thinking that I would be impressed. Just the general mentality of people made it seem like they were more serious about the sick side of things than we were. To us, the graphic lyrics were kind of a joke. We took the band seriously, but we didn't take the imagery seriously. It was more like a silly horror movie, and after we broke up in 1986, I thought that was that. Then I was working at a record store and this kid pulled the Napalm Death record [*Scum*] out of a box of imports that had just come in. I heard one of our riffs, note for note. At first I thought it was a bizarre coincidence until I picked up the album cover and started seeing [photos of] homemade Repulsion T-shirts and hats. I was like, "Wow, we actually influenced another band that has a record out." Bill Steer and Jeff Walker of Carcass were actually instrumental in getting our album released on Earache three years after it was recorded.

There's no question that Napalm Death was the reigning pioneer of grindcore. Its debut album, 1987's *Scum*, was influenced by Repulsion, Massachusetts band Siege, and Florida's Terrorizer, yet it was explosively original, blindingly fast, and poignantly political, igniting a powder keg across England that set their careers and the grindcore scene in motion. Never mind that it was written with two almost completely different lineups.

JUSTIN BROADRICK (ex–Napalm Death, ex-Godflesh, Jesu): I knew Nik Bullen because we worked on my [eighties] noise band, Final, together. Two weeks after our first session, he came over and heard me playing guitar. At the time, he was having some problems with Napalm Death and invited me over. We jammed some of their songs and were like, "Wow, this is great." I replaced the other two guys, [guitarist Graham Robertson] and [Finbar Quinn], and we became a trio with a drummer named Rat.

BARNEY GREENWAY (Napalm Death): In the really early days, Napalm were as influenced by My Bloody Valentine and Swans as [much as] anything metal—especially when [drummer] Miles ["Rat" Ratledge] was in the band.

JUSTIN BROADRICK: Early in '85, someone gave me a tape of Metallica's *Kill 'Em All* and we were blown away. I brought some of those types of riffs to Napalm Death, and Nik got into it as well. That led to hearing Slayer, which made us want to really ramp it up. And basically, Rat couldn't play fast enough, so he left and we got Mick Harris, who could reach this hyper speed.

JIM WELCH: Mick Harris has a nickname—the Human Tornado—because he's the fucking Tasmanian devil—on the drums, personality-wise, humor-wise, everything. He is definitely the drummer of Napalm Death and you couldn't have scripted it better.

JUSTIN BROADRICK: If we were rehearsing for two hours in a room, we'd only be making music for twenty minutes and the rest of the time Nik and Mick would be rolling around the floor fighting. Once at a party, they started arguing and spat in each other's faces, and that turned into a bout of fisticuffs. And Nik, at that time, would get absolutely slaughtered both on drink and drugs. It was almost a part of his onstage personality to be this fucking train wreck. By contrast, Mick was totally in control, especially playing beats that fast. But there was an air of extreme tension both within the group and what it caused offstage. There was a lot of fighting in the crowd and we would stop the show whenever it turned into a bloodbath, which happened fairly frequently at the Mermaid in Birmingham, where we'd play eighteen times every weekend.

BARNEY GREENWAY: They were magnificent in concert. They were my favorite band before I joined them [in 1989]. They totally blew me away, not only with the intensity, but the songwriting.

JUSTIN BROADRICK: A lot of the catchiness came after we discovered Celtic Frost, almost by accident. We'd go to the thrash metal sections at the record stores and literally laugh at the way the bands looked on the sleeves. We had punk backgrounds, so metal to us was still fuckin' hilarious, even though we liked Metallica and Slayer. We weren't used to geezers in spandex and long hair pulling poses. We literally picked up the Celtic Frost sleeve and were laughing at the way they looked. Next thing you know, Mick Harris actually bought one of these records, played it to me, and I was like, "Fucking shit, this is amazing. This is like punk." It was so maximal in its attack, but so minimal in terms of riffing. So I started coming up with these Celtic Frost rip-off songs, where it was like, "Let's have these slow breakdowns with these super-heavy riffs. And then let's go into this really hyperspeed shit influenced by Siege and Discharge." And that's how we ended up with side A of *Scum*.

NIK BULLEN: We played a show in Leeds with Justin just before he left, and after every song, all the people did was shout, "Play faster!" I felt like we were performing bears in a zoo and that nobody was listening to the content of the songs in terms of the politics.

JUSTIN BROADRICK: I got fed up and gave the tape of side one of *Scum* to Digby [Pearson] at Earache [Records] and said, "Just take it off my hands," because at the moment it seemed like no one was interested. Nik and Mick had a falling out; it looked like the band was over. I was offered the chance to join Head of David playing drums, and I viewed that as a safer option and something I was a bit more musically interested in.

Unable to get along with Mick Harris and feeling isolated without Broadrick, Bullen quit Napalm Death. Undeterred, Harris hired greenhorn vocalist Lee Dorrian and started writing new material. At the end of 1986, Pearson contacted Harris and offered to put Napalm Death back in the studio to record side B of *Scum*. In February 1987, Harris recruited guitarist Bill Steer, and the revitalized Napalm practiced in Steer's parents' house for a few weeks before heading back into the studio on Pearson's dime. To say they were flying by the seat of their pants would be an understatement. At first, Dorrian didn't even want to make the record.

LEE DORRIAN (ex–Napalm Death, Cathedral): I never wanted to sing. I had no intentions on joining a band. We were friends, and I just got asked and I thought, "Well why not?" I had zero experience. I had been a fanzine writer and a concert promoter in Coventry when I was sixteen. So I had booked Napalm Death and written about them. But I didn't know how to sing for them. My obvious [vocal] influences were [Kelvin] "Cal" [Morris] from Discharge and Pete [Boyce] from Antisect. So I kind of copied their style and tried to make it deeper, more extreme and manic, with some Japanese hardcore thrown in.

When we did the B-side of *Scum*, I was totally unprepared.
Mick had to cue me when to come in.

DAN LILKER: I was working at Important Distribution, which
gave me and [Nuclear Assault vocalist] John Connelly jobs at
the warehouse picking records for the distributor when we
weren't on tour. *Scum* had just come in and somebody ran it
to the warehouse and said, "Man you gotta hear this." And I
was like, "Holy shit." I had heard stuff like Repulsion before,
which, ironically, Napalm had taken a lot of influence from.
But to hear it presented in that context—even faster and
noisier, with forty songs on a record—that was a big moment
for me, almost as huge as the first time I heard Black Sabbath.

LEE DORRIAN: I made my mind up [to quit Napalm Death] in
Japan, [which] was one place I had always wanted to visit. I got
so drunk on the plane going home; I was awakened by a Japanese air hostess who was shaking me whilst I was asleep with
my head in the toilet, my hair and face covered in puke. The
next half of the journey back to the UK was quite possibly the
most painful twelve hours of my life.

Napalm Death didn't just lead the charge for UK extreme metal;
the members it shed along the way started their own equally influential outfits. Broadrick played in Head of David and launched
pioneering industrial metal group Godflesh and post-rock outfit
Jesu; Dorrian formed doom band Cathedral and launched Rise
Above Records; Mick Harris created isolationist ambient bands
Scorn and Lull. And perhaps most significantly for the continued
development of grindcore and death metal, Bill Steer started
Carcass, a gory grindcore outfit whose lyrics were culled from
medical texts.

JEFF WALKER (ex-Carcass): In 1985, I was in Electro Hippies,
which was a crossover hardcore band like Siege, MDC, and
D.R.I. The guitarist [Andy Barnard] was a total metalhead,

and I was a punker who had started getting back into metal again. I got ejected from that band because they said I wasn't contributing enough, but I think it was really because the drummer, Simon, who was originally the vocalist, wanted to be a vocalist again. So I met up with [guitarist] Bill [Steer], who was playing in a Discharge-type punk band called Disattack. They asked me to join, and they went in a more metal direction. Then we had a coup d'état by getting rid of the drummer and the vocalist, and we got Ken [Owen] in, and that's how Carcass was born [in 1986].

MATT HARVEY (Exhumed): When Carcass came out, that total medical gore fascination was just perfect. I thought, "Fuck, why didn't I think of that when I was fourteen."

JEFF WALKER: My sister was a nurse, and she had a medical dictionary. I used to sit there and try to sound articulate and intelligent by using this dictionary as a source of inspiration. Carcass was meant to be a scientific approach to death metal because it was so boring listening to lyrics that would say "I'm gonna kill you" in fifty different ways.

BILL STEER (ex-Carcass): The intention from the start was to take advantage of the English language. There's a lot of vocabulary there. Perhaps early on we felt it was a compliment if people read our lyrics and then picked up a dictionary to try and figure out what they meant.

JEFF WALKER: An English journalist came up with the idea that we all went to medical school then formed a band, and for the longest time people really believed it. In reality, 1988's *Reek of Putrefaction* was meant to be the ultimate death metal album, the album that killed Slayer's *Reign in Blood*. But, of course, no one ever said that because the production was so raw. In fact, the only good reviews we got in the beginning were from [late BBC radio legend] John Peel. And I think part of that was because Bill and Ken are from the same area where he grew up, and he wanted to support us.

ANGELA GOSSOW (Arch Enemy): I worked as a journalist for a while, and the reason I did it was just so I could interview Carcass. I loved them more than anything else. And they were slagged off by almost everyone.

JEFF WALKER: All the heavy metal mags hated us. Our second album, *Symphonies of Sickness*, got such a bad review in *Metal Forces*—1 out of 100. The woman who reviewed it was so offended.

JIM WELCH: Bill went on a mission to become the most amazing guitar player and that's when Mike [Amott of Arch Enemy] joined the band, which gave them a dual guitar approach, and that's when their musicianship got noticed by metal bands all over the world—not just grindcore bands and death metal bands. Carcass became one of the most important metal bands of that time.

JEFF WALKER: Our music was extreme, but we weren't these maniacs. We were very boring. We should have been out partying, getting girls, and doing drugs, but we weren't. Everyone in that [British grindcore] scene was the same. We used to go to the Mermaid in Birmingham to the gigs and just see bands. I was so poor I couldn't afford to drink.

BARNEY GREENWAY: For a band and the scene that we came from that was never meant to have icons or put people on pedestals, they sure made a big song and dance about Lee [Dorrian] not being in Napalm Death anymore, and about me stepping into his shoes [in 1989]. People were like, "Oh, it's not Lee and Bill anymore. That was the band." It used to really get to me in the old days because I was like, "I'm really trying my hardest to contribute to the ethos and the musical heritage of the band,"

and I was being met with this negativity. The lesson I learned from that was, "Fuck those people."

The only way to upstage the ferocity of UK grindcore was to take the violence and brutality from the music directly into the crowd. For better or worse, Massachusetts brawler Seth Putnam was the master. While his band, Anal Cunt, wrote sloppy, unremarkable songs that dripped with bad riffs and sick humor, their performances were filled with palpable danger—brief, sonic melees of chaos and destruction that often ended in riots.

SETH PUTNAM (1968–2011) (Anal Cunt): When we started in 1988, we wanted to be the least musical band possible. If you take death metal and hardcore to its furthest extreme, that's basically what we were doing. The original lineup from '88 to '90 [which featured Putnam, guitarist Mike Mahan, and drummer Tim Morse] was really intense, but the shows weren't as violent as when we reformed in '91 [with guitarist Fred Ordonez replacing Mahan]. During the year we had off I became a total alcoholic. And the new shows basically were just me and the guitarist going out and punching everyone in the crowd in the face while the drummer kept playing. The guitar would get unplugged and my mic would get broken. That's why we got a second guitarist [John Kozik]—so we could keep the noise going when Fred's guitar became unplugged and my mic wasn't on.

ALBERT MUDRIAN: Musically, I don't have much time for Anal Cunt. I have one record because the song titles crack me up. But it's just button-pushing. I will never have the urge to listen to any music Seth Putnam created.

KEVIN SHARP (Primate, Brutal Truth): Anal Cunt were the masters of blur grind. It was chaotic and noisy and no one will ever touch them, not any gore grind or porno grind band—no one.

SETH PUTNAM: We used to beat up people who took videos of us because they never sent us copies of the videos. Once there was a guy standing on a bar stool videotaping, and I went to Fred [Ordonez], "Okay, I'll get him from the left, you get him from the right." We fuckin' crunched him. The guy fuckin' fell on the ground, his camera broke, and we kicked his camera and kicked him in the face.

RANDY BLYTHE (Lamb of God): Anal Cunt was on tour with Eyehategod, and I took a road trip to see them in Winston Salem, North Carolina. Seth had this 10-foot-tall stepladder. He opened it up, sang two songs on top of the ladder. Then he got down, closed the ladder, and threw it feet first at the bartender, who was this fifty-year-old woman. It smashed her head into the glass mirror behind the bar and the mirror shattered everywhere. I was like, "Dude, you are fucked up!" I'm not advocating violence towards bartenders or women. I love both of them, but it *was* pretty intense.

MIKE WILLIAMS (Eyehategod): One time I saw them, the band starts playing the first song, and he comes out and punches this girl in the face and that was the show. He even attacked me on that tour. We were in Charlotte, North Carolina. I'm standing out in the crowd just watching A.C., and the next thing I know, Seth fucking picks up a chair and swings it wrestling style into my back. I had a beer in my hand, apparently. He knocked me completely unconscious, and as soon as I came to, I was asking, "Where did my beer go?"

SETH PUTNAM: After we reformed in '91 I played every show fuckin' wrecked. I blacked out at half the shows. I don't remember what happened. Some of the best stuff we ever came up with happened when I was blacked out. The alcohol and drugs were a huge part of what I did. Mostly, I was doing coke, speed, or meth. I was really into shooting cocaine. I'd usually only shoot heroin after being up for five days straight shooting cocaine. I just wanted to come down because I was bored of being up for five days. Or I'd do speedballs. I just did heroin every now and then, but it wasn't one of my main choices.

KEVIN SHARP (Brutal Truth): I saw Seth throw a mic stand like a javelin at [guitarist] Terry [Savastano] from Grief—flattened his face like a fuckin' coin. Seth was an original. PC he wasn't. Get over it. He wasn't claiming to be anything other than what he was—a fuckin' lunatic.

SETH PUTNAM: In Somerville, Massachusetts, in 1998, I OD'ed on heroin and was pronounced dead. An ambulance came and the paramedics [used a defibrillator] on me, and it didn't work. They tried it again for the fuck of it and I woke up in my kitchen with no idea where the fuck I was. On the ambulance ride to the hospital, one of the paramedics said, "You'll probably have brain damage for the rest of your life." And by the time I got to the hospital my thoughts were completely back to normal and I saw a shitload of cops in the hallway, so I ran away from the hospital and went home because I thought they would arrest me for having heroin. I've been arrested ten times. The first time was in San Francisco for punching a lesbian in the face. Back then we weren't really getting paid for shows. We just fucked up every place we played and punched out a bunch of people because we knew we weren't getting any money. I almost ripped a guy's ear off with a mic stand. I broke some girl's arm. After a while, we made a plan. We'd pick a place three blocks away where I'd hide when the cops came. The band would tell the cops, "Sorry, he's already left," and then they'd pick me up and we'd leave.

MIKE WILLIAMS [2010 interview]: Seth is not a nice guy. He's a fucking son of a bitch and he's an asshole. He fucked up a lot of people, and I don't agree with any of that. And I don't agree with any of his racist shit either. He's just stupid and I can't take him seriously at all.

SETH PUTNAM: That racist accusation is bullshit. We have a song "Hitler Was a Sensitive Man," and I can imagine someone hearing that and getting all pissed off. But the lyrics are all true. Hitler went to art school when he was young. He wanted to be a painter. He was a vegetarian. He was a nonsmoker. So how can you get mad at that? And the song "Into the Oven" is about cooking a turkey. Everybody thinks it's about Jews in the Holocaust. Yeah, we've got songs like "I Sent Concentration Camp Footage to America's Funniest Home Videos" and "Ha-Ha Holocaust" just because we thought that was funny. I'm trying to be as offensive as possible, but fuck, I have friends who are gay and Jewish, black and Jewish, female and gay. I naturally hate everyone until I somehow get along with them.

The Nazi ideology might have been a joke for A.C.—just another way to antagonize listeners—but in 1990s Europe, the neo-Nazi movement was on the rise, and some of its followers flooded shows by Napalm Death. At the same time, thugs also became interested in the music, and rival gangs waged war at its concerts.

BARNEY GREENWAY: Even though our message was very left-wing and pro-vegetarian and pro-choice, we used to get Nazi boneheads who would turn up en masse without any warning, and start fights. At one point, the Mermaid put iron bars across the door, and the Nazi skinheads would literally be barred out. They'd kick the shit out of the doors, but they didn't get in. The same thing happened in America. A ton of them turned up on the Sheer Terror tour, and they kicked the shit out of kids and beat up the promoter as well, who was a white Rastafarian guy. Another time, a guy drove up in his car. He opened up the back and he had this rack of guns. He looked at us, looked at the guns, then closed the trunk and drove off again. Clearly, that was meant to send some kind of message.

LEE DORRIAN: A lot of people missed the political messages of the band. Some bands played fast but had racist or sexist lyrics. That wasn't us. We were totally against violence and discrimination of any kind.

BARNEY GREENWAY: In Los Angeles there was a gang called Killed the Liars that attached itself to Napalm. Kids would get stabbed in the crowd when we used to play certain songs, which really saddened me. The gang used signals when they were about to attack someone.

As the intensity and speed of grindcore gained popularity, former thrash and death metal musicians started forming their own grindcore bands. Leading the charge was Brutal Truth, which was anchored by Dan Lilker (ex-Anthrax, ex-S.O.D., Nuclear Assault) and music journalist Kevin Sharp.

DAN LILKER: By 1990, thrash was stale and boring and I consequently couldn't create it anymore. So I formed Brutal Truth. The two bands, Brutal Truth and Nuclear Assault, overlapped for a bit but that was too hectic. Brutal Truth started as a side project but became legit, and I had to make a choice.

KEVIN SHARP: In America, there were only a handful of people doing this kind of music back then, and that's when the music was at its purest, because it was original.

DAN LILKER: Jim Welch hooked up Kevin and I. Kevin was a scenester who worked at *CMJ*. And Brutal Truth had gone on for almost a year without a vocalist. I was doing most of the vocals, ex-drummer Scott [Lewis] was doing some of 'em. And it got to the point where we wanted to speed up ridiculously and it was getting too hard to do both at once. Jim suggested

Kevin, who had a nice roar and mixed in the influence from Japanese hardcore bands [such as Hanatarash and GISM]. The shows were kind of extreme. We used to have a car door that we brought onstage and bashed with a crowbar, then we took a grinder that made sparks, which caught a few people in the crowd, but that was part of the show. It's just a nice, natural, healthy way to purge the bad emotions.

KEVIN SHARP: This is a crazy business, and anything can happen. You stick around, you see your share of tragedies and overdoses. Everybody was abused at that time, and in turn, everybody abused. CDs were flying out the door and the labels were holding on to every last dime and not paying you, and instigating the mayhem. We were totally exploited. We had to run out and tour eight, ten months of the year, come [back] broke while they sat around and counted their money. The exploitation game drives the self-abuse game, drives the madness. It's a miracle that more people didn't overdose. Why do you think you always get two cases of beer on the fuckin' rider? So you're completely obliterated and don't fuckin' realize you're getting stunted by everybody—all the fuckin' people digging in your pants giving you the pull and tuck. When *Extreme Conditions Demand Extreme Responses* was selling 100,000 copies, we didn't get dime fuckin' one. We'd play to 3,600 people at the Palladium, $20 tickets. We got paid $50.

SETH PUTNAM: In October 2004, I went to Rob Williams, the drummer for Siege's, birthday party. I got $200 worth of crack. I smoked that. Shot a bunch of heroin, drank a huge bottle of whisky. And then I got a hotel room the next day and I actually considered killing myself, but I decided that would be gay. I was taking Ambien at the time. And a lot of people who take Ambien sleepwalk or forget what they did. I had gotten a two-month supply before I went to Rob's house. So, I'm pretty sure I took all that because there were no pills left when the cops came. I don't think it was a suicide attempt. But I was in a coma for a month and when I woke up, I couldn't move any part of my body except my eyes and my mouth. I couldn't walk for eight months.

BARNEY GREENWAY: [Ex–Napalm Death guitarist, ex-Terrorizer] Jesse [Pintado] was a severe alcoholic for a long time and it got progressively worse. He got very unpredictable. It got to the point where we had studio time booked, which costs money, and Jesse just didn't turn up. We gave him more chances after that happened. But in the end, it was just too much. We couldn't do anything without fear of Jesse disappearing when we were booked to go play gigs. We tried to help as much as we could as friends. I love Jesse to bits, but we couldn't help him, because he didn't want to help himself.

JESSE PINTADO (1969–2006) (ex–Napalm Death, Terrorizer) [2006 interview]: The other day I was browsing the Internet, and they stated I was dead! I thought, "Oh shit, I'm dead!" I really don't pay much attention to that.

BARNEY GREENWAY: The whole structure of a touring band didn't help Jesse because free booze is there—a couple of cases of beer on a rider a night. And there you go, instant damage. I guess Jesse succumbed to it. [He died on August 27, 2006.]

Beginning in 2007, a new style of death metal emerged in America—deathcore. These extreme bands borrow the styles of nineties grindy death metal bands like Suffocation, Dying Fetus, and Cattle Decapitation and blend them with the sounds of newer, more popular groups, including Job for a Cowboy and the Red Chord. Then they present their digitally enhanced music on flashy websites adorned with spiky, illegible logos. Adored by the young, ridiculed by their elders, these bands are stuck in a vacuum between trendiness and credibility. For this reason, most, including Carnifex and Emmure, object to being called deathcore, but it seems the most appropriate tag for bands that blend death metal brutality with multiple hardcore breakdowns.

CHRIS BRUNI (owner, Profound Lore Records): There seems to be a real surge in technical, polished, digital-sounding death metal. That's getting really huge. I don't really like most of it. But there's also an underground movement in death metal now where the darkness and sinister vibe of classic death metal is making a comeback. Some of that is really cool.

BRIAN SLAGEL: I love the fact that a lot of these [deathcore] guys are influenced by that older stuff, like Morbid Angel and Cannibal Corpse. They're all doing something interesting and a bit different from everyone else.

JIM WELCH: We used the word *deathcore* when we were writing fanzines in the eighties. It's not like it was a movement; it was just a cool fucking word. But it's a good marketing term for labels like Victory Records to describe the next step after metalcore.

ALEX WADE (Whitechapel): We're not afraid of admitting we're a deathcore band. But we have three guitarists, so that gives us a different flavor than deathcore bands that just focus on slammy riffs all the time. We try to make the guitar work really interesting.

SCOTT LEWIS (Carnifex): I think Between the Buried and Me was the first deathcore band. As progressive as they are, they were one of the earlier bands to combine traditional death metal with metalcore breakdowns in a really cool way.

FRANKIE PALMERI (Emmure): Deathcore is a genre that has always sort of existed but just recently become really popular. But I don't care. We can be deathcore. Or we can be power slop. Whatever you want to call us.

MONTE CONNER: At least bands like Job for a Cowboy and Suicide Silence aren't just regurgitating the same old death metal. They're putting a fresh twist on it and combining it with other things to give it a new feel. And I think that's why that stuff is working. They're taking their influences and modernizing it to reach a new generation of kids.

GUY KOZOWYK (Red Chord, Black Market Activities Records): There's definitely bands out there that are doing deathcore in a decent way, but there's this whole wave of trendy, fuckin' sixteen-year-old kids with scratchy logos who scarcely know how to play their instruments and have plugged into a microphone and are doing pig squeals. I just want to publicly apologize to the world for having any part in influencing any of that garbage.

11

IN THE NIGHTSIDE ECLIPSE: BLACK METAL, 1982–PRESENT

The international media thrived on it. Fans obsessed over it. And musicians made it not just their career, but their calling—one that, for some, led to arson and murder. Black metal, the most controversial and titillating metal scene, is steeped in history, mythology, and demonology. For some, the occult was a vehicle for expression, not a platform for worship. But for others, the glorification of man's dark side and exultation in anti-Christian deities is as important as the blazing guitars, crushing beats, and banshee vocals. Much of the metal community scoff at or dismiss black metal's excesses—the sweeping, symphonic keyboards, stage theatrics, and ghoulish face painting. Yet for those who take it seriously, black metal is a complex, emotional, and transcendent form of music, and many of the champions of the genre, regardless of their extremism, are talented songwriters and gifted players.

VEGARD SVERRE "IHSAHN" TVEITAN (Emperor, ex-Peccatum): Being very intense and dark, black metal enables us to roar out of the dark atmospheres at high energy, giving it a very strong appeal to those of us who enjoy these kinds of emotions. Our intention is to bring the listener on a journey into those nightside landscapes we describe in our songs.

JOSE MANGIN: Black metal is a static wall of noise with shrieking vocals. It's church-burning music. It can be symphonic, but it's usually low-fi. When I think of black metal I think of corpse paint and Norwegians in freezing-cold forests with torches. It's depressed music for people that have no hope.

KORY GROW: Black metal reintroduced the minor third and major third back into extreme metal, which death metal wasn't using so much. Death metal was still very much about power chords. Black metal guitarists were more interested in two-note chords that had a little bit more melody, and they would emphasize those minor keys more within the tonality.

GRUTLE KJELLSON (Enslaved): The so-called first movement of black metal started with Venom, because they called their second album *Black Metal*. That was in the early eighties, and there were other bands that took the lead from Venom [such as] Bathory and Celtic Frost.

OLVE "ABBATH" EIKEMO (Immortal): Bands like Iron Maiden, KISS, and Black Sabbath always ran into trouble with Christian people who complained about rock and roll. And they would all say, "No, we're not Satanists." But Venom didn't give a fuck. They just said, "Praise Satan," which was a statement to all these people like, "Fuck you all."

STIAN TOMT "SHAGRATH" THORESEN (Dimmu Borgir): I didn't like the music of Venom so much, but the imagery and lyrics were fascinating.

CRONOS: Look, I don't preach Satanism, occultism, witchcraft, or anything. Rock and roll is basically entertainment, and that's as far as it goes. It's always nice to hear that we came up with the phrase *black metal*. A long time ago I had an idea for a band, and I thought that idea was only mine and the two guys I was with. But when I realized that there are so many millions of people around the world who also like that style of music, well, that's just the most amazing thing in the world.

DAVE GROHL: I went to England to see Cronos from Venom, and he really *is* that guy. I don't know if he's really Satanic, but we went to dinner and he drank like a Viking and ate a piece of meat that was almost still alive. The outside was kind of brown, but it was cold and bloody. And he told us about going into supermarkets and eating raw meat when he didn't have any money. I told that to Lemmy [Kilmister (Motörhead, ex-Hawkwind)] and he said, "Yeah, well I used to suck the meat out of raw sausages." It was like a contest for who could be more metal.

Venom's influence on black metal can't be underestimated, but the band's sound is light-years away from that of the most revered black metal bands, including Burzum, Mayhem, Darkthrone, Emperor, and Immortal. Three other early European bands had a far greater impact on the sonic development of the genre: Hellhammer was a sloppy Swiss group that existed from 1982 to 1984 before changing its name to Celtic Frost and recording far more experimental and majestic compositions. Bathory was a Swedish outfit that launched in 1983 and recorded three Satanic, extreme thrash records, then shifted gears in the late eighties, embracing Viking themes and epic arrangements. And Mercyful Fate was an accomplished New Wave of British Heavy Metal–style band from Denmark whose front man, King Diamond, wrote Satanic lyrics and wore face paint, which he punctuated with an inverted cross on his forehead.

THOMAS GABRIEL FISCHER (Triptykon, ex–Celtic Frost, ex-Hellhammer): Hellhammer started as a clone of Venom. The first songs we wrote were complete copies of Venom material, including the Satanic lyrics. Then in the final month of Hellhammer, we reached a stage where we were good enough to write our own material. The lyrics became more dignified and dealt with occultism in a historical manner, a researching manner, not a Satanic manner. That's really when we became our own band. When Hellhammer existed, the band was ripped apart by everybody—fans, media, record companies. Ninety-five percent of all of the reviews of the demos and [1984] EP [*Apocalyptic Raids*] were obliterating. The words journalists found to destroy Hellhammer are beyond belief. Nobody understood what Hellhammer was doing at the time. The myth of Hellhammer only happened later, after the band was gone.

THOMAS "QUORTHON" FORSBERG (1966–2004) (Bathory): I went to London with a friend about a year prior to forming Bathory. In the London Dungeon—a sort of wax museum of horror—there was [a] display built to resemble a medieval chamber. In the middle of the room, reclined in a bathtub filled with blood, we spotted this naked female figure. Above the tub, three or four also naked female figures were hanging upside down suspended in chains, throats cut and blood flowing. After finding out the woman in the tub's name was Countess Elizabeth Bathory, a sixteenth-century Hungarian noblewoman and serial killer who bathed in the blood of female virgins in an effort to retain her youthful looks, I realized her life story was as close to a Bathory lyric as can be; the name was, of course, perfect for the band. As for my name, Quorthon, during the winter of 1983, I was reading this book on Satanic rituals and there were a bunch of names of dark princes banished from Heaven and now in the service of Satan. These guys were supposedly supreme princes of darkness and evil, destined to fight at Lord Satan's side in the final battle between the forces of light and dark. I stopped at one name and felt instinctively that this was it: Quorthon.

KJETIL-VIDAR "FROST" HARALDSTAD (Satyricon): When I was thirteen, I lived in the countryside, so I had to travel quite a distance to get to town and buy albums, and the first one I bought was the first Bathory album. I remember I was drawing the goat on the front cover and the pentagram on the back of the cover, and then I'd turn off the lights and turn on the album, and I was never the same after that experience. That was the first time I got a connection with something deeper and darker in music.

QUORTHON: All I knew about metal when I started Bathory in 1983 was Motörhead and Black Sabbath. But I knew that what I wanted to do sure as hell was a lot closer to metal than Oi! [punk]. So the little metal I knew became all the more important for the sound of early Bathory. The energy and speed was obviously Oi!, but the sound was absolutely Motörhead, and the gloom was, of course, Black Sabbath.

IHSAHN: Even though Venom invented the term *black metal*, not much black metal sounds like Venom. At the time, no bands really sounded like Celtic Frost either, even though they had the same image and were a hugely respected band from having influenced the scene when they called themselves Hellhammer. But the vocals and epic style of black metal with keyboards originated from Bathory. I have only one idol when it comes to black metal vocals and that's Quorthon. That's the only reference I need.

QUORTHON: My vocal style at the time must have been something nobody had ever heard before. It was once described as reminiscent of a dog choking to death on a goat's head.

PER YNGVE "DEAD" OHLIN (1969–1991) (ex-Mayhem): Why is Quorthon talked about so often? I don't think he invented occultism or the death way of singing. I can listen to the early stuff by Bathory, only, like, the first LP. Later he lost all that ability to crush and kill.

QUORTHON: The fanzines and magazines back in the early eighties had a field day reviewing our first album. The only thing that came to their mind was Venom, and we were called Venom clones for years, when in fact we hadn't even heard Venom at that point and couldn't see or hear any resemblance at all once we actually got to listen to them. The funny thing is, when I told people I heard Venom for the first time after the release of the first Bathory album, they wouldn't believe me. And when I mentioned GBH was an influence, nobody knew what the hell I was talking about.

VARG "COUNT GRISHNACKH" VIKERNES (Burzum): When I started Burzum I hadn't even heard about Venom, so naturally Burzum is not—like some have claimed—influenced by Venom, in any way. The other guys in the band liked Entombed and Morbid Angel, but I have never liked or listened to them. But in late 1991 we began listening to our old Celtic Frost, Destruction, Kreator, and the older Bathory records as well.

QUORTHON: When every second band in interviews refer to Bathory as their main source of inspiration or influence, that's when you realize you've been doing at least some things right. But all Bathory was trying to do was make interesting metal and paint with words.

CRONOS: To me, Venom [guitarist] Mantas and [drummer] Abaddon were just living the image in Venom. These are guys who would always use blasphemous phrases and wear crucifixes around their necks—that's hypocrisy to me. Once,

Abaddon went on some TV show in England and the guy asked him if he was a Satanist, and when he said yes, the guy interrogated him and Abaddon fell flat because he couldn't answer any of the questions.

KIM BENDIX "KING DIAMOND" PETERSEN (ex–Mercyful Fate): When I wrote [the Mercyful Fate EP] *Nuns Have No Fun*, I had a lot of questions about Christianity. The song is about a cult raping a nun and crucifying her, and there's an image on the cover depicting that. You may ask, "Where is the good in that?" Well, I'm not saying it's good, but isn't it funny that a lot of people freaked out about a drawing on a record? After we released it, I was on a Saturday night TV show in Denmark having a discussion with a priest about this record cover. He was there to confront me. He had been after Mercy's ass since we started. He wanted us banned from the radio and had a personal vendetta against us. I was so fed up with this guy. He tried to slaughter us with all these accusations, and the first thing I said was, "You know what? I really like your tie. I think you are very nicely dressed for this occasion. I will compliment you on the way you are dressed." He got totally silent, and then he said, "Well, thank you," not knowing what else to do. Then I said, "Oops, pride. Isn't that one of your sins? Why are you dressed up for this? Shouldn't you just come in as you are normally? Okay, forget that, let's talk a little bit about the Inquisition? Wouldn't that be nice to talk about now that we've talked about the cover of my record. Because those are the things your faith did for real. They didn't just draw it on a little cover. They did it for real to how many people?" He left the studio and never interfered with us again.

DANI "FILTH" DAVEY (Cradle of Filth): I heard *Don't Break the Oath* by Mercyful Fate when I was thirteen, and it felt like I was listening to ghosts captured on vinyl. I was elated because it seemed like something I had been searching for. I grew up in a witch county, so it was like Halloween most of the year.

People would come to our village to try to find the graves of Matthew Hopkins, the Witchfinder General, and Christian martyrs that were burned. We'd feel that vibe, but you could never quite put your finger on it. At the time, I was listening to horrible eighties pop music like Ultravox, which I thought was dark. Then somebody introduced me to metal. A few weeks later I heard *Don't Break the Oath* and that was the trigger for everything else.

ADAM "NERGAL" DARSKI (Behemoth): When I was ten, I was getting into metal, and I remember my brother's friend said, "Hey, I have this record of music made by Satan. It's a black mass." I was scared when he put it on, and it was the intro to the first song on Mercyful Fate's *Don't Break the Oath* ["A Dangerous Meeting"]. He never said what band it was, and when I bought the record years later, all the memories came back.

KING DIAMOND: I always liked to be scared. I must have been eight years old and I'd fall asleep thinking vampires and monsters would come out from under the bed and take me away; that was very exciting.

QUORTHON: In 1983, there were no places in Stockholm for a band like Bathory to perform. And even if there had been such a place, given the quality or appearance of Bathory in those days, there was not a shot in hell that [we] would have been booked or allowed an inch of a stage. By the time we did have the money, we weren't interested in anything beyond the studio.

THOMAS GABRIEL FISCHER: In the eighties, Hellhammer were shunned. We never played live. Nobody would give us a chance. Promoters, fans, musicians, they all laughed at us. They said, "This is not even music." They told us we had to play like Dio or AC/DC, and we did exactly the opposite. No one would book us, so we resorted to private shows for friends in a nuclear-hardened bunker underground where we practiced.

QUORTHON: In the late eighties people began to send letters written in blood. These were the frantic days of HIV hysteria, and it was sometimes necessary to wear plastic gloves when reading fan mail. Prisoners that really shouldn't have had access to pen and paper where they were locked away began to write the band commenting on some of our lyrics that, to the apparent joy of these cannibals and molesters, coincided almost in detail with crimes they had committed earlier—crimes that had rendered them a triple life sentence. The most bizarre photos would arrive, depicting everything from a young female fan dressed up as a nun masturbating with a crucifix to a young male fan munching on a dead rat. Fans would slice the band's name into their arms and happily snap a shot or two of themselves proudly displaying their arms spelling out the word *Bathory* in fresh cuts, with blood splattered all over the floor.

THOMAS GABRIEL FISCHER: We got the unwelcome attention of National Socialist Satanists, which became quite dangerous. Maybe to some, that sounds like a joke. It certainly wasn't. There was an early heavy metal–related Satanic movement in the Scandinavian black metal scene. And there were exponents of that in Switzerland because Hellhammer was one of the very few bands that dealt in occult topics. They tried to indoctrinate the band. We did not want to be associated with that. We wrote absurd lyrics, but the lyrics didn't represent our way of life. That was one of the reasons Hellhammer dissolved and Celtic Frost took shape.

GYLVE FENRIS "FENRIZ" NAGELL (Darkthrone): Hearing Celtic Frost's "Dawn of Megiddo" from 1986's *To Mega Therion* was insane—like going to another dimension. Celtic Frost was one of the bands that pushed me into forming my own band on Christmas of 1986. I bought *Bathory* in '87, but I was young and didn't get the harsh sound right away. But it was good enough to buy [their next album], *Blood Fire Death*, in '88, and I listened again and again. Suddenly I realized the [low-fi production] was the perfect sound for Darkthrone. And so the seed of black metal was planted, growing slowly but steadily in me.

QUORTHON: The money reserved for the [first Bathory] record was around $600. We knew about this place in Stockholm that was a garage turned into a demo studio. It had primitive recording equipment, a homemade 8-track table, two small recording machines in one room, plus this switchboard thing on the wall. It was best suited for acoustic and vocal material and maybe light pop music. Nothing like Bathory had ever been recorded there. We had to adapt to the place and its limitations, [which is why the music sounds so low-fi].

KING DIAMOND: When the early Mercyful Fate stuff was written I had a lot of experiences with the supernatural, especially in this apartment in Copenhagen. One time me and King Ross, the drummer, were waiting for the other guys in Mercy to come by and my brother's beer glass rose two feet in the air and came down very slowly. The song "A Dangerous Meeting" is actually a warning not to mess with the occult. If you don't have someone in there that can really interpret things the right way, it is way too dangerous for young teenagers to fool around with because you don't know what's speaking to you. And if it feels mocked or disrespected, it can give you answers back that will ruin your life. After my first experiences with the supernatural, I went to the library and read a lot about the occult and I realized that most of those books were written from one specific viewpoint, where Satanism was always depicted as these maniacs sacrificing virgins. That's insanity.

CRONOS: I believe in nothing. My philosophy is this: you're born and one day you're in a box, and what you do in between is your own choice. And to live by a dogma that tells you that you can't do this and you can't do that is one of the most absurd things I've ever heard.

KING DIAMOND: I would be stupid to say, "I don't believe in anything, so there is no God." I would be the last to say there is no God. There might be fifteen, there might be a hundred, there might be none. No one can say.

The seeds of black metal spread across the world in the eighties. The antiauthoritarian and antireligious views of the genre's pioneers struck a particularly strong chord in the rural youth of Norway, who felt stifled by small-town conservatism and Christian ideologies. By the end of the decade, a second wave of black metal, initially bred from the bowels of thrash and death metal, expanded upon the rhetoric and blasphemous lyrics of the genre's forefathers. Venom may have coined the phrase *black metal*, but the first band to create a misanthropic, macabre, chaotic aesthetic for the music was Mayhem; they were followed shortly thereafter by Darkthrone, Burzum, and Immortal.

JORN "NECROBUTCHER" STUBBERUD (Mayhem): I was coming from a place in Norway called Langhus, and I went to a town called Ski five kilometers from the center of the county in 1984 to try out for a band. There was this guy who was going to meet me at the train station who was going to guide me to the house of this band, and this was Øystein [Aarseth], this was Euronymous. Walking there, we realized we liked the same music: Venom, German electronica, punk. We were both seeking the extreme, and we were amazed that we could have been living so close together without already knowing each other. Since I had another band and a rehearsal space already, I asked him to join my band immediately, even before we got to the audition. Me and my drummer [Manheim] had a band called the Musta, which is "black" in Finnish. Euronymous had come up with the name Mayhem for a band that he put together to play songs for his [high school] graduation ceremony. The name was taken from the Venom song "Mayhem with Mercy" from the *Welcome to Hell* album, and we decided to keep that name, because we felt it was better than Musta.

ØYSTEIN "EURONYMOUS" AARSETH (ex-Mayhem): I'd like to think that we would have been the first evil band if the older bands wouldn't have existed. Venom was our first and major influence, later Bathory, Hellhammer, Sodom, and Destruction. I'm sure [if it weren't for them] we would sound very different.

NECROBUTCHER: We were into dark music and horror movies, especially ones by the Italian directors [Dario] Argento and Lucio Fulci. We liked the splatter, the thinking about death, anti-Christian, anti-religious, antisocial lyrics. But we were not religious in any way. Many people have misunderstood us. They called us Satanists, but we were so far from that—as far as you could possibly be. Satan is mentioned in the Bible, so if you're a Satanist you're also a Christian, and we are *anti*-religious. Religion is for weak people who need something to explain the bigger picture—why they are living. We didn't need any help from any religion to be able to cope with reality.

EURONYMOUS: I will never accept any band which preaches [Anton LaVey's] Church of Satan ideas, as they are just a bunch of freedom- and life-loving atheists, and they stand exactly the opposite of me. I believe in a horned devil, a personified Satan. In my opinion, all the other forms of Satanism are bullshit. Satanism comes from religious Christianity, and there it shall stay. I'm a religious person and I will fight those who misuse his name. People are not supposed to believe in themselves and be individualists. They are supposed to *obey*, to be the *slaves* of religion.

FENRIZ: Lyrically, I was influenced by Danzig and writings from the Church of Satan as much as anything else—although

I knew distinctly that affiliation with the Church of Satan was
out of the question. We formed our own aesthetic. We all had
a contempt for organized religion since we were mere toddlers,
combined with a natural interest for the *opposite* of that—and
a morbid hunger for the sickest sounds of underground metal.
Sounding angry or aggressive was also important, but the
bands we got the black metal vibes from were original and had
evil atmospheres and sounded twisted—they certainly weren't
overproduced.

The first wave of Norwegian black metal bands shared similar
influences and perspectives, so their music had common threads.
The bands were almost all fast and frantic, and their songs were
more minimalistic and atmospheric than most extreme metal.
Many emphasized repetitive, minor-key riffs and eschewed traditional start-stop metallic crunch, opting instead for a monochro-
matic, mesmerizing buzz.

BRANDON GEIST: These guys were trying to one-up what was
previously the most extreme style of metal. Death metal
seemed like it was as extreme as it could get, and black metal's
like, "That's bullshit. You're wearing sweatpants and your
production's too good. We're gonna make this way more
evil and way more extreme." One way they did that was by
making the production more low-fi and genuinely disturbing
in this visceral way that's a little more mysterious.

TOM CATO "KING ov HELL" VISNES (ex-Gorgoroth): The American
death metal scene was going on when the Norwegian black
metal scene started. So as the [American] death metal scene
got more and more attention and [the playing became] more
technical and the albums were [more sonically polished], the
Norwegian scenes relied not so much on playing as fast as
you can, but more on presenting a lot of atmosphere [in the
music]. [Low-fi] production in the beginning made the music
more ugly sounding, and the attitude got more real and brutal.

Euronymous said it very precisely; he said, "What Venom talked about and used as a shock factor, we actually mean." The Satanic part got more real.

As the bleak, morbid ideologies and raging, despairing sounds of Norwegian black metal started to congeal, so did the look. Inspired by the theatricality of Alice Cooper, KISS, and King Diamond, Norway's outcasts painted their faces white, with jagged smears of black encircling their eyes. The first band to adopt this horror-zombie look was Norway's Mayhem, whose singer at the time, Per Yngve Ohlin (aka Dead), had already worn corpse paint in his old death metal band, Sweden's Morbid.

NECROBUTCHER: The term "corpse paint" was actually not introduced before Dead. Back in Morbid, he was very fascinated by death, and wanted to look like he was dead, so he would paint his face like he was a corpse. But he didn't join Mayhem until 1988, after we had already worked with other singers and released our first record [*Deathcrush*].

COUNT GRISHNACKH (Burzum): The corpse paint thread [dates] back to KISS and further, all the way to Alice Cooper. . . . [But] when you look at it from a different, non-metal perspective, you need to follow a completely different thread all the way back to antiquity. In European cultures it was custom to see the world as being for all beings: man, spirits, and later, deities, too. However, only the initiates could see the spirits, and in order to do so they needed to put on a mask. We know from the older traditions, from sorcery. On certain festivals, the sorcerer hung his clothes in the holy tree, so that it looked as if he had hanged himself. He then covered his entire naked body and face with ash from a sacred fire. When he did [this] he was able to see [the spirits and deities], and thus communicate and interact with them. The ash was the mask. The ash was the "corpse paint."

NERGAL: The costume, the mask, the spikes help me express the inner strength I feel. So I might be fucked up or tired or want to go back to sleep, but when I put the shit on it empowers me.

SVEN ATLE "SILENOZ" KOPPERUD (Dimmu Borgir): I'm sure it would be nice to not put on corpse paint and spikes every night. But we're so used to it and it's such a huge part of our look that it would be totally wrong to abandon it. We got a new guitar tech and he thought the spikes weren't real and scratched himself pretty bad. Now he stands a few feet further away from us. Some stagedivers have gotten hit in the head and the neck with the spikes. It's anti–stage diving regalia.

The first Norwegian black metal band, Mayhem, didn't stop with corpse paint, decorating the stage with animal heads on stakes and engaging in dangerous acts of self-mutilation. Capitalizing on all the chaos and hysteria was Euronymous, who embraced his role as figurehead of the emerging movement. As much a salesman as he was a Satanist, the guitarist hyped drama and barbarism to promote his band and scene.

NECROBUTCHER: Øystein first painted his face in 1985. Then we wanted to do another gig and we were going to rent the community house for cultural events in Ski, the town we came from. We wanted a scary, dramatic stage show, so we went to the butcher shop and got ourselves four big pig heads, but the community center canceled us. They didn't find out about the pig heads, but they didn't want a heavy metal concert at a place where they held bingo for seniors. We were living at home at the time, so we had these pig heads in our mom and dad's freezers, and of course mom and dad didn't like that. They were saying, "When the fuck are you going to get rid of these pig heads?"

COUNT GRISHNACKH: Black metal [as a movement] was a name given by [Mayhem guitarist] Euronymous to the music of

Darkthrone and Burzum in 1991, to describe our revolt against the trendy death metal scene, and he used it because he knew the term from a Venom album, a band he, for some incomprehensible reason, cared [too] much for. The term quickly became popular, and after a while a lot of bands were using it to describe their music—for all the wrong reasons, of course, and not knowing what it really was all about.

GRUTLE KJELLSON: Everybody was talking about death metal in the late eighties and the first one to say, "Okay, we don't really play death metal, we play black metal," was Euronymous. He painted his face, he inspired loads of other bands to quit playing death metal and start this new thing that would later become a huge trend.

BÅRD "FAUST" EITHUN (ex-Emperor, ex-Thorns, Blood Tsunami, Aborym): Euronymous was very articulate, very calm, and you always had the impression everything he said was thought through many times before he expressed it. His philosophy towards music inspired many people. The Mayhem lineup with Euronymous, Necrobutcher, Dead, and Hellhammer was unbeatable, and the two songs they recorded for a [1991] Swedish compilation *Projections of a Stained Mind*, ["Freezing Moon" and "Carnage"], the [1993] *Live in Leipzig* live album, and [1994's] *De Mysteriis Dom Sathanas* are among the most fierce and powerful black metal there is.

NECROBUTCHER: Euronymous was a visionary, for sure. I don't want to take anything away from him, but I was more the bandleader. I invited him to my band. He didn't even have a rehearsal space, and I already had been playing in a band for four years. When we started out, he was the one who got our music out and built the network. Right after we recorded the demo *Pure Fucking Armageddon* [in 1986], we bought rail tickets which let you go wherever you like in Europe, and we went out to establish contacts with other bands, record stores, and magazines. We went to Germany to see Kreator, Sodom, Assassin; in England we saw Napalm Death and Extreme Noise Terror; Aggressor and Monumentum in Italy. We found the markets for our music to build a network and he got more and more into that over the years, and we started our own record label [Posercorpse Music].

AUDREY EWELL (director): Euronymous was like the advertising executive of the movement. He took a businesslike approach to the whole scene and saw a marketable element, and really tried to advertise based on those elements.

In addition to being the first band to perform, Mayhem was also the first to release an actual record—1987's *Deathcrush*. The album was rooted in thrash and death metal but featured the shrill vocal howls that became a blueprint for black metal and sparked the development of the nascent scene.

FENRIZ: *Deathcrush* was insanely inspirational. It could be bought on tape under the counter at Hot Records in Oslo in early 1987. The vinyl came out later that year. It was by far the rawest band in Norway. Just looking at the logo was godly. After I heard it, I got in touch with them, and even though I was a greenhorn they took some interest in me. I had my own crew to build in Darkthrone. So my contact with Euronymous and Necrobutcher between 1987 and 1990 was sporadic, but memorable. But there wasn't a scene. Everyone was just pen pals, more or less. I think Mayhem showed a lot of us that we had to fend for ourselves, DIY-style.

SHAGRATH: I really liked *Deathcrush*; it was so raw and heavy. It was Euronymous who introduced me to it. I wanted to buy it from him and I couldn't. It was a limited edition—that's before it was reprinted.

FROST: Mayhem would say [1994's] *De Mysteriis Dom Sathanas* was a much more important album, and of course it was. But to me, *Deathcrush* was really significant, and especially that saw blade guitar sound. It's the first proper release by a really extreme Norwegian band, and that gave Mayhem cult status.

FAUST: Many people were directly inspired to make riffs the same way as Euronymous did. For example, Snorre Ruch from Thorns was very inspired by it, and, in fact, he did it so well that his kind of riffing in turn inspired Euronymous again, and it eventually became the trademark riffing of what became known as Norwegian black metal. Today, Thorns is a well-kept secret from the more superficial black metal fans, and little do they probably realize that this loner from Trondheim influenced bands like Darkthrone, Dimmu Borgir, Burzum, Emperor, and even Mayhem. I didn't leave Thorns as such, but we more or less decided to put it down [in 1992] since Snorre joined Mayhem and I joined Emperor.

EURONYMOUS: Most people hated us. It was something so raw and evil [that chills ran down your back], and you really got a kick from listening to it [if you were into black metal]. Now death metal is commercial, and bands like Cadaver have even played gigs for their parents. This is not good. This does not help the underground. Real death metal should be something normal people are afraid of, not something mothers listen to.

Darkthrone, launched under the name Black Death in 1986, evolved into one of the most influential bands in Norwegian black metal. Unlike some of their peers, the band began as a death metal group, as reflected in their 1991 debut, *Soulside Journey.* But it was 1992's *A Blaze in the Northern Sky* that marked their transformation and became a landmark for the genre. Chilling and evil—and so tinny-sounding the songs seemed to be playing on damaged speakers—the music resonated with the lunatic conviction of a group dedicated to darkness and determined to sign a pact with the devil.

FENRIZ: We started out as a band that [just] *tried* to play. Inspired by the primitive riffs of Celtic Frost and the [sloppiness] of [crossover punk band] Cryptic Slaughter, I thought, "I can start playing as well." Then in the autumn of '87 I formed Darkthrone and our sound developed into trying out anything, from Napalm Death's crusty grind/punk with Celtic Frost riffs thrown in for good measure to softer, epic acoustic bits probably inspired by Metallica instrumentals. So we were a metal/punk band in '87 and '88, just as we have been since 2005. But in '89 we turned into death-thrashers, and by the end of the year we were fully fledged technical horror death metal fiends with a record deal to match. I had been listening to death metal since I discovered Possessed as early as '86, and in the underground, death metal riffs flourished. In those days, thrash, death, and black were often mixed together, as there were luckily no real niches yet. It was when death metal became streamlined that I didn't feel it anymore. Plus we had been rediscovering blacker vibes since 1989, hearing our old Destruction albums, for instance, in a new way. And we were worshipping Bathory and Hellhammer combined with Motörhead and Black Sabbath. Of course, in 1990 we were a technical, evil death metal band, but this had to change. In early '91 we decided to start rocking out the black metal vibes and tone down the slinky death metal stuff.

KORY GROW: One reason Darkthrone is so important is because [1992's] *A Blaze in the Northern Sky* was the first record that got across the whole idea of taking back Norway from the Christians. They were saying, "A thousand years ago you invaded Norway and you raped us of our religion and our culture. So why are we continuing to follow these rules that the English brought to us when they took so much from us?"

Darkthrone followed up *A Blaze in the Northern Sky* with two more harrowing and hellish black metal releases—1993's *Under a Funeral Moon* and 1994's *Transylvanian Hunger*—before Mayhem finally released the seminal follow-up to *Deathcrush*: *De Mysteriis Dom Sathanas*. That album's creation was, to say the least, fraught with complications, including member shifts, suicide, and murder, which explains why it took six years to complete. Going into the project, Mayhem wanted a more dramatic front man than either of their former vocalists, Eirik Nordheim (aka Messiah) and Sven Erik Kristiansen (aka Maniac, who returned to the band between 1994 and 2004). So they recruited Per Yngve Ohlin (aka Dead), whose volatility and aesthetic made Mayhem's performances visceral and terrifying. The band also replaced drummer Manheim with Jan Axel Blomberg (aka Hellhammer), who remains one of the genre's fastest and most aggressive players.

NECROBUTCHER: Dead really took his role in the band seriously. He buried his stage clothes in the ground so they would decompose and smell. He also collected dead squirrels and roadkill and kept them in this cooler bag without cooling elements, so the stench was very foul. He always took that in a plastic bag to gigs or to the studios, where he could open up the bag and smell it before he sang to get the right feeling of death.

JAN AXEL "HELLHAMMER" BLOMBERG (Mayhem): I joined Mayhem in 1988. I took my name from Celtic Frost's previous project Hellhammer, and I thought it was a shame that such a good name had to disappear. My friends introduced me to Euronymous and Dead. Soon after [I joined] we got into the dark side of life and Satanism. I would always like those things in spite of the fact that I was born in a Christian family. Only years after, I realized how weird and how harmful it was for us. But I was too young to resist my temptation for darkness. I found some books where different rituals were described. Later on, we put our knowledge into real life practice. Euronymous was the most deeply involved. He was our teacher. Now I realize he went too far. And Dead followed his lead. Frankly speaking, I didn't completely understand Satanism. I was attracted by the dark, sinister imagery, but I didn't feel any anger for Christianity. Euronymous and Dead hated it. "Christianity is evil," they used to say. But I asked them: "Ain't it evil what we are doing?" I never got an answer.

NECROBUTCHER: One of the reasons we had dead animals on-stage was because Dead liked that kind of image; it fit with his stage show. The first time we used it was in late '88. I'd say 50 percent of the people at the show liked the visuals and thought it was cool—like performance art. The other 50 percent of the crowd were disgusted. But Dead always said he'd like to take it a step further. His dream was to play in Stockholm and slaughter a goat with a chainsaw onstage, but we never got to do that.

DEAD: My mum told me when I was a baby I slept so deeply I turned white. She had to check me all the time to see if I was still alive. Maybe the whole thing started there? And maybe it started before that. My great-great-grandmother was a sorcerer but only practiced white magic. I have never been into fuckin' white magic. I have always hated Christianity, and when I discovered Satanism I became insanely interested in that.

HELLHAMMER: When Dead entered the show he just became Dead. I don't know why he was cutting himself, but he did it a lot. He cut his arm so bad with a bottle once that he almost fainted onstage.

NECROBUTCHER: For [Dead], the stage was the place where he could live out everything you couldn't do in normal life. You don't cut yourself when you're in the supermarket. But when he performed he could really show off his bizarre ideas about this character, Dead. He was an antisocial guy, more into being alone and reading books and drawing. When we met, he was smiling. He had a great sense of humor, black humor that we shared. Other people didn't know him. He didn't open up easily, so people thought he was depressed. But he wasn't at all. He just was not interested in interacting with new people, or listening to other people's opinions.

HELLHAMMER: In the beginning of the nineties we rented an old deserted house in the forest to rehearse. Everybody [in town] hated us, but we enjoyed it. Dead would lock himself in his room, permanently depressed. Euronymous and Dead didn't get along. Dead didn't trust Euronymous. The verbal fights turned into real bloody beatings. I got tired of their quarrels and moved to my grandmother's, coming back mainly to rehearse. One day I decided to go to Oslo with my friends. Before the departure, I met Dead. He was grim and depressed: "Look, I bought a big knife. It's very sharp." Those were the last words I heard from him.

NECROBUTCHER: We had a lot of plans, but things weren't moving so fast. Tours were canceled, the songs for *De Mysteriis Dom Sathanas* were more or less finished, but we didn't have a budget to enter the studio. We had some setbacks. On top of that, all of Dead's friends were still in Sweden and that depressed him a little bit. And his family was constantly on him about the choices he had to make in his life, pushing him all the time to go back to school and get a real job. Ultimately, after living together for a while, he and Euronymous were no longer friends. Also, he was morbidly [obsessed with the] afterlife. All his lyrics were about this, and I think that came from an episode that happened to him when he was ten years old and he was ice skating and he fell on the ice. His [spleen] sprung open and he was rushed to the hospital, and then he had this vision. What he told me was that he was actually dead, but they got him back to life. And [while he was unconscious] he heard some music and saw a tunnel with a light at the end of it, and then when he found out that people had similar visions after near-death experiences he read all the books on the subject that he could get. He [felt that] there was an afterlife, and fuck anyone who didn't believe in it. It was not religious; it was a spiritual thing. His solution [to proving there is an afterlife] was just to kill himself. So he did.

HELLHAMMER: Euronymous was leaving with me that day. He went to town on some business for his label [Deathlike Silence Productions]. Several days later, when he came back, the house looked deserted. The front door was locked and there was no key in our secret place. Euronymous went round the house and noticed that the window to Dead's room was opened. He got to the house and saw Dead lying on the floor: a part of his head was blown away by [a] gunshot. Euronymous hitchhiked to the nearest town to buy film for his camera. Then he returned and made a shot of Dead's corpse. When Euronymous called me, he was not talkative. "Dead went back home," he said. "Back to Sweden?" I wondered. "No, he's blown his head [off]." Then I realized that Dead was dead. Police took Dead's body, and we lived in the house for a few more weeks. Dead's blood and pieces of his skull were all over the room. Once I looked under his bed and found two big pieces of skull. I took one piece and Euronymous took the other. We made amulets out of them.

EURONYMOUS: Although I was the one who found him and had to crawl through his brains to get into his house, I don't think it affected me very much. Of course, he was a friend, but I know he wanted to die, and the only right thing he could do was to give his life to the darkness. It would have been wrong to prevent him from doing it. Besides, when I say I'm into death metal, I mean it! I hate when people say that they're into death, and when it comes down to it they're really just life-loving, humanitarian false trendies. Of course I took photos—wouldn't you? It's not every day you get to mess around with a real corpse. Unfortunately.

NECROBUTCHER: Øystein called me and said that Dead had done something cool. I said, "What's up?" Euronymous said, "He blew his brains out," and I said, "What the fuck?" He told me about the pictures [he had taken of Dead's corpse], and I told him, "You burn those pictures before you even call me again. You're sick in your head." I was completely angry and knocked out by grief. When somebody close to you kills himself, that's the worst grief you can have because it doesn't explain anything. It's almost like a betrayal. You start to think, "Was there something I could do, was it something I said?" When somebody dies in a car accident, you can accept, "Yeah, he was in a car, they came off of a road, hit a tree, it was sad—but it has an explanation." This wasn't like that. So I was full of grief and was the only one from the band who went to Sweden for the funeral. My dear brother, Euronymous—the guy I met when I was sixteen and was together with every day for ten years, sharing information, talking about plans—his reaction to Dead's death was a betrayal to me, and I got very pissed off. He didn't get rid of the pictures, and he took advantage of the situation because now he could be the leader of Mayhem.

HELLHAMMER: After Dead killed himself, the police removed the corpse, but all the blood and this shit was lying around the floor and the walls of this old house they were living in. I was there with Euronymous, and he took a piece of Dead's brain and put it in some Mexican stew. It was just a small piece that had been lying on the floor. When Euronymous was eating Dead's brain, that was pretty strange. I didn't eat it because I really enjoy good food, and I wouldn't destroy my senses eating this kind of shit. I don't think he enjoyed eating it either, but he just wanted to taste human flesh, so he did. I think it was cool, but I would never have done something like that.

NECROBUTCHER: After that, Euronymous moved to Oslo so he could be in a bigger city and present himself as the evil character he had always envisioned. He would rather have people fear and hate him than respect him. He wrote shitloads of letters to me the first year. I was still grieving after Dead's suicide, so I wrote him back and told him to fuck off. That's around the time he started the Helvete record store where he held these meetings with members of other bands.

In no time, Helvete became ground zero for Norwegian black metal bands. Musicians in the so-called "inner circle" met not just to jam and hang out but also to share antisocial thoughts about politics and religion. After playing with Abbath and ex-Immortal guitarist Demonaz in Old Funeral, Count Grishnackh became a regular at Helvete, and when Mayhem needed a new bassist he volunteered to step in.

HELLHAMMER: Dead's death didn't stop us. We decided to find a new vocalist, [Attila Csihar, who left after 1994's *De Mysteriis Dom Sathanas*, then rejoined in 2004 and continues to sing for Mayhem]. I liked Grishnackh from our first meeting: He was an intelligent guy. He stood out from other musicians. He was modest and polite.

COUNT GRISHNACKH: In 1988 or 1989, when I had played guitar for a year or two, I formed a band called Kalashnikov, named after my favorite assault rifle. One of our songs was named "Uruk-Hai." The chorus was "Uruk-Hai! / You will die." We soon changed the name of the whole band to Uruk-Hai. As most Burzum fans should know, Uruk-Hai was the name of the High Orcs of Sauron [from J. R. R. Tolkein's *Lord of the Rings* trilogy], and it translates as "Orc Race," from Black Speech, the language of Mordor [the fictional city created by Tolkien]. I knew the drummer from an earlier encounter, when we were somewhere between twelve and fifteen years old, and he had put a loaded .375 Magnum revolver to my forehead on New Year's Eve, because he thought I had called him "fatso." I had actually called not him, but his friend, a "fatso," and told him that. In 1989, I met the guys in Old

Funeral, who were excellent and serious musicians, and we dropped the whole Uruk-Hai project. The two other Uruk-Hai members were already fighting over a girl, and we had stopped rehearsing, so it was not hard to put Uruk-Hai to rest. I played with Old Funeral for two years.

ABBATH: I asked Varg [Count Grishnackh] to join Old Funeral when we needed another guitar player. He was very dedicated. At the time he seemed good to work with.

COUNT GRISHNACKH: During the time I was with Old Funeral, the band turned from a really cool techno-thrash band to a boring death metal band. This was the reason I eventually left Old Funeral, as I wanted to play my own type of music.

FENRIZ: Varg and me had a huge amount of mutual respect, but I don't think anyone in the scene were close friends. That would be anathema—black metal people being friends. It wasn't a cozy scene.

HARALD "DEMONAZ" NÆVDAL (Immortal): Varg had a lot of passion for what he did, but he wanted to go by himself and do Burzum, and we did Immortal.

COUNT GRISHNACKH: If people knew that Burzum was just some teenager's band, that would have ruined the magic. For that reason I felt that I needed to be anonymous. So I used a pseudonym, Count Grishnackh, and used a photo on the debut album that didn't look like me at all to make Burzum itself seem more out-of-this-world, and to confuse people.

Although it arrived after the first wave of black metal bands (Mayhem, Darkthrone, Burzum, and Immortal), Emperor became a fixture of black metal in the early nineties. *In the Nightside Eclipse* rivals Mayhem's *De Mysteriis Dom Sathanas* as one of the best early black metal albums, a whirlwind of high-velocity rhythms, majestic arrangements, and atmospheric keyboards.

IHSAHN: Samoth and I met in 1989 at a local blues seminar where kids come together from different parts of the country to get tutored and put together bands and have a go at playing the blues. Samoth was already in a band. He was fourteen. They needed a second guitarist. I had long blond hair and my jacket had Iron Maiden patches on it. So I joined his band. He was always good at tape trading, so quite early on he had a huge network around the world and [the band evolved] really quickly. We grew from heavy metal through thrash and death metal.

FAUST: I knew Samoth from the scene and I was hoping and believing he would ask me to join as Emperor's drummer. He started out on drums and I think that was an emergency solution because he is really a guitarist and not a drummer. What distinguished Emperor from the rest of the bands was that Ihsahn was an experienced synth and keyboard player. He could actually play, not just use it to create a layer of sound.

FENRIZ: I think Emperor is kind of *overly* liked in the U.S. I mean, the whole Norwegian black metal thing really didn't hit the USA until 1998, and the chronology and what counted was all jumbled up. Emperor was really from the after-wave, like Gorgoroth, Satyricon, and Gehenna. We, in Darkthrone, fed on the eighties international releases. When we made our two "black metal" releases as a whole band [1992's *A Blaze in the Northern Sky* and 1993's *Under a Funeral Moon*], the only Norwegian black metal we had heard were Mayhem, Burzum, Thorns, and Immortal.

IHSAHN: We were in touch with other metal bands quite early. We went to meet up with Darkthrone and even sat in on rehearsals where they rehearsed for the [1996] *Goatlord* album that they originally planned to release after [1991's] *Soulside Journey*. We had contact with the Old Funeral guys and some people who are now in Enslaved. The first time we got Ivar [Bjornson] from Enslaved drunk, he was twelve.

FAUST: It was a chaotic time to say the least. When we did *In the Nightside Eclipse* [in 1993], the material was well rehearsed and tight as hell, but at the same time we had a very relaxed feeling to it all. We had no idea of the importance of what we were about to record, nor did any of the other bands at the time who ended up recording albums which would later be deemed as seminal or legendary. The recording alone took one or two weeks. Ihsahn was seventeen years old at the time and couldn't get into the bars so he just stayed in the studio working. I used to say that all the great vocal work on the album was thanks to his being underage because Ihsahn had so much time to work on it.

As more bands entered the scene, including Enslaved, Marduk, Satyricon, and Gorgoroth, the power and influence of black metal grew; but the core of the movement continued to be controlled by Euronymous and Count Grishnackh, who served as the scene's ambassadors. Euronymous's approval could lead to an invitation into the "inner circle" and a deal with Deathlike Silence. Members of bands as far away as Germany (Marduk) and Japan (Sigh) sought approval from the black metal messiah.

MORGAN "EVIL" STEINMEYER HÅKANSSON (Marduk): Marduk began in 1990 to make brutal, antireligious metal. Together, the message and the music became dynamite. Even though we weren't from Norway, Euronymous was selling our demo tape in his record store. You knew everybody in every country that was connected to the same scene and you shared ideas and visions. Of course, I was part of the Inner Circle, but I don't think that's anything anyone should speak about even now.

FAUST: I first met Euronymous outside a gig with Anthrax and Suicidal Tendencies in Oslo on the *Among the Living* tour. He and Dead were selling some Metallica bootlegs they had pressed themselves called *Phantom Lord*. I realized instantly who they were. They both made a tremendous impression on me and they both seemed like serious outcasts, even amongst the metal audience waiting to get into the venue.

GRUTLE KJELLSON: When I met Euronymous back in '91 when we started Enslaved, I thought he was a very polite and intelligent man. He and I didn't necessarily share the same ideology when it came to Satanism and politics, but we shared the same love for Pink Floyd, the Residents, psychedelic music, and early seventies electronic groups. He was completely different from what you see in pictures and what you hear about. Yeah, he had an image because he was running a company and was trying to build a band and his record label. But in private he was polite and intelligent, a nice person and a cool guy.

FENRIZ: The greatest misconception is people think we only listened to black metal and we didn't have senses of humor. People without humor are garish company. Simply put, if you are a loner with no social skills that wants to sulk, it's possible to make black metal, but you might want to choose another arena.

AUDREY EWELL: What people don't understand is these guys were really smart. There was a tongue-in-cheek aspect to what they were doing. People in their time didn't understand that and took everything at face value, and that's where so much of the black metal mythos actually came from—an inability to assess statements these guys made and see any sort of humor in them.

FROST: Euronymous helped a lot of creative people meet and eventually form constellations. All the bands went for the best and only accepted the best, and challenged themselves. And the healthy competition fueled the quality of the bands.

SILENOZ: We frequently visited Euronymous's record shop and he always gave us advice. He guided us to the more evil and brutal side of metal. He sold the albums for very little money, too, so you usually came home with a stack of CDs and vinyl.

FAUST: Helvete was the first real physical manifestation of something that was *ours*. Euronymous made the shop look really old, dirty, and dark. This, together with his magnetic force on younger metalheads, made the shop a place where guys into dark death and black metal could crawl into, discuss big topics, listen to music, and get drunk.

GRUTLE KJELLSON: Euronymous was kind of funny. On the one hand he was a leader, but he was also very absent-minded. He could drive for hours and suddenly go, "Where the hell am I?" He was kind of a dreamer. He enjoyed a good laugh, you could tell stupid jokes and drink beer and have a great time.

FROST: When people were gathered at Helvete there was this weird atmosphere that was almost palpable. I had no reference for it, no words for it, and then I felt it, and it was an instant connection. I belonged somehow to this thing, and I wanted to dedicate myself to it. The common denominator was the fascination with extreme music that brought us there in the first place. If you didn't have an affinity for the music and the darkness you wouldn't feel well in those surroundings.

GRUTLE KJELLSON: Euronymous was very much into dictators, and outside the store he had national flags from horrible regimes around the world. One day we were sitting there drinking and a bunch of Iranians came in. They had seen the Iranian flag on the outside and thought it was a cafe. So there were twenty confused Iranians walking into a very dark room with dim lights and five people sitting there in black leather jackets.

GLEN BENTON (Deicide): [When I met Euronymous] he was carrying a mace, but it looks like he stole the table leg off his mom's kitchen table and put nails through it. He was wearing this cape that you'd buy at the dollar store during Halloween. They brought me backstage and they said, "Uranus"—or whatever—"from Mayhem is here and wants to meet you." So I went out there and in his broken English, he said, "I did not have problem with you, but this band Gorguts [a death metal band that came out of the same nineties scene as Benton], they are not true death-metal/black-metal band." I was just sitting there with a big shit-eating grin on my face like, "Yeah, that's cool, man." I really didn't know the importance of the guy. To me he looked like another goofball fan.

FAUST: As bands started recording great albums and became recognized as a vital force of music and ideology both within and outside of Norway, it became more important to Euronymous to maintain an image and wear a mask, especially to people who were outside of the inner core but still wanted to know more about the underground music phenomenon. This is not entirely Euronymous's fault, but was merely a result of a group psychosis where everything became more serious, dark, and sinister. He was a well-read and fascinating guy, but I think Euronymous was caught in his own game, and we all know how that ended.

Even today, members within the Norwegian black metal community continue to debate whether the black metal genre ever practiced or promoted Satanic worship. Most Norwegian metal bands were anti-Christian, but not all of them embraced Satanism. And those that did had varying beliefs in what the religion meant.

DEMONAZ: When I started writing lyrics for the first Immortal album I didn't want to write about politics or religion. I wanted to have something more evil and based on the Northern darkness and the inspiring black forests and the snow and winters that we have. I think it's a little like Conan the Barbarian. His God is Krum, who doesn't care about him, but still, he wants to have a relation to Krum. I have a relation to nature, to the dark path. I never sought God, I never saw Satan, but I saw the darkness that creeps over my house. Nature is everything for humans. We are bound to it. We need it. It doesn't need us. And that makes it the power. That makes it the God.

COUNT GRISHNACKH: Burzum had an occult concept, but it is more correct to say it was a concept built on fantasy magic. Everything with Burzum was out-of-this-world—even the name. When the Christians called the gods of my forefathers "demons," "trolls," "goblins," and, not least, "evil," I naturally felt attracted to everything that was seen as evil by the Christians. As most [J. R. R.] Tolkien fans should know, *burzum* is one of the words that are written in Black Speech on the One Ring of Sauron. As far as I remember, the last sentence is *"Ash nazg durbabatulûk agh burzum ishi krimpatûl,"* meaning "one ring to bring them all and in the darkness bind them." The "darkness" of the Christians was, of course, my "light." So all in all it was natural for me to use the name Burzum.

DAVE PYBUS (Cradle of Filth): These guys in Scandinavia were taking the *Lord of the Rings* and Venom at face value. [We were from England], and the more we giggled, the more earnest and desperate they were to be taken seriously.

IHSAHN: That which in Christian eyes would be categorized as evil would not necessarily be seen as cruel or destructive in the eyes of those who are not chained to the narrow path of Christianity. Evil is more or less controlled by the beast in man, also known as free will. Satan is the personification of free will, individualism, and intelligence, so building one's ideology on values categorized as evil does not make you a ruthless maniac. Just like the beast, one has to adapt to one's environment.

ABBATH: The Satan part of black metal has never been our true belief. We follow our own path. We don't experiment with that kind of stuff. Maybe in the beginning we did, but we quickly found our own road where we were our own gods. But still the dark side of life is very important to us. We created Blashyrkh, our own hell. And that's where we find inspiration—and it can be anywhere in nature. Blashyrkh is always following us. It's just our thing.

KRISTIAN EIVIND "GAAHL" ESPEDAL (GORGOROTH): [Satan] means opponent—as long as the world speaks in a Christian language. I have to be Satan—the opponent of this—the opponent to slavery basically, which the rest of the world is [bound by]. Therefore, Satan means freedom.

COUNT GRISHNACKH: My hope would be that Burzum could inspire people to wish for a new and better reality in the real world and hopefully do something about it. Maybe revolt against the modern world by refusing to participate in the rape of Mother Earth, by refusing to participate in the murder of our European race, by refusing to become a part of any of these artificial media-created "rock-and-roll" subcultures, and by building new and healthy communities, where the Pagan culture—and magic if you like—can be cultivated.

In addition to being a think tank to combat the evils of Christianity, the Inner Circle was a musical breeding ground that encouraged cross-pollination. Euronymous played a guitar solo on Burzum's 1992 self-titled debut, and released it and its follow-up—1992's *Aske* (which featured bass by Emperor's Samoth)—on Deathlike Silence Productions. And Vikernes wrote lyrics for Darkthrone's 1994 album *Transylvanian Hunger* and 1995's *Panzerfaust*. But musical and artistic exchanges weren't all that went down at Helvete, and over time, several of its denizens moved away from philosophy—and gravitated toward crime. While Euronymous was more of the spiritual leader of the group, Grishnackh held more radical views and believed in action over contemplation. To express his contempt for Christian culture, Vikernes advocated church-burning. On June 6, 1992, the Fantoft Stave church in Bergen was torched and seriously damaged. The remains of the building appear on the cover art of Burzum's *Aske*. After conducting what he claims was supposed to be an off-the-record interview with a Norwegian newspaper about the crime, Vikernes was arrested for arson.

COUNT GRISHNACKH: When I did the anonymous interview in January 1993, I exaggerated a lot, and when the journalist left we—a girl and I—had a good laugh, because he didn't seem to understand that I was pulling his leg. He took everything dead serious. Unfortunately, he went to the police the next day and had me arrested, and his newspaper printed his version of what I had said while I was in a holding cell and unable to tell anybody that it was just a load of crap I had said to create some interest in a musical genre—to help Euronymous get some customers [in Helvete] for a change.

MORGAN HÅKANSSON: In the middle of the night Euronymous called and told me, "Today the war has begun," when the first church burning was a reality. It was something we had talked about many times and we were very excited about it. The problem was, people wanted to brag about what they did instead of just doing it for a specific cause. And that's their undoing. That's how they got caught.

FROST: I never took part in any such acts. I do not support crime. I don't think we owe anything to Christianity and the Church, but to try to destroy them would not be a constructive way to move forward. It will backfire.

By early 1993, four more churches had been torched, two in Bergen—Åsane Church and Storetveit Church—Vindafjord's Skjold Church, and Oslo's Holmenkollen Chapel. After a thorough police investigation, Emperor guitarist Tomas Thormodsæter Haugen (aka Samoth) was sentenced to sixteen months in prison for burning down the Skjold Church with Vikernes. In total, seven churches in Norway were set aflame by black metal musicians.

COUNT GRISHNACKH: Originally, [Skjold Church] was an old pagan holy site where our forefathers used to celebrate the sun. And what the Christians did was move this church from another place and put it not close to this holy site but on top of it in the midst of the circle, actually breaking up the circle. And on the pagan site they put a big stone cross. So if they have no respect for the Norwegian culture, why on earth should Norwegians respect *their* culture?

CRONOS: Look, civilized creatures on this planet who have all gone to school and learned about society should know the difference between burning churches and fantasy. We are entertainers—if I wanted to be a murderer or a Satanist, I'd do that full time instead of playing songs for a living.

ALICE COOPER: Now, if you're in Norway and you want to have any kind of authority or credibility in metal, you have to eat your lead singer. It's like rap: if you don't shoot somebody you can't really be a rapper. I love these advertisements in metal magazines for all these bands that are trying to be more evil than the other band, or they're trying to be more Celtic or more occult. It's just hysterical. These guys are role-playing for a couple years, and then they turn into something else. They go, "We are Gothora, and we are Vikings!" No, you're not. You're not Vikings at all. Vikings don't go to McDonald's.

IHSAHN: Metal has always been about the opposition, breaking with the rules. That's why metal has always been associated

with the devil. For each decade, when something gets accepted
you need to go to more extreme forms to create the same
effect—the break from conformity. We were all influenced
by each other, then someone took the leap with the church
burnings, and the flame ignited. You have to remember, we
were teenagers. Euronymous was twenty-three and the rest of
us were late teens, and some were twenty. You're very impressionable at that age.

In the mid-nineties, Emperor was temporarily crippled by the
extracurricular activities of the Inner Circle. In 1994, in addition
to Samoth's jail sentence, bassist Terje Vik Schei (aka Tchort) was
arrested for burglary, knife assault, and grave desecration, and sentenced to two years. And in August 1994, drummer Bård Eithun
(aka Faust) was sentenced to fourteen years in jail for killing a
stranger, Magne Andreassen, in the woods outside of Lillehammer.
He was released in 2002 after serving nine years and four months
of his sentence.

FAUST: I was walking back home again [after going out to
drink]. This man approached me. He was obviously drunk and
obviously a faggot. He asked me if we could leave this place
and go up to the woods. So I agreed, because already then I
had decided that I wanted to kill him. I [had] a black knife
with a handgrip. He was walking behind me and I turned
around and stabbed him in the stomach. He went down on his
knees. I started stabbing him in the neck and face. Then he lay
down and I was standing over him stabbing.

IHSAHN [1994 interview]: I was not surprised at all when Samoth
was involved in the church burnings and Faust was accused of
murder. Faust has been obsessed with serial killers and murder
for quite some time, so when this homosexual made a pass
at him in a park in Lillehammer, he took the opportunity to
experience the thrill of the kill. Personally, I think human life

has very little value in itself, and that it's the relationship you have to people that give them value. One can only experience emotional affection through one's own senses. Thus, the death of someone outside my range of personal relations has no emotional effect on me.

FAUST: All I care about now is making flesh-ripping metal again with Mongo Ninja, Blood Tsunami, and Aborym.

The most infamous and dramatic crime in black metal history took place on August 10, 1993, when Count Grishnackh murdered Euronymous. While the two extreme musicians started as comrades, some believe they became locked in a power struggle to control the Inner Circle. Others claim Grishnackh was irate because Euronymous owed him money. Grishnackh insists he was acting in self-defense and that Euronymous was already planning to kill him.

FROST: At first, Varg and Euronymous seemed to be the best of friends. Varg even recorded all the bass parts on Mayhem's excellent *De Mysteriis Dom Sathanas* [after Necrobutcher left the band]. The rivalry started later. Irritation became anger and just escalated.

GRUTLE KJELLSON: People felt threatened by Euronymous because of the controversial things he said in interviews on radio and, obviously, because he was trying to establish this so-called "black circle." But it was more or less just a PR stunt. I don't think he had any actual enemies—well, except for one, obviously.

HELLHAMMER: I didn't believe that it was going to such extremes, but to other people it could likely have gone the other way. Euronymous told *me* that he was going to have Grishnackh killed.

COUNT GRISHNACKH: In 1991, most of the metal musicians in Norway believed Euronymous was a so-called cool guy, but in mid- or late 1992, most of us realized that he was not. When his label released the Burzum debut album in March 1992, he had to take a loan to pay for it; he [borrowed] the money from me. When he sold all the Burzum albums he paid his private bills rather than print more records—or pay me back the money he owed me—and I never saw any royalties either. When the record sold out, he had no money to print more records. This is probably the reason why some people think I killed him for money, but certainly I wouldn't have gotten my money back by killing him. Breaking his legs would probably have worked, but not killing him.

HELLHAMMER: I didn't see Varg very much at the end. But he was writing letters to Euronymous. I know he and Euronymous were angry at each other. I just didn't know how angry.

COUNT GRISHNACKH: For some months this dislike for Euronymous spread in the metal scene, as more and more people understood what a moron he was, and he blamed me for all of this and started to hate me. He believed it was my fault people lost their respect for him. In a sense he was right, as I certainly didn't keep my opinions a secret, but I think he brought that upon himself. He had made a fool of himself. Further, when the media wrote all that crap about me it made him feel less important. Suddenly he was no longer the main character in the hardcore metal scene. As he saw it, that, too, was all my fault.

HELLHAMMER: One night, Count Grishnackh broke into Euronymous's house and stabbed him, like, thirty times. He stabbed him in the face right under the eye, and he had to put his foot on his face to get the knife back out again.

DANI FILTH: Before that happened, no one outside of a small following in Norway knew who Mayhem were, and then suddenly he went from Anonymous to Euronymous all over the world.

KERRANG! MAGAZINE (August 1993): Euronymous, 25, died from multiple stab wounds. He was found dead on the staircase outside his Oslo flat at 5:15 a.m. on August 10.

COUNT GRISHNACKH: Euronymous had begun to plot against my life. He wanted to kill me. In his view I was the problem, so by killing me he believed the problem would go away. His problem was that he included a few metal people in his plot to kill me, and they told me. He had told them because he trusted them, but obviously they had warmer feelings for me than for him. At one point he phoned Snorre [Ruch], who lived in my apartment, and Snorre let me listen to what Euronymous had to say. He told Snorre, "Varg must disappear for good" and similar, confirming the plans others had told me about earlier.

TOM ARAYA: For a lead singer of one band to kill the leader of another band—where does that come from? They're in another mind frame. They're tapped into something else and everything they see is different. Those people have issues.

COUNT GRISHNACKH: A lot of people claimed that I overreacted because Euronymous was such a wimp and didn't have the guts to kill me. Sure, he was a wimp, but I took the threats seriously in this instance because instead of telling everyone like he usually did, he only told a very few people he trusted, his closest friends—or those he believed were his closest friends. On top of that, he'd been convicted of injuring two people with a broken bottle because they had "looked at his girlfriend" at a bus stop and was about to go to prison for four months. With his back against the wall he was capable of executing his plans. If scared enough, even the biggest cowards become dangerous.

LEE BARRETT (head of Candlelight Records, ex–Extreme Noise Terror): Euronymous' death was harsh and brutal, which reflects perfectly on his life. He will be missed by some, but remembered by all.

COUNT GRISHNACKH: The same day [Euronymous] told Snorre about his intentions to kill me, I received a letter from him, where he pretended to be very positive and wanted to meet me to discuss a contract I had not yet signed. This was the only excuse he had to contact me, and it seemed like he was trying to set me up. According to his friends, the plan was to meet me, knock me out with a stun gun, tie me up, and put me in the trunk of a car. He would then drive into the countryside, tie me to a tree, and torture me to death while videotaping everything. My reaction to this was naturally anger. Who the hell did he think he was? The same day I decided to drive to Oslo, hand him the signed contract, and tell him to fuck off, basically, and by doing so take away all the excuses he had to contact me ever again.

KERRANG! MAGAZINE: Police suspect that Euronymous knew his killer or killers, and had admitted them into his apartment. Euronymous' body was found dead only in underwear.

COUNT GRISHNACKH: [Snorre and I] went to the front door of the building block and I rang his doorbell. Euronymous was sleeping. You might think that visiting people in the middle of the night was a bit strange, but it was perfectly normal for us. A lot of people in the metal scene were nocturnal creatures. He said, "I am sleeping. Can't you come back later?" I said, "I got the contract. Let me in," and he buzzed me in. His flat was on the fourth floor and I began climbing the stairs. Snorre wanted to have a cigarette, and since he couldn't smoke in Euronymous's apartment or my car, he waited downstairs to have one.

KERRANG! MAGAZINE: According to police, the act of murder began in the victim's fourth-floor apartment. Blood tracks began in Euronymous' hallway.

COUNT GRISHNACKH: Euronymous was waiting for me in the entrance looking very nervous, and I handed him the contract. Of course he was nervous. The guy he planned to murder showed up at his doorstep in the middle of the night. I then asked him what the fuck he was up to, and when I took a step forward, he panicked. He freaked out and attacked me with a kick in the chest. I simply threw him to the floor, and was a bit stunned. I wasn't stunned by his kick, but by the fact he had attacked me. I didn't expect that. Not in his apartment, and not like that. He had just started to train in kickboxing, and like all beginners, thought he had become Bruce Lee overnight.

FAUST: That's bullshit. There's no reason why Øystein would attack Vikernes after he'd just woken up, still in his underwear. He wouldn't do it. I can understand [the self-defense claim] though, because Vikernes wanted to get away from a twenty-one-year first-degree murder sentence. It's a natural move—it was the same with me in court. [When I committed murder] I tried to get away from it by claiming self-defense.

COUNT GRISHNACKH: He jumped from the floor and dashed for the kitchen. I knew there was a knife lying on the kitchen table. I jumped in front of him and managed to stop him before he got his hands on it. He ran for the bedroom, and I figured he was going for another weapon. He had some weeks earlier told people he would soon get the shotgun back from the police that Dead used to shoot himself, so I figured he was going for that or his stun gun. I gave chase and stabbed him with my pocketknife with an 8-centimeter blade. I was a bit surprised when he ran out of the apartment. It made no sense to flee, and it made me angry to know that he had started the fight, but the moment it didn't go his way he decided to flee instead of fighting like a man.

KERRANG! MAGAZINE: Several of the victim's neighbors were awakened by the sound of a struggle at approximately 3 a.m. but had dismissed the noise as a drunken brawl.

COUNT GRISHNACKH: Outside, we ran into Snorre, who had finished his cigarette. All the doors looked the same, and Snorre was pretty absent-minded and ended up one floor up by mistake. Confused, he had gone back down and used his lighter to try to read the door sign and figure out if this was the right apartment. As he was doing so, Euronymous came running out in his underwear, bleeding and screaming like a madman.

SNORRE RUCH (Thorns, ex-Mayhem): [I think one reason Varg killed Euronymous is because] he was envious of Bard [Faust] because Bard had killed a man and Varg hadn't. Varg was saying that what Bard had done was uncool, but inside the scene, Bard's actions commanded respect. . . . The Count said it was no big deal to kill someone.

COUNT GRISHNACKH: Euronymous ran down a flight of stairs and stopped to ring the neighbor's doorbell. He quickly real-ized that I had come after him, so he continued to flee down the stairs, knocking on the walls, trying to ring the doorbells as he ran past them, screaming for help. I stabbed him three or four times in his left shoulder as he ran—that was the only part I could hit while we were running. He stumbled and broke a lamp on the wall and fell into the glass fragments in his underwear. I ran past him and waited. Snorre was so surprised and terrified he looked like a ghost and as if his eyeballs were about to fall out of his head. He had a blackout and didn't remember anything until I later asked him if he was okay. By then Euronymous was back on his feet. He looked resigned and said, "That's enough," but then he tried to kick me again, and I finished him off by thrusting the knife into his forehead through his skull, killing him instantaneously. His eyes rolled back in his head and he moaned as his lungs emptied and he fell to a sitting position with the knife still stuck in his forehead. I held him up as I held on to the knife and when I jerked it out he fell forward and rolled down a flight of stairs like a sack of potatoes, making enough noise to wake up the whole neighborhood. He had intended to kill me, and I did not feel bad for killing him. His cowardice made me angry and I saw no reason to let him live. Had I, he only would have made another attempt on my life later on.

HELLHAMMER: On the day of Euronymous's death I called him at the office. Nobody picked up the phone. Then I called his parents, hoping to reach him there. I was told that Euronymous was murdered the night before. I was shocked. I didn't know who did it, but I was sure it could be the Swedes. There were constant conflicts among Norwegian, Swedish, and Finnish clans. Dead bodies were found everywhere. My friends and I got knives and guns and prepared to defend ourselves. We were waiting for the worst to happen. But soon we learned that Grishnackh had murdered Euronymous. That shy boy turned out to be a killer. The police had their suspicions. They watched him and watched him, and one day while he was walking down the street in Bergen with some friends they arrested him.

SILENOZ: The day Euronymous was murdered I went to the post office to pick up a package he had sent me with some T-shirts and a new CD. As I'm walking into the convenience store I see the story all over the front page of the newspapers. It was kind of weird to experience that at age seventeen.

FROST: Lives turned upside down, and it was a while before I was able to take in what had happened. But I had started to go down a pretty dark alley of my own, and it was impossible to really shock me at that point. As a young person, I felt such an affinity for darkness that I wasn't able to separate what was constructive and what was destructive.

MORGAN HÅKANSSON: One of the basic ideas of the Inner Circle was that we should send a message that we were not like them. There are no limitations when you have an enemy. Why should you limit yourself from doing certain things? If you have to commit murder as part of your ideology, then so be it. To Varg, it was an internal problem that got solved.

HELLHAMMER: For all the new bands, it was kind of sad because they didn't have Euronymous to lead them anymore. And that was a shame. When Euronymous was alive it was his duty to see that all the bands coming from Norway were authentic. Posers were told to quit, and a couple of bands did. The Norway scene has been blown out of proportion. There are hundreds of black metal bands coming out of Norway made of sixteen-year-olds. I laugh about it, but Euronymous really had done something to keep the music pure. The positive thing about it is it's clear that he got Mayhem very much attention, PR-wise. It was the same thing when Dead died. Euronymous said band-wise it wasn't so great, but the hype for us was cool. It was the same with Euronymous. We were friends, but I wasn't upset when he was killed.

I think that death is only natural. I don't think death is sad or anything to be upset about. I was thinking about it after he died and I think he maybe didn't have that much more to give, so maybe he just died at the right point.

Count Grishnackh and Faust weren't the only black metal musicians to commit murder. In July 1997, the front man of Swedish death/black metal band Dissection, Jon Nödtveidt, was convicted of helping to kill thirty-eight-year-old Algerian Josef Ben Meddour, a gay man, and of possessing an illegal firearm. The story of the murder was chronicled in the movie *Keiler's Park*. Nödtveidt was released from prison in 2004 and relaunched Dissection, but committed suicide in August 2006, claiming he had accomplished all he set out to do with the band and had nothing left to live for. It would be easy to dismiss Nödtveidt as a sadistic, homophobic Satanist, but like Count Grishnackh and Faust, he was a musical pioneer, creating a fiery hybrid of melodic, symphonic black metal on two highly influential albums: 1993's *The Somberlain* and 1995's *Storm of the Light's Bane*.

JON NÖDTVEIDT (1975–2006) (Dissection) [2006 interview]: My lifestyle was always about breaking boundaries and reaching beyond a normal level of existence. I always put the emphasis on Satanism, since that's the reason why I'm playing music.

ANDERS BJÖRLER (ex–At the Gates, Haunted): Dissection were really close friends. In the mid-nineties they moved down to Gothenburg [Sweden]. Jon was a good musician and a really nice guy. He was like the prankster in the class. The image that's being presented doesn't fit because he was so friendly. There was a shimmer of darkness somewhere inside of him, especially when he was writing and listening to music. You noticed that side sometimes, but overall he was very positive and very bright. He loved to make prank calls—picking up the phonebook, pointing at a name, and pretending to be from the electric company—just stupid, funny stuff. I didn't think he was homophobic. I think they were high on amphetamines and drunk. I don't think [he would have committed murder] if he was sober. Never. It was like 4 a.m. and they had been up for 24 hours partying, and one thing led to another. Of course, the reports said they had planned this sort of ritualistic murder, but I never knew that side of him.

JON NÖDTVEIDT: No matter how you twist and turn it, [what I did] can't be undone. I must move forward with my life. I have taken responsibility for my actions by having served my time in prison. I'm not proud of the fact that I have to watch my mother cry, but I'm working with new strength and looking ahead.

ANDERS BJÖRLER: I talked to Jon a couple of weeks after he got out of prison and he was a totally changed person. He was strange and very cold. I wasn't very shocked when I found out he killed himself.

EXPRESSEN NEWSPAPER, August 19, 2006: At 7:21 p.m. CET [Central European Time] on Wednesday [August 16], a police patrol reported to the police communication center in Stockholm that a man had been found dead, the apparent victim of a self-inflicted gunshot wound. According to several of *Expressen*'s sources, the singer had placed an open copy of *The Satanic Bible* in front of him before pulling the trigger. "He shot himself in the head and lay dead in a ring of lit candles," says a police source. At 5:44 p.m. on Wednesday, the police received a 911 call from Jon Nödtveidt's family, who hadn't been able to establish contact with him for a couple of days.

It's hard to imagine that an underground music scene that ignited in Scandinavia yielded at least two suicides, three murders, seven church burnings, and numerous incarcerations and lawsuits. It would be easier to understand if the musicians had been gang members or condemned sociopaths. But for the most part they were just naïve young men whose foolish, impulsive actions had dire consequences.

GRUTLE KJELLSON: I guess it's kind of easy for a young and somewhat disturbed mind to commit crimes in order to be accepted and looked up to. That's not only happening in black metal. It's happened many times before in history. There are lots of equivalents to such actions. So there was nothing special about this.

SILENOZ: People were really impressionable and it felt like it was a competition to see who could be more extreme than the next guy. Sooner or later that's going to turn into action somehow, and that's exactly what happened. I'm glad we kept our heads cool, so to speak. We subconsciously made a decision to concentrate on the music and stay away from trouble.

IHSAHN: The whole philosophy and idealism within the black metal scene was about feeling nothing, which is kind of a paradox because in your teens you feel absolutely everything. You're in emotional turmoil and you have an ideal where you want to handle everything with absolute control and not feel remorse, not feel regret, not feel anything. There's this idea of absolute coldness.

Along with the rash of hate, church burnings, and murders came a flood of media attention. After the first wave of arson, the UK's weekly *Kerrang!* ran a six-page story on black metal that sparked public interest, and after Euronymous was murdered, the story of the crime spread throughout Europe, and then to America. The bizarre nature of the Inner Circle crimes and the extreme quality of the music appealed to audiences seeking more intensity in metal; the harsh reality of black metal proved too tempting to resist. Some argue that the media attention stripped the scene of substance, but it certainly didn't affect the music's popularity. Black metal became Norway's leading musical export; existing bands across the globe gained popularity, and new bands spread across the landscape like a virus.

COUNT GRISHNACKH: I am no friend of the modern so-called black metal culture. It is a tasteless, lowbrow parody of Norwegian so-called black metal circa 1991–1992, and if it was up to me it would meet its dishonorable end as soon as possible. However, rather than abandon my own music because others have soiled its name by claiming to have something in common with it, I will stick with it. The "black metallers" will probably continue to get loaded, get high, and in all other manners, too, behave like the stereotypical Negro; they will probably continue to get foreign tribal tattoos, dress, walk, talk, look, and act like homosexuals, and so forth. Some of the "black metallers," their fans, and accomplices will probably even continue to pretend—and actually believe—they have something in common with Burzum, but let me assure you they don't.

DANI FILTH: Black metal became a cliché because the whole thing started with passionate bands that probably didn't have enough money to get a great production. So that's been the formula for wave upon wave of bands to imitate. And when you're imitating bands, you're not putting your own distinctive mark on your music.

FROST: There have been times we felt that the whole scene was heading the wrong way, like '97, '98, '99. The scene was permeated by this goth influence, and black metal was suddenly all about synthesizers and these large, pompous orchestrations and female vocals and harmonies and melody, and everything was so soft and so gothic and so romantic. It felt like black metal was becoming some sort of anachronism, and there was this general misunderstanding of what the genre was about and where it came from.

FENRIZ: Wherever there is money, people want a part of it. For me, that killed it—like a party that's cool and then all the idiots arrive.

IHSAHN: If you look at the scene as an artistic movement, and see the music, the imagery, the makeup, the crimes, the church burnings, and the murders as an expression, it's all really, really extreme, and it affected a lot of people and got lots of attention. We had this youthful confidence and energy when we were doing *In the Nightside Eclipse* [in 1993] and *Anthems to the Welkin at Dusk* [in 1997], and that empowerment shines through even today.

GRUTLE KJELLSON: Everybody opened their eyes to the Norwegian metal scene [after the arsons and the murders]. Everyone was in shock and everything from Norway was suddenly exciting. But after a while, when the media lost interest, a lot of bands disappeared and people thought that most of the bands coming out of Norway had no quality and were mostly copycats, so a lot of bands lost followers. The remaining bands from Norway are mostly the same ones who started the whole thing. We suffered for a long time because the press did not pay attention to the music. We were labeled as criminals and Satanists—the whole bunch of us, all the bands. It was like that until 2002 or 2003. Then the press opened their eyes and discovered that there was actually some musical quality overshadowed by all of those crimes.

SILENOZ: We got discriminated against a lot. We got in trouble with the police unfairly. They stopped us on the street when we were wearing bullet belts and had the biggest upside down crosses we could carry. They said, "Hey, you come with us," and we were like, "Why?" And they just spit in our face. [Our vocalist] Shaggy was in jail for two days and I was in an interrogation room for eight hours. It was horrible, but it just made us stronger.

ABBATH: When the music got more popular again, some of the fans got more crazy, too. This guy in a club in Germany cut his wrist just to get attention from the band. He went to the hospital and he never got to see the band at all [*laughs*].

FAUST: There are many groups that have turned black metal into a parody, but a few bands still manage to create that magic fire. . . . I know a band like Deathspell Omega would be something of a wet dream for Euronmyous; 1349 are doing it well, and so are Slagmaur, Forgotten Tomb, Impiety, Urgehal, Watain, Necrophobic, Wolves in the Throne Room, Blut Aus Nord, Malfeitor, and Black Witchery.

One of the most popular Norwegian black metal acts today is Dimmu Borgir, but despite their heaviness and dedication to darkness, some members of the old guard consider them charlatans. Dimmu released their debut, *For All Tid*, in 1994. Eleven years later they were one of the highlights at America's leading summer metal music festival, Ozzfest, playing a style of grandiose, orchestral black metal that capitalized on the achievements of Emperor and Cradle of Filth.

FENRIZ: After people started calling bands like Dimmu Borgir and Cradle of Filth black metal, the most black metal thing to do was to quit playing black metal, and since 2005 we have our own style, freestyle, mostly speed metal/heavy metal-punk.

SILENOZ: I don't care if anyone has a problem with us. We've always looked at ourselves as the odd one, the black sheep in the family. But I always considered us a lot more than just black metal, even since the beginning. Of course, everything was simpler and straight to the point back then, but I think we've shown a huge progression that leads beyond any borders or categorization.

NERGAL: Dimmu are still honest and they still do what they feel like doing. There's nothing wrong with becoming big in the black metal scene and spreading the word. Those who think that black metal should stay in the garage and that the message should remain very hermetic and be spread to just a small amount of people are narrow-minded. The whole point is to spread your music to the people that don't know what the message is. How many times can you repeat the same shit to the same people?

12

WHEN DARKNESS FALLS: METALCORE, 1992–2006

In the early 2000s, a batch of bands from opposite coasts combined thrash and death metal rhythms, virtuosic guitar leads reminiscent of Iron Maiden and Judas Priest, and vocals that veered from ferocious hardcore to soaring melodic eighties metal. After nearly a decade of gestation, Killswitch Engage, All That Remains, Shadows Fall, Underoath, Atreyu, and Avenged Sevenfold arose from the underground and gained varying degrees of mainstream acclaim. Still, it's too simple to describe metalcore as a mere hybrid of metal and hardcore. The progenitors of the movement were just as inspired by the dissonance of American post-punk and noise-rock. Other bands incorporated avant-metal prog rock, straight-edge, and/or screamo. What they all shared was a commitment to inspire crowds on an emotional and physical level.

KEITH BUCKLEY (Every Time I Die): The whole metalcore thing started [in the late eighties and early nineties] with bands like Earth Crisis, Deadguy, Converge, Coalesce, and Cave In. On a disharmonic, technical level, the music had a frenzied feel to it that was totally new. They abandoned song structure and took their own approach to making music, and they really paved the way for bands like us.

STEVE AUSTIN (Today Is the Day): Whenever I see guys playing odd–time–signature–, heavy–type noise, I feel a sense of pride of being an old cat. We came around at a strange time in music. After Nirvana got big, there wasn't really a band that took superextreme elements of Earache–type [grindcore] and infused them with the weird off–time rhythms of bands like Jesus Lizard and Big Black. I think our [1993] album *Supernova* is the first one that did that. When we came through Connecticut, kids in the band Deadguy said that we really threw a loop in the hardcore scene as far as what could be done and what couldn't.

KARL BEUCHNER (Earth Crisis): I grew up loving the power of metal and connecting with a lot of the positive, straight–edge ideas that were being put forward by hardcore bands in the early eighties. So when [guitarist] Scott [Crouse] and I started writing and composing [in Syracuse, New York, in 1991], we put together what we felt were the best aspects of both of those genres. And we had lyrics about terrorism or wars for resources or territory, animal rights, and environmentalism. Plus, we were drug–free and committed to the straight–edge idealism, which made us different than a lot of bands.

RYAN DOWNEY (band manager, journalist): The first true metalcore band was [Cleveland, Ohio's] Integrity, which drew equally from Cro-Mags and Judge. They formed in 1988 and they were very influential to Killswitch Engage and a lot of other bands. And they had a totally punk rock fuck-you attitude.

DWID HELLION (Integrity): I am a personally focused terrorist of destructive artistic creation. [I'm] not interested in acceptance, conformity, nor praise. If and when my music begins to rub the world the wrong way, then I am truly in my element. My musical interest has always been aggressive, metallic punk with noise and other extreme elements intertwined within—threatening sounds for hopeless souls. Whatever it has been misconstrued as by the mainstream is not of my own design. There are those who know and feel what I am creating, and there are those who only hear loud music.

BRIAN FAIR (ex-Overcast, Shadows Fall): When Overcast started [in Boston] in 1990, we were stealing ideas from Integrity and Starkweather. They were some of the first bands I heard who had amazing melodic singing *and* brutal screaming, and I loved Coalesce and Converge. It was an exciting time for music because that was before anyone was getting trapped into a formula.

JACOB BANNON (Converge): We've been doing this for twenty years, so we don't align ourselves with anyone. We have always been on the outer fringes of the community, as much as we are responsible for unintentionally influencing a lot of it. We don't see ourselves as peers of a lot of the bands we get credit for influencing. Some of them in spirit, sure, and in heart and approach, but certainly not in sound.

JESSE LEACH (Killswitch Engage, Times of Grace): Converge was great, but New Jersey's Rorschach was also there [in 1989] right when hardcore was starting to fuse with metal. And I'd have to say they were probably the biggest influence for any of the bands in the scene. They did it before anyone else, and didn't get the credit they deserved.

CHARLES MAGGIO (Rorschach): We were all coming out of a scene of bands like Youth of Today and Bold, who were pissed off by people not being straight-edge. Then I got sick with cancer—Hodgkin's disease—and it opened up a whole new slew of anger trigger points: cigarette smoking, socialized medicine, mortality, death. Things got darker. I had eight months of chemotherapy. It was two treatments a month, and I scheduled them on Mondays so that I would be recovered to go to the shows on weekends. I came out of it a changed man. I felt invincible, impervious to the petty things that affect mortal people. . . . And we were lucky enough to have generated enough in-band ill will toward each other to break up while we were still doing something seemingly valid. A lot of bands don't have that kind of luck.

As the late nineties gave way to the new millennium, two distinct scenes emerged that were more musically focused and that often incorporated strong doses of melody. The first developed around a region that extended from Boston to Western Massachusetts, and the other was in the far smaller area of Orange County in Southern California. The former adhered to the sounds, but generally not the straight-edge ethic, of Earth Crisis and Rorschach, while most Cali bands, including Eighteen Visions, Throwdown, and Bleeding Through—at least at first—were clean, sober, and sonically brutal.

MIKE D'ANTONIO (Overcast, Killswitch Engage): Western Massachusetts is the little scene that could. It's absolutely bizarre that so many bands made it so far, given that we were all just playing music for the love of it. You'd be playing with these other bands and then the next week you'd find out that a member left one band to go to another band, and members would swap out all the time. It seems like this big thing, but it's really been a core of about fifty or sixty kids that were all friends that played together that intermingle and are very incestuous.

MATT BACHAND (ex-Exhumed, Shadows Fall): We were all kids and we didn't have cars, and Boston was two hours away, so we had to create our own scene with shows at the Green Field Grange and Katina's and Pearl Street and all these clubs that were around in Western Massachusetts.

ADAM DUTKIEWICZ (Aftershock, Killswitch Engage): I listened to a lot of DC and New York hardcore. But I was also way into early Metallica and Slayer, so for Aftershock, I took all that stuff and squished it together.

SYNYSTER GATES (Avenged Sevenfold): We liked hardcore, but we *loved* the classics: Iron Maiden, Guns N' Roses, Metallica, Pantera. We were also into progressive stuff like Mr. Bungle and Dream Theater. That's where we get our crazy musical transitions.

BRIAN FAIR: One cool thing about this scene is I don't think it's based on anger, like death metal. Even when I was younger and I was into hardcore, I wasn't angry, I was just into this aggressive release of youthful energy. Some people played football, I went to hardcore shows. I had a nice suburban life. I was getting laid, so I was having a good time. But there was this aggression that I released whether I was skateboarding or listening to hardcore or metal. Even at our shows, we're trying to have as much fun as possible onstage. It's not about smash, kill, destroy. It's more like let's fuckin' drink beer and rock out.

BRANDAN SCHIEPPATI (ex-Eighteen Visions, ex-Throwdown, Bleeding Through, I Am War, Sorrows): I've gotten to where I have today because of my anger about things that I have gone through and the damage of everyday life. We play an angry, scary type of music, and that's exactly how we feel. I use emotional strife as a driving point for everything I do, especially in Bleeding Through.

ALEX VARKATZAS (I Am War, Atreyu): I'm a really high-stressed, crazy person. I lose my mind sometimes and the anger keeps me going when I'm too tired and depressed. I just rely on being fucking mad. I'd rather be pissed off than be happy with a shit-eating grin on my face.

MIKE D'ANTONIO: Everything was an extension of skateboarding. You look at all the other skateboarders wearing shirts with skulls on them, then you follow that trail to find out who the band is, and it turns out to be the Misfits or Cro-Mags, and you go out and buy their records. A lot of the punk and metal album art really helped me gravitate towards that style of music. When I was a kid, I went to a technical high school and joined the graphics program so I could help my friends with their demo and seven-inch covers, getting them printed for free and making paper stickers for my buddies who needed promo items for their bands. That's what motivated me to go into the art industry.

RYAN CLARK (Demon Hunter): My brother [and former guitarist] Don and I have a design company [in Seattle] called Invisible Creatures. I do most of the stuff on Tooth & Nail and Solid State, and Don has done Bullet for My Valentine, Foo Fighters, Chris Cornell. We got asked to design a Cradle of Filth record, but we turned them down because we're devout Christians and we knew it was gonna get into some pretty weird territory.

Revisionist historians tend to lump the biggest New England metalcore bands together. But the members of Killswitch Engage, Shadows Fall, and All That Remains grew up in different bands in various areas of Massachusetts. Boston's Overcast, which often toured Western Massachusetts, and Westfield's Aftershock were the scene's pioneers. The former was more chaotic and hardcore-based, with a definable metal edge, and the latter was more firmly rooted in thrash and melodic death metal.

MIKE D'ANTONIO: I went to a high school graduation party for someone I didn't know and [Overcast vocalist] Brian [Fair] was there as well as drummer Jay Fitzgerald. Brian and I got along and we started to skateboard together. I asked him if he wanted to go to a Leeway show at the Channel in Boston the next day. He was only a sophomore in high school, so his mom called me to make sure I wasn't some weirdo taking her son away from her. We began hanging out a lot. He was playing bass and singing in a punk rock band called Frenzy. I recorded them and said, "Hey, there's this other stuff out there that we could try playing if you want to do something when we're not skateboarding." That's how Overcast started in [1990].

PHIL LABONTE (ex–Shadows Fall, All That Remains): Western Mass. was pretty tame. There are multiple dudes in bands from the area that didn't lose their virginity until they were far older than twenty. We were not the ragers. We were the nerds practicing our instruments for hours and hours.

MIKE D'ANTONIO: The funny thing is, we didn't have a musical direction at all when we were writing songs [for Overcast]. We were putting things together almost at random, so it took quite a few years to figure out where we wanted the band to go. We took on that evil Integrity attitude about hating the world and being down on your luck. Then bands started popping, like Starkweather in Philadelphia. They were huge for us. We looked up to the way they jumped from one type of a genre to another in an instant and gave the listener a bit of whiplash. Also, [Brooklyn's] Candiria was a force to be reckoned with. They were throwing as many different styles of music into their songs as possible, and that's something that Overcast got a little *too* caught up in—the breakneck swerves and turns that we tried to purposely put into our music so that the listener didn't know what was coming next.

Even as they combined various American music styles, early Massachusetts metalcore bands were also inspired by emerging Swedish melodic death metal groups, including At the Gates, In Flames, and Dark Tranquility, all of which combined raw musicality with uplifting harmonies. Once Aftershock's Adam Dutkiewicz blended these ingredients with soaring melodic choruses, almost every other band in the scene followed suit.

BRIAN FAIR: As we all got to be better musicians, we all wanted to try to do this tricky, crazy stuff we were hearing from these Swedish bands. The Massachusetts sound really came from that transition from being a traditional hardcore band to playing more in a metal style and straight up improving as musicians. You may have wanted to do some of that shit when you were younger, but the only thing you could play was a simple E chord chug mosh part. I listen to early Overcast shit now and I'm like, "Wow, we were lucky if we could pull off the world's worst Cro-Mags cover when we started." Back then, people were just like, "Get the fuck off the stage. Why are you singing and screaming? You guys suck. Your guitar player has long hair."

ADAM DUTKIEWICZ: My brother Toby was the vocalist in Aftershock and everyone [else] went to the same high school and grew up in the same area. We were all friends anyway, so we started playing music together. By late junior year of high school, I discovered melodic death metal, and that had a huge effect on my songwriting. My gateway drugs were Carcass and At the Gates, which got me into the whole melodic style of riffing, and after that I fell in love with that whole European style of melodic death metal.

PHIL LABONTE (All That Remains): If you want to boil all of Western Mass. down to one dude, you can do it, and his name's Adam D. Every single successful band that's come out of Western Massachusetts somehow is connected to Adam. When Adam was sixteen, he was in Aftershock with Jon Donais, who's now in Shadows Fall. I filled in on guitar for Aftershock for a while. Adam produced two Unearth records, including their biggest one [*The Oncoming Storm*]. He's done the Acacia Strain and three All That Remains records [and the latest Shadows Fall album]. He'll deny it all day long, but it all comes back to him.

MATT BACHAND: I've never met a more talented dude in my life. The guy can pick up an instrument he's never seen before and play it fluently in ten minutes. One time, Aftershock's drummer couldn't get to Connecticut for a gig, and Adam said, "Fuck it, I'll just play drums." I filled in on guitar for that show. I remember rehearsing in his bedroom in his parents' house when he was a high school senior. And the kid is just nailing it on the kit. I was thinking, "I didn't even know you *played* drums." And he's got a stand-up bass in the corner. I was like, "Jesus Christ, who *is* this guy?"

ADAM DUTKIEWICZ: It's so funny. People sometimes come up and say, "I used to see you in Aftershock. You guys were so influential." I'm like, "Influential? Dude, really? You weren't in our shoes, trust me." We'd play anywhere in the Northeast, and we were guaranteed to *not* have more than ten people there who would be into it. We played basements that had just one light bulb for illumination. It was one tragedy after another. My brother, [vocalist] Tobias, got hit in the head and had to get stitches. We had tons of van breakdowns, and we got all of our drum gear stolen. It felt like we were cursed from the start.

BRIAN FAIR: We had to have an "all for one and one for all" vibe because we were literally playing for the guys in the other bands that were also playing the show. Mike [D'Antonio] used to have shows in his living room. We would get four bands together and drag over three or four of our other close friends and get a case of beer. It wasn't even underground. It was underwater, for chrissakes. But that's what made it really special. And it's special that people still give a shit about it. It makes you feel like those long rides in a Ford Escort pulling a trailer out of a kit we built from Home Depot were totally worth it.

MIKE D'ANTONIO: There were lots of times in Overcast when we'd drive for eight hours and play a house show for five kids, or show up to a place and the door would be locked. No one even cared to put up flyers or cancel the show. It was rough, but fun at the same time. It felt like we were paving a new way for ourselves, learning as we went. We didn't know anything about booking agents or riders; we were lucky if we got water onstage in cups, poured from a tap.

PHIL LABONTE: I was playing guitar in Perpetual Doom [starting in 1992] and then nu metal happened. Those guys wanted to play nu metal, and I said, "No way. I want to do death metal." So I quit, and for a year I worked in an auto parts store, but I was also hanging around with Matt [Bachand], who formed Shadows Fall [in 1995, with guitarist Jon Donais after Aftershock broke up]. I went to their second show with a buddy of mine, and I remember telling him, "Dude, that band's going to be big." And by "big," I meant they were going to be signed and sell ten thousand or twenty thousand records someday.

MATT BACHAND: Our old singer Damien [McPherson] was gravitating more towards nu metal. The way he was putting shit together seemed more Korn/Limp Bizkit to me, which was the most unappealing thing in the world because I was trying to start a *metal* band. I immediately thought of replacing him with Phil [Labonte], who I had been hanging out with. It's so funny, because originally Phil didn't *want* to sing. He just wanted to play guitar. He used to do backup vocals with Perpetual Doom a lot, so I said, "Look, man, you can sing. You've got a front man's personality. Give it a shot."

PHIL LABONTE: When Damien quit in 1996 they asked me to join and I said, "Well hell yeah." It's funny 'cause later, they were like, "Yo, can you do stuff like Brian from Overcast?" I should have seen the writing on the wall.

Early metalcore tours were sparsely attended, but musicians seeking action and misadventure (rather than fame and fortune) usually came home with great stories—some humorous, others horrific.

MATT BACHAND: Shadows Fall did a mini-tour with Overcast when Phil [Labonte] was still singing for us. We got strip-searched in Canada. They ripped the van apart and threw shit everywhere. Then they found a pebble or something and claimed it was a pot seed. It could have been anything. They were just looking for an excuse to fuck with us because they knew we were coming into the country to play shows, and whoever booked the tour gave us paperwork that said we were going there to record an album. So we see this guy come around the corner with a rubber glove on. Phil was the first one to go in. He went into the room and came out with a miserable look on his face, but he couldn't tell us what happened. He had to sit on the other side while we went in one by one. When it was my turn I was expecting the worst. They said, "Well, we can't touch you." But they made me drop my drawers, bend over and they looked up my asshole with a flashlight. And we still didn't get into the country because one of the band members had a rap sheet longer than he was tall, filled with stupid childhood breaking-and-entering and arson charges that we didn't know about. We got fined $500 and we had to turn around and go home.

BRIAN FAIR: One time, Overcast was out with Jasta 14 and we were going to Ithaca to play with Madball. I met up with some friends who went to college there. We were raging, getting so loaded-drunk. Our drummer Jay [Fitzgerald] went out with the two guitar players for Jasta 14 and they were on a rampage, going into frat houses and stealing CDs, smashing shit and causing trouble. They wanted a case of beer but didn't have any money, and nobody was twenty-one. So they decided to try and steal beer from this convenience store. Jay ran in, grabbed a case, tripped on his way out, and smashed it right into the doorway. He realized he fucked up and took off running. They finally made it back to the apartment where we were staying, and I went, "Dude, people are looking for you. You gotta stay here and find a place to hide. Do not leave." We all passed out, but Jay woke up later and decided he needed cigarettes. So he walked back to the same fucking store while the cops were watching the footage of him smashing the case of beer. He put a pack of Marlboros down on the counter, and they look at him like, "Are you fucking kidding me, dude?" They arrested him on the spot. The next day, we didn't know where he was, so we started looking in ditches. We finally called the police station and they called us back a couple hours later and said, "Oh, you're looking for the drunk kid. Yeah, we got him." We didn't have any bail money because we were broke. So we called his mom back in Massachusetts and she said, "Just fuckin' leave him there. I'll be there Monday." This was Friday. So she just let him stew and we went home and missed the shows.

KARL BEUCHNER: We were coming down out of the mountains in Yakima, Washington, and our van rolled four times. Everybody smashed out of the windows and was lying in the snow except for me and the driver. I went into the back of the van and was lifting up all of our gear—we had it all packed in there with us, which was an insane way to travel. I thought everyone was crushed under it, so it was a miracle to see everyone alive outside. Our fill-in guitarist had one of his ears partially detached. Our drummer Dennis [Merrick] got hurt the worst. He had collapsed lungs and a broken collarbone and broken ribs and a concussion. I didn't know what was going to happen to him. Incredibly, he was playing drums again six months later.

DEREK YOUNGSMA (Bleeding Through): It was about 7 a.m. and we had just left Salt Lake City on our way to Denver. The ground was covered in snow and I was driving. [Vocalist] Brandan [Schieppati] was sitting shotgun and most of our other band members were in the back of the van lying down. I was coming down a hill and noticed there was an accident in the center of the highway about a quarter mile ahead. I could see the highway patrol cars and some people standing around. As I drove closer, I crossed a bridge and the trailer started to slide and just pulled the van right along with it. We spun 360 degrees and slid into the center of the road, and just as the van began to tip, we hit the truck that crashed in front of us. When we hit, the van came to a stop but the trailer broke off and flipped, throwing gear and merch everywhere. The cops were all running and diving out of the way and thankfully no one was hit. The van and trailer we borrowed were completely totaled and we were stranded in Salt Lake for a few days, but we all walked away and most of our gear survived, though we did have to cancel the rest of the tour. The cops were actually very cool considering what they had been through. The reason we got so much notoriety out of the crash was because the dashboard camera in one of the police cars caught the whole thing. We ended up all over the news: *Inside Edition, Wildest Police Videos.* And most of the news shows were cool enough to include some of our music and live footage in their stories.

For most veteran Massachusetts metalcore bands, wild rides couldn't make up for the continued lack of commercial acclaim. Overcast was first to break up, in 1998, followed by Aftershock a year later (though they continued to put out previously unreleased material posthumously on Devil's Head Records). The fragmentation of the pioneering bands was ultimately beneficial for the growth of metalcore. Members of Aftershock and Overcast launched Shadows Fall, Killswitch Engage, and, eventually, All That Remains—all three of which would grow exponentially in popularity, selling out clubs and performing at stadium festivals, including Ozzfest and the Rockstar Energy Mayhem Fest.

ADAM DUTKIEWICZ: We got an offer to play Japan, and that's actually how we ended Aftershock. We were playing these clubs there with five to six hundred capacity. They were sold out, and we were like, "This is freaking crazy. We had to fly halfway across the world to play shows in front of a bunch of people who are into us." At that point, going back to playing shows for fifty people again didn't make sense.

MIKE D'ANTONIO: We had just done our first major U.S. tour as Overcast; it took about seven years to get to that point and we struggled the whole time. We had put out *Fight Ambition to Kill* [in 1997], and it was doing okay. So we started talking about writing another record, and our drummer Jay [Fitzgerald] said, "I don't know if I can do this anymore. It's costing more for us to get to a show than we're getting paid." That was a big blow to me because Overcast was my baby. I had a stronghold on that band—a stranglehold, probably. It meant everything to me.

BRIAN FAIR: We did our last tour together [in 1998] with Section 8, Shai Hulud, and Disembodied. Pretty much every band on that tour broke up except Shai Hulud, and they lost every member except Matt Fox; we called it the Tour to End All Bands. Mike D had been keeping track of the money we were making for every show, and there were definitely a few zeros, but what's even funnier is there's actually a $7 and an $8, and then there's a $32. And on one, we made $102. And that was the *big* tour. We were getting to California with three other bands who all had records out. We all thought, "This is gonna be huge!" Yeah, right. "Here's $32."

MIKE D'ANTONIO: One of our last shows was at the Rathskeller in Kenmore Square [in Boston]. We get there and the floor is covered in kitty litter, which was really weird. When we started playing the pit got going and a big cloud of kitty litter dust arose. You couldn't see the audience at all.

BRIAN FAIR: All the bouncers were wearing surgical masks, which should have been a sign we should pack up and leave. We found out later that the night before, a sewage pipe had blown up, and, in classic Rat style, they didn't clean it. They dumped all this kitty litter on the floor to absorb it all. My throat was torn apart with each breath.

MATT BACHAND: I started my own label, Lifeless Records, just to put out our first [Shadows Fall] album, [1997's] *Somber Eyes to the Sky*, and make it look professional. That record featured Phil [Labonte] on vocals and, at the time, Phil's thing was death metal. He didn't want to do any clean singing. Most of the clean singing on that album is me. His main focus was the growl and the aggressiveness. That's the main reason we started looking for another singer.

PHIL LABONTE: I got kicked out of Shadows Fall [in 1999] because Brian from Overcast became available. I actually drove [Shadows Fall bassist] Paul [Romanko], [guitarist] Matt [Bachand] and [guitarist] Jon [Donais] to Overcast's last show at the Espresso Bar in Worcester, Massachusetts. I was like, "I'll be designated driver." I didn't know they'd spend all night talking to Brian about how they were going to kick me out of Shadows Fall.

BRIAN FAIR: Phil was into more brutal death metal and they were getting more melodic, so it was really a common parting of the ways. Matt, being the ambitious one, asked me to join the band literally as I was coming offstage from the last-ever Overcast set in Connecticut. I was like, "Dude, gimme a minute. I'm burying one of my best friends now."

MATT BACHAND: The crazy thing is we kicked out Phil because he didn't want to sing, and now if you listen to what he's doing in All That Remains, it's exactly what *we* wanted him to do.

PHIL LABONTE: I had already started writing stuff for All That Remains. I had written "Follow," "Shading," and "Ace," which are off our first record. I wrote the music because I had planned on playing guitar again and not just singing. Everything worked out in the end.

Since Unearth's breakthrough album was 2004's *The Oncoming Storm*, many casual metalcore fans consider them latecomers to the scene. In actuality, the band was there almost from the start.

TREVOR PHIPPS (Unearth): In 1998, I ruptured my appendix and had to have it removed. I was trapped in my house for a week and I couldn't really move. [Unearth guitarist] Ken [Susi] came over every day to try to convince me to leave my old band, Second Division, and join their project. Finally, I agreed to go to their practice space to hear their songs. I thought they were pretty fuckin' killer, so I agreed to join.

KEN SUSI (Unearth): Unearth is one of the first bands to play metalcore as it's known today, and that started a huge trend. We're very big fans of classic thrash, and we wanted that to be a major part of our music because no one was doing that at the time. And we've never tried to sell hits. A lot of metalcore bands go straight from a mosh riff to a bright, shiny chorus to make their music more commercial, and I just think if people keep watering down metal with clean vocals, it's going to be nu metal all over again. So we went all-out in the other direction.

As the Massachusetts metalcore scene was heating up, on the other side of the country, in insular Orange County, California, another batch of musicians—some of whom were influenced by Shadows Fall and Converge—were forming new groups. Like the Massachusetts bands, they often featured a revolving door of players from other bands. The most popular were Avenged Sevenfold and Atreyu, but the first to strike were straight-edge adherents Eighteen Visions, which was formed in 1996 by front man James Hart and guitarists Ken Floyd and Dave Peters. In the beginning, Eighteen

Visions was primarily influenced by Thousand Oaks' straight-edge metalcore band Strife, one of the early staples of Victory Records, and San Diego's Unbroken. In contrast to many of the outfits they spawned, the first California metalcore bands were unapologetic teetotalers.

DAVE PETERS (ex–Eighteen Visions, Throwdown): I started out as a metal kid. The only shows I had seen before I got into hardcore were when I was a teenager and I got $60 of allowance from my mom to go see Metallica, Guns N' Roses, and Motörhead. Then I went to see Unbroken and I was standing two feet from the band. I was like, "Wow, I can get this close? I thought you had to sit an acre away to see a concert, like at Metallica."

MICK MORRIS (Eighteen Visions, xCLEARx): I grew up in Salt Lake City, and I was really into Slayer and Pantera, but once I discovered the early Victory [Records] bands, it all made sense to me because it had that heavy vibe that was metal but it was a whole new scene. One of the first shows I saw in 1995 was Integrity, Earth Crisis, and Bloodlet, which was a life changer. I could relate to the crowd, I could relate to the straight-edge lyrics, and I could relate to the intensity of the music. I started xCLEARx, and our two biggest influences were Overcast and Converge. We were on a label called Life Sentence that had some popular bands in the metalcore scene in the late nineties, including Eighteen Visions, which I later joined.

BRANDAN SCHIEPPATI: We're all straight-edge. We're not militant about it. If people want to drink or whatever, cool. But it's really maintained my focus on what I want to do. If I was doing something where I didn't have control over myself, I don't know if I could accomplish anything.

KEITH BARNEY (Eighteen Visions, ex-Throwdown): I never did drugs, drank, or smoked. When I got out of high school, someone on my baseball team showed me some hardcore bands and gave me a few tapes, and I got into it from there. The straight-edge attitude came along with that, so it was a natural fit.

DAVE PETERS: Orange County is a weird place. There's definitely this element of materialism. There's a lot of money in the area and in high school, the norm on the weekend for rich kids was to get drunk out of their parents' liquor cabinets and have these parties at Edward's Hill, which was the expensive area. More than anything, our music and our brand of straight-edge was a reaction to that.

Bassist Mick Morris joined Eighteen Visions in 1999. Unlike the other members, he grew up in Salt Lake City, where straight-edge had an entirely different vibe. Musicians and fans were more militant about their beliefs, and their conviction sometimes erupted in chaos. Cigarette smokers were beaten up, meat eaters were threatened, and drug users faced severe bodily harm. After several violent outbreaks and dangerous protests, local law enforcement started to crack down on the scene.

MICK MORRIS: We were looked at as a gang, like the Bloods and the Crips. Actually, we were looked at as terrorists since some straight-edge groups have burned down McDonalds and released animals from labs. There were lots of stabbings at shows, and in high school if you wore a shirt that said "Drug Free" you would get sent home because it was considered gang-related. We'd go to shows and there'd be forty eighteen-year-old vegan straight-edge kids there who all weighed 110 pounds, and the majority of them were there to fight. There were two Slayer shows that had to be stopped because there were stabbings in the pit and the riot police came. Three or four people got stabbed at a Hatebreed show because of a beef within the scene, and TV shows like *20/20* and *America's Most Wanted* did specials on the movement.

[In 1997], a group of kids [who called themselves the Animal Liberation Front] went out and bombed the biggest fur plant right outside of Salt Lake, the Fur Breeders Co-Op]. They released the minks, which ended up running onto the highway and dying anyway. But the bombing cost millions of dollars in damage. After that, you couldn't really have normal straight-edge shows in Salt Lake.

DAVE PETERS: We drove twelve hours to play our first show in Salt Lake City. We watched xCLEARx play, then out of nowhere we see a cop come in wearing full riot gear and then another and another. There were fifty to seventy-five cops with shields, masks, and tear gas guns standing shoulder to shoulder inside the perimeter of the building, and they shut the show down. We ended up playing in xCLEARx's practice space.

Eighteen Visions was the Aftershock/Overcast of the Orange County metalcore scene, the tree trunk from which other bands would sprout. Since 1997, the group has featured vocalist James Hart (who later formed Burn Halo), guitarists Brandan Schieppati (who played guitar in Throwdown and launched Bleeding Through), Dave Peters (who now fronts Throwdown), bassist Javier Van Huss (who has played in Bleeding Through, Throwdown, and the Mistake), and drummer Ken Floyd (who has toured in Throwdown).

DAVE PETERS: Ken and I grew up together. We were sixteen in 1996, when we started Eighteen Visions with James [Hart]. James went to Huntington High and was sitting in my English class one day when I got to the room. He was wearing braces and a Baltimore Orioles baseball hat and had this ugly-ass backpack. He had written "Earth Crisis" and "Chokehold" and all these hardcore bands from that era on it in Wite-Out with, like, three hundred X's. What was funny was that he wasn't actually in the class; he'd just go there to hang out with us. After five days, the teacher said, "Are you even in this class?" James said, "No," and they kicked him out. He was always great for comic relief and he was always extreme. You could say, "Hey man, go throw this full 2-liter bottle of Pepsi at that group of fifteen people over there?" And he'd do it. One day me and Ken were jamming and just joking around about getting James to sing. We were like, "I don't know if he can sing, but he's crazy." So we asked him and he was super stoked.

BRANDAN SCHIEPPATI: The Eighteen Visions guys lived in Huntington; I lived in Newport Beach, so I went to a different high school. But one of my older high school friends, Javier Van Huss, met James and Dave and joined the band as their bassist. They needed another guitar player so Javier suggested me. I had literally been playing guitar for six months and could just play well enough to fake it. I told them I had been playing for a few years and tried out for them, and I did well enough to get the spot. I was fifteen, and basically the first songs I ever learned on guitar were Eighteen Visions songs.

DAVE PETERS: We wanted to sound like the Florida band Bloodlet when we started. Everything I wrote sounded like a rip-off of them or Sepultura, which isn't a far cry from what I'm doing today in Throwdown. Our first show as 18V was in 1996 at a skating rink and we were pretty awful. Back then James would always completely blow his voice out every practice after two or three songs because he didn't realize you have to learn to breathe correctly when you sing. He had no voice for at least three days out of every week because we'd practice over the weekend. James was kind of a loose cannon. At one show, he smashed his head with the microphone over and over again until he was bleeding everywhere. That was his attempt to be metal and scary. We actually played a show with Bloodlet and James did that and was bleeding all over. We figured, "Well, these Bloodlet guys are weirdos. They're gonna think this is cool." But after the show the drummer looked at him like he was a total asshole.

BRANDAN SCHIEPPATI: Dave and James were both very alpha male and they butted heads all the time. It seemed to me that they both wanted to be the focal point of the band. Dave would say he wanted to quit all the time because he didn't like the way things were going. We'd say, "No, don't quit." Then James would get mad. They were both fishing for compliments or reinforcements that they *were* the band. They meshed really well from a writing standpoint. The five of us together were writing some really incredible music. But egos got in the way.

DAVE PETERS: A lot of people didn't like James. I always got along with pretty much everyone. Before I even joined Throwdown, the guys who formed the band, [vocalist] Keith Barney and [bassist] Dom [Macaluso] made it clear that they did not like James and they wouldn't be caught dead at an Eighteen Visions show.

JAMES HART (Eighteen Visions): Dave wanted to feel like he was a necessity to the success and growth of our band, and I got tired of that. One day he said, "I don't want to do it anymore, I quit." I think that he expected us to say, "No, no, no. Wait, wait, wait." But we sat down and said, "You know what, let's move forward. Let's just see how it goes and how we can do on our own." It was definitely unexpected and a weird and ballsy move considering that he was *the* talent in the band as far as guitar playing went. But we stuck it out as a four-piece until we got Keith [Barney, in 1999].

DAVE PETERS: I was trying to show Ken this riff I came up with. James listened to it and then did this ridiculous dance. It drove me insane. I was like, "You motherfucker!" He was just kidding around, but I got so offended and that ended the practice session. The last few months of the band, the dudes would fall all over the drums and end up on the floor in a mess like the San Diego hardcore bands. Even at the tender age of seventeen, that looked weird to me. So when we played this show at Ken's house, they ended up writhing around the floor. I thought, "This is not cool, this is silly." So I blew a snot rocket at Ken and it hit his drums. That's when everything fell apart and I quit.

Even with its revolving-door lineup, Eighteen Visions played a major role in changing the look of California metalcore. During their peak years in the early 2000s they dressed sharply, wore makeup, and styled their hair like glam musicians. The band was musically innovative as well, changing styles over the course of their career from bruising hardcore metal to melodic alternative rock, predating similar moves by Atreyu and Avenged Sevenfold.

BRANDAN SCHIEPPATI: Since Javier was in hair school, his whole thing was wanting to cut everybody's hair. So we all had freaky haircuts. We modeled ourselves a little bit after Unbroken, who were very sharply dressed because they were the heaviest band around and they didn't look it, which we thought was fuckin' cool.

RYAN DOWNEY: If anyone is responsible for what became fashioncore, it's Javier. He went to cosmetology school; he was a hair stylist. James Hart was also a hair stylist at a salon in Orange County. Brandan Schieppati was going to cosmetology school, which he eventually dropped out of. But Javier really led the charge with crazy hairstyles and pink and blond and blue chunks in their hair. A lot of the guys were fit and really into working out, and they had this sexual energy onstage, which was very much taboo in the hardcore scene.

JAMES HART: When we were doing *Yesterday Is Time Killed* in 1999, we were working at the mall in some boutiques, where we were introduced to different clothing. We started getting into that stuff and we took on this attitude that we're not just getting up there playing our songs to a crowd. We gotta put on a show and look different and stand out from the people we're playing to. And if it meant putting on a dress shirt and a tie, that's what we did. So, by the time we put out *Until the Ink Runs Out* in 2000 we started dressing a little slicker and combing our hair and putting on more of a show.

MICK MORRIS: I hadn't seen those dudes in a year, and then my band xCLEARx toured with them. The first show of that tour was in Chicago and they looked completely different. When they went on I was like, "This might be the fuckin' coolest thing I've ever seen." After touring with them for a couple weeks, I said, "Hey, if you guys ever need a guitar or bass player I'll move to California." I was kind of joking, but I kind of meant it.

JAMES HART: Things weren't panning out with Javier. He was showing up really late to practice or leaving really early, or both. His lack of interest or lack of commitment to the band was holding us back. We had written an entire record and were ready to record it, and he was like, "I don't like that part, I don't like that song." We were like, "Dude, that's too bad. You weren't here at all for the writing process." He played on part of *Until the Ink Runs Out*. Then on some of it, Keith [Barney] had to play bass because Javier didn't know the songs well enough because he wasn't showing to practice or couldn't play them.

MICK MORRIS: The summer of 2000, xCLEARx broke up and me and some friends flew up to Hellfest in Syracuse, which was a giant hardcore festival. Brandan took me aside and said, "Hey dude, wanna join the band? We're kicking out our bass player." I thought about it for a day and then accepted. A few weeks later I learned all the songs in my bedroom, packed up my car, broke up with my girlfriend, quit my job, left my roommate, and drove to California.

BRANDAN SCHIEPPATI: At one point, Eighteen Visions had so many collectively strong personalities—even myself. It got to the point where I was a tenured person in the band responsible for a lot of the material. I carried a lot of the weight. I decided I wanted to make decisions and take the band heavier. I really wanted my opinion to be heard, and by that time, nobody wanted to hear it. They had the whole Guns N' Roses and Stone Temple Pilots crush going, and I was listening to At the Gates and Dissection.

Schieppati wasn't the only one unhappy with the band's new look and sound. After the image makeover, they were targeted by local rednecks and even some former fans. But they had the courage and attitude—and fighting skills—to stick to their guns. And eventually their image paid off—especially for female fans.

RYAN DOWNEY: A lot of other guys were still wearing backwards baseball caps and basketball jerseys and camo shorts. Just looking like James and Brandan did was a bold move, and invited trouble.

MICK MORRIS: We never started crap, but we would get a lot of grief within the hardcore scene from kids who went, "Who are these faggots?" And we'd get the occasional asshole that would punch us or spit at us. If it wasn't from people in the crowd, it was outside. We would go to Del Taco and get in fights with big bro dudes who would give us a hard time for having styled hair, wearing eyeliner, or having tattoos. I've heard many, many times that we ruined the hardcore scene, and it's funny because a lot of bands today have the look that we introduced.

RYAN DOWNEY: Most of those guys' vice was women. Pre-MySpace, there was a website called makeoutclub.com which enabled bands to go on tour and physically encounter the girls they met online. 18V very much put across this rock star image and these girls responded.

MICK MORRIS: I had never been on the Internet before I moved to California. In '99, I lived with James and his mother, and he had AOL Instant Messenger. I had no idea what that was. He was like, "Dude, you have to make a screen name and start talking to chicks." It was a whole new world to me. Since I was new blood in Orange County, these girls swarmed me. Then I discovered makeoutclub.com in 2001. Then Friendster came out, then MySpace, which was the be-all, end-all of sleaze for the entire world, but especially for bands.

JAMES HART: The biggest mistake I ever made was introducing Mick to the Internet.

MICK MORRIS: The first time we went to Europe, we brought out this Dutch dude and he was very shy. He was good-looking, but scared to meet girls. One night, it was us and Throwdown on our first European tour, and we got our roadie out in a van with two girls. I guess they gave him a hand job. Then the next day, the girls are on the message board saying Eighteen Visions raped them! We still had a month left in Europe, and promoters threatened to cancel our shows because we're rapists. We were hearing this shit back home from friends and family and girlfriends. We were like, "That's not true at all. We weren't even involved with any of this." We soon discovered there are a lot of girls going out of their way to sabotage band dudes.

JAMES HART: That tour was such a mess. Our driver split on us, saying he got robbed in Rome, and the backpack that had all the money in it and passports was stolen. But I can tell you right now, rape is not something that's fun to be accused of.

That's why I always try to stay away from the Internet. We've had crew members in the past say some stupid things online, and people find out what band they work for and it comes back to us. Then people say, "Oh, you guys hire racists and KKK members." You end up having to fire good people and good friends because of the way it affects your band on tour and the way people perceive you as individuals.

MICK MORRIS: No matter what we did, girls seemed to cling to us. A handful of times I'd come on the bus sweaty as hell, completely drenched, and have naked girls in my bunk waiting for me. Once we evolved from the metal scene to the radio rock scene, it was a whole different world in every aspect, but especially with women. But you have to take the good with the bad. Sometimes girls would get mad and throw shit at you because you were with them the first time they came to your town and when you came back you didn't want to be with them. Some of these chicks, especially in Europe, would claim that they were pregnant. I would always call bullshit about that. They never had proof.

Throwdown featured many of the same members as Eighteen Visions, so it's no surprise that they experienced similar instability. Not only were the personalities volatile, some of the members did double- and triple-duty in other groups.

DAVE PETERS: In November 1999, when Brandan left Throwdown, he recommended me to replace him on guitar. I was stoked to be in a band again playing shows. The songs were tongue-in-cheek at first and poked fun of the tough-guy hardcore subgenre. The lyrics for "Box Your Face In" were "Box your face in fuckface / I'll put you in your place." The first time you play it you're like, "This is really funny and people are singing along and it's a big joke." Then it gets to a point when you can write real lyrics and real music and you're still playing "Box Your Face In." People want you to play it and they want to hear "Get Sick," where all you say is "Get sick motherfucker." It became kind of tiresome.

BRANDAN SCHIEPPATI: I played in Throwdown from 1998 until 2000. At one point, I was in Bleeding Through, Throwdown, and Eighteen Visions all at the same time. But Bleeding Through was really my thing. I had filled in a show for Throwdown singing because Keith [Barney's] voice was ripped up. So he played guitar and I sang, and Scott [Danough] came up to me afterwards and said, "Listen, I need you to sing in a band and I'm gonna play guitar and I have these guys that will play with us." That's how I met [original Bleeding Through guitarist] Chad [Tafolla] and drummer Troy [Born]. We tried a bunch of different bass players and guitar players. We even had Dave Peters come in, but he only lasted for one practice. Finally we got some people that stuck: [bassist] Ryan [Wombacher], [guitarist] Brian [Leppke] and [drummer] Derek [Youngsma]. And while I was writing and recording with Bleeding Through and Eighteen Visions, we actually played a couple shows where all three bands played and I played during each set, which was tiring but fun. For the first two Bleeding Through tours, Throwdown brought us out and then Eighteen Visions took us out, so I got to play double sets each night. That's how incestuous it was.

MICK MORRIS: Everybody was all over the place because Ken and Keith were both in Throwdown. Ken was playing drums in Throwdown and Brandan asked me to play bass in Bleeding Through. That was in 2002. So I was in Bleeding Through for a summer [and played on the 2002 Bleeding Through album *Portrait of the Goddess*]. Ken and Keith were out with Throwdown and we were swinging back and forth between both bands. James would fly out and we would do an 18V set, then a Bleeding Through set. Then Eighteen Visions' [2002 album]

Vanity came out, which Brandan was a part of and tracked on and wrote half of. At the end of the next Bleeding Through tour there was an 18V tour coming up. Me and Brandan sat down and said, "Dude, we've got to figure this out." I said, "I moved out here to be in 18V. I love Bleeding Through. I love everybody in the band, but my priority is 18V." And he's like, "Well, I'm one of the original members of 18V, but Bleeding Through is my thing now."

DAVE PETERS: Keith decided he wasn't going to sing for Throwdown anymore. He sang straight through his throat and blew it out. He only wanted to play guitar. I said, "Okay, but then who's singing and who's not playing guitar? We already have two guitar players." He said, "Well, you've been in the band the least amount of time, so we're gonna find another singer and you're not in the band anymore." I went, "Well hold on. I can still play guitar just fine. You're the one who can't sing anymore. Why are you still in the band and I'm not?" I was really insulted, but in an attempt to make lemonade out of lemons I said, "Let me try and sing." I ended up trying it and I was kind of shaky at first, but in ret-rospect it's the best thing that could have happened because when it comes to performing there's nothing I like more than singing and interacting with a crowd. Being thrown overboard without a dinghy forced me into the position that suited me best.

By 2000, with the release of its second album, the scabrous *Of One Blood,* and the addition of charismatic vocalist Brian Fair, Massachusetts band Shadows Fall started making inroads with the U.S. metalcore community. Killswitch Engage followed soon after.

MATT BACHAND: One of the first times Shadows Fall ever left New England was in 2000 when we played the Milwau-kee Metal Fest, where we made friends with some people at

Century Media. We handed them our disc and they liked it and signed us. Our first few tours were with bands we didn't fit in with. We went out with Dismember, Kataklysm, and Krisiun, which were all death metal bands, but it kind of worked out. We were the lightest bands on the bill, and we were getting $50 a night and sleeping on whoever's floor we could find. Maybe we'd eat a slice of pizza once a week. And coming up with the money to fill the tank to get to the next show was rough. But it was fun as hell.

BRIAN FAIR: We realized we could do these tours opening for death metal bands because these crowds across the country and world started responding to our music. We went, "Holy shit, we might be able to quit our day jobs someday." But even after we had done four full records, I was still working as a gourmet ice cream chef for a few days a week in Cambridge, [Massachusetts], [bassist] Paul [Romanko] was working in a grocery store, Matt was working in a shoe store, [guitarist] Jon [Donais] was at a Hot Topic in the mall, and [drummer] Jason [Bittner] was working in the IT field.

MIKE D'ANTONIO: Nine months after we started Killswitch we still didn't have a singer. We had tried out thirty or forty guys and nothing was working. Then Adam [Dutkiewicz's] brother, [Toby], who was the vocalist in Aftershock, suggested we try Jesse Leach. Toby had put out a record of Jesse's old band, Current, who were from Rhode Island. And it was pretty much, "If this guy Jesse doesn't work, we should probably just say forget it, because this is lame. We're playing the same songs over and over with no singer. Why should we write more if we don't have something to let us move forward?" So I was told that this new singer guy was going to come to my house and we were going to drive to a practice space in Westfield. I was living in Worcester at the time, and he shows up at my door. I didn't quite know who Jesse was until he came over and then I was like, "Oh yeah, I've seen you moshing at shows.

Let's do this, this should be really fun." And he worked out perfectly—for a while.

JESSE LEACH (Killswitch Engage, Times of Grace): One day Adam called me out of the blue and said, "Hey I'm jamming with Mike D. from Overcast and we've been looking for a vocalist for a long time for this side project. Do you want to audition?" I went over there and after the first song, Killswitch was born.

MIKE D'ANTONIO: Overcast and Aftershock had gone in such crazy directions, we were throwing a million genres into one song, and these songs started to be, like, twelve minutes long. For people with ADD, it wasn't making sense anymore. You'd play a show and no one would get it unless they'd seen you thirty times. So we took a step back and looked at what else was going on. We saw what was going on with Hatebreed, who had been together for quite a while. They had this simplistic style and they sold a million records on Victory [Records]. So we took our whole book of writing songs and threw it out the window and started from scratch and stripped everything down, and added these guitar harmonies inspired by Swedish melodic death metal.

JAMEY JASTA (Jasta 14, Hatebreed, Kingdom of Sorrow; ex-host, MTV's *Headbangers Ball*): With the Massachusetts bands following right behind us, we knew they were going to have a lot of success, too. With Hatebreed, we always had everything going against us. We're not the greatest players; I can only hold a couple of different notes. But what we lacked in talent, we more than made up for with sheer animalistic drive and ambition. Whereas with the Massachusetts bands, these guys were seriously talented. When Killswitch first started bubbling up on *Alive or Just Breathing*, those riffs, the drums, Jesse's vocals—we all knew it was going to be very big.

MIKE D'ANTONIO: Killswitch got signed pretty easily. I was doing graphic design for Ferret [Records], and I just happened to say, "Hey, I have a new band," and [label founder Carl Severson] said, "Send it to me." So I sent him the demo and he really liked it and wanted to put it out. Suddenly we had a self-titled album.

ADAM DUTKIEWICZ: Even with Killswitch, in the beginning we were in our van, making really terrible guarantees. We'd come home from tours with no money, stay on people's floors, eat pizza every day, rent vans that would break down every hundred miles. Once, we drove five hundred miles to play a show in Tallahassee, Florida, and when we got to the club no one was there, so we called to find out what was up. They came down and said, "Oh, we didn't tell you? The whole place is flooded with feces." The sewer had backed up in the club, so they canceled the show without telling us.

MATT BACHAND: We had so many weird shows. We played with Hatebreed and Diecast in Brockton, [Massachusetts], and a box of merch got stolen, which was like a box of gold bars to a band like us at that time. We weren't even getting paid for the show. It was a three-hour drive. And then we find out the promoter left with all of the money. He just took off. We had $50 coming to us. So at 3 a.m. the Hatebreed crew went to his house and the rest of the story I don't know and I don't want to know. I'm pretty sure they got their money, though.

MIKE D'ANTONIO: Carl Severson was working at Roadrunner as the new media manager, which is a fancy word for website guy. Any time he'd have a release on his record label, he'd hand it out to all the A&R guys at Roadrunner, as if to say, "Hey, here's what I'm doing, maybe you should think about going in a different direction." At the time, Roadrunner was pretty nu metal. He handed our record to A&R man Mike Gitter, who called me up at my parents' house. I couldn't believe that this guy from Roadrunner was calling me. It was never anything we aspired to, and when I brought it up to the guys, everyone laughed at me, literally. They were like, "That's stupid. Why would they want to have anything to do with us?"

MIKE GITTER (Razor & Tie; ex-A&R, Roadrunner): When Carl gave me that first [self-titled] Killswitch record [in 2000], it blew my mind. I went and saw the band at a tiny art gallery in Western Mass. called the Flywheel. There were, maybe, fifty people there. Unearth was the opener. Adam D. was still on drums. I loved the passion behind it all—Jesse's emotional vocals and spiritual lyrics with riffs that wouldn't be out of place on a Carcass or In Flames record.

MIKE D'ANTONIO: Mike Gitter actually lied to Roadrunner and told them that we sold a lot more records than we did when they signed us, otherwise I'm not even sure we would have gotten the deal. I think we were at about two thousand records for [2000's *Killswitch Engage*], and he probably told them ten thousand. He made me swear never to tell Roadrunner how many records we initially sold so he didn't look bad. It was basically a big dupe.

ADAM DUTKIEWICZ: Working on our second Killswitch Engage album, [2002's] *Alive or Just Breathing*, was incredibly difficult. I would drive two hours to Jesse's place in Providence with a mobile digital recording rig, and we'd work on his vocals in his living room. There were nights where he'd literally sing for five minutes and then say his throat hurt and he couldn't do it. Then I'd drive two hours back home. It was a bad situation for everyone. He didn't know how to prevent throat fatigue and it ended up cornering and overwhelming him.

JESSE LEACH: I had all these misconceptions about my voice. I didn't know how to sing properly. I had no technique. So I would get up there and bleed my soul through a microphone and force my voice out and my vocal chords would smash together.

ADAM DUTKIEWICZ: There was literally this gradual self-implosion that started with Jesse around the time when we signed to Roadrunner. Not to point fingers, but when we worked on the first Roadrunner record [*Alive or Just Breathing*], Jesse was getting a lot of outside pressure from the label, most notably our A&R guy Mike Gitter, who would make phone calls saying, "You should try to sound like this" or "Maybe you should use this for inspiration." A lot of people are able to deal with that kind of stress, but Jesse internalized all of it. He took everything to heart, and I think that was the beginning of the destruction of Jesse being a front man in the band. His concentration was scattered all over the place and his confidence was crushed.

MIKE GITTER: Was there pressure on Jesse to deliver the best vocals he could? Absolutely. Was this one of the contributing factors to Jesse leaving the band? Sure. That wasn't the only factor. Jesse had just gotten married and felt a responsibility to his wife. He also felt the pressure of everything that was going on around Killswitch at the time. It wasn't an easy time for the guy. I don't think that with Jesse, Killswitch would have become as big as they did. They would have done well, but not become the commercial band that they became with Howard Jones.

JESSE LEACH: Our first official tour was with Soilwork, and those guys had a ritual of doing beer bongs. When Adam and [guitarist] Joel [Stroetzel] got seasoned by them, it was ridiculous. They would get so drunk, and I would get irritated. If I was in a better place, I'm sure I would have laughed a lot harder at some of the hilarity. Adam is still one of the funniest guys I know, and the banter between him and Joel when they were drunk in the van was hilarious. They were like the two old guys from the Muppets who could take any situation and pick it apart and make it funny.

ADAM DUTKIEWICZ: I played drums straight through the release of the first Roadrunner record, [2002's] *Alive or Just Breathing,* which was at least a year and a half. As soon as the record was released, that's when we decided to be a five-piece instead of a four-piece, just for a bigger sound. That, and I was tired of setting up the drum kit. So we got our friend Tom [Gomes] in to play [drums] and I moved to guitar.

MIKE D'ANTONIO: Playing with Adam has always been hilarious. Even in the beginning, he'd wear a Viking helmet onstage behind his drum set and blow horns and play kazoos and do everything he could to make people look at him. It's so funny because he started out as a really timid guy and he just blew up into this dude ready to get nuts.

ADAM DUTKIEWICZ: We've always liked getting our drink on, just bro-ing down and being goofy. Jesse didn't really vibe with that. I've always found that a bunch of drinks before a show tames the jitters. Joel says that if he doesn't have drinks before he goes on, he can't remember how to play the songs. There's definitely been nights where I've been less than tight, but I think for the most part I'm pretty good at remembering stuff, somehow. I don't know how I do it. Muscle memory, I guess.

JESSE LEACH: When we toured, I did my best to stay completely sober. No beers, no nothing, because I had read that alcohol is bad for your voice and it dries you out. Back then, a lot of the clubs allowed smoking. So I'd be in these smoky rooms and I would be freaking out, which is part of the reason I would hide out all the time. Basically, while they were all having fun, I kept to myself in the van. I thought not talking between shows was good. I was way wet behind the ears.

Nu-metal icon Korn gears up at the Anaheim NAMM (National Association of Music Merchants) show. Photograph by Stephanie Cabral.

When he's not fighting capitalist pigs, Tom Morello likes to Rage on his guitar. Photograph by Stephanie Cabral.

Limp Bizkit's Fred Durst tries to recall what he "did it all for." Oh yeah, he remembers, "the nookie." Photograph by Stephanie Cabral.

After the 2001 anthrax terrorist attacks, Anthrax, the band, refuses to back down. Photograph by Stephanie Cabral.

Deftones singer Chino Moreno "dreads" being called nu-metal. Photograph by Stephanie Cabral.

Korn's Jonathan Davis gets intimate with his H. R. Giger mic stand. Photograph by Kevin Hodapp.

George "Corpsegrinder" Fisher joins the ranks of the mighty Cannibal Corpse.
Photograph by Jeremy Saffer.

Late death metal pioneer and Death front
man Chuck Schuldiner.
Photograph by Jeff Kitts.

Obituary: one of Florida death metal's first and finest. Photograph by Bill O'Leary.

After leaving Cannibal Corpse, Chris Barnes butchered new victims in Six Feet Under. Photograph by Stephanie Cabral.

Eyehategod vocalist Mike Williams boozes it up onstage. Photograph by Jon Wiederhorn.

Swedish black metal band Marduk vocalist Daniel "Mortus" Rostén sings psalms of blasphemy and destruction. Photograph by Greg Cristman.

UK black metal band Cradle of Filth front man, Dani Davey guts it out. Photograph by Stephanie Cabral.

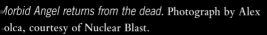

Morbid Angel returns from the dead. Photograph by Alex Solca, courtesy of Nuclear Blast.

Godfathers of goregrind Carcass refuse to smile for the camera. Photograph by Jeremy Saffer.

Adam "Nergal" Darski, front man of Poland's Behemoth, picks out the faithful among the crowd. Photograph by Stephanie Cabral.

Dimmu Borgir guitarist Tom "Galder" Rune Andersen falls victim to the black metal zombie invasion. Photograph by Stephanie Cabral.

Current Mayhem vocalist Attila Csihar sings to his good-luck charm and former best friend. Photograph by Jon Wiederhorn.

Gorgoroth's Gaahl: evil is as evil does. Photograph by Kristell Gathoye.

Dimmu Borgir worships at the temple of . . . Dimmu Borgir. Photograph courtesy of Nuclear Blast.

Norwegian progressive black metal band Enslaved reveals the rock. Photograph by Jeremy Saffer.

Black metal pioneers Immortal stand guard against the Christian infidels. Photograph by Peter Beste, courtesy of Nuclear Blast.

Watain's fork-tongued vocalist and bassist Erik Danielsen. Photograph by Ester Segarra, courtesy of Nuclear Blast.

Eighteen Visions: The first name in straight-edge metalcore. Photograph by Jeremy Saffer.

All That Remains: armed and ready for battle (and dessert). Photograph by Jeremy Saffer.

Ave.
guit
Ven
Syn
Pho
Step

Bleeding Through flexes its Orange County metalcore muscle. Photograph by Jeremy Saffer.

Boston-based metalcore pioneer Overcast. Photograph by Jeremy Saffer.

Killswitch Engage guitarist Joel Stroetzel and ex-vocalist Howard Jones try to restrain guitarist Adam Dutkiewicz from trashing another art gallery. Photograph by Stephanie Cabral.

Early Throwdown: metalcore with the emphasis on "core." Photograph by Jeremy Saffer.

Megadeth bassist Dave Ellefson returns to the fold with a new lineup featuring lead guitarist Chris Broderick and drummer Shawn Drover. Photograph by Stephanie Cabral.

Unearth rockin' the house. Photograph by Jeremy Saffer.

Mastodon: new masters of prog-metal (left to right) *Brent Hinds, Troy Sanders, Bill Kelliher, Brann Dailor.* Photograph by Stephanie Cabral.

System of a Down guitarist Daron Malakian checks whether his deodorant is still working while John Dolmayan keeps the beat. Photograph by Stephanie Cabral.

Tool vocalist Maynard James Keenan never has a bad hair day. Photograph by Stephanie Cabral.

Metallica joins Motörhead legend Lemmy Kilmister at L.A.'s Whisky for a special set dressed as The Lemmys, in honor of their idol's fiftieth birthday. Photograph by Stephanie Cabral.

Early Slipknot shot of vocalist Corey Taylor flipping the crowd the bird. Photograph by Stephanie Cabral.

Disturbed front man David Draiman gets down with the sickness. Photograph by Stephanie Cabral.

Hatebreed: warriors of the wasteland. Photograph by Jeremy Saffer.

Lamb of God vocalist Randy Blythe promotes Aboriginal Living Skills School while rocking the crowd back to the Stone Age. Photograph by Kristell Gathoye.

Rock royalty lineup: Metal lover Dave Grohl, System of a Down vocalist Serj Tankian, Henry Rollins, Tony Iommi, and Bill Ward. Photograph by Stephanie Cabral.

Atreyu breaks "The Curse," becomes metalcore darlings. Photograph by Jeremy Saffer.

Meeting of the minds: Alice In Chains bassist Mike Inez and guitarist Jerry Cantrell pose with metal legends Ronnie James Dio and Rob Halford. Photograph by Stephanie Cabral.

Mastodon's Brent Hinds rocks the New York crowd at Terminal 5. Photograph by Jon Wiederhorn.

Modern metal offers something for everybody: (left to right) Trivium's Matt Heafy, Machine Head's Robb Flynn, Slipknot's Joey Jordison, Fear Factory's Dino Cazares. Photograph by Stephanie Cabral.

Slipknot cofounder, songwriter, and bassist Gray. Photograph by Kevin Hodapp.

Machine Head front man Robb Flynn clenching the fist of dissent. Photograph by Stephanie Cabral.

Avenged Sevenfold's late drummer, Jimmy "The Rev" Sullivan. Photograph by Stephanie Cabral.

Faith No More backstage at RIP *magazine party with Ozzy Osbourne and Metallica's James Hetfield.* Photograph by Nick Charles.

ADAM DUTKIEWICZ: It got to a point [in 2002] where Jesse was miserable. He felt like he couldn't talk, he missed his wife, his throat was always a gamble. We canceled two or three shows because of his throat problems. By the end of the first tour, we had played all these gigs in these terrible venues with nobody showing up, and finally we were in Seattle, about to play our last show. There was a great turnout, the club was amazing. We were so amped up. Great vibes, great city. Then all of a sudden Jesse goes, "You know what, I can't do this. I'm leaving." He packed his stuff and hopped the plane home to go be with his family.

JESSE LEACH: Everything came crashing down on me, so I literally disappeared on the second-to-last day of the tour. I had my brother pick me up in Seattle, where he lives, and I got a flight straight home. I didn't even say goodbye to those guys. I went into hiding for a month. Then I had to pay my bills, so I ended up working three jobs and I became a total workaholic.

MIKE D'ANTONIO: I received an e-mail from him about two days after he left saying he didn't want to do it anymore. We had just started driving back home, and our van broke down in the middle of South Dakota. The wheelbase fell off and we were just sitting there at our lowest point. We had just put out our record on Roadrunner, and all of a sudden we find out we don't have a singer.

BRIAN FAIR: Back in '91 or '92, Overcast played with Howard Jones's old band, Driven. Howard was actually the first person I suggested to Mike D. when he told me Jesse was leaving the band. At first they thought, "Well, he's already got a solid band going on with Blood Has Been Shed," and they didn't want to steal him away. Then *he* actually ended up getting in touch with *them*.

PHIL LABONTE: After Jesse [Leach] left [in 2002], I tried out for

Killswitch a couple of times. Once, they had me ride down with them to New York City's SIR Studios. I had a leg up, and I thought, "Ah, I got this." I did the tryout. Mike Gitter from Roadrunner was there and he said, "It was great. You nailed it." But the day before we did that, I heard that Howard [Jones] had called them up and I thought, "Uh-oh." Because I had heard Howard sing, and he's really talented. After that, I had another tryout, and a week later I called Adam and he said, "Yeah, we're gonna go with Howard." I was like, "Fuck!" But man, I wasn't mad. Because one thing people may not know about Adam is he's funny and he's a jokester, but he's the most straight-shooting and legit dude that I know. There are no pulled punches and he doesn't mince words when he has to be straight. You have to respect that.

ADAM DUTKIEWICZ: We auditioned a bunch of people, and several were pretty good, including Phil. But Howard just had that *thing*, he had the magic. He can sing his nuts off and he's really great at melody and great at projecting.

MIKE GITTER: When Howard came in, a lot of things about the band and its sound broadened. He's *bigger*. His voice is bigger. *Physically*, he's bigger. He is the kind of front man that can stand in front of a crowd of fifteen thousand people and be utterly commanding. He's also spontaneous and is the straight man to Adam D's tomfoolery.

HOWARD JONES (ex–Killswitch Engage): Adam is hysterical. He's funny, period, but when he's drinking it's even better. I don't drink. My beverage of choice is protein and soy milk. Adam drinks enough for everybody.

In February 2010, after releasing their self-titled fifth album, Killswitch Engage announced that Jones was taking time off from the band to sort out personal issues. Labonte filled in for a tour.

Then, in 2012, Jones announced that he was battling type 2 diabetes and was leaving the band. Moreover, he stated that his heart was no longer in the music. Having worked again with Dutkiewicz in the side project Times of Grace, original Killswitch singer Jesse Leach was invited to rejoin the band. Killswitch Engage wasn't the only Massachusetts metalcore pioneer to struggle with lineup changes; Unearth also had its share of personnel shake-ups.

BUZ McGRATH (Unearth): In 2002, we had to replace [bassist] Chris "Rover" Rybicki with [bassist] John ["Slo"] Maggard, who used to be in a Western Mass. band called Flatlined. Chris just wasn't ready to commit to how far we wanted to take the band.

TREVOR PHIPPS: We remained friends with Chris, [who died in 2009 when his scooter was hit by a drunk driver]. He had a really funny, dark sense of humor. And he was a bit perverted. We were shopping the band to get to a bigger label and we were on tour and this label guy put us up for the night. He has a guest house/gym that had a couple couches. I was sleeping the next morning, and this guy's wife and her friend were working out in the next room and I woke to see Rover filming this label guy's wife with a video camera. We had to tell him to stop and delete the footage because it could have gotten us in trouble. That wasn't all he filmed. We had good friends of ours who were girls, and out of the blue Chris would show us videos of him having sex with them. We wouldn't have thought the girls would do that with him, but sure enough, he could convince them. He used to walk up to a girl in a bar or at a show and say something really dirty that he wanted to do to her. He told us, "If you do that to a hundred girls, you might get slapped ninety-eight times, but there'll be one or two girls who will be psyched for it." He'd have sex with these girls in club bathrooms or stairwells. The rest of us were just in awe.

BUZ McGRATH: After we got rid of Rover our original drummer, Mike Rudberg, quit. We had about half of [2004's] *The Oncoming Storm* written when that happened. [Drummer] Mike Justian came in around then and learned what we had written and made it his own and wrote the rest. That was a big record for us and it really brought us into our own as more of a thrash band and less of a metalcore group.

TREVOR PHIPPS (Unearth): Mike Rudberg was a very reserved, shy, quiet guy. He wouldn't do anything crazy, ever. But we were playing this sold-out show at Emo's in 2003 with Evergreen Terrace, at South by Southwest, and for some weird reason Mike stripped down naked and played the entire set nude. After the show he was psyched for about five minutes. Then he took a long walk and came back and told us he was leaving the band because he didn't want to tour.

For groups that weren't already insiders, the Orange County metalcore scene was hard to break into. Ironically, the two acts that had the hardest time being accepted by the metalcore elite, Atreyu and Avenged Sevenfold, would later become the most successful bands in the scene. Atreyu, who named themselves after a character from the children's movie *The Neverending Story*, formed in 1998 and fought relentlessly to win over metalcore fans with vocals that were alternately acerbic and syrupy, and guitars that combined elements of thrash, post-hardcore, and eighties metal.

DAN JACOBS (Atreyu): I was a big fan of Warrant and Queen back when I was ten or eleven years old. I went off in a punk direction for a while; then when I was fifteen, my friend played me Def Leppard's "Pour Some Sugar on Me" and I was like, "Oh, my God, this is awesome." From there, I discovered Ozzy, Twisted Sister, Bon Jovi, and the more I looked into it, the more I discovered how over-the-top eighties metal was, how big the live shows were, and how every musician ripped. I manage to get a little bit of that flavor in the music of Atreyu.

ALEX VARKATZAS: Dan and I met in eighth grade. [Drummer] Brandon [Saller] had just started seventh grade, but I knew his older brother Ryan, who introduced me to Brandon, and it just clicked. Our first band practice was me, Dan, and Brandon. We were in a little punk band in high school and we practiced in Brandon's apartment and covered Black Flag's version of "Louie, Louie."

BRANDON SALLER (Atreyu): When we started Atreyu, I was kind of scared because Alex and Dan were both older than me, and Alex was this gnarly punk dude who knew so much more about music than I did. I was like, "Shit, what if we play and they think I suck?" But it worked out. I had been play-ing drums for two years at that point. I was not good by any means. I could work my way around some Green Day songs; it wasn't anything special, but it was good enough.

ALEX VARKATZAS: We started out as a crappy punk band. And we realized that wasn't what we wanted to be, so we changed our sound and became more hardcore metal-y. We liked the change and became determined to be one of those bands that constantly evolves.

BRANDON SALLER: Our high school was in Anaheim, Califor-nia, right on the border of Yorba Linda. Once a year they had a battle of the bands called "Creative Impulse." You'd pay to get in, and we'd play those shows and only our friends would understand what we were doing. Every other band was ska or pop, and then we'd get up there and people were like, "What the fuck?" Once we got to play at lunch at school on this square cement 2-foot platform. There were a lot of people watching us, but a big portion of the school were thugged-out dudes and jocks and preppy girls, and they all thought we sucked. Alex had a cordless mic and he left the stage and walked around the school screaming. He'd go 100 yards away to the bathroom and take a piss in the middle of our songs.

Everyone saw him as this weird tattooed guy with big ear plugs, lip rings, and painted nails screaming at people while they were eating lunch.

ALEX VARKATZAS: I got picked on a lot, which is where a lot of my anger came from. When I was a freshman I got pushed into the pool at a big party. And once, I was running to class because I was late, and this big dude tripped me and I fell flat on my face. That kind of shit really formed who I am now. But I look at what most of those people are doing now and I'm like, "Fuck you guys. Who's laughing now?"

BRANDON SALLER: When we started our first demo CD [1999's *Visions*], a lot of our songs were pissed-off, screamy kind of stuff. But as we evolved, I realized that I could actually *sing*, which I never knew because I had never done it before. There weren't a lot of bands doing that screaming and singing mix; I'm not saying we pioneered it, but we took our own approach to it.

ALEX VARKATZAS: We started as a metalcore band, but we *changed*. People have compared us to Poison the Well and Killswitch Engage, which is really funny to me because we were around just as long as both of those bands. They just got more well-known first. I had sent our first demo CD to the owner of Tribunal Records, Matt [Rudzinski], and he e-mailed me back making fun of the name of our band. And I was like, "Look, we have a four-song EP done. It's mastered, it's mixed. All you have to do is put it out. It's mint for you. Just duplication." He agreed but said he wasn't going to do shit to promote it. So we pressed a thousand in 2001 and it took us a year to sell those.

DAN JACOBS: I was the only guitarist back then and we were getting way more into hardcore and metal. We went, "Gosh, all these bands have two guitar players and they just sound so much heavier live and can do so much more." So we got Travis [Miguel] to fatten up our sound.

TRAVIS MIGUEL (Atreyu): I joined in early 2001. Alex and I used to work at Hot Topic together. He pulled me aside one day and said, "I think we need another guitar player, so if you want to come by and jam with us, you're more than welcome." The next thing I know, I'm signing a record contract [with Victory]. I had a semester of college left to finish. So it was kind of either do the responsible thing, finish up school and lead the normal life, or sign this record contract, which could go down in flames. I haven't been back to school since.

JAMES HART: Our relationship with Atreyu was not great at first. Their old bassist [Chris Thomson] liked to talk a lot of shit and was constantly running his mouth about us, Avenged Sevenfold, Bleeding Through, Throwdown, and Adamantium, who we got along with really well. It got to a point where none of our bands would play local shows with them.

ALEX VARKATZAS: We were really on the outside of the Orange County scene. A big fight happened at one of our early shows between some of our friends and some dudes from Eighteen Visions. People had beef from it for years. Afterwards, a lot of people didn't like our band and we had a hard time getting shows because I knew that none of those bigger bands were gonna put us on a show.

BRANDON SALLER: It was extremely annoying. We were just like, "Why? What makes these other bands so special? What makes it so difficult for us to be accepted?" But we kept pressing on, and little by little we started seeing results. We didn't get a lot of shows until our first record, *Suicide Notes and Butterfly Kisses*, came out in 2002. After that we'd book shows at Chain Reaction in Anaheim and put on our own shows at parties.

DAN JACOBS: When we started getting more popular than bands like Eighteen Visions, I think people started to hate on us, and I think a lot of that came from jealousy. People who weren't necessarily our biggest fans in the beginning saw us starting to do okay, and they said, "Why is this band, which I don't really like, doing really well, and these other bands that I love are not doing as well?" I think that pissed people off and fueled their fire.

ALEX VARKATZAS: I found out about this supposed rivalry with Avenged Sevenfold through *Kerrang!* They sent me an e-mail saying, "This is what this band said about you in an article." They accused us of stealing a song from them. I got mad about it for a second and then I thought about it a little. It was curiously right around the time the Avenged record *City of Evil* came out [in 2005]. I think that was an interesting maneuver and a total fantasy. We never stole a song. If you're cool with Atreyu, thank you, and if you're not, go fuck yourself.

M. SHADOWS (Avenged Sevenfold): All that shit gets so blown up in the press. We never had a real problem with Atreyu. Those guys are our friends. But I will say this: Atreyu get more shit talked about them than anybody.

BRANDON SALLER: We decided that since we weren't a part of the cool scene, we weren't going to even *try* to be. We don't want to be a metalcore band because that puts limits on you. We don't want people to be able to put a name on us, so the more we can do to be able to make that happen, the better for us.

In the early 2000s, Atreyu had more pressing concerns than squabbles with metalcore bands. Having suffered through a series of dysfunctional relationships that left him disillusioned and bitter, Varkatzas became a problem drinker. His spirits improved considerably after he hooked up with current wife Hollie Anne; they got married on October 4, 2009. But back in 2004, the singer felt ready to burst.

ALEX VARKATZAS: I had a couple of really big betrayals from people that were supposed to be my friends. It hardened my heart to everyone. I had this inner anger and mistrust towards anyone I didn't know. At the time, I was drinking a good amount every day, and I lost it. I punched a palm tree and really messed up my left hand. I didn't break any bones, but I ripped up all my knuckles and fingers and I poured Jack Daniel's on it afterwards, which was stupid and hurt like a motherfucker. I was running away from some bad shit and I realized it's hard to run when you're drunk. I wasn't performing how I should and I was letting my band down, the kids down, and myself down. The last straw came after we played a show at Carnegie Mellon [University, in Pittsburgh], with Taking Back Sunday. I had way too much to drink before we went on, and when we played, I couldn't talk between songs. The songs come off from memory, so I just do it naturally. But afterwards, I was practically incoherent and puking all over the place. I stopped drinking pretty much right after that and found other ways to deal with my anger, like martial arts.

TRAVIS MIGUEL: When I party too hard, something stupid always happens. We played a show in Ottawa, Canada. It was freezing cold, and like clockwork, I ended up at the bar after the show. The next thing I know, I'm in this apartment at this party and I didn't recognize anybody there. I lost my jacket. I had no cell phone. I didn't know the name of the venue or how to get back. I'm in a daze, and this girl comes up to me and goes, "Who the fuck are you?" I'm like, "Well, sorry, I thought I was invited." She's like, "No, no, fuck that! Lock the door behind him! Make sure he doesn't leave." And she storms into another room. I was like, "Fuck, what did I do?" This guy next to me whispers in my ear, "Dude, you better get out of here while you still can." So I left real quick and ran down this totally empty street. By some divine act of God, I was able to hail a cab. I couldn't tell him where to go. But as luck turned out, I saw our bus while we were driving and said, "Oh, my God, stop. We're here."

Atreyu released their last straight metalcore album, *A Death Grip on Yesterday*, in 2006, then harnessed their creativity in more creative directions. Varkatzas screamed less and sang more on 2007's slicker, more experimental *Lead Sails Paper Anchor* (which included pop-punk riffs, horns, cowbell, and handclaps), and 2009's *Congregation of the Damned* (which featured storming riffs and crushing breakdowns but lacked the clawing intensity of the band's first three albums). At the same time, Avenged Sevenfold was evolving from a Maiden-obsessed metalcore band into a hybrid of Guns N' Roses, Metallica, Mötley Crüe, and Dream Theater. Unlike Atreyu, Avenged Sevenfold wanted to be rock stars from the moment they started jamming together in 1999, and they were largely motivated by the promises of celebrity— free booze, abundant drugs, and decadent sex. But while they earned the key to the backstage liquor cabinet while they were still young, their success came from their talent as players and songwriters, not their antics (some of which rivaled those of their heroes). Actually, the members insist they were more deviant *before* they formed the band.

JIMMY "THE REV" SULLIVAN (1981–2009) (Avenged Sevenfold): I was a psychotic child. I was fucked-up when I was young. When I was eight, I used to kill cats, and now I love them more than anything, so when I think about it, it makes me sick. I'd beat them or run over them with my bike. Throwing them in the air used to be funny. I watched my friend James put his dog on the stove and turn it on. I broke my neighbor's leg for fun because we were playing WWF. Then I turned into kind of a psychopath and did a bunch of acid and thought I was the smartest kid in the world.

SYNYSTER GATES: If I had to do anything else in the world, I would be a failure. I couldn't hold a job, I couldn't stay in school. But one thing I never let up on was music. I was an honors student until fourth grade, when I got a guitar in my hand. Then I quickly became an educational failure. This is all I can do now and I want to be the best.

DAVE PETERS: Matt [M. Shadows] and Jimmy went to Huntington High School with [Eighteen Visions members] James, Ken, and I. I actually went to middle school with Jimmy, too. Back then his nickname was Boner. One day, Boner brought his whole drum kit to school and set it up on the baseball diamond and played during recess. People went out and watched this sixth-grader shredding on the kit. Then the teachers came out. Everybody thought, "Oh, well this must have been approved. There's no way he just came here with his drums," which is exactly what he did. Finally, somebody figured out he didn't have permission and they made him stop.

M. SHADOWS: Freshman year, when we were fifteen or sixteen, we burned down a school that we can't name because we could still get in trouble for it. We did millions of dollars of damage. We were fucking around and burning shit, drinking underneath the fucking school, just being assholes. And we set some shit on fire. All of a sudden it's out of control. So, we're like, "Okay, we gotta go now." As we're leaving, you hear the fucking fire engines. We were like, "Dude, we can't shake this. They're gonna catch us!"

THE REV: At school I was kind of bragging about it. Then someone in my school said it was me.

M. SHADOWS: The cops came to the Rev's house, but he got out of it. One time before, when we stole stuff, I told the cops, "Hey, I didn't really steal stuff. I just told everyone I did because I wanted them to think I was cool." So the Rev did the same thing. He said, "No, we didn't really burn down the school. We just said we did." It was scary, but they let him off.

SYNYSTER GATES: Before we started the band, we all had crazy long nights of binge drug using and excess drinking—just thinking you're gonna die. You've been up for a fucking day and a half and you just can't go to bed even though it's been a while since you've slept, and you're having heart seizures and panic attacks. I think we've learned our limitations and have a good time now. Me and the Rev and Zack used to do a lot of fucking coke. If I ever thought of doing as much coke now, I would freak out. But you're young, you're naïve, and you don't know the repercussions. You keep going more and more and more until finally you fuck yourself up. Then you fuck yourself up twice, and then you start to learn. I had a bad incident with shrooms where I puked up a lot of blood. I was passing out and my friends had to keep me awake. I've woken up after puking in my sleep and that's not cool either. But that only happened when I was really, really young. I've calmed down a lot since then.

M. SHADOWS: When you're growing up and going to the bar and your friend is the bartender and there's blow on the fucking bar every night and there are shrooms and GHB and it's do-whatever-you-want-and-everything's-free all-night and you have no responsibilities, well that's a different story. But that's not our situation now. We play shows every night and the people that come are paying money to see a good show. We don't want to go on wasted and be all sloppy. We want to impress them.

THE REV: I've been in county jail twice, dog. Two years of probation for armed robbery, which I plea bargained. We robbed a store and the security guard jumped onto the car. We drove away with the security guard hanging half out of the car, trying to make us stop. The cops threatened us with attempted manslaughter, but it didn't stick. Other times I had minor offenses for fights and drinking in public. The most I ever got was a week. You never appreciate anything more than when you get out of jail. You're like, "Shit, I can walk around for 5 feet if I want to or fucking go get some cigarettes."

Considering their reckless, fast-paced childhoods, it's a minor miracle that Avenged Sevenfold were able to focus long enough to learn to play, form a band, write songs, and practice. As it turned out, music was their salvation, and their love for gigging equaled their penchant for partying. From the start they were convinced that if they became a killer band, stardom would follow. So they took their music incredibly seriously, analyzing each riff, taking every opportunity to adapt and improve. At first they tried to fit into the Orange County scene by playing blazing Eighteen Visions–style metalcore seasoned with guitar ripping solos. Around the same time, Eighteen Visions was trying to break out of the metalcore mold, integrating more hard rock elements into its music, ironically paving the way for Atreyu and Avenged Sevenfold.

JAMES HART: There were straight-up rock riffs on [2000's] *Until the Ink Runs Out* and nobody batted an eyelash because there was screaming over it. Once we made a couple albums, we decided to emphasize the melodic guitar parts and rock-oriented songs. I started developing my voice and we explored some of our more melodic ideas. That started on [2002's] *Vanity* and got more pronounced on [2004's] *Obsession*. And the hardcore kids gave us hell for it.

M. SHADOWS: When we first started [in 1999], we were really young and we wanted to do a mix of punk and metal, and it came off as metalcore. After that, everyone jumped on the bandwagon.

ZACKY VENGEANCE: When you've got a dollar-a-day food budget, life's hard, but we were always focused to take over the world. We went through more self-bought fog machines than any band in the history of music. In the beginning, we'd put on another band's shirt that we toured with because we could get them for free. We'd be the opening band on a hardcore bill playing in front of ten kids and playing through all this fog. Maybe the ten kids hated our guts and laughed. But fuck them. Look at what we're doing now. They can suck my dick.

At its peak, the metalcore movement most closely resembled the thrash metal scene. With the exception of the straight-edge bands, there was plenty of drinking and tomfoolery, and while the shows could get violent, the crowds were usually not mean-spirited. Of course, there were exceptions.

BRANDAN SCHIEPPATI: We were playing a floor show in Long Island and this kid broke his leg in the pit. He just lay there and he was still singing along and people were moshing over him and he refused to be moved. He was there for two songs before he let the paramedics take him out.

MATT BACHAND: In 2003, Shadows Fall did the Headbangers Ball Tour, which was a triple-headliner with Lamb of God and Killswitch. Unearth and God Forbid were the support bands. That was the tour where Adam D. got drunk and shot some bottle rockets out of his ass in the parking lot of the Alrosa Villa in Columbus, Ohio. That year we also did [the second stage of] Ozzfest with Killswitch, and one day we painted Adam like Paul Stanley. Everyone else in Killswitch just looked defeated. He came off our bus like that right before the show, and they all groaned.

BRANDAN SCHIEPPATI: Bleeding Through did the Headbangers Ball Tour 2004 and it was a disaster. A couple of our friends got in a fight and there were security guards in the middle, and one of the guards pulled out a knife and stabbed two of my friends. One was in critical condition and had to get surgery. We got fuckin' blamed for it and almost got kicked off the tour.

BRIAN FAIR: Those summer tours like Ozzfest are crazy because your day is done so early that you don't know what to do with yourself. And all your alcoholic friends are there. So they're all enabling you and even if you're just like, "Okay, let's take the day off drinking," you run into your friends from Arch Enemy, and you're like, "Oh, well. Time for some liver push-ups and 12-ounce curls." There was one show on the King Diamond tour and our old drummer imbibed a bit too much and he was playing with his eyes closed; when you're a drummer that's not a very good thing to do. There's a video of it on YouTube, and you can hear him hitting the microphone.

ADAM DUTKIEWICZ: One of my favorite tours was Ozzfest with Cradle of Filth, because I got on really well with [keyboardist] Martin Powell, who also liked a bit of the drink. One night I saw him in the parking lot throwing up through a traffic cone. I told him I would give him a dollar if he picked up his vomit and ate it and he agreed. That was disgusting. That was the same tour where he and I ended up drinking so much that I wound up not being able to play half the set. I was just on the ground. And by the time he got onstage directly after us, he passed out on his keyboard. You just hear this sustained note over the speakers, and they had to drag him out. The Cradle guys were pretty upset about that.

MIKE D'ANTONIO: Adam took a golf cart with Matt [DeVries, guitarist] from Chimaira and one of the guys from Cradle of Filth, and they were driving around the parking lot, drinking and knocking over trash cans. When you're on a golf cart it seems like it's going super fast, but when you watch it, it looks like you're moving in slow motion. So they're having this great time running over things and all of the bands are watching them and laughing. And they decide to drive over this table that kind of looks like a ramp, but they miss it, and two wheels go up on the table and then it flips the entire golf cart on its head. Adam has his beer and he's hanging on to it, and even with the flip, he doesn't spill a drop. The roll cage landed on his arm and he still had the beer upright. They pushed the golf cart over and he just started drinking again.

MICK MORRIS: In 2004, we played a skate park in a really bad part of Buffalo with the German band Caliban, Scars of To-morrow, Evergreen Terrace, and It Dies Today. After the show, we were all hanging out at 2 a.m., talking, packing up our trailers, and this car sped through the little alley we were in. One of the dudes tapped the car, like, "Hey, slow down." Ten minutes later we see ten teenage kids walking towards us. They said, "Yo, who the fuck hit my mom's car?" They were these little black gangbangers and they had no fear. They prob-ably had knives or guns. I was telling everyone, "Let's just pack up and leave." The singer of Evergreen Terrace said something and somebody threw a punch and it turned into a massacre. The guys from Caliban jumped in their van and took off and the rest of us were punching out all these kids in this dark alley, half expecting to get shot or stabbed. A week later, we got an e-mail from the principal of the school where these kids went, saying one of the kids got his head split all the way open and they're gonna take us to court, and possibly jail.

JAMES HART: We were out with Killswitch Engage in 2004 right in between *Vanity* and *Obsession*. I was signing autographs and some guy was like, "Hey, will you sign my ticket?" I'm like, "Sure man." He rips his ticket up and throws it at me and says, "I fuckin' hate your band. You guys suck." Imagine having fifteen or twenty of your fans waiting in line and seeing somebody disrespect you like that. I went after him and got surrounded by him and five of his bigger buddies.

MICK MORRIS: The five guys dumped beer on James's head and he literally fought them all and destroyed them.

BRANDAN SCHIEPPATI: We were in Calgary with Cradle of Filth, and I was down in the pit with [Seattle metal band] Himsa trying to get the crowd going and get the guys the love they deserved. This guy kept grabbing my hood and pushing me. I was like, "Okay, whatever. I don't really care about your pit beef." So I pushed him away and said, "Fuck off." He did it again and I threw a left at him and knocked him out. It was meant to get him the hell away from me, but he went down on the ground. It was funny because his friends looked at me and said to him, "That's the singer of Bleeding Through." He came up to me after the show and said, "Oh, I'm so sorry I did that. I love you guys." I said, "Well, I'm sorry I punched you."

The turning point in metalcore history came with Avenged Sevenfold's 2005 album, *City of Evil*, which marked the band's total departure from the scene. They abandoned harrowing screams in favor of powerful singing, and went for classic rock, metal, and prog riffs in lieu of hardcore-based rhythms, unleashing infectious rockers like "Bat Country" and "Beast and the Harlot" as well as ballads like "Seize the Day." With strong support from their label, Warner Bros., *City of Evil* steadily gained steam, and in January 2006, about six months after its release, the album went gold. In August 2009 it sold platinum, garnering one million in U.S. sales, the largest number of any modern Orange County band. By that time 2003's *Waking the Fallen* and 2007's *Avenged Sevenfold* had also gone gold. The next most popular metalcore act was Killswitch Engage, whose 2004 album, *The End of Heartache*, and 2006's *As Daylight Dies* have both gone gold.

JAMES HART: I've always liked Avenged Sevenfold, even when they were the punching bags of that world. I never looked at them as a hardcore band. I saw them more like a metal punk band, but they were always something different. And they brought different people to the shows that your typical hardcore kid didn't like—guys that just wanted to surf and party. Those dudes didn't really mix well with your stuck-up straight-edge hardcore kids back then.

JAMEY JASTA: In one of the first Avenged videos, the main character is wearing a Hatebreed shirt. That was really smart because it showed how different walks of life were into their music. They had the hardcore kids *and* the Guns N' Roses fans. They showcased their talent in their music with these amazing guitar parts and went on to incorporate clean singing, which is always going to take you places.

M. SHADOWS: When we were doing [2005's] *City of Evil*, all we were listening to was Sonata Arctica, a European power metal band, and Blind Guardian and Queen, where it's all built around pop melodies with lots of backup vocals. Musically it's more of a Pantera-, Metallica-, Iron Maiden-type thing. That's what we were going for, and to be completely honest, we knew it was going to be more commercial. We changed our sound because we wanted to play the kind of music we liked, but we were smart enough to want to be accessible for people. We knew the metalcore thing had a cap on it. But the funny thing is, Warner Bros. *wanted* us to do a metalcore record because major labels like to jump on the bandwagon. Thrice was signed and Thursday, so Warner Bros. was like, "Well *we* got Avenged Sevenfold." Then we were like, "Okay, but we're not gonna give you that type of record." So at first it was kind of weird for them.

ZACKY VENGEANCE: We've always looked at things as us versus everyone else and we'll take our fans along for the ride. We're determined to be the biggest thing out there. There's a lot of people that don't see our vision and try to fuck with us, be it the press or label people who don't care about us. We could be the happiest guys in the world, and as soon as somebody tries to cross us we'll bite their heads off because we've worked too hard for years to make this thing work.

M. SHADOWS: We met [Pantera's] Vinnie Paul in Dallas and he came up to us and said, "Hey, I was driving from Dallas to Vegas, and I heard your shit on the radio and I dug it so much I went right out and bought it. Your drummer is killer. He stole some of my chops, but that's okay." Then we met [Pantera bassist] Rex Brown after our show in Irvine, California. He said, "You guys are waving the flag of metal now. Fucking run with it, dude."

DAVE PETERS: At first when I saw those bands blowing up I felt this combination of disbelief and envy. I went, "Fuck, these guys are doing so well." At that time, we didn't see their music for what it was so it was easier to write it off. Then when you step back and really look at it you go, "That band is big because those dudes can write circles around most people in Orange County. They're these phenomenal musicians."

Avenged Sevenfold doesn't have a slogan, but if it did it would be: "work hard, play hard." Guitarists Zacky Vengeance and Synyster Gates hone their chops for hours at a time, and M. Shadows spent a mint on vocal training with one of the best coaches in the business. They continue to play concerts sober and are reliable about making promotional appointments. But when their work is done for the day, Avenged Sevenfold like to let loose. They drink heavily; they've experimented with pills, acid, and coke; they gamble; they visit strip clubs; and they have gotten involved in messy brawls. At times, especially around the *City of Evil* era, it looked like their appetite for destruction just might take them out.

M. SHADOWS: The last time we got into a bar fight we were just sitting there drinking and some asshole goes, "If I don't get a drink in the next five minutes, I'm gonna punch the next person that walks in the door." So he doesn't get his drink and my friend walks in, so the guy shoves my friend. The Rev walks up with a beer bottle and just, *boom!* across the guy's face. All I remember is kneeing someone in the face over and over and not stopping.

JOHNNY CHRIST (Avenged Sevenfold): I got arrested for a DUI in 1994. I had just bought my Crown Victoria and I went out. I wasn't planning on going anywhere. I just had a bottle of Jack sitting next to me and I was drinking, watching TV, and a friend came over. I had just got back from a tour. So I showed him the car and I was drinking some more. I ended up blacking out. And for whatever reason, I wanted to go for a spin. Next thing I know, I wake up and I've driven my car underneath a parked Dodge pickup truck. I found out later I had put the pedal all the way down and at the last second I fishtailed and went right underneath the truck. So I'm trying to back out and this guy runs out in his underwear and starts screaming. I tried settling it, but there was already a cop there. I went to jail and had a pretty hefty fine.

SYNYSTER GATES: People are saying we're the next Mötley Crüe. They say our way of life is over-the-top and crazy, but to us *their* way of life is pretty crazy—to not be human and indulge in things when you want to do them. People are animals. We like to explore and we're daring, and to stifle that is unnatural.

ROXANA SHIRAZI (groupie, writer): [One time], Synyster put down his beer and unzipped his heavy metal pants, full of chains, studs, and assorted accessories. He unleashed his hot pee like a fountain all over my breasts. I held my head back to expose my neck. [Back on the band's bus] the Rev tried to fuck me. M. Shadows watched. When Synyster showed up, though, the Rev's dick died. He kept trying to fuck, but his dick was spaghetti limp. He tried to shove it in again and again. Because of all the chemical substances he'd consumed, he began foaming at the mouth. All of a sudden, his face went pale and twisted in deranged psychosis, and he slammed me onto the ground. I hit my head, then stood back up in a daze. I was angry, but mostly because I hadn't gotten proper sex.

SYNYSTER GATES: When we went to Atlantic City on the *City of Evil* tour there were a couple of girls we met at our meet-and-greet. We were supposed to play strip poker, and while we were there, we got a little crazy. We filled up a bucket with urine and dumped it all over one of the girls and she was freaking out. She was soaked head to toe in the band's urine. So Johnny said, "Don't worry, baby. It's just alcohol." So she picks up a bottle of Patrón [tequila] and says, "I can't believe you wasted this bottle of Patrón on me." We're just busting out because she's covered with piss.

THE REV: We had a day off in New Mexico [in 2006] and there was nothing to do, so me and [guitarist] Zacky [Vengeance] were drinking. It was just me and him in the bathroom at this tequila bar. We got drunk to the point where it felt like we were on crazy drugs because it was, like, 100 degrees outside and we were out of our minds. So Zack thought it was fuckin' hilarious to start pissing on the floor. I was like, "Yea-eah!" I fuckin' dropped to my knees and started fuckin' lickin' it up.

M. SHADOWS: Everyone thinks I'm the craziest one in the band because my temper has an on/off switch, so when I drink certain alcohols I get out of my mind worse than anyone else on drugs. I'm going around trying to kill everybody or I'm just going nuts. I've whipped cards in the faces of casino dealers when I've lost, I've grabbed knives and tried to stab people and had to be talked down. That's how I get my bad rep—just from my temper.

THE REV: I'm not a drug addict, but I'm a total sex addict. I'm also probably an alcoholic. I mean, shit, when you're sitting around the tour bus every night driving to the next town, what the fuck else is there to do but drink and take drugs? But I'm not into ruining my life. I never had to go to the hospital or anything. The closest I got was being on a lot of cocaine and then snorting Oxycontin pills. That was really dumb, and I don't remember anything after that.

ZACKY VENGEANCE: I once saw Jimmy walking down the street holding his arm up and fucking wheezing. Like, "I gotta put my arm up, it's hurting my heart. It hurts really bad." Like the dude's about to have a heart attack. Then he walked back to the room and I see these lines of coke cut on a mirror that are literally the size of four pencils stuck together. Each line was seriously like a gram and a half. I looked at him and started laughing. I'm all, "That's enough to last a fucking month."

THE REV: We have this term *cross-eyed drunk* for Johnny. He gets so drunk that any other one of us or any normal human being would pass out and get sick. But his body will never make him pass out, so he never has to stop. He's not conscious at all and he's doing the most unspeakable things. He'll be buck naked, puking on himself. He was trying to get drunk enough to do stand-up comedy and improvise. He pukes and we're like, "You didn't drink enough." So he goes, "I know, I know. I can still see." He downs three more full glasses of tequila and does more stand-up comedy. It's the most disturbing thing. We filmed it, and watching the video is like watching *Faces of Death*. There's one point where he lay down, he got pulled out of his bunk, and it looked like a dead body being dragged across the floor. Then he covered himself in suntan lotion and started trying to tell jokes again.

For Jimmy "the Rev" Sullivan, the good times came to an end on December 28, 2009. Avenged Sevenfold were well into the writing process for their 2010 album, *Nightmare,* when the drummer died unexpectedly at his home in Huntington Beach, California. Toxicology reports determined that his death was caused by acute polydrug intoxication due to combined effects of the prescription drugs oxycodone, oxymorphone, diazepam/nordiazepam, and alcohol. The coroner's report also indicated that Sullivan suffered from an enlarged heart, which may have contributed to his premature death.

LARRY JACOBSON (manager): To all of us who loved Jimmy, the only thing relevant about December 28 is that this is the night we lost, too soon, a son, brother, friend, and one of the most talented artists in the world. Every day, his parents and sisters, and his brothers in Avenged Sevenfold smile at the many memories they have of Jimmy, and his fans around the world revel in the musical legacy he left them.

M. SHADOWS: I came home [from playing golf when my wife called me with the news] and there were probably fifty people [there], just crying. [We were] camping at each other's houses. We'd order in food and sleep and watch videos. We didn't want to go anywhere or do anything or talk to anybody.

SYNYSTER GATES: A week or two after the Rev passed, some fans gave us this huge book of thousands of stories of the band and [personal] notes and pictures. It was the first therapeutic thing that happened and it was just unreal.

JOHNNY CHRIST: After Jimmy passed, we didn't think we were going to continue. We couldn't imagine Avenged Sevenfold without the Rev. But [the fans] sent letters and videos and there was this tremendous outpouring over the Internet, and they asked us if we could continue. After a while we realized that this thing that we created with Jimmy is a little bit bigger than we are at this point.

ZACKY VENGEANCE: *Nightmare* is the darkest, the coldest, most numb album I've ever heard, because we went there during the hardest time, basically with tears in our eyes, and recorded the songs our friend had helped write. Having to listen to the demos he played on, we put up a shield. We turned the rest of the world off, marched in there, and went to work. Looking back, I don't even know how we did it.

13

ΠEW AMERICAΠ GOSPEL: MİLLEΠΠİAL MEΤAL, 1992–PRESEΠΤ

The nineties and aughts have been a strange time for those who found grunge and alternative rock too lightweight, nu metal too trendy or stereotypically macho, and death metal too brutal. Yet the era yielded some of the most creative and iconoclastic bands formed by artists who wanted to play a combination of sounds they liked and weren't hearing from existing bands. While Tool, System of a Down, and Mastodon didn't set out to be rock stars, they each imbued underground sounds with commercial elements that took the mainstream by surprise. Others, such as Lamb of God, Machine Head, Slipknot, and Hatebreed also wrote bracing, original material, yet these bands featured striking and charismatic musicians that couldn't have stayed out of the headlines if they wanted to, often because their offstage lives were as chaotic as their onstage performances. Then there were rockers like Disturbed and Godsmack, who drew influence from classic metal and wrote heavy, melodic songs that were easily digestible and that turned them into willing celebrities, at least until they craved anonymity and family lives.

MAYNARD JAMES KEENAN (Tool, Puscifer, A Perfect Circle): I moved to LA in December of 1989 and immediately noticed that people playing music clearly were taking cues from A&R guys or marketing people. It seemed all upside-down. They had clever gimmicks, and the music was suffering. I'm kind of an opinionated guy, so I kept expressing myself, and a bunch of people said, "Well, if you think you can do better, *you* form a band."

ADAM JONES (Tool): I met Maynard through an old friend he was dating. I was working in Hollywood on special effects for movies, and my hobby was playing guitar. Maynard played me a tape of a joke band that he was in back on the East Coast, and I went, "Maynard, you can sing! You sing good." I kept bugging him to start a band on the side with me. Danny [Carey] lived downstairs from Maynard, and was playing in Green Jellÿ. He originally didn't want to play with us. Then we had a practice session and the guy that was supposed to drum for us didn't show up. Danny felt sorry for us and agreed to play. He said, "Well, I'll sit in on the sessions, but that's it." Afterwards, he went, "Wow, we should jam again."

DANNY CAREY (Tool): We weren't trying to *be* anything. We were just trying to stay open and experiment and find out what our personality was as a band. I was really into prog-rock at that time and Adam was more into rock and roll like Black Sabbath. Maynard was into Joni Mitchell and singer/songwriters. [Bassist] Paul D'Amour was more the grunge guy. We really did just throw everything into the pot and let it develop.

MAYNARD JAMES KEENAN: It wasn't hard for Tool to get signed. We were four pissed-off, relatively talented musicians, and we got a record deal after about seven shows. Nirvana helped open the door because after they hit, most music guys around town were chasing their tails trying to find the next big thing. Here we come along and we don't sound like most of the other stuff going on, so for them, they don't really get it, but they knew that it was different and that Nirvana was selling lots of records, so they knew they had to grab whatever it was, just in case.

ADAM JONES: The most important thing for us at that point was to have creative control. When we got signed [to Zoo Records], we went, "Okay, if we take less money can we have control of the music?" and the label went, "Yeah. No problem." We said, "If we take even less money can we have final say over the videos?" And so on. So we got artistic control, but there was a lot of banging heads with the record company anyway because they wanted to do things in the traditional way. They'd go, "If you're not gonna be in your video, we're not gonna pay for it." Typical slimy shit. We really wanted to take the importance of who *we* were and stress what we were doing instead—just the music and the art. We signed a three-album deal and the first thing we wanted to do was an EP. They went, "Yeah, do an EP. That'd be great!" We kind of got burned from it because it wasn't a full-length so it didn't count as a record on our contract, which is why they were so agreeable when we suggested it in the first place.

DANNY CAREY: We were broke, and we knew that even if the record company was willing to pay for studio time we were going to have to pay it all back. So we recorded *Opiate* in four days because we knew if we were there longer it was gonna get expensive. But we also had a live recording and we were happy with the way it sounded. So we thought, "We've got all these great live tracks, let's just mix them and add them to the record." That's how "Cold and Ugly" and "Jerk-Off" got on there.

ADAM JONES: We felt like no one would take us seriously unless we pushed the more heavy metal ideas, and that explains *Opiate*. We got typecast as a metal band right off the bat. It's kind of funny because the least aggressive song, "Opiate," was the most popular one.

MAYNARD JAMES KEENAN: After *Opiate* came out, we found ourselves in some place like Akron, Ohio, playing some club that looks like it holds five hundred people, but there are only five people there and those are the guys that are playing after us. But it didn't matter because we were still getting to know each other. Being on a stage like that, hearing what things sound like in different venues, getting used to traveling—I think that was a very important step in our growth.

DANNY CAREY: We got thrown into the whole grunge thing, which was weird. Everyone was into that stuff so heavily, so just because we had sort of a heavy sound and we didn't look like a spandex-wearing hair band, they instantly assumed we were one of those Seattle-type bands.

Tool delivered their music with artistic flair and drama that equaled their aggression. Other bands, however, focused more intently on sheer rage born of challenging upbringings, chemical imbalances, or just plain contempt for society and/or themselves. Robb Flynn, the force behind Machine Head, had an abusive childhood, but he was able to turn his negativity and depression into inflammatory songs rooted in thrash and incorporating aspects of nu metal. Flynn actually cut his teeth in the Bay Area's late thrash band Vio-Lence (as did current Machine Head lead guitarist Phil Demmel). At the time, Flynn and bassist Adam Duce were young, hostile, and trying to survive in an industry that had grown antagonistic toward thrash.

ROBB FLYNN (ex–Vio-Lence, Machine Head): Vio-Lence was a second-wave Bay Area thrash band that I was with [from 1986 to 1992], and it was reaching its end. The shows were down to about a hundred people. I told them I'd stay, but I wanted to start another band called Machine Head. The end of my time with the band came a year before they broke up. We went to a Deftones show and left roaring drunk with a crazy friend who loved to fight. The three of us would drink a fifth of vodka and then either get laid or fight somebody for no particular reason. This night we were getting gas and beer at the AM/PM, and this big white dude walks up and starts shit with my friend. We're watching them fight, then these two black girls from the neighborhood walk up to see what's going on. Seeing two white guys fight was pretty entertaining to them. All of a sudden, three carloads of black dudes roll up and they're like, "What are you doing fucking with our black girls?" They were fucked up and wanted to start shit. They surrounded us, the girls scatter. The dude who's fighting our friend bails. I could see there was no talking. I had a handful of these gnarly rings and I swung and felt this guy's nose break under my fist and he dropped. It was on. We're fighting five dudes. They're kicking and beating on me, and in the end, three of these guys got stabbed [by my crazy friend] and we bailed.

ADAM DUCE (Machine Head): I came out of the mini-mart with a six-pack and I see Robb and the other guy we were hanging with squaring off with six guys. I put my beer down on the curb and I thought, "Oh, fuck. We are about to die," 'cause there's about fourteen of them. They kicked Robb to the ground and surrounded him. I came over and I'm swinging on whoever, not looking. I'm hitting people in the ear as hard as I can from behind. Next thing I know, I'm picking myself up off the ground 'cause I got knocked out. I wake up and start hitting people again 'cause they didn't surround me. And I got knocked out again. I wake up and look up, and these [black dudes] are screaming and running. I was like, "What the fuck happened and now how do we get out of here?"

ROBB FLYNN: We had a show coming up and I started getting death threats at the club. People were calling in and saying,

"We're gonna throw grenades onstage." This was the real deal, so I told the band, "This is too fucked-up. I'm not gonna play the show." They took that to mean I was quitting. For the next month, Adam and I lived every second terrified. These gang guys had gotten our number and were calling and threatening our lives. Eventually it all passed over because they ended up finding somebody else to fight. Over the next six months almost every single person in that gang was killed through their own internal shit.

ADAM DUCE: Me and [ex–Machine Head guitarist] Logan [Mader] used to score weed and hang out with [Vio-Lence guitarist] Phil [Demmel] all the time. Then in 1990 we all moved into the same apartment building. We'd sit around playing acoustic guitars and get wasted. So when Robb approached us to say, "Hey, I want to do this other thing," we had already started doing something.

ROBB FLYNN: Before Machine Head, I was doing a lot of drugs and I sold speed at shows. Slayer shows were always the big score 'cause I could send my trolls off and make $700 in one night. I used to do a lot of speed, but after I left Vio-Lence, I completely stopped. I just wanted to sell drugs to make money because I needed to live. I was basically just drinking at that point.

ADAM DUCE: I was at rock bottom. I'd panhandle $20 so I could buy a $20 bag of speed and cut it in half and sell both of them for $40. I'd do it again and again. To live in the Bay Area was a real struggle. I did it for several years, and then I rented a warehouse to grow weed, and that was a huge job.

ROBB FLYNN: The first Machine Head record, *Burn My Eyes*, was fueled mostly by alcohol, rage, and hunger.

ADAM DUCE: I was a pissed-off nineteen-year-old kid starving to death, deciding whether I should go down to the store and buy a sandwich or buy a pack of cigarettes, and choosing the cigarettes because cigarettes are going to last all day and I won't be hungry. There wasn't a chance in hell the four guys that did *Burn My Eyes* could burn that hot for that long.

ROBB FLYNN: At first, no one liked us. One reviewer wrote, *"Burn My Eyes*: pretty good if you've never heard Prong." I was like, "Dude, fuck you!" We opened for Napalm Death and Obituary and at 85 percent of those dates the crowds hated us so much dudes were trying to fight us onstage. They were shouting, "Go back to Oakland, pussies" and spitting on us. At the end of the Denver show we had to take cymbal stands off the drum riser and use them like shields to defend ourselves. I thought Chicago was gonna be sick because Vio-Lence did pretty well there. We played there, and when we stopped "Davidian" there were just two people sarcastically clapping. I said, "You suck, fuck you Chicago."

While alternative and grunge incapacitated thrash and nu metal, it didn't have the same effect on hardcore, largely because many of the popular bands of the day—Nirvana, Pearl Jam, Rage Against the Machine—all claimed to be rooted more in punk than metal. Ironically, one of the most popular hardcore bands, Hatebreed, was influenced as much by Slayer as Minor Threat. The front man for the band, Jamey Jasta, started in the music industry in Connecticut in his early teens, playing in the well-respected band Jasta 14 and booking local hardcore and metal shows. Like Flynn, Jasta came from a dysfunctional family and sought music as an escape.

JAMEY JASTA: I was thirteen when I was in my first band, Dreadnaught. We had to change the name when I was fourteen because there were other Dreadnaughts, so we went with Jasta 14 and started to play out and do trade shows. I loved every part of it, whether it was handing out flyers a week before the shows or making the demos and photocopying at the Food Bag down the road from my house, cutting them with scissors or buying the tapes for demos at the dollar store. We could draw two or three hundred kids in some places, and we sold a lot of demos. We were kind of like a mix between mosh metal and bands like Burn or Quicksand. The other guys were older than me, but I grabbed the mic because I was determined to be the singer. I don't think they necessarily wanted me to do the vocals, but I didn't know how to play an instrument so they went with it. We practiced in the middle of the night in a band room in downtown New Haven above an old woman's clothing store. It was not what a normal fourteen-year-old should have been doing. I missed a lot of school to play shows out of state, and I made it to the end of the ninth grade before I dropped out. I lived at home on and off and I lived with the drummer of High on Fire, Des [Kensel]. My crackhead Uncle Paulie, God rest his soul, used to take us to gigs. He didn't have car insurance, but he had a license, so he convinced Ryder to rent us a truck. One tour, it was us and Dive in the back of a Ryder truck, which you're not supposed to have people in the back of. We're drinking Mad Dog, we're smoking weed. Matt [Kelly] from Dive, who is now the drummer of Dropkick Murphys, was in the back with us, and we were telling stories about the hookers that my uncle used to fuck—that he'd bring to my house. Talk about debauchery. We didn't believe in karma. Shoplifting was the norm, being a scumbag, being an asshole. Eventually it caught up with me.

BRIAN FAIR: Jamey was the hardest-working man in hardcore. He saw the possibility of making a career out of this long before anyone else I knew did. But he knew that meant multitasking and having a million irons in the fire. He booked shows, he had a 'zine, he started a small record label, he had Jasta 14. We were all like, "Who is this little chubby kid that's running the Connecticut hardcore scene?" It's weird because he was totally responsible with the business, but totally crazy. We had some great times with Jasta 14, but you never knew if they were gonna make it to the show or end up in jail that night.

JAMEY JASTA: I worked hard booking and promoting shows and getting the band noticed, but I also did a lot of fucked-up shit. We'd steal equipment from band rooms and get in fights all the time, when I was still in New Haven. Because you're in Yale, you feel this intense divide with the upper class. You're on the street, you have no money, and you're high or drunk. We thought it was a good idea to do fucked-up shit to Yale students. One time at three in the morning, my friend was wearing this Judge shirt and somebody had made a comment about his shirt and it started this whole melee between these football player Yale students and us. The Judge shirt was white and it ended up being almost completely red with [other people's] blood by the end of the fight. One night we were all camped out at a friend's apartment, and a buddy of mine went downstairs to answer the door and got shot in the leg. He came up bleeding and we called 911, but you don't want to tell them exactly what happened because there was some illegal activity going on. I kind of learned my lesson when I was arrested in New Britain in '92. I got into a fight in a diner with a guy who ended up being an off-duty cop, and I spent Thursday through Sunday in jail. When you're fifteen and you think you're tough and you're drunk and this grown man hands your ass to you and then you end up spending four days in jail and no one will bail you out, it's kind of humbling. You realize you're not such a badass. At the time, New Britain jail was bad. They were calling me Kurt Cobain and I'd hear people crying in other cells. After that, I just said "I'll never go back to jail." And I never did.

In 1994, Jasta was fired from Jasta 14 for missing a band meeting and started Hatebreed with some friends in Bridgeport: guitarist Matt McIntosh, bassist Chris Beattie, and ex-drummer Dave Russo.

JAMEY JASTA: We made a joke demo tape with studio time Jasta 14 had already paid for. We worked that to get a lot of shows. Kids started coming to the shows and taking part in this positive, energetic experience. Even though the music was always loud and aggressive and we were sometimes violent as fuck, the message has always been positive.

CHRIS BEATTIE (Hatebreed): [Our band has] always been about having a good time. I like to see kids up front. I don't want to see them standing in the back because they're afraid to come see us.

JAMEY JASTA: In Jasta 14 everyone was so talented and had so many great ideas, but when you're trying to make a simple recipe it just doesn't work. It would be like having Paul Prudhomme, Emeril Lagasse, and Bobby Flay trying to make one little simple dish; you have too many cooks in the kitchen. With Hatebreed, I felt like, "Let's make this meat and potatoes. Let's try and be like the AC/DC of metallic hardcore and write songs that any kid can pick up and learn." By the end of '95, we had a real three-song demo. But Chris and [guitarist] Matt McIntosh had day jobs and I didn't. I was trying to be fully about the band, promoting it, booking shows. Matt eventually quit. He needed to get a stable day job and didn't think this crazy hardcore band from Connecticut was ever gonna amount to anything. But he did record on our first EP, *Under the Knife*. We sold it as a 7-inch through the Victory distribution system, and it was just a phenomenon. We sold 50,000 copies and it got the label's attention. We did a deal with them in early '97.

In 1992, vocalist Randy Blythe was Lamb of God to the core, and he hadn't even joined the band yet. Rugged, daring, unpredictable, and a little bit unstable, Blythe grew up as a hardcore kid and didn't even embrace metal until he joined Lamb of God (then called Burn the Priest) in 1994. But at heart, he was all metal.

Whether a sign or mere coincidence, both the swaggering Blythe and Mastodon's maverick, loose-cannon guitarist/vocalist Brent Hinds rode freight trains like hobos before they hooked up with their main bands.

RANDY BLYTHE (Lamb of God): I hopped trains for two or three summers to California and back [to Virginia] just to see America. My grandfather had done it and my mom would always tell me stories about it. I had a romantic view of what it must have been like to ride the rails in the Depression era. I wanted to see if you could still do it. I discovered that you can if you know what you're doing, but I wouldn't recommend it, 'cause if you try, you'll more than likely get killed. I had a rail partner, Tyler, and the first night of the second summer we rode out, we carried this girl along with us. She wanted to ride freight and we were like, "Well, all right." We had done it the previous summer, so we kind of knew what we were doing. We told her to pack light. So Tyler jumps up on the train and I jump on the train and it's moving out. And this girl is getting on the train. All of a sudden she's dragging her feet, holding the ladder, trying to get up, and she's slipping. We were like, "Aw, shit, we gotta pull this chick up!" We grabbed her and she was a little girl so it shouldn't have been too hard. We start pulling her up and she was heavy as fuck. All three of us almost got yanked overboard. We would have been chewed to pieces by the rails. But we got up there. We're panting, and I said, "Gimme your backpack." I opened it, and she had books, makeup, toiletries, and all this fucking girl shit—a nice dress. So we're just throwing stuff off the train left and right and she's freaking out, going, "But I need that. I'm a *girl*." We were like, "You're not a girl out here. You're a liability." I knew a girl in Minneapolis who lost her foot because she was drunk and she tried to hop out and didn't make it and the train chopped off her foot. You don't fuck around with freight trains drunk. You'll lose.

BRENT HINDS (Mastodon, Fiend Without a Face, Four Hour Fogger):
When I turned seventeen I decided to try the hobo life for
a while—hopping freight trains and drinking whisky. That
didn't last; I got arrested and went to jail in New Orleans. I
had walked out of a bar and I was tripping pretty hard on acid.
I had taken my shirt off. At this point, my torso wasn't fully
tattooed, but I had a huge bat on my chest and some tattoos
on my forearms. I was staggering down the street dragging my
jacket behind me. I was obviously drunk. So I walked over to
this horse. I started bridling the horse and walking away with
him. This cop comes up to me and says, "Hey, what the hell
do you think you're doing?" I said, "Oh, I'm taking this horse
with me." He said, "No, you're not. What the hell are you
on?" I went, "I'm on the sidewalk, motherfucker, what are you
on?" I went to jail for a couple months for that one. I called
my mom. She went, "God, I haven't heard from you in two
years. I want you to come home." I went, "Okay, cool, 'cause
I'm in jail and I need you to come get me out." Then I went
down to Birmingham, Alabama, and saw my buddy Gary
Lindsey's band Knuckle. And that's how I met [their bassist]
Troy Sanders [now in Mastodon].

TROY SANDERS (ex–Four Hour Fogger, Mastodon): Brent is like a
smart homeless guy or a mad scientist, but he's mostly mad.
He's 75 percent mad, 25 percent scientist. But he's a great musician and a great guy if you stay on his good side.

BILL KELLIHER (ex-Lethargy, ex–Today Is the Day, Mastodon): Sometimes Brent is the nicest guy on earth, other times he's . . . a
little volatile. You just gotta be careful of what you say around
him. It's like playing with fire. I've seen him pour beer on
people's heads just for fun. But he's Brent. He just gets away
with stuff like that. He lives for the moment and doesn't really
think about the future.

JOHN CAMPBELL (Lamb of God): We all met at Virginia Commonwealth University [in 1990]. Randy went there, too. Chris [Adler] learned how to play drums. [Guitarist] Mark [Morton] was in [indie rock band] Hgual. Then [in 1994] we got together and started Burn the Priest as an instrumental band. There was no heat at the house. We would freeze our asses off, get really drunk on Black Label beer, and hang around the kerosene heaters trying to write metal songs. But we practiced five days a week out of necessity. The bands in Richmond can flat outplay you and if you don't rehearse they will blow you off the stage. They inspired us to raise the bar musically and taught us the work ethic we needed to succeed.

MARK MORTON (Lamb of God): These really off-time, rhythmically powerful instrumental bands—like Breadwinner, the Alternatives, Brainflower, Ladyfinger—that's who we saw at parties and clubs and that stuff was a big influence on us. We were a heavy metal version of that. Randy wasn't in the band yet, but I knew him from around Richmond. Friends of mine were in a band called hose.got.cable. Every once in a while, Randy would hop onstage and do a song with them. He had this crazy death metal growl. But then I left Burn the Priest to go to graduate school, and during that time, they got Randy and [guitarist] Abe [Spear] to join.

RANDY BLYTHE: [When I first saw Burn the Priest in 1995] they were loud as fuck and awesome. And the cops came. They were playing in this garage behind this house and the cops were shining their lights in, so they just ducked down and kept playing. I was like, "That is fucking punk rock!" I looked at my girlfriend and I said, "This is the band I'm going to sing for." She's like, "Whatever, Randy." A week later I'm in the band.

MARK MORTON: When I came back after grad school, they were this grindcore/thrash band with some of the riffs I had written. But I was certainly happy to come back to it, and that's when things started taking off. It's not like we went from the Richmond college scene to doing big shows. In the mid-nineties, when we were in that basement in Richmond pooling our money for a case of cheap beer, we weren't thinking about being nominated for Grammys and touring the world. We were just thinking about having enough money for that beer. I was a roofer for six or seven years before the band broke. There was a time when I thought, "If I can go roofing full time I can make really good money." I had bought a little house for myself and was living a cool bachelor's life. We were just playing weekend shows. We'd show up at the practice space, load up the van, everybody would throw a twenty or two down and that would be our gas money. Then we'd go and try to make it back. If we did good, we came back with a couple extra bucks and that was all it ever was. As it got more serious, the business stuff started creeping in and it became harder to balance making the right decisions for the band versus keeping my life going. I never wanted to gamble everything I had built for myself on the band, which at the time seemed really far-fetched. It was tricky walking that fine line for a while. 'Cause on my own, doing construction, I was fine. In the band full-time, I was broke. There were definitely times I was selling CDs so my power wouldn't get cut off and saving scrap copper from jobs in a bucket so every couple weeks I could turn that in and get a hundred bucks for it to put towards the bills.

E. J. JOHANTGEN (president, Prosthetic Records): We were just starting out as a label and I heard about Burn the Priest from a friend and I thought there was nothing else like them at the time. I thought they sounded a little bit like Brutal Truth, but there was something unique and different. I heard no one would sign them because they were called Burn the Priest and they refused to change their name. So I called them up and said, "I don't want you to change your name." After three days of negotiation we signed them. Then right before that they decided to change their name because they thought the name Burn the Priest would hold them back.

From the moment he joined, Blythe was both Lamb of God's greatest asset and the hurricane force that threatened to rip it to pieces. Misanthropic, belligerent, and accident-prone, he provoked controversy and drama wherever he went. But he was always amazing onstage, captivating crowds with the fury of Phil Anselmo and the attitude of Jello Biafra.

RANDY BLYTHE: The first time we toured with Gwar, I got pass-out drunk. We were staying at this house, and I got up in the middle of the night to take a leak and walked out a second-story door off the roof and woke up on the ground with a broken arm. When I was onstage performing and getting really worked up, the blood would just rush to my arm and the part I broke at the wrist hurt like a motherfucker.

MARK MORTON: Randy is one of my best friends in the world. When we've gotten drunk and gotten in fights and I've punched him in the face, he was still one of my best friends. I hang out with him as a friend socially and I would tomorrow if the band broke up. He's my compadre and my partner in crime. But because we *are* that close, we fight like brothers.

RANDY BLYTHE: The worst fight Mark and I ever got into was in Glasgow and it was documented on our *Killadelphia* DVD. I was drunk as shit and we were fuckin' sick of each other after being on the road for so long and we just went at it. I picked him up and threw him on the ground and I think I cracked his shoulder. I woke up with a sideways nose so I went into the bathroom and popped that back into place, and my pinky was broken and my eye was swollen shut. The next morning after that was not a good morning.

MARK MORTON: I think it scared everyone else worse than it scared us. Fifteen minutes after the fight, I walked off and got my head back together and came back and everyone was in the back lounge like there was this big crisis. Me and Randy were in the front lounge and he handed me a beer and I popped it and we kept on going and laughed about the whole thing. It certainly wasn't the first time we've come to blows. It's just that someone happened to have a camera there to document it.

In Des Moines, Iowa, in the heart of what some consider America's Midwestern wasteland, one of the most artistic, chaotic, eclectic, and popular contemporary metal bands evolved like a creature from a prehistoric swamp. All nine members of Slipknot were too bored, furious, determined, and subversive not to change the cultural landscape of their hometown, and later the entire metal scene. Aside from becoming one of the strangest and most disturbing bands to break into the mainstream, the members of Slipknot have been involved with other popular and artistically praised groups, including Stone Sour (vocalist Corey Taylor and guitarist Jim Root), the Murderdolls (drummer Joey Jordison), Dirty Little Rabbits (percussionist Shawn "Clown" Crahan), and DJ Starscream (turntablist Sid Wilson).

PAUL GRAY (1972–2010) (Slipknot): Before Slipknot, I was in a band called Body Pit with Andy [Colsefni] on vocals, and Mick [Thomson] and Donnie Steele on guitars. I had played with Joey in a band called Anal Blast. The basic idea of Slipknot started in '92 and we didn't have a name. We just knew we wanted to do something with extra percussion. [Percussionist] Shawn [Crahan] started jamming, but then I moved to California with an old girlfriend, which didn't work out. So Shawn was like, "You wanna come back and do this?" I told the chick I was leaving, got on a plane, and went back to Iowa.

SHAWN CRAHAN (Slipknot): Paul and I used to get together in his mom's basement and we'd write songs and drink beer, with me on drums. Then I reached out to Andy, and he had

a death-growl that slays to this day. It was Paul, Andy, and I.
But the truth is, I always knew they were going to call Joey
[Jordison] to play drums. It was part of the plan. I was molding
this sickness. I was like the sun on the water boiling the shit.
We had all these other people who came in and out. We even
called Jim [Root]. He was supposed to be the original guitarist because spiritually we were trying to get all these people
aligned. But he said no. Jim's place wasn't until later.

JOEY JORDISON (Slipknot, Murderdolls): The first time I met Shawn
was when he was in his old band, Heads on the Wall. My
band, Modifidious, played on a bill with them and [guitar-
ist Jim Root's old band] Atomic Opera. I watched Shawn
play, and the dude was kicking over his hi-hat stand, pissed as
shit. I was like, "I wanna be in a band with that guy." After
Modifidious broke up, I was talking to Paul [Gray] about
doing something, and he said, "Come see what me and Shawn
are working on." I went over and they played me four songs.
The first was "Slipknot" [later rewritten as "Sick"]. From that
second on, I knew they would be the biggest fucking band
ever. I said to myself, "I'm gonna either join this band or I'm
gonna destroy it."

JIM ROOT (Slipknot, Stone Sour): In 1985, Atomic Opera fell apart
so I started jamming with some other friends, including [bassist]
Shawn Economaki. He said, "Why don't you come over and
hear what Corey and I have been doing with Stone Sour?"
I'd heard some of their stuff on local radio before and I wasn't
into it. They sounded almost like Tesla. So I put it off, but then
one day after I was practicing with Economaki I stuck around
to watch a Stone Sour rehearsal, and they sounded completely
different than when I had last seen them three years ago. So I
called them up and said, "Hey, I'd like to be a part of this."

PAUL GRAY: We had a show booked and we didn't have a name.
But we had the song "Slipknot," which rolled off the tongue

pretty easy. So we used it. One day we were in rehearsal and Clown had this clown mask. He put it on and would not take it off. At first, it pissed us off. You couldn't even see if he was serious. We went, "Dude, please take that fuckin' thing off," and he sat there and laughed. After a while we went, "Man, that is actually creepy. Maybe we should *all* get masks." It was cool because after the shows we could go back in the club in our normal clothes and talk to people in the crowd to find out if they liked us or hated us, and no one knew the dudes they were talking to were in the band.

COREY TAYLOR: I was at the first Slipknot show with my buddy Denny and about twenty other people. It started with this crazy circus of masked freaks walking from the outside through the crowd up on the stage. It was so ominous and inspiring, and as much love as I had for Stone Sour, I thought, "Someday I'm gonna sing for this band." After the show, we all went to what has gone down in Des Moines history as the House Destruction Party of '95. There were a lot of people from Slipknot there and this house that some of my friends lived at was being condemned. So we thought, "Well, if they're gonna tear it down the next day, let's trash it." We started destroying everything. When the cops showed up we were trying to go through a wall to the outside with the railing from one of the staircases. Water was shooting up out of the bathroom. I had plaster in my hair. I'm wasted. I was beating on the wall with a portable barbecue. Somehow, I ended up sneaking away and went home with these two girls. I woke up the next day and everybody was in jail, including Denny. So I went down to bail him out as his birthday present, and there's Clown and Paul and they're bailing out Paul's brother, Tony. That was the beginning of my weird relationship with Slipknot.

PAUL GRAY: We decided to go in the studio and do a CD right away, which was crazy because we had only done a couple shows. It took forever to make, it was expensive, and we paid for it ourselves—a couple hundred bucks an hour. Andy and I were doing concrete to pay for it. We borrowed a lot of money from Shawn's wife, who actually had a job. The producer, Sean McMahon, was super Christian, and he was in turmoil because he thought we were Satanic. We were in the studio day and night. We'd sleep there and watch porn and videos of people killing themselves or getting killed. The producer walked in while we were watching this stuff, and he stood there for a couple minutes and then had a mental breakdown and locked himself in the bathroom for a few hours. We were getting charged for him to sit in there and cry. He ended up getting [guitarist] Donnie [Steele] to quit because he convinced him that what we were doing was evil. Donnie was supposed to play all the leads and he started not showing up. That record took so long to make that by the time we were finally done, it didn't really represent us.

JOEY JORDISON: Everything was a work in progress. We experimented a lot because we weren't really sure where we wanted to go. The cover of that album—*Mate.Feed.Kill.Repeat*—is me naked in this cage contraption that Shawn welded together. It's 20 degrees out and I'm in the middle of a fucking cornfield freezing to death. In the picture you can see my foot looks like a goddamn devil hoof. That wasn't intended, but we saw it and went, "Fuck, we're onto something." It was all about misery, and that's what we love—the misery, the hurt, and the pain. We're gonna kill ourselves more than any other band. Slipknot is absolutely the most painful thing you could ever endure.

MICK THOMSON (Slipknot): They had already recorded *Mate. Feed.Kill.Repeat* when Paul asked me to play with them. It was weird because Joey and I had this personal beef going from before Slipknot. It was a stupid, childish thing. He once gave me a look I didn't appreciate, and I don't think he appreciated the look I gave back to him. So we were both like, "Yeah, fuck that guy." It's funny. Talking about it to him years later, it was like, "Wow, we were stupid because we were *wrong.*"

PAUL GRAY: We got a wake-up call when we were in a battle of the bands hosted by the local radio station. We went up against Stone Sour and we won. Show-wise, we blew them away, but Corey's voice was killer. We read back what the judges wrote and they raved about our performance and music. The only negative thing they would say was about our vocalist. He could do death metal, but he would try to *sing,* too, and it just sounded horrible. We knew something had to change.

ANDY COLSEFNI: Right before Corey came in there were no feelings of negativity in my mind at all. We were constantly in the studio re-recording things or putting something else down for Roadrunner, trying to seal that deal. I was walking on clouds. I thought we were actually going to make it work. It wasn't until after I came back from a long weekend vacation with my family that I found out that without ever talking to me, they had Corey come in and record over a bunch of my vocal tracks.

SHAWN CRAHAN: I bought a bar because we got banned from playing everywhere else. We used to saw on things and make sparks, and we'd go into the crowd and put a noose over fans' heads and drag them around with it. No one wanted that in their place. Andy helped get that world going. But we knew we had to replace him with Corey. If we were smart and mature, we would have said, "Andy, play the drums." But he wanted to be the lead singer so he quit, and I don't think he made a mistake. I absolutely know he's not supposed to be in this band. It's no offense to him, but this is *Slipknot.* He was throwing fits and not growing, not evolving, and we were on the fuckin' bulldozer and there was a maniac driving it. We were frightened, all of us. Scared to death. But it felt good.

JOEY JORDISON: Me, Mick, and Shawn came into the porn shop Corey worked at one night and circled the DVDs and looked at them a little bit. Corey was almost ready to piss his fuckin' pants. He thought we were there to beat him up since he was in Stone Sour. We went up to him and said, "All right man, straight up: You wanna join Slipknot?"

COREY TAYLOR: I know there's a big legend about how they threatened to kick my ass if I didn't join the band. It's completely untrue. They were so nervous it was fucking adorable. Clown was constantly moving around, couldn't stand still. He went, "Hey, you know . . . I'm just gonna be straight up with you. . . . We want you to join the band. . . . " Joey was mumbling something and Mick was going, "Look, man, I just wanna do whatever we gotta do to make it." I was like, "Holy shit!" I was still doing Stone Sour and I was very devoted to that band. So I said, "Well, gimme a little time to think about it," but in the back of my head I knew.

PAUL GRAY: At first, the plan was to keep Andy, too, and have him just play the percussion and scream the heavier stuff. We actually did one show like that and it was good. But Andy wanted to be the singer so he announced at his second show with Corey that he was quitting the band. We didn't even know that was coming, but we were relieved because he was so unhappy we brought Corey in. It took us from being a really big local band to a place where we knew we could get a record deal. It was definitely Corey's vocals that changed it.

JIM ROOT: I was pissed at Corey when he joined Slipknot. Shit was going really well for Stone Sour so I couldn't understand why he'd leave.

It wasn't just Taylor's vocals—which can grate like a tire spinning on gravel or flow like a troubadour singing tales of heartbreak—that brought Slipknot sudden attention. It was their ugly aesthetic, which included macabre costumes, conceptual approaches to albums and shows, multimedia presentations, and the type of performance art antics usually reserved for experimental industrial bands.

COREY TAYLOR: We had this bootleg videotape that we had named "Sex, Death and Mayhem." It had all this crazy animation, snuff shit, and real death. We decided to splice together an hour of footage from that for a Halloween show, and the footage culminated with the Bud Dwyer suicide. [Dwyer was the former treasurer of Pennsylvania who, in 1987, after being accused of accepting a bribe, held a press conference in which he removed a .357 Magnum from a manila envelope, inserted the loaded revolver in his mouth, and pulled the trigger.] We looped it, so at the end of "Scissors," there's Bud Dwyer popping himself over and over. I watched people's faces staring in absolute horror because not only did we loop it, we slowed it down [*laughs*]. We were fucked-up at the time—so angry and so hungry and willing to do anything to make a statement. We lost half of our fans at that show. I had a friend who still, to this day, will not talk to me. She looked at me straight in the face and said, "This is disgusting, this is not gonna go anywhere. You are not the person I thought you were."

SHAWN CRAHAN: I came up with the name "maggots" for our fans, and it's simple. I had a dead bird that was given to me. I watched the maggots come and I studied them. We used to inhale the fumes from this bird before we played and just— death, man. When you inhale it into your lungs there's just this sickness that overtakes you and makes you throw up, and we'd walk onstage with that. I'd watch this thing and I'd see the maggots grow and they'd die in the liquid 'cause it was in a jar and they'd drown and didn't get to be flies. I was watching the fans one day and they were all pushed together. Once in a while one of them would get on top. I was like, "Wow. Maggots burrow themselves straight up and down like that and they eat, and when they're done they fall on top and they literally roll to the back." I was like, "Maggots. You feed off of us. Then hopefully you get your life going. One day you will get the wings of flies and fly away."

At first glance, System of a Down was as unlikely to become famous in LA as Slipknot was in the Midwest. Yet for a period of time they were the darlings of the Los Angeles scene. The band, which re-formed in 2010 after a six-year hiatus, was composed completely of Armenian musicians who eschewed traditional metal in favor of something more bizarre. Their influences were all over the place—Dead Kennedys, Black Sabbath, Slayer, Mr. Bungle, Frank Zappa, Parliament/Funkadelic, Middle Eastern and Armenian music—and they shifted rythmic gears multiple times between songs. Yet their chemistry was so strong, their melodies so clever, and their lyrics so compelling—a combination of politics, angst, and nonsense—that they demanded attention.

DARON MALAKIAN (System of a Down): We started playing out at the late end of the whole grunge thing—end of '95—and we didn't really know what was going on in the metal scene in LA, to be honest. We had never been those guys who go out on Sunset Strip. So when we went to LA to play shows it was a weird shock to the scene; the other bands were like, "Who the hell are these dudes?" We were four Armenian guys, and in the early days a lot of Armenian kids came out and supported us. But we never really felt like a part of any scene.

SERJ TANKIAN (System of a Down): I wouldn't say we were grounded in the Armenian community. We're proud of our heritage and it's definitely an influence that we don't want to deny. But it's not specifically something we've tried to incorporate in our music and say, "Hey look, we're Armenian."

DARON MALAKIAN: The two or three years that we were selling out clubs and had a huge buzz in LA, nobody wanted to sign us *because* we were Armenian. We were told, "Yeah, you know you guys have a big buzz. There's a big Armenian community in LA. But who's gonna get you in Texas? Who's gonna get you in Germany? Who's gonna get you in these places where they don't even know what an Armenian is?" We never considered the Armenian thing to be such a big deal; it just was.

SERJ TANKIAN: When we write new songs, we try not to sound like System of a Down, let alone anyone else. That keeps us not only a step ahead, but a step ahead of ourselves. The reason we do a lot of different things in the same song is because you don't wake up in the morning and think about one thing during your whole day. You think about love for a second, you think about hate, you get angry at your boss. With System of a Down, we want to bring all of that kind of life emotion into the music.

DARON MALAKIAN: After years of having every record company shut their doors on us, we finally got a manager who knew someone who knew [American Recordings president] Rick Rubin, and Rick ended up coming to see us at the Viper Room, and he loved it.

SERJ TANKIAN: We had a couple lineup shifts before we got signed. We had a bassist [Dave Hakopyan] who was a great player, but he didn't really fit in with our vision, so we got Shavo [Odadjian], who had been hanging out with us for a long time and was a guitarist in our previous band, Soil. Plus he and Daron vibed better. They both grew up on KISS and they played really well together. [Hakopyan later joined the Armenian metal band Apex Theory.]

DARON MALAKIAN: We were on the verge of getting signed and had been talking to [drummer John Dolmayan], whose own band was falling apart. We shared studios with him and we noticed there were personal issues that [our drummer] Andy [Ontronik Khachaturian] was having that were getting in the way of the band. He was a great player, but he was unstable. We told John, "Look, if something happens, we might need your help." Next thing we know, Andy gets into a fight and punches a wall, shattering every bone from his fingers all the way up to his elbow. I was hanging out with Shavo that day, and he goes, "Hey man, Andy just broke his arm," and right away I said, "Call John." I didn't even stutter. Then we went in and did the record.

When its self-titled debut came out in 1998, System of a Down hit the road with more traditional metal bands and eventually won over Slayer's fans and other tough crowds. The album eventually went platinum, and the band's second record, 2001's *Toxicity*, which featured the radio hit "Aerials," has gone triple platinum. Morally, if not musically, System of a Down had a similar vibe to Tool. Neither band partied especially hard, the members valued their privacy, and their primary goal was to make music, not trouble. Tool was even more popular than System. To date, all its releases have gone platinum or double platinum, except for 1996's *Ænima*, which is triple platinum. In 2012, Tool was working on its fifth release. Despite its financial success, the band has experienced various growing pains and personality conflicts.

MAYNARD JAMES KEENAN: Near the recording of *Undertow*, you're really starting to figure each other out and see the nuances and hang-ups and emotional and mental obstacles. I think we went from zero to jaded in under thirty seconds. The honeymoon was definitely over and we started to see what was happening out there with bands coming and going. Toward the end of the tour we were watching amazing bands like Fishbone struggling to make it. We used to think Fishbone was gonna be around forever.

ADAM JONES: We got asked to do all these strange things. Once this girl asked us to play an anti-vivisection show at the [Hollywood] Palladium, and she was talking about how killing animals is wrong—but she was wearing leather Doc [Martens]! We said, "Okay, we'll do it," but we went the other way with it because we feel that life feeding on life is very natural.

MAYNARD JAMES KEENAN: We came out with acoustic guitars and started playing "Maynard's Dick" for this sold out crowd that wasn't even there to see us. The chorus goes, "Slide a mile six inches at a time on Maynard's dick." So we're already trying to be offensive. Then right in the middle of the song, we started picking up all these $5 acoustic guitars we got from Tijuana that we had stacked by the side of the stage and we began smashing them. We pulled out chainsaws and tore the hell out of these things.

ADAM JONES: That performance was the birth of "Disgustipated," which is the industrial track at the end of *Undertow.* We also bought two pianos for $100 a pop through *The Recycler* and [while recording] at Grand Master Studios, we shot them up with shotguns, bashed the shit out of them, and then we [played them and] had a guy come in and help us with sampling, which was really a new thing at the time.

MAYNARD JAMES KEENAN: I had a shotgun with blanks in it and I'm shooting it off inside the Palladium, flames leaping up out of the barrel towards the curtain. There were all these horrified people there to save the bunnies, and here we are screaming, "Life feeds on life!"

ADAM JONES: After we finished, the girl with the leather Docs went, "Oh, that was *so* great!" She totally missed the point [*laughs*].

DANNY CAREY: After we put out *Undertow* we went on tour with the Rollins Band and we could tell we were winning over hundreds of fans every night. Then we were lucky enough to have a connection that got us on Lollapalooza. So suddenly,

MTV had to pay attention to us. They played our [surreal stop-action] video [for "Sober"] one time and they got bombarded with requests. We watched our record go from nowhere to number 50 on the charts, and it stayed there for two years. Suddenly we go from playing for 100 people in a club to performing for 20,000 people a night on Lollapalooza.

MAYNARD JAMES KEENAN: A lot of my songs are very personal, so one of the biggest obstacles for me was overcoming the emotional and physical drain of being on the road trying to perform those songs every night in front of huge crowds.

ADAM JONES: "Prison Sex" was the second single and the record company was getting all geared up for that. Contractually, they were supposed to talk to us about any sort of publicity stunt they pulled on our behalf. But without telling us, they made little kid T-shirts with our Tool wrench logo on there, which is actually a phallic symbol; it looks like a penis with testicles. So, the label was going to send the shirts to all the radio stations to promote "Prison Sex" because Nirvana sent T-shirts for one of their songs. Maynard goes, "Do you know what that song's about?" They went, "Uhhh, no." He said, "It's about getting fucked in the ass and being a little kid and then that child abuse cycling [to the next generation]." They went, "Oh my god" and the shirts never went out.

MAYNARD JAMES KEENAN: The tragic part of that is they didn't get the joke they had accidentally made. They were just *that* stupid. We had to go, "*This* is funny. I don't think you *know* it's funny, but it's *funny* and, *no*, we can't send these to people."

Tool's traumas may have been mostly silly and superficial; Machine Head was dealing with real problems caused by dysfunction and overindulgence.

ROBB FLYNN: By the time I was writing for the [1997] album

[*The More Things Change . . .*] I was too fucked-up to care as much as I should have. I was drinking a lot and getting into a self-destructive phase. I put on a bunch of weight and got very insecure about it. I started making myself throw up after every meal and became a full-blown bulimic. Now, when I listen to the lyrics, it takes me right back there. That was the beginning of this manic partying. There were times we'd have sixty people on our bus blinded out of their heads. The VOD guys introduced us to Special K and we fucking loved that. It was elephant tranquilizers. Adam [Duce] and I did that and we were fucking crushed.

DAVE McCLAIN (ex–Sacred Reich, Machine Head): Ozzy canceled his set at Ozzfest in Columbus, Ohio, right before he came out. Sharon was telling Phil [Anselmo] "You've gotta go out and tell the crowd Ozzy's not gonna be here." Phil said, "I'm not gonna go out there unless Robb's with me." Then they started getting people to sing. So, all the singers who knew Ozzy's songs sang with his backing band.

ROBB FLYNN: Phil and I do "I Don't Know" and Manson and I do "Crazy Train." Then they just wanted me to stay up there. But by the fifth or sixth song, everyone was like, "What the fuck's going on?" So you start to see from the back of the amphitheater all these little fires pop up. The grass is frying and part of the fence goes up. It's like, "Holy shit there's gonna be a riot!" So Anselmo, who's got the most undesirable job in the world at that point, comes out and says, "All right, Ozzy's not gonna be fucking. . . . " Boo-oo-oo-oo! Next thing we know, the police helicopters are there.

DAVE McCLAIN: If Robb didn't perform, the crowd definitely would have rioted. He really saved the day. So we're getting ready to go, and I go outside to take a piss. Robb's lying there looking like he's half dead. His fucking shirt's off and the word "METAL" is carved into his chest. There's a knife out and he's bleeding. We were like, "Dude, what's up? We're here for you. We're fucking proud of you, you got up there and saved the day."

ROBB FLYNN: Here's what happened. I called my dad, thrilled about this thing I had done. He literally said, "Oh, cool. I gotta go to bed right now." And he hung up. I was drunk, but I was trying to keep it together, and that was my way of dealing with the lack of support of my father.

After some bands have a few albums under their belts, they calm down and curtail their self-destructive ways. Not Machine Head. It wasn't until the members started having families that they cut back on the decadence and debauchery.

ADAM DUCE: There are giant blocks of time—like years—that I just don't remember. During our first year and a half of touring for [1994's] *Burn my Eyes*, I was so drunk that when we toured the same places for *The More Things Change*, I didn't remember any of the venues.

ROBB FLYNN: Adam and I were drinking too much at that point, but [guitarist] Logan [Mader] had gone into raging drug mode. He was doing booze, weed, Valium, Percocets [a prescription narcotic that combines Tylenol with oxycodone], Ecstasy, and coke. By the end of that tour cycle, we'd go onstage and he'd be playing the wrong riffs and we'd be arguing with him onstage. In our last conversation, he was convinced the government had placed robot cats on the fence outside his window, and they had fiber-optic eyes that broadcast his every move back to the CIA.

LOGAN MADER (ex–Machine Head, ex-Soulfly; Dirty Icon Productions): Clearly, we were all out of control drinking and taking drugs all the time. I don't think I was any worse than any of the other guys, but it became clear that I couldn't keep doing that, so I left the band. And yes, I probably said something about robot cats with camera eyes, but I must have been joking. I wasn't crazy.

ADAM DUCE: I did meth for a couple years, but I couldn't handle the fucking painful comedown. I eventually came to the conclusion that the only way to never come down again is to not go up. So I just quit and went back to mostly drinking.

ROBB FLYNN: [1999's] *Burning Red* was the most drugs I had ever done during a record session or a tour. I was gacked out of my brain on coke, and boozed out every night. The night before I ended all coke use, eight people had an eight ball each, and we went through seven and a half of them in a thirty-six hour period. It was like *Boogie Nights*.

DAVE McCLAIN: At two o'clock in the afternoon, they were sitting around the pool buck-ass naked and then Robb's gacked out of his mind, and he has to get on the phone with our label to ask for tour support.

ROBB FLYNN: I can't even focus on the numbers and I was on the phone exploding in a rage to get another $50,000. And I fuckin' *got* it.

Though they shared the same thrash influences, Hatebreed's music wasn't as complex as Machine Head's, which is probably a good thing since, for a number of years, Jasta and his bandmates started drinking 40s at 11 a.m. and kept going until they passed out. Hatebreed wasn't the tightest band on the planet. But no matter how hammered they were in writing sessions, onstage, or after a gig, the band delivered surging, savage riffs and gut-roaring vocals with the fortitude and ferocity of frontline soldiers storming enemy lines. In many ways, Hatebreed *was* battling to survive. Even when their albums sold, even when they landed high-profile tours, their demons threatened to outrun them, and poor business decisions kept the group on the verge of collapse. Since they knew they weren't going to get rich, they settled for getting shit-faced, touring the globe, and coming home with outrageous stories and a few war wounds.

JAMEY JASTA: Victory Records signed us and put out *Satisfaction Is the Death of Desire* in 2007. We were on fire. We sold a hundred thousand records and we thought that was insane, but it didn't stop. We went on to sell two hundred thousand copies—and didn't see a penny.

FRANKIE PALMERI (Emmure): *Satisfaction Is the Death of Desire* is the greatest hardcore album ever. So many bands use that as the blueprint of what they're going to sound like, even today.

JAMEY JASTA: There's a reason we toured that album for four years. We were broke. We were worse than broke. I was young when I signed both a bad record deal and a terrible publishing deal. There was a point where we had a merch bill that was over $30,000. We had so many vehicles breaking down and practice rooms we didn't pay, and we used merch money for gas. There was a lot of borrowing from one empty pot to fill another. I used to start drinking at noon, then go to the club and sell dime bags of weed out front before the show. Then at the wrong times, I'd fight someone and we'd get banned from a club. We got a reputation for being this out-of-control band. When we did Warped Tour '98 we were thrown off multiple times. I have memories of [ex-guitarist] Lou "Boulder" Richards riding around naked on a bike. We were sharing a bus with Carey Hart and these [other] big-time motocross riders, and those guys were big drinkers, too. [Warped Tour founder] Kevin Lyman wound up kicking us off the bus with the motocross guys. But he said, "Look, get to Jacksonville, Florida, and you can stay on the tour." He never expected us to make it there. So we took Greyhound, split the gear up in other people's vans, and when we showed up he was like, "How the hell did you get here?"

LOU "BOULDER" RICHARDS (1970–2006) (ex-Hatebreed): People assume we are tough guys or something. Put it this way: we are only tough when we absolutely have to be, and you don't want to see that side of us. Musically we bury any band out there. There isn't any band as heavy as us, not to dis any other bands. I think we are definitely the heaviest and most brutal.

JAMEY JASTA: We had some great times with Lou. But he was battling depression and drugs. It just got to the point where there was always some new major issue with him. He was just one of those guys who always had—not bad luck—but if it wasn't one thing it was another. He had a very hard upbringing; we all did. We just chose to do different things about it. . . . We were ready to shoot the "I Will Be Heard" video [for 2002's *Perseverance*]. This was the biggest moment in the band's career, and Lou told us, "I can't do this. I'm quitting the band." We were like, "Dude, you've gotta be in the video." But Lou said, "No, this is my last show and I'm quitting." Then he started telling people that we kicked him out. We have him on film telling people it's his last show. So when we had Frank [Novinec] join the band, we don't know what Lou was thinking. We knew that he had a drug problem. But the guy's dead. He can't speak for himself. With him, I just try to remember the fun times. Because there were so many good times, and before the drugs and depression got really bad there was a great guy there.

Sully Erna didn't look like a biker or a badass when he was sporting long, curly hair and drumming for Boston alt-metal band Strip Mind and old-school thrash band Meliah Rage. Like others before him, including his heroes in Alice in Chains and Pantera, he was paying his dues, scrambling from band to band in order to inch his way up in the heavy metal hierarchy and escape a life of street brawling and a landscape of urban decay. He never expected that his calling wasn't as a drummer but as the front man of what would become one of the best-selling metal groups of the aughts.

SULLY ERNA: I grew up in a very violent neighborhood in Lawrence, Massachusetts. There were cop chases, drugs, and gang fights. You could hear gunshots at night, and I got in my fair share of trouble. I was arrested a couple times for fighting or being drunk in public. I never went to prison, but I was going nowhere, so I moved away from that lifestyle and focused on Godsmack.

TONY ROMBOLA (Godsmack): It started out small. We'd play Boston and the surrounding towns, but nothing more. Then, bang, we got lucky. [Radio station] WAAF started playing our song "Keep Away." Over the next six months it got to where our gigs were sold out and we were selling a ton of CDs completely on our own. Newbury Comics [record store chain] picked it up and they were selling, like, a thousand a week. That's when the labels started calling *us*.

By the time Tool started working on their second full album, *Ænima*, which came out in 1996, the members could barely stand each other. Too many days touring together without a significant break had exacerbated their differences. They fought constantly in the studio, and despite their efforts to keep the band together, they seemed to constantly be at an impasse. The creative tension of the period helped the band sound tightly wound and claustrophobic even when playing meandering rhythms, but it took its toll on the members' psyches. Before the album was completed, original bassist Paul D'Amour was out of the band.

DANNY CAREY: When we were writing for *Ænima*, Paul was frustrated about not playing enough guitar. He really wanted to be a guitar player and get another bass player in the band. We said, "We have a guitarist and there's no way we're getting another asshole in this band to have to deal with."

MAYNARD JAMES KEENAN: We spent a lot of time chasing our tails, and things weren't happening with Paul. Outside of that space, it was great: we're friends, we talk. But in there it wasn't working and we had to part ways and let him do his own thing. I think he was caught up in that indie guilt thing. The band was getting bigger than he was comfortable with and he was so much the "anti" guy that he wasn't allowing himself to enjoy the success. To save face we told everybody that he quit, but he didn't. He was let go.

PAUL D'AMOUR (Tool): It was a bad marriage. Any three of us would be talking shit about the one that wasn't there. It went all around. Maynard and I used to be roommates. We were like two peas in a pod for a while, but the demise came from that last year of writing from *Ænima*. It took us a year to put together three songs. There was zero communication. Everybody blamed everybody else for why it was dysfunctional. We had typical sophomore album jitters, and I just couldn't do it.

ADAM JONES: [Bassist] Justin Chancellor [ex-Peach] was the missing link for Tool, completely. We tried out other guys that were really great and maybe even technically better, but Justin had the writing, he had the ideas, he was really artistic, he was great to get along with. So it was kind of like the new, improved Tool, and the other records were like Coke Classic.

JUSTIN CHANCELLOR (ex-Peach, Tool): When they put out *Opiate*, my brother and I took a trip to New York to see them play at CBGBs because we liked it so much. And because we knew Matt Marshall, who signed them, we were introduced to the band and became friends. In 1995 I did a gig in London with my old band Peach, and we were loading our amps out of the van back into the singer's flat, and my flatmate called me at the house and said I had to call Adam in America. I did, and he said Paul left the band and they wanted me to try out. They sent me a demo of "Pushit," "Ænima," and "Eulogy," which were all in their infant stages, and had me learn them for the audition. Those were the first things we finished up after I joined and from then on it was on to new material, which was incredibly challenging and intimidating.

DANNY CAREY: Working Justin into the band made a huge difference. Once we had a different personality, everything completely changed. The whole dynamic, the chemistry that goes down in the room when we write—everything. There were even more possibilities because Justin's such a great musician and has so many vibrant ideas coming out of his space. It pushed us in a whole new way.

MAYNARD JAMES KEENAN: The first couple of records for me were the primal scream. As a lyricist and performer, the idea was to work out some issues and then move the fuck on. So here you are in your third year of telling the same story over and over again, which was a negative story to begin with, and impacted your life in a negative way. And having to retell it every night is not so healthy. So right around the time of *Ænima* I was trying to figure out a way to transmute that stuff and let it go—finding different paths to disperse that negativity. I did a lot of esoteric, spiritual, and religious research. I read a lot of mathematical and psychological books and did a lot of introspection. That stuff helped take the record in a more esoteric, spiritual direction.

DANNY CAREY: We all were doing psychedelics during that era—not that we hadn't for our whole lives. We were able to dig a little deeper and expose those parts of our personalities and psyches and be a little bit more bold about it and more revealing. That's where the music automatically went.

JUSTIN CHANCELLOR: I remember lots of makeup. I think Maynard was getting into cross-dressing at the time. It was pretty crazy for me because all of that was a brand new thing. I'd never been in a big band or played these giant venues. I'd just played in the toilets in England.

MAYNARD JAMES KEENAN: I painted myself blue for about three years. It was a lot of work, but it was something to take you outside of yourself. That's part of what *Ænima* was to me—just to put on some of the craziest, eyesore costumes I've ever worn in my life, and it kind of frees you up. I'm a bit of a reserved, quiet person and it's very difficult for me to open up, and to open up onstage in front of that many people, you kind of need a costume. Being painted up like that helped, but eventually you're onstage trying to do your thing and your pores are clogged with paint. Your skin can't breathe, and after a while it takes its toll. I'll still go through my closet and find pieces of clothes or shoes covered in blue paint. We toured too much and I started to realize that I've got this responsibility the other guys don't have. You've got these two little flaps of skin in your throat that are very volatile and you have to take care of them. As time goes on this creates a weird kind of tension that starts to slip out. You're like the pregnant girl who can't go into the smoky pub. Everyone else wants to go in, and you're like, "No, I really can't," and they go, "Oh, right, you can't go in there. Okay, well we'll find someplace that's not as fun so the pregnant woman can hang out with us."

During the years Tool spent touring for *Ænima*, Keenan had just a small taste of what all nine guys in Slipknot experienced on a nightly basis—masks, coveralls, paint, sweating to death in sweltering clubs and at radio station summer festivals. Like Tool, Slipknot was on a never-ending quest to find new ways to present their art. But while Tool was dark and cryptic but ultimately life-affirming, Slipknot thrived on filth and degradation, and excelled in a landscape of chaos, pain, and destruction. To some, it was a sign of how debased mainstream entertainment could be and how low the public was willing to stoop. For others, the music was a reflection of how ugly the world itself was and a reaction against those who seek to censor artistic expression. Regardless, Slipknot was real, frightening—and almost immediately popular.

PAUL GRAY: We had talked to Roadrunner Records in the past and sent them all kinds of demos with Andy [Colsefni] singing. They really liked the music, but they were hesitant. Then we did "Spit It Out" with Corey [Taylor] singing and it started getting spins in Des Moines and record people started noticing. We were working with Sophia John at the time, who worked at a radio station, and one day she asked us, "If you could have anybody hear you, who would it be?" We said, "Ross Robinson." It just so happened that she was on the phone one day talking to John Reese, [who birthed the Warped Tour and Rockstar Energy Mayhem], and, at the time, John managed Ross. So Ross heard the demo and flew out to see us. He said he would produce the album without a record label. But by that time, we had an offer on the table from Sony. They came out to Vegas to see us do a show at the Eden Festival, but when we got home the fucking deal was null and void. One of the [artist development] guys from the label named Vince Bannon had seen us and he said, "If this is the future of fucking music, I don't want no part of it." So that was it. We went with Ross and he signed a deal with Roadrunner for the record. I think Vince Bannon missed out on that one.

CHRIS FEHN (Slipknot): I knew Slipknot from when I played in the band Shed, and I had heard they had just signed a record deal and I thought, "Here's my chance to get the fuck out of Iowa." So I went up to Shawn [Crahan] at a show and said, "Hey man, if you need a roadie or a drum tech I'm ready to go." The next week he called and said, "Do you still want to be a drum tech?" I said, "Hell yeah." He went, "Well, how about trying out for the band instead?" I started rehearsals with them the next day. My first show with the band, I shoved everything off the bar, kicked everyone's drinks over, and knocked a huge espresso machine off the counter and it exploded like a bomb. The cops were trying to arrest me afterwards. I was trying so hard to show the band I was worthy.

JOEY JORDISON: We worked on the first album with Ross Robinson and he's the most intense person I've ever met in my life besides the nine of us. We completely gelled. We were out for blood and Ross saw that in us. I would track my drums and we would all be headbanging, throwing our headphones off, punching the fucking walls. He would take plants and throw them at me while I was playing and I'd have to duck them, then they'd smash against the wall. He knocked the guitars out of people's hands and he made Chris Fehn drink two gallons of water to where he was totally bloated and on the verge of throwing up just to get a miked mallet sound out of his stomach.

ROSS ROBINSON: The most hungry record [was that] first Slipknot record: pure hunger. Clown had kids already, he's just barely surviving, these other dudes had no money, they came out here before the record deal was even done. We started rehearsing, they were sleeping on the floor in my house. Nothing got in the way. If anybody drank or did any kind of drug, they were kicked out of the band. They were absolutely militant and full on. It was heaven on earth for me. Joey would play and his hands were completely blistered and bleeding and shaking. They deserve everything they have; I don't care what anybody says.

COREY TAYLOR: I've never screamed or sang like that in my life. Ross pushed me every day to the point where by the end of the day I was literally broken completely in half and wide open and bawling, and I couldn't stop crying. I was throwing up all over the fucking place and the vocal booth smelled awful.

There was a dead rat we couldn't find. That stench just kept me going. It was fantastic.

SHAWN CRAHAN: Working with Ross, I wound up being the guy who would take people down to Melrose [to sightsee]. "Hey, there's too many people in here, we can't get anything done. Clown, why don't you take everyone down to Melrose." So for me it was two thumbs down. I played on the record. I'm all over it, but I didn't have a say in *anything*.

COREY TAYLOR: A lot of the songs on that record were inspired by my exes and my life. I just wanted to feel loved, and I didn't care where it was from. I grew up without a dad and I had no idea it was my mom who was keeping him out of my life. When you grow up like that, you automatically assume, "There's gotta be something wrong with me. My father didn't want to be there or didn't even contact me. It's gotta be my fault." It was something that I really struggled with and still do.

JOEY JORDISON: [Guitarist] Josh [Brainard] got lonely or something and didn't know if he wanted to deal with what lay ahead, so he quit. He's a great guitar player and a great friend, but he quit out of the fuckin' blue. So we called Jim [Root] again and we were like, "Hey, man, would you like to join?"

JIM ROOT: A year after I vowed not to join Slipknot, they called me to replace Josh. At first I told them no because I made a promise to my band, Death Front, that I would never join. But they called me two times that day and I slept on it and decided to give it a shot. I literally went from playing weekend gigs and working six in the morning until six at night silk-screening T-shirts to giving my boss notice and a week later showing up in Malibu to record "Spit It Out" and "Purity." The first record had already been recorded by the time Josh left the band. So when they called me there were only two songs to mess with.

Everything happened so fast I didn't have time to think about whether or not I felt comfortable or fit, and part of the thing with Slipknot was not feeling comfortable anyways.

JOEY JORDISON: I was staying there mixing the record after Ross had left. I always had a heater by me because it was always really cold. One night I knocked over one of the pillows I was sleeping on and it fell onto the heater. Next thing I know, I'm smelling something so I jumped up. I almost burned Indigo Ranch studio completely down. The whole thing was filled with smoke and flames. Rich Kaplan, the guy who owns the place, came in and we had to use fire extinguishers all over the place and open all the windows. It took about a week to get the smell out.

SID WILSON (Slipknot; DJ Starscream): We did a warm-up show at First Avenue [in Iowa City] before Ozzfest '99, and I was head-butting my beer keg right before "Eeyore." I was wearing my first gas mask, which had three holes in it and there were metal rings where the eye lenses used to be. I did two good hits into it with my head and you could hear the keg echo even though there were no mics on it. The lights went out. My knees buckled and I hit the floor. When the lights went back on I couldn't get up. Blood was gushing like crazy all down my face and pouring out of the mask. I hobbled over to our security guy at the side of the stage and when he saw all the blood, he turned white. He took me to the dressing room. I took the mask off and looked at the wound, which was wide open. I could see my skull. He sat me down and pressed my head with a towel, and every time he took the towel off it would gush blood again. He said, "You need to sit down and chill out until they're done playing." I said, "No, there's a song coming up. I've got parts." I put the towel on my head and strapped the mask over my towel really tight to try to stop the bleeding. I go back out onstage and I get there on my knees and do my part at the beginning of "Prosthetics." I go over to Clown and he's looking at me funny. He doesn't know I've split my head open. He's giving me this look that says, "You look like a fucking idiot with that towel." He thought I did it to look cool. So he punches me in the head right in the gaping wound. The world turns white and I'm seeing stars. I pushed him away and waved my hand. I thought, "Fuck, man. I gotta get somewhere safe. I crawled over to Corey because he had never beat on me during a show. He grabs me by the head and bangs my head onto the floor to the beat of the music. I went to the hospital after the show feeling drained and nauseous and I got sixteen stitches to close the gash.

COREY TAYLOR: There were a lot of times during Ozzfest when it was so hot and I was raging so hard that I threw up in my mask and the slit was too small to spit it out so I'd choke on it. And I broke my mouth so many fucking times just coming up too hard on the mic. I went from puking and having to swallow that to having to swallow blood.

As impulsive and explosive as they were onstage, backstage and offstage Slipknot were just as crazy. And their handlers made sure they had enough booze, drugs, and girls to satisfy their every desire.

PAUL GRAY: The craziest groupie I ever met was this girl who wound up on our bus. We went into the back lounge and started messing around. Everybody else was in their bunks sleeping. So, we're going at it and then all of a sudden she tells me to hit her and I said, "What? No." So she fuckin' punches me in the face. Then she says it again. "Hit me." And I'm like, "No, I ain't gonna hit you." And she kept fucking punching me. Finally, after getting hit in the fucking face ten times, I said, "Seriously, I will fucking hit you if you do it again." So she hit me again and I fucking slapped her. That's totally what she wanted. It turned into this full-on Wrestlemania with us fighting and getting it on. It was the weirdest thing. When it was all done it was, like, four in the morning, and I'm trying to get her off the bus. I'm thinking everyone's still asleep, and when we step out of the back everyone's sitting there in the front lounge clapping. It was definitely a walk of shame for me.

CHRIS FEHN: We had a no-drugs policy for years, and then when we went to Amsterdam we said, "Okay, you can do a little something if you want." That opened the door for a little here, a little there. Then it was, "Okay, everything's fine. Do whatever you want."

JIM ROOT: I got wasted constantly. Suddenly, you're like twenty-seven, and you're in this lifestyle where you can show up to work fucked-up. Nobody's gonna tell you any different because everybody's working for you and it's handed to you and sometimes people expect it. I went for it against my better judgment. The first four or five years of us touring I was in a bad spot and really depraved and doing some fucked-up shit and hurting people and being a horrible person. It started out as a fun partying thing and then it turned into a medication thing. You have to do it to deal with this lifestyle because you're constantly away from your family and your friends, if you even have any left after being away from them for so long.

PAUL GRAY: One night we were in Cincinnati and Chris, who's not a big drinker, had been drinking with [Deftones bassist] Chi [Cheng] all night, and he's fucking wasted. In the middle of the night he gets out of his bus bunk to take a piss and he thinks his bunk is actually the bathroom. He sticks his dick in between the mattress and the railing of the bunk, lifted his mattress like it was the toilet seat and just started pissing and it all starts dripping down on Sid, who's below him. Sid starts screaming, "What the fuck. What the fuck! *What the fuck?*" He smelled it and tasted it, and he's like, "It's fuckin' *piss!*"

CHRIS FEHN: We had been drinking full glasses of rum all night so I had no idea what was happening. I woke up with Sid yelling, "You pissed in my bunk." I said, "I did not. Shut the fuck up." But I totally did. Before I die, I have to let Sid piss on me.

Along with Lamb of God and High on Fire, Mastodon was tagged by the press as one of the three great hopes for an emerging New American Metal movement—a nod to the New Wave of British Heavy Metal. Although it was a more ludicrous tag than "metalcore" and a more manufactured scene than grunge, it broadly defined a new generation of bands with eccentric members and the potential to be rock stars. Mastodon, while not the most successful, has become the most inventive of the bunch. With time, their sound has progressed from pulverizing, rhythmically complex noise metal to heavy, psychedelic prog, and in every (largely conceptual) album they've expressed the need to escape through a sonic odyssey driven by stunning musicianship and cinematic performances.

BRENT HINDS: My buddies Gary Lindsey and Troy Sanders brought me to Atlanta when I was nineteen. Their band Knuckle was playing at the Nick in Birmingham, Alabama. I came up to them after the show and went, "Man, you guys are awesome—except for your guitar player. He fuckin' sucks. You need a good guitar player, like me." They're like, "He's just filling in until we can find someone good." I went, "Well, look no further. I'm right here." A week later I knocked on the warehouse door, and I've been in Atlanta ever since.

TROY SANDERS (Mastodon, Four Hour Fogger): Four Hour Fogger [started in 1995 and] lasted until December 1999. In January 2000, Brent and I were at a High on Fire show at the Parasite House, and it seemed like a fresh time to pursue anything new and exciting. At that High on Fire show we met [guitarist] Bill [Kelliher] and [drummer] Brann [Dailor], and they were looking for a second guitar player and a bass player. Brent said,

"Well, I'm your second guitar player. There's Troy. He's my bass player."

BILL KELLIHER (ex–Today Is the Day, Mastodon, ex-Lethargy): [Drummer] Brann [Dailor] was a scenester. He hung out in the square in [Rochester, New York] and was always wearing Elvis sunglasses with his hair all bouffanted up and a wifebeater so you could see his tattoos. I thought he was kind of this showoff with platform shoes. But then I started playing with him in [technical death metal band] Lethargy, and we became friends. Then in 1997 Brann got a call saying [Nashville noisecore band] Today Is the Day is looking for a drummer. I had just seen Today Is the Day play and Troy and Brent's band Four Hour Fogger had opened for them. So Brann got the gig. Six months later their bass player wasn't working out so Brann called me and said, "Come out to Texas and try out. I know you'll get the gig." So I went out there and I got the job.

STEVE AUSTIN: I started Today Is the Day in 1992. We've had a lot of great players over the years, like Bill and Brann and [drummer] Derek Roddy [ex-Nile, ex-Hate Eternal]. A lot of people are finding out about us through these other bands, and that's great because they're going, "Wow, this seems like a seminal thing. I wonder what this shit's about?" My music is disturbing yet lulling at the same time, and that's because it's pretty much what my life is like.

BRANN DAILOR (ex-Lethargy, ex–Today Is the Day, Mastodon): Our first Mastodon rehearsal was a disaster. Brent was extremely inebriated. He could barely play guitar. He just started hitting open droning notes. And before we went into the practice space he almost got into a fight with the cook at [Atlanta restaurant] Elmyr. A lot of people said, "Don't be in a band with him. He's got a lot of baggage." I thought, "Well, we'll see what happens." But there were red flags all over the place. So then he came over the next day with an acoustic guitar and ripped out all this crazy shit. I think he kind of knew the night before didn't go so well. But he definitely proved himself to be an amazing guitar player. Bill and I had three or four songs, and he had five or six songs he had already recorded with Four Hour Fogger. So we started working on those. They hadn't done any vocals over them. We changed some of the stuff around and before you know it we had all of the elements for *Call of the Mastodon*, what became known as "The Nine-Song Demo."

BRENT HINDS: Bill and Brann moved into town and were asking people, "Is there anyone around here who's crazy and a really good guitar player?" Someone went, "Yeah, this guy Brent Hinds. But don't mess with him because he's crazy, for real. He's on, like, every drug in the world and he'll just take your life in a spiral down to hell." They found me at a Four Hour Fogger show. I had an Iron Maiden shirt and jacket on and Brann loves Iron Maiden. We got along really good and I wasn't drunk or fucked-up 'cause I had just played a show. They said, "Hey, man, meet us at Elmyr tomorrow at about six and we'll have a drink and go down to the practice pad and jam. So I get to Elmyr the next day and lo and behold, the Patrón Silver girls are there and they're handing out Patrón Silver for free, and I was like, "Yes, I think I will." I had about seven shots and then I went, "Okay, let's go jam." I sparked up a big joint on the way down there. By the time I got to the practice pad I could hardly walk. I went, "Yeah, I'm into *this* kind of stuff." I played this one droning chord over and over. I was way ahead of Sunn O))). I was doing that kind of stuff ten years ago. I was using a didgeridoo with Tibetan monk singing and playing heavy chords over it. And I was sincere when I was telling Bill and Brann that's the kind of music I wanted to do. It wasn't 'cause I was drunk or fucked-up. But they just weren't into that. So I said, "Okay, whatever. What do you guys have?" And they played me some stuff they did in Lethargy and I went, "I ain't playing that shit. That's just crazy." So that was it. They went their way and I went mine. The next day Brann calls and goes, "Hey man, why don't you come over to my house sober. Everyone I talked to says you're a really good guitar player and I just want to see you play." I said "Sure. Sorry about last night, man. I was totally wasted." So, I played all this classical guitar for him and they decided to give it another shot. So Mastodon is kind of a toned down version of Lethargy with me as a heavy influence.

BRANN DAILOR: In Today Is the Day, we were on Relapse Records and they heard our demo, so they were excited about seeing us live. We played the Robot House in West Philadelphia in one of the worst neighborhoods. The show was in the basement. You'd got down the stairs and the audience had to be on one side of the stairway and watch the band through the banister. [Relapse president] Matt Jacobson and [the retail and marketing guy] Pellet were staring at us, which was pretty weird. But they signed us and put out our EP *Lifesblood* in 2001. We released our first full-length, *Remission*, the next year.

Many musicians have side projects. Tool's Maynard James Keenan has taken the practice to a new extreme that at times has left him gasping for air and unsure of his identity. He has been involved with A Perfect Circle, which recorded three platinum albums, and formed the performance art band Puscifer. Outside of music, he owns the Arizona wine companies Merkin Vineyards and Caduceus Cellars, and starred in the 2010 documentary *Blood into Wine*. Maynard's inability to focus on just one artistic endeavor both jeopardized and saved Tool. *Lateralus* was created in an environment of discord and distrust. Keenan couldn't stand being with his bandmates while they composed, and ultimately bailed to work with his former guitar tech Billy Howardel on A Perfect Circle. Ultimately, Tool benefited from the front man's departure, as it enabled them to compose in an unorthodox manner without pressure from Keenan about each song's vocal demands.

MAYNARD JAMES KEENAN: We found we definitely have different ways of processing information and being creative, and I was frustrated. I like to capture the emotion and have fun. At that point, the other guys in Tool were really taking their time. I understand that the method they have to go through involves taking every avenue possible and going down them to see if they get anywhere and then coming back and starting over at another avenue. It's a very tedious and long process that doesn't really lend itself to telling a story. I need some of the foundation there before I can start telling a story because if the foundation keeps changing, the story's gonna keep changing. So I had to step back, but if I was going to go through an entire two- or three-year process of trying to write this stuff while they were working that way I was going to go out of my mind. So that's when I took a break and I worked with my roommate Billy Howardel on A Perfect Circle. I had no idea it was gonna blow up as big as it did, but I went along willingly, and that caused a lot of tension with the Tool camp. "Where were you? You're off with your *mistress*." We've navigated that, but it was always a sore spot. So getting into *Lateralus* was a little bit of a chore. But I believe that friction and juxtaposition makes for good art.

DANNY CAREY: When Maynard went to do A Perfect Circle, that added gasoline to the fire. His heart was in the right place, I think, but he went, "I'm going to go out and do this while you guys figure this out because I can't be in the next room while you are getting this meticulous over these stupid things." It was a healthy split, but I don't know if I could recommend the process it took to get it out of us—to say the least.

ADAM JONES: We stopped recording at one point because we were so frustrated. We took some time off, and then we met and talked it out and things got better. Sometimes you need to go through really awful experiences to get to a place that's better. We're basically married to each other and we have to put up with the fact that this guy doesn't wash his dishes and that guy doesn't brush his teeth every day. The reason we've outlasted all of our peers is we split everything four ways and we compromise, compromise, compromise.

Compromise and unity in the Slipknot camp would be a pipe dream. Throughout their careers, the Iowa nine-piece have thrived on discord and unhappiness, and in the process they've repeatedly demonstrated that beauty can be found in ugliness, and that destruction is sometimes necessary to create. After their first Ozzfest, the band was on an upward trajectory. "Spit It Out" and "Wait and Bleed" were all over the radio, and audiences were hungering for more. When they finished the tour, Slipknot went right back into the studio with producer Ross Robinson to record *Iowa*, the record that nearly broke up the band and exposed each member to his scariest demons.

JOEY JORDISON: Doing a Slipknot record is fucking prison. You're trapped until it's done. I'm in a band with the best singer, the best percussion players, the best guitar players, bass player, sampler, DJ in the fucking world. I'm so blessed. But at the same time, when we get together—even though we have so much love for each other—we fuckin' want to kill each other. When we did *Iowa*, it was a very dark time for the band. We hated each other. We were all on drugs. We were all fucking drunk and it sucked.

JIM ROOT: With the first album all this stuff was happening and we didn't have time to think about it. Then all of a sudden here we are recording the second album and I'm seeing the way Ross works. I'm down *in* it. I'm seeing the band coming together, but not coming together. It was an angry time and the songs reflected that. People expected us to come out with an album of "Wait and Bleed"s or "Spit It Out"s. That would have been the safe thing to do, and I don't think we've ever done anything to be safe. To us it made more sense to come out with all this brutal shit.

COREY TAYLOR: I was drinking a lot. I was in a relationship that wasn't good for me and I didn't want to realize it at the time. We went out to LA and that's where I really started to get into the booze and the philandering. I was doing anything I could to feel good because everything else felt really bad. But I knew we had a responsibility and that's why *Iowa* is so dark.

MICK THOMSON: I should dig up [our former manager] Steve Richards and beat his fucking corpse. I'm an atheist, but every once in a while I think there may be a God that put a cyst on his brainstem and caused him to be a fuckin' zombie. The dude stepped into our lives and tried his best to cause rifts. There was a divide-and-conquer attitude that I could see a mile away, but no one wanted to listen. He'd pit one person in the band against another because as long as you've got them occupied you can be raping them and stealing from them and they're not noticing because they're too caught up in stupid shit to see a bigger picture. I tried to show people in the band his true colors for years and they wouldn't listen because he would buddy up with them and do special things and treat certain people like they were important. He basically corrupted and pissed on the beautiful thing we had done. He did a lot of fucking damage for his own financial gain.

COREY TAYLOR: I was at parties with orgies in the room. The last night we were staying at the Oakwoods [corporate housing], we were having "patio furniture Olympics," throwing shit through the patio doors into the LA River. We threw chairs, all my dishes, we tried to get the bed over there. It culminated with a threesome in somebody's hotel room. I was so angry and there was so much darkness. I was cutting myself in the studio vocal booth, bleeding everywhere and screaming my fucking head off. I just wanted to feel *something*. I didn't care what it was.

SHAWN CRAHAN: Life was a disaster because outside forces were interfering with our art. Drugs, women, idiots saying, "Whoa, you guys are gonna be *huge*." Everybody wants our money. Everyone wants our souls. We've got forty-eight fuckin' employees. No one's worth a shit. Use, use, use. So I hate *Iowa*, but it *is* brutality at its finest. We almost all died. There were chemicals. I was probably the worst, man. Happily married. My wife was very ill [with Crohn's disease] during those times. I felt really isolated because I couldn't be with her. We're being lied to about money by our former manager and we're still broke.

PAUL GRAY: The week our record comes out is the same week [pop star] Aaliyah died. We thought we were going to have the number one record. Aaliyah had only sold 20,000 records the week before, but she opened with like 400,000, and Mary J. Blige's sales went up too because of that, and then we ended up with the number 3 record. We went to start the Pledge of Allegiance tour with System of a Down and the date we were gonna start, that's when 9/11 happened.

COREY TAYLOR: It wasn't a good time for the country, but it wasn't a good time for us, either. We got banned at a lot of radio stations and MTV wouldn't touch us. So here we were with our finest work to date and nobody would give us the time of day. We were working our asses off and we weren't getting paid shit. We were going, "Where's the fucking money?" and no one could give us a fucking answer. The sunshine from the first album was totally fucking gone. It was a total eclipse for a very fucking long time.

JIM ROOT: There were always random women hanging around on that tour. At the time I was pretty naïve and I would think, "Oh, this chick really likes me." But no, she doesn't really like me. She likes the *idea* of me. It took me a while to figure that one out. Then I just withdrew and did more drugs.

COREY TAYLOR: We didn't like each other. There was a lot of screaming and animosity, and that's a big reason the tour only lasted seven or eight months. Jim and I went off and did Stone Sour because we had to get the fuck away from Slipknot. And that was a little better. But at the same time I was not being fulfilled musically anymore because I had too many problems.

PAUL GRAY: I was pissed at Corey and Jim. I thought, "Fuck, we should be working on Slipknot." During the downtime I started doing some really heavy drugs. Heavy, heavy, heavy drugs. Heroin. I was shooting speedballs every day. And then pills. I was on everything, man. We were working on the *Disasterpieces* DVD. That was the only thing that was really happening with Slipknot. In the beginning I kind of had my shit under control, but after a while, no. I became an addict and always will be.

CHRIS FEHN: I moved to Lake Tahoe with my girlfriend at the time. No one was talking and Corey was doing Stone Sour. I didn't know if we were ever gonna get back together. I would wait for a call from Slipknot every day and it never came, and that drove me deeper into depression. I'd be driving home up the mountain and I would hear Corey on the radio with Stone Sour. It was a really good song. I'd be bummed out and happy for him. So, what would I do? I'd just go get fucked-up and try to make it through the night. I was going through mental torture. I did a lot of drugs, and there were a couple nights where I'd wake up on the bathroom floor and not know if I was gonna see tomorrow morning.

The idea that stardom leads to boozing, drugging, and sexual excess is a fallacy. But for those seeking depravity and cheap thrills, the opportunities are there. Some, like Tool and System of a Down, prefer not to talk about it. Others, like Slipknot and Machine Head, reel off both joyous and devastating tales of decadence and debauchery, refusing to be judged for their actions.

ROBB FLYNN: We like to drink and rage and put on diapers and pee in them. It's fun. Depends are fucking classic, dude, peeing in your pants when you're wasted is the fucking best. The last night of our Pantera tour was the biggest Depends-mania scenario. We tried the generic Depends on the bus in the kitchen area. No one wanted to test 'em, so I did and it was like, "Ohh no, these leak. Aww, right into my shoe." I had a squishy shoe for the rest of the night. I was so wasted I didn't even think to change my shoe. We had our bus driver pull over at that Walmart. [Ex-guitarist] Logan [Mader] was wearing a red fireman's hat and red cowboy boots and a diaper. I'm wearing a giant afro and Elvis shades and nipple tape. I go in there and they're like, "Y'all in a band?" Logan's like, "Yeah, we're in a band. Wanna see my cock?" An hour later, we're championing how we fucking flashed this girl. We drank until eleven the next morning. I passed out in my bunk in the new Depends. Woke up pruned and shriveled and urined. And happy.

SULLY ERNA: I went from partying heavily to partying like a fuckin' maniac. I drank so much that I sometimes felt like I would overdose on fuckin' booze. I was lying in my bunk going through Europe, and I would wake up at seven or eight in the morning and I would have my hand on my pulse. I'd fall asleep listening to my heart beat because I felt like it was going to stop, it was beating so slowly.

JIM ROOT: There were times I'd be sitting on the bus and I'd done so much coke and my heart was beating so fast I was like, "Oh shit, I'm having a heart attack. I'm freaking out." Fortunately, I never got into heroin. I think I purposely stayed away from that because I knew I'd like it if I tried it.

COREY TAYLOR: When we were doing *Vol. 3: The Subliminal Verses*, I would keep a bottle of Jack next to my fucking bed every day. I had cab companies in my fucking phone so if I couldn't get a ride to the bar I was still going to the fucking bar.

JIM ROOT: I was pretty good at hiding my drug addiction from people. But at one point, I was up for a few days partying and I had a breakdown—I couldn't handle it, mentally. I was spun out from too much cocaine and drinking and just hanging around generally bad people. All that negative energy built up inside of me and I finally freaked out. I wouldn't go into the studio for a few days and one of the guys from our management company had to drive me out to Topanga Canyon and put me on a crystal table to try to mellow me out. I'm laying on this table going, "What the fuck am I doing? Is this table gonna do anything for me other than maybe straighten my back out?" I was at the bottom of my hole and was really starting to build a wall up around myself. I'd go into the studio as early as I could so I could get my tracking done and leave before anyone else in the band showed up.

DAVID DRAIMAN: Before I settled down, I was absolutely a hedonist in every way. I don't think it's a secret to anyone that I am an incredible admirer of the female form. I'm not a big drinker. I do love marijuana, but I would say that if there's one thing I was truly addicted to it would be women.

SULLY ERNA: I used to be out of control with women and alcohol—just full-blown. Me and [drummer] Shannon [Larkin] alone would go through two cases of beer a night on our bus and at least a bottle and a half of Crown Royal. For every show, we'd have a case of Pedialyte on our rider because you drink a bottle of that and the hangover's gone. Then before you go onstage you drink a bottle of wine, the buzz kicks in, and you're ready to roll. Then *after* the show I'd drink heavily again, and that was a vehicle to sleeping with two or three women a night. It was a vicious cycle.

DAVID DRAIMAN: Some of my favorite sexual experiences don't involve a multitude of women. Those situations are fun, but there isn't necessarily always the same sort of intensity as there can be with a one-on-one. But I've seen everything that you can possibly imagine. I've seen girls stick things into parts of their bodies that they do not belong in—things that you would never dream would fit—just for the amusement of people around them. I've seen women get on their hands and knees and bark like dogs while attached to a collar and chain. I've seen girls take on a team of men. Once, in the back lounge of our bus at Ozzfest, this girl was just such a champ, and literally there was a line of people on our bus—band guys, crew guys—who were just being serviced. It's wonderful to see that someone can be that free with themselves and actually still enjoy it. But that's not really, to me, what women and the sensuality and the power and the sexuality that they harness are all about. When you start getting into crazy numbers of women at the same time and crazy numbers of guys on one woman at the same time, then it kind of becomes more foolish, more of a game.

STEVE "FUZZ" KMAK (ex-Disturbed): The best line that a girl on the bus can ever say is, "I've never done this before." That's the best.

DAVID DRAIMAN: Especially because they always seem to know the rules of the bus. They know where everything is, they know you can't poop in the toilet [or the septic system has to be drained].

ZAKK WYLDE: Black Label Society's soundman, Dave, had some fuckin' chick in the back lounge of the bus. The rest of us are sitting up in the front packed in there. It was like fuckin' *Animal House* on fucking crack cocaine and steroids. The majority of guys were all single, so it was like a *Caligula* fuckfest. There was this one chick that all the guys were fucking. She was riding two guys, trying to fit both of their fat-ass cocks in her fuckin' mouth and getting pounded by one of the other guys. I grabbed our driver, Mike, and went, "Dude you gotta see this shit!" Then there was the girl in the back that Dave was banging. She only knew him as Soundman Dave. So she's yelling, "Fuck me, Soundman Dave!" because she didn't know his last name. And the next thing you know [bassist] John "JD" DeServio is sitting there and he's, like, five-foot-three. So she goes, "Soundman Dave, I'm done with you. Lemme fuck the little guy." I'm going, "What the fuck?" The next day at sound check JD's playing "Riders on the Storm," Dave's out front. And in a voice like Jim Morrison, JD goes, "Fuck me, Soundman Dave / Your throbbing cock I crave." For the next fuckin' month and a half everyone called him, "Fuck Me Soundman Dave." We'd be in a bar, and when I'd introduce him to someone I'd go, "This is Fuck Me Soundman Dave. It's fuckin' crazy his parents named him that."

SULLY ERNA: There were times where there were forty or fifty people jammed on the bus. My bus used to be nicknamed the Combat Zone [after Boston's Red Light District]. There's a vision you have when you're not signed yet about what it's like to be a rock star. When you jump into it and you start to live it, you're like, "Cool, this is what I wanted to do." Then all of a sudden it consumes you and turns into this awful fuckin' creature and it takes over your life.

MICK THOMSON: No one knows who they are until they're in a different situation. People think, "Oh, I'm really grounded. I'm faithful. I would never cheat on my girlfriend or my wife." Oh, really? Ever had extremely hot pussy dangling in front of your face every fucking night willing to give it up? No. What you're saying is you don't go to a bar and chase tail. But when you're faced with that shit right in front of you and it's there every single fucking day, those are usually the people that are first to cave.

SULLY ERNA: You go out and play the show. You hit the bottle. You're drunk. The chicks are back there. The party's back there. You're the center of the whole thing. The next thing you know, you wake up in the morning and you got some stranger in your fucking bed that you don't give a fuck about, and you can't wait for her to get the fuck out of there. Then there's a new chick, so you go, "Oh, she's fucking hot." And you're banging her. There's no satisfaction in it, and it becomes an addiction. You see the next girl and you go, "Whoa, look at her! I haven't fucked *her* yet." So you fuck her and then you're like, "Eaagh! I don't really like you. And I'm starting to not really like myself." You start to feel like Bill Murray in *Groundhog Day.* In the end I came clean with my old lady and told her about every fucking girl I ever cheated on her with.

DAVID DRAIMAN: Now I'm very happy and monogamous. But since I've been on the road, I've had a handful of meaningful relationships, all of which left me fairly badly wounded. I had an ex-fiancée leave me. I lost my unborn child four or five years ago while my ex was in the middle of her second trimester. That's what "My Child" [on the *Asylum* CD] is about. I wanted a family so badly, I didn't see that she and I were not meant to be together. But she had an epiphany when we were in Amsterdam and literally, within twenty-four hours of coming home from Europe, she was gone.

SULLY ERNA: To be able to tell your girl that you've been cheating on her for three fucking years on the road and all the suspicions she had about you were true, that's heavy. I don't know any fuckin' dude that's done it. Well, I know James Hetfield did it. When he told me I went, "Wow, that's pretty awesome, but I would never fucking tell." But eventually I decided I had to. Before I told her, I went to the desert for two weeks and worked with these Native American medicine men—these people I've known that do some amazing rituals and ceremonies. It was magical in a sense, and it allowed me to open the door and realize what my problem was, and it was just that I wasn't being honest and I wasn't living an honest life.

MICK THOMSON: Our old manager and everyone around him were invading our fucking shit going, "Hey, dude, try some of this. Hey dude, there's a chick over here who wants to fuckin' blow you." I'm like, "You just smiled and said goodbye to his girlfriend and now you're trying to get him to fuck somebody *else?*" That's who these people are. They'd try that shit with me and I'd go, "You know what, dude. You don't need to worry about my dick. My dick will go wherever my dick wants to go. But you don't need to fuckin' come over and try to urge me to go into some room and tag some fuckin' chick." I almost found it gay. Like, "What, are you gonna sit there and beat off thinking about how I'm just destroying some pussy in there? What the fuck is wrong with you?" To me, if my pants are off, that's my private life and you don't need to be involved with it in any way, shape, or form.

COREY TAYLOR: When we went in to do *Vol. 3: The Subliminal Verses*, we were in the studio three months and I hadn't laid down a stitch of vocals. I was gonna quit the band and I was actually on the phone buying a plane ticket home. I was wasted at the time and it took Clown to fuckin' talk me down. Clown has always been kind of my father figure in a weird way, even though we're only four years apart. There were a few guys I was close to at that time, but for the most part I pushed everybody away. I was just going through a constant cycle of abuse and it culminated with me at the Hyatt on Sunset almost jumping out of an eight-story window. If my buddy Tommy and my ex-wife hadn't been there, I'd be dead. The next morning I had my little moment of fucking clarity. I quit drinking for three years until my wife and I split up.

JAMEY JASTA: The low point for Hatebreed came when we were doing a festival with Kid Rock, Static-X, and Staind in Wisconsin. We made an agreement not to drink. One night we decided to break the whisky out, and that ended up with me, [bassist Chris] Beattie, and ex-guitarist Sean [Martin] all fighting each other individually, cage-match style, outside the bus in front of all the other bands, agents, and managers. It was terrible. We broke the windshield out of the bus, which cost us over $15,000. We missed shows. I woke up in a bathtub filled with blood. And my elbow was cracked open from Sean body-slamming me onto these rocks. It was full-blown—the hardest you can punch, the hardest you can smash someone's face into the ground. Everybody witnessed this and it was just a disgusting display of drunken idiocy. But it made us all better friends. Fortunately, I cleaned up my act and got sober. But I'll always have an addictive personality. I have mental illness, depression, alcoholism, and drug addiction in my family for generations going back. So with an addictive personality, anything can be a problem—food, booze, pills, women. All that stuff comes out in the music.

ZAKK WYLDE: Once, some of the guys in the back were getting blowjobs from some chick. There was this whole running joke that went this chick's gotta blow the whole crew, the Doom Crew, before she gets to the band. So she's blowing some dudes in the back. Next thing you know I hear, *ba-boo-oom!* I go up to the fuckin' front and the windshield of the bus is shattered. Someone threw a brick at it and took off running. I saw him and chased this motherfucker down, beat the living fuck out of him, and then walked back to the bus. One of my guys goes, "Man, did you talk to him?" And I said, "No, I beat the living fuck out of the motherfucker." And he goes, "Aw, dude.

It wasn't his fault. His girlfriend was the one who came on the bus." I go, "Are you kidding me? Well, he shouldn't have thrown a brick. He should have gotten her out and dealt with her or just left her there." The poor fuckin' bastard pays for the two tickets, probably brought her out to dinner. And what does he get? Does he get a blowjob? No. Does he get laid? No. He gets his ass handed to him and his fucking girlfriend sucks off the Doom Crew. God bless heavy metal.

RANDY BLYTHE: I'm not a big fighter, but I'm definitely accident prone. The last day of the Unholy Alliance tour in 2006 with Slayer I bought a really sharp machete. Some kids asked me for an autograph and the machete came off the belt of my sheath and landed right on my toe. Blood started fountaining everywhere. I asked the fans to get me some Super Glue. If a cut's not too deep, you can glue the wound right back together, but it was way too late for that. I had to get stitches right away. More recently, we were playing in Osaka, [Japan], and I was visiting with my tattoo artist. I had forty-five minutes before I had to be onstage. He said, "My buddy has a clothing store. He wants to flow you some cool gear." I went and got some hats and a cool jacket and he asked me to put the jacket on so he could take a picture of me wearing it for the store. So I whipped it on and a tag was hanging out. I busted out my knife to remove the tag. I cut the tag off, closed the knife and I wasn't paying attention so I closed it on my thumb and split it wide open. I should have had stitches, but I had to be onstage early. I went back to the club bleeding like a stuck pig. Everyone looks at me and shakes their head like, "Oh, there goes Randy again."

When Lamb of God arrived in Prague on June 27, 2012, to play a show at Rock Café with Skeletonwitch and All Shall Perish, to everyone's shock Blythe was cornered by police at the airport, arrested, and charged with manslaughter, stemming from an incident in 2010 in which nineteen-year-old Daniel N. died. After the fan rushed the stage, Blythe allegedly pushed him back into the crowd, where he fell and hit his head. Two weeks later, N. died from injuries sustained from the fall. Even after posting US$200,000 bail, Blythe was held at Pankrác Prison through August 2, 2012.

RANDY BLYTHE [in a press statement]: If it is deemed necessary for me to do so, I *will* return to Prague to stand trial. While I maintain my innocence one hundred percent, and will do so steadfastly, I will *not* hide in the United States, safe from extradition and possible prosecution. The family of a fan of my band [still] suffers through the indescribably tragic loss of their child. They have to deal with constantly varying media reports about the circumstances surrounding his death. I am charged with maliciously causing severe bodily harm to this young man, resulting in his death. While I consider the charge leveled against me ludicrous and without qualification, my opinion makes no difference in this matter. The charge exists, and for the family of this young man, questions remain. The worst possible pain remains.

For many years, Mastodon front man, guitarist and vocalist Brent Hinds tempted fate. On September 9, 2007, insane partying and juvenile antics almost ended his career. Hinds was swinging around a wet shirt when he accidentally hit someone with it. The guy blindsided him and Hinds's head smashed against the cement, causing severe internal bleeding. Ironically, the trauma fueled his creativity for the band's 2009 psychedelic prog-metal epic *Crack the Skye*.

BRENT HINDS: I got run over pretty hard by this dude, and if I would have seen it coming it never would have happened. He sucker punched me out of nowhere and he's a coward for doing it. If he would have said, "Hey, I'm about to punch you," it would have been a different story. It's like, "Dude, grow some balls and fuckin' face me. It was an accident that I hit you. I was fuckin' wasted drunk." Me and [Queens of the Stone Age front man] Josh Homme had just played with the Foo Fighters on MTV. We were hanging out with Lemmy. I was just having too much fun. That's why he punched me. [System of a Down guitarist] Daron [Malakian, who was there], said I hit the back of my head [on the ground] so hard it sounded like someone had hit a homerun. I went into convulsions and seized out and had blood coming out my ears and mouth and nose and brain hemorrhaging and a brain aneurysm. I was holding the fuckin' Grim Reaper's hand. It's a miracle I made it through.

TROY SANDERS: Bill [Kelliher], Brann [Dailor], and I were in my room real late and we got a phone call and found out Brent was beaten on and had head injuries, and next thing you know our party vibe got turned into us sitting in this deluxe hotel room crying together because we were scared that brain injury means possible death, possible coma, possible motor skills lost for life. It was incredibly scary. That element of the unknown terrified us, and that was the first step of us for the next twelve or eighteen months becoming more solid as a family. It takes those kinds of moments for you to step back and reassess your life personally, and your career and your bandmates and the brotherhood you've been sharing for the past nine years.

BRENT HINDS: While I was out, I had all these dreams. I was asleep for three days. I went a lot of places. It's really hard to explain because of how vivid it is and all the stuff was—just complete sensory overload. I was there physically, but mentally I was not there at all. I was out in the universe. I'd be in Thailand or Bali or Hawaii or all these paradise-type places and everything was really mellow and I was happy. When I woke up three days after I was sucker punched I looked at everybody in my family and projectile vomited water, blood, and alcohol on everyone. It looked like sangria going everywhere. The fucker who sucker punched me had rings on his finger. He broke my nose so bad I had to wait eight months until the vertigo stopped and I could go back into the hospital under anesthesia and have them re-break my nose again so I could breathe. It was really crazy how it made me want to play guitar more. I was just really grateful to have a second lease on life. I was like, okay, I'm just gonna play. I'm not gonna change my ways, but I am gonna play more and maybe that will change my ways more.

TROY SANDERS: Thankfully, Brent was able to overcome his in-juries after eight months of truly being in a haze. Thankfully, he was able to pick up a guitar and become as creative or more creative than he ever has been in his life. Physically and emo-tionally, we were more united as a team and as friends, more so than ever. That's probably why [2009's *Crack the Skye*] was the most cohesive piece of art we've ever crafted together.

From the beginning, Slipknot's chosen path was infused with darkness. They thrived on hate and relished the acclaim it brought (from their largely disenfranchised fans). Aside from Corey Taylor's suicide attempt, no one in the band had a public near-death experience. There were broken bones, assorted burns and cuts, and thousands of bruises, but nothing life-threatening. Then, on May 24, 2010, bassist and songwriter Paul Gray died in a hotel in Urbandale, Iowa. An autopsy revealed he had overdosed on a combination of morphine and a stronger but shorter-lasting narcotic called fentanyl. While Gray had a history of heroin use, he had reportedly cleaned up after meeting his girlfriend, Brenna, who was pregnant at the time of his death.

PAUL GRAY: For *Vol. 3: The Subliminal Verses*, I wrote a bunch of stuff—like I do every record—but I would spend half the time in the bathroom [doing drugs]. And I'd be trying to play and I'd fall out of my chair a couple times and fall asleep in the middle of tracking a fucking song. It was pretty bad. I was get-ting depressed that the band might break up. I was like, "What would I do?" This has been the best thing that ever happened to me. So I've never wanted to leave this. Maybe that was partly the reason for the drug use. I'd hear someone say, "Fuck it, I'm quitting. I'm out." That would fucking freak me out. I'd be like, "What the fuck? What are we gonna do now?" And I'd just dig myself in deeper holes. All that had to stop. But once you get to a certain point, it's fuckin' so hard going through withdrawal. It's so bad. It's not that you don't want to quit. You just can't. Going through rehab kept me good for a little while and then we got back out on the road and I just knew too many people and I started using a lot again. I would clean up and then I'd do shit again. I had some near-death experiences and a few stints of rehab here and there. I got left in rehab at the end of the arena tour with Shadows Fall and Lamb of God. It was the same place Lindsay Lohan went. I missed the last six shows of the tour. That's when I really started going, "Fuck, I need to figure my shit out." When we got done with the whole *Subliminal* tour, well, idle hands do the devil's work. I met my wife and she stayed with me and helped me. But then I'd full-on run with it again. Finally she said, "I can't sit around and watch you kill yourself." So we moved back to Iowa and I went to my doctor and got straightened out. I have friends, though, who pushed it just the same way, and they *are* dead.

JIM ROOT: I had just driven home from the studio in Nashville to my place in Florida when I got a call from our manager. At the same time, Clown called me. That's how I found out Paul was dead. We were done with Stone Sour's 2010 album *Audio Secrecy* and I got the call the next morning. I was home for less than twenty-four hours before I was on a plane to go to Iowa to say goodbye. Then less than a week after that we were on a plane to Europe to start a European tour. I didn't even have a chance to sit down and really think about it. We had even talked about getting together to start writing some shit for the next Slipknot record. When Stone Sour was on a festival with Metallica, James Hetfield was really helpful. He came out of nowhere when we were in Greece and sat down and talked to me for about an hour about what happened to Paul. He said, "If you need an ear, if you need somebody to talk to, you know where I am." They went through the same thing with [late bassist] Cliff [Burton], so James *knows*. He said in some ways they really didn't deal with it. He wanted to make sure we didn't make some of the same mistakes they made through-out their grieving process.

COREY TAYLOR: James did the same thing with me. For him to reach out was really, really cool. That was absolutely reassuring. He and Lars were both very cool about it. But honestly, it was still uncomfortable to talk about, even two years after it happened. It's one of those things I wear close to my chest and still try to process.

ANDY COLSEFNI: [Paul] was staying at that hotel for a couple of weeks and he was going there to meet up with Donnie [Steele] to write music for a new Body Pit CD they were planning after Slipknot's next tour. Paul must have had this room reserved to try to keep all that [drug] crap away from his wife.

JIM ROOT: What do we do now? Some people say it will never be the same. Now that I've had a little time to think about it [I wonder], do we kill an entire band, an entire culture, over something that took Paul? Paul just wanted to jam. That's all he ever wanted. He was *that* dude. He was a talented mother-fucker and he would think we were a bunch of fucking idiots if we didn't keep jamming.

In 2011, Slipknot did a short European tour, headlining the So-nisphere Festival, among other European festivals. Taylor called the gigs a "celebration" and tribute to Gray. Original Slipknot guitarist and Body Pit bandmate Donnie Steele filled in for Gray on the tour, though he was hidden from the audience's view. In 2012, Slipknot headlined the Rockstar Energy Mayhem Festival with Slayer.

COREY TAYLOR: After we were able to grieve for a while we decided that we were going to keep going. And by the time we agreed to headline the 2012 Mayhem festival, we knew we were going to do another record. I've already got some ideas and Joey sent me some stuff he's been writing. But it's gonna be a couple years before we'll be able to get together and do it. It's nothing any of us want to rush into.

DES MOINES REGISTER (September 6, 2012): Des Moines physician Daniel Baldi was charged with eight counts of involuntary manslaughter for allegedly prescribing large amounts of narcotic painkillers to patients who later died of overdoses. One of the eight patients was identified in court papers as Paul Gray.

SLIPKNOT STATEMENT (September 6, 2012): As the loss of our brother Paul Gray is still very fresh for us in the Slipknot family, this new development has us all in a state of anger and sadness. The fact that this person took advantage of our brother's illness while he was in a position to help others has outraged everyone in our family. We can only hope that justice will be served so this can NEVER happen to anyone else ever again.

THE END COMPLETE

The development of metal is like the evolution of a virus. Microscopic organisms replicate inside living cells, and to ensure their survival, they adapt and mutate over generations. Not that headbangers are afflicted with a debilitating disease. On the contrary, the relationship between metal fans and the "metal virus" is symbiotic, and once infected, the host becomes empowered and, for a while at least, thrives on the chaos, aggression, and sense of individuality and community that metal provides. Various metal bands understand the contagious quality of the music they create: Anthrax named its second album *Spreading the Disease* in 1985; Carcass called its 1989 record *Symphonies of Sickness*. Then there was Disturbed's career-skyrocketing single "Down with the Sickness" in 1999.

The base musical and cultural elements motivating the current crop of young metalheads is different than those that inspired fans of Blue Cheer and Alice Cooper in the sixties, but the core compounds are the same. Those who harbor the metal virus know that the music they love is rooted in intensity, nonconformity, and escapism, regardless of the era in which it spawned. And, unbeknownst to its adversaries, who seem to view metal fans as a single mass of knuckle-dragging troglodytes, metal affects men and women of all races, creeds, and social classes. There are metalheads with academic degrees who seek solace in the stress relief and mathematical intricacies of the genre, and middle-class adults who still cling to the music's volume and power, either because it keeps them feeling young or because they still revel in the bursts of energy it provides. There are soldiers who rely on metal's aggression and muscle to give them strength in life-threatening situations and help them survive post-traumatic stress disorder. Then there are those the metal virus feeds upon most ravenously—the young.

Metal speaks to young people like nothing else can, and it convinces them that, with their favorite bands and albums as an anchor, they can survive pain, depression, and almost any type of adversity and then revel in their rebellion, partying and tearing shit up simply because they can. It doesn't have to be a life-or-death thing. They might just be regular suburban teens disenfranchised in a society of conformists, jocks, and cheerleaders. Regardless, for each subtype infected or enlightened by metal, it's the music no one else understands or appreciates, filled with "heroes" the mainstream regards as degenerates or morons because they can't relate to the thunderous release the music provides. To those untouched by the metal virus, the music is "just a bunch of noise," it "all sounds the same," "has no musical value," or "sends out negative messages that warp minds and promote violence."

What the ignorant consistently fail to realize is that the more they dismiss the music, the more passionate metal's followers become about the force that gets them through the day. Like a virus, metal has grown so rapidly and gone through so many permutations that all metalheads don't even fit under the same umbrella. You won't find many Deicide fans listening to Mötley Crüe, while Tool followers aren't lining up to catch Napalm Death at their local dive.

But that's just fine; infection is strengthened by adversity, and the necessary cross-pollination of metal's subgenres over the years has kept the music vital, even as record labels and other corporate entities struggled to contain, stamp, and commodify it. Metal is an infectious disease; a beast to be respected, not caged. In a way, it's like the Terminator. "It can't be reasoned with. It doesn't feel pity, or remorse, or fear. And it absolutely will not stop—ever."

Throughout the past four decades, fans of other styles of music have repeatedly declared that metal is dead. It was supposed to be supplanted by punk in the seventies, by New Wave in the eighties, and by grunge in the nineties. Yet even during eras when it was least popular, the music continued to evolve and gain power in the underground. Then when the masses were angry enough at the state of the world—and disgruntled by the lack of passion and substance in popular music—metal rose from the dirt to inspire once again.

Of course, predicting when that will happen is like guessing when massive earthquakes will obliterate major cities. It's hardly a perfect science. But until then, the current crop of metal will continue to affect and infect. Survivors from past eras will keep kneeling at their respective altars of noise, while new generations of sonic terrorists—be they metalcore, deathcore, avant-black metal, or a subgenre as yet undiscovered—will keep forming and mutating to make their mark and struggle for survival. As long as there is anger, disenfranchisement, corruption, abuse, and angst, the heavy metal microbe will continue to multiply and seek new, willing hosts.

—JON WIEDERHORN

DEFENDER
OF THE FAITH

BY ROB HALFORD

"It stimulates, regenerates / It's therapeutic healing. / It lifts our feet up off the ground /
and blasts us through the ceiling. . . . Heavy Metal / What do you want? / Heavy Metal."

"HEAVY METAL," *RAM IT DOWN*—JUDAS PRIEST

Having experienced and performed through four-plus de-cades of the music we now know as heavy metal, there are several things I can say with confidence. Metal was not born; it evolved from other existing sounds, ideas, and technologies. It can therefore never die. Over the years, its popularity has risen and fallen, but metal always bounces back, usually better than before. And those who choose to write and play it always find ways to de-construct or modify it for a new audience. Whether it's New Wave of British Heavy Metal, thrash, death metal, black metal, nu metal, or metalcore, discovering a new subgenre of metal music is like finding the key to an exotic kingdom. Open the door and excite-ment, empowerment, and enjoyment wait on the other side. Why does metal have the ability to touch its audience so profoundly? Because metal gives people an identity and a cause, a motivation to come together—especially in a live arena—and be united with other people who share the love for metal's power.

From the overdriven volume to the crunching intensity, metal is a catalyst, offering the ability to let go, be explosive, and let out that primal scream. It's a universal experience that means as much to a teenager with angst as it means to a middle-aged person in a midlife crisis. At a metal show these days, particularly one by a band that has had a long career, you see fifteen-year-olds and fifty-year-olds—and they're giving each other the devil horns, the universal metal salute. It's a shared and meaningful moment, one that will last long after Judas Priest, Metallica, and Korn—or whatever bands are dominating the scene at any given moment—have come and gone.

Metal isn't just defined by the music artists create. From one decade to the next, it's about signature looks, styles, and attitudes that unify a generation and differentiate them from ones that came before. "Oh, you think that band is fast and brutal? Well, check *this* one out!"

Metal is music for the ages, and as it continues, metal bands will continue to break boundaries and defy barriers. Each subgenre offers its own set of codes and conduct, and its fans absorb these mannerisms as if by osmosis, slamming, stage-diving, and moshing their way toward both the end of the world and the next evolution of the art form. It's like a religion, such believers, such followers are the people who love metal. It's more than a passion: it's a lifestyle. And it's a lifestyle for life. Once a metalhead, always a metalhead.

At its primitive core, the way metal makes us feel touches us at the most basic, animalistic level. It's different from any other kind of music because of the power and influence it possesses, and it will be another forty years before we can truly trace the many paths and forks in the road musicians will take to create new variations on the common themes of rebellion, aggression, and unification.

CAST OF CHARACTERS

ABBATH (OLVE EIKEMO): Multi-instrumentalist for black metal bands Old Funeral and Immortal.

VINNIE PAUL ABBOTT: Drummer for Pantera and Damageplan.

MARK "PSYCHO" ABRAMSON: Vice president of promotions for Roadrunner Records.

STEVEN ADLER: Ex–Guns N' Roses drummer.

MICHAEL ALAGO: ex-A&R for Geffen, Interscope.

GENE AMBO: Photographer.

JONATHAN ANASTAS: Bassist for Boston hardcore bands DYS, Slapshot.

IAN ANDERSON: Singer/flautist for Jethro Tull.

TOM ANGELRIPPER: Singer, bassist, founder of German thrash band Sodom.

PHILIP ANSELMO: Ex-Pantera singer, 1987–2003; Down, 1991–present; ex-singer, Superjoint Ritual, 1993–2004; guitarist for Arson Anthem.

CARMINE APPICE: Drummer for Vanilla Fudge, Cactus, Beck, Bogart & Appice.

VINNY APPICE: Ex-drummer for Black Sabbath, Dio, Heaven & Hell.

TOM ARAYA: Singer/bassist for thrash band Slayer.

STEVE AUSTIN: Founder, guitarist, vocalist for experimental noise band Today Is the Day.

TREY AZAGTHOTH: Guitarist for Florida death metal band Morbid Angel.

SEBASTIAN BACH: Singer, ex–Skid Row, solo artist.

MATT BACHAND: Guitarist for Boston metalcore pioneers Shadows Fall.

SUSAN BAKER: Cofounder of the Parents Music Resource Center (P.M.R.C.), 1985.

PAUL BALOFF (b: 1960, d: 2002): Singer for Exodus, 1981–1986, 1997–2002.

FRANKIE BANALI: Drummer for Quiet Riot.

JACOB BANNON: Vocalist for hardcore band Converge.

PAUL BARKER: Ex-bassist for The Blackouts, Ministry, Revolting Cocks, Lard, USSA; solo artist.

CHRIS BARNES: Ex-vocalist for Florida death metal band Cannibal Corpse; singer, Six Feet Under.

KEITH BARNEY: Ex-guitarist for Orange County metalcore band Eighteen Visions, ex-vocalist for Throwdown.

LEE BARRETT: Head of Candlelight Records.

GEOFF BARTON: British journalist, ex-editor of *Sounds*, founder of *Kerrang!*.

CHRIS BEATTIE: Bassist for hardcore metal band Hatebreed since 1994.

TOM BEAUJOUR: Ex-editor of *Revolver*, editor of *Guitar Aficionado*.

JEFF BECCERA: Front man for thrash band Possessed.

BURTON C. BELL: Vocalist for industrial band Fear Factory, Ascension of the Watchers.

JOEY BELLADONNA: Singer for Anthrax, 1984–92, 2005–06, 2010–present; ex-Belladonna.

CHARLIE BENANTE: Drummer for Anthrax, S.O.D.

CHESTER BENNINGTON: Vocalist for Linkin Park.

GLEN BENTON: Front man for Florida death metal band Deicide.

PETER BESTE: Photographer.

KARL BEUCHNER: Singer for metallic hardcore band Earth Crisis.

CHUCK BILLY: Singer for thrash band Testament.

MARTIN BIRCH: British rock and metal record producer.

BETSY BITCH: Singer of Bitch.

RITCHIE BLACKMORE: Ex-Rainbow, ex–Deep Purple guitarist; Blackmore's Night.

RANDY BLYTHE: Vocalist for Lamb of God.

MARS BONFIRE: Canadian rock musician/songwriter.

WES BORLAND: Guitarist for Limp Bizkit, Black Light Burns, Big Dumb Face.

NICK BOWCOTT: Guitarist for New Wave of British Heavy Metal band Grim Reaper.

KURT BRECHT: Vocalist for crossover

metal band Dirty Rotten Imbeciles (D.R.I.).

JUSTIN BROADRICK: Ex-guitarist for Napalm Death; ex-drummer for Head of David, Fall of Because; front man for Final, Techno Animal, Godflesh, Jesu.

CHRIS BRODERICK: Megadeth guitarist, ex-Nevermore, ex-Jag Panzer.

REX BROWN: Bassist for Pantera, Kill Devil Hill; ex-Down.

KEITH BUCKLEY: Vocalist for experimental metalcore band Every Time I Die.

NIK BULLEN: Ex-Napalm Death bassist and vocalist, 1981–1987.

SCOTT BURNS: Ex-producer at Florida's Morrisound Studios.

WILLIAM BURROUGHS (b: 1914, d: 1997): American author. Wrote *Naked Lunch* and *Junky*, both of which referenced the term "heavy metal."

CLIFF BURTON (b: 1962, d: 1986): Metallica bassist, 1982–1986.

JOHN BUSH: Armored Saint vocalist; ex-Anthrax vocalist, 1992–2005, 2009–2010.

GEEZER BUTLER: Cofounder and bassist of Black Sabbath, Heaven & Hell, GZR.

BIFF BYFORD: Singer for New Wave of Heavy Metal band Saxon.

JOHN CAMPBELL: Bassist for Lamb of God.

CARL CANEDY: Drummer for The Rods, ex-Manowar, ex-Thrasher; record producer.

JERRY CANTRELL: Guitarist, backup singer, co-founder for Alice in Chains; solo artist.

DANNY CAREY: Drummer for Tool, ex-Green Jellÿ.

SCOTT CARLSON: Vocalist and bassist for Repulsion, ex-Death, Genocide.

STEPHEN CARPENTER: Cofounder and guitarist for Deftones, Kush, Sol Invicto.

IGOR CAVALERA: Cofounder and former drummer for Sepultura, currently with Cavalera Conspiracy, Mixhell, ex-Nailbomb.

MAX CAVALERA: Cofounder and former front man of Sepultura, currently front man of Soulfly, Cavalera Conspiracy, ex-Nailbomb, ex-Fudge Tunnel.

CARLOS CAVAZO: Guitarist of Ratt (2008–present), ex-Quiet Riot (1982–2000), ex-Snow.

ROB CAVESTANY: Guitarist, co-founder of thrash band Death Angel.

PHIL CAIVANO: Ex-Monster Magnet guitarist.

DINO CAZARES: Cofounder and guitarist of industrial metal band Fear

Factory, Divine Heresy, Asesino, Brujeria.

JACKIE CHAMBERS: Guitarist for New Wave of British Heavy Metal band Girlschool.

JUSTIN CHANCELLOR: Bassist for Tool, ex-Peach.

CHI CHENG: Bassist for Deftones, currently in semiconscious state following 2008 car accident.

BOB CHIAPPARDI: Founder of Concrete Marketing/Foundations Forum/F-Musicfest.

STEFFAN CHIRAZI: Journalist, editor of Metallica magazine *So What?*

JOHNNY CHRIST: Bassist for Avenged Sevenfold.

RICHARD CHRISTY: Drummer, ex-Death, ex–Public Assassin, Charred Walls of the Damned; radio personality, *The Howard Stern Show.*

MIKE CLARK: Guitarist for crossover band Suicidal Tendencies.

RYAN CLARK: Vocalist for Christian metalcore band Demon Hunter; art director.

BRIAN COGAN: Professor, author.

RICHARD COLE: Ex–Led Zeppelin road manager.

JAZ COLEMAN: Front man for punk/industrial pioneers Killing Joke.

PHIL COLLEN: Guitarist for Def Leppard, ex-Girl.

ANDY COLSEFNI: Ex-Slipknot vocalist, Painface.

MONTE CONNOR: Ex-VP of A&R, Roadrunner Records.

ALICE COOPER: Front man for the Alice Cooper Band, solo artist, pioneer of "shock rock."

CANDY COOPER: Journalist.

COUNT GRISHNAKH (VARG VIKERNES): Front man of Norwegian black metal band Burzum, ex–Old Funeral.

ANTHONY COUNTEY: Bad Brains manager.

SHAWN "CLOWN" M. CRAHAN: Percussionist of Slipknot, ex–To My Surprise, Dirty Little Rabbits; filmmaker, photographer.

JEANNIE CRANE: Groupie.

PETER CRISS: Ex-KISS drummer; solo artist.

CRONOS (CONRAD LANT): Venom singer and bassist, 1979–87, 1995–present; ex-Cronos.

ROBBIN CROSBY (b: 1959, d: 2002): Ex-Ratt guitarist.

ABE CUNNINGHAM: Deftones drummer.

BRANN DAILOR: Mastodon drummer, ex-Lethargy, ex–Today Is the Day.

PAUL D'AMOUR: Ex-bassist for Tool, soundtrack composer, front man of Feersum Endjinn.

MIKE D'ANTONIO: Bassist for Overcast, Killswitch Engage.

GLENN DANZIG: Ex-singer/founder for the Misfits, ex-Samhain, Danzig front man.

TERRY DATE: Producer.

DANI "FILTH" DAVEY: Front man for UK black metal band Cradle of Filth.

JONATHAN DAVIS: Vocalist of Korn.

KATON W. DE PENA: Front man of crossover thrash band Hirax.

DEAD (PER YNGVE OHLIN) (b: 1969, d: 1991): Ex-vocalist of Norwegian black metal band Mayhem.

MIKE DEAN: Bassist for crossover band Corrosion of Conformity (C.O.C.).

WARREN DeMARTINI: Ratt guitarist; touring and session guitarist, solo artist.

DEMONAZ (HARALD NAEVDAL): Vocalist and guitarist for Norwegian black metal band Immortal.

AMIR DERAKH: Guitarist, keyboardist, ex-Orgy, ex–Rough Cutt, ex-Firehouse.

MIKE DeWOLF: Guitarist for Taproot.

PAUL DI'ANNO: Ex–Iron Maiden singer, 1978–81.

BRUCE DICKINSON: Iron Maiden singer, 1981–93, 1999–present; ex-Samson.

"DIMEBAG DARRELL" ABBOTT (b: 1966, d: 2004): Ex-Pantera and Damageplan guitarist.

RONNIE JAMES DIO (b: 1942, d: 2010): Singer for Elf, Rainbow, Black Sabbath, Dio, and the revamped Black Sabbath group Heaven & Hell.

DON DOKKEN: Dokken singer and founder.

JON DONAIS: Guitarist for metalcore bands Aftershock, Shadows Fall.

LEE DORRIAN: Ex-vocalist for grindcore band Napalm Death, founder of doom band Cathedral; owner of Rise Above Records.

RYAN DOWNEY: Band manager; journalist.

K.K. DOWNING: Ex–Judas Priest guitarist.

DAVID DRAIMAN: Vocalist for Disturbed, Device.

DR. KNOW: Bad Brains guitarist.

KEVIN DuBROW (b: 1955, d: 2007): Quiet Riot singer.

ADAM DUCE: Machine Head bassist.

FRED DURST: Front man of nu metal band Limp Bizkit.

ADAM DUTKIEWICZ: Drummer and

guitarist for former band Aftershock, ex-drummer, guitarist for Killswitch Engage, Times of Grace.

SUSANNA EDWARDS: Film director.

DAVID ELLEFSON: Bassist and co-founder of Megadeth, ex-F5.

JOE ELLIOTT: Vocalist for Def Leppard.

BOBBY "BLITZ" ELLSWORTH: Singer for thrash band Overkill.

SULLY ERNA: Vocalist for Godsmack, solo artist.

RICK ERNST: Director, executive producer, at Roadrunner Records.

TOBIN ESPERANCE: Bassist for Papa Roach.

EURONYMOUS (ØYSTEIN AARSETH) (b: 1968, d: 1993): Founder and guitarist of Norwegian black metal band Mayhem. Murdered by Burzum's Count Grishnackh.

DAVE EVANS: Ex-singer for AC/DC.

EVIL (MORGAN STEINMEYER HAKANSSON): Guitarist for Swedish black metal band Marduk.

AUDREY EWELL: Movie director.

BOB EZRIN: Record producer.

DEZ FAFARA: Vocalist for nu metal band Coal Chamber, death/thrash band DevilDriver.

BRIAN FAIR: Vocalist for

Massachusetts metalcore pioneers Overcast and Shadows Fall.

PHIL FASCIANA: Guitarist for Malevolent Creation.

FAUST (BARD EITHUN): Ex-drummer for Emperor, Blood Tsunami, Aborym.

CHRIS FEHN: Percussionist for Slipknot.

FENRIZ (LEIF GYLVE NAGELL): Drummer for Darkthrone.

MARIA FERRERO: Ex-Megaforce publicist, Adrenaline PR founder.

FIELDY (REGINALD ARVIZU): Bassist for Korn.

THOMAS GABRIEL FISCHER: Front man for Triptykon, ex–Celtic Frost, ex-Hellhammer.

HARLEY FLANAGAN: Ex-drummer for The Stimulators, ex–Cro-Mags, Harley's War.

TONY FLETCHER: Journalist.

ROBB FLYNN: Ex-guitarist for thrash bands Forbidden, Vio-Lence; front man for Machine Head.

LITA FORD: Ex-guitarist for The Runaways, solo artist.

RAYNA FOSS: Bassist for Coal Chamber.

ACE FREHLEY: Ex-KISS guitarist, Frehley's Comet, solo artist.

JAY JAY FRENCH: Guitarist and co-founder of Twisted Sister.

DAVID FRICKE: Journalist.

LONN FRIEND: Journalist, ex-*RIP* magazine editor, author.

FROST (KJETIL VIDAR HARALDSTAD): Drummer for Satyricon.

GAAHL (KRISTIAN EIVIND ESPEDAL): Ex-vocalist for Norwegian black metal band Gorgoroth, God Seed, ex-Trelldom, ex-Gaahlskagg, ex-Warduna.

JOHN GALLAGHER: Singer, bassist and cofounder of Raven.

RONNIE "NASTY" GALETTI: Front man for Nasty Savage; ex-professional wrestler.

SYNYSTER GATES: Guitarist for Avenged Sevenfold.

BRANDON GEIST: *Revolver* editor in chief.

BARRY GIFFORD: Journalist, author, screenwriter.

IAN GILLAN: Singer for Deep Purple; ex-singer for Black Sabbath; solo artist.

BRAD GILLIS: Guitarist of Night Ranger, ex–Ozzy Osbourne guitarist.

JOE GIRON: Photographer.

MIKE GITTER: Ex-A&R for Road-runner, Razor & Tie.

TERRY GLAZE: Ex-vocalist for Pantera, Lord Tracy.

JAY GORDON: Vocalist for Orgy.

ANGELA GOSSOW: Vocalist for Arch Enemy.

BILLY GOULD: Bassist for Faith No More.

PAUL GRAY (b: 1972, d: 2010): Bassist, songwriter and cofounder of Slipknot.

BILLY GRAZIADEI: Guitarist for Bio-hazard, ex–Suicide City.

BARNEY GREENWAY: Vocalist for Napalm Death.

DAVE GROHL: Ex-Nirvana drummer; singer, guitarist, and founder of Foo Fighters.

ADAM GROSSMAN: Front man for Skrew, ex–Angkor Wat.

KORY GROW: Journalist.

TRACII GUNS: Ex-guitarist for Guns N' Roses; founder of L.A. Guns.

ROB HALFORD: Vocalist for Judas Priest, 1974–1991, 2003–present; ex-Fight, ex-2wo, ex-Halford.

CHRISTOPHER HALL: Vocalist for industrial band Stabbing Westward.

VICKY HAMILTON: Music executive, ex-Geffen A&R, manager.

KIRK HAMMETT: Guitarist for

Metallica, 1983–present, ex-Exodus, 1980–1983.

CONNIE "SWEET CONNIE" HAMZY: Famed groupie.

RITA HANEY: Longtime girlfriend of Dimebag Darrell.

JEFF HANNEMAN: Guitarist for Slayer.

STEVE HARRIS: Iron Maiden cofounder, songwriter, and bassist.

JAMES HART: Vocalist for Eighteen Visions.

MATT HARVEY: Vocalist and guitarist for Exhumed, Dekapitator, Gravehill.

JOE HASSELVANDER: Drummer for Raven, ex-Pentagram.

HEAD (BRIAN WELCH): Ex-guitarist for Korn, solo artist.

WILLIAM HEIN: Cofounder of Enigma Records.

HELLHAMMER (JAN AXEL BLOMBERG): Drummer for Mayhem, Arcturus, Winds, Nidingr, Mezzerschmitt, Death of Desire, Age of Silence.

DWID HELLION: Vocalist for Integrity.

RAYMOND HERRERA: Ex-drummer for Fear Factory, Arkaea.

JAMES HETFIELD: Front man, cofounder of Metallica.

BOBBY HEWITT: Drummer for Orgy.

KENNY HICKEY: Guitarist for Type O Negative.

IAN HILL: Bassist for Judas Priest.

BRENT HINDS: Guitarist and vocalist for Mastodon, Fiend Without a Face; ex–Four Hour Fogger.

KEVIN HODAPP: Photographer.

GENE HOGLAN: Drummer for Dethklok, ex–Strapping Young Lad, Dark Angel, Fear Factory.

GARY HOLT: Exodus guitarist.

JOSH HOMME: Queens of the Stone Age guitarist, vocalist, ex-Kyuss guitarist, Them Crooked Vultures; record producer.

H.R.: Front man for Bad Brains.

EARL HUDSON: Drummer for Bad Brains.

GLENN HUGHES: Ex-vocalist for Deep Purple, ex–Black Sabbath, Black Country Communion.

SCOTT IAN: Guitarist, cofounder of Anthrax, ex–Stormtroopers of Death (S.O.D.), The Damned Things.

ICE CUBE: Body Count front man, rapper; actor.

IGGY POP: Vocalist of The Stooges, solo artist.

IHSAHN (VEGARD SVERRE TVEI-TAN): Front man of Emperor, ex-Peccatum, solo artist.

INFERNUS (ROGER TIEGS): Ex-guitarist for Gorgoroth, ex-Orcustus, ex-Desekrator.

TONY IOMMI: Cofounder and guitarist for Black Sabbath, Heaven & Hell.

DAN JACOBS: Guitarist for Atreyu.

LARRY JACOBSON: Band manager.

JAMEY JASTA: Jasta 14, Hatebreed, Kingdom of Sorrow, Jasta; ex-host, MTV's *Headbangers Ball.*

DARRYL JENIFER: Bassist for Bad Brains.

EJ JOHANTGEN: President of Prosthetic Records, ex–Metal Blade radio promo, ex-Columbia radio promo.

JOHN 5: Guitarist for Rob Zombie, ex–Marilyn Manson, ex-DLR band.

BRIAN JOHNSON: Singer for AC/DC.

ADAM JONES: Cofounder and guitarist for Tool.

HOWARD JONES: Ex-vocalist of Massachusetts metalcore band Killswitch Engage, ex–Blood Has Been Shed.

JOHN PAUL JONES: Bassist for Led Zeppelin, Them Crooked Vultures.

JOEY JORDISON: Drummer for Slipknot, Murderdolls.

JOHN JOSEPH: Ex-vocalist for New York crossover band Cro-Mags.

NEAL KAY: London-based DJ who coined "New Wave of British Heavy Metal"; Soundhouse club manager.

MAYNARD JAMES KEENAN: Cofounder and vocalist for Tool, A Perfect Circle, Puscifer.

PEPPER KEENAN: Down guitarist, front man for Corrosion of Conformity (C.O.C.).

BILL KELLIHER: Guitarist for Mastodon, ex-Lethargy, ex–Today Is the Day.

A. B. KILLHEFFER: Connecticut-based teacher, researcher.

LEMMY KILMISTER: Singer and bassist for Motörhead, ex-Hawkwind.

KING DIAMOND (KIM BENDIX PE-TERSEN): Front man for Mercyful Fate, solo artist.

KERRY KING: Cofounder and guitarist of thrash band Slayer.

KING Ov HELL (TOM CATO VISNES): Ex-bassist of Gorgoroth, ex–Ov Hell, God Seed, Sahg, ex-Jotunspor, ex–Audrey Horne.

ALISTAIR KINNEAR: Australian musician, friend of late AC/DC vocalist Bon Scott.

GRUTLE KJELLSON: Bassist and vocalist for Enslaved.

STEVE "FUZZ" KMAK: Ex-Disturbed bassist.

SASCHA KONIETZKO: Front man of KMFDM, ex–Excessive Force, ex-MDFMK.

GUY KOZOWYK: Front man of The Red Chord; owner of Black Market Activities.

WAYNE KRAMER: Guitarist of MC5.

RICHARD KRUSPE: Guitarist of Rammstein.

PHIL LABONTE: Ex-vocalist of Shadows Fall, All That Remains.

PATRICK LACHMAN: Vocalist of Damageplan, ex-guitarist of Halford.

CORKY LAING: Drummer for Mountain.

MORGAN LANDER: Front woman of Kittie.

JANI LANE (b: 1964, d: 2011): Singer of Warrant.

PAUL LARSON: 5AD radio reporter.

BLACKIE LAWLESS: Front man of W.A.S.P.

JESSE LEACH: Vocalist for Killswitch Engage, Times of Grace.

JAKE E. LEE: Ex-guitarist for Ozzy Osbourne, ex-Ratt, ex-Badlands, solo artist.

KAM LEE: Ex-vocalist for Death, ex-Massacre, Bone Gnawer.

TOMMY LEE: Drummer for Mötley Crüe, solo artist.

BILL LEEB: Programmer for Front Line Assembly, ex–Skinny Puppy.

BOB LEFSETZ: Music biz blogger, author of "The Lefsetz Letter" e-mail.

AARON LEWIS: Vocalist of Staind.

PHIL LEWIS: Singer of L.A. Guns, ex-Girl.

SCOTT LEWIS: Vocalist for Carnifex.

JOSEPH LIEBERMAN: Former Connecticut senator.

BOBBY LIEBLING: Vocalist for Pentagram.

DAN LILKER: Ex-bassist for Anthrax, ex–Nuclear Assault, ex-S.O.D., Brutal Truth.

KURT LODER: Ex-MTV News anchor; author, journalist.

DAVE LOMBARDO: Drummer for Slayer, ex–Grip Inc.

COURTNEY LOVE: Front woman for Hole, ex–Faith No More.

MITCH LUCKER (b: 1984, d: 2012): Vocalist for Suicide Silence.

GEORGE LYNCH: Ex-Dokken guitarist, Lynch Mob guitarist, solo artist.

IAN MACKAYE: Vocalist and guitarist

for Minor Threat, Fugazi, ex–Pailhead; producer, owner of Dischord Records.

CHARLES MAGGIO: Vocalist for Rorschach.

DARON MALAKIAN: Guitarist for System of a Down, front man for Scars on Broadway; producer.

YNGWIE MALMSTEEN: Guitarist, ex-Steeler, ex-Alcatrazz, ex–Rising Force; solo artist.

JOSE MANGIN: Sirius XM on-air talent, MTV *Headbangers Ball* host.

MARILYN MANSON: Vocalist, Marilyn Manson.

JIM MARTIN: Ex-guitarist for Faith No More, ex-solo artist.

PAUL MASVIDAL: Guitarist for Florida death metal band Cynic, ex-Death.

PAUL MAZURKIEWICZ: Drummer for Cannibal Corpse.

NICKO McBRAIN: Drummer of Iron Maiden.

DAVE McCLAIN: Drummer of Machine Head, ex–Sacred Reich.

RON McGOVNEY: Ex-Metallica bassist.

BUZ McGRATH: Guitarist for Massachusetts metalcore band Unearth.

MARK McGRATH: Vocalist for Sugar Ray; TV host, DJ.

DUFF McKAGAN: Ex-Guns N' Roses bassist, ex-Velvet Revolver, solo artist.

BRET MICHAELS: Cofounder and vocalist of Poison, solo artist, TV personality.

TRAVIS MIGUEL: Guitarist for Atreyu, Fake Figures.

ROGER MIRET: Vocalist for Agnostic Front, Roger Miret and the Disasters.

MICHAEL MONROE: Singer and cofounder of Hanoi Rocks, ex–Jerusalem Slim, ex–Demolition 23, solo artist.

TOM MORELLO: Founder and guitarist for Rage Against the Machine, Audioslave, Street Sweeper Social Club; front man for Nightwatchman.

CHINO MORENO: Vocalist for Deftones, Team Sleep, Crosses.

MICK MORRIS: Guitarist for Eighteen Visions, ex-xCLEARx.

TOM MORRIS: Owner of Morrisound Studios.

MARK MORTON: Guitarist of Lamb of God.

CHUCK MOSLEY: Ex-vocalist for Faith No More, solo artist.

ALBERT MUDRIAN: Author, *Decibel* editor.

MIKE MUIR: Singer/founder, Suicidal

Tendencies, Infectious Grooves, Cyco Miko.

REED MULLIN: Drummer for Corrosion of Conformity (C.O.C.).

MUNKY (JAMES SHAFFER): Guitarist and cofounder of Korn.

JAMES MURPHY: Ex-guitarist for Death, Disincarnate.

DAVE MURRAY: Guitarist for Iron Maiden.

DAVE MUSTAINE: Ex-Metallica guitarist, front man and cofounder of Megadeth.

NECROBUTCHER (JORN STUBBERUD): Cofounder and bassist for Mayhem.

VINCE NEIL: Singer of Mötley Crüe.

NERGAL (ADAM DARSKI): Founder and front man of Behemoth.

JON NÖDTVEIDT (b: 1975, d: 2006): Founder and front man of Dissection.

TED NUGENT: Ex-guitarist for Amboy Dukes, ex–Damn Yankees, solo artist.

SHAVO ODADJIAN: Bassist for System of a Down.

KEVIN "NIVEK OGRE" OGILVIE: Vocalist of industrial band Skinny Puppy.

HARALD OIMOEN: Bassist, Dirty Rotten Imbeciles (D.R.I.); photographer.

MATT OLIVO: Guitarist of Repulsion, Dejecta, ex-Death.

OZZY OSBOURNE: Founding vocalist for Black Sabbath, solo artist, TV personality.

SHARON OSBOURNE: Ozzy Osbourne's manager/wife; TV personality.

JIMMY PAGE: Guitarist for Led Zeppelin, ex-Yardbirds.

FRANKIE PALMERI: Vocalist of Emmure.

CHUCK PALAHNIUK: Author.

RICHARD PATRICK: Filter front man, ex–Nine Inch Nails.

MIKE PATTON: Vocalist for Faith No More, Tomahawk, Fantomas, Lovage, Peeping Tom, ex–Mr. Bungle; owner of Ipecac Records.

STEPHEN PEARCY: Singer for Ratt.

DAVE PETERS: Ex-guitarist for Eighteen Visions, vocalist, ex-guitarist for Throwdown.

DICKIE PETERSON (b: 1964, d: 2009): Blue Cheer singer/bassist.

ERIC PETERSON: Guitarist for Testament, ex-front man for Dragonlord.

MILLE PETROZZA: Front man of Kreator.

TREVOR PHIPPS: Vocalist of Unearth.

MATT PIKE: Front man and founder of High on Fire, Sleep.

MATT PINFIELD: TV, radio personality.

JESSE PINTADO (b: 1969, d: 2006): ex-guitarist for Napalm Death, Terrorizer.

CYNTHIA PLASTERCASTER: Groupie, penis sculptor.

MARTIN POPOFF: Author, journalist.

SETH PUTNAM (b: 1968, d: 2011): Front man of grindcore band Anal Cunt.

DAVE PYBUS: Guitarist for Cradle of Filth, ex-Anathema, Dreambreed.

RON QUINTANA: KUSF San Francisco Radio DJ, ex-fanzine editor.

QUORTHON (TOMAS FORSBERG) (b: 1966, d: 2004): Founder and front man of Bathory.

RIKI RACHTMAN: DJ, VJ, Cathouse nightclub founder.

TWIGGY RAMIREZ: Ex-bassist, current guitarist for Marilyn Manson.

MEEGS RANSCÓN: Guitarist for nu metal band Coal Chamber, Glass Pinata, NEO GEO, We Are the Riot.

CHRIS REIFERT: Drummer for Autopsy, ex-Death, ex-Abscess, ex–The Ravenous, ex–Burnt Offerings.

REVEREND RUN: Rapper for Run-DMC.

TRENT REZNOR: Front man for Nine Inch Nails, ex-2wo, solo artist.

DELORES RHOADS: Randy Rhoads's mother, owner of Musonia music school.

KELLI RHOADS: Brother of Randy Rhoads, classical musician, composer.

RANDY RHOADS (b: 1956, d: 1982): Guitarist for Ozzy Osbourne, ex–Quiet Riot.

LOU BOULDER RICHARDS (b: 1970, d: 2006): Ex-Hatebreed guitarist.

RIPPER (TIM OWENS): Ex-vocalist of Judas Priest, ex–Iced Earth, Charred Walls of the Damned, Dio's Disciples.

ROSS ROBINSON: Producer.

BOB ROCK: Producer.

HENRY ROLLINS: Vocalist for Black Flag, Rollins Band, writer, poet.

TONY ROMBOLA: Guitarist for Godsmack.

JIM ROOT: Guitarist for Slipknot, Stone Sour.

W. AXL ROSE: Singer/founder of Guns N' Roses.

RICK ROZZ: Ex-guitarist and co-founder of Death, Massacre. M. Inc.

SNORRE RUCH: Guitarist for Thorns, ex-Mayhem.

PHIL RUDD: Drummer for AC/DC.

ERIK RUTAN: Ex-guitarist for Morbid Angel, front man of Hate Eternal; producer.

BRANDON SALLER: Drummer of Atreyu, front man of Hell or Highwater.

ED SANDERS: Front man of The Fugs, poet, social activist.

TROY SANDERS: Bassist and vocalist for Mastodon, ex–Four Hour Fogger.

RUDY SARZO: Ex-bassist for Ozzy Osbourne, ex-Whitesnake, ex–Quiet Riot.

MARK SAWACKIS: Guitarist for Impetigo.

RUDOLF SCHENKER: Guitarist of Scorpions.

BRANDAN SCHIEPPATI: Ex-guitarist for Eighteen Visions, ex-Throwdown, vocalist of Bleeding Through, I Am War.

CHRISTOPH "DOOM" SCHNEIDER: Drummer of German industrial band Rammstein.

CHUCK SCHULDINER (b: 1967, d: 2001): Guitarist and vocalist of Death, ex–Control Denied, ex-Voodoocult.

BON SCOTT (b: 1946, d: 1980): Ex-Singer for AC/DC.

EVAN SEINFELD: Ex-bassist and cofounder of Biohazard, ex-Spyderz,

Attika 7; actor, adult film performer and director.

JACOBY SHADDIX: Vocalist for Papa Roach.

M. SHADOWS: Cofounder and vocalist of Avenged Sevenfold.

KELLY SHAEFER: Guitarist and vocalist of Atheist, ex-Neurotica.

SHAGRATH (STIAN TOMT THORESEN): Front man of Dimmu Borgir, guitarist for Chrome Division, ex–OV Hell.

KEVIN SHARP: Vocalist of grindcore band Brutal Truth.

MIKE SHINODA: Rapper for Linkin Park.

ROXANA SHIRAZI: Groupie, author.

RYAN SHUCK: Guitarist for Orgy, ex-Sexart, Julian-K, Dead by Sunrise.

DEREK SHULMAN: President of 2PLUS Music & Entertainment, ex-President/CEO, Atco & Roadrunner Records.

SILENOZ (SVEN ATLE KOPPERUD): Guitarist for Dimmu Borgir.

JOSH SILVER: Keyboardist of Type O Negative.

GENE SIMMONS: Bassist/singer for KISS.

RAT SKATES: Ex-drummer and co-founder of Overkill.

ALEX SKOLNICK: Guitarist for Testament, Alex Skolnick Trio, Trans Siberian Orchestra.

BRIAN SLAGEL: Founder of Metal Blade Records.

SLASH: Ex-guitarist for Guns N' Roses, Velvet Revolver, solo artist.

ROD SMALLWOOD: Sanctuary Management.

ADRIAN SMITH: Guitarist for Iron Maiden.

NEAL SMITH: Ex-drummer for Alice Cooper.

DEE SNIDER: Front man of Twisted Sister, Widowmaker, solo artist, actor, radio and TV personality.

DAN SPITZ: Ex-guitarist for Anthrax, Red Lamb.

PAUL STANLEY: Singer/guitarist for KISS.

WAYNE STATIC: Front man of Static-X, solo artist.

PETER STEELE (b: 1962, d: 2010): Singer, bassist, and founder of Carnivore and Type O Negative.

BILL STEER: Guitarist of Carcass, Firebird, Gentleman's Pistols, Angel Witch.

IZZY STRADLIN: Ex–Guns N' Roses guitarist, solo artist.

LYNN STRAIT (b: 1968, d: 1998): Vocalist for Snot.

DANNY SUGERMAN (b: 1954, d: 2005): Author, band manager.

KEN SUSI: Guitarist for Unearth.

MICHAEL SWEET: Singer, guitarist, and cofounder of Stryper.

SERJ TANKIAN: Vocalist for System of a Down, solo artist.

JOHN TARDY: Vocalist for pioneer death metal band Obituary.

GEOFF TATE: Ex-singer for Queensrÿche (1981–2012).

BRIAN TATLER: Guitarist and cofounder of Diamond Head.

COREY TAYLOR: Vocalist for Slipknot and Stone Sour.

THE REV (JIMMY SULLIVAN) (b: 1981, d: 2009): Founding drummer for Avenged Sevenfold.

MICK THOMSON: Guitarist for Slipknot.

GLENN TIPTON: Guitarist for Judas Priest.

BOBBY TONGS: Pantera videographer.

ROBERT TRUJILLO: Ex-bassist for Ozzy Osbourne, ex–Suicidal Tendencies, Metallica.

EDDIE TRUNK: Former VP of Megaforce Records, radio DJ, host of VH1's "That Metal Show," author of *Eddie Trunk's Essential Hard Rock and Heavy Metal.*

NEIL TURBIN: Ex-vocalist of Anthrax, Death Riders, solo artist.

LARS ULRICH: Metallica drummer and cofounder.

ALEX VAN HALEN: Drummer and cofounder of Van Halen.

EDDIE VAN HALEN: Guitarist and cofounder of Van Halen.

JAVIER VAN HUSS: Ex-bassist for Eighteen Visions, Throwdown.

ALEX VARKATZAS: Vocalist for Atreyu, I Am War.

ZACKY VENGEANCE: Guitarist for Avenged Sevenfold.

JOEY VERA: Bassist for Armored Saint, Fates Warning, ex-Anthrax bassist, producer, solo artist.

TOMMY VICTOR: Front man of Prong, guitarist for Ministry, Danzig.

DAVID VINCENT: Vocalist for Morbid Angel, ex-Terrorizer, ex-Genitorturers.

EERIE VON: Ex–Rosemary's Babies drummer, ex-Samhain bassist, ex-Danzig, solo artist.

ALEX WADE: Guitarist for deathcore band Whitechapel.

JEREMY WAGNER: Author, guitarist for Broken Hope.

JEFF WALKER: Bassist and vocalist for grindcore pioneers Carcass.

MICK WALL: Author, journalist.

RICK WARTELL: Guitarist for Trouble, Wet Animal.

ALEX WEBSTER: Bassist for Cannibal Corpse.

JIM WELCH: Ex-head of Earache U.S.

LESLIE WEST: Singer and guitarist for Mountain.

MIKE IX WILLIAMS: Singer for Eyehategod.

JAMES WILLIAMSON: Guitarist for The Stooges.

SID WILSON: DJ for Slipknot; DJ Starscream.

WINO (SCOTT WEINRICH): The Obsessed ex-singer, guitarist, Saint Vitus.

ZAKK WYLDE: Ex-guitarist for Ozzy Osbourne, guitarist, front man for Black Label Society.

DAVE WYNDORF: Front man of Monster Magnet.

ANGUS YOUNG: Guitarist for AC/DC.

MALCOLM YOUNG: Guitarist for AC/DC.

DEREK YOUNGSMA: Drummer for Bleeding Through.

SEAN YSEULT: Bassist for White Zombie.

FRANK ZAPPA (b: 1940, d: 1993): American composer, singer, producer, guitarist.

JONNY ZAZULA: Rock 'n Roll Heaven record store owner; Megaforce Records founder, along with his wife, Marsha.

NEIL ZLOZOWER: Photographer.

ROB ZOMBIE: Ex–White Zombie front man, solo artist.

ACKNOWLEDGMENTS

Without whose help and encouragement this book would not have been possible:

JON WIEDERHORN AND KATHERINE TURMAN: Stephanie Cabral, Anne Killheffer, Penny Rosen, Greg Cristman, Robert Matheu, Jeremy Saffer, Tresa Redburn, Alex Solca, Philip Raskin, Chris Steffen, Mark Yarm, Sean McDevitt, Kevin Hodap, Matthew Oppenheim, Jayne Andrews, Chip Ruggieri, Mick Wall, Mark McGrath, Scott Ian, Rob Halford, Todd Nakamine, Philip Anselmo, Alice Cooper, Heidi Ellen Robinson, Jason Elzy, Sean "Pellet" Pelletier, Paula Hogan, Robyn Doreian, Brad Tolinski, Brandon Geist, Kory Grow, Josh Bernstein, Slash, Zakk Wylde, Jeremy Wagner, Tom Beaujour, Jeff Kitts, Jeff Perlah, Ray Van Horn, Jennifer Clay, Erin Amar, Brian Cogan, Jeff Gilbert, Bill O'Leary, Rat Skates, Michele Matz, Michael Duncan, Brian Slagel, Bill Meis, Jim Baltutis, Mike Gitter, Ian Christie, Mike Newman, Charrie Foglio, Andy Denemark, Toby Mamis, Mitch Schneider, Marcee Rondan, Erik Toms, Full Metal Jackie Kajzer, Lauren Stockner, Karen Sidlow, Barbara Rice, Gregg Journigan, Jamie Shen, Janiss Garza, Matt Pinfield, Kristine Ashton-Magnuson, Roxy Myzal, hardDrive Radio, Don Kaye, Rich Glinnen, Eddie Trunk, Jose Mangin, Richard Christy, George Vallee, Veronique Cordier, Cory

Brennan, Kimberly Zide Davis, Rick Ernst, Liz Ciavarella-Brenner, Loana Valencia, Kelli Malella, Maria Ferrero, Riki Namm, Larry Getlen, Steffan Chirazi, Jennifer Vineyard, Natalie Camillo, Seth Werkheiser, Donna Hahner, Benjamin Wagner, Jody Gilsman-Best, Nils Bernstein, Cheryl Rixon, James Fitzgerald, Mauro DiPreta, Denise Oswald, Steve Joester, Stephen Stickler, E. J. Johantgen, *This is . . . Spinal Tap*, Dmitry Basik, Neil Zlozower, Jason Buhrmester, Monica Seide, Hannah Verbeuren, Rachel Tatler, WWNSD, Kristell Gathoye . . . and the devoted metalheads the world over! \m/

JON WIEDERHORN: Hap and Miriam Rust, Jean Cecile Wiederhorn, Amy Wilk Sides, Frank and Carole Kaplan, Ken Micallef, Jeff Perlah, Shawn Crow, David Fricke, Michael Azerrad, JG Ballard, J. Edward Keyes, Dave Marchese, Scott Ian, Christopher Weingarten, Shawn "Clown" Crahan, Al Jourgensen, Angie Jourgensen, Philip Raskin, Erin Amar, Barry Appleton, PF Dumanis, Jack Falla, Norman Moyes, *Revolver, Guitar World*, Loudwire.com, Noisecreep.com, *Kerrang!, Metal Hammer*, Matthew Oppenheim, Elizabeth Oppenheim, Lucky 13, Walter White, Dexter Morgan.

KATHERINE TURMAN: Jennifer Clay, Antonia Turman, Herbert Turman, Eleanor Oland, Michael Whitehead, Rod Bradley, Stephanie Cabral, Tresa Redburn, Amy Zaret, Babs MacDonald, Diana Tanda, Claire Carter, Larry Turman, Jackie Terrell, Alice Cooper, Erik Toms, Mike Newman, Christine Jordan, Lonn Friend, Jeremy Wagner, Kym Foglia, Dawn Riddle, Mark Whitehead, Rachel Whitehead, Chrissy Shannon, Vicky Hamilton, Carl Canedy, Budgie Werner, Andy Denemark, Bill Holdship, Jennifer Schwartz, Robert Matheu, Bruce Haring, Chris Broderick, Tracy Vera, Joey Vera, Adrianne Stone, Bernadette Duncan, Barbara Wilson, Josh Sindell, Roxy Myzal, Vanessa Cajucom, Hilary Kaufman, Nights with Alice Cooper, Ronnie Champagne, Suzanna Turman, Elizabeth Kaplan, Robert Hilburn, 93 KHJ, Virginia

Jorgensen, Norman Corwin, Timothy Ferris, *Rip* magazine, *BAM* magazine, *Metal Hammer UK*, *Guitar One*, The Owl's Head, Small's, The Rainbow, Lucky 13, my Muse, Maggie May Burbank, Nancy Drew, Jack Daniels, Hank Moody, Charles Bukowski.

CREDITS

Prologue: Heavy Metal Thunder

William Burroughs, p. 1, from *Burroughs Live: The Collected Interviews of William S. Burroughs, 1960-1997* by William Burroughs and Sylvere Lotringer, Semiotext(e), MIT Press, p. 72

Mars Bonfire, p. 2, from *Heavy Metal: The Music And Its Culture*, Revised Edition, by Deena Weinstein, Da Capo Press, 2000, p. 19

Barry Gifford, p. 2, from interview with Anne B. Killheffer, property of interviewer

Bob Lefsetz, p. 4, from "The Last in Line" by Bob Lefsetz, The Lefsetz Letter: First in Music Analysis, http://lefsetz.com/wordpress/index.php/archives/2010/05/19/the-last-in-line/

Gene Simmons, p. 4, from "Your Letters," Genesimmons.com, http://www.genesimmons.com/fanstories/letters7/index609.html

Kick Out the Jams: Proto Metal, 1964–1970

Jimmy Page, p. 8, from "Heavy Friends" by Brad Tolinski, *Guitar World Presents Guitar Legends*, March 2004 (p. 57)

Ritchie Blackmore, p. 9, interview by Jeff Perlah, property of interviewer

Iggy Pop, p. 11, from "Naughty Little Doggie" by Jennifer Clay, *RIP* magazine, April 1996

Iggy Pop, p. 12, ibid

Iggy Pop, p. 13, ibid

Ritchie Blackmore, p. 16, interview by Jeff Perlah, property of interviewer

Jimmy Page, p. 18, from "The Greatest Show on Earth" by Brad Tolinski, *Guitar World Presents Guitar Legends*, March 2004 (p. 72)

Richard Cole, p. 18, from *Hammer of the Gods: The Led Zeppelin Saga* by Stephen Davis, Harper Collins, p. 87

Iggy Pop, p 19, from "Naughty Little Doggie" by Jennifer Clay, *RIP* magazine, April 1996

Jimmy Page, p. 20, from "The Greatest Show on Earth" by Brad Tolinski, *Guitar World Presents Guitar Legends*, March 2004 (p. 75)

Ritchie Blackmore, p. 23, from interview by Jeff Perlah, property of interviewer

Jimmy Page, p. 24, from "The Greatest Show on Earth" by Brad Tolinski, *Guitar World Presents Guitar Legends*, March 2004 (p. 75)

Masters of Reality: Sabbath, Priest, and Beyond, 1970–1979

Sharon Osbourne, p. 31, from "Against All Ozz: Ozzy Osbourne Bites Back" by Jon Wiederhorn, *Penthouse*, Nov. 1998, p. 48

Tony Iommi, p. 33, from *Iron Man: My Journey Through Heaven & Hell With Black Sabbath* by Tony Iommi with TJ Lammers, Da Capo Press, 2011, p. 22

Ozzy Osbourne, p. 39, from "Against All Ozz: Ozzy Osbourne Bites Back" by Jon Wiederhorn, *Penthouse*, Nov. 1998, p. 47

Paul Stanley, p. 50, from *Kissology, Vol. 1: 1974-1977* Starring Kiss, 2006

Gene Simmons, p. 52, from *Kissology, Vol. 1: 1974-1977* Starring Kiss, 2006.

Gene Simmons, p. 53, ibid

Gene Simmons, p. 57, from *Kiss and Make-Up* by Gene Simmons, Crown, 2001, p. 4

Ace Frehley, p. 59, from interview with Jeff Kitts, property of interviewer

Gene Simmons, p. 59, from *Kissology, Vol. 1: 1974-1977* Starring Kiss, 2006

Gene Simmons, p. 60, ibid

Gene Simmons, p. 60, from *Kiss and Make-Up* by Gene Simmons, Crown, 2001, p. 130

Dave Evans, p. 61, from *AC/DC High-Voltage Rock 'N' Roll: The Illustrated History* by Phil Sutcliffe, Voyageur Press, 2010, p. 31

Angus Young, p. 62, from *Highway to Hell: The Life and Death of AC/DC Legend Bon Scott* by Clinton Walker, Verse Chorus Press, 1994, p. 127

Malcolm Young, p. 62, from "AC/DC Celebrate their Quarter Century" by Sylvie Simmons, *Mojo* Magazine

Peter Criss, p. 70, from "Peter Criss" by Gary James, Famousinterview.com, http://www.famousinterview.ca/interviews/peter_criss_2.htm

Gene Simmons, p. 70, from *Kiss and Make-Up* by Gene Simmons, Crown, 2001, p. 139

Ace Frehley, p. 70, interview by Jeff Kitts, property of interviewer

Alistair Kinnear, p. 71, from "Alistair Kinnear's recollection of 19th February 1980" by Alistair Kinnear, "Metal Hammer and Classic Rock Present AC/DC Special," 2005

Angus Young, p. 72, from "Brian: The Baptism of Fire" by Michel Rémy, Let There Be Light, 1994

Phil Rudd, p. 72, from *AC/DC High-Voltage Rock 'N' Roll: The Illustrated History* by Phil Sutcliffe, Voyageur Press, 2010, p. 94

British Steel: New Wave of British Heavy Metal Shapes the Future, 1980–present

Ozzy Osbourne, p. 83, from "Against All Ozz: Ozzy Osbourne Bites Back" by Jon Wiederhorn, *Penthouse*, Nov. 1998, p. 48

Sharon Osbourne, p. 84, from "Against All Ozz: Ozzy Osbourne Bites Back" by Jon Wiederhorn, *Penthouse*, Nov. 1998, p. 48

David Fricke, p. 86, from "AC/DC Back in Black" review by David Fricke, *Rolling Stone*, July 1980

Steve Harris, p. 90, interview by Mick Wall, property of interviewer

Dave Murray, p. 91, ibid

Steve Harris, p. 91, ibid

Neil Kay, p. 92, ibid

Geoff Barton, p. 94, ibid

Jackie Chambers, p. 99, interview by Ray Van Horn, property of interviewer.

Martin Birch, p. 101, ibid

Adrian Smith, p. 102, ibid

Steve Harris, p. 102, ibid

Glenn Danzig, p. 110, from "Danzig: Mother's Finest" by Katherine Turman, *Rip* magazine, Sept. 1994, p. 45

Phil Caivano, p.111, from "Pussy Magnet" by Jon Wiederhorn, *Penthouse*, Aug. 1999, p. 62

Phil Caivano, p. 112, ibid

Dave Wyndorf, p. 116, from "Dave Ling's Diary" by Dave Ling, Dave Ling Online, July 2007, http://www.daveling.co.uk/diaryjuly07.htm

Youth Gone Wild: Metal Goes Mainstream, 1978–1992

Eddie Van Halen, p. 122, from "Van Halen Family Values" by Jon Wiederhorn, *Penthouse*, Sept. 1998, p. 126

Kevin DuBrow, p. 123, interview by Ray Van Horn, property of interviewer

Kevin DuBrow, p. 124, from "Van Halen Family Values" by Jon Wiederhorn, *Penthouse*, Sept. 1998, p. 127

Eddie Van Halen, p. 124, ibid

Kevin DuBrow, p. 125, ibid

Kevin DuBrow, p. 130, ibid

Jake E. Lee, p. 135, from "How to Succeed Without Really Whammying" by Steven Rosen, *Guitar World*, Nov. 1986

Kevin DuBrow, p. 146, interview by Ray Van Horn, property of interviewer

Randy Rhoads, p. 147, from "Randy Rhoads: A Biography by Family, Friends and Fellow Musicians" by Jas Obrecht, *Guitar Player*, Nov. 1982

Ozzy Osbourne, p. 148, ibid

Ozzy Osbourne, p. 149, from *I Am Ozzy* by Ozzy Osbourne with Chris Ayres, Grand Central Publishing, p. 240

Brad Gillis, p. 151, from "Dear Guitar Hero: Night Ranger's Brad Gillis and Joel Hoekstra," GuitarWorld.com, March 2, 2010, http://www.store.guitarworld.com/dear-guitar-hero-night-rangers-brad-gillis-and-joel-hoekstra

Jake E. Lee, p. 151, from "How to Succeed Without Really Whammying" by Steven Rosen, *Guitar World*, Nov. 1986

Eddie Van Halen, p. 161, from "Van Halen Family Values" by Jon Wiederhorn, *Penthouse*, Sept. 1998, p. 127

Alex Van Halen, p. 162, ibid

Sweet Connie Hamzy, p. 162, from "The Howard Stern Show," Dec. 8, 2010, http://groupieblog.wordpress.com/2010/12/09/connie-hamzy-on-howard-stern-show/

Jeannie Crane, p. 162, from Australian TV program *Hard Copy*, ep. "Groupies," 1988 http://www.youtube.com/watch?v=f6wZoYMS2HM&feature=player_embedded#!

Frank Zappa, p. 164, from the Record Labeling Hearing before the Committee on Commerce, Science and Transportation in the United States Senate, Sept. 19, 1985, http://www.joesapt.net/superlink/shrg99-529/toc.html

Susan Baker, p. 164, from the Record Labeling Hearing before the Committee on Commerce, Science and Transportation in the United States Senate, Sept. 19, 1985, http://www.joesapt.net/superlink/shrg99-529/toc.html

Vince Neil, p. 176, *Mötley Crüe: The Dirt – Confessions of the World's Most Notorious Rock Band* by Mötley Crüe with Neil Strauss, Regan Books, p. 130

Eddie Van Halen, p. 180, from "Van Halen Family Values" by Jon Wiederhorn, *Penthouse*, Sept. 1998, p. 127

Eddie Van Halen, p. 182, from "Van Halen Family Values" by Jon Wiederhorn, *Penthouse*, Sept. 1998, p. 126

Robbin Crosby, p. 184, from "VH1 Behind the Music: Ratt," Ep. 198, May 11, 2006

Caught in a Mosh: Thrash Metal, 1981–1991

Lars Ulrich, p. 196, from *Get Thrashed*, directed by Rick Ernst, produced by Rat Skates, Saigon 1515 Productions, 2006

Lars Ulrich, p. 199, from "Metallica: The MTV Icon Interviews" by Erica Forstadt, MTV.com, 2003, http://www.mtv.com/bands/m/metallica/news_feature_030506/

Lars Ulrich, p. 200, ibid

Dave Mustaine, p. 201, from *Mustaine: A Heavy Metal Memoir* by Dave Mustaine with Joe Layden, It Books, 2011, p. 48

Conrad "Cronos" Lant, p. 203, interview by Jeff Kitts, property of interviewer

Conrad "Cronos" Lant, p. 204, ibid

James Hetfield, p. 205, from "Metallica: The MTV Icon Interviews" by Erica Forstadt, MTV.com, 2003, http://www.mtv.com/bands/m/metallica/news_feature_030506/

Lars Ulrich, p. 205, from "Metallica: The MTV Icon Interviews" by Erica Forstadt, MTV.com, 2003, http://www.mtv.com/bands/m/metallica/news_feature_030506/

Kirk Hammett, p. 206, from *Get Thrashed*, directed by Rick Ernst, produced by Rat Skates, Saigon 1515 Productions, 2006

Dave Mustaine, p. 207, from *Mustaine: A Heavy Metal Memoir* by Dave Mustaine with Joe Layden, It Books, 2011, p. 75

Kirk Hammett, p. 207, from *Get Thrashed*, directed by Rick Ernst, produced by Rat Skates, Saigon 1515 Productions, 2006

Cliff Burton, p. 208, interview by Harald Oimoen, property of interviewer

Dave Mustaine, p. 215, from Lydverket interview, NRK, 2009, http://www.youtube.com/watch?v=WW8NgXZWotM&playnext=1&list=PLDADF01BEB3FE51A7&feature=results_video

Dave Mustaine, p. 216, from "Bending Metal: Megadeth's Transformation" by Jon Wiederhorn, *Penthouse*, May 2000, p. 44

Kirk Hammett, p. 217, from "Metallica: The MTV Icon Interviews" by Erica Forstadt, MTV.com, 2003, http://www.mtv.com/bands/m/metallica/news_feature_030506/

Kirk Hammett, p. 217, ibid

Dave Mustaine, p. 222, from "Bending Metal: Megadeth's Transformation" by Jon Wiederhorn, *Penthouse*, May 2000, p. 45

Dave Ellefson, p. 226, ibid

Dave Mustaine, p. 226, ibid

Dave Ellefson, p. 227, ibid

Dave Mustaine, p. 227, ibid

Paul Baloff, p. 242, from "Tales From the Pit No. 3" video magazine produced by Jerry Allen, 1985 http://www.youtube.com/watch?v=aDE25qgkUW4

Lars Ulrich, p. 245, from "Masterpiece" by Mick Wall, Guitar World Presents Guitar Legends: Metallica—25 Years of Heavy Metal Thunder, March 2009, p. 33

Lars Ulrich, p. 246, ibid

Kirk Hammett, 246, from "Masterpiece" by Mick Wall, Guitar World Presents Guitar Legends: Metallica—25 Years of Heavy Metal Thunder, March 2009, p. 34

James Hetfield, p. 246, from "Metallica:

Talkin' Trash" by Richard Bienstock,
guitarworld.com

Lars Ulrich, p. 246, from "Metallica:
The MTV Icon Interviews" by Erica
Forstadt, MTV.com, 2003, http://
www.mtv.com/bands/m/metallica/
news_feature_030506/

James Hetfield, p. 247, from "Metallica:
Talkin' Trash" by Richard Bienstock,
guitarworld.com

Dave Mustaine, p. 248, from *Mustaine: A
Heavy Metal Memoir* by Dave Mustaine
with Joe Layden, It Books, 2011

Lars Ulrich, p. 250, from "Metallica:
The MTV Icon Interviews," by Erica
Forstadt, MTV.com, 2003, http://
www.mtv.com/bands/m/metallica/
news_feature_030506/

Kirk Hammett, p. 257, from "Playboy
Interview: Metallica," by Rob Tannenbaum, *Playboy*, April 2001

Lars Ulrich, p. 257, ibid

Dave Mustaine, p. 258, from "Bending Metal:
Megadeth's Transformation" by Jon Wiederhorn, *Penthouse*, May 2000, p. 45

James Hetfield, p. 258, from "Playboy
Interview: Metallica," by Rob Tannenbaum, *Playboy*, April 2001

The Age of Quarrel: Crossover/
Hardcore, 1977–1992

Glenn Danzig, p. 269, from "New Music
Preview: Glenn Danzig" by Legs
McNeil, *Spin*, Jan. 1991, p. 29

Glenn Danzig, p. 269, "Glenn Danzig:
Resurrection of a Misfit" by Mike
Gitter, *Rip* magazine, Oct. 1987

Glenn Danzig, p. 269, from "New Music
Preview: Glenn Danzig" by Legs
McNeil, *Spin*, Jan. 1991, p. 29

New York Daily News, p. 278, from *Daily
News*, "Webster Hall pulls plug on
hardcore show after punk rockers
battle," by Kerry Burke, Shayna Jacobs,
July 7, 2012

Peter Steele, p. 287, from "Death Metal: A
Documentary" written and directed by
Bill Zebub, Bill Zebub productions, 2002

Far Beyond Driven: Thrash Revisited
and Revised, 1987–2004

Sharon Osbourne, p. 328, from "Against
All Ozz: Ozzy Osbourne Bites
Back" by Jon Wiederhorn, *Penthouse*,
Nov. 1998, p. 47

Ozzy Osbourne, p. 328, ibid

San Luis Obispo Tribune, p. 332, from "Elyse
Pahler: Killed in Nipomo in 1995"
by newspaper staff, *San Luis Obispo
Tribune*, April 14, 2010, http://www.san
luisobispo.com/2010/04/14/1102851/
elyse-pahler-killed-in-nipomo.
html#storylink=cpy

San Francisco Examiner, p. 333, from
"Subliminal Messages, Heavy Metal
Music and Teenage Suicide" by Candy
Cooper, *San Francisco Examiner*, Sept.
29, 1989

Lars Ulrich, p. 337, from "Metallica:
The MTV Icon Interviews" by Erica
Forstadt, MTV.com, 2003, http://
www.mtv.com/bands/m/metallica/
news_feature_030506/

Kirk Hammett, p. 337, ibid

Bob Rock, p. 338, ibid

Lars Ulrich, p. 338, ibid

Dave Mustaine, p. 343, from "Bending Metal:
Megadeth's Transformation" by Jon Wiederhorn, *Penthouse*, May 2000, p. 44

Dave Ellefson, p. 343, ibid

Nicko McBrain, p. 344, interview by Mick
Wall, property of interviewer

Steve Harris, p. 344, ibid

Phil Anselmo, p. 347, from 1996 press release issued by Elektra Records

Steve Harris, p. 352, interview by Mick Wall, property of interviewer

Rob Halford, p. 353, from "MTV News 1515" interview by Jim Fraenkel, Feb. 6, 1998

Phil Anselmo, p. 361, self-released Internet video statement about the death of Dimebag Darrell, philanselmo.com, Dec. 16, 2004, http://www.youtube.com/watch?v=QpX3I-cx0CA

High-Tech Hate: Industrial, 1980–1997

Trent Reznor, p. 366, from "Nine Inches of Love" by Jim Greer, Spin, March, 1992

Tony Fletcher, p. 367, from "Killing Joke" by Anthony Blampied and Tony Fletcher, Jamming 12, 1981

Kevin Ogilvie, p. 370, from "Skinny Puppy Radio Interview" by Joe Radio, December 9, 1989

Trent Reznor, p. 378, from "To Hell and Back" by Stevie Chick, Kerrang!, March 30, 2005

Trent Reznor, p. 379, from "Nine Inch Nails With Teeth" by Paul Gargano, Maximum Ink, Oct. 2005

Trent Reznor, p. 380, from "Nine Inch Nails: The Upward Spiral" by Corey Moss, MTV.com, May 2005

Trent Reznor, p. 381, ibid

Trent Reznor, p. 381, from "Portrait of a Nine Inch Nail" by Stacey Sanner, Alternative Press, July 1990

Chuck Pahlaniuk, p. 386, from "The Fragile: Album of the Year" by Chris Norris, Spin, Dec. 1999.

Marilyn Manson, p. 388, from "Marilyn Manson Interview" by Jeff Jolley, Radio Alternative Digital Magazine, 1994

Trent Reznor, p. 388, from "Reznor Resurrected" by Simon Price, Metal Hammer, July 2005, p. 38

Marilyn Manson, p. 390, from The Long Hard Road Out of Hell by Marilyn Manson with Neil Strauss, Regan Books, 1998, p. 229

Trent Reznor, p. 392, from "Trent Reznor Says Marilyn Manson Has Become a Dopey Clown" by Daniel Kreps, Rollingstone.com, June 2, 2009

Marilyn Manson, p. 393, from "Marilyn Manson Back on the Road" by Cameron Adams, Melbourne and Victoria Herald Sun, July 30, 2009

Alec Empire, p. 404, "Atari Teenage Riot's Alec Empire Questions Rammstein's Sincerity" by MTV staff, MTV.com, Nov. 9, 1998

Til Lindemann, p. 405, from "Playboy Interview" by Rob Tannenbaum, Playboy, January 2006

All for the Nookie: Nu Metal, 1989–2002

Mike Patton, p. 413, from "Faith No More: Artist of the Year" by Frank Owen, Spin, Dec. 1990

Jonathan Davis, p. 420, from "Kornucopia: Nu-Metal Band's Disturbing—And Successful—Vision" by Jon Wiederhorn, Penthouse, Oct. 2002, p. 82

Fieldy, p. 420, from "Testing Their Metal" by Jon Wiederhorn, Penthouse, March 1999, p. 90

Jonathan Davis, p. 421, from "Kornucopia: Nu-Metal Band's Disturbing—And Successful—Vision" by Jon Wiederhorn, Penthouse, Oct. 2002, p. 83

Fieldy, p. 421, ibid

Jay Gordon, p. 432, from "Grope Therapy: Orgy Lives Up to Its Name" by Jon Wiederhorn, *Penthouse*, April 2001, p. 83

Bobby Hewitt, p. 433, ibid

Jonathan Davis, p. 433, from "Kornucopia: Nu-Metal Band's Disturbing—And Successful—Vision" by Jon Wiederhorn, *Penthouse*, Oct. 2002, p. 84

Lynn Strait, p. 434, from "Lynn Strait Interview" by Ro, Snotmerch.com, May 1997

Fred Durst, p. 435, from "Testing Their Metal" by Jon Wiederhorn, *Penthouse*, March 1999.

Jonathan Davis, p. 435, from "Kornucopia: Nu-Metal Band's Disturbing—And Successful—Vision" by Jon Wiederhorn, *Penthouse*, Oct. 2002, p. 87

Fieldy, p. 436, from "Kornucopia: Nu-Metal Band's Disturbing—And Successful—Vision" by Jon Wiederhorn, *Penthouse*, Oct. 2002, p. 84

Fred Durst, p. 436, from "Testing Their Metal" by Jon Wiederhorn, *Penthouse*, March 1999, p. 135

Jonathan Davis, p. 437, from "Kornucopia: Nu-Metal Band's Disturbing—And Successful—Vision" by Jon Wiederhorn, *Penthouse*, Oct. 2002, p. 85

Ice-T, p. 437, from "Ice-T: Still the Original Gangster" by Jon Wiederhorn, *Penthouse*, Sept. 2004, p. 50

Ice-T, p. 438, ibid

Fred Durst, p. 444, from Steven Richards's answering machine message posted by Stephen Richards, 1999, http://www.youtube.com/watch?v=v5KHWBiWXOk

Courtney Love, p. 457, statement to crowd at Edgefest in Dallas, May 6, 2010, http://www.youtube.com/watch?v=DWbtO4aEGJo&feature=related

Hammer Smashed Face: Death Metal, 1983–1993

Jeff Beccera, p. 460, from "Possessed," by Shan Shiva, Batttlehelm.com, http://www.battlehelmarchives.com/interviews/Possessed.html

Jeff Beccera, p. 461, from *Choosing Death: The Improbable History of Death Metal and Grindcore* by Albert Mudrian, Feral House, 2004, p. 70

Chuck Schuldiner, p. 464, interview by Jeff Kitts, property of interviewer

Joseph Lieberman, p. 475, from "Music Violence: How Does it Affect Our Children?" Hearing before the Subcommittee on Oversight of Government Management, Restructuring, and the District of Columbia of the Committee on Governmental Affairs, United States Senate, One Hundred Fifth Congress, first session, Nov. 6, 1997, http://www.gpo.gov/fdsys/pkg/CHRG-105shrg45594/pdf/CHRG-105shrg45594.pdf

Nik Bullen, p. 492, from *Precious Metal: Decibel Presents the Stories Behind 25 Extreme Metal Masterpieces,* edited by Albert Mudrian, quote by Kory Grow, DeCapo, 2009

Lee Dorrian, p. 492, from "Lee Dorrian interview by Dan Tobin," Wicked World, http://webcache.googleusercontent.com/search?q=cache:http://www.earache.com/WickedWorld/interview/lee_dorrian/lee.html

Lee Dorrian, p. 493, ibid

In the Nightside Eclipse: Black Metal, 1982–Present

Tomas "Quorthon" Forsberg, p. 508, from "Becoming the Sons of the

Bloodcountess: The Story of Naming the Band" by Quorthon, Official Bathory Website, http://www.bathory. nu/htmlbathory/03_kap.htm

Quorthon, p. 509, from "The Birth of a Legend: From the Forming of Bathory on the 16th of March 1983 to a Scandinavian Metal Attack in January 1984" by Quorthon, Official Bathory Website

Per Yngve "Dead" Ohlin, p. 510, "Interview with Dead" by fanzine staff, Battery #5, 1990

Quorthon, p. 510, from "The Birth of a Legend: From the Forming of Bathory on the 16th of March 1983 to a Scandinavian Metal Attack in January 1984" by Quorthon, Official Bathory Website

Varg "Count Grishnackh" Vikernes, p. 510, from "A Burzum Story: Part I—The Origin And Meaning" by Varg Vikernes, Official Varg Vikernes Website, www.Burzum.org

Cronos, p. 510, interview by Jeff Kitts, property of interviewer

Quorthon, p. 513, from "Names Rumors Legends Music and Image," by Quorthon, Official Bathory Website

Quorthon, p. 514, ibid

Quorthon, p. 514, from "Recording the Debut Album" by Quorthon, Official Bathory Website

Cronos, p. 514, interview by Jeff Kitts, property of interviewer

Euronymous, p. 516, from "Interview with Euronymous" By Esa Lahdenpera, *Kill Yourself!*, Issue No. 2, 1993

Count Grishnackh, p. 518, from "Interview with Varg Vikernes" by James Minton, *Terrorizer* magazine, March 2010, http://www.burzum.org/eng/library/2010_interview_terrorizer.shtml

Count Grishnackh, p. 519, ibid

Euronymous, p. 522, from "Euronymous and Dead Interview" by Jon Kristiansen, *Slayer* issue 8, 1991, http://www.cultofaraluen.com/2011/euronymous-and-dead-interview-in-slayer-issue-8-1991/

Jan Axel "Hellhammer" Blomberg, p. 524, interview by Dmitry Basik, property of interviewer

Dead, p. 525, from "Interview with Dead by Jon Kristiansen, *Slayer* #6, 1988

Hellhammer, p. 526, interview by Dmitry Basik, property of interviewer

Hellhammer, p. 527, ibid

Euronymous, p. 527, "Interview with Euronymous," *Battery*, 1992

Hellhammer, p. 528, interview by Dmitry Basik, property of interviewer

Count Grishnackh, p. 529, from "A Burzum Story: Part I—The Origin And Meaning," by Varg Vikernes, Official Varg Vikernes Website, www.Burzum.org

Count Grishnackh, p. 530, ibid

Count Grishnackh, p. 530, ibid

Kristian Eivind "Gaahl" Espedal, p. 537, from "Contemplating Infamy: An Interview with Gaahl of Trelldom and Gorgoroth" by Kenneth Morton, Highwiredaze.com, http://www.gorgoroth.com.pl/english/art-interview_with_gaahl_for_highwiredaze_com

Count Grishnackh, p. 537, from "A Burzum Story: Part I—The Origin And Meaning" by Varg Vikernes, Official Varg Vikernes Website, www.Burzum.org

Count Grishnackh, p. 538, Count Grishnackh from "A Burzum Story: Part II—Euronymous" by Varg Vikernes, Official Varg Vikernes Website, www.Burzum.org

Count Grishnackh, p. 539, from *Until the*

Light Takes Us, written and directed by Aaron Aites and Audrey Ewell, Gravitas Ventures, 2008

Cronos, p. 539, interview by Jeff Kitts, property of interviewer

Faust, p. 540, from *Lords of Chaos: The Bloody Rise of the Satanic Metal Underground* by Michael Moynihan and Didrik Soderlind, Feral House, 1998, p. 120

Count Grishnackh, p. 542, Count Grishnackh from "A Burzum Story: Part II—Euronymous" by Varg Vikernes, Official Varg Vikernes Website, www. Burzum.org

Kerrang! magazine, p. 543, from "Euronymous Murdered!: Black Metal 'Godfather' Stabbed to Death; Rival Swedish Satanists Suspected" by Tore Dien, Paul Elliott, *Kerrang!,* Aug., 1993, p. 6

Count Grishnackh, p. 543, Count Grishnackh from "A Burzum Story: Part II—Euronymous" by Varg Vikernes, Official Varg Vikernes Website, www. Burzum.org

Lee Barrett, p. 544, from Candlelight Records Press Release by Lee Barrett, August, 1993

Count Grishnackh, p. 544, Count Grishnackh from "A Burzum Story: Part II—Euronymous" by Varg Vikernes, Official Varg Vikernes Website, www. Burzum.org

Kerrang! magazine, p. 544, from "Euronymous Murdered!: Black Metal 'Godfather' Stabbed to Death; Rival Swedish Satanists Suspected" by Tore Dien, Paul Elliott, *Kerrang!,* Aug., 1993, p. 6

Count Grishnackh, p. 544, Count Grishnackh from "A Burzum Story: Part II—Euronymous" by Varg Vikernes,

Official Varg Vikernes Website, www. Burzum.org

Kerrang! magazine, p. 545, from "Euronymous Murdered!: Black Metal 'Godfather' Stabbed to Death; Rival Swedish Satanists Suspected" by Tore Dien, Paul Elliott, *Kerrang!,* Aug., 1993, p. 6

Count Grishnackh, p. 545, Count Grishnackh from "A Burzum Story: Part II—Euronymous" by Varg Vikernes, Official Varg Vikernes Website, www. Burzum.org

Faust, p. 545, from *Lords of Chaos: The Bloody Rise of the Satanic Metal Underground* by Michael Moynihan and Didrik Soderlind, Feral House, 1998, p. 130

Count Grishnackh, p. 545, Count Grishnackh from "A Burzum Story: Part II—Euronymous" by Varg Vikernes, Official Varg Vikernes Website, www. Burzum.org

Kerrang! magazine, p. 546, from "Euronymous Murdered!: Black Metal 'Godfather' Stabbed to Death; Rival Swedish Satanists Suspected" by Tore Dien, Paul Elliott, *Kerrang!,* Aug., 1993, p. 6

Snorre Ruch, p. 546, from *Lords of Chaos: The Bloody Rise of the Satanic Metal Underground* by Michael Moynihan and Didrik Soderlind, Feral House, 1998, p. 140

Count Grishnackh, p. 546, Count Grishnackh from "A Burzum Story: Part II—Euronymous" by Varg Vikernes, Official Varg Vikernes Website, www. Burzum.org

Hellhammer, p. 547, interview by Dmitry Basik, property of interviewer

Jon Nödtveidt, p. 549, from *Rebirth of Dissection* DVD, Escapi, 2006

Jon Nödtveidt, p. 550, ibid

Expressen newspaper, p. 550 from "Swedish

Hard Rock Star Jon Nödtveidt Took His Life" by Anna Wahlgren, Lars Johansson, and Niclas Rislund, *Expressen* newspaper, August 19, 2006

Count Grishnackh, p. 552, Count Grishnackh from "A Burzum Story: Part II—Euronymous" by Varg Vikernes, Official Varg Vikernes Website, www.Burzum.org

When Darkness Falls: Metalcore, 1992–2006

Dwid Hellion, p. 558, from "Dwid Hellion of Integrity Rare Exclusive Interview" by Joshua T. Cohen, Blowthescene.com

Charles Maggio, p. 559, from "Charles Maggio from Rorschach," by Ryan Duffy, Vice.com, 2009

Roxana Shirazi, p. 610, from *The Last Living Slut: Born in Iran, Bred Backstage* by Roxana Shirazi, Igniter, 2010, p. 179

M. Shadows, p. 613, from "For Avenged Sevenfold, 'Nightmare' album is part of the grief" by Mikael Wood, *Los Angeles Times*, July 29, 2010

Synyster Gates, p. 613, from AOL Noisecreep "Creep Show" interview with Amy Sciarretto, Aug. 4, 2010

Johnny Christ, p. 613, from radio interview with Mistress Carrie of WAAF, Boston, Jan. 22, 2011

Zacky Vengeance, p. 614, from "Avenged Sevenfold Wrap First Disc Since Drummer's Death" by Chris Harris, Rolling Stone.com, July 2, 2010

New American Gospel: Millennial Metal, 1992–present

Chris Beattie, p. 624, from "Hatebreed interview with: Beattie [Bass]. Matt [guitar]. Lou [guitar]" by John Vista, April 19, 1996

Lou "Boulder" Richards, p. 646, from "An Interview with Lou of Hatebreed" by John Vista, April 19, 1996

Sully Erna, p. 666, from "Living in Sin: Godsmack's Sully Erna" by Jon Wiederhorn, *Penthouse*, June, 2006, p. 44

Sully Erna, p. 667, ibid

Sully Erna, p. 669, ibid

p. 679, *Des Moines Register,* "We'll help ensure doctor pays for Paul Gray's overdose death" (September 6, 2012)

All other interviews not credited here were conducted by and are property of Jon Wiederhorn and Katherine Turman.